Philip the Good

The Dukes of Burgundy

Some press opinions

Philip the Bold

Richard Vaughan writes well, with a thorough command of his sources and a sharp eye for the witty asides of contemporary chroniclers... [the] first volume of an important study.

DAILY TELEGRAPH

The author's power of narrative writing ... sweeps the reader along so spiritedly that one is surprised to discover how much information has been imparted on the way.

CONTEMPORARY REVIEW

John the Fearless

With its predecessor it must become prescribed reading for all who wish to understand that important and fascinating phenomenon, the rise of Burgundy to be a major European power in the fifteenth century.

HISTORY TODAY

It is good to have a work of English scholarship on such a scale in the European field.

TIMES EDUCATIONAL SUPPLEMENT

A broad and scholarly narrative.

ENGLISH HISTORICAL REVIEW

Philip the Good

Not only of great value to the professional historian and student: it should be of much interest to the general reader.

HISTORY TODAY

1. Philip the Good

Philip the Good

THE APOGEE OF BURGUNDY

RICHARD VAUGHAN

THE BOYDELL PRESS

First published 1970
Longman, London and New York

New edition 2002
The Boydell Press, Woodbridge
Reprinted 2004, 2008, 2010, 2011, 2012

ISBN 978-0-85115-917-1

The Boydell Press is an imprint of Boydell & Brewer Ltd
PO Box 9, Woodbridge, Suffolk IP12 3DF, UK
and of Boydell & Brewer Inc.
668 Mt Hope Avenue, Rochester, NY 14620, USA
website: www.boydellandbrewer.com

A CiP catalogue record for this book is available
from the British Library

Papers used by Boydell & Brewer Ltd are natural, recyclable products
made from wood grown in sustainable forests

Printed in Great Britain by
CPI Antony Rowe, Chippenham and Eastbourne

Contents

Plates

Maps

Genealogical Tables

Nos. 1, 2, 4, and 5 are based on tables in von Isenburg, *Europäischen Stammtafeln*.

Abbreviations

AAAB	*Annales de l'Académie d'archéologie de Belgique*
AB	*Annales de Bourgogne*
ABSHF	*Annuaire-bulletin de la Société de l'histoire de France*
ACFF	*Annales du Comité flamand de France*
ACO	Archives départementales de la Côte-d'Or, Dijon
ADN	Archives départementales du Nord, Lille
AFH	*Archivum Franciscanum historicum*
AGR	Archives générales du royaume, Brussels
AIPHOS	*Annuaire de l'Institut de philologie et d'histoire orientales et slaves*
AM	*Annales du Midi*
AMA	*Akademie der Wissenschaften und der Literatur im Mainz. Abhandlungen der Geistes- und Sozialwissenschaftlichen Klasse*
AMSL	*Archives des missions scientifiques et littéraires*
AOGV	Archiv des Ordens vom Goldenen Vliesse
APAE	*Anciens pays et assemblées d'États*
ARH	Algemeen rijksarchief, The Hague
ASEB	*Annales de la Société d'émulation de Bruges*
ASHAG	*Annales de la Société d'histoire et d'archéologie de Gand*
BARB	*Bulletin de l'Académie royale de Belgique*
BARBL	*Bulletin de l'Académie royale de Belgique. Lettres*
BCHDN	*Bulletin de la Commission historique du département du Nord*
BCRH	*Bulletin de la Commission royale d'histoire*
BEC	*Bibliothèque de l'École des Chartes*
BEP	*Bulletin des études portugaises*
BGN	*Bijdragen voor de geschiedenis der Nederlanden*
BHPTH	*Bulletin historique et philologique du Comité des travaux historiques*, continued under the title *Bulletin philologique et historique*
BIAL	*Bulletin de l'Institut archéologique liégeois*
BIHBR	*Bulletin de l'Institut historique belge de Rome*

BIHR	*Bulletin of the Institute of Historical Research*
BIMGU	*Bijdragen van het Instituut voor middeleeuwsche geschiedenis der Rijksuniversiteit te Utrecht*
BM	British Museum, London
BMHGU	*Bijdragen en mededelingen van het historisch Genootschap te Utrecht*
BN	Bibliothèque Nationale, Paris
BPIAA	*Bulletin of the Polish Institute of Arts and Sciences in America*
BSAB	*Bulletin de la Société royale d'archéologie de Bruxelles*
BSBB	*Bulletin de la Société des bibliophiles belges*
BSEPC	*Bulletin de la Société d'études de la province de Cambrai*
BSHAG	*Bulletin de la Société d'histoire et d'archéologie de Gand*
BSHP	*Bulletin de la Société de l'histoire de Paris*
BVGO	*Bijdragen voor vaderlandsche geschiedenis en oudheidkunde*
CDIHF	Collection de documents inédits sur l'histoire de France
CHF	Classiques de l'histoire de France au moyen âge
CRAIBL	*Comptes rendus de l'Académie des inscriptions et belles-lettres*
CRH	Commission royale d'histoire
DRA	*Deutsche Reichstagsakten*
EHR	*English Historical Review*
FRADA	Fontes rerum Austriacorum. Diplomataria et acta
GBM	*Gelre. Bijdragen en mededelingen*
HBKD	*Historisch-politische Blätter für das katholische Deutschland*
HG	*Hansische Geschichtsblätter*
HKOM	*Handelingen van de koninklijke Kring voor oudheidkunde, letteren en kunst van Mechelen*
IAB, etc.	Printed inventories of archives, see below, pp. 416–17
IG	*L'Intermédiaire des généalogistes*
JBHM	*Jahrbuch des bernischen historischen Museums in Bern*
JMH	*Journal of Modern History*
JS	*Journal des savants*
JSG	*Jahrbuch für schweizerische Geschichte*
LFCL	*Les Facultés catholiques de Lille*
MA	*Le Moyen Âge*
MAB	*Mémoires de l'Académie des sciences, belles-lettres et arts de Besançon*
MAD	*Mémoires de l'Académie des sciences, arts et belles-lettres de Dijon*
MAM	*Mémoires de l'Académie nationale de Metz*
MAMB	*Mededelingen der Akademie van marine van België*
MARB	Mémoires de l'Académie royale de Belgique
MARBBA	Mémoires de l'Académie royale de Belgique. Beaux-arts

MARBL	Mémoires de l'Académie royale de Belgique. Lettres
MAWL	*Mededelingen der koninklijke Akademie van wetenschappen, Amsterdam. Afdeling letterkunde*
MCACO	*Mémoires de la Commission des antiquités du département de la Côte-d'Or*
MCMP	*Mémoires de la Commission départementale des monuments historiques du Pas-de-Calais*
MIOG	*Mitteilungen des Instituts für österreichische Geschichtsforschung*
MKVAL	*Mededelingen van de koninklijke Vlaamse Academie voor wetenschappen, letteren en schone kunsten van België. Klasse der letteren*
MSAB	*Messager des sciences et des arts de la Belgique*
MPSALH	*Mémoires et publications de la Société des sciences, des arts et des lettres de Hainaut*
MSE	*Mémoires de la Société éduenne*
MSED	*Mémoires de la Société d'émulation du Doubs*
MSHA Beaune	*Mémoires de la Société d'histoire, d'archéologie et de littérature de Beaune*
MSHAC	*Mémoires de la Société d'histoire et d'archéologie de Chalon-sur-Saône*
MSHB	*Messager des sciences historiques de Belgique*
MSHDB	*Mémoires de la Société pour l'histoire du droit et des institutions des anciens pays bourguignons, comtois et romands*
MSHP	*Mémoires de la Société de l'histoire de Paris et de l'Île-de-France*
MSSL	*Mémoires de la Société des sciences de Lille*
MVP	Maetschappy der Vlaemsche bibliophilen te Gent
NEBN	*Notices et extraits des manuscrits de la Bibliothèque Nationale et autres bibliothèques*
NGWG	*Nachrichten von der königlichen Gesellschaft der Wissenschaften zu Göttingen. Philologisch-historische Klasse*
PCEEBM	*Publications du Centre européen d'études burgondo-médianes*
PH	*Provence historique*
PHG	*Pfingstblätter des hansischen Geschichtsvereins*
PSHIL	Publications de la section historique de l'Institut grand-ducal de Luxembourg
PTSEC	*Positions des thèses soutenues à l'École des Chartes*
RB	*Revue bourguignonne*
RBAHA	*Revue belge d'archéologie et d'histoire de l'art*
RBG	*Revue historique de Bordeaux et du département de la Gironde*
RBN	*Revue belge de numismatique*
RBPH	*Revue belge de philologie et d'histoire*

RCC	*Revue des cours et conférences*
RDT	*Revue diocésaine de Tournai*
RH	*Revue historique*
RLC	*Revue de littérature comparée*
RN	*Revue du Nord*
RNum	*Revue numismatique*
RNHB	*Revue nobiliaire, héraldique et biographique*
RQH	*Revue des questions historiques*
RS	Rolls Series
RSS	*Revue des Sociétés savantes*
SFW	*Souvenirs de la Flandre wallonne*
SHF	Société de l'histoire de France
TG	*Tijdschrift voor Geschiedenis*
VKAWL	*Verhandelingen der koninklijke Akademie van wetenschappen. Amsterdam. Afdeling letterkunde*
VSW	*Vierteljahrschrift für Social und Wirtschaftgeschichte*
VVATL	*Verslagen en mededelingen van de koninklijke Vlaamse Academie voor taal- en letterkunde*
WG	*Werken Gelre*
WZGK	*Westdeutsche Zeitschrift für Geschichte und Kunst*

Acknowledgements

Without the assistance of numerous scholars, librarians and others this book could never have been written. I thank them all. My friend and colleague Dr. F. W. Brooks has read the typescript and made many valuable suggestions; Dr. Peter Spufford has helped me with monetary matters; Dr. M. H. Tweedy was kind enough to translate two of Philip the Good's letters for me; Mr. Brian Morris answered a Spanish query for me and Professor G. Griffith helped with an Italian problem. Others have been kind enough to lend me useful material, and I wish particularly to thank Professor Dr. H. Heimpel for letting me see and use the proofs of volume xix of the *Deutsche Reichstagsakten*; Professor R. Weiss for lending me a microfilm of Frulovisi's *Humfroidos*; Miss J. M. Backhouse, of the Department of Manuscripts of the British Museum, for lending at short notice a microfilm of the hitherto unknown section of Chastellain's chronicle, from 1458 to 1461; and Mlle N. Grain, of the Centre Régional d'Études Historiques at Lille University, for lending me microfilms of several unpublished theses. Other scholars have most generously given me copies of their papers or other material of value to me. In this respect I am especially indebted to Professor J. Richard at Dijon, Professor E. Lousse, Mr. C. A. J. Armstrong, M. Y. Lacaze, Dr. P. Spufford, M. G. Dogaer and M. Henri Dubois. I am also grateful to Mme G. Milis-Proost, M. A. Grunzweig, M. R. Robinet of the Archives du Nord, Lille, and some of the above-mentioned, for kindly replying to my queries. But above all I must record my gratitude to the younger generation of scholars who have unselfishly placed their unpublished work at my disposal. I thank the author of every one of the fifteen or more theses I have been permitted to borrow, and I would like to mention in particular those of Drs. Schwarzkopf and von Dietze on the Burgundian court and Luxembourg respectively; of Mme Milis-Proost and M. P. Cockshaw on the duke's financial officers and secretaries; of Dr. Spufford on monetary affairs; of M. Y. Lacaze on Jehan Germain and Mme D. Hillard on Franco-Burgundian relations; and of Mlle L. Régibeau on the Croy. I would like to thank the authorities of the archive repositories who have permitted me to use microfilms of unprinted material in their possession; also Mr. A. C. Wood and other members of the staff of the University Library, Hull, who have taken endless trouble in obtaining films and books for me. Finally, my special thanks go to Miss Susan Appleton, who has typed the entire manuscript and, in the process, removed many errors.

RICHARD VAUGHAN

November 1968

A note on coinage and moneys of account mentioned in this book

The gold coins in use in Philip the Good's Burgundy were partly French, partly Burgundian and partly Rhenish or imperial. Of French coins, the two most important were the crown or *écu à la couronne*, valued at £1 2s 6d of Tours or 40 groats, and the salut, valued at 48 groats, which was the standard gold coin of Lancastrian France. In the early part of Philip's reign Flemish nobles of the same value as a pound of Tours and Dutch crowns or clinkarts, valued at 40 groats, were current in the Netherlands. In 1433 Philip introduced the philippus, cavalier or rider, of the same fineness and weight as the salut and likewise valued at 48 groats. The rider was issued concurrently in Flanders, Brabant, Holland and Hainault and, from 1433, the Burgundian Netherlands possessed in it a common gold currency. The principal imperial gold coin in circulation in the Netherlands in Philip the Good's reign was the florin or gulden of the Rhine, current at 38 or 40 Flemish groats. The English noble, which was worth 6s 8d or one-third of a pound sterling, was valued at 92–96 Flemish groats. The groat had been the standard Flemish silver coin but, by Philip the Good's reign, the double groat had largely taken its place.

Numerous systems of money of account, nearly all based on pounds, shillings and pence, were used in Burgundy; the accounts of the receipt-general of all finances employ eleven of them between 1433 and 1444. But two were dominant: one based on the pound groat, which comprised 240 Flemish groats, the other based on the pound of 40 groats. In France, and in Philip the Good's southern territories, the system based on the pound of Tours or franc, current at 32–36 Flemish groats, was prevalent. The pound of Tours (*livre tournois*) was four-fifths of the pound of Paris (*livre parisis*). In what follows, the symbol £, unqualified, refers to pounds of 40 groats.

THE HOUSE OF BURGUNDY

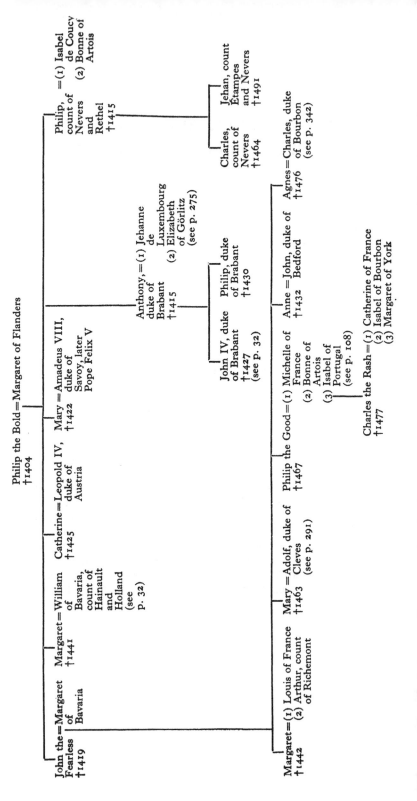

Introduction to the 2002 Edition

Several important surveys of the 'Burgundian phenomenon' have appeared in the thirty-one years since Richard Vaughan first published his study of Philip the Good, but no scholar has yet attempted to reappraise this central reign in a monograph-length study.[1] The extent of Professor Vaughan's achievement was immediately apparent to reviewers, among whom André Leguai noted that 'with the exception of Paul Bonenfant, no-one has had the courage to attempt a general account of the career and achievement of this figure'.[2] To the latest generation of Burgundian scholars the master narrative of Philip's reign still seems indispensable for its 'scale, its commanding view and its completeness'.[3] The durability of the work is partly attributable to its extensive use of archival material, chronicle accounts and

---

[1] I borrow the phrase from an important historiographical survey, A. Jongkees, 'Une génération d'historiens devant le phénomène bourguignon', *Bijdragen en mededelingen betreffende de Geschiedenis der Nederlanden*, vol. lxxxviii (1973), pp. 215–32; repr. in his *Burgundica et varia* (Hilversum, 1990). E. Bourassin, *Philippe le Bon, le grand lion des Flandres* (Paris, 1983) is a popular account of the reign. For general histories see *Algemene Geschiedenis der Nederlanden, G: Middeleeuwen*, vol. 4 (Haarlem, 1981); W. Blockmans and W. Prevenier, *The Burgundian Netherlands* (Cambridge, 1986), and their *The Promised Lands. The Low Countries under Burgundian rule, 1369–1530* (Philadelphia, 1999); W. Prevenier (ed.), *Prinsen en poorters. Beelden van de laat-middeleeuwse samenleving in de Bourgondische Nederlanden 1384–1530* (Antwerp, 1998); and a shorter survey by B. Schnerb in C. Allmand (ed.), *New Cambridge Medieval History, 7: c. 1415–c. 1500* (Cambridge, 1998) – but see also n. 3 below. For a recent short survey of all four dukes see: A. Brown, *The Valois dukes of Burgundy* (Oxford, 2002). For a part of Philip's reign see also B. Schnerb, *Les armagnacs et les bourguignons: la maudite guerre* (Paris, 1988).

[2] *AB*, vol. xliii (1971), pp. 278–83, at p. 278 (my translation). Paul Bonenfant's general study of Philip's reign and a number of his shorter pieces on the duke were republished in *Philippe le Bon. Sa politique, son action. Études présentées par A.-M. Bonenfant-Feytmans* (Brussels, 1996).

[3] A comment applied to all four volumes of Professor Vaughan's study of

other narrative sources, some of which have only been published in recent years.[4] However, the book is also a remarkable work of synthesis, drawing together for the first time a vast literature in several languages devoted to the reign of the third Valois duke. The welcome reappearance in print of *Philip the Good: apogee of Burgundy* inevitably calls for a brief account of the relevant research which has appeared in the last three decades of late medieval Burgundian studies.[5]

Beginning with the prince himself, it is worth noting that a judgement first formulated by Johan Huizinga in 1932 remains surprisingly valid: Philip the Good is an ambiguous figure.[6] Although the duke's prayer book and some of his religious foundations have been studied, for instance, the more general matter of his piety – if we may set aside for the moment the question of the crusade – has not been the subject of detailed studies to compare with those devoted to Burgundian duchesses in general, to Isabella of Portugal in particular, or even to his chancellor, Nicolas Rolin.[7] The in-

the dukes: B. Schnerb, *L'État bourguignon 1363–1477* (Paris, 1999), p. 7 (my translation).

4 For example, Professor Vaughan was the first to use unpublished fragments of the chronicle of George Chastelain discovered by John Armstrong and Janet Backhouse, and published in J.-C. Delclos (ed.), *Georges Chastellain, Chronique: les fragments du Livre IV révélés par l'Additional manuscrit 54156 de la British Library* (Geneva, 1991). The Brynmor Jones Library of the University of Hull still has an extensive collection of microfilms of Burgundian archival material from Professor Vaughan's time there.

5 Cf. J.-M. Cauchies, 'Le prince territorial au bas Moyen Âge dans les anciens Pays-Bas. Quinze années de recherches en Belgique (1975–1990)', in *Les princes et le pouvoir au moyen âge. XXIIIe Congrès de la Société des historiens médiévistes de l'enseignement supérieur public. Brest, mai 1992* (Paris, 1993), pp. 35–48; idem, 'Autour de 1996: une année "Philippe le Bon"'. *Chronique ducale bourguignonne'*, in C. Thiry (ed.), *'À l'heure encore de mon escrire': aspects de la littérature de Bourgogne sous Philippe le Bon et Charles le Téméraire* (Louvain-la-Neuve, 1997), pp. 253–62.

6 J. Huizinga, 'La physionomie morale de Philippe le Bon', *AB*, vol. iv (1932), pp. 101–39.

7 M. Thomas, 'Le livre de prières de Philippe le Bon', *Dossiers archéologiques*, no. 16 (1976), pp. 84–95; M. Sommé, 'Une fondation de Philippe le Bon dans l'église collégiale Saint-Barthélemy de Béthune en 1455', in G. Deregnaucourt (ed.), *Société et religion en France et aux Pays-Bas, XVe–XVIe siècle. Mélanges en l'honneur d'Alain Lottin* (Arras, 2000), pp. 391–402; M. Cheyns-Condé, 'Expressions de la piété des duchesses de

fluence of psychoanalytical approaches to historical subjects in the seventies did not make much of an impression on the study of Philip the Good: perhaps he seemed a less promising case for investigation than his son.[8] It is nonetheless the case that the duke himself, a prince whom Professor Vaughan and others have shown to be closely involved in the political acts of his reign, could still benefit from further consideration.[9]

Studies of members of the ducal family have continued to appear in considerable number, however. In addition to the monograph devoted to the duke's third wife mentioned above, the entourage and other aspects of the early life of Charles of Charolais, Philip's only legitimate heir to reach adulthood, have received renewed attention.[10] We may note the appearance of studies of Philip's sister, Agnes of Bourbon; of his daughter-in-law, Isabelle of Bourbon; and of some of his many bastard children, notably Antoine (the Great Bastard), Baudouin and Philip.[11] This body of research reminds us that

Bourgogne au XVe siècle dans la vie quotidienne et dans l'art. Essai de synthèse', *PCEEB*, vol. xxix (1995), pp. 47–68; M. Sommé, *Isabelle de Portugal, duchesse de Bourgogne. Une femme au pouvoir au XVe siècle* (Villeneuve d'Ascq, 1998), with a full bibliography; H. Kamp, *Memoria und Selbstdarstellung: die Stiftungen des burgundischen Kanzlers Rolin* (Sigmaringen, 1993).

8 W. Paravicini, *Karl der Kühne. Das ende des Hauses Burgund* (Göttingen, 1976).

9 There is however an edition and commentary of an important source on this matter: M. Prietzel, 'Guillaume Fillastre d.J.: über Herzog Philipp den Guten von Burgund. Text und Kommentar', *Francia*, vol. xxiv (1998), pp. 83–121.

10 M. Sommé, 'La jeunesse de Charles le Téméraire d'après les comptes de la maison de Bourgogne', *RN*, vol. lii (1970), pp. 183–97; idem, 'Une mère et son fils: Isabelle de Portugal après son départ de la cour (1457–1471) et Charles le Téméraire', in G. et P. Contamine (eds.), *Autour de Marguerite d'Écosse: reines, princesses et dames du XVe siècle* (Paris, 1999), pp. 99–121; H. Kruse, *Hof, Amt und Gagen: die täglichen Gagenlisten des burgundischen Hofes (1430–1467) und der erste Hofstaat Karls des Kühnen (1456)* (Bonn, 1996); B. Groothuis, 'Karel van Charolais in Holland, 1457–1465', doctoral thesis, Leiden (1990).

11 A. Leguai, 'Agnès de Bourgogne, duchesse de Bourbon (1405?–1476)', *Études bourbonnaises*, 15th series, no. 276 (1996), pp. 405–17; D. Verdonck, 'Isabelle de Bourbon, comtesse de Charolais et mère de Marie de Bourgogne', *Mémoire de maîtrise*, Lille III (1989); J. Clement, 'Antoine de Bourgogne, dit le Grand bâtard', *PCEEB*, vol. xxx (1990), pp. 165–82; A. Comines, ' "Nul ne s'y frote". Een biografische schets van Antoon, Bastaard

ducal politics was not simply the business of one man whose
character at times appears obscure: it was often a family affair,
as well as a partnership of husband and wife.

Ducal politics was also the business of Philip's collaborators
among the nobilities of his various lands. In an important
article which in some respects rejects the image of Philip the
Good created in the present volume by Richard Vaughan,
Yvon Lacaze described the third Valois duke as 'a political
mind surrounded by political minds'.[12] The comment finds
echoes in an observation made by John Armstrong, whose
own study of Valois Burgundy may yet appear posthumously:
'Burgundian power was something of a syndicate in which
people took stakes so as to share in the fortunes of the
house'.[13] Among Philip's servants the great men have continued to attract much interest, as witnessed by the appearance of three studies devoted to Nicolas Rolin alone.[14] The
Croÿ and Lalaing families have been the subject of attention,
as have Louis de Bruges, Jean de Créquy, Jacques de Brégilles

van Bourgondië' in *Excursiones Mediavales: Opstellen aangeboden aan Prof.
Dr. A. G. Jongkees door zijn leerlingen* (Groningen, 1979), pp. 59–76;
J.-M. Cauchies, 'Baudouin de Bourgogne (v. 1446–1508), bâtard, militaire
et diplomate: une carrière exemplaire?', *RN*, vol. lxxvii (1995), pp. 257–81;
J. Sterk, *Philips van Bourgondië (1465–1524), bisschop van Utrecht, als pro-
tagonist van de Renaissance* (Zutphen, 1980); H. Cools, 'In het spoor van "de
grote bastaard" ', in *Het Land van Beveren*, vol. xxiv (1981), pp. 9–23 and
Het Land van Aalst, vol. xxxiii (1990), pp. 42–55; S. Gilloen, 'La vie et le
statut des enfants illégitimes: l'exemple des bâtards de Philippe le Bon',
Mémoire de maîtrise, Lille III (1992); M. Carlier, 'Onwettige kinderen in de
Bourgondische Nederlanden. Determinaten van hun plaats binnen de
familie en binnen de maatschappij', doctoral thesis, Ghent (1998–9).
12 Y. Lacaze, 'Philippe le Bon et l'Empire: bilan d'un règne', *Francia*, vol.
ix (1981), pp. 133–75; vol. x (1982), pp. 167–227, at p. 227 (my translation).
13 C.A.J. Armstrong, 'The golden age of Burgundy: the dukes that outdid
kings', in A. Dickens (ed.), *The courts of Europe: politics, patronage and
royalty, 1400–1800* (London, 1975), pp. 55–75, at p. 60. See also his collected works: *England, France and Burgundy in the fifteenth century*
(London, 1983); and an important essay published posthumously: 'Les ducs
de Bourgogne, interprètes de la pensée politique du XVe siècle', *AB*, vol.
lxvii (1995), pp. 5–34.
14 R. Berger, *Nicolas Rolin, Kanzler der Zeitenwende im burgundisch-
französischen Konflikt (1422–61)* (Fribourg, 1976); H. Pridat, *Nicolas Rolin,
chancelier de Bourgogne* (Dijon, 1996; in German, Berlin, 1995); M.-T.
Berthier and J. Sweeney, *Le chancelier Rolin (1376–1462): ambition, pouvoir
et fortune en Bourgogne* (Précy-sous-Thil, 1998).

and Philippe Pot, the latter a central character of the reign.[15] Alongside monographs devoted to leading figures it is possible to trace another tendency in Burgundian historiography since the publication of Professor Vaughan's work: the study of lesser nobles, of noble families or of networks of families whose fortunes and influence were affected by the stunning growth of ducal power under Philip the Good. The duchy of Burgundy has been the subject of a particularly wide-ranging inquiry of this kind.[16] In the Boulonnais we might mention a study of the Bournonville family as a case in

[15] W. Paravicini, 'Moers, Croy, Burgund. Eine Studie über den Niedergang des Hauses Moers in den zweiten Hälfte des 15. Jahrhunderts', *Annalen des historischen Vereins für den Niederrhein*, vol. clxxix (1978), pp. 7–113; J.-M. Roger, 'Le don de Bar-sur-Aube à Antoine de Croy (1435–1438)', *104e Congrès national des sociétés savantes. Philologie et histoire*, vol. 1 (Bordeaux, 1981), pp. 161–215; C. Thiry, 'Les Croy face aux indiciaires bourguignons: George Chastelain, Jean Molinet', in J.-C. Aubailly et al. (eds.), *'Et c'est la fin pour quoy sommes ensemble: hommage à Jean Dufournet*, vol. iii (Paris, 1993), pp. 1363–80; R. Born, *Les Croÿ: une grande lignée hennuyère d'hommes de guerre, de diplomates, de conseillers secrets, dans les coulisses du pouvoir, sous les ducs de Bourgogne et la maison d'Autriche (1390–1612)* (Brussels, 1981); idem, *Les Lalaing: une grande "mesnie" hennuyère (1096–1600)* (Brussels, 1986); M.P. Martens (ed.), *Lodewijk van Gruuthuse: mecenas en Europees diplomaat, ca. 1427–1492* (Bruges, 1992); R. Lesage, 'Un grand seigneur bourguignon: Jean de Créquy, chevalier de la Toison d'Or (1400–1471)', *Bulletin historique du haut pays*, vol. 12 (1995), pp. 35–51; J. Paviot, 'Jacques de Brégilles, garde-joyaux des ducs de Bourgogne Philippe le Bon et Charles le Téméraire', *RN*, vol. lxxvii (1995), pp. 313–20; H. Bouchard, *Philippe Pot (1428–1493), grand sénéchal de Bourgogne* (Châteauneuf, 1998: see *Position des thèses de l'École des chartes*, 1949, pp. 23–7).
[16] M.-T. Caron, *La noblesse dans le duché de Bourgogne, 1315–1477* (Lille, 1987). We should also mention the same author's 'Vie et mort d'une grande dame: Jeanne de Chalon, comtesse de Tonnerre (vers 1388–vers 1450)', *Francia*, vol. viii (1980), pp. 147–90; 'La fidélité dans la noblesse bourguignonne à la fin du Moyen Âge', in P. Contamine (ed.), *L'État et les aristocraties (France, Angleterre, Écosse), 12e–17e siècles: table ronde. Maison française d'Oxford, 26 et 27 septembre 1986* (Paris, 1989), pp. 103–27; and her *Noblesse et pouvoir royal en France (XIIIe–XVIe siecles)* (Paris, 1994). For other ducal territories, see: R. van Uytven, 'De Brabantse adel als politieke en sociale groep tijdens de late middeleeuwen', in J. Verbesselt et al. (eds.), *De adel in het hertogdom Brabant* (Brussels, 1985), pp. 75–88; M. Margue, 'La noblesse du duché de Luxembourg au XVe siècle', *Hémecht. Zeitschrift für luxemburger Geschichte*, vol. xxxvi (1984), pp. 339–41.

point;[17] in Flanders, the Uutkerkes, the de la Kethulles or the van Massemines;[18] in Hainaut, the example of Engelbert II d'Enghien.[19] The lifestyle of the nobility, their status and their presence in urban society have also been the subject of interesting work.[20] Thanks to this type of research it is clear that the process of state formation under Philip the Good did not simply depend on the actions or personal qualities of the prince, but also, and in very large part, on the integration and the participation of the nobilities of his dominions.[21]

[17] B. Schnerb, *Enguerrand de Bournonville et les siens: un lignage noble du Boulonnais aux XIVe et XVe siècles* (Paris, 1997).

[18] M. Boone, 'Une famille au service de l'état bourguignon naissant: Roland et Jean d'Uutkerke, nobles flamands dans l'entourage de Philippe le Bon', *RN*, vol. lxxvii (1995), pp. 233–55; H. Douxchamps, *La famille de la Kethulle* (Brussels, 1996: *Recueil de l'Office généalogique et héraldique de Belgique*, nos. 44–6); E. Balthau 'La famille van Massemen/de Masmines. Aspects sociaux et matériels de la noblesse flamande ca. 1350–ca. 1450', *PCEEB*, vol. xxxvii (1997), pp. 173–194.

[19] M. Cheyns-Condé, 'Un seigneur hennuyer face à Jacqueline de Bavière et Philippe le Bon: Engelbert II d'Enghien, seigneur de Rameru et de la Follie', *PCEEBM*, vol. xix (1978), pp. 25–33.

[20] P. de Win, 'Adel en statspatriciaat in het hertogdom Brabant in de 15e eeuw', *Spiegel Historiael*, vol. xvi (1981), pp. 407–11; idem, ' "Queeste" naar de rechtspositie van de edelman in de Bourgondische Nederlanden', *Tijdschrift voor Geschiedenis*, vol. liii (1985), pp. 223–74; idem, 'The lesser nobility of the Burgundian Netherlands', in M. Jones (ed.), *Gentry and lesser nobility in late medieval Europe* (Gloucester, 1986), pp. 95–118; A. Janse, 'Marriage and noble lifestyle in Holland in the late Middle Ages', in W. Blockmans and A. Janse (eds.), *Showing status. Representation of social positions in the late Middle Ages* (Turnhout, 1999), pp. 113–38; M. Boone, M.-C. Laleman and D. Lievois, 'Van Simon sRijkensteen tot Ryhove. Van erfachtige lieden tot dienaren van de centrale Bourgondische staat', *Handelingen der Maatschappij voor geschiedenis en oudheidkunde te Gent*, n.s., vol. xliv (1990), pp. 47–86. J. Dumolyn and F. Van Tricht, 'Adel en nobiliteringsprocessen in het laatmiddeleeuwse Vlaanderen. Een status quaestionis', *Bijdragen en mededelingen voor de geschiedenis van de Nederlanden*, vol. cxv (2000), pp. 197–222; idem, 'De sociaal-economische positie van de laatmiddeleeuwse Vlaamse adel. Enkele trends', *Handelingen van het Genootschap voor geschiedenis te Brugge*, vol. cxxxvii (2000), pp. 3–46; A. Naber, 'Bourgondische ridderethiek: ontwikkeling en verspreiding', *Millennium*, vol. viii (1994), pp. 109–16; idem, 'Bourgondische edelen en hun opvoeding', in R. Stuip and C. Vellekoop (eds.), *Scholing in de middeleeuwen* (Hilversum, 1995), pp. 239–256.

[21] See especially W. Paravicini, 'Expansion et intégration: la noblesse des Pays-Bas à la cour de Philippe le Bon', *Bijdragen en mededelingen betreffende de geschiedenis der Nederlanden*, vol. xcv (1980), pp. 298–314.

Under Philip the Good there existed two valuable means of integrating the nobility. The first, founded by Philip himself, was the Order of the Golden Fleece, an institution which (in its early years at least) served to tie together the higher nobility of Philip's lands by means of a common chivalric bond. The history and importance of the Order have been clarified by the publication of a valuable series of short articles devoted to each of its members in the fifteenth century;[22] by studies of the chapters and the officers of the Order;[23] and by more general histories of the institution and its various roles.[24] Ongoing editorial work on the protocol books of the Order demonstrates the continuing importance of the subject in Burgundian studies.[25]

The second tool for integrating the nobility of the ducal dominions also served to protect the prince, to magnify his prestige, and to organise his daily life: the court, a less exclusive organism than the Order of the Golden Fleece, but one which also played a key role in the development of

[22] R. de Smedt (ed.), *Les chevaliers de la Toison d'Or au XVe siècle* (Frankfurt, 1994; second edition, revised and with corrections, 2000).

[23] F. Koller, *Au service de la Toison d'Or* (Dison, 1971); B. Janssens de Bisthoven, 'Het feest van het Gulden Vlies in Sint-Donaas op 1 en 2 december 1432', *Handelingen van de 'Société d'émulation' te Brugge*, vol. cviii (1971), pp. 238–44; F. de Gruben, *Les chapitres de la Toison d'Or à l'époque bourguignonne (1430–1477)* (Leuven, 1997).

[24] D'A.J.D. Boulton, *The knights of the crown. The monarchical orders of knighthood in later medieval Europe, 1325–1520* (Woodbridge, 1987; second edition 2000); P. Cockshaw and C. van den Bergen-Pantens (eds.), *L'Ordre de la Toison dOr de Philippe le Bon à Philippe le Beau (1430–1505): idéal ou reflet d'une société?* (Brussels-Turnhout, 1996); G. Jones, *The Order of the Golden Fleece: form, function and evolution, 1430–1555* (Ann Arbor, 1988); G. Melville, 'Rituelle Ostentation und pragmatische Inquisition. Zur Institutionalität des Ordens vom Goldenen Vlies', in H. Duchhardt and G. Melville (eds.), *Im Spannungsfeld von Recht und Ritual: soziale Kommunikation in Mittelalter und früher Neuzeit* (Cologne, 1997), pp. 215–71; L. Horowski, '*xxxi chevaliers sans reproche*. Der Orden vom Goldenen Vlies als Instrument burgundischer Elitenpolitik, 1430–77', *Sacra Militia*, vol. i (2000), pp. 187–234. See also J. de la Croix Bouton, 'Un poème à Philippe le Bon sur la Toison d'Or', *AB*, vol. xlii (1970), pp. 1–29; and A. van Buren-Hagopian, 'The model roll of the Golden Fleece', *The Art Bulletin*, vol. lxi (1979), pp. 359–76.

[25] S. Dünnebeil (ed.), *Die Protokollbücher des Ordens vom Goldenen Vlies. I. Herzog Philipp der Gute, 1430–1467* (forthcoming).

Burgundian power under Philip the Good.[26] Professor Vaughan devoted an entire chapter to this topic and it remains a popular subject for research. Many of the sources which have been edited for Philip's reign concern the court in some way or other: the impressive series of household ordinances;[27] the *Honneurs de la cour* by Aliénor de Poitiers (which, although written long after the duke's death, frequently refers to his reign);[28] the dispatches of Milanese ambassadors at Philip's court in the fifties and sixties;[29] the previously unknown passages of the chronicle of the court historian, George Chastelain;[30] the work of the court poet Michel Taillevent;[31] and an important collection of sources, rendered into modern French, organised around the theme of the

[26] W. Paravicini, 'Structure et fonctionnement de la cour bourguignonne au XVe siècle', *PCEEB*, vol. xxix (1989), pp. 67–73. See also idem, 'Soziale Schichtung und soziale Mobilität am Hof der Herzöge von Burgund', *Francia*, vol. v (1977), pp. 298–314.

[27] See in general H. Kruse, 'Éditions de textes et banques de données servant à l'histoire de l'hôtel des ducs de Bourgogne au XVe siècle', in W. Paravicini (ed.), *Les ateliers de l'Institut historique allemand* (Paris, 1994), pp. 57–72; Professor Paravicini's edition of the *ordonnances* in *Francia*, vol. x (1982), pp. 131–66; vol. xi (1983), pp. 257–301; vol. xiii (1985), pp. 191–211; vol. xv (1987), pp. 183–231; vol. xviii (1991), pp. 111–23; and H. Kruse, 'Die Hofordnungen Herzog Philipps des Guten von Burgund', in idem and W. Paravicini (eds.), *Höfe und Hofordnungen 1200–1600* (Sigmaringen, 1999), pp. 141–65.

[28] J. Paviot (ed.), 'Eléonore de Poitiers. *Les États de France* (*Les Honneurs de la cour*)', *Annuaire-bulletin de la Société de l'histoire de France. Année 1996* (Paris, 1998), pp. 75–136.

[29] P.M. Kendall and V. Ilardi (eds.), *Dispatches with related documents of Milanese ambassadors in France and Burgundy, 1450–1483*, vol. i (1450–60) (Athens, Ohio, 1970); vol. ii (1460–1) (Athens, Ohio, 1971); vol. iii, edited by V. Ilardi and F. Fata, for the period 11 March–29 June 1466 (Dekalb, Illinois, 1981). On this source see also G. Soldi-Rondinini, 'Aspects de la vie des cours en France et en Bourgogne par les dépêches des ambassadeurs milanais (seconde moitié du XVe siècle)', in *Adelige Sachkultur des Spätmittelalters* (Österreichische Akademie der Wissenschaften, no. 452) (Vienna, 1982), pp. 195–214; and R. Walsh, 'Relations between Milan and Burgundy in the period 1450–1476', in *Gli Sforza a Milano e in Lombardia e i loro rapporti con gli stati ed europei (1450–1535)* (Milan, 1982), pp. 369–96.

[30] Delclos (ed.), *Georges Chastellain, Chronique* (see above, n. 4).

[31] R. Deschaux, *Un poète bourguignon du XVe siècle, Michault Taillevent (édition et étude)* (Genève, 1975).

splendours of the court.[32] The study of the Burgundian court has worked outwards from these and other base texts to consider afresh certain fundamental questions: where did the court reside, and under what circumstances?[33] What did one eat/drink/wear/hunt at the court of Philip the Good?[34] Who

[32] D. Regnier-Bohler (director), *Splendeurs de la cour de Bourgogne* (Paris, 1995).

[33] A survey is to be found in W. Paravicini, 'Die Residenzen der Herzöge von Burgund, 1363–1477', in *Fürstliche Residenzen im Spätmittelalterlichen Europa* (Sigmaringen, 1991), pp. 209–63. Since the very full bibliography of that work we may note the appearance of the following on the major residence of Philip's reign: K. de Jonge, 'Het Paleis op de Coudenberg te Brussel in de vijftiende eeuw', *Revue belge d'archéologie et de l'histoire de l'art*, vol. lx (1991), pp. 5–38; idem, 'Le palais de Charles-Quint à Bruxelles. Ses dispositions intérieures aux XVe et XVIe siècles et le cérémonial de Bourgogne', in J. Guillaume (ed.), *Architecture et vie sociale. Actes du colloque tenu à Tours du 6 au 10 juin 1988* (Paris, 1994), pp. 107–25; A. Smolar- Meynart, 'Le palais de Bruxelles: des origines à Charles-Quint', in idem and A. Vanrie (eds.), *Le palais de Brussels. Huit siècles d'art et d'histoire* (Brussels, 1991), pp. 15–90. On lesser residences and their attractions (or drawbacks) see B. Francke, 'Gesellschaftsspiele mit Automaten- "Merveilles" in Hesdin', *Marburger Jahrbuch für Kunstgeschichte*, vol. xxiv (1997), pp. 135–58; V. Maliet, 'Valenciennes: La Salle-le-Comte', in P. Beaussart and A. Salamagne (eds.), *Châteaux-chevaliers en Hainaut au Moyen Âge* (Brussels, 1995), pp. 134–7; M. Boone and T. de Hemptinne, 'Espace urbain et ambitions princières: les présences matérielles de l'autorité princière dans le Gand médiéval (12e siècle–1540)', in W. Paravicini (ed.), *Zeremoniell und Raum. 4 Symposium der Residenzen-Kommission der Akademie der Wissenschaften in Göttingen* (Residenz-forschung, 6) (Sigmaringen, 1997), pp. 279–304; *Het prinselijk hof ten Walle in Gent* (Ghent, 2000) (with a remarkable survey by D. Lievois based on the archival sources).

[34] M. Sommé, 'L'alimentation quotidienne à la cour de Bourgogne au XVe siècle', *Bulletin philologique et historique (jusqu'à 1610) du Comité des travaux historiques et scientifiques*, vol. i (1968; publ. 1971), pp. 103–17; idem, 'Les approvisionnements en vin de la cour de Bourgogne au XVe siècle sous Philippe le Bon', *RN*, vol. lxxix (1998), pp. 949–68; M.-T. Caron, 'Les choix de consommation d'un jeune prince à la cour de Philippe le Bon', in E. Rassart-Eeckhout et al. (eds.), *La vie matérielle au Moyen Âge* (Louvain-la-Neuve, 1997), pp. 51–64; idem, 'La noblesse en représentation: vêtements de parade', *PCEEB*, vol. xxxvii (1997), pp. 157–72; S. Jolivet, 'Se vêtir pour traiter: données économiques du costume de la cour de Bourgogne dans les négotiations d'Arras de 1435', *AB*, vol. lxix (1997), pp. 5–35; idem, 'La vie quotidienne à la cour de Bourgogne', *L'Histoire*, no. ccii (1998), pp. 70–4; M. Aymard and M. Romani (eds.), *La cour comme institution économique* (Paris, 1998); C. Niedermann, *Das*

visited the duke's court, and how were visitors received there?[35] How did the Burgundian court or its satellite households function on their travels in the ducal dominions and further afield?[36]

It is possible to detect at least three further tendencies in the historiography of the court since Professor Vaughan's study of the subject, all drawing on the remarkable body of archival material available to the Burgundian historian.[37]

Jagdwesen am Hofe Herzog Philipps des Guten von Burgund (Brussels, 1995); W. Paravicini, 'Alltag bei Hofe', in idem (ed.), *Alltag bei Hofe. 3. Symposium der residenzen-Kommission der Akademie der Wissenschaften in Göttingen* (Sigmaringen, 1995), pp. 9–30.

35 The most studied visitor is still Leo of Rozmital: A. van Crugten, 'Un voyageur de Bohème à la cour de Bourgogne', *Cahiers bruxellois*, vol. xxi (1976), pp. 60–8; J. Huesman, 'Über einige Aspekte des Aufenthaltes Leos von Rozmital am Hof Philipps des Guten von Burgund', *Stredocesky sbornik historicky*, vol. xxv (1999), pp. 49–61. See also the latter's 'Hospitality at the court of Philip the Good, Duke of Burgundy (c. 1435–1467)', D.Phil. thesis, Oxford (2001).

36 B. Schwineköper, 'Das "Große Fest" zu Freiburg (3.–8. Juli 1454)', *Festschrift Clemens Bauer* (Berlin, 1974), pp. 73–91; W. Paravicini, 'Charles le Téméraire à Tours', in M. Bourin (ed.), *Villes, bonnes villes, cités et capitales: mélanges offerts à Bernard Chevalier* (Tours, 1989), pp. 47–69; idem, 'Philippe le Bon en Allemagne (1454)', *RBPH*, vol. lxxv (1997), pp. 967–1018; P. Ehm, 'Der reisende Hof und die Gabe. Zur Geschenkpraxis Philipps des Guten auf seiner Reise 1454 in das Reich', in U.C. Ewert and S. Selzer (eds.), *Ordnungsformen des Hofes: Ergebnisse eines Forschungskolloquiums der Studienstiftung des Deutschen Volkes* (Residenzen-Kommission, Sonderheft 2) (Kiel, 1997), pp. 67–78; U.C. Ewert, 'Die Itinerare der burgundischen Herzöge aus dem Hause Valois. Eine empirische Untersuchung zum Zusammenhang zwischen Itinerarstruktur und Herrschaftserfolg im 14. und 15. Jahrhundert', doctoral thesis, Kiel (1998); M. Sommé, 'Vie itinérante et résidences d'Isabelle de Portugal, duchesse de Bourgogne (1430–1471)', *RN*, vol. xxix (1997), pp. 7–43.

37 For archival inventories which have appeared since 1971, see under the relevant rubric of the 'Bibliographie de Belgique' published in *RBPH*. Three volumes deserve particular mention: R.-H. Bautier, J. Sornay and F. Muret, *Les sources de l'histoire économique et sociale du Moyen Âge. Les états de la maison de Bourgogne, I. Archives des principautés territoriales. 2. Les principautés du Nord* (Paris, 1984); and *Archives centrales de l'état bourguignon (1384–1500). Archives des principautés territoriales 1. Les principautés du sud 2. Les principautés du nord (supplément), comtés de Hollande et Zélande et duché de Gueldre par Michel van Gent* (Paris, 2001); J. Rigault, *Guide des archives de la Côte d'Or* (Dijon, 1984). For a valuable discussion of the subject see W. Paravicini, 'L'embarras de richesse: comment rendre accessibles les archives financières de la maison de Bourgogne-Valois',

There has been continued interest in the structures of the court, its offices and the rewards associated with them, as evinced in the edition of household ordinances mentioned above and in other related research.[38] Some of the occupants of these offices have also been studied, either through biographies such as those discussed above, or through prosopographies which sometimes throw up rather different conclusions.[39] Among the latter we may cite the data assembled from the *escroes* which primarily concerns the household, along with work on the membership of the councils of Flanders and Holland, and on the personnel of the chancellery and the chancellors of Flanders, some of whom had their place at court.[40] Finally, the willingness of historians of the Burgundian

Bulletin de la Classe des lettres et des sciences morales et politiques de Belgique, 6th series, vol. vii (1996, publ. 1997), pp. 21–68. Useful observations on financial records may be found in E. Aerts, 'De inhoud der rekeningen van de Brabantse algemeen-ontvangerij (1430–40): moeilijkheden en mogelijkheden voor het historisch onderzoek', *Bijdragen tot de Geschiedenis*, vol. lxi (1978), pp. 13–95; U.C. Ewert, 'Langfristige Struktur und kurzfristige Dynamik: Ein Längsschnittuntersuchung der Einnahmen der burgundischen *recette générale de toutes les finances* (1383–1476)', in H. von Seggern and G. Fouquet (eds.), *Adel und Zahl* (Ubstadt-Weiher, 2000), pp. 165–196.
38 U. Schwarzkopf, *Die Rechnungslegen des Humbert de Plaine über die Jahre 1448 bis 1452. Eine Studie zur Amtsführung des burgundischen Maître de la Chambre aux Deniers* (Göttingen, 1970); idem, 'Zum höfischen Dienstrecht im 15. Jahrhundert: das Burgundische Beispiel', in *Festschrift für Hermann Heimpel zum 70. Geburtstag am 19. September 1971*, vol. ii (Göttingen, 1972), pp. 422–42; F. Cattez, 'Les chambellans au début du principat de Philippe le Bon', *Mémoire de maitrise*, Lille III (1992); M. Kintzinger, '*Physicien de Monseigneur de Bourgogne*. Leibärzte und Heilkunst am spätmittelalterlichen Fürstenhof', *Francia*, vol. xxvii/1 (2000), pp. 89–116; M. Sommé, 'Que représente un gage journalier de 3 sous pour l'officier d'un hôtel ducal à la cour de Bourgogne au XVe siècle?', in J.-P. Sosson (ed.), *Les niveaux de vie au Moyen Âge* (Louvain-la-Neuve, 1999), pp. 297–315.
39 Cf. M. Boone, 'Biografie en prosopografie, een tegenstelling? Een stand van zaken in het biografisch onderzoek over Pieter Lanchals (ca.1430/1440–1488): een bruggeling in dienst van de Bourgondische staat', *Millennium*, vol. vii (1993), pp. 4–13; H. de Ridder-Symoens, 'Prosopographical Research in the Low Countries concerning the Middle Ages and the Sixteenth Century', *Medieval Prosopography*, vol. xiv (1993), pp. 27–120.
40 J. Dumolyn, 'Het hogere personeel van de hertogen van Bourgondië in het graafschap Vlaanderen (1419–1477)', doctoral thesis, Ghent (2001); M. Damen, *De staat van dienst? De gewestelijke ambtenaren van Holland en*

30

court to embrace other methodologies is also found in the growing influence of sociological and anthropological approaches – two areas in which Huizinga proved to be a pioneer in Burgundian studies.[41] The Feast of the Pheasant and court banquets more generally have been investigated in detail since 1970.[42] Several of these studies have concentrated

---

Zeeland in de Bourgondische periode (1425–1482) (Hilversum, 2000); W. Paravicini, ' "Ordonnances de l'hôtel" und "Escroes des gaiges": Wege zu einer prosopographischen Erforschung des burgundischen Staats im fünfzehnten Jahrhundert', in *Medieval lives and the historian: studies in medieval prosopography* (Kalamazoo, 1986), pp. 243–66; P. Cockshaw, *Le personnel de la chancellerie de Bourgogne-Flandre sous les ducs de Bourgogne de la maison de Valois (1384–1477)* (Kortrijk-Heule, 1982) (data for a prosopographical study of the secretaries of the chancellery is also being assembled in a related project); M. Boone, 'Kanselier van Vlaanderen en Bourgondië (1385–1530)', in E. Aerts et al. (eds.), *De centrale overheidsinstellingen van de Habsburgse Nederlanden (1482–1795)* (Brussels, 1994), pp. 217–33. The existence of an important long-term prosopographical project, the *Prosopographia burgundica*, should also be mentioned here: see *Francia*, vol. xxiv/1 (1997), pp. 147–8.

[41] Philip the Good's reign was often the focal point of Huizinga's work on Burgundy: for a survey of recent work see E. Peters and W. Simons, 'The new Huizinga and the old Middle Ages', *Speculum*, vol. lxxiv (1999), pp. 587–620. The appearance of gender studies in the field of Burgundian studies is also worth noting: E. Bousmar, 'Een historisch-antropologische kijk op gender in de Bourgondische Nederlanden (15de eeuw)', *Verslagen van het RUG-Centrum voor Genderstudies*, vol. viii (1999), pp. 35–53; idem, 'La place des hommes et des femmes dans les fêtes de cour bourguignonnes (Philippe-le-Bon et Charles-le-Hardi)', *PCEEB*, vol. xxxiv (1994), pp. 123–43 (repr. in J.-M. Cauchies [ed.], *À la cour de bourgogne. Le duc, son entourage, son train* [Turnhout, 1998]); idem, 'Le "gender" dans les anciens Pays-Bas méridionaux. Entre Moyen Âge et Renaissance: un modèle de subordination tempérée par la subsidiarité. Vers une nouvelle lecture des faits', in *Women's studies. Bilan et perspectives de la recherche et de l'enseignement en Belgique* (Brussels, 1998), pp. 54–7; idem and M. Sommé, 'Femmes et espaces féminins à la cour de Bourgogne au temps d'Isabelle de Portugal (1430–1471)', in J. Hirschbiegel and W. Paravicini (eds.), *Das Frauenzimmer* (Stuttgart, 2000), pp. 47–78.

[42] A. Lafortune-Martel, *Fête noble en Bourgogne au XVe siècle: le Banquet du Faisan* (Paris, 1984); D. Quéruel, 'Des entremets aux intermèdes dans les banquets bourguignons', in *Banquets et manières de table au Moyen Âge* (Aix-en-Provence, 1996), pp. 141–57; M.-T. Caron, '17 février 1454: le Banquet du Faisan: fête de cour et stratégies de pouvoir', *RN*, vol. lxxviii (1996), pp. 269–88; idem and D. Clauzel (eds.), *Le Banquet du Faisan 1454: l'Occident face au défi de l'Empire ottoman* (Arras, 1997).

INTRODUCTION TO THE 2002 EDITION xxxi

on ceremonies, protocol and the role of ritual at court.[43] Even if it is no longer possible to simply affirm that the court of Philip the Good served as a model for those of later *Ancien Régime* Europe, it is clear that the Burgundian example, with its pronounced sense of hierarchy and marks of respect, prefigured the complex court society of the time of Louis XIV as studied by Norbert Elias.[44]

It would be impossible to leave the subject of the court without some comment on its role as a stimulus for creative activity, a matter which Professor Vaughan touches upon briefly in the present study. Georges Doutrepont's remarkable account of Burgundian court literature has not yet been surpassed, although aspects of his subjet have been explored in considerable detail:[45] we know more about some (but far from all) of the Burgundian court chroniclers, for instance,[46]

---

[43] P. Arnade, *Realms of ritual: Burgundian ceremony and civic life in late medieval Ghent* (Ithaca and London, 1996); J. Paviot, 'Les marques de distance dans les *Honneurs de la cour* d'Aliénor de Poitiers', in W. Paravicini (ed.), *Zeremoniell und Raum* (Sigmaringen, 1997), pp. 91–6; W. Paravicini, 'Zeremoniell und Raum', in ibid., pp. 11–36.
[44] W. Paravicini, 'The court of Burgundy – a model for Europe?', in R.G. Asch and A.M. Birks (eds.), *Princes, patronage and the nobility: the court at the beginning of the early modern age, c. 1450–1650* (Oxford, 1991), pp. 69–102; N. Elias, *The Court society*, trans. E. Jephcott (Oxford, 1983).
[45] G. Doutrepont, *La littérature française à la cour des ducs de Bourgogne* (Paris, 1909).
[46] On historians generally see M. Zingel, *Frankreich, das Reich und Burgund im Urteil der burgundischen Historiographie des 15. Jahrhunderts* (Sigmaringen, 1995). For individuals or particular works connected to Philip's reign see (with bibliographies) C. van den Bergen-Pantens (ed.), *Les Chroniques de Hainaut ou les ambitions d'un prince bourguignon* (Brussels, 2000); R. Stein, *Politiek en historiografie: het onstaansmilieu van Brabantse kronieken in de eerste helft van de 15de eeuw* (Leuven, 1994); D. Boucquey, 'Enguerran de Monstrelet, historien trop longtemps oublié', *PCEEB*, vol. xxxi (1991), pp. 113–25; G. Barner, 'Jacques du Clercq und seine *Mémoires*. Ein Sittengemälde des 15. Jahrhunderts', doctoral thesis, Düsseldorf (1989) (and see important comment by Nicole Pons in *Francia*, vol. xviii [1991], pp. 319–20); G. Halligan, 'La *Chronique* de Mathieu d'Escouchy', *Romania*, vol. xc (1969), pp. 100–10; J.-C. Delclos, 'Jean Lefèvre: l'une des sources du Livre II de Georges Chastellain', *Rencontres médiévales en Bourgogne (XIVe–XVe siècles)*, vol. i (1991), pp. 7–18; idem, *Le témoignage de Georges Chastellain* (Geneva, 1980); G. Small, *George Chastelain and the shaping of Valois Burgundy* (Woodbridge and Rochester, N.Y., 1997); C. Thiry, 'Ville en fête, ville en feu: présences de la ville dans les *Mémoires* de Jean de

and literary scholars and historians have worked on the prose
romances and other literary genres which the court is thought
to have enjoyed.[47] The cultivation of letters extended beyond
the duke, and some of Philip's servants have emerged as
significant patrons in their own right.[48] Recent work has
altered the all-too common perception – stemming from
Huizinga and Kilgour among others – that Burgundian court
culture was almost exclusively preoccupied with chivalric
values which had lost their relevance. The court is now
thought to have encouraged the development of political

Haynin', *RBPH* vol. lxxviii (2000), pp. 423–43; J. Blanchard, *Commynes
l'européen: l'invention du politique* (Geneva, 1996). The 2000 and 2002 conferences of the *CEEB* have considered aspects of Olivier de La Marche's
work (with relevant bibliographies), and Alistair Millar wrote a doctoral
thesis on the subject at the University of Edinburgh (1997). Livia
Visser-Fuchs is working on Jean de Wavrin.

[47] R. Morse, 'Historical fiction in fifteenth-century Burgundy', *Modern
Language Review*, vol. lxxv (1980), pp. 48–64; R. Stuip, 'Le public de
l'*Histoire des seigneurs de Gavre*', in K. Busby and E. Cooper (eds.), *Courtly
literature: culture and context* (Amsterdam and Philadelphia, 1990),
pp. 531–7; C. van den Bergen-Pantens, 'Traditions généalogiques et
héraldiques troyennes à la cour de Bourgogne', *Revue française d'héraldique
et de sigillographie*, vol. lx–lxi (1990–1), pp. 83–97; W. Keesman, 'Troje in
de middeleeuwse literatuur. Antiek verleiden in dienst van de eigen tijd',
Literatuur: Tijdschrift over Nederlandse letterkunde, vol. iv (1987), pp.
257–65; D. Quéruel (ed.), *Les manuscrits de David Aubert, 'escripvain' bourguignon* (Paris, 1999); R. Straub, *David Aubert, 'escripvain' et 'clerc'*
(Amsterdam, 1995); E. Gaucher, *La biographie chevaleresque: typologie d'un
genre (XIIIe–XVe siècle)* (Paris, 1994); idem, 'La confrontation de l'idéal
chevaleresque et de l'idéologie politique en Bourgogne au XVe siècle:
L'exemple de Jacques de Lalaing', *Rencontres Médiévales en Bourgogne
(XIVe–XVe siècles)*, vol. ii (1992), pp. 3–25. On the *Cent nouvelles nouvelles*
which Richard Vaughan comments on here, see J.B. Diner, 'The courtly
comic style of the *Cent nouvelles nouvelles*', *Romance Philology*, vol. lxviii
(1993), pp. 48–60 (with bibliography). Edgar de Blieck is writing a doctoral
thesis on the subject at Glasgow.

[48] See for instance A. Naber, 'Les manuscrits d'un bibliophile bourguignon
du XVe siècle, Jean de Wavrin', *RN*, vol. lxxii (1990), pp. 23–48; M. Gil,
'Le mécénat littéraire de Jean V de Créquy, conseiller et chambellan de
Philippe le Bon: exemple singulier de création et de diffusion d'oeuvres
nouvelles à la cour de Bourgogne', *Eulalie*, vol. i (1998), pp. 69–95; C. van
den Bergen-Pantens, 'Héraldique et bibliophilie: le cas d'Antoine Grand
Bâtard de Bourgogne (1421–1504)', in *Miscellanea Martin Wittek* (Leuven
and Paris, 1993), pp. 323–54.

thought and humanistic learning,[49] and most historians today would be less willing to accept the clear line which Doutrepont imagined there existed between court and civic culture in the Burgundian Netherlands under Philip the Good.[50] The court was of course a great centre for music and

[49] R. Bernard, 'The intellectual circle of Isabel of Portugal, duchess of Burgundy, and the Portuguese translation of *Le Livre des trois vertus*', in G.K. McLeod (ed.), *The reception of Christine de Pizan from the fifteenth through the nineteenth centuries: visitors to the city* (Lewiston, NY, 1991), pp. 43–58; C.C. Willard, 'The patronage of Isabel of Portugal', in J.H. McCash (ed.), *The cultural patronage of medieval women* (Athens, Georgia, 1996), pp. 306–20; C. van Leeuwen, *Denkbeelden van een vliesridder. De l'instruction d'un jeune prince van Guillebert van Lannoy* (Amsterdam, 1975); and a number of important works by Professor A. Vanderjagt, including: *"Qui sa vertu anoblist". The concepts of* noblesse *and* chose publicque *in Burgundian political thought* (Groningen, 1981); 'Burgundian political ideas between Laurentius Pignon and Guillaume Hugonet', *Fifteenth-Century Studies*, vol. ix (1984), pp. 197–213; *Laurens Pignon, O.P., confessor of Philip the Good. Ideas on jurisdiction and estates* (Venlo, 1985); 'Frans-Bourgondische geleerde politici in de vijftiende eeuw', *Theorestische Geschiedenis*, vol. xvi (1989), pp. 401–19; and 'Classical learning and the building of power at the fifteenth-century Burgundian court', in J.W. Drijvers and A.A. Macdonald (eds.), *Centres of learning: learning and location in pre-modern Europe and the Near East* (Leiden and New York, 1995), pp. 267–77. Aspects of the work of Pignon are also considered in J. Veenstra, *Magic and divination at the courts of Burgundy and France: text and contexts of Laurens Pignon's "Contre les devineurs" (1411)* (Leiden and New York, 1998).
[50] Cf. W. Prevenier 'Court and city culture in the Low Countries from 1100 to 1530', in E. Koopers (ed.), *Medieval Dutch Literature in its European Context* (Cambridge, 1994), 11–27; J. Koopmans, 'Rhétorique de cour et rhétorique de ville', in J. Koopmans et al. (eds.), *Rhetoric – Rhétoriqueurs – Rederijkers* (Amsterdam, 1995), pp. 67–81; R. van Uytven, 'Scènes de la vie sociale dans les villes des Pays-Bas du XIVe au XVIe siècle', in *Actes du Colloque sur la sociabilité urbaine en Europe du Nord-Ouest du XIVe au XVIIIe siècle, 5 février 1983* (Douai, 1983), pp. 11–31; A.-L. Van Bruaene, *De Gentse memorieboeken als spiegel van stedelijk historisch bewustzijn (14de tot 16de eeuw)* (Ghent, 1998); F. van Oostrom, *Court and culture: Dutch literature, 1350–1450* (Berkeley, Los Angeles and Oxford, 1992); H. Pleij, *Op belofte van profijt. Stadsliteratuur en burgermoraal in de Nederlandse letterkunde van de middeleeuwen* (Amsterdam, 1991); G. Small, 'Chroniqueurs et culture historique', in L. Nys and A. Salamagne (eds.), *Valenciennes aux XIVe et XVe siècles* (Valenciennes, 1996), pp. 271–96; idem, 'Les origines de la ville de Tournai dans les chroniques légendaires du bas Moyen Âge', in *Les grands siècles de Tournai (12e–15e siècles)* (Tournai–Louvain-la-Neuve, 1993), pp. 81–113.

art, although the many publications relating to these vast subjects cannot be treated in any detail here.[51] Beyond the court, the government of the ducal dominions has remained a popular topic for research. In a significant contribution to this subject Professor Jean-Marie Cauchies has described the reign of Philip the Good as one in which 'new institutional structures blossomed, exercising their authority throughout the Low Countries as a whole and heading up the instruments of authority and administration which already existed in the different Burgundian domin-ions.'[52] Among the mechanisms of government to have received close scrutiny since 1970 are the Great Council and the regional Council of Brabant.[53] Analysis of governmental

---

[51] See for instance L. Campbell, *The fifteenth-century Netherlandish schools* (London, 1998); B. Bousmanne, '*Item a Guillaume Wyelant aussi enlumineur*'. *Willem Vrelant. Un aspect de l'enluminure dans les Pays-Bas méridionaux sous le mécénat des ducs de Bourgogne Philippe le Bon et Charles le Téméraire* (Brussels and Turnhout, 1997); J.C. Smith, 'The artistic patronage of Philip the Good, Duke of Burgundy', doctoral thesis, Colum-bia (1979); idem, 'Portable propaganda: tapestries as princely metaphors at the courts of Philip the Good and Charles the Bold', *Art Journal*, vol. xxviii (1989), pp. 123–8; R. Eikelmann, 'Goldschmiedekunst am Hof der Herzöge von Burgund', in B. Franke and B. Welzel (eds.), *Die Kunst der burgundischen Niederlande: Eine Einführung* (Berlin, 1997), pp. 85–101; R. Strohm, *Music in late medieval Bruges* (Oxford, 1985); W. Edwards, 'Burgundian verse sung', *RBPH* vol. lxxviii (2000), pp. 339–58; R. Hoyoux, 'L'organisation musicale à la cour des ducs de Bourgogne', *PCEEB*, vol. xxv (1985), pp. 57–72.
[52] J.-M.Cauchies, 'Le droit et les institutions dans les anciens Pays-Bas sous Philippe le Bon (1419–1467). Essai de synthèse', *Cahiers de Clio*, no. 123 (1995), pp. 33–68, at p. 33 (my translation). Cf. R. Stein, 'Burgundian bureaucracy as a model for the Low Countries? The *Chambre des comptes* and the creation of an administrative unity', in *Powerbrokers in the late Middle Ages. The Burgundian Low Countries in a European context* (Turnhout, 2001), pp. 3–25.
[53] See generally J. van Rompaey, 'De Bourgondische staatsinstellingen', in *Algemene geschiedenis der Nederlanden*, vol. iv (Haarlem, 1981), pp. 136–55. On the Great Council see idem, 'Het onstaan van de Grote Raad onder Filips de Goede', *Handelingen van de Koninklijke Zuidnederlandse Maatschappij voor Taal – en Letterkunde en Geschiedenis*, vol. xxv (1971), pp. 297–310; idem, *De grote Raad van de hertogen van Boergondië en het Parlement van Mechelen* (Brussels, 1973). For Brabant see P. Godding, 'L'activité judiciaire du conseil de Brabant sous le règne de Philippe le Bon: premiers jalons de recherche en cours', *RN*, vol. liv (1972), pp. 107–8; idem, 'De opkomst van de Raad van Brabant (1427–72)', *Noordbrabants*

personnel includes a number of studies organised by region, profession or office.[54] Important questions have been posed concerning princely legislation, the process of political decision-taking, and the means and speed of communication within governmental circles.[55] The functioning of the estates

historisch jaarboek, vol. ii (1985), pp. 1–16; idem, *Le conseil de Brabant sous Philippe le Bon (1430–1467)* (Brussels, 1999).
54 In addition to studies of secretaries and chancellors of Flanders mentioned above, see W. Prevenier and B. Augustyn (eds.), *De gewestelijke en lokale overheidsinstellingen in Vlaanderen tot 1795* (Brussels, 1997); A. Smolar-Meynart, *La justice ducal du plat pays, des forêts et des chasses en Brabant (XIIe–XVIe siècles). Sénéchal, maître des bois, gruyer, grand veneur* (Brussels, 1991); J. Bovesse, 'Le personnel administratif du Comté de Namur au bas Moyen Âge: aperçu général', *Revue de l'Université de Brussels*, mai–juillet 1970, pp. 432–57; G. Baurin, *Les gouverneurs du comté de Namur de 1430 à 1794* (Brussels, 1984); H.J.P. Jansen, 'Modernization of government: the advent of Philip the Good in Holland', *Bijdragen en mededelingen betreffende de Geschiedenis der Nederlanden*, vol. xcv (1980), pp. 254–64; W. Blockmans, 'Privaat en openbaar domein. Hollandse ambtenaren voor de rechter onder de Bourgondiërs', in J.-M. Duvosquel and E. Thoen (eds.), *Peasants and townsmen in medieval Europe. Studia in honorem Adriaan Verhulst* (Gand, 1995), pp. 707–19; M. Damen, 'De Raad volgens Rosa. De vorming en samenstelling van de Raad van Holland en Zeeland (1428–1447)', in R. Huijbrecht (ed.), *Handelingen van het eerste Hof van Holland Symposium gehouden op 24 mei 1996 in het Algemeen Rijksarchief te Den Haag* (The Hague, 1997), pp. 29–41; P. Spufford, 'The general officers of the Burgundian mints in the Netherlands in the fifteenth century', *Jaarboek voor Munt- en Peningkunde*, vol. 65–6 (1978–9), pp. 5–14; J.-M. Cauchies, 'L'intérêt des comptes des officiers de justice pour l'étude de la législation monétaire: l'exemple du Hainaut sous la régence de Philippe le Bon', *Bulletin du Cercle d'études numismatiques*, vol. x (1973), pp. 46–58; idem, 'Un officier comtal hainuyer mal connu: le prévôt forain du Quesnoy (deuxième quart du XVe siècle)', in J.-M. Duvosquel and A. Dierkens (eds.), *Villes et campagnes au Moyen Âge. Mélanges Georges Despy* (Liège, 1991), pp. 143–57; M. Jollant, 'Philippe le Bon et les officiers ducaux', *AB*, vol. lv (1983), pp. 137–9; M. Boone, 'De soeverein-baljuw van Vlaanderen: breekijzer in het conflict tussen stedelijk particularisme en Bourgondische centralisatie', *Handelingen van de 'Société d'émulation' te Brugge*, vol. cxxvi, 1989, pp. 57–78; idem, 'Les juristes et la construction de l'Etat bourguignon aux Pays-Bas. Etat de la question, pistes de recherches', in J.-M. Duvosquel et al. (eds.), *Les Pays-Bas bourguignons. Histoire et Institutions. Mélanges André Uyttebrouck* (Brussels, 1996), pp. 105–120; idem and J. Dumolyn, 'Les officiers-créditeurs des ducs de Bourgogne dans l'ancien comté de Flandre: aspects financiers, politiques et sociaux', *PCEEB*, vol. xxxix (1999), pp. 225–41. There is also interesting and relevant comment in Stein (ed.), *Powerbrokers in the late Middle Ages*.
55 J.-M. Cauchies, *La législation princière pour le comté de Hainaut. Ducs de*

is now better understood, at the regional level – the representative assemblies of Flanders, Hainaut or Burgundy, for
example – or on the level of the estates-general, the origins of
which lie in the reign of Philip the Good.⁵⁶ A series of studies
on corruption, patronage and bribes reminds us that the political process often worked through informal channels in the

Bourgogne et premiers Habsbourg (1427–1506) (Brussels, 1982); idem, 'La
législation dans les Pays-Bas bourguignons: état de la question et perspectives de recherches', *Tijdschrift voor rechtsgeschiedenis*, vol. lxi (1993), pp.
375–86; P. Godding, 'Lettres de justice, instrument du pouvoir central en
Brabant', in *Miscellanea Roger Petit (Archives et bibliothèques de Belgique*,
vol. lxi [1990], pp. 293–564), pp. 385–402; J.-M. Cauchies and H. de
Schepper, *Justice, grâce et législation. Genèse de l'état et moyens juridiques
dans les Pays-Bas (1200–1600)* (Brussels, 1994: *Cahiers du Centre de recherche en histoire du droit et des institutions*, no. 2). See also idem, 'Le processus
de la décision politique à travers quelques actes des ducs de Bourgogne
(1427–1472)', *PCEEB*, vol. xxiv (1984), pp. 33–42; idem, 'Indices de
gestion, formules de décision. Les mentions de service dans les actes
princiers pour les Pays-Bas au XVe siècle', in *Décisions et gestion. Septièmes
rencontres, 26 et 27 novembre 1998* (Toulouse, 1999), pp. 15–24; idem (ed.),
Les ordonnances de Jean sans Peur (1405–19) (Brussels, 2001) (including
ordonnances for Philip's time as count of Charolais); idem, 'La terminologie
dans les ordonnances des ducs de Bourgogne', *RBPH*, vol. liii (1975), pp.
401–18; idem, 'Messageries et messages en Hainaut au XVe siècle', *MA*
(1976), pp. 301–41; T. Kanao, 'L'organisation et l'enregistrement des
messageries du duc de Bourgogne dans les années 1420', *RN*, vol. lxxvi
(1994), pp. 275–98; idem, 'Les messagers du duc de Bourgogne au début du
XVe siècle', *Journal of Medieval History*, vol. xxi (1995), pp. 195–226;
J. Richard, 'La Lorraine et les liaisons internes de l'État bourguignon', *Le
pays lorrain*, vol. lviii (1977), pp. 113–22; A. Dubois, 'Techniques et coûts
de transport terrestres dans l'espace bourguignon aux XIVe et XVe siècle',
AB, vol. lii (1980), pp. 65–82. On monetary matters, one of the areas in
which one may speak of general ducal legislation evolving under the third
duke, see P. Spufford, *Monetary problems and policies in the Burgundian
Netherlands, 1433–1496* (Leiden, 1970).
⁵⁶ R. Wellens, *Les états généraux des Pays-Bas des origines à la fin du règne
de Philippe le Beau (1464–1506)* (Heule, 1974); idem, 'Les états et
l'accession de Philippe le Bon au gouvernement du comté de Hainaut', in
Recueil d'études d'histoire hainuyère offertes à Maurice A. Arnould, vol. ii
(Mons, 1982), pp. 101–8; W. Blockmans, *De volksvertegenwoordiging in
Vlaanderen in de overgang van Middeleeuwen naar Nieuwe Tijden, 1384–1506*
(Brussels, 1978); idem, 'Flemings on the move. A profile of representatives,
1384–1504', in idem, M. Boone and T. de Hemptinne (eds.), *Secretum
scriptorum. Liber alumnorum Walter Prevenier* (Leuven and Apeldoorn,
1999), pp. 307–26; J. Richard, 'Les états de Bourgogne dans la politique des
ducs Valois', *PCEEB*, vol. xxiv (1984), pp. 11–15.

Burgundian Netherlands, and that in political history, the study of institutions is but part of a wider picture.[57] Last but not least under the heading of government, there has been a large number of studies devoted to ducal finances under Philip the Good – an understandable development given the relevance of the matter to the duke's role in the formation of a Burgundian state.[58] Professor Vaughan considered the healthy finances which Philip left to his son as one of the few undisputable achievements of his reign. The duke's

[57] A. Derville, 'Pots-de-vin, cadeaux, racket, patronage. Essai sur les mécanismes de décision dans l'État bourguignon', *RN*, vol. lvi (1974), pp. 341–64; W. Blockmans, 'Corruptie, patronage, makelardij en venaliteit als symptomen van een ontluikende staatsvorming in de Bourgondisch-Habsburgse Nederlanden', *Tijdschrift voor sociale geschiedenis*, vol. xi (1985), pp. 231–47 (for an English version, see 'Patronage, brokerage and corruption as symptoms of incipient state formation in the Burgundian-Habsburg Netherlands', in A. Maczak and E. Müller-Luckner [eds.], *Klientelsysteme im Europa der frühen Neuzeit* [Munich, 1988], pp. 117–126); M. Boone, 'Dons et pots-de-vin, aspects de la sociabilité urbaine au bas Moyen Âge. Le cas gantois pendant la période bourguignonne', *RN*, vol. lxx (1988), pp. 471–87. On other aspects of the phenomenon see W. Paravicini, 'Invitations au mariage, pratique sociale, abus de pouvoir, intérêt de l'État à la cour des ducs de Bourgogne au XVe siècle', *Comptes-rendus des séances de l'Académie des inscriptions et belles-lettres*, 1995, pp. 687–711.
[58] M.-A. Arnould, 'Une estimation des revenus et des dépenses de Philippe le Bon en 1445', *Acta historica Bruxellensia. Recherches sur l'histoire des finances publiques en Belgique*, vol. iii (1973), pp. 131–219; D. Deneuville, 'Quelques aspects des finances bourguignonnes en 1437', *RN*, vol. lxi (1979), pp. 571–9; Y. Coutiez, 'La part du comté de Hainaut dans les resources financières de Philippe le Bon', *Mémoires et publications de la Société des sciences, des arts et des lettres du Hainaut*, vol. xci (1980), pp. 105–38; F. Desbarbieux, 'L'administration des finances en Flandre sous Philippe le Bon', *Mémoire de maîtrise*, Lille III (1985); J. Sornay, 'Les états prévisionnels des finances ducales au temps de Philippe le Bon', in *109e congrès des sociétés savantes, Dijon 1984. Histoire médiévale*, vol. ii (Paris, 1986), pp. 35–94; A. Derville, *Enquêtes fiscales de la Flandre wallonne, 1449–1549, 1. L'Enquête de 1449* (Lille, 1983); H. Kruse, 'Les malversations commises par le receveur général Martin Cornille à la cour de Philippe le Bon d'après l'enquête de 1449', *RN*, vol. lxxvii (1995), pp. 283–312. More generally see also W. Blockmans, 'Finances publiques et inégalité sociale dans les Pays-Bas aux XIVe–XVIe siècles', in J.-P. Genet and M. Mené (eds.), *Genèse de l'état moderne: prélèvement et distribution* (Paris, 1987), pp. 77–90; M. Boone, 'Overheidsfinanciën in de Middeleeuwse Zuidelijke Nederlanden', *Tijdschrift voor fiscaal recht*, no. cxvii (1993), pp. 105–15.

wealth can be explained in two manners: the relative prosperity of many of his lands at a time when the economies of
much of Western Europe were in contraction; and the ability
of central authority to extract an increasing proportion of its
subjects' revenues through domain rights, indirect taxation
and the like.[59] The first of these explanations was considered
in a famous article by Raymond Van Uytven on the 'Promised
Lands' of Philip the Good a few years before Professor
Vaughan's work. A rich synthesis of research in this field was
recently produced by Professors Prevenier and Blockmans.[60]
However, if the Valois regime under Philip did indeed benefit
from a favourable set of economic circumstances, it remains
the case that he and his collaborators were able to exploit
them. The reign of Philip the Good has been described by
Maurice Arnould as one in which permanent taxation was
established, for example – a crucial step in the firming-up of
state power in the Low Countries. The study of 'aides'
('beden') voted by representative assemblies is important in
this respect, as exemplified by recent work on Flanders and
Holland.[61] There have also been several studies of municipal
finances,[62] a good number of which have emphasised financial

[59] E. van Cauwenberghe, *Het vorstelijk domein en de overheidsfinanciën in de Nederlanden, 15de–16de eeuw* (Brussels, 1982).
[60] W. Blockmans and W. Prevenier, *The promised lands: the Low Countries under Burgundian rule, 1369–1530*, trans. E. Fackelman, ed. E. Peters (Philadelphia, 1999).
[61] A. Zoete, *De organisatie en betekenis van de beden in het graafschap Vlaanderen onder de hertogen Jan zonder Vrees en Filips de Goede (1405–1467)* (Brussels, 1994); J.A.M.Y. Bos-Rops, 'Van incidentele gunst tot jaarlijkse belasting: de bede in het vijftiende-eeuwse Holland', in J. de Smidt (ed.) *Fiscaliteit in Nederland* (Zutphen and Deventer, 1987), pp. 21–32.
[62] C. Dickstein-Bernard, *La gestion financière d'une capitale à ses débuts: Brussels, 1334–1467* (Brussels, 1977: *Annales de la Société royale d'archéologie de Bruxelles*, vol. liv); J.W. Marsilje, *Het financiële beleid van Leiden in de laat-Beierse en Bourgondische periode, c. 1390–1477* (Hilversum, 1985); C. Pétillon, 'Les finances de Saint-Omer dans la première moitié du XVe siècle (1417–1446)', *Mémoire de maîtrise*, Lille III (1988); W. Mertens, 'Financieel beheer en economische politiek te Mechelen tussen 1439 en 1490', *Handelingen van de Koninklijke Kring voor oudheidkunde, letteren en kunst van Mechelen*, vol. xc (1986), pp. 129–76; M. Boone, 'Stratégies fiscales et financières des élites urbaines et l'État bourguignon naissant dans l'ancien comté de Flandre (XIVe–XVIe siècle)', in *L'argent au Moyen Âge*.

relations between city and state in particular.[63] Scholars have not always agreed on the intensity or the consequences of the fiscal pressure exerted by ducal government on the towns.[64] However, it does seem to be generally accepted that this same pressure contributed to the formation of the Burgundian state, and that the reign of Philip the Good, especially after the Treaty of Arras, represented a key phase in that process.[65] The study of Philip the Good's dominions has continued to develop along regional lines, with important source editions and valuable surveys appearing for the counties of Flanders, Hainaut, Namur and Holland since the completion of Professor Vaughan's monograph.[66] However, given the densely

---

28e congrès de la Société des historiens médiévistes de l'enseignement supérieur public (Paris, 1998), pp. 235–53.

[63] L. Coulon, 'Un emprunt forcé à Arras en 1433', RN, vol. lxix (1998), pp. 939–48; M. van Gent, 'The dukes of Burgundy and Dordrecht: a financial account of their relationship from 1435 to 1482', PCEEB, vol. xxii (1993), pp. 61–74; J. Paviot, 'Tournai dans l'histoire bourguignonne', in Les grands siècles de Tournai (12e–15e siècles) (Tournai, 1993), pp. 59–80; G. Small, 'Centre and periphery in later medieval France: Tournai, 1384–1477', in C.T. Allmand (ed.), War, government and power in late medieval France (Liverpool, 2000), pp. 145–74.

[64] Cf. D. Clauzel, Finances et politique à Lille pendant la période bourguignonne (Dunkerque, 1982); A. Derville, 'La fiscalité d'État dans l'Artois et la Flandre wallonne avant 1569', RN, vol. lxxiv (1992), pp. 25–32; and D. Clauzel again, 'Le roi, le prince et la ville: l'enjeu des réformes financières à Lille à la fin du Moyen Âge', PCEEB, vol. xxxiii (1993), pp. 75–90.

[65] M. Boone, Geld en macht. De Gentse stadsfinanciën en de Bourgondische staatsvorming (1384–1453) (Ghent, 1990).

[66] For Flanders see in particular the rich material of W. Blockmans, Handelingen van de Leden en van de Staten van Vlaanderen (1419–1467), I: tot de onderwerping van Brugge (4 maart 1438); II (Vanaf de onderwerping van Brugge (4 maart 1438) (Brussels, 1990–5); D. Nicholas, Medieval Flanders (London and New York, 1992); M. Haegeman, De anglofilie in het graafschap Vlaanderen tussen 1379 en 1435: politieke en economische aspecten (Kortrijk-Heule, 1988). For Hainaut sources see J.-M. Cauchies, 'Liste chronologique provisoire des ordonnances de Philippe le Bon, duc de Bourgogne, pour le comté de Hainaut, 1425–1467', Bulletin de la Commission royale des anciennes lois et ordonnances de la Belgique, vol. xxvi (1973–4), pp. 35–146. Studies include G. Sivery, 'L'entrée du Hainaut dans la principauté bourguignonne', RN, vol. lvi (1974); idem, 'La fin de la Guerre de cent ans et les malheurs du Hainaut', Revue d'histoire économique et sociale, vol. lii (1974), pp. 312–38. For other principalities see H. Douxchamps, 'La vente du comté de Namur à Philippe le Bon (16

urbanised nature of the Burgundian Low Countries it is
perhaps not surprising that the history of the towns and cities
has tended to dominate recent research.[67] Considerable attention has been paid to municipal government and urban institutions, and to the composition and conduct of urban elites –

janvier 1421)', *Annales de la Société archéologique de Namur*, vol. lxv (1987),
pp. 119–75; C. Douxchamps-Lefèvre, 'L'organisation politique du comté
de Namur sous les ducs de Bourgogne', in *Recht en instellingen in de oude
Nederlanden tijdens de Middeleeuwen en de Nieuwe tijd. Liber amicorum Jan
Buntinx* (Leuven, 1981), pp. 199–210; R. Fietier (dir.), *Histoire de la
Franche-Comté* (Toulouse, 1977); P. Gresser, *La Franche-Comté au temps de
la Guerre de Cent ans* (Besançon, 1989); idem, *Le crépuscule du Moyen Âge
en Franche-Comté* (Besançon, 1992); J. Richard, 'Les pays bourguignons
méridionaux dans l'ensemble des États des ducs valois', *Bijdragen en
Mededelingen voor de Geschiedenis der Nederlanden*, vol. xcv (1980), pp.
335–48; A. Jongkees, 'La Hollande bourguignonne: son intérêt pour les
ducs Valois', *PCEEBM*, vol. xviii (1977), pp. 65–75; J.G. Smit, *Vorst en
Onderdaan. Studies over Holland en Zeeland in de late Middeleeuwen*
(Leuven, 1995); K. Spading, *Holland und die Hanse im 15. Jahrhundert*
(Weimar, 1973); M.J. van Gent, *"Pertijelike saken": Hoeken en Kabeljauwen
in het Bourgondisch-Oostenrijkse tijdperk* (The Hague, 1994); D. Seifert,
Kompagnons und Konkurrenten: Holland und die Hanse im späten Mittelalter
(Cologne and Vienna, 1997). For a wide-ranging social history that concentrates on the south-eastern area of Holland, see P. Hoppenbrouwers, *Een
middeleeuwse samenleving. Het Land van Heusden (ca. 1360–1515)*
(Wageningen, 1992).
[67] For a valuable survey of themes see W. Prevenier and M. Boone, 'Les
villes des Pays-Bas méridionaux au bas Moyen Âge: identité urbaine et
solidarités corporatives', *Bulletin trimestriel du Crédit communal de Belgique*,
no. 183 (1993/1), pp. 25–42. Broader studies which touch on Philip's period
include W. Prevenier, 'La démographie des villes du comté de Flandre aux
XIVe et XVe siècles', *RN*, vol. lxv (1983), pp. 255–75; M. Boone and W.
Prevenier, '1300–1500: the "city-state" dream', in J. Decavele (ed.), *Ghent:
in defence of a rebellious city* (Antwerp, 1989), pp. 81–104; M. Boone, *Gent
en de bourgondische hertogen, ca. 1384–ca. 1453* (Brussels, 1990); Y.-M.
Hilaire et al., *Histoire d'Arras* (Dunkerque, 1988); M. Martens (ed.),
Histoire de Bruxelles (Toulouse, 1976); J. Stenghers (ed.), *Brussel, groie van
een hoofdstad* (Antwerp, 1979); H. Platelle (dir.), *Histoire de Valenciennes*
(Lille, 1982); L. Nys and A. Salamagne (eds.), *Valenciennes aux XIVe et
XVe siècles* (Valenciennes, 1996); H. Servant, *Artistes et gens de lettres à
Valenciennes à la fin du Moyen Âge (vers 1440–1507)* (Paris, 1998); L.
Trénard (dir.), *Histoire de Lille* (Lille, 1970); M. Rouche (dir.), *Histoire de
Douai* (Dunkerque, 1985); J.A. van Houtte, *De geschiedenis van Brugge*
(Tielt, 1982); V. Vermeersch (ed.), *Bruges and Europe* (Anvers, 1993); W.
Tyler, *Dijon and the Valois dukes of Burgundy* (Norman, Oklahoma, 1971);
R. van Uytven, *Leuven, de beste stad van Brabant. I: De geschiedenis van het
stadsgewest Leuven tot omstreeks 1600* (Leuven, 1980).

or, to use a possibly more appropriate term, urban groups in power.[68] Relations between cities, as well as the network of smaller urban communities, have been studied too.[69] It would be no exaggeration to say that relations between cities and the state in the Burgundian Netherlands have come under the greatest scrutiny since Professor Vaughan's work appeared – indeed, this may even be the most extensively worked field in the political history of Philip's reign.[70] Since Henri Pirenne

---

[68] H. Brand, *Over macht en overwicht. Stedelijke elites in Leiden (1420–1510)* (Leuven and Apeldoorn, 1996); idem, 'Urban elites and central government: co-operation or antagonism? The case of Leiden at the close of the Middle Ages', *PCEEB*, vol. xxxiii (1993), pp. 49–60; idem, 'Les élites de Leyde et leurs famille à la fin du Moyen Âge', *RH*, vol. cccv (2001), pp. 603–37; D. Clauzel, 'Le renouvellement de l'échevinage à la fin du Moyen Âge: l'exemple de Lille', *RN*, vol. lxxvii (1995), pp. 365–85; idem, 'Les élites urbaines et le pouvoir municipal: le "cas" de la bonne ville de Lille aux XIVe et XVe siècles', *RN*, vol. lxxviii (1996), pp. 241–67; A. Derville, 'Les échevinages de Lille et de Saint-Omer: étude comparée', in *Actes du 1er congrès de l'Association des cercles francophones d'histoire et d'archéologie de Belgique* (Comines, 1980), pp. 33–44; idem, 'Les échevins de Douai (1228–1527)', *Mémoires de la Société centrale d'agriculture, sciences et arts du Département du Nord*, 5th ser., vol. viii (1984), pp. 39–48; idem, 'Les élites urbaines en Flandre et en Artois', in *Les élites urbaines au Moyen Âge. 27e congrès de la Société des historiens médiévistes de l'enseignement supérieur public* (Paris, 1997), pp. 9–27; C. Joly, 'Dijon sous le principat de Philippe le Bon: une singulière coutume électorale', *AB*, vol. liii (1981), pp. 113–5; C. Pauwelyn, 'Lijsten van de gegoede burgers van Kortrijk en de struktur van hun vermogens in 1440 en 1447', *Standen en Landen*, vol. lxiii (1973), pp. 9–45. See also P. Arnade, 'Urban elites and the politics of public culture in the late-medieval Low Countries', in M. Carlier, A. Greve, W. Prevenier and P. Stabel (eds.), *Core and periphery in late medieval urban society* (Leuven-Apeldoorn, 1997), pp. 33–50; and J. Baerten, 'De politieke evolutie te Brussel in de 15de eeuw', *Tijdschrift voor Brusselse geschiedenis*, vol. ii (1985), pp. 111–22.

[69] W. Prevenier, J.-P. Sosson and M. Boone, 'Le réseau urbain en Flandre (XIIIe–XIXe siècle): composantes et dynamique', in *Le réseau urbain en Belgique dans une perspective historique (1350–1850). Une approche statistique et dynamique (15de Internationaal Colloquium, Spa, 4–6 september 1990)* (Brussels, 1992), pp. 157–200; P. Stabel, *De kleine stad in Vlaanderen (14de–16de eeuw)* (Brussels, 1995); idem, *Dwarfs among giants: the Flemish urban network in the late Middle Ages* (Leuven-Apeldoorn, 1997).

[70] See for example A. Leguai, 'Relations between the towns of Burgundy and the French crown in the fifteenth century', in J. Highfield and R. Jeffs (eds.), *Crown and local communities in the fifteenth century* (Gloucester, 1981); idem, 'Les ducs valois et les villes du duché de Bourgogne', *PCEEB*, vol. xxii (1993), pp. 21–33; P. Godding, 'Le Conseil de Brabant au XVe

historians have often insisted on the conflictual nature of relations between city and state in the Burgundian Netherlands
in Philip's reign, and this dimension has not been neglected:
there are now valuable studies of the Bruges revolt, of the
important episode of the Ghent war and the campaigns
against Liège towards the end of the reign.[71] However, there
has also been a legitimate emphasis on cooperation between
'calculating townsmen' and 'conquering princes' in the era of
Philip the Good, and upon the related 'contribution of urban
networks to the process of state formation'.[72] In this context it

siècle, instrument de pouvoir ducal à l'égard des villes?', in Duvosquel and
Dierkens (eds.), *Mélanges Georges Despy*, pp. 335–54; A. Uyttebrouck, 'Le
rôle politique des villes brabançonnes au bas Moyen Âge', *Bulletin
trimestriel du Crédit communal de Belgique*, no. 116 (1976), pp. 115–30.

[71] For revolts in general see W. Blockmans, 'La repression des révoltes
urbaines comme méthode de centralisation dans les Pays-Bas
bourguignons', *PCEEB*, vol. xxviii (1988), pp. 5–20; and M. Boone, 'Destroying and reconstructing the city: the inculcation and arrogation of
princely power in the Burgundian-Habsburg Netherlands (14th–16th centuries)', in M. Gosman et al. (eds.), *The propagation of power in the medieval
west* (Groningen, 1998), pp. 1–33. For Bruges, see J. Dumolyn, *De Brugse
opstand van 1436–38* (Kortrijk - Heule, 1997). For the other episodes see M.
Boone, 'Diplomatie et violence d'état: la sentence rendue par les
ambassadeurs et conseillers du roi de France, Charles VII, concernant le
conflit entre Philippe le Bon, duc de Bourgogne, et Gand en 1452', *Bulletin
de la Commission royale d'histoire*, vol. clvi (1990), pp. 1–54; M. Populer, 'Le
conflit de 1447 à 1453 entre Gand et Philippe le Bon: propagande et
historiographie', *Handelingen der Maatschappij voor geschiedenis en
oudheidkunde te Gent*, vol. xliv (1990), pp. 99–123; P. Arnade, 'Crowds,
banners and the marketplace: symbols of defiance and defeat during the
Ghent war of 1452–3', *Journal of Medieval and Renaissance History*, vol.
xxiv (1994), pp. 471–97; P. Harsin, 'Liège entre France et Bourgogne au
XVe siècle', in *Liège et Bourgogne* (Paris, 1972: *Bibliothèque de la Faculté de
philosophie et lettres de l'Université de Liège*, no. 203), pp. 193–256; J.-P.
Peters, 'De militaire-strategische situatie van de steden en vrijheden in
Oost-Brabant in de invloed van het konflict Luik-Bourgondië tijdens de
jaaren 1465–8', *Eigen Schoon en de Brabander*, vol. lix (1976), pp. 269–90.
[72] W. Blockmans, 'Princes conquérants et bourgeois calculateurs: le poids
des réseaux urbains dans la formation des états', in N. Bulst and J. Genet
(eds.), *La ville, la bourgeoisie et la genèse de l'état moderne (XIIe–XVIIIe
siècles)* (Paris, 1988), pp. 167–81 (my translation). For an example of townsmen who found their way into ducal service see M. Boone, 'De la ville à
l'état: les Tolvins, clercs de la ville de Gand, serviteurs des ducs de
Bourgogne', in Blockmans, Boone and de Hemptinne (eds.), *Secretum
scriptorum*, pp. 327–50.

is worth noting the fecundity of the concept of a Burgundian 'theatre state', a term borrowed from the work of the anthropologist Clifford Geertz as a means of characterising the role of ceremony in relations between the prince and urban groups in power.[73] In fewer than twenty years the number of studies devoted to princely entries under Philip the Good,[74] and even to the Ghent entry of 1458 alone, has been remarkable.[75] We now have detailed studies of particular aspects of such ceremonies, including the use of light and sound, street decorations and the role of dramatic and para-dramatic representations.[76] Urban jousts and processions have also received close

---

73 Blockmans and Prevenier, *The Burgundian Netherlands*, p. 223. For an effective survey of the literature see Arnade, *Realms of Ritual*.
74 J. Hurlbut, 'Ceremonial entries in Burgundy: Philip the Good and Charles the Bold (1419–1477)', doctoral thesis, Indiana (1990) (a revised version of this thesis is to be published by Brepols); D. Nicholas, 'In the pit of the Burgundian theater state', in B. Hanawalt and K. Reyerson (eds.), *City and spectacle in medieval Europe* (Minneapolis–London, 1992), pp. 271–95; J. Murray, 'The liturgy of the count's advent in Bruges, from Galbert to Van Eyck', in ibid, pp. 137–52; G. Kipling, *Enter the king: theatre, liturgy and ritual in the medieval civic triumph* (Oxford, 1998); N. Mosselmans, 'Les villes face au prince: l'importance réelle de la cérémonie d'entrée solennelle sous le règne de Philippe le Bon', in *Mélanges Georges Despy*, pp. 533–48; M. Populer, 'Les entrées inaugurales des princes dans les villes. Usages et significations. L'exemple des trois comtés de Hainaut, Hollande et Zélande entre 1417 et 1433', *RN*, vol. lxxvi (1994), pp. 25–52, M. Mestayer, 'Les fêtes et cérémonies à Douai, 1450–1550', *Mémoires de la Société d'agriculture, sciences et arts de Douai*, 5th series, vol. viii (1980–2), pp. 103–10. The 1992 Lausanne meeting of the *CEEB* was given over to the theme of *Fêtes et cérémonies aux XIVe et XVe siècles* (*PCEEB*, vol. xxxiv [1993]).
75 Detailed comment in Arnade, *Realms of ritual* and Hurlbut, 'Ceremonial entries', plus: J.C. Smith, '*Venit nobis pacificus Dominus*: Philip the Good's triumphal entry into Ghent in 1458', in B. Wisch and S. Munshower (eds.), *'All the world's a stage . . .': art and pageantry in the Renaissance and Baroque, I* (Pennsylvania, 1990), pp. 259–90; B. Ramakers, '13 April 1458: De blijde inkomst van Filips de Goede in Gent. De theatrale versiering van vorstelijke intochten', in R. Erenstein (ed.), *Een theatergeschiedenis der Nederlanden. Tien eeuwen drama en theater in Nederland en Vlaanderen* (Amsterdam, 1996); E. Dhanens, 'De blijde inkomst van Filips de Goede in 1458 en de plastische kunsten te Gent', *Mededelingen van de Koninklijke Academie van Wetenschappen, Letteren en Schonen Kunsten van België*, vol. xlviii (1987), pp. 53–8.
76 E. Lecuppre-Desjardin, 'Les lumières de la ville: recherche sur l'utilisation de la lumière dans les cérémonies bourguignonnes (XIVe–XVe

attention.[77] Ceremony can no longer be seen as a mere auxiliary of the political process; rather, it was an integral part of relations between city and state, capable of modifying conduct and the course of events and, in doing so, of contributing to the formation of a Burgundian state.[78]

Within the boundaries of his dominions and beyond, Philip the Good's actions were determined in large part by his continuing status as a peer of the French realm; by his increasing presence as a prince of the Empire; and by his standing as the Christian prince most consistently associated with the Crusade in the middle years of the fifteenth century. All three areas of the reign have received scholarly attention since the publication of *Philip the Good*.

A number of biographies of Philip's French royal contemporaries consider the duke's role within the kingdom to some extent.[79] The period of the reign which has attracted the

siècles)', *RH*, vol. ccci (1999), pp. 23–43; idem, 'Un modèle de scénographie urbaine: l'exemple des Pays-Bas bourguignons au XVe siècle', *RN*, vol. lxxxi (1999), pp. 679–88; M. Clouzot, 'Le son et le pouvoir en Bourgogne au XVe siècle', *RH*, vol. cccii (2000), pp. 615–28; J. Hurlbut, 'The city renewed: decorations for the "Joyeuses entrées" of Philip the Good and Charles the Bold', *Fifteenth-century studies*, vol. xix (1992), pp. 73–84; D. Eichberger, 'The *tableau vivant*: an ephemeral art form in Burgundian festivities', *Parergon*, vol. vi (1988), pp. 37–64; B. Ramakers, *Spelen en figuren. Toneelkunst en processiecultuur in Oudenaarde tussen Middeleeuwen en Moderne Tijd* (Amsterdam, 1996); G. Nijsten, 'Toneel in de stad. Op zoek naar culturele uitingsvormen van stedelijk bewustzijn in de Noordelijke Nederlanden', in Carlier et al. (eds.), *Core and periphery*, pp. 105–30.

[77] E. van den Neste, *Tournois, joutes, pas d'armes dans les villes de Flandre à la fin du Moyen Âge (1300–1486)* (Paris, 1996); A. Brown, 'Civic ritual: Bruges and the counts of Flanders in the later Middle Ages', *English Historical Review*, vol. cxii (1997), pp. 277–99; idem, 'Bruges and the Burgundian theatre state: Charles the Bold and Our Lady of the Snow', *History*, vol. lxxxiv (1999), pp. 573–89; idem, 'Urban jousts in the later Middle Ages: the White Bear of Bruges', *RBPH* (2000), pp. 315–30.

[78] Cf. W. Blockmans and E. Donckers, 'Self-representation of court and city in Flanders and Brabant in the fifteenth and early sixteenth centuries', in Blockmans and Janse (eds.), *Showing status*, pp. 81–111.

[79] J. Ehlers, H. Müller and B. Schneidmüller (eds.), *Die französischen Könige des Mittelalters von Odo bis Karl VIII, 888–1498* (Munich, 1996); F. Autrand, *Charles VI. La folie du roi* (Paris, 1986); R. Famiglietti, *Royal intrigue: crisis at the court of Charles VI* (New York, 1986); M. Vale, *Charles VII* (London, 1974); P.M. Kendall, *Louis XI* (London, 1971); P.-R. Gaussin, *Louis XI, roi méconnu* (Paris, 1976).

greatest interest falls understandably between the treaties of Troyes (1420) and Arras (1435), when Philip's actions helped determine English and French royal fortunes in the later stages of the Hundred Years' War.[80] After Arras, however, the influence of the *Parlement* of Paris was one of a series of significant issues which continued to shape the relationship between the duke and his sovereign, as Professor Van Caenegem's edition of sources and a number of valuable studies demonstrate.[81] While the War of the Public Weal (1465) has received more attention in recent years, significant episodes in Philip's relationship with the French crown, such as his dealings with other French princes in the early 1440s, could benefit from further exploration.[82] However, we may

[80] P. Duparc, 'La conclusion du traité de Troyes', *Revue historique de droit français et étranger*, vol. xlix (1971), pp. 50–64; Y. Lacaze, 'Aux origines de la paix d'Arras (1435). Amédée VIII de Savoie, médiateur entre France et Bourgogne', *Revue d'histoire diplomatique*, vol. lxxxvii (1973), pp. 232–76; A.C. Reeves, 'The Congress of Arras (1435)', *History Today*, vol. 22 (1972), pp. 724–32; G. Thompson, 'Le régime anglo-bourguignon à Paris: facteurs idéologiques', in *La "France anglaise" au Moyen Âge: colloque des historiens médiévistes français et britanniques, ACNSS 111, Poitiers 1986, PH*, vol. 1 (Paris, 1988), pp. 53–60; idem, *Paris and its people under English rule: the Anglo-Burgundian regime, 1420–1436* (Oxford, 1991); M. Warner, 'The Anglo-French dual monarchy and the house of Burgundy: the survival of an alliance', *French History*, vol. 11 (1997), pp. 103–30.
[81] R.C. Van Caenegem, *Les arrêts et jugés du Parlement de Paris sur appels flamands conservés dans les registres du Parlement 1320–1521*, 2 vols (Brussels, 1965–77); S. Dauchy, 'Le Parlement de Paris, juge contraignant ou arbitre conciliant? Les conflits entre Philippe le Bon et ses bonnes villes de Flandre', *PCEEB*, vol. xxxiii (1993), pp. 143–52; idem, *De processen in beroep uit Vlaanderen bij het Parlement van Parijs, 1320–1521. Een rechts-historisch onderzoek naar de wording van staat en souvereiniteit in de Bourgondisch- Habsburgse periode* (Brussels, 1995); idem (ed.), *Les appels flamands au Parlement de Paris. Regestes des dossiers de procès reconstitués d'après les registres du Parlement et les sources conservées dans les dépôts d'archives de Belgique et du Nord de la France* (Brussels, 1998). See also W. Blockmans, 'La position du comté de Flandre dans le royaume à la fin du XVe siècle', in B. Chevalier and P. Contamine (eds.), *La France de la fin du XVe siècle* (Paris, 1985), pp. 71–89.
[82] J. Krynen, 'La rébellion du Bien public (1465)', in M.-T. Fögen (ed.), *Ordnung und Aufruhr im Mittelalter* (Frankfurt, 1995), pp. 81–98; J.-Y. Mariotte, 'La Guerre du Bien public vue de Strasbourg (1465)', in *Mélanges offerts à Jean-Yves Ribault* (Bourges, 1996), pp. 231–4; M. Rimboud, 'La paix du Bien public: démesure et marchandages (août–novembre 1465)', in *109e congrès national des sociétés historiques et scientifiques, Amiens 1994. I:*

note that one scholar has attempted a broad reappraisal of ducal intentions with regard to the kingdom. In an important series of articles André Leguai pointed out that the severance of the umbilical cord to France, which was first posited in the work of Pirenne and dated by him to the murder of John the Fearless in 1419, was in fact far from complete by the time of Philip's death in 1467.[83]

The remarkable expansion of ducal power within the Empire has been the subject of sustained and detailed analysis since Professor Vaughan considered it in 1970, including an important work of synthesis which emphasises the duke's realistic pursuit of his goals and his skilful expoitation of

La guerre, la violence et les gens au Moyen Âge (Paris, 1996), pp. 333–44. We may note in this context a number of studies which consider aspects of the military history of Philip's reign: J. Doig, 'A new source for the siege of Calais in 1436', *English Historical Review*, vol. cx (1995), pp. 404–16; M. Sommé, 'L'armée bourguignonne au siège de Calais de 1436', in P. Contamine, C. Giry-Deloison and M. Keen (eds.), *Guerre et société en France, en Angleterre et en Bourgogne, XIVe–XVe siècle* (Lille, 1991), pp. 197–219; J.-M. Cauchies, 'Les "écorcheurs" en Hainaut, 1437–1445', *Revue belge d'histoire militaire*, vol. xx (1974), pp. 317–39; idem, 'La désertion dans les armées bourguignonnes de 1465 à 1476', *Revue belge d'histoire militaire*, vol. xxii (1977), pp. 132–48; N. Michael, *Armies of medieval Burgundy (1364–1477)* (London, 1977); and the work of Bertrand Schnerb, including 'Un plan de guerre anglo-bourguignon en 1430', *Mémoires*, no. 5 (1986), pp. 106–11; idem, 'Un thème de recherche: l'exercice de la justice dans les armées des ducs de Bourgogne (fin XIVe– fin XVe siècle)', *PCEEB*, vol. xxx (1990), pp. 99–115; idem, 'La préparation des opérations militaires au début du XVe siècle: l'exemple d'un document prévisionnel bourguignon', in Contamine, Giry-Deloison and Keen (eds.), *Guerre et société en France*, pp. 189–96; idem, *Bulgnéville (1431): l'état bourguignon prend pied en Lorraine* (Paris, 1993); and idem, *L'honneur de la Maréchaussée. Maréchalat et maréchaux en Bourgogne des origines à la fin du XVe siècle* (Turnhout, 2000).

[83] A. Leguai, 'La "France bourguignonne" dans le conflit entre la "France française" et la "France anglaise" (1420–1435)', in *La 'France anglaise' au Moyen Âge*, pp. 41–52; idem, 'Royauté française et état bourguignon de 1435 à 1477', *PCEEB*, vol. xxxii (1992), pp. 65–75; idem, 'Royauté et principautés en France aux XIVe et XVe siècles: l'évolution de leurs rapports au cours de la guerre de Cent Ans', *MA*, vol. ci (1995), pp. 121–36. Further important comment in P. Contamine, 'La Bourgogne du XVe siècle', in *La bataille de Morat. Un événement suisse d'histoire européenne entre le Moyen Âge et les temps modernes (1476–1976). Actes du colloque* (Fribourg and Bern, 1976).

circumstance.[84] Some of the many imperial princes affected by the encroachment of ducal ambitions have been studied in their own right.[85] Philip's desire to expand his influence in the Empire and to clarify the tenure of his territories there emerges strongly from such work, but historians have also continued to reflect on whether the duke might have entertained wider ambitions. Given the fact that conferment of a crown upon Philip the Good by the emperor was discussed more than once in his reign, not to mention the survival of the ancient idea of Lotharingia and other imperial themes in Burgundian historical culture, such speculation is understandable.[86] However, new evidence relating to an early proposal to put forward Philip's candidature for the crown of King of the Romans in 1438 tends to confirm Professor Vaughan's

[84] Lacaze, 'Philippe le Bon et l'empire' (see above, n. 12).

[85] See for instance W.J. Alberts, *Geschiedenis van Gelderland tot 1492* (Zutphen, 1978); idem, *Overzicht van de Geschiedenis van de Nederrijnse territoria tussen Maas en Rijn, 2: 1288–c.1500* (Assen, 1982); H.-J. Brandt, 'Klevisch-märkische Kirchenpolitik im Bündnis mit Burgund in der ersten Hälfte des XV. Jahrhunderts', *Annalen des historischen Vereins für den Niederrhein*, no. clxxviii (1976), pp. 42–76; D. Kastner, *Die Territorialpolitik der Grafen van Kleve* (Düsseldorf, 1972); W. Maleczek, 'Österreich – Frankreich – Burgund. Zur Westpolitik Herzog Friedrichs IV in der Zeit von 1430 bis 1439', *Mitteilungen des Instituts für österreichische Geschichts- forschung*, vol. lxxix (1971), pp. 111–55; Paravicini 'Moers, Croy, Burgund'; P. Pégeot, 'Bourgogne et Wurtemberg, 1397–1477: esquisse de leurs relations', in *Cinq-centième anniversaire de la bataille de Nancy (1477)* (Nancy, 1979), pp. 339–59. See also R. Stein, 'Philip the Good and the German Empire: the legitimation of the Burgundian succession to the German principalities', *PCEEB*, vol. xxxvi (1996), pp. 33–48.

[86] R. Stein, 'Recht und Territorium. Die lotharingischen Ambitionen Philipps des Guten', *Zeitschrift für historische Forschung*, vol. xxiv (1997), pp. 481–508; M. de Roos, 'Les ambitions royales de Philippe le Bon et Charles le Téméraire: une approche anthropologique', *PCEEB*, vol. xxxvi (1996), pp. 71–87; J. Schneider, 'Lotharingie, Bourgogne ou Provence? L'idée d'un royaume d'entre-deux aux derniers siècles du Moyen Âge', in *Liège et Bourgogne*, pp. 15–44; Y. Lacaze, 'Le rôle des traditions dans la genèse d'un sentiment national au XVe siècle: la Bourgogne de Philippe le Bon', *Bibliothèque de l'École des chartes*, vol. cxxix (1971), pp. 303–85; A. Hagopian-van Buren, 'Philip the Good's manuscripts as documents of his relations with the Empire', *PCEEB*, vol. xxxvi (1996), pp. 49–69.

impression that such projects were, on the whole, ephemeral in quality.[87]

Some have been tempted to form a similar judgement of Philip the Good's crusading plans, although as Professor Vaughan point out here, and as subsequent research has emphasised, the 'business of Christ' was very much at the forefront of the duke's thoughts, particularly in the later stages of his reign.[88] Among the undoubted benefits of Philip's crusading stance were improved relations with the church at home and more broadly throughout Christendom.[89]

[87] W. Paravicini, 'Zur Königswahl von 1438', *Rheinische Vierteljahrsblätter*, vol. xxxix (1975), pp. 99–115.

[88] See especially J. Paviot, 'La dévotion vis-à-vis de la Terre sainte au 15e siècle: l'exemple de Philippe le Bon, duc de Bourgogne', in M. Balard (ed.), *Autour de la première croisade* (Paris, 1996), pp. 401–11. For relevant general histories see N. Housley, *The later crusades: from Lyons to Alcazar, 1274–1580* (Oxford, 1992) and H. Müller, *Kreuzzugspläne und Kreuzzugspolitik des Herzogs Philipp des Guten von Burgund* (Göttingen 1993). Philip did not only consider crusading against the Turk: see Y. Lacaze, 'Philippe le Bon et le problème hussite: un projet de croisade bourguignon en 1428–1429', *RH*, vol. ccxli (1969), pp. 69–98; A. vanTuch, 'La participation liégeoise à la croisade contre les Hussites en 1421, d'après Jean de Stavelot', in *Liège et Bourgogne*, pp. 45–54.

[89] Since Professor Vaughan's chapter on the subject, see 'Kerkelijk en godsdienstig leven circa 1384–1520', in *AGN* IV, 378–439; J. Helmrath, *Das Basler Konzil 1431–1449, Forschungsstand und Probleme* (Cologne and Vienna, 1987); H. Müller, ' "Cum res ageretur inter tantos principes": Der Streit um das Bistum Tournai (1433–1438)', in J. Helmrath, H. Müller and H. Wolff (eds.), *Studien zum 15. Jahrhundert: Festschrift für Erich Meuthen*, vol. 1 (Munich, 1994), pp. 231–53; idem, *Die Franzosen, Frankreich und das Basler Konzil (1431–49)* (Paderborn, 1990); idem, 'Konzil und Frieden. Basel und Arras (1435)', in J. Fried (ed.), *Träger und Instrumentarien des Friedens im hohen und späten Mittelalter* (Sigmaringen, 1996), pp. 333–90; A.J. Jongkees, 'Pie II et Philippe le Bon, deux protagonistes de l'union chrétienne', *PCEEBM*, vol. xx (1980), pp. 103–15. The 1996 Dijon colloquium of the *Centre européen d'études bourguignonnes* considered *Hommes d'église et pouvoirs à l'époque bourguignonne (XIVe–XVIe siècles)*. For churchmen and ecclesiastical institutions in the Burgundian dominions see also E. Brouette, 'Bénéficiers du diocèse de Thérouanne de 1431 à 1475', *Bulletin trimestriel de la Société des antiquaires de la Morinie*, vol. xxii (1977), pp. 576–82; M. Prietzel, 'Jacques Maes († 1465). Lebensführung und Wirkungskreis eines flämischen Kanonikers', *Zeitschrift für historische Forschung*, vol. xxiii (1996), pp. 325–54; idem, *Guillaume Fillastre der Jüngere (1400/1407–1473). Kirchenfürst und herzoglich-burgundischer Rat* (Stuttgart, 2001); C. Märtl, *Kardinal Jean Jouffroy. Leben und Werk* (Sigmaringen, 1996); R. de Keyser, 'Chanoines séculiers et universités: le

Philip's presence on the international stage, not least among Mediterranean powers, was also greatly enhanced.[90] Whatever the practical benefits which support for the crusade brought to the duke, the enterprise was of course not the fruit of his ideals and ambitions alone: the Burgundian court included a good number of crusade enthusiasts throughout the reign, including Guillebert de Lannoy, Geoffrey de Thoisy,

cas de Saint-Donatien de Bruges (1350–1450)', in *Les Universités au Moyen Âge* (Leuven, 1978), pp. 584–97; J. Pycke, 'De Louis de la Trémoïlle à Ferry de Clugny (1388–1483): cinq évêques au service des ducs de Bourgogne', in *Les grands siècles de Tournai*, pp. 210–38; O. de Waele, 'Étude prosopographique des chanoines de Tournai (1378–1460)', *Mémoire de licence*, Louvain-la-Neuve (1992–3); *Monasticon belge*, 7 vols. (Liège, 1961–89). Among studies devoted to other aspects of contemporary belief see Walter Prevenier, 'Les triangles "Église-État, société" et "Église, famille, société laïque" dans les Pays-Bas bourguignons du XVe siècle', in F. Alvarrez-Peyrere (ed.), *Le politique et le religieux. Essais théoriques et comparatifs* (Jerusalem, 1995), pp. 119–37; P. Trio, *Volksreligie als spiegel van een stedelijke samenleving: de broederschappen te Gent in de late Middeleeuwen* (Leuven, 1993).
90 J. Richard, 'Louis de Bologne, patriarche d'Antioche et la politique bourguignonne envers les États de la Méditerranée orientale', *PCEEBM*, vol. xx (1980), pp. 63–9; idem, 'La Bourgogne des Valois, l'idée de croisade et la défense de l'Europe', in Caron and Clauzel (eds.), *Le Banquet du Faisan*, pp. 16–27; Y. Lacaze, 'Perse et Bourgogne dans la seconde moitié du XVe siècle', *Revue d'histoire diplomatique* (1975), pp. 77–82; R. Degryse, 'Les expéditions bourguignonnes à Rhodes, Constantinople et Ceuta', *Revue de la Société dunkerquoise d'histoire et d'archéologie*, no. 21 (1987), pp. 39–49; H. Taparel, 'Un épisode de la politique orientale de Philippe le Bon: les bourguignons en Mer Noire (1444–1446)', *AB*, vol. lv (1983), pp. 5–29. J. Paviot has worked extensively in this field. His studies include 'La piraterie bourguignonne en Mer noire à la moitié du XVe siecle', in H. Dubois, J.-C. Hocquet and A. Vauchez (eds.), *Horizons marins et itinéraires spirituels: Mélanges M. Mollat du Jardin*, vol. 2 (Paris, 1987), pp. 203–14; idem, ' "Croisade" bourguignonne et intérêts génois en Mer Noire au milieu du XVe siècle', *Studi di Storia medioevale e di Diplomatica*, vols. xii–xiii (1992), pp. 135–62; idem, 'Oliviero Maruffo et la cour de Bourgogne', in *Atti del convengo internazionale di studi sui ceti dirigenti nelle istituzioni della republica di Genova, maggio 1989* (Genoa, 1990), pp. 369–93; idem, *La politique navale des ducs de Bourgogne, 1384–1482* (Lille, 1995); idem, 'Les navires du duc de Bourgogne Philippe le Bon (1440–1465)', *Atti del V. Convengo internazionale di studi colombiani (Navi e navigazione nei secoli XVe XVI)* (Genoa, 1987), pp. 169–95; idem and M. Chauney-Bouillot (eds.), *Nicopolis, 1396–1996: actes du colloque international de Dijon, 18 octobre 1996* (published Dijon, 1997, and as fasc. 3 of *Annales de Bourgogne*, vol. lxviii [1996]).

Walleran de Wavrin and even Philip's wife, Isabelle of Portugal.[91]

What, finally, of the image of Philip the Good which Richard Vaughan left to posterity? Despite the sub-title of the present volume, and although he acknowledged a number of enduring and important achievements which Philip left for his son, Professor Vaughan's estimation of the third duke's qualities was mixed to say the least. An earlier volume had established Philip's grandfather as the founder of Burgundian power; a later volume would attempt to restore the reputation of Philip's son; but in the present study, Philip is found to be 'no diplomat', a 'poor statesman' whose 'failings . . . became more and more apparent as he grew older'. It is important to remember how different this image of Philip the Good was from many – although not all – previous interpretations: the prince depicted here was no founder of Belgium as he had seemed to Henri Pirenne and others before him; nor was he the French prince who sought primarily to retain a dominant role in the kingdom, as Paul Bonenfant had argued.[92] The Philip the Good that emerges here in fact resembles that presented by Johan Huizinga: 'a great lord whose vices, like his virtues, were those commonly found among the aristoc-

[91] R. Arié, 'Un seigneur bourguignon en terre musulmane au XVe siècle: Ghilebert de Lannoy', *MA*, vol. lxxxiii (1977), pp. 283–302; H. Taparel, 'Geoffroy de Thoisy: une figure de la croisade bourguignonne au 15e siècle', ibid., vol. xciv (1988), pp. 381–93; G. Le Brusque, 'Des chevaliers bourguignons dans les pays du Levant: l'expédition de Walleran de Wavrin contre les Turcs ottomans (1444–6) dans les *Anchiennes Cronicques d'Engleterre* de Jean de Wavrin', ibid., vol. cvi (2000), pp. 255–75; A. Bertrand, 'Guillebert de Lannoy (1386–1460): ses "Voyages et ambassades" en Europe de l'Est', *PCEEB*, vol. xxxi (1991), pp. 79–92; W. Schulz, *Andreaskreuz und Christusorden. Isabella van Portugal und der burgundische Kreuzzug* (Fribourg, 1976); C.C. Willard, 'Isabel of Portugal and the fifteenth-century Burgundian crusade', in B. Sargent-Baur, *Journeys towards God: pilgrimage and crusade* (Kalamazoo, 1992), pp. 206–14.
[92] On the historiographical context generally see Jongkees above, and: P. Carlier, 'Contribution à l'étude de l'unification bourguignonne dans l'historiographie nationale belge de 1830 à 1914', *Belgisch Tijdschrift voor nieuwste Geschiedenis*, vol. xvi (1985), pp. 1–24; A. Uyttebrouck, 'Henri Pirenne et les ducs de Bourgogne', in G. Despy and A. Verhulst (eds.), *La fortune historiographique des thèses d'Henri Pirenne* (Brussels, 1986) (*Archives et bibliothèques de Belgique*, extra no. 28), pp. 87–111. See also Bonenfant, *Philippe le Bon. Sa politique, son action*, pp. 3–18, 22–104.

racy'.[93] Like Huizinga, Professor Vaughan also felt that one could not speak of a Burgundian state under Philip the Good.[94] While it is difficult to predict how interpretations of the duke's personal role may develop, it seems fair to say that more recent scholarship has looked differently on this last point. The reign of Philip the Good appears today as an important stage in the process of state formation in the Low Countries in the late Middle Ages.

Graeme Small
University of Glasgow
October 2001

93 Huizinga, 'La physionomie morale de Philippe le Bon', p. 128. Compare some of Professor Vaughan's judgements ('Philip was by no means a successful dynast. . . . In the pursuit of pleasure and renown [he] had enjoyed a measure of success given to few rulers of his time but, in spite of his early territorial successes, he had done little to consolidate his dynasty's power' [pp. 399–400]) with those of Huizinga ('he does not seem to us to have merited the title of statesman. It is likely that his personal qualities have played a far smaller role than is commonly imagined in the fortunes of his dynasty' [pp. 124–5]; 'a wise prince he certainly was not: a fortunate prince, sometimes a skilful prince, perhaps. Everything fell into place for him'. [p. 127] – my translations).

94 Cf. J. Huizinga, 'L'état bourguignon, ses rapports avec la France, et les origines d'une nationalité néerlandaise', *MA*, vol. xl (1930), pp. 171–93; vol. xli (1931), pp. 11–35, 83–96 and R. Vaughan, 'Hue de Lannoy and the question of the Burgundian state', in R. Schneider (ed.), *Das spätmittelalterliche Königtum im Europäischen Vergleich* (Sigmaringen, 1987), pp. 335–45. Professor Vaughan's reflections on the existence of a Burgundian state must be seen in the context of contemporary discussion of the applicability of the term in a late medieval context: see for instance S. Ehler, 'On Applying the Modern Term "State" to the Middle Ages', in J.A. Watt (ed.), *Medieval Studies presented to Aubrey Gwynn* (Dublin, 1961), pp. 492–501; B. Guenée, 'L'histoire de l'Etat en France à la fin du Moyen Âge vue par les historiens français depuis cent ans', *RH*, vol. ccxxxii (1964), pp. 331–360; idem, 'État et nation en France au Moyen Âge', ibid., vol. ccxxxvii (1967), pp. 17–30; idem, 'Y a-t-il un État des XIVe et XVe siècles?', *Annales ESC*, vol. xxvi (1971), pp. 399–406; J. Strayer, *On the Medieval Origins of the Modern State* (Princeton, 1970); or R. Fedou, *L'État au Moyen Âge* (Paris, 1971).

CHAPTER ONE

Burgundy, England and France: 1419–35

On 10 September 1419, at about five o'clock in the afternoon, John the Fearless, duke of Burgundy and count of Burgundy, Artois and Flanders, was hacked to death on the bridge of Montereau during a diplomatic parley. But this assassination, which had been contrived and carried out by the sixteen-year-old dauphin of France and his advisers, did not significantly disrupt the administration of John the Fearless's territories, nor even the government of that part of France which was under his control.

At this time France was virtually divided into three parts. Extensive areas in the north, including Normandy in particular, had succumbed to the triumphant military progress of Henry V since Agincourt. This was Lancastrian France. To the south, other territories supported the dauphin, the inhabitants having transferred their loyalties from King Charles VI to his son Charles. North-east of dauphinist France, in Champagne and Picardy, the Burgundians reigned supreme. They had set up a makeshift government and court at Troyes. Burgundian France was being ruled in name by King Charles VI and Queen Isabel, and in fact by John the Fearless. Isabel now took over *de facto* rule with an energy and decision which contrasted with the lunatic nonchalance of her mad husband. She was informed of Duke John's murder on 11 September. By the twelfth, couriers were off to Nevers, La Charité-sur-Loire, Bar-sur-Aube, Langres, Beauvais, Amiens and Châlons to 'induce the inhabitants to remain loyal to the king', and clerks were at work in the chancery day and night for the next four days, drawing up copies of letters and instructions.[1] This energetic start was well maintained.

[1] Bonenfant, *Meutre de Montereau*, 19. For this chapter as a whole I have leaned heavily on Monstrelet, *Chronique*; Plancher, iv; du Fresne de Beaucourt, *Charles VII*; Petit-Dutaillis, *Charles VII, Louis XI, et les premières*

Burgundian France continued to be effectively governed from Troyes until, as a result of the prolonged Anglo-Burgundian negotiations of 1419–20, most of it was ceded to Henry V.

Apart from a three-month visit to the duchy of Burgundy in summer 1418, John the Fearless had been absent from his own territories since August 1417. During this time he had pursued his interests in France and become ever more deeply involved in French affairs. His lands had been ably ruled by his only legitimate son, and successor in all of them, Philip, count of Charolais, and by his wife, Margaret of Bavaria. While Philip at Ghent looked after the northern counties of Flanders and Artois, Margaret, at Dijon or Rouvres, administered the duchy and county of Burgundy. It was this convenient arrangement which permitted the government of the Burgundian state to continue smoothly without hiatus or disruption, in spite of the tragedy of Duke John's death.

News of this was brought to Philip on 14 September by messengers who had thus covered the 200 miles from Troyes to Ghent in a mere three days.[1] The court chronicler, George Chastellain, whose powers as a rhetorician and journalist somewhat outshine his historical talents, describes in a famous passage how the twenty-three-year-old Philip threw himself onto a bed gnashing his teeth and rolling his eyes with grief. The cold but clearer light of historical record does confirm that Philip's anguish was real enough to occasion a temporary breakdown in the administration, witness the letter written by his councillors at Ghent to their colleagues of the Lille *chambre des comptes* on Sunday, 17 September.

> You wish to obtain instructions from my lord of Charolais. Be pleased to know that the piteous news was fully confirmed this evening, after we had received your letters, by certain of the dead duke's people and servants who were present when the murderous deed was perpetrated. After delaying as long as we decently could, we have broken this news to my lord of Charolais, who has suffered and is suffering extreme grief and distress, as one would expect. Because of this, and until he has somewhat recovered, it is quite impossible for him to deal with the matters men-

années de Charles VIII; Calmette and Déprez, *France et Angleterre en conflit*; Bossuat, *Gressart et Surienne*; Perroy, *Hundred Years War*; d'Avout, *Armagnacs et Bourguignons*; Bonenfant, *Philippe le Bon*; Armstrong, *AB* xxxvii (1965), 81–112; and, for the early part, Bonenfant, *Meutre de Montereau* and Wylie and Waugh, *Henry V*, iii.

[1] Bonenfant, *Meutre de Montereau*, 43–4 and de Lichtervelde, *Grand commis*, 282. For what follows, see Chastellain, *Oeuvres*, i. 49 and *IADNB* 1 (2), 75, whence the extract.

tioned in your letter, nor with any of his other affairs. So we have agreed that you should adjourn for a fortnight today's conference at Lille with the bailiffs of Flanders, for the audit of their accounts. Meanwhile my lord will take advice on this and his other affairs and see to them as soon as possible.

The practical demands of diplomacy and administration must soon have deflected the attention of the new ruler of Burgundy from his father's assassination. As early as 20 September we find him being sworn in as count of Flanders at Ghent. But Philip was in no hurry to comply with the pressing appeals for his immediate presence, or intervention, in French affairs, which he received before the end of September, both from the court at Troyes and from the royal officials in Paris. Instead, he made a tour of the Flemish towns in order to be installed as count in each of them; he held a family council at Malines on 8–10 October; and he presided over a conference at Arras later in the month which was attended by a large gathering of captains and noblemen, ecclesiastics, and urban representatives from Flanders and from Burgundian France. On Sunday 22 October a solemn memorial service for the soul of John the Fearless was held in the church of St. Vaast. The choir stalls were filled, according to a carefully arranged seating plan, by the clergy of Flanders and Artois and the councillors of the dead duke and, after the service, twenty-four monks from assorted Orders went through the entire Psalter, each receiving a half-franc tip for his pains.[1]

Meanwhile, negotiations with England, and deliberations of councillors, had been initiated. Philip certainly did not become 'king Harry's man', as an English chronicler later put it, overnight. The arguments for and against an outright alliance with Henry V against the dauphin were weighed and examined. No sentimental or emotional considerations of revenge were permitted to influence the councillors' logic, nicely displayed in a memorandum drawn up at the time. It was argued, in favour of rejecting the alliance with England, that the duke of Burgundy was principal vassal of the crown of France and it was his duty to protect, not alienate, it; that he was the senior peer of France and ought to summon the three Estates of the realm in this crisis; that he could not risk making war in France on the king of England's behalf without the authorization of the court at Troyes, for such a course of action might cause Queen Isabel to seek a settlement with the dauphin. Finally it was urged that an alliance

[1] ADN B1602, fos. 68b–69b. For what follows, see *English chronicle of the reigns of Richard II*, 50 and Bonenfant, *Meurtre de Montereau*, 216–21.

with England would benefit the king of England much more than the duke of Burgundy.

But the councillors found more compelling reasons for accepting the English alliance and recognizing Henry as king of France. They thought that this would avoid further warfare in France, for Henry V had declared his intention of having the crown of France in any case, by military conquest if necessary. Furthermore, they argued that if Duke Philip rejected the English offers, someone else would take them up to his disadvantage and that he might just as well allow Henry V to have the crown of France. Otherwise, after the death of the present king, Charles VI, it would surely pass to Philip's enemy the dauphin; or possibly to the duke of Orleans, likewise enemy of Burgundy.

While Philip the Good's councillors were coolly deliberating on the best course of action for him to take, and during the period of over a month, when as we may suppose, he was revolving these important problems in his mind, his mother's considerable energies and administrative skill had been instantly mobilized in the cause of revenge. Action of every conceivable kind, diplomatic, legal, military, was initiated or demanded by the bereaved duchess, Margaret of Bavaria.[1] The court at Troyes, centre of Burgundian influence in France, naturally received most attention. Letters demanding help in punishing the murderers were followed up by an embassy, and this in its turn by a contingent of her councillors. The mechanism of Burgundian interest thus established at the French court was subsequently lubricated, by the thoughtful duchess, with a consignment of wine. She sent an embassy to her son, insisting on revenge. She sent messengers, letters or embassies, appealing for support, to the pope and 'the Emperor', to the king of Navarre and the duchess of Bourbon, to the duke of Lorraine, to Strasbourg, to Avignon, to Paris, to the count palatine of the Rhine and the countess of Württemberg and to many other towns, princes and ecclesiastics. She even collared some astrologers and held them under arrest until they had been interrogated on the subject of her husband's death. Nor were the legal aspects of the case forgotten: secretaries and lawyers were hard at work before the end of September. One of them, the ducal secretary Baude des Bordes, started placing the 'treasons, machinations and evil deeds' perpetrated against Duke John on record on 21 September 1419, and worked for 194 days, only completing his task in April 1420.

As a matter of fact, John the Fearless's murderers never were

[1] Plancher, iv. 5–6; *Mémoires*, i. 226–30; *Comptes généraux*, ii (2), 734–8, 757–9, 779–80, 824–5 etc.

brought to justice. The guilty dauphin protected and even favoured his accomplices long after he became King Charles VII.[1] At a somewhat bizarre trial, held in Paris in December 1420, the ducal advocate, Nicolas Rolin, accused the dauphin and his associates of the crime and demanded a sentence which seems mild, though involved. The offenders were to be carried bare-headed on tumbrils through the streets of Paris, on three successive Saturdays. Holding lighted wax tapers in their hands, they were to make loud and public confession of their crime in every square they passed through. Thence to Montereau, where the same rigmarole was to be enacted, and where they were to build and endow a collegiate church for twelve canons, six chaplains and six clerks. An inscription explaining why this church was built was to be carved in stone over its main entrance, and similar inscriptions were to be set up in Rome, Paris, Ghent, Dijon, Santiago de Compostela and Jerusalem. But nothing came of this turgid penal rhetoric. When the duchess did manage to arrest a person suspected of helping in the assassination, the sentence actually carried out was savage in the extreme, though still intricate. The victim was dragged alive on a hurdle through the streets of Dijon; his severed head was exhibited for eight days at a street corner; his body was quartered and the pieces attached to the four gates of Dijon, high enough to be seen from all sides; and what remained of the trunk was burnt outside the ducal palace.

If the dauphin was beyond the reach of the law, he might still be crushed by means of a political combination against him. The terms of the treaty signed at Troyes on 21 May 1420, which consummated agreements made between Duke Philip and King Henry during the previous winter, seem to have been specially devised to secure his utter destruction. King Henry V, married to Catherine of France, was now made sole heir of her parents King Charles VI and Queen Isabel. Not only was he to succeed Charles VI as king of France, but the government of France was handed over to him there and then. He and his heirs were to become joint rulers of France and England. Neither Charles VI, nor Henry V, nor Duke Philip of Burgundy was permitted to enter into separate negotiations with the dauphin. The text of this document speaks for itself. Yet a dauphinist chronicler finds it necessary to attach additional disrepute and even more partisan stigma to it, by describing it as witnessed in the royal council by 'Charles de Savoisy, Renier Pot, and Pierre de Fontenay, knights;

[1] Mirot, *AB* xiv (1942), 197–210. For what follows, see Monstrelet, *Chronique*, iv. 17–20, and Plancher, iv. 38–9.

by Master Philippe de Morvilliers president in the *Parlement* of Paris; Guillaume le Clerc, *maître des comptes*; Michel de Lallier; Guillaume Sanguin; Jehan Legoix and other burgesses, merchants, butchers, brigands and murderers of Paris'.[1]

It is fallacious to discover in the treaty of Troyes the basis of an alignment of great powers, and fallacious too, to think of the western European scene in the years 1420–35 in terms of an Anglo-Burgundian alliance against France. For these were attitudes rather than real alliances, and personal not national, in their scope. It goes without saying that for Henry V, and even more for his successor, John, duke of Bedford, private ambition was the mainspring of their French policies. Individual princes, not systematic policies, were involved, both in France and in Burgundy. Philip may have regarded the dauphin as a personal enemy, but he never made all out war on France. Some of his territories were never affected at all; others were protected by local truces. Franco-Burgundian warfare was sporadic and mostly peripheral, Franco-Burgundian negotiation began as early as 1422. The English alliance was only a by-product of Philip's pursuit of his own material interests, and only a part of a much wider system of connections which he developed in 1420–3 on the basis of that brought into existence by his father John the Fearless.

Of more immediate importance to Philip than the alliance with England, especially at a time when everyone seemed to be at war or on the brink of it, were his relations with the duchy of Bourbon and its dependent territories.[2] The duke, John I, had been a prisoner of war of the English since Agincourt, but his lands were in the capable hands of his wife, Marie de Berry, who ruled them with a skill and vigour matched by her neighbour in Burgundy, the duchess Margaret of Bavaria. It seems to have been Margaret of Bavaria, rather than Philip the Good, who in 1419–20 took the initiative in maintaining and developing John the Fearless's policy of a local truce and a marriage alliance with Bourbon. The truce, which created a demilitarized zone on the south-western frontier of the duchy of Burgundy embracing the counties of Charolais, Forez, the lordship

---

[1] *Geste des nobles*, 178. The best text of the treaty of Troyes is in *Grands traités*, 100–15.
[2] In general, see Leguai, *Ducs de Bourbon*, 92–5 and 115–19, and Plancher, iv. nos. 14 and 16, and pp. 11, 26, 45, 52 etc. The truce of 8 May 1420 is printed in *Mémoires*, i. 326–33. For Margaret of Bavaria's initiative, see *Comptes généraux*, ii (2), 731, 742–4, 752; and for the early marriage alliance negotiations Gachard, *Rapport sur Dijon*, 55, *IACOB* i. 154, and ADN B1925, fos. 39b–40.

of Beaujolais and much else besides, was signed at Bourbon-Lancy in May 1420. The marriage alliance, planned since 1412 between Charles, count of Clermont and Agnes of Burgundy, Philip the Good's youngest sister, was taken up again in 1422. Before it was formalized the truce of 1420 had been developed, in February 1422, into an elaborate treaty, the provisions of which show that the primary purpose of the prevention of warfare had been reinforced by commercial considerations.

While thus to the south of Burgundy a potential enemy was neutralized and a potential area of warfare with France was eliminated, to the north and east a similar policy was applied. Relations with the duchy of Bar were improved by a truce and negotiations in 1420.[1] The ruler of the neighbouring duchy of Lorraine, Duke Charles, visited Dijon in May 1422 and, recognizing King Henry V of England as 'heir and regent' of France, promised to support Philip against his enemies. Negotiations with the most powerful of Philip's Burgundian neighbours, his uncle Duke Amadeus VIII of Savoy, concerning minor disputes, led in October 1420 to the treaty of St. Claude which provided for the release of prisoners on either side, the return of stolen goods and money, and the appointment of commissioners to investigate other contentious incidents. Meanwhile, directly after John the Fearless's assassination, Margaret of Bavaria had appealed to the duke and duchess of Savoy to prohibit the dauphin from recruiting forces in, or passing troops through, Savoy; and on 1 October Philip instructed ambassadors to ask Amadeus for his 'aid, counsel and support' in avenging the death of his father. But the duke of Savoy refused to be drawn into French affairs: he neither attended the Burgundian family assembly at Malines nor the dauphin's rally of French princes at Lyons.

Nevertheless, from 1419 onwards Amadeus of Savoy was the pivot of Philip the Good's system of connections. Not only did he arrange a series of truces, from 1423 on, in Mâconnais and along the southern borders of Burgundy,[2] but he also made strenuous efforts to achieve

[1] BN Coll. de Bourg. 95, pp. 589–90. For the next sentence, see Plancher, iv. 26, 51–2 and no. 17. For what follows on Savoy, see José, *Amédée VIII*, i. 316–32; Cognasso, *Amedeo VIII*, ii. 45–54; Guichenon, *Savoie*, iv. 35 etc.; Plancher, iv. nos. 8 and 20; Blondeau, *MSED* (10) x (1940–2), 61–3; *Comptes généraux*, ii (2), 732–3, 738; and Gachard, *Rapport sur Dijon*, 112–13.

[2] Déniau, *Commune de Lyon*, 472–3, 497, etc. For what follows, see du Fresne de Beaucourt, *Charles VII*, i. 339 and ii. 318–36, etc.; Plancher, iv. no. 29. Rolin's rôle at Bourg-en-Bresse is discussed by Valat, *MSE* (n.s.) xl (1912), 65–75 and Marc, *MSBGH* xxi (1905), 375–8.

a reconciliation between Philip and the dauphin which might lead to a Franco-Burgundian settlement. He met Philip at Geneva in March, 1422. It was he who organized the first tentative discussions between diplomats at Bourg-en-Bresse in winter 1422–3, and the two dukes met again at Chalon-sur-Saône a year later. These conferences, which were taken up and continued in subsequent negotiations, modified Philip's position in an important way. Far from appearing an outright English partisan, as in the treaty of Troyes, he now emerged as a sort of *tertius gaudens*, prepared to negotiate seriously with either side, and intent on extracting material advantages for himself by playing one off against the other. The architect of this diplomacy may have been the new chancellor, Nicolas Rolin, who conducted the early negotiations with Savoy and reported in detail on them to Duke Philip.

Philip the Good's first wife was Michelle of France, daughter of Charles VI and sister of Henry V's wife Catherine, the bride of 1420. When Michelle died at Ghent, probably not by poisoning as some suspected,[1] on 8 July 1422, she left Philip without heir, though they had been married in 1409 and she was approaching thirty when she died. In these circumstances the duke could hardly delay his remarriage. His choice, which was guided by Duke Amadeus of Savoy, fell on his aunt Bonne of Artois, countess of Nevers, who had been widowed at Agincourt. The trouble and expense of obtaining dispensation from Rome for this purpose was repaid in a twofold manner, for Philip thereby consolidated his French connections and also improved his grip over the county of Nevers. This territory, which lay next to the duchy of Burgundy on the side of France, had been virtually a Burgundian adjunct since 1415. But the marriage was not destined to last, for Bonne died less than a year after it, on 15 September 1425, leaving behind her a reputation for beauty and gentility celebrated by a contemporary poet, who praised her for eschewing outlandish clothes, especially tassels and long sleeves; for not being a gourmand; and for not drinking wine laced with spices.

Thus in the years after 1419 Philip employed his diplomacy to protect and improve his political situation on the borders of France.

---

[1] See, for example, on this, Monstrelet, *Chronique*, iv. 118–19, Chastellain, *Oeuvres*, i. 341–4, de Fauquembergue, *Journal*, ii. 100–2; Fris, *Gand*, 110 and Plancher, iv. 56–7. For what follows, see Plancher, iv. 89, and nos. 38 and 39; José, *Amédée VIII*, ii. 332; Armstrong, *AB* xl (1968), 124; Mirot, *JS* (1942), 73; de Flamare, *Nivernais*, 397, etc.; de Lespinasse, *Nivernais*, iii. 184, 207–8, etc.; and Baudot, *MAD* (1827), 194–6.

But he did not neglect the English alliance, for Henry V's successor as ruler of Lancastrian France, his brother John, duke of Bedford, was persuaded or permitted by Philip to marry his sister Anne.[1] When the negotiations were initiated in October 1422, she was eighteen, but a contemporary has stated that she and her sisters were as plain as owls. In any case the bait which attracted Bedford was financial and territorial: the marriage-treaty accorded him a personal gift of 50,000 gold crowns and the promise of the county of Artois if Philip died childless. Politically too, this further consolidation of the Anglo-Burgundian alliance was clearly desirable. The marriage was a success. John and Anne set up house together in Paris and apparently became fond of each other, and it is a reasonable supposition that, in the years that followed, she was in part responsible for maintaining Philip the Good's support for the English in France.

It was at the time of the negotiations for the marriage of Bedford and Anne that the so-called Triple Alliance, or treaty of Amiens, was signed on 17 April 1423, by Philip the Good, John, duke of Bedford and John V, duke of Brittany. The last of these was an irresolute intriguer who managed to keep himself out of serious trouble and promote his own interests by shifting in and out of alliances with each of his powerful neighbours, and double-crossing them one after the other. The treaty he signed with Philip in December 1419 was drawn up in the chancery of John the Fearless. The draft text had been taken to Brittany by Guillaume de Champdivers, who arrived there four days after John's death. In 1421 John V swung the other way and signed an alliance with the dauphin. While one of his brothers was sent to give military aid to the dauphin, the other was encouraged to fight for the English. This latter, Arthur, count of Richemont[2], was married in 1423 to Philip's sister Margaret, and thus the Triple Alliance was buttressed by two marriages between the families of the signatories: John of Lancaster married Anne, Arthur of Britanny married Margaret, of Burgundy.

[1] For this and what follows on the Triple Alliance, see Plancher, iv. 66–71; Pocquet, *BEC* xcv (1934), 284–326; Armstrong, *AB* xxxvii (1965), 83–5; Williams, *Bedford*, 97–105. The marriage treaty is printed by Plancher, iii. no. 313; the text of the alliance is in Monstrelet, *Chronique*, iv. 147–9, and de Fauquembergue, *Journal*, ii. 94–7. See too Plancher, iv. no. 23.

[2] Richemont was the French spelling of Richmond, a Yorkshire earldom which Richard II had restored and confirmed to Duke John IV of Brittany in 1398. While the title was thereafter transferred by John IV to his son Arthur, the lands and castle were granted in 1399 by Henry IV to Ralph Neville, earl of Westmorland.

The eldest child of John the Fearless, Margaret had been engaged at the age of two to a dauphin of France. She had married another dauphin, Louis, duke of Guienne, when she was eleven, and, on his death in 1415, she had returned from Paris to the duchy of Burgundy to live with her unmarried sisters. She showed no enthusiasm whatsoever early in 1423 to re-enter the married state. Indeed, she made all sorts of difficulties. She complained that Arthur still had a ransom to pay to the English, who had taken him prisoner at Agincourt, and that all her sisters had married dukes. Moreover she had been a dauphine and still used the title duchess of Guienne. How could she marry a mere count? Philip had to send a special ambassador, the trusted ducal servant Renier Pot, to bring her round. He pointed out to her that her father needed to consolidate his alliance with Brittany; that Arthur was at least a titular duke of Touraine; and that he was 'a valiant knight, renowned for his loyalty, prudence and prowess, well-loved and likely to enjoy much influence and authority in France'. Renier Pot was also instructed by Philip to point out to Margaret that she was still young, had been a widow for some years, and really ought to get married and have children soon, especially since Philip himself had none.[1]

Margaret submitted to these persuasions and was married to Arthur on 10 October 1423. Sure enough, he very soon became a dominant figure at the French court and Philip found in him a constant friend and invaluable supporter in French affairs. Not so his brother Duke John V, who was soon back at his old game of changing diplomatic horses: in the course of the year 1425 he signed a treaty with Philip the Good in the spring, and another, with the dauphin, in the autumn.

For the Burgundian chroniclers, and perhaps for the participants, Philip the Good's French campaigns of the years after 1420 seemed of paramount interest. But for us, viewing the whole long reign in the perspective of history, these military activities assume a secondary importance. It was the diplomatic system just outlined which ensured the peace and security of Philip's lands in these years, not the battles and sieges.

What a contrast there was between the two companions in arms

[1] Renier Pot's instructions, quoted here, are partly printed in *IADNB* i (1), 293 (see Pot, *Pot*, 239–40). For this and what precedes I have used Gruel, *Chronique*, 25–32; Pocquet, *AB* vii (1935), 309–36; Pocquet, *RCC* xxxvi (1) (1934–5), 439–51; *Lettres et mandements de Jean V*, v and vi; Cosneau, *Connétable de Richemont* and Knowlson, *Jean V*. The marriage treaty of Arthur and Margaret is printed in Plancher, iii. no. 311.

who set out, in the early summer of 1420, after the junketings of Troyes to conquer dauphinist France! Henry V was a seasoned military leader of thirty-two, victor of the most famous battle in western Europe between Hastings and Waterloo, and architect of the first systematic military occupation since the Roman Empire. A ruler who was experienced, ambitious and, above all, a ruthless soldier. Witness his dictum when someone complained that he ransacked every place he conquered: 'War without fire is worth nothing—like sausages without mustard.'[1] Compared to him, Philip cut a poor figure indeed. A mere duke; only twenty-four years old and lacking altogether in military experience. On his own confession he was 'as yet but slightly equipped' with the virtue of martial courage.[2]

In the summer of 1420 this ill-assorted pair embarked on the joint conquest by siege and assault of Sens, Montereau and Melun. At Sens, in spite of quarrels between the English and Philip's Picards, victory came easily, for the town surrendered within a week. At Montereau, John the Fearless's body was disinterred and sent off spiced and salted to Dijon in a lead coffin, while the vacant grave was conveniently used to dispose of the body of one of Philip's soldiers who had been killed in the assault. At Melun, serious resistance was encountered which prolonged the siege for eighteen weeks while subterranean deeds of arms were performed in mines and counter-mines.

The result of these operations was important, for they ensured communication between Lancastrian France, with its capital Paris, and the duchy of Burgundy. But subsequent campaigns were desultory, indecisive and severely limited in scope. The few pitched battles only served to maintain stability or stalemate. Thus at Baugé, in Anjou, on 22 May 1421, Henry V's offensive was halted by the dauphin; and at Cravant, on 30 July 1423, the dauphin's offensive against Champagne was cut short by Philip. The dauphin, or Charles VII, as he became after his mad father's death in 1422, had neither the resources nor personal inclination in these years to conduct an effective campaign. His army, such as it was, was destroyed at Verneuil, on 17 August 1424, by the English. But they too were incapable of mounting an all-out offensive: all they managed to do was to hold on to their conquests and maintain their garrisons.

[1] Juvenel des Ursins, *Charles VI*, 565.
[2] *IADNB* i (2), 272. For the next paragraph and what follows, see especially Monstrelet, *Chronique*, iv, de Fenin, *Mémoires*, *Chronique des Cordeliers*, le Févre, *Chronique*, i, and Juvenel des Ursins, *Charles VI*.

Philip the Good's military posture in these years was wholly defensive. He could on occasion make a gesture towards offensive cooperation with the English but in fact, after 1420, he normally took the field only to defend his own frontiers in wars which were mainly local in significance. Thus, in June 1421, when he held council of war at Montreuil with Henry V, who had just landed at Calais with 'the largest army he has so far brought to France',[1] he left the king of England to conduct the main offensive against the dauphinists, while he himself remained in Artois in order to besiege the town of St. Riquier near Abbeville, on the borders of his northern territories, which was held against him by the local nobleman Jaques d'Harcourt. A dauphinist force, which marched from Compiègne to d'Harcourt's relief, was intercepted by Philip and forced to do battle. No history of Burgundy can afford to omit the chronicler Monstrelet's account of the battle of Mons-en-Vimeu which followed, the first personal military victory of the new duke.[2]

On Saturday, the 31st of August, the two armies kept advancing with much courage, and halted about eleven o'clock in the forenoon, at three bow-shots' distance from each other. During this short halt, many new knights were hastily created on both sides. In the number was the duke of Burgundy, by the hand of Sir Jehan de Luxembourg, when the duke did the same to Philippe de Saveuse. . . .

When this ceremony was over, the duke sent the banner of Philippe de Saveuse, with six-score combatants, under the command of Sir Mauroy de St. Léger and the bastard of Coucy, across the plain to fall on the flank of the dauphinists. Both armies were eager for the combat; and these last advanced with a great noise, and fell on the division of the duke with all the strength of their horses' speed. The Burgundians received them well; and at this onset there was a grand clattering of arms, and horses thrown to the ground in a most horrible manner on each side. Both parties now began to wound and kill, and the affair became very murderous; but during this first shock of arms one-half of the duke's forces were panic-struck and fled to Abbeville, where being refused admittance they galloped on for Picquigny. The duke's banner was carried away with them; for in the alarm the varlet who had usually borne it forgot to give it to some other person, and in his

---

[1] ACO B11942, no. 38, ducal letter of 27 June 1421 to Dijon *chambre des comptes.*
[2] Monstrelet, *Chronique*, iv. 59–63; I have used T. Johnes's translation, i. 465–6, with minor changes. On the battle, see Huguet, *Aspects de la Guerre de Cent Ans*, i. 141–3 and references given there, and Pius II, *Commentaries*, 581–3.

flight had thrown it on the ground, where it was found and raised by a gentleman called Jehan de Rosimbos, who rallied about it many of the runaways who had until that day been reputed men of courage and expert in arms. They had, however, deserted the duke of Burgundy, their lord, in this danger, and were ever after greatly blamed for their conduct. Some pretended to excuse themselves by saying that seeing the banner they thought the duke was with it. It was also declared, on the authority of Flanders King-of-Arms, that to his knowledge the duke was either killed or made prisoner, which made matters worse; for those who were most frightened continued their flight across the Somme at Picquigny to their homes, whence they did not return.

Some of the dauphin's forces, perceiving them running away from the duke's army, set out in pursuit after them, namely, Jehan Raoulet and Peron de Lupe, with about six-score combatants, and killed and took a good many of them. They imagined they had gained the day, and that the Burgundians were totally defeated; but in this they were mistaken, for the duke, with about five hundred combatants of the highest nobility and most able in arms, fought with determined resolution, insomuch that they over-powered the dauphinists, and remained masters of the field of battle.

According to the report of each party, the duke behaved with the utmost coolness and courage; but he had some narrow escapes, for at the onset he was hit by two lances, one of which pierced through the front of his war-saddle and grazed the armour of his right side; he was also grappled with by a very strong man, who attempted to unhorse him, but his courser, being high-mettled and stout, bore him out of this danger. He therefore fought manfully, and took with his own hands two men-at-arms, as he was chasing the enemy along the river-side. Those nearest his person in this conflict were the lord of Longueval and Guy d'Arly, and some of his attendants, who, though few in number, supported him ably. It was some time before his own men knew where he was, as they missed his banner; and when Jehan Raoulet and Peron de Lupe returned from their pursuit of the Burgundian runaways, expecting to find their companions victorious on the field of battle, they were confounded with disappointment on seeing the contrary, and instantly fled toward St. Valéry, and with them the lord of Moy; others made for Airaines.

The duke of Burgundy, on coming back to the field of battle, collected his men, and caused the bodies of those to be carried off who had fallen in the engagement, particularly that of the lord of la Viesville. Although all the nobles and great lords who had remained with the duke of Burgundy behaved most gallantly, I must especially notice the conduct of Jehan Vilain, who had that day been made a knight. He was a nobleman from Flanders, very tall and of great bodily strength, and was mounted on a good horse, holding a battle-axe in both hands. Thus he pushed into the thickest part of the battle, and, throwing the bridle on his horse's neck, gave such blows on all sides with his battle-axe that whoever was struck was instantly unhorsed and wounded past recovery. In this way he met Poton de Saintrailles, who, after the battle was over, declared the wonders he did, and that he got out of his reach as fast as he could.

The chronicler hazards no estimate of the number of Burgundian troops engaged at Mons-en-Vimeu, but it was only a skirmish by Agincourt standards. On the size and composition of Philip's army at this time, an interesting document has survived.[1] It is a report made to the duke by Hue de Lannoy on the recruitment of troops for a campaign in Picardy, which, though it has been attributed to 1422, must surely have been drawn up in the spring of 1421. Four hundred and fifty-one men-at-arms were to be made available from Flanders (109) and Artois (342). To these could be added fifty from the ducal court, twenty from Hainault, and twenty from Rethel. Total, 541 men-at-arms. As to crossbowmen, Lille, Douai, Orchies and the towns of Artois each owed a contingent at their own expense. Malines would provide ten, and twenty Flemish bailiffs would each provide two, to be financed out of the receipts of their offices: total, 245 crossbowmen. Besides these, 200 archers were to be assembled. Such was the diminutive army with which Philip set out, in the summer of 1421, to clear Picardy of enemies.

The victory of Mons-en-Vimeu was only just a victory, but Burgundian poets and propagandists used it to celebrate the military renown of Philip the Good and strategically it placed the scattered dauphinist or royalist elements which still held out in north-east France, in places like Le Crotoy and Guise, firmly on the defensive. Other Burgundian military operations were conducted at this time in the south, where the French threatened, especially after their seizure of La Charité in June 1422, to invade the duchy of Burgundy from across the Loire. Here, Philip was able to obtain English help, and in July 1422 the dying Henry V sent Bedford to his assistance at Cosne. In the following summer a hastily assembled Anglo-Burgundian force checked at Cravant the advance of a body of Scottish mercenaries hired by Charles VII, as the dauphin must now be called. The rendezvous before this battle was Auxerre, where the English and Burgundian captains conferred in the cathedral and drew up battle orders which seem to betray English predominance, or

[1] Printed B. de Lannoy, *Hugues de Lannoy*, 201–11 and in part in Chastellain, *Œuvres*, i. 274–7.

superiority, in military affairs, since it is English tactics which are here adopted.[1]

1. They would set out with their men at 10.0 a.m. next day, Friday (30 July 1423), and advance towards Cravant.

2. Two marshals were appointed to look after the troops, the lord of Vergy for the Burgundians and Gilbert Halsall for the English.

3. English and Burgundians to be ordered to live together in amity and not to quarrel, on pain of punishment at the discretion of the captains.

4. They would all ride together, but 120 men-at-arms, sixty English and sixty Burgundians, with as many archers, were to be sent ahead.

5. It was agreed that, when they arrived at the battlefield, they would all dismount promptly on the word of command. Those who refused to be put to death. The horses to be led half a league to the rear. Any found nearer would be confiscated.

6. Every archer to provide himself with a pole, sharpened at both ends, to fix in front of him as necessary.

7. No one, of whatever rank, may take prisoners during the battle until victory is completely assured. Any prisoners thus taken to be executed, along with their captors.

8. Everyone must provide himself with food for two days. The citizens of Auxerre to be asked to send provisions to the army which will be paid for.

9. On pain of death, no one is to ride in front or behind of his appointed place without leave of the captains.

10. Tonight, everyone is to pray as devoutly as possible, while awaiting life or death next day according to the grace of God.

Cravant, like Mons-en-Vimeu, was fought to protect the frontiers of Philip the Good's lands. In this essential task he showed commendable vigilance. In 1424 he took the field in person to drive the enemy out of Mâconnais where Imbert de Grôlée, the royal bailiff of Mâcon, had counterattacked after Cravant. But Philip's attention was being diverted more and more from French affairs. One only has to look at his itinerary[2] to appreciate what was

[1] Text in Monstrelet, *Chronique*, iv. 159–60; de Waurin, *Croniques*, iii. 64–6; le Févre, *Chronique*, ii. 77–8 (in part only), and Pot, *Pot*, 242–4. On the battle itself, see too *Livre des trahisons*, 169–71; Jouffroy, *Oratio*, 135–6, and Vallet de Viriville, *Charles VII*, i. 380–5.

[2] Published, though incompletely and with many errors, by Vander Linden in 1940.

B

happening. In 1420 he spent the whole year in France, and even found it necessary to be present throughout the protracted siege of Melun at the end of the year. But in 1421, apart from a brief Picardy campaign culminating in the battle of Mons-en-Vimeu, he spent the entire year in his northern territories. In the winter of 1421–2 Philip remained engrossed in his own affairs or pleasures, and paid only a brief visit to his ally King Henry V, who suffered the rigours of camp life in siege before Meaux from October 1421 until May 1422. True, he did dally in Paris during January 1422, but only to indulge in nocturnal gallantries and riotous living (he had left his duchess behind in Flanders), which shocked the respectable burgess-chronicler into some very uncomplimentary entries in his journal.[1] Installed in his duchy of Burgundy in February 1422, Philip stayed there till August, when news of Henry V's death brought him to Paris. Though regarded by many as the natural choice for the regency of France on behalf of the infant Henry VI, Philip allowed John, duke of Bedford, brother of Henry V, to arrogate this title to himself, and left Paris in October for the Low Countries. When Charles VI died on 22 October Philip was at Lille. He neither troubled to return to Paris for the funeral, nor did he take any notice of the invitation to come to Paris and concern himself with French affairs which he received at the end of the year from the authorities there.[2]

Philip the Good had never been seriously interested in French affairs. Moreover, he must have appreciated the weakness of Burgundy when compared to the growing political power of Charles VII, or to the military might of England. In consequence, his French interests were limited to negotiations and local truces with the former and the maintenance of alliances with the latter. From 1422 onwards, as he became more and more involved in the conquest of Holland and the unification of the Low Countries under himself, he only visited France on occasional passage to and from his southern territories. But, while Philip thus turned his back on France, he did not by any means neglect to pursue his own material advantage there, whether territorial or financial, on every possible occasion or pretext.

It must not be imagined, for example, that the duke of Burgundy paid for his own military expenses in France. Far from it. He charged Charles VI 10,000 francs for the military operations which accompanied his visit to Troyes in April 1420.[3] In 1421 his accounting

[1] *Journal d'un bourgeois de Paris*, 165.
[2] See de Fauquembergue, *Journal*, ii. 68–70.
[3] ADN B1929, f. 33b. For what follows in the next two paragraphs, see

officers refer to him, militarily speaking, as being 'in the service of the king of France', and, among the revenues of the receipt-general of all finances that year are sums of 3,000 and 10,000 gold crowns, paid by Charles VI towards Philip's expenses in helping to recover Compiègne and St. Riquier for the king. Thus Charles VI was made to pay for the defence of Philip's northern territories. But this almost traditional ransacking of the French royal treasury by the dukes of Burgundy was cut short in 1421–2, when control of the French revenues not accruing to the dauphin's government at Bourges passed to the English administration in Paris. Henceforth Philip's military ardour cooled. He let the English take Le Crotoy in autumn 1423 and retake Compiègne early in 1424, and he obtained considerable English help in the conquest of Guise in the summer of that year. Thereafter, until 1429, there is scarcely any mention in the pages of the chronicler Monstrelet, who never missed a battle, of Burgundian military operations in France.

When in 1429 Bedford desperately needed Burgundian help, Philip insisted on full payment for all his services, and a special account was kept which shows that, by 1431, he had been paid £150,000, though he was still owed £100,000. This account records payments for two excursions to Paris in 1429, the despatch of Burgundian reinforcements to Paris in January 1430, the siege of Compiègne in the summer and autumn of 1430, and the establishment of Burgundian garrisons in certain towns of Vermandois. Subsequently, a further statement was submitted to the king of England, detailing outstanding debts to the tune of 113,075 francs for services mostly in connection with the siege of Compiègne, and including the value of artillery abandoned there by Philip when he withdrew in haste in the autumn of 1430. Conversion of English into Burgundian currency sometimes involved Philip in a financial loss. For instance, in March 1430 Henry Beaufort delivered to him at Lille 15,565 English nobles. These were sent to the mint at Zevenbergen to be converted into Dutch clinkarts, but £700 was lost in consequence.

By 1431 Philip was in receipt of a regular English pension of 3,000 francs per month. His attitude had become increasingly mercenary by this time, witness the treaty he signed with Henry VI on 12 February

ADN B1923, fos. 30–1; a separate account attached to ADN B1942; Gachard, *Rapport sur Lille*, 360 and 362–3; ADN B1942, f. 17b; and *IADNB* i. (1), 229. See too, *Letters and papers*, ii. (1), 101–11, and, on the English subsidies in 1430, below, p. 25.

1430, in which he promised to serve Henry against 'the dauphin' with 3,000 men for two months, in return for 50,000 gold saluts and the county of Champagne.

As a matter of fact Champagne was granted to Philip by the English on 8 March 1430, but they had lost control of it the year before and it was firmly in the hands of Charles VII, who is said indeed to have offered it to Philip in August 1429 as part of a projected peace settlement.[1] But Philip did make some important territorial acquisitions as a result of his intervention in France in these years. In particular, he saw to it that the ill-gotten gains of John the Fearless were confirmed or legalized. The county of Boulogne was seized in 1423 after it had been briefly returned to its legal owner George de la Trémoille from whom John the Fearless had confiscated it in 1416. The towns of Péronne, Roye and Montdidier, with their surrounding territories, were confirmed to Philip by Charles VI in 1420 and by Henry VI in 1423; and the territories of Auxerre, Mâcon and Bar-sur-Seine, adjoining the duchy of Burgundy, were officially transferred to him by Henry VI's letters of 21 June 1424. Auxerre and Bar-sur-Seine were new gains of Philip's, and to these must be added the county of Ponthieu, with Abbeville and St. Valéry in the north. Possession of all these territories was confirmed to Philip the Good by the treaty of Arras in 1435.

In the case of the French city of Tournai, which became after 1430 an enclave in Philip's northern territories, significant financial gain followed ineffective or nominal territorial concession.[2] Philip the Good's relations with Tournai were based on friendly contacts with the patrician elements who were in control there when he succeeded his father in 1419. These people refused to subscribe to the treaty of Troyes and paid 500 crowns for exemption from doing so. The old historians thought that they were inspired by French

[1] Boutiot, *Troyes*, ii. 512–13 and 518 and Boussat, *AB* ix (1937), 18. For what follows in general, see Armstrong, *AB* xxxvii (1965), 85–91; Vaughan, *J. the Fearless*, 236–7; and Plancher, iv. nos. 7, 25, 34 and 35. For Boulogne, see Héliot and Benoit, *RN* xxiv (1938), 29–45; for Abbeville, Prarond, *Abbeville*; for St. Valéry, ADN B1931, f. 65b and Huguet, *Aspects de la Guerre de Cent Ans en Picardie maritime*, i.

[2] For this paragraph and the next, see *Extraits analytiques, 1385–1422* and *1422–1430; Chronique des Pays-Bas et de Tournai; Collection de documents inédits*, i. 16–20; Houtart, *Les Tournaisiens et le roi de Bourges*; and Champion and de Thoisy, *Bourgogne–France–Angleterre*. For sums recorded in the receipt-general of all finances, see, for example, ADN B1931, fos. 36a–b; B1942, fos. 16b–17; B1951, fos. 18–19.

patriotism or royalist sentiment. In fact, the burgesses of Tournai merely consulted their own interests. When in 1423 Charles VII asked them for an *aide* of £30,000 or £50,000 of Tours, they responded with a loan of £250 of Tours. But they had willingly paid Philip 4,000 crowns in 1421 in return for commercial privileges and exemption from military service. In 1423 they tried to secure, from him, their exemption from the jurisdiction of the Paris *Parlement*. They demonstrated no enthusiasm to be subjects of the king of France, nor of anyone else for that matter.

The attitude of the new government which was temporarily established in Tournai as a result of a popular revolution in 1423 was not greatly different, even though this new régime enjoyed the support of Charles VII. But the situation was changed by the issue, on 8 September 1423, of English royal letters granting Tournai to Philip. Though he promised in writing to do his best to reduce the city to the obedience of the king of England before next July, 1424, Philip could have had no serious aggressive intentions. Patrician elements regained power at the end of 1423, and Philip merely used his grant of Tournai by the English to increase the price demanded for his inaction or neutrality. Every year a treaty was signed, or rather sold, in which Philip promised not to molest Tournai. And every year the price was increased. It was 2,000 crowns in 1424; 7,000 in 1426; 15,000 in 1427. In 1428 Philip sold Tournai a six-year treaty for a total of 73,500 crowns. And the ducal accounts show that these sums were actually paid: over 100,000 saluts were received from Tournai in the period 1430–5.

One important advantage which Philip might reasonably have hoped to gain from his English connection was a juridical one. Owing to its extensive appellate jurisdiction, the Paris *Parlement*, or royal high court of France, was a thorn in the flesh of every judicial authority, and therefore of every town and ruler, west of the Schelde, upper Meuse and Saône, as well as some others beside. With his allies the English in control of Paris, Philip may have hoped to find support in the *Parlement* there for his encroachments on royal jurisdiction, not to mention favourable treatment in the litigation in which he was constantly involved. But the *Parlement* resisted his attempts to usurp royal rights, especially in the territories ceded to him by the English. Moreover, its attitude, in so far as ordinary litigation was concerned, was uncompromising, and the ducal *procureur* and *soliciteur des causes* there were kept as busy as ever. The abbey of St. Peter, Ghent, the municipal authorities of Bruges, the inhabitants of the castellany of Cassel, even a ducal official: all appealed against judgments of ducal courts to the *Parlement* of Paris. Far from benefiting from the English occupation of Paris, Philip seems to have had more trouble with the Parisian lawyers than either of his predecessors. While the English permitted Normandy to be withdrawn from these irritations, Burgundy and Flanders continued to suffer them, and it is hardly surprising that formal, though ineffectual, complaint was made by Philip to Bedford in November 1430 over the *Parlement's* support of the rebellious peasants of Cassel.[1]

The somewhat meagre material advantages which Philip obtained from his English allies by no means encouraged him to support them systematically in France. Instead, he prolonged and extended truces with those parts of France nearest his own territories while at the same time continuing his negotiations with Charles VII for a general pacification. In fact, during the late 1420s, Philip approached nearer and nearer to the complete abandonment of that aggressive posture towards Charles VII in which he had been placed by the tragedy of Montereau. The truce with Tournai, inaugurated by the neutrality treaty of 1424, was accompanied by another, signed at Chambéry in September of that year and watched over by the duke of Savoy, which embraced practically all Philip's southern frontiers. In approving it Philip for the first time accorded official recognition to Charles VII by referring to him as 'king of France'.[2] In the years following, the system of truces covering Philip's southern territories was maintained and even extended under the patronage of the duke of Savoy, while the dukes of Brittany and Savoy, the pope, and other interested parties, ensured that negotiations between Philip and Charles VII would continue. By 1428, in spite of the fall from power at the French court of Arthur, count of Richemont, the two sides had quite ceased to question the existence of the truce, and were arguing instead about infringements of its terms.

There were at least two reasons why the Franco-Burgundian settlement, which seemed to be a logical development from these truces and negotiations, was delayed so long. One was personal:

[1] For this paragraph, besides A. Bossuat, *RH* ccxxix (1963), 19–40 and Armstrong, *AB* xxxvii (1965), 91–101 and the references given there, see *Chartes et documents de l'abbaye de Saint-Pierre à Gand*, ii. 188; *IAB* iv. 357–61; *IAY* iii. 160–2 and 168; ACO B15, f. 198; and, above all, *Les arrêts et jugés du Parlement de Paris sur appels flamands*.
[2] Perroy, *Hundred Years War*, 273. The Chambéry truce is printed in Plancher, iv. no. 37; other truces are nos. 55, 57 and 66, and the negotiations are documented in nos. 47, 48, 51, 53, 54 and 68.

Philip's sister Anne was married to John, duke of Bedford. The other was political: until Philip had gained firm control of Holland–Hainault, the friendship and support of Bedford was essential to him. After all Bedford's brother, Humphrey duke of Gloucester, had done his utmost to acquire those territories for himself. While these two reasons were operative, Philip remained an ally of the English in France. But Anne died in 1432 and Holland was definitively acquired for Burgundy by 1433. The long expected Franco-Burgundian settlement was made at Arras in 1435.

King Charles VII's willingness to negotiate with Philip in the late 1420s is undisputed. The offers his ambassadors made in August 1429 were generous enough and probably sincere. They point to the existence of a third reason for Philip's reluctance to come to terms with Charles. A reason which was essentially a matter of sentiment. He found the notion of an alliance with his father's murderer utterly repugnant. These French offers, made through the mediation of the duke of Savoy's ambassadors, conceded nearly everything that was later conceded at Arras. They were in substance as follows:[1]

1. The king promised in principle that, on the conclusion of peace, he would make suitable spiritual reparation for the crime of Montereau. Philip had insisted that he denounce the crime and abandon the criminals.

2. The king offered to submit to arbitration Philip's demand that he should establish various religious foundations as an act of penance.

3. The king offered Philip 50,000 gold crowns in compensation for the jewels and belongings which his father had had with him at the time of his murder.

4. The king was prepared to grant to Philip certain lands which he already occupied and which had been granted to him by the English government in France: the counties of Mâcon and Auxerre; the towns and castellanies of Péronne, Roye and Montdidier; and the castellany of Bar-sur-Seine.

5. Philip would be personally excused from doing homage to the king of France.

6. The king promised to pay compensation for damages sustained by Burgundian personnel at Montereau.

7. The king would grant a general pardon and promulgate a general truce.

---

[1] *Grands traités,* 180–2; du Fresne de Beaucourt, *Charles VII,* ii. 405–10; Plancher, iv. no. 70. Compare Monstrelet, *Chronique,* iv. 348–9 and 352–3.

Nothing came of these diplomatic exchanges, except that a 'northern' truce was added, in 1429, to the 'southern' one, covering the two Burgundies, already in existence. While Philip parleyed with Charles VII, he remained in constant touch with John, duke of Bedford, and he even reluctantly accepted from him, in autumn 1429, the title of royal lieutenant in France for King Henry VI.[1] But his visit to Paris on that occasion was brief enough to show that he had no intention of taking his duties seriously. In the spring of 1430 his councillors or military advisers, prominent among them probably Hue de Lannoy, who had far more faith in the Anglo-Burgundian alliance than Philip, drew up a plan of campaign, which was agreed to in substance by both Philip and the English though the former was evidently only interested in this military collaboration with his allies in order to obtain Compiègne for himself at their expense, and possibly also Champagne. This plan of action runs in part as follows:[2]

Advice, subject to modification by others, on the strategy to follow when the king of England and his army disembark in France. In the first place, the following points must be borne in mind:

1. At the moment, the enemy holds a great deal of territory and many towns and castles on this side of the rivers Loire, Yonne, Seine, Marne and Oise, and most of his troops are in this area.

2. It is likely that few or no provisions will be available in this enemy-occupied countryside, yet such provisions are essential to undertake sieges and keep armies in the field.

3. The situation of the city of Paris, which is the heart and capital of the realm, must be carefully considered. Its citizens, conducting themselves well and loyally, have remained firm, though Paris has been for a long time, and still is, surrounded by the enemy and in great danger. . . . Moreover, as things are at the moment, it looks as though the loss of Paris would entail the loss of the whole kingdom. . . .

It follows that first priority ought to be given, in the strategy of the king and my lord of Burgundy, to clearing the enemy from around Paris, and they must advance to do this through areas where provisions are available, i.e. Normandy and Picardy. . . . It would be a good plan, too, to attack the enemy somewhere on and beyond the river Loire in order to distract his attention and cause him to withdraw forces from nearer here. Indeed, the king could send an army to Guienne, in order

---

[1] De Fauquembergue, *Journal*, ii. 327.
[2] Printed in Champion, *Flavy*, no. 30 from BN MS fr. 1278, fos. 12–14. See G. de Lannoy, *Œuvres*, 486–7 and A. Bossuat, *Gressart et Surienne*, 124–6.

to engage the counts of Foix and Armagnac and the lord of Albret in the defence of their own territories.

It has been suggested that, after the king disembarks in France, he should advance with his army direct to Rheims with my lord of Burgundy in his company, in order to conquer that town and be crowned there . . . leaving garrisons to defend Paris and other loyal towns and castles. Against this may be argued, subject to correction, as follows:

1. Rheims is a strong, well-fortified and well-provisioned city and, if it is garrisoned properly, will require a prolonged siege by a very large army. . . .

2. The king's power and authority would be severely undermined if he and the duke of Burgundy met with prolonged resistance at Rheims, or if things turned out badly for them there.

3. It is quite possible that Paris . . . would be unable to go on sustaining the oppressions and hostilities of the enemy during the length of time the king would be occupied at and around Rheims.

4. As to placing garrisons in and around Paris to defend it securely during the king's absence, under correction, it seems likely that this would contribute more to the destruction than the salvation of the said town, for, while the countryside would be ransacked for provisions, the enemy would neither be defeated nor forced to retreat. . . .

Thus, taking these points into account, and assuming that the king crosses to France with a minimum of 10,000 combatants, it seems, subject to correction, that the best course of action for him to take to shorten the war, drive back the enemy, make the best use of the available time and the best possible use of his army, and to ensure its provisioning, would be the following:

1. An advance party of 1,000 combatants, expert on horseback and under reliable captains, to be sent to Perrinet Gressart on the Loire frontier. These, together with 200 men-at-arms from the duke of Burgundy's lands and the troops that Perrinet Gressart can himself raise, to campaign against the enemy in Berry, Bourbonnais, Forez, Beaujolais, Auvergne, and towards Orleans . . . , at their own discretion and taking into account the enemy's dispositions. . . .

2. The king should send 700 or 800 combatants immediately, to besiege Aumale, to avoid the possibility of it refusing to surrender on his arrival. . . .

3. My lord of Burgundy, with 1,200 picked Burgundian and Picard men-at-arms, 1,000 Picard archers and 200 crossbowmen . . . , together with 1,000 English archers under a good captain provided by the king of England, should advance towards Laon and Soissons to conquer this area and prepare a route for the king to go to Rheims

for his coronation if he should choose to do so. Thence the duke of Burgundy may embark on the conquest of Champagne.

4. God willing, the sieges of Torcy and Château-Gaillard will soon be over. Then the English in Normandy will be powerful enough to lay siege to Louviers. If they are not, the king could send over some fresh troops from England.

5. The rest of the English army should advance to Beauvais to see if it can be induced to submit. The small castles around it should be conquered, and garrisons placed in them, in order to cut off its supplies, for the strength of Beauvais and its existing provisions would make it difficult to take it by siege. . . . On completion of these operations, which ought not to take long, this army should advance into the Île-de-France, besieging the town of Creil on the way, fortifying the bridge leading to Beauvais, and relieving the castles thereabouts, such as Luzarches and others. The siege of Creil once finished, this army should continue with the liberation of the Île-de-France, which will be of much comfort and help to Paris.

6. As to Compiègne, if my lord of Burgundy gets hold of the bridge at Choisy-au-Bac, takes the monastery at Verberie, blockades the bridge at Compiègne, and establishes garrisons roundabout, the town of Compiègne would be so closely invested that no supplies would be able to reach it. . . .

In the event, this carefully thought out scheme came to nothing. After besieging Compiègne throughout the summer of 1430, Philip was forced to retreat in haste and with the loss of much of his artillery. Inevitably, the English were blamed for this military setback. Philip expressed his dissatisfaction in a strongly worded letter to Henry VI, which was reinforced by diplomatic representations. The letter ran in part as follows:[1]

Most redoubted lord, I recommend myself to you in all humility. I imagine that you and your councillors remember that it was at your urgent request that I took part in your French war. For my part, I have so far accomplished everything that I agreed to and promised in the indenture made between . . . the cardinal of England [Henry Beaufort], acting in your name, and myself. It is a fact that, as a result, all my lands both in Burgundy and Picardy have been and are at war and in danger of destruction. . . . Moreover, it was at your request and command that I undertook the siege of Compiègne, though this was contrary to the advice of my council and my own opinion. For it had seemed to us better for

[1] *Letters and papers*, ii (1), 156–64. For the siege of Compiègne, see Champion, *Flavy*, 42–58 and 162–82.

me to advance towards Creil and Laon, as appears in the recommendations drawn up on this and sent to Calais by our secretary Master
Jehan Milet.[1]

It is also true, most redoubted lord, that, according to the agreement
drawn up on your part with my people, you ought to have paid me the
sum of 19,500 francs of royal money each month for the expenses of my
troops before Compiègne, as well as the cost of the artillery; while my
good cousin the earl of Huntingdon with his company ought to have
remained with me before the said town of Compiègne. . . . It was under
the impression that this would be done on your part, and especially that
the said payment would be made without fail, as agreed, that I had my
men stationed before Compiègne all the time.

But, most redoubted lord, these payments have not been kept up by
you, for they are in arrears to the tune of two months. The same goes
for the artillery, for which I have myself paid out over 40,000 saluts. . . .
Likewise, my good cousin of Huntingdon has been unable, according
to him, for want of payment, to keep his forces in the field any longer. . . .

My most redoubted lord, I cannot continue these [military operations]
without adequate provision in future from you . . . and without payment
of what is due to me, both on account of the two months above-
mentioned, and for the artillery. Thus, most redoubted lord, I ask and
entreat you most humbly to see that the said sums are paid over at once
to my people at Calais who have been waiting there for this purpose for
some time. . . .

Written in my town of Arras, 4 November 1430. Your humble and
obedient uncle, Philip, duke of Burgundy, of Brabant and of Limbourg.

Military operations were resumed by Philip almost at once, but in
a very half-hearted manner. Within a few days of writing this letter
he assembled another army and advanced into Picardy to avenge his
defeat at Compiègne, but this counterattack was by no means pressed
home. Monstrelet describes how the troops of the Burgundian van,
incautiously advancing in separate groups without scouts and in some
cases without wearing armour, and with considerable hooting and
holloing after hares they put up on their way, were surprised and cut
to pieces by the French.[2] Though Philip interrupted his dinner at
Péronne on receipt of the news of this disaster, he or his councillors
resolved not to do battle with the French, for it was considered unwise
and improper for the duke of Burgundy to risk his person in combat
with mere rank and file who had no leader of rank comparable to his.
Instead, they informed the French that Sir Jehan de Luxembourg

---

[1] This is the plan of action quoted above, pp. 22–4.
[2] *Chronique*, iv. 422–5, and see Chastellain, *Œuvres*, ii. 122.

would be sent next morning to do battle with them. But the French insisted that they would only fight the duke of Burgundy in person. Thus, after the armies had been drawn up for some hours in order of battle on either side of an impassable swamp, they both dispersed homewards.

Not long after these curious but indecisive military antics another truce intervened, which was ratified by Charles VII in September 1431, and further pacificatory documents were exchanged between Philip and Charles in December.[1] Meanwhile, Philip's attitude towards the English had changed from indifference or disillusion to outright discontent. In April 1431 another Burgundian embassy conveyed to London a gruesome picture of the horrors, and the expenses, of the war their master claimed to be waging on behalf of the king of England. Burgundy and Charolais were currently threatened by hostile forces; Rethel, which belonged to Philip's cousin, was devastated; Artois had been invaded and damaged; Burgundy, Charolais, the towns of Péronne, Roye and Montdidier and other lands had much diminished in value because of the war; Namur had been invaded; many ducal subjects were dead or had had to be ransomed at great expense. The duke was indeed so impoverished that he simply could not afford to continue the war. However, he would keep troops in the field for a further two months. After that, either the king of England must pay all his debts and expenses or, his ambassadors hinted, the duke would make a separate peace with France.[2]

These flights of diplomatic hyperbole had some effect on the English, who promised to provide more troops to help in the defence of Philip's lands. But it was events, rather than English bribes, which now served to nourish Philip's waning loyalty to them. On 30 June 1431 a small Burgundian force which had been sent by Philip to help Anthony of Lorraine, count of Vaudémont, in his struggle for the succession of the duchy of Lorraine with René, duke of Bar and titular king of Naples, was surprised by René's French army. The battle took place at Bulgnéville, and the Burgundians, fighting defensively in prepared positions and making excellent use of their artillery, won the day. Not only was the French army scattered, but René fell into Philip's hands. He was escorted to Talant near Dijon as a prisoner of war.[3]

[1] Plancher, iv. nos. 79, 90 and 91.
[2] For this paragraph, see the ambassador's instructions in Plancher, iv. no. 75.
[3] *Chronique de Lorraine*, xxv–xxvi; Monstrelet, *Chronique*, iv. 459–65; le

The Burgundian victory of Bulgnéville avenged the defeat of the prince of Orange at Anthon in Dauphiny the year before, it strengthened Philip's military and political situation *vis-à-vis* Charles VII, and it placed in his hands an invaluable diplomatic instrument. Indeed, it enabled him to delay still further the long-awaited peace settlement with Charles VII, while continuing to threaten Henry VI with this eventuality.[1] Fruitless Franco-Burgundian conferences took place at Auxerre in 1432. In June 1433 an Anglo-Burgundian conference was arranged at St. Omer, but though both Philip and John, duke of Bedford, arrived in the town, neither was prepared to suffer the indignity of going to visit the other. In spite of determined mediatory efforts by Henry Beaufort, Bedford's uncle, they never even met.[2] Philip's ambassadors, one of them Hue de Lannoy, were in London in July, but their efforts were of no avail. Nothing could now restore Philip's waning loyalty to the English, nor stimulate his interest in French affairs. Growing commitments in his own territories coincided with a growing appreciation in Burgundian court circles, of the need for a peace settlement. True, there was no very serious war to bring to an end, but ever since 1429 the duchy of Burgundy had been under intermittent attack. As early as 1423 the peace of Arras was in sight; ten years later, it was imminent.

Under Philip the Bold, Burgundy had successfully exploited France, but John the Fearless only succeeded in continuing this exploitation by becoming inextricably involved in French politics. In the years reviewed in this chapter, Philip the Good enjoyed, but never grasped, countless opportunities for French intervention. In 1419-20, for example, he abandoned Languedoc, where his father had asserted Burgundian influence.[3] Not once did he try to secure the city of Paris, possession of which had been the basis of his father's political situation in France, nor did he make any serious attempt to keep aflame there the flickering embers of Burgundian sentiment, which had been first lit by his grandfather. No wonder the anonymous burgess of Paris, disillusioned at last, accused him in 1431 of not

Bouvier, *Croniques*, 383–4; Germain, *Liber de virtutibus*, 31–3; Jouffroy, *Oratio*, 141–4; and Lecoy de la Marche, *René*, i. 83–92. For the next paragraph, see Déniau, *Commune de Lyon*, 550–4 and Payet, *Bulletin de l'Académie delphinale* (6) xxiv–vi (1957), 39–51.
[1] For example, in his letters of 29 December 1431, Plancher, iv. no. 93.
[2] Monstrelet, *Chronique*, v. 57–8. For the next sentence, see *Letters and Papers*, ii (1), 218–49.
[3] Dognon, *AM* i (1889), 483–95.

caring for the welfare of Paris and its people.[1] In reality, Philip's interest in Paris, in the years of English government there, was limited to the maintenance of a caretaker in his hôtel d'Artois, the protection of his own interests in the *Parlement*; and the currying of favour with the University, on whose behalf, for instance, he wrote in 1432 or 1433 to the king of England, asking him not to permit the establishment of a rival university at Caen.

The fact is that Philip's policy in these years was one of withdrawal from France. His aims there were virtually limited to securing his own frontiers by means of alliances and sporadic warfare, and to minor territorial acquisitions made by diplomacy. His attitude was dictated by the lure of ambition and by the ferment of circumstances elsewhere. The history of Burgundy was being made in Holland, not France.

[1] *Journal d'un bourgeois de Paris*, 274. For what follows, see *Chartularium univ. Parisiensis*, iv. 536–7.

CHAPTER TWO

Conquest and Expansion:
1420–33

The expansion of Burgundy in the early years of Philip the Good's reign was so dramatic and extensive that some historians have scarcely admitted the existence of a Burgundian polity before these years. In adding Brabant, Hainault and Holland to Flanders and Artois, Philip has been credited, not only with the unification of the Low Countries under himself, but also with the foundation of the Burgundian state. Other historians have emphasized the hidden forces at work behind the façade of personality, and it has even been suggested that no more than a series of lucky coincidences linked to a policy of territorial expansion inherited from earlier counts of Flanders and others, brought these territories into the Burgundian orbit.[1] However, in the pages which follow, evidence will be submitted which may convince the reader that in Philip's acquisition of these territories we have a notable example of a ruler's determination, and ambitions, impinging significantly on the course of events.

This is not to deny, of course, that accidents, and traditional policies, played their part. These influences are perhaps more apparent in the limited fields of expansion in which Philip found himself involved at the very start of his reign. I refer to the counties of Namur and Ferrette. Philip's efforts to obtain these territories, successful only in the case of the former, constituted a prelude to the struggle for Hainault and Holland.

In a sense, the acquisition of Namur was a complete accident. Its count, John III, found himself in need of cash, embarrassed by disputes with his next-door neighbour, Liège, and without an heir. In November 1420 Philip, 'wishing to enlarge' his territories, and 'considering that the said county lies next to' his land of Flanders,

[1] Bonenfant, *BMHGU* lxxiv (1960), 18–20.

appointed proctors to effect the purchase of Namur from John III.[1]
The price was high: 132,000 gold crowns; 25,000 down, and the
remainder in three annual payments. But Philip's instructions to his
officers show that he was determined not to miss this opportunity of
territorial aggrandizement.

Paris, 7 January 1421

Philip, duke of Burgundy, etc. . . . Greetings to all those who receive
these letters. In order to acquire certain large and important lordships
and territories, which will be extremely useful and profitable to us and
to our lands, we must at once raise a considerable sum of money.
Moreover, owing to the very heavy military expenses we have had to
meet since the death of our . . . father . . . , especially for the sieges of
Crépy-en-Laonnois, Sens, Montereau and Melun, which we undertook
in person with large forces of men-at-arms and archers, as well as those
of Roye in Vermandois and Allibaudières in Champagne, which were
very costly, we cannot find this money from our rents and revenues.
Instead, we must of necessity borrow on the security of some of our
jewellery and gold and silver plate, and mortgage certain parts of our
domain. Be it known that we, desiring this payment to be made, have
ordered and appointed, and do order and appoint by these present
letters, our well-loved and loyal servants Sir Jaques de Courtiamble,
lord of Commarin, our chamberlain; Master Dreue Mareschal, *maître*
of our *comptes* at Dijon; and our treasurer and governor-general of
finances, Jehan de Noident, empowering them or any two of them to
borrow on our behalf from our redoubted lady and mother madam the
duchess of Burgundy and others what sums of money they can.

One important condition was attached to the sale of Namur:
John III was to remain in possession and enjoy the usufruct until his
death. Nevertheless, Philip took the trouble to convoke the Estates
in June 1421 in order to secure their allegiance to his succession and,
as if to make assurance double sure, he appointed commissioners in
July with instructions to be ready to take over Namur in his name
in the event of John III's death. It was only after the succession to
Namur had thus been confirmed to him that Philip set out on the
campaign in Picardy which led to the battle of Mons-en-Vimeu. He

[1] ADN B1602, f. 149b, and see fos. 149–59 for other documents concerning
the purchase of Namur. For what follows, see *Chronique de l'abbaye de
Floreffe*, 88–93; Plancher, iv. 26–7 and no. 11 (whence the quotation); *IAB*
iv. 371–2 and *Coutumes de Namur*, i. 287–8; Muller, *Études . . . F. Courtoy*,
483–98; and Champion and de Thoisy, *Bourgogne–France–Angleterre*,
246–7.

had certainly spared no effort to obtain this territory which, however, did not finally become his until John III's death in 1429.

Whereas the acquisition of Namur was an isolated act by a single duke, all four of the Valois dukes of Burgundy made efforts, one way or another, to lay their hands on the rights and possessions of the Habsburgs in Upper Alsace, centred on the county of Ferrette. This had been ceded to Catherine of Burgundy as her dowry when she married Leopold IV of Austria in 1393. After Leopold's death in 1411 his brother Frederick seized all Catherine's possessions except a castle or two which John the Fearless garrisoned on her behalf. But Catherine stoutly maintained her rights to the county of Ferrette, not to mention her jewellery, which had been impounded in Vienna. This was the situation which Philip the Good inherited, and which he tried to exploit in the early years of his reign. He first struck a bargain with his aunt in 1420, whereby he promised to continue her 3,000 francs per annum pension, and to help her recover her lost property, on condition she made him her heir. Next, he opened negotiations with Duke Frederick of Austria with a view to the restoration of Catherine's jewels and lands. But in spite of these efforts, which were reinforced in 1422-3 by threats of war from Philip and actual hostilities from Catherine, Frederick IV remained unmoved. He even bullied Catherine into ceding him the Burgundian-held castle of Belfort and, when she died in 1426, in spite of Philip's claims as her heir, Ferrette remained a Habsburg possession. Philip had tried, and failed, but he had at least strengthened the Burgundian claims to this area, and thus indirectly contributed to the annexation of Upper Alsace by Burgundy in 1469.[1]

Namur and Ferrette were mere crumbs compared to the veritable feast which had been rousing the territorial appetites of the Valois dukes of Burgundy ever since 1385, in the form of Holland, Zeeland and Hainault. For it was in that year that Philip the Bold had married his daughter Margaret to Count William VI of Hainault, Holland and Zeeland. But the first Philip had not only staked his claims to these territories, he had also acquired the duchy of Brabant for his son Anthony. In the years that followed, events reinforced the efforts of John the Fearless to extend Burgundian influence in the Low Countries. Duke Anthony died at Agincourt, leaving Brabant in the unsteady hands of an aristocratic junta and under the nominal rule of a boy duke, Anthony's son John IV. Two years later, in 1417, on

[1] Stouff, *Catherine de Bourgogne*, is the main authority for this paragraph. See too *DRA* viii. 251-2.

Count William's death, Hainault, Holland and Zeeland passed to his only child Jacqueline, then aged sixteen. Within weeks of William's death, John the Fearless was helping to arrange the marriage of his nephew of Brabant and his niece of Holland, and John IV and Jacqueline were engaged on 1 August 1417.[1]

THE SUCCESSION TO BRABANT AND TO HAINAULT, HOLLAND AND ZEELAND

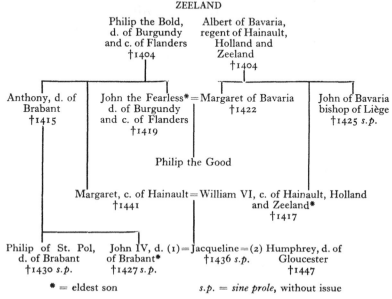

* = eldest son   s.p. = *sine prole*, without issue

Jacqueline was not the only claimant to the succession of Hainault, Holland and Zeeland and, soon after her engagement to John IV, her father's brother, John of Bavaria, stepped into the arena with the encouragement of King Sigismund, the Emperor-elect. This John had been foiled by the citizens of Liège in his attempt to use his position as bishop-elect of Liège to further his own ends and increase his own personal power. He now saw an opportunity to establish himself as ruler of his dead brother's territories. Abandoning his bishopric, he installed himself in Dordrecht and appealed to the other

---

[1] *Algemene geschiedenis*, iii, ch. 9, is the best modern account of this and what follows. The documentary material is in *Groot charterboek*, iv; *Boergoensche Charters; Cartulaire de Hainaut*, iv; and von Löher, *Beiträge*. On Jacqueline and Philip the main authorities used here are (in declining order of importance) von Löher, *Jacobäa von Bayern*; van Riemsdijk, *VKAWL* (n.s.) viii (1906), 1–82; de Potter, *Geschiedenis van Jacoba van Beieren*; le Blant, *Les quatres mariages*; and Putnam, *A medieval princess*.

Dutch towns to support his claim to the guardianship of his niece's lands. Before the end of 1417, manifestoes had been distributed on his behalf; Sigismund had promised him imperial investment with Hainault, Holland and Zeeland; the Fathers of the Church assembled at Constance had been asked to prevent the issue of the necessary dispensations for the marriage of John IV and Jacqueline; and Holland had been set ablaze with civil war.

In spite of the efforts of Sigismund and John of Bavaria to stop it, the marriage of the duke of Brabant, John IV, and the heiress of Holland, was celebrated as planned at Easter 1418, in The Hague. Whether, canonically speaking, it was acceptable and valid is a moot point. The pope, Martin V, had issued dispensations on 22 December 1417 and revoked them, under pressure from Sigismund, on 5 January 1418! Later, on 27 May 1419, he officially confirmed the marriage.

The intervention of John of Bavaria, and the war of succession in Holland which followed it, may have been approved by John the Fearless. But in 1418 and 1419 that ruler was far too busy in France to concern himself closely with the intricacies of Dutch politics. It therefore fell to his son Philip, then stationed at Ghent, to try to achieve a settlement. He arranged a truce, acted as mediator, and initiated negotiations. But the peace settlement published under his auspices at Woudrichem on 13 February 1419 was so favourable to John of Bavaria that Jacqueline refused to accept it. Not only was John allowed to remain in possession of those parts of Holland, including Dordrecht and Rotterdam, which he already occupied; he was to share the government of Jacqueline's territories with her for a five-year period, and he was recognized as Jacqueline's heir. Moreover, in compensation for the abandonment of his claim to be count of Holland, John of Bavaria was to be paid the sum of 100,000 nobles by Duke John IV of Brabant.

When Philip succeeded his father as duke of Burgundy in September 1419 the succession to Holland, Hainault and Zeeland was still in dispute. Evidently it was in his interests to maintain the *status quo* while seeking to prevent open warfare. But the weakness, or incompetence, of Duke John IV made the implementation of this policy increasingly difficult. Instead of intervening forcefully in Holland on his wife's behalf, John IV mortgaged Holland and Zeeland to John of Bavaria, in April 1420, by the treaty of St. Maartensdijk in Tholen. Instead of enlisting the support of his own subjects in Brabant, he alienated their sympathies; and, worst of all, instead of living amicably with his wife, he actually caused her to desert him.

Although the terms of the treaty of St. Maartensdijk were extremely unwelcome to Jacqueline, the reasons for her flight from Brussels on 11 April 1420 were complex. The human element was probably more important than politics and, to domestic or sexual incompatibility between herself and her husband, must be added a whole series of grievances. The last straw came when Duke John IV excluded a number of Jacqueline's ladies-in-waiting from dining at court and, if we may believe the ducal secretary Edmond de Dynter, even reduced her allowance of soup and wine. She summoned her redoubtable mother from Le Quesnoy in Hainault and, when redress was not forthcoming, mother and daughter decamped angrily from Brussels.[1]

At first, the situation resulting from this marital disaster was scarcely dangerous for Philip, though he did his best to reconcile the estranged couple. But Jacqueline's dramatic flight to England early in 1421 and, above all, her marriage to Duke Humphrey of Gloucester late in 1422, raised the spectre of immediate English intervention in the Low Countries, and the possibility of future English rule in Hainault, Holland and Zeeland. What made these events even more sinister, from Philip's point of view, was that Jacqueline had travelled to England with the help of King Henry V, and that he paid her expenses while she was there.[2] By the spring of 1423 Humphrey was using the title count of Hainault, Holland and Zeeland, while Pope Martin V's commission of cardinals was still examining the validity of Jacqueline's first marriage. Since Rome dithered, Jacqueline had her second marriage confirmed at Peñiscola, where the half-forgotten anti-pope, Benedict XIII, still obstinately maintained his own supremacy.

Even a most cursory inspection of the accounts of the Burgundian receipt-general of all finances demonstrates Philip's acute concern in these affairs. The sections devoted to messengers' expenses betray, throughout the years 1420-3, constant comings and goings between Philip and Humphrey, duke of Gloucester, and others in England; between Philip and Duke John IV; and, especially, between Philip and John of Bavaria in Holland. Though the intricate mesh of circumstance revealed no obvious opening for Burgundian expansion, Philip nevertheless kept in close touch with events. Thus, while the future

---

[1] De Dynter, *Chronique des ducs de Brabant*, iii. 388–9 and Gysels, *Miscellanea van der Essen*, 413–27.
[2] Wylie and Waugh, *Henry V*, iii. 291 n. 5 and Bonenfant, *Meutre de Montereau*, 125 and n. 4.

of Hainault, Holland and Zeeland was doubtful and subject to dispute, Burgundian intervention there was firm and constant. Moreover Burgundian influence was significantly extended on 6 April 1424,
when the childless and middle-aged John of Bavaria made Philip heir
to his extensive Dutch estates.[1]

It was in the second half of 1424 and the first few months of 1425
that the course of events took a dramatic and critical turn which
intensified Burgundian intervention in both Hainault and Holland.
Far from merely watching these developments, Philip grasped with
vigour and decision the very opportunities for which he had waited.
In these momentous months he moulded the destiny of the Low
Countries to suit his own ambitions by decisively extending Burgundian power in the disputed territories.

As early as July 1424 John of Bavaria had heard rumours of an
impending English attack in the Low Countries. Duke Humphrey of
Gloucester was in fact raising troops in England with a view to
seizing or conquering Hainault from John IV of Brabant. While
Philip the Good and John, duke of Bedford, were still trying to
achieve a diplomatic settlement, Humphrey and Jacqueline crossed
the Channel to Calais. They actually left Dover at 10.0 a.m. on
16 October and, aided by favourable wind and weather, reached
Calais between 2.0 and 3.0 p.m. on the same day.[2] The ever watchful
Four Members of Flanders[3] had sent to Calais as early as 21 September to try to ascertain the truth of reports that Humphrey was bringing
an army to invade Hainault and when he arrived at Calais their
representative greeted him with the request not to traverse Flemish
territory. Philip's immediate reaction was equally mild: his deputies
asked Humphrey if he would be kind enough to avoid passing through
Artois. But the English army could scarcely reach Hainault except by
crossing Burgundian territory, and in fact it marched past Hesdin
and across Artois in November, apparently without incident. It was
not until the middle of December, when much of Hainault was in the
hands of Humphrey and Jacqueline and several of its towns had been
occupied by English garrisons, that Philip abandoned his conciliatory
efforts and pacific intentions or pretences. Having waited until
John IV had shown himself utterly incapable of defending his own

[1] Plancher, iv. no. 22.
[2] These details are recorded in the letter of a participant, printed in *Letters
and papers*, ii (2), 396–400. For what follows see *Précis analytique* (2) ii. 21
and ADN B1931, f. 68b. See too, Vickers, *Humphrey, duke of Gloucester*.
[3] Ghent, Bruges, Ypres and the Franc or castellany of Bruges.

territories, Philip the Good persuaded John's brother Philip, count of St. Pol, to lead a joint Burgundian–Brabantine army into Hainault. In view of subsequent events, the conclusion is inescapable, that Philip the Good's delay was deliberately contrived to enable him to gain control of Hainault for himself.

Just at the moment when Philip the Good's troops, acting officially on Duke John IV of Brabant's behalf, were preparing to rescue Hainault from the English aggressor, an event occurred which transformed the whole situation. John of Bavaria, effective ruler of Holland, died on 6 January 1425, murdered, it was claimed by some, and actually confessed under duress by one of the suspects, with a poisoned prayer-book. The intensity of Burgundian governmental activity at this juncture, revealed above all in the records of messengers sent out by the ducal council in Flanders, betrays Philip's deep concern and unalterable determination to extend his grasp over the counties of Holland and Zeeland, which John of Bavaria had been ruling as governor and mortgagee for Duke John IV and Jacqueline. When John of Bavaria died, Philip was on a visit to Burgundy, where he had married his second wife, Bonne of Artois, on 30 November 1424. In the north, he had left a council of regency to look after Flanders and Artois. These self-styled 'messeigneurs du gouvernement' despatched the following messages in January 1425.[1]

6.1.1425. Letters close to Philip at Dijon, reporting John of Bavaria's illness. His doctors at The Hague despaired of his life.

7.1.1425. Letters to Philip at Dijon, reporting John of Bavaria's death, stating that Humphrey, duke of Gloucester, had already learnt the news, and asking Philip to return at once to his northern territories.

12.1.1425. Letters sent to Enghien in Hainault, asking for information about the duke of Gloucester's situation and intentions.

13.1.1425. Letters to the maritime bailiff at Sluis, which show that he had been ordered to arrest all Dutchmen and Zeelanders passing through Sluis and confiscate any letters they might be carrying addressed to Humphrey and Jacqueline.

19.1.1425. Messengers sent to the receiver-general of Flanders at Bruges, to see about payments for a certain embassy which the regency council had sent to Holland 'concerning the succession and inheritance recently fallen to my lord of Burgundy in Holland and Zeeland through John duke of Bavaria's death'.

27.1.1425. Messenger sent to the ambassadors going to Holland, then at Sluis, with copies of letters from 'the duke of Gloucester and Lady

---

[1] AGR CC21800, fos. 42b–44b.

Jaque of Bavaria' to the people of Holland and Zeeland, asking them to accept them as their rulers. These letters had been intercepted near Ghent by the bailiff of Ghent, and sent to the council.

Meanwhile, an embassy had been sent on 12 January from Ghent to John IV of Brabant, to remind him that Philip was heir to John of Bavaria's extensive estates in Holland, Zeeland and Hainault, 'and to seek his advice, help and good counsel in this matter'.[1] As a matter of fact, Philip and his councillors hoped not only to inherit John of Bavaria's private possessions in Holland, but also to step into his political shoes there, but the war in Hainault, and a bizarre personal quarrel between Philip and Humphrey, now intervened.

Humphrey and Jacqueline had gained control of most of Hainault in the autumn of 1424 without even using the army they had brought from England. They set up their government at Mons, the citizens of which had somewhat reluctantly accepted these new rulers.[2] In January 1425 Humphrey was voted a subsidy or *aide* by the Estates of Hainault for his military expenses, but he was unable for long to use with any conviction the proud title 'count of Hainault, Holland and Zeeland'. Early in March, the Burgundian-Brabantine army advanced into his newly won but weakly held territories and laid siege to the town of Braine-le-Comte, on the main road from Brussels to Mons. Humphrey did nothing and, within a few days, the town with its English garrison surrendered. The sudden collapse of resistance there was afterwards attributed by some English prisoners to defeatism, engendered among them by the appearance on the besiegers' side of St. George, fully armed and riding on a white horse. As a matter of fact, their excuse was not quite as extravagant or improbable as it seems, for a Brabantine knight, with arms similar to those of St. George, had taken part in the siege mounted on a white horse.

After the fall of Braine-le-Comte, in the middle of March 1425, Duke Humphrey of Gloucester and Philip, count of St. Pol, each led or sent out his army as if to do battle in earnest. According to one chronicler, the armies were actually drawn up in battle order opposite one another on either side of a small stream, when news of a truce was brought to them. But neither was prepared to suffer the indignity of being first to leave the field. The two armies therefore remained in

[1] ADN B1931, f. 70.
[2] For this and what follows, see *Particularités curieuses*; Monstrelet, *Chronique*, iv; de Waurin, *Croniques*, iii; de Dynter, *Chronique des ducs de Brabant*, iii; le Févre, *Chronique*, ii; and de Fenin, *Mémoires*.

full array until after dark, when a nocturnal, if not simultaneous, withdrawal was effected by them both.

The truce which occasioned this minor military farce had itself been brought about by something equally farcical. In January Duke Humphrey had written to Philip complaining of his warlike intentions in summoning troops to help John IV of Brabant to recover Hainault. Philip replied in early March, challenging Humphrey to a single combat with either King Sigismund or John, duke of Bedford, as judge, and pompously hinting that young knights like themselves should settle their differences by personal combat rather than by waging public war, with all the slaughter it entailed. In mid-March the date of the contest was fixed for St. George's Day next, 23 April 1425, and Humphrey, furnished with suitable safe-conducts by Philip, abandoned both his newly won county of Hainault and his wife Jacqueline, and returned to England. His exact motives for this desertion of wife and territory are obscure, but he took with him to England one of Jacqueline's ladies-in-waiting, the beautiful Eleanor Cobham, whom he subsequently married. Jacqueline was left more or less besieged in Mons, in a situation which was politically and militarily hopeless. Hainault was slipping from her grasp.

How serious were Philip the Good's martial intentions against the duke of Gloucester? Did his horrified councillors really find it impossible to dissuade their duke from this bizarre and perilous adventure? Can we believe Monstrelet and the others, who describe Philip retiring in April 1425 to his castle of Hesdin in Artois, and going into strict training for this heroic single combat? No one surely would have been better placed to know the truth than the ducal herald Charolais, Jehan Lefèvre.[1]

> In order to be ready on St. George's day, the duke withdrew to Hesdin and summoned several armourers to make the necessary armour and equipment. He took exercise every morning in the beautiful park of Hesdin, which is one of the finest in the country, and he had certain secret places where he practised fencing and took lessons. . . . As to the gear the duke had made for the day of the combat, I think that no other prince had anything so fine by way of pavilions, horses' caparisons and coats of arms. And, to demonstrate the truth of this, I appeal to those who have seen these things in the castle of Lille in Flanders, where they still are in 1460.

Bizarre as it may seem, Lefèvre was right. The accounts prove to the hilt that Philip really was naïve or impetuous enough to entertain

[1] Le Févre, *Chronique*, ii. 106-7.

serious duelling intentions.[1] His friends and allies were pressed into service. The bishop of Liège sent one of his people to Hesdin to teach Philip 'certain tricks and stratagems in the art of fencing', and some fine large war-horses were sent by the count of Virneburg. Armourers, painters, other craftsmen and materials, were brought from Paris and elsewhere. Nearly £14,000 was spent on the ornate accoutrements mentioned by Lefèvre, which included seven horse-blankets embroidered in gold thread. On one were the ducal arms, on another, the arms of the duchy of Burgundy, another had the arms of Flanders, two others, of blue velvet, supported the arms of Artois and the county of Burgundy, another, of blue and white patterned satin, bore Philip's favourite device all over it, of a steel and flint with sparks and flames, and the seventh displayed that favourite Burgundian emblem, the cross of St. Andrew. There were standards and pennons too, and a magnificent tent of blue and white patterned satin embroidered all over with coats of arms, steels, flints, flames and sparks.

News of the great fight thus preparing spread abroad. At Mainz, Eberhard Windecke heard all about it and recorded it in his chronicle.[2] But, of course, the duel was never fought. The pope banned it in May; the English Parliament resolved to stop it at all costs in July; and John, duke of Bedford, solemnly forbade it in September. Other important matters soon engaged Philip's attention. In the summer of 1425 a concentrated diplomatic offensive directed against the deserted and beleaguered Jacqueline culminated in a striking, if temporary, Burgundian victory. It was agreed that Philip, having got hold of Jacqueline's person, should keep her in his care, and therefore virtually a prisoner, until the pope had decided whether she was married to Humphrey or to John IV of Brabant. Meanwhile she was to be excluded from the government of her own territories. At the same time Philip persuaded John IV to share the administration of Hainault with him and to transfer that of Holland to him for at least twelve years.

So far circumstances had played into Philip's hands. But Jacqueline was a woman of determination and resource. She had appealed to Humphrey early in June for his immediate intervention on her behalf. There was no response, and she had to submit to being placed under

[1] ADN B1931, fos. 107, 112, 113, 152, 160 and 182–94. Partly printed in de Laborde, *Ducs de Bourgogne*, i. 201–4.
[2] Windecke, *Denkwürdigkeiten*, 216. For what follows, see *Letters and papers*, ii (2) 412–14; *Rotuli parliamentorum*, iv. 277; and Plancher, iv. no. 46.

house arrest at Ghent while Philip prepared to take control of
Holland. At 5.0 a.m. on 2 September 1425, the very moment when
Philip was arranging her transfer to Lille,[1] where she would have been
far more securely in his power, Jacqueline contrived a dramatic
escape from Ghent dressed as a man. Galloping thence to Antwerp,
she made her way to Gouda to rally and inspire the forces of opposition, in Holland, to the Burgundian seizure of the country.

From September 1425 until April 1428 Philip never once visited
France. The war in Holland occupied his person, his armies, his
finances, to the exclusion of other interests. Hitherto, the military
annals of Burgundy had comprised a mixed assortment of campaigns,
sieges, and pitched battles. Now, for the first time, the duke waged
a real war. A war of conquest and military occupation; a war which
was in large measure a civil war, fought between places like Gouda,
Oudewater and Schoonhoven and the aristocratic, feudal elements of
the population, supporting Jacqueline, against the merchant cities
and burgesses of Rotterdam, Amsterdam and Haarlem. Above all,
it was a long, hard, costly war, which was only won because of the
energy and determination of Philip the Good himself.

Philip was in Bruges when he had news of Jacqueline's escape. His
reactions were swift. On 4 September, apparently thinking that she
was making for England, he sent couriers to the Flemish ports and
Calais to ask if 'madam the heiress of Hainault, who had left Ghent,
had passed that way'.[2] But on 6 September he was already writing to
the knights and squires of Oudenaarde, to Courtrai, Lille, and elsewhere, as well as to the bishop of Liège, ordering them to come at
once in arms to Sluis to accompany him to Holland and Zeeland. By
October he was receiving the oaths of allegiance of Alkmaar, The
Hague and other places in Holland loyal to him, while spies were
despatched from Bruges to England, to try to ascertain if there were
plans for English intervention on Jacqueline's behalf. Rotterdam,
Leiden and the other towns favourable to Philip were strongly garrisoned, and some of the most experienced and famous Burgundian
captains, veterans like Jehan de Villiers, lord of l'Isle Adam, and the
Flemish knight, Roland d'Uutkerke, were now stationed in Holland.
But these precautions, and this activity, did not stop Philip's spirited
and resolute cousin from striking the first blow. On 22 October

[1] ADN B1933, f. 49. The time and date of her flight is given in AGR
CC21801, f. 10.
[2] For this and what follows, see ADN B1931, fos. 162a-b and 167b; and
B1933, fos. 62b, 77, 147 ff., etc.

1. Holland, Hainault and Zeeland

1425 Jacqueline's partisans attacked and defeated near Alphen a Burgundian army, consisting mainly of the citizen levies of Haarlem, Amsterdam and Leiden, which was advancing towards her stronghold of Gouda.

The battle of Alphen was a serious setback for Philip, who was compelled to spend the next few weeks carefully rallying the spirits of the Dutch towns by collecting reinforcements, confirming their privileges, and visiting them in turn. We find him at Dordrecht, Rotterdam, Delft and Leiden before the end of the year. Meanwhile, there was no need for Philip's spies to reveal the growing English threat to him: John, duke of Bedford, had tipped him off early in December, by informing him of Humphrey's aggressive intentions,[1] and confirmation that an English force had actually set sail for Holland was sent to Philip on 30 December 1425. He himself takes up the story of subsequent events in a letter written in January 1426 to the council and *chambre des comptes* at Dijon.

Middelburg, Zeeland.
19 January, 1426.

Dear and well-beloved, since you always like to know of our health and to have our news, we now inform you, to your consolation and gratification, that, at the time of writing, and thanks to Our Lord, we are in excellent health and doing very well.

At about two o'clock in the morning of Saturday, the 5th of this month, when we were at Leiden in Holland, definite news reached us that Lord Fitzwalter, self-styled lieutenant of the duke of Gloucester in the lands of Holland and Zeeland, had arrived near Zierikzee in Zeeland with 1,500 English soldiers, intending to join forces with the duchess of Brabant [Jacqueline] and make war in Holland and Zeeland. Consequently, in order to resist this English expedition, we left Leiden at dawn and reached Rotterdam the same day. Next day we took ship, accompanied by people from our own lands as well as Dutchmen and Zeelanders, with the intention of contacting and fighting the English at sea.

While at sea, our people came across some of the English, numbering about 300, all of whom were taken or killed. We then pursued the other English forces to the port of Brouwershaven in Zeeland, where they had retreated and disembarked. As we were anchored off the town and port of Brouwershaven, they sent the herald Gloucester to us, to state on behalf of their captain Lord Fitzwalter that if we would like to fight him, he would offer us a time and place for the battle. But we sent our

---

[1] AGR CC21801, f. 16b. The letter which follows is printed by Gachard, *Rapport sur Dijon*, 116–17, from ACO B11942, no. 48.

herald Burgundy to reply to Fitzwalter, that it was hardly up to him to choose the battlefield, since we were strong enough to station ourselves, and to offer battle, wherever and whenever we chose.

After that, because of the weather, which was very windy, we stayed at sea, taking care to keep them blockaded, until last Sunday, 13th day of this month, when the winds died down sufficiently. Then we and our people, numbering about 4,000 combatants, disembarked at the port of Brouwershaven, and attacked the English, with whom were the lord of Heemstede and his cousin the count of Heemstede, accompanied by 3,000 combatants from Zeeland. In all, counting English and Zeelanders allied to them, there must have been over 4,000 enemy.

By the grace of God, they were defeated. A good many were put to flight, and we chased these into the sea, so that few escaped. This in spite of the fact that, at the moment when battle was joined with the English, only about two-thirds of our people had got on shore. For the English advanced to attack us, and began to fight us, before all our men had disembarked. On our side, no one of note was killed, except for Sir Andrieu de Valines (God have mercy on him), but several were wounded. Of the enemy, the captains and principal men are dead, except for the lord of Heemstede, who is a prisoner, and a good 200 English also prisoners. The rest are dead or dispersed, either on the battlefield or in pursuit. Nevertheless, with regard to the said Fitzwalter, we still haven't ascertained if he is dead or taken, but part of his armour, which he wore in the battle, has been found, also his banner, flung to the ground. And several people claim that he fled.

Dear and well-beloved, pass on this news to the good subjects of our towns in the duchy and county of Burgundy, and of Mâcon and Auxerre, to give them cause to rejoice, and so that they can give thanks and praise to Our Lord for our victory.

A solitary and anonymous chronicler provides further information, evidently from a participant, about the battle of Brouwershaven, confirming the accuracy of Philip's account, just quoted.[1] He tells how, during those days of gales, when the ducal fleet was immobilized off Brouwershaven, the enterprising citizens of neighbouring Zierikzee did excellent business with both armies, by selling them provisions. He describes the disembarkation of the Burgundian army, which consisted mainly of the municipal levies of the Dutch towns loyal to Philip. The men of Dordrecht, with their red and white hoods, were in the van, followed by the citizen-soldiers of The Hague and Delft, in black and white. Disembarkation was hampered by an ebbing tide, but, for some reason, the English did not try to prevent Philip's troops from leaving their boats and coming ashore. English discipline

[1] *Livre des trahisons*, 181–3.

apparently impressed and possibly dismayed the Dutch. For the English advanced marching in step, ignored a brief salvo fired at them by a cannoneer from Dordrecht, and then suddenly emitted a frightening yell and a fanfare of trumpets and bugles. Holding their fire till the armies were well within range, the Dutch 'shot simultaneously at the English with over a thousand crossbows. But these did about as much harm to them as a shower of rotten apples:' they returned fire with their deadly long-bows and drove the Dutch back in disorder. However, arrows could make no impression on Philip and his heavily-armed knights, who now arrived on the scene. The chronicler points out that Andrieu de Valines was killed by an arrow in the eye because he was not wearing a helmet. Duke Philip was there in person, his banner carried by the lord of l'Isle Adam, whose armour, and the shaft of the banner he was carrying, were soon festooned with numerous arrows that had lodged in them; and arrows dented or damaged many a cuirass. Eventually the English were driven back onto, and then along, a dyke, where the Dutchmen slaughtered them mercilessly, so that scarcely a single one escaped. 'The poor English archers leapt into the ditches and were either drowned, or else they were cut down as they tried to clamber out of them.' So ended the battle of Brouwershaven, a little-known chapter in English history, but the first resounding victory of Burgundian arms in Holland.

This victory was followed up by further energetic action on Philip's part. Throughout January and February 1426 he was at Middelburg in Zeeland, and the whole of this county, including the town of Zierikzee, now went over to him. When he sailed back to Flanders at the end of March he may have congratulated himself on the fact that most of Holland and Zeeland was in his hands. If so, he was soon disillusioned, for his departure was the signal for a renewed offensive by Jacqueline and her partisans. Moreover, while they laid siege to Haarlem and defeated a contingent of Flemish reinforcements in a second battle of Alphen on 30 April 1426, the town of Alkmaar and with it the whole of Kennemerland raised the standard of revolt against Philip and went over to Jacqueline. By July Philip was back again in Holland with a large army, and he now embarked on a carefully prepared campaign, which soon resulted in the reduction of the Kennemerlanders, who had to pay over 100,000 gold crowns in reparations, while the town of Alkmaar forfeited its walls, gates and privileges. But, when Philip left the country once more, in October 1426, no significant military progress had been made, except that more Burgundian garrisons had been installed in the towns, and more Burgundian blockhouses constructed at strategic points. Jacqueline still held Gouda, Oudewater, Zevenbergen, and Amersfoort in the bishopric of Utrecht. Indeed, in this last area, Philip had lost ground in the summer of 1426, for the aspirant to the episcopal succession there, Zweder van Culemborg, who enjoyed Burgundian support, had been all but driven out by the superior forces, and popularity, of his rival Rudolf von Diepholz, who became in March 1427 a formal ally of Jacqueline.[1]

Philip's only aim, in leaving Holland in the autumn of 1426, seems to have been to return with reinforcements. He sailed once more from Sluis shortly before Christmas, taking with him 427 men-at-arms from Artois, well provided with armed varlets, and 1,210 cross-bow-men and archers.[2] More troops were assembled in Holland and siege was laid in mid-winter to Jacqueline's stronghold and naval base of Zevenbergen, a place which Philip had already attacked in the autumn. Its defender and lord was Gerrit van Strijen, who proudly unfurled the imperial banner from the battlements, though the only help he obtained from King Sigismund was a series of imperial letters inviting other Dutch towns to come to his aid. Since the great inundation of the sea in 1421, the town and castle of Zevenbergen had been an island, and the Burgundian siege of it, which lasted some four months, was conducted by sea, Philip's ships, some with towers erected on them, being anchored in a circle offshore. Surrender was eventually forced on Gerrit van Strijen by the townspeople in April 1427. We are told that in the early stages of the siege the castle had been supplied with food from the town. Later, when provisions were short in the town and more abundant in the castle, Gerrit refused to help the citizens. It was this internal quarrel which led the town to open its gates, and the castle fell with it. The luckless Gerrit had to give the place to Philip and suffer imprisonment at Lille, and the burgesses of Zevenbergen were made to swear an oath of allegiance to their conqueror.

Within a few days of the surrender of Zevenbergen, on 11 April 1427, Philip's attention was deflected to Hainault by an event which was dangerous, yet potentially advantageous, for him. After surviving

---

[1] For Utrecht, see especially *Utrechtsche jaarboeken*, i; de Hullu, *Utrechtsche schisma*; and Post, *Utrechtsche bisschopsverkiezingen*.
[2] ADN B1935, 154b ff. For this paragraph, see de Dynter, *Chronique des ducs de Brabant*, iii. 472–3; O. van Dixmude, *Merkwaerdige gebeurtenissen*, 116–17; and Lambin, *MSAB* v (1837), 13–16.

a plot of Margaret of Hainault to kill or imprison him, Duke John IV of Brabant died a natural death on 17 April. In Brabant he was succeeded automatically by his brother Philip, count of St. Pol; but his death left the succession of Hainault wide open. True, Philip the Good had more or less taken it over from John IV in 1425, but this was because John IV, as its rightful ruler in right of his wife Jacqueline, had accepted Philip as partner in its administration. Now John IV was dead, Hainault in theory reverted to Jacqueline, who might be expected to persuade her English husband, Duke Humphrey of Gloucester, to try again to seize it for her by force of arms. What made the situation doubly dangerous for Philip was the presence in Hainault of his aunt, the dowager countess Margaret, whose main interest in life was to further her daughter Jacqueline's career. She used the title 'duchess of Bavaria, countess of Hainault, Holland and Zeeland', and certainly hoped to see Jacqueline, rather than Philip, ruling in Hainault and Holland. Nor was she herself lacking in political ambition.

It so happened that, just before the surrender of Zevenbergen and the death of John IV, Jacqueline had launched an intensive diplomatic campaign to obtain English help. Her opening salvo was a rhetorical but outspoken letter addressed to the English Privy Council, parts of which ran as follows:[1]

> Most noble, very reverend, reverend fathers in God, my most honourable lords and special friends, I recommend myself to your highnesses, worships and gracious lordships as humbly as I can. . . .
> Concerning my desolate self, be pleased to know that, at the writing of this, I am in reasonable health, but, on the other hand, in great anxiety, fear, danger and grief. . . . Most noble, very reverend, reverend fathers in God, my most honourable lords and special friends, I am sending to your noblenesses, fatherships and discretions, and to my most redoubted lord and husband, my friends and loyal councillors Louis de Montfort and Arnault de Gand, knights, bearers of this letter, to humbly explain my urgent and pressing affairs, which are for the most part already known to you, in order to refresh your most noble memories and to bring to your notice the monstrous outrages, oppressions and injuries, which my cousin of Burgundy has perpetrated against me in the last two years in pursuing me from one of my countries to another in order to disinherit me, and in cruelly spilling the blood of my poor but loyal subjects. . . .
> I have also instructed my above-mentioned councillors to explain to

---

[1] Von Löher, *Beiträge*, ii. 220–2.

you that I cannot endure much longer without your help and my husband's. . . . So I, a poor disconsolate woman, entreat you most humbly that it may please you to consider this matter sympathetically. Have pity on my grievous suffering and bring it to the notice of my most redoubted lord and husband without any further delaying with messages and embassies. . . . Written in my town of Gouda, 8 April 1427.

As a matter of fact, encouraged no doubt by news of John IV's death, Humphrey, duke of Gloucester, did make some attempt in the summer of 1427 to intervene once more in the Low Countries. Rumour had it at Ghent, in June, that he was on his way to Holland in force; and in July Philip's councillors at Ghent reported that he had been sighted at sea with his fleet.[1] But John, duke of Bedford, who feared that an Anglo-Burgundian breach would seriously jeopardize the whole English position in France, managed to persuade the English government, and his brother Humphrey, to do nothing, in spite of further urgent communications from Jacqueline.

Thus it was that the destiny of Hainault was settled without any reference to Jacqueline, who was rebuffed by England and hopelessly involved in any case with the war in Holland. The surrender of Zevenbergen left Philip free to visit Hainault in person, to convoke the Estates and, after some resistance from Mons, to persuade them to accept him as governor until such time as Jacqueline abandoned her English husband and alliance. Her ambassadors had been tricked or ignored; her mother was side-tracked; her claims to Hainault were shelved. Philip the Good now took over its administration and its revenues and, on 24 June 1427, Guillaume de Lalaing was sworn in as first Burgundian bailiff of Hainault.

In the summer of 1427 Jacqueline's military situation was by no means desperate. Although, since the fall of Zevenbergen, she had altogether lost control of Zeeland and southern Holland, her fleet, under the command of Willem van Brederode, still cruised undefeated in the Zuiderzee. Furthermore, though she had failed to bring the English into Holland in her support, she had found a more useful and nearer ally in the person of Rudolf von Diepholz, on whom Philip the Good formally declared war at the end of May 1427. Hostilities were thus extended to include Utrecht and, when Philip returned to the struggle in September 1427 for yet another winter campaign, the centre of operations had shifted eastward to the southern shore of the Zuiderzee. At first Burgundy was successful.

---

[1] AGR CC21802, fos. 6 and 7. For Duke Humphrey's parliamentary subsidy in aid of Jacqueline, see *Foedera*, x. 374–5.

c

Willem van Brederode was captured and his fleet dispersed at the naval battle of Wieringen, which was then an island, though now forming part of mainland Holland. But on land, in spite of the fortified bridgeheads which Philip established on the shores of the Zuiderzee at Naarden, at the mouth of the Eem, and at Harderwijk, he could make little progress. The five-hour assault on Amersfoort, on 1 November 1427, which he directed in person, was a failure. Instead of a triumphant mid-winter conquest of the episcopal principality of Utrecht, the immediate aim of which was to expel Jacqueline's ally Rudolf and leave in his place, on the episcopal throne there, the Burgundian candidate Zweder van Culemborg, Philip was forced to concentrate his military resources on defending his Zuiderzee bridgeheads, while Zweder, far from recovering the capital city of Utrecht which he claimed was his, was driven out of his own ancestral town and castle of Culemborg by a successful nocturnal assault on 23 January 1428. Soon after this, Philip's floating blockhouse at the mouth of the Eem was wrecked by the combined destructive agencies of enemy artillery and ice-floes, and he was forced to withdraw altogether. So ended one of the most elaborate of Burgundian military undertakings, Philip's fourth consecutive campaign in Holland since September 1425.

It must have long been apparent to Jacqueline that coming to terms with her cousin Philip the Good would mean abandoning her territories to him. The possibility of continuing the war indefinitely, especially with the help of Utrecht, was a real one; but Jacqueline could scarcely hope for an outright victory against the military might of Burgundy. At best, she might hope to achieve a sort of military stalemate, costly in lives and suffering, and not enabling her to enjoy possession of any significant part of her lands. She was determined and resourceful, but not obstinate. Her only hope of achieving her aim of obtaining possession of Holland or Hainault lay in English help; for Philip, had he been deserted by John, duke of Bedford, in France, and attacked by Humphrey, duke of Gloucester, in the Low Countries, would surely have been forced to sue for peace and to make significant territorial concessions to Jacqueline.

In the early months of 1428 the whole basis of Jacqueline's position, the sole justification of her endeavour, her English connection, was severed. The first blow, bitterest of all perhaps, was the final papal judgment in the affair of her double marriage, first to Duke John IV of Brabant, then to Duke Humphrey of Gloucester. On 9 January 1428 Pope Martin V ruled, finally and irrevocably, that her marriage to Duke John IV was alone valid. As if this were not enough, Humphrey took advantage of the sentence to marry his mistress, Eleanor Cobham, and demonstrated his complete loss of interest in Jacqueline's affairs by cancelling an advance that was to have been made to him on the parliamentary subsidy granted in the previous summer to enable him to help her. The last straw, for Jacqueline, must have been the news that the earl of Salisbury was sailing with his army to France, instead of Holland, coupled with the siege that Philip laid, in the spring of 1428, to her headquarters at Gouda. She surrendered and, on 3 July 1428, signed the treaty of Delft, the main provisions of which were as follows:[1]

1. Jacqueline renounced an appeal she had lodged at Rome against the papal judgment of 9 January 1428.
2. Philip recognized his 'dear cousin, Lady Jacqueline, duchess in Bavaria', as countess of Hainault, Holland and Zeeland.
3. Jacqueline recognized Philip as her heir in these territories and appointed him their guardian and governor, with possession of all the castles.
4. If Jacqueline married again, without the consent of her mother Margaret of Hainault, of Philip, and of the Estates of the three lands, or of any one of them, her subjects were to cease obeying her and give their allegiance to Philip.
5. A regency council of nine persons was to be established, six to be appointed by Philip, and three by Jacqueline.
6. The revenues of Holland, Hainault and Zeeland were to be shared between Philip and Jacqueline.

The treaty of Delft was followed by a separate settlement between Philip and Jacqueline's Utrecht ally, Rudolf von Diepholz, now fully established as bishop, which was signed in January 1430. Philip recognized Rudolf as bishop of Utrecht, and Rudolf recognized Philip as ruler of Holland. The inhabitants of the bishopric were granted free access to Philip's lands for purposes of trading and, in return, Philip's banner was to be displayed for three days over the town hall at Utrecht and on the walls of Rhenen and Amersfoort. Moreover, it was stipulated that when Philip or his representative visited Utrecht he was to be met half-a-mile outside the city gate by Rudolf von Diepholz, who must kneel to seek and receive Philip's pardon for his misdeeds.

No single date can be attached to Philip's acquisition of Hainault,

[1] Text in *Groot charterboek*, iv. 917–22 and *Cartulaire de Hainaut*, iv. 666–75.

Holland and Zeeland, for the process was a gradual one. Long before the treaty of Delft, the Dutch administration was effectively Burgundian and a large part of the Dutch revenues was being paid into Philip's receipt-general of all finances.[1] Philip appointed Boudewijn van Zweten treasurer of Holland in October 1425; and in September 1426 a Brabanter, a Frenchman and a Fleming were appointed his joint captains and governors in Holland: these were Jacob, lord of Gaasbeek, Jehan de Villiers, lord of l'Isle Adam, and Roland d'Uutkerke. Nor was the settlement of Delft by any means definitive. It was modified in January 1429 by an agreement made at Valenciennes, according to the terms of which Jacqueline renounced her share of the Dutch revenues in return for a fixed annual payment of 24,000 crowns, and abandoned all part in the administration. But this arrangement did not work satisfactorily and in October 1430 Philip leased out the administration of Holland for eight years, in return for part of the revenues, to the lords of Borselen, Frank, Filips and Floris.

The events that followed, which culminated in the final and complete transference of Hainault, Holland and Zeeland to Philip in April 1433, have not yet been rescued by historians from the attentions, and fabrications, of romancers and biographers. It seems that in the summer of 1432 Jacqueline secretly married Frank van Borselen and, when Philip discovered this at The Hague in November 1432, he resolved to implement the terms of the treaty of Delft by depriving her altogether of her territories. Her husband Frank was arrested, and only released after she had solemnly abdicated at The Hague and recognized Philip as count of Hainault, Holland and Zeeland. At last, Holland and Zeeland could follow the fate which had already overtaken Hainault in 1427: they were incorporated into the Burgundian state, under the able rule of a ducal stadholder, Hue de Lannoy, lord of Santes, assisted by a group of councillors at The Hague, and a receiver-general. Jacqueline retired to her own estates to indulge in hunting and perhaps pottery. She lived long enough to quarrel with her new husband and died in 1436, just too soon to exploit the Anglo-Burgundian war which broke out in that year, and which brought Duke Humphrey once more to the Low Countries at the head of an English army.

Holland and Zeeland were only added to the Burgundian state as

[1] E.g. ADN B1935, f. 15. For what follows, see van Riemsdijk, *Geschiedkundige opstellen . . . R. Fruin*, 183–208 and *Tresorie en kanselarij*; *Memorialen van het Hof*, i–xii; and Blok, *BVGO* (3) ii (1885), 319–48 and Frederiks, *BVGO* (3) viii (1894), 47–70.

CONQUEST AND EXPANSION 51

a result of prolonged military effort. Brabant, by comparison, almost fell into Philip's lap. Yet, without considerable vigilance and repeated diplomatic initiatives, this important territory would certainly not have become Burgundian.

When Philip became duke of Burgundy in 1419 Brabant was ruled by the youthful John IV, elder son of John the Fearless's brother, Anthony. He was scarcely robust in health or character, but he had an heir in the form of his brother Philip, count of St. Pol, who was at that time Burgundian governor of Paris and a prominent figure at the Burgundian court. The turbulent internal affairs of Brabant, made even more chaotic by the incompetence of John IV, soon claimed Philip the Good's attention and permitted his intervention. In July 1420 a messenger from the council of Flanders brought to Philip, who was then engaged, with Henry V, in the siege of Melun, 'a huge paper scroll containing the demands, responses, replies and counter-demands of the duke of Brabant on the one side, and the nobles, with Louvain, on the other', together with the advice of the council on what should be done.[1] Things went from bad to worse and, to avoid open revolution or civil war, Philip the Good arranged or supported the appointment, later in 1420, of Philip of St. Pol as governor of Brabant for his brother and in March 1421 he visited Brussels in person. But fresh trouble broke out in the capital of Brabant soon after Duke Philip had left and the commotions and executions which followed led to a conference at Bruges between Philip the Good, John IV, and Philip of St. Pol. The last of these remained acting governor of Brabant for most of the rest of 1421.

We have already seen how, when Duke John IV of Brabant died unexpectedly on 17 April 1427, Philip the Good intervened swiftly and successfully in Hainault to take advantage of the absence in Holland of the rightful ruler, Jacqueline. But no opportunity for intervention occurred in Brabant, where the Estates readily recognized John IV's brother, Philip of St. Pol, as their new duke. If Philip hoped to convert Brabant, with his relative, protégé, and partisan on the ducal throne, into a Burgundian client state, he was sadly mistaken. Philip of St. Pol, childless, did make Philip the Good his heir in an act of 3 September 1427[2] but, in other respects, he showed no inclination towards Burgundy. Indeed his projected marriage with a French princess of the house of Anjou is said to have infuriated

---

[1] AGR CC21798, f. 16. For what follows, see de Dynter, *Chronique des ducs de Brabant*, iii. 398–401 and 415–17, etc.
[2] *ICL* iv. 198–9.

Philip the Good. Whether he would in fact, as Chastellain suggests, have been prepared to use force against Philip of St. Pol, we shall never know, for, while Philip of Burgundy was busy with the siege of Compiègne, Philip of St. Pol died suddenly on 4 August 1430. Chastellain, who was a student at the University of Louvain at the time, says that the accusing finger of rumour pointed at Philip the Good, but he rightly absolves him from all blame, for documents prove that the duke of Brabant had been ill for some time, and that he died a natural death.[1]

But Brabant was not yet Burgundian. There were other claimants besides Philip the Good, and it was for the Estates to decide between them. His aunt Margaret, countess of Hainault, was nearest at hand. She made an immediate journey from Le Quesnoy to Louvain, to try to persuade the Estates to accept her; and at least two German princes, Otto, count palatine of Mosbach, and Duke Frederick IV of the Tirol, approached Sigismund with a view to their investment with the vacant duchy. But King Sigismund had grandly resolved to keep Brabant for himself by allowing it to revert to the Empire! He even wrote to Philip the Good early in October 1430 solemnly warning him to leave the duchy well alone. But Philip, withdrawing from the siege of Compiègne, had already arrived at Louvain to be installed as duke of Brabant, the Estates having resolved to accept him after protracted negotiations. On 8 October 1430 he made his 'joyous entry' into Brussels, a city which was later to become the virtual capital of the Burgundian state.

Thus Margaret, countess of Hainault, was brushed aside by her triumphant nephew, and deprived of her Brabant inheritance, just as her only child, Jacqueline had been robbed of her patrimony. Chastellain and others hint that her anger and humiliation may have hardened into vindictiveness, and imply that Margaret and Jacqueline even attempted to have Philip murdered at a tournament in Hainault in summer 1433.[2] Is it conceivable that these two women were already practised murderesses, having poisoned John of Bavaria and tried to kidnap, or possibly actually murdered, John IV of Brabant?

[1] Chastellain, *Œuvres*, ii. 72–7. Unfortunately, Madame J. Scarcez was unwilling to lend me her thesis on Philip of St. Pol. For the next paragraph, see especially ADN B10394, f. 67; Chastellain, *Œuvres*, ii. 79–83; de Dynter, *Chronique des ducs de Brabant*, iii. 500–2; Gachard, *Rapport sur Dijon*, 148–50; Gross, *MIOG* xli (1926), 150–8; Galesloot, *BCRH* (4) v (1878), 437–70; and Poullet, *Constitution brabançonne*.

[2] Chastellain, *Œuvres*, ii. 85 and n. 1; *Livre des trahisons*, 196; Monstrelet, *Chronique*, v. 67.

All this seems unlikely. One thing we do know is that Philip had made reasonable financial provision for his aunt, for in 1430 she was being paid 8,000 clinkarts per annum from the revenues of Hainault. In 1434, in return for a substantial sum, she finally renounced her claims to Brabant, as well as those to the county of Ferrette.[1]

The incorporation of the counties of Holland, Zeeland and Hainault, and the duchy of Brabant, into the Burgundian state, was the culmination of a gradual process. Not only had French or Burgundian influences and institutions been disseminated throughout Brabant and Holland for fifty years and more, but numerous steps had been taken, here and there, towards the unification of the Low Countries under a single ruler. Burgundy had been allied by marriage with Holland since 1385; a junior branch of the Burgundian ducal house had ruled in Brabant since 1405. Nevertheless, the acquisition of these territories was of the utmost significance in the history of Burgundy. In mere size, and material resources, Philip's state was increased by more than one-third. Moreover, it was shifted further away from France, and towards the German-speaking world of the Holy Roman Empire. As duke of Brabant, Philip inherited two houses in, as well as close economic connections with, the German city of Cologne, which he visited in 1440. As the political interests of Burgundy swung to the east, so the geographical balance of the Burgundian territories was weighted more heavily than ever towards the north. Furthermore, while the European stature of the duke of Burgundy was now immeasurably enhanced, the significance of that first and original title was diminished by his new status as ruler of the Low Countries.

[1] ADN B10394, f. 38b and *Cartulaire de Hainaut*, v. 275–83.

CHAPTER THREE

The Critical Decade: 1430-40

In the first decade of his reign, that is, in the years before 1430, Philip the Good had been a reasonably successful ruler. A combination of good fortune, military advantage, sound policy and clever diplomatic manipulation, had enabled him to confer the benefits of peace and prosperity on his subjects in Burgundy and Artois, in spite of the danger of French aggression. Moreover, he had managed, by 1430, greatly to increase the size of his own territories by adding to them Hainault, Holland and Brabant. By means of a sort of diplomatic tightrope walk, he had contrived to fight against the English in the Low Countries although remaining their ally in France, and to pose as an enemy of France while maintaining a system of Franco-Burgundian truces. These initial successes culminated, at the very beginning of 1430, in two splendid events which, by utilizing the glittering ceremonial of the court, served to proclaim the new-found greatness of Burgundy throughout Europe. I refer to the marriage of Philip the Good and Isabel of Portugal, and the founding of the Order of the Golden Fleece.

The choice of a Portuguese princess for Philip the Good's third wife need occasion no surprise. Not only was there a longstanding tradition of diplomatic and courtly contact between Burgundy and Portugal, witness the comings and goings between John the Fearless and King John I;[1] but also, the names of the limited number of eligible young ladies were already well known, and Isabel had, for some years at least, figured among them. Indeed, she had been seriously considered in 1424, before Philip married his seond wife, Bonne

---

[1] Vaughan, *John the Fearless*, 259 and Lousse, *La Nation Belge*, nos. 21–32 (1961–2). For the next sentence, see Morosini, *Chronique*, ii. 274 and 275 n. 4. The extract that follows is from Stouff, *Catherine de Bourgogne*, ii. 180.

of Artois. It must have been of some concern and anxiety to Philip's councillors, if not to the duke himself, that, at the age of thirty, and after two weddings, he was still without a legal heir, though two flourishing bastards proclaimed his sexual potency. On 6 October 1425, within weeks of the death of Bonne of Artois, a *maître des comptes* at Dijon, Jehan Gueniot, wrote thus to Philip's aunt Catherine of Burgundy, duchess of Austria.

> I wish that . . . my lord [the duke] was well married, so that he could have an heir. It's said that there are five marriageable young women, hearty and handsome. That is to say, Robert of Bar's daughter; the two sisters of the king of Navarre; the king of Portugal's daughter; and a noble English lady. If you, my redoubted lady, know of any others, do put forward their names alongside these, because a choice has got to be made in this case, which is like a battle, where one party must remain in possession of the field.

In spite of this active speculation Philip was evidently in no hurry to marry again. In 1427 he negotiated inconclusively with King Alfonso V of Aragon for a matrimonial alliance.[1] In September 1428 he received a petition from the Four Members of Flanders asking him to get married as soon as possible so that he could have an heir. But by this time a decision had been made, for an embassy embarked for Portugal at Sluis on 19 October 1428, with a firm request to King John I for the hand of his daughter Isabel, sister of Henry the Navigator and grand-daughter of John of Gaunt.[2] This choice marked a distinct break with Philip's previous marital policy, for his first two wives had represented close relations with France, while this third wife implied independence in that respect, though she had dynastic, and not insignificant, ties with England.

The marriage treaty of Philip and Isabel was signed in Lisbon in July 1429,[3] and the ducal embassy now acted as her escort on their return journey. In November, Philip was at Bruges anxiously awaiting his bride's arrival. A Venetian merchant there wrote home on

---

[1] Van Puyvelde, *VVATL* (1940), 20; Marinesco, *CRAIBL* (1956), 410; and du Fresne de Beaucourt, *Charles VII*, ii. 491 and n. For the next sentence, see *Précis analytique*, (2) ii. 35 and, for what follows, Armstrong, *AB* xxxvii (1965),106–7 and *AB* xl (1968) 40–4. For the Portuguese embassy, see below, pp. 178–84.

[2] See the genealogical table on p. 108 below.

[3] Analysed in *IADNB* 1 (i), 294. For what follows, see Morosini, *Chronique*, iii. 236–8 and 254–5; O. van Dixmude, *Merkwaerdige gebeurtenissen*, 125; Plancher, iv. 134; and, above all, le Févre, *Chronique*, ii. 158–72.

20 November 1429 with news that the duke of Burgundy was expecting Isabel's arrival at Sluis 'day by day and hour by hour'. Her small fleet of some twenty ships had been scattered by storm; two of them had arrived at Sluis, six had reached Southampton, and nothing was known of the others, nor of Isabel herself. She arrived at last on Christmas Day, and put up for a fortnight in Sluis in the house of one Godevaert Wilden where, among others, she received a deputation from the Four Members of Flanders. The actual marriage ceremony took place quietly at Sluis on 7 January, and it was only on 8 January that Isabel made her entry into Bruges, welcomed by a fanfare of silver trumpets and a huge crowd, for the start of a week of elaborate festivities.

Preparations for this court occasion had been made long in advance. A 400-man escort had been provided for the convoys of carts which wound their laborious way northwards from Dijon and Lille, to Bruges, carrying the raw materials for courtly entertainment and luxury. There were fifteen cart-loads of tapestries; one hundred wagons of Burgundian wine; fifteen cart-loads of arms and armour for tournaments, specially made at Besançon; and fifty loads of furnishings and jewels.

Fortunately, an exact account of Philip's wedding-feast and the tournaments which followed was set down by the observant and punctilious ducal herald Jehan Lefèvre. He describes how the ducal palace at Bruges was transformed by the construction of a whole range of elaborate, but only temporary, buildings in wood, which were set up in the main courtyard. Three spacious kitchens, three ovens, and six larders, one each for soups, boiled meats, jellies, roast meats, pastries and fruit, were arranged around a single banqueting hall, which was 150 feet long. A beautifully painted wooden lion on the exterior façade of the palace poured wine from its paw into a basin below it. Inside the courtyard, a stag and a unicorn dispensed hippocras and rose-water in the same manner. Inside the banqueting hall, a minstrels' gallery held sixty heralds, trumpets, and musicians; and on a gilded tree were hung the coats of arms of the duke's lands and gentry. Isabel of Portugal was met outside the town and escorted through streets hung with crimson, to the sound of a fanfare from seventy-six trumpets. The herald tells us exactly who was present at the banquet and where they sat at table. He describes how each dish was accompanied on the table or sideboard by a sort of tableau or spectacle. There were women holding unicorns, goats and pennons bearing the ducal arms. There were men, also with the ducal arms, fitted out as savages or wild beasts, riding on roast pigs. Next to one dish was a castle, with a 'wild man' in the central tower, holding the inevitable ducal banner, while in each corner tower a woman held a pennon decorated with the arms of one of the ducal territories. But the *pièce de résistance* was a huge pie, containing a live sheep dyed blue with gilded horns and yet another man got up as a wild beast.

This extravagant and memorable banquet was followed by a series of tournaments held, on successive days, in the market-place of Bruges; and the whole jamboree was brought to an end, in appropriate manner, by the announcement on 10 January of a new Order of chivalry to be called the *Toison d'Or*, or Golden Fleece. A kind of Burgundian Garter, membership of this Order was limited to twenty-four knights, men of noble and legitimate birth and without reproach, chosen by the duke from among the gentry of Artois, French-speaking Flanders, and the two Burgundies.[1]

The pomp and splendour of the festivities which accompanied the inauguration in January 1430 of a new duchess and a new Order of chivalry at the Burgundian court contrasted forcefully with the actual state of affairs. For, behind this splendid façade, Duke Philip the Good was already beginning to experience the dangers and difficulties of a critical decade. As the year 1430 wore on, an almost explosive mixture of internal discontent and external menace became apparent. And in subsequent years the pattern repeated itself, so that for a time the entire fabric of Burgundian power seemed threatened.

On 13 January 1430, within a few days of Philip's wedding and the foundation of the Golden Fleece, a curious and seemingly unimportant incident occurred, which indicated that all was not well in Philip's lands. A royal official from the bailiwick of Amiens appeared in the market-place at Thérouanne in Artois and read out in public a summons issued by the *Parlement* of Paris, citing Colard de Commynes, the ducal bailiff of Cassel, and his three lieutenants, to appear without fail by 10 February next at the supreme court of France, to answer for certain excesses they were reputed to have perpetrated against the rights and privileges of the inhabitants of the castellany of Cassel.[2]

What was the meaning of these legal histrionics? Unfortunately much of the history and significance of the rebellion of the rural

[1] Vienna, AOGV, Regest i. f. 1, le Févre, *Chronique*, ii. 172–4, and de Reiffenberg, *Histoire de l'Ordre de la Toison d'Or*, xvii–xxiv. See below, pp. 160–2.
[2] On this and what follows, see Desplanque, *ACFF* viii (1864–5), 218–81.

inhabitants of this part of Flanders remains obscure. The trouble seems to have started in 1427, as a result of the too vigorous attempts of the bailiff to stamp out certain judicial procedures which he and Philip the Good's government regarded as abuses, but which the local populace cherished as time-honoured customs. They lost no time in appealing against the bailiff to the Paris *Parlement*, an institution which specialized in meddling with other people's affairs, and which was only too glad to intervene. Hence the summons mentioned above, which the ducal officers named in it wisely ignored. But the situation deteriorated during 1430. The rebellious peasants seized some close relatives of two ducal officials and, when they escaped, entered Bailleul one night and kidnapped the bailiff himself, after breaking into the Angel inn, where he had taken refuge. Worse was to come, for the rebels laid siege to the castle of Renescure, which belonged to the bailiff, in spite of the ducal pennon with which it was adorned and by which it ought to have been protected, and razed it to the ground. Thus, right through the year 1430, an important part of rural Flanders was in turmoil and active rebellion against its Burgundian government. Things only quietened down in January 1431, when a combination of mediatory efforts by the Four Members of Flanders, a show of military strength, and a personal visit by Philip himself, caused the mutineers to submit. They had to undergo the customary pantomime of a public apology, kneeling barefooted before the duke in the January mud of Flanders. They had to hand over their arms, formally renounce their appeal to Paris, and pay over 50,000 nobles in reparation to Philip, Colard de Commynes and the church of Cassel. There were only a few executions.

The quarrel with Liège which came to a head in 1430 had really started the year before. Of course, the dukes of Burgundy had had relations with the ecclesiastical principality and city of Liège ever since John the Fearless had supported the bishop-elect, John of Bavaria, against his rebellious subjects on the battlefield of Othée in 1408.[1] But these relations had been more or less personal, that is, they resulted from the fact that John of Bavaria was a relative and political ally of John the Fearless. In 1418 John of Bavaria resigned the bishopric and turned his attention to Holland. His successor lived only a year and, immediately after his death in May 1419, Philip the Good, who was then count of Charolais, tried to persuade the chapter of Liège to elect Louis de Luxembourg, bishop of Thérouanne.[2]

---

[1] Vaughan, *John the Fearless*, 49–66.
[2] *Comptes généraux*, i. 311 (where the date is wrongly printed as 1420) and 335.

Instead, they chose Jehan de Heinsberg, the son of a local nobleman. Although Philip succeeded in persuading the new bishop to sign a treaty of alliance with him in 1421,[1] relations remained somewhat distant. Then, early in 1429, an event occurred which resulted in the sudden involvement of Burgundy with Liège.

The towns of Dinant and Bouvignes stand nearly opposite one another on either bank of the river Meuse. Throughout the later Middle Ages the bitter rivalry between them intermittently took the form of savage warfare. In 1319, taking advantage of the absence of many of the inhabitants of Bouvignes, who were attending a local religious festival, the citizens of Dinant sallied across the Meuse and virtually destroyed their hated rival. But, in the following February, the Bouvignois contrived to wreak a bloody revenge after luring the Dinanters into an ambush. This rivalry was partly commercial, and partly political. Dinant was in the episcopal principality of Liège; Bouvignes formed part of the county of Namur. Philip the Good became directly involved in 1421, when he bought the county of Namur from John III. For, though John was to enjoy possession of it till his death, Philip was permitted at once to garrison three places in Namur, one of which was Bouvignes.

After their defeat at Othée in 1408 at the hands of John the Fearless, the Liègeois had accepted a peace settlement which, among other things, required the demolition of the fortifications of Dinant. These included a tower, called Montorgueil, which the Dinanters had constructed so that they could overlook Bouvignes from across the river, and fire down into it. But, far from demolishing this tower, they actually rebuilt it during the 1420s, in open defiance of Philip the Good, son of the author of the peace settlement of Othée and future ruler of Namur and therefore of Bouvignes. No wonder he made repeated representations to the Dinanters to dismantle their tower; no wonder, eventually, he lost patience and decided on the use of force. During the night of 4/5 February 1429, at a time when both the bishop of Liège, Jehan de Heinsberg and the count of Namur, were Philip's guests at the Burgundian court in Brussels, a small detachment of some twenty men crossed the Meuse and assaulted the

[1] ADN B1925, f. 37 and *Cartulaire de St. Lambert de Liège*, v. 75. For what follows on the Liège war of 1430, the most important chroniclers are Chastellain, *Œuvres*, ii. 56-63; O. van Dixmude, *Merkwaerdige gebeurtenissen*, 126-7; le Févre, *Chronique*, ii. 180-1 and 187-92; Monstrelet, *Chronique*, iv. 392-5; d'Oudenbosch, *Chronique*, 5-12; de Stavelot, *Chronique*, 243-81; and Zantfliet, *Chronicon*, cols. 420-3. See, too, Daris, *Liège pendant le xvᵉ siècle* and Kurth, *Cité de Liège*, iii, 98-102.

tower of Montorgueil. But the guards were alerted, and the marauders were forced to flee, leaving their ladders behind them. Dinant complained to Liège; Liège complained to Philip, who did not deny responsibility, and also to his guests, the count of Namur and the bishop of Liège.

Before this matter could be satisfactorily sorted out, the count of Namur died on 1 March and Philip, already involved with Liège over the Montorgueil incident, now inherited or took over from John III certain other disputes with Liège. Nor was the situation improved by a conference held by Philip in person at Namur on 13 March 1429. Further acts of hostility occurred and at the beginning of 1430 only an uneasy truce protected Philip's newly obtained county of Namur from devastation and warfare at the hands of Liège.[1] But these disasters were not long in coming, though the exact reason for the outbreak of war in summer 1430 remains obscure. Were French agents active in Liège at the time, encouraging the Liègeois to stab Philip in the back, as it were, while he was busy besieging Compiègne? This seems unlikely, and the scanty evidence is of doubtful value.[2] It is much more probable that the war was started by a local incident, just as its origins lay in local quarrels, especially the age-old dispute of Dinant and Bouvignes, and in certain time-honoured boundary disputes between Liège and Namur.

The opening of hostilities was accompanied by the traditional flourish of letters of defiance. Thus Bishop Jehan de Heinsberg, who was evidently on friendly personal terms with Philip, was persuaded or compelled by the Liègeois to send an official declaration of war. But he contrived this in the mildest and politest manner possible:[3]

> Most high, most noble, and most puissant prince Philip, duke of Burgundy, count of Artois, Flanders and Burgundy, etc.
> Notwithstanding that I, Jehan de Heinsberg, bishop of Liège and count of Looz, in virtue of certain statements that have passed between us, have made frequent applications to you for reparation according to the claims declared in these aforesaid statements, which have been but little attended to, and that divers great and abominable outrages have been committed by your captains and servants on my country and subjects, which, if it may please you to remember, have been fully detailed in the complaints that were made to you thereon; nevertheless,

---

[1] Morosini, *Chronique*, iii. 238–40.
[2] Heuterus, *Rerum burgundicarum libri VI*, 108.
[3] Monstrelet, *Chronique*, iv. 393–4. I have used T. Johnes's translation, i. 574–5. The text is also given by Chastellain, *Œuvres*, ii. 58–60.

most high, noble and puissant prince, although your answers have been very gracious, and although you declare your intentions of preserving a good understanding between us, your promises have hitherto been without effect; and these matters are now so much entangled with others, no wise concerning them, that it is very grievous to us, and most highly displeasing.

Most high, noble and puissant prince, you must, in your wisdom, know, that by reason of my oath to remain faithful to my church and country, it behoves me to support and defend their rights against all who may attempt to infringe them, with the whole force I shall be possessed of. For this reason, most high, noble, and puissant prince, after my humble salutations and excuses, I must again inform you of these things, and, should they be continued, opposition will be made thereto, so that my honour may be preserved.

Given under my seal, appended to these presents, the 10th day of July, in the year 1430.

Hostilities began in earnest in the middle of July 1430, not before Philip had had time to send reinforcements to Namur under an experienced captain, Anthoine, lord of Croy. The character of the war is well illustrated by the chronicler's claim or boast that the citizen-army of Liège, which was in the field between 20 July and 1 September 1430, had burnt down 300 houses, thirty-three fortified places, and seventeen windmills, in the county of Namur. The principal military event was the siege of Bouvignes by the men of Liège, who were enthusiastically assisted by the citizens of Dinant. They constructed an enormous wooden cat with ten pairs of wheels which carried 200 men under cover close up to the walls of Bouvignes. We are told by a chronicler that they omitted to oil the wheels of this engine and that, had it not been for the noise of shouting and trumpets, this cat could have been heard meeowing from Dinant.[1] But the siege was a failure. The cat was set on fire by incendiary missiles shot from the walls of Bouvignes, and many of its occupants were burnt to death before they could escape.

The Liège war had broken out at a critical moment in Philip's affairs. When it started, he was engaged in the siege of Compiègne, whence troops had to be detached for Namur. Soon after this, the death of the duke of Brabant on 4 August 1430 introduced a further complication, for Philip had to conduct a series of delicate negotiations with the Estates of that duchy before he was recognized in October as its new duke. Some of the chroniclers suggest that Liège

---

[1] *Livre des trahisons*, 201.

accepted a truce with Philip at the end of September because of its new-found fear of him as duke of Brabant. But the explanation given by the ducal herald Lefèvre, that it was the outbreak of plague which ended hostilities, is much more plausible. That the peace which followed in 1431 was so favourable to Burgundy, seems largely to have been due to the pro-Burgundian arbitration of the count of Mörs and his brother the archbishop of Cologne.[1] Montorgueil had to be demolished and Liège had to pay 100,000 English nobles in reparation. So ended the second of the fifteenth-century wars between Burgundy and Liège.

On 11 June 1430, when Jan van Hoerne, councillor and official of Brabant, set out for Flanders, Holland, Guelders and Utrecht to seek military aid against the menacing Liègeois,[2] on this very day, Philip's captain, Louis de Chalon, prince of Orange, suffered a crushing defeat at the hands of the French. He had invaded Dauphiny, partly on his own behalf and partly on the duke's, but his territorial ambitions were abruptly cut short on the road from Anthon to Colombier, not far from Lyons, when he marched his invading column into a cleverly contrived forest ambush. Attacked simultaneously in the van and rear, the Burgundian army dispersed, panic-stricken, into the woods. The prince himself earned renown for his heroic escape: though badly wounded, he is said to have crossed the Rhone on horseback, fully armed. Several of his men were killed and their bones are still uncovered from time to time when new vines are planted near the village of Janneyrias. One of his soldiers, hiding in a hollow oak tree in his armour, got stuck. He was found there in 1672, when the tree was felled.

The defeat of Anthon may have served as a sharp reminder to Philip, at a time of increasing military commitments in the north, that the war in the south, in and around the duchy of Burgundy, was by no means going well for him. In the years leading up to 1430 the duchy of Burgundy had been protected by a system of local truces, while the French, especially in Berry, had been kept on the defensive by a succession of raids, often in violation of the truces, conducted from La Charité on the Loire by a formidable freelance mercenary captain, Perrinet Gressart, who worked for both the English and the Burgundians. Meanwhile, the policy of the French government to-

---

[1] For the peace treaty, see *Régestes de Liège*, iii. no. 775 and references given there.
[2] AGR CC2409, f. 65b. For what follows, see Payet, *Bulletin de l'Académie delphinale* (6) xxiv-vi (1957), 39–51.

2. Presentation of the *Chroniques de Hainault* to Philip the Good in the presence of Charles, count of Charolais, Nicolas Rolin and other courtiers

3.   Isabel of Portugal, duchess of Burgundy

wards Philip's southern territories had been one of non-aggression. After all, its attention, and resources, were fully occupied in the war against the English. Thus in 1429 Joan of Arc's main effort was directed against the English, and a subsidiary French offensive towards La Charité in the autumn was easily repelled by Perrinet Gressart. But this policy, so favourable to the duchy of Burgundy, was relinquished by the French government in May 1430, when a royal manifesto, inaugurating a period of intermittent and extremely damaging warfare in and around the duchy of Burgundy which continued throughout the 1430s, was circulated to the French towns.

'Our adversary of Burgundy' was accused of having 'diverted and deceived us for some time with truces', while, behind this mask of good faith he had consistently favoured the English, and obviously lacked any genuine peaceful intentions.[1] As a matter of fact, the French captain Forte-Espice had already invaded the extreme north of the duchy in January 1430, but was forced to withdraw in March. In August, Charolais, to the south of the duchy, was invaded; in the autumn, French forces attacked the northern frontiers again in the region of Auxerre and Tonnerre, advancing along the valleys of the Yonne and Seine. In December, the Burgundians were defeated in a pitched battle at Chappes near Bar-sur-Seine, and much of their artillery was lost. This assault on the duchy was pressed home in the spring of 1431, when part of Charolais was conquered and occupied by the count of Clermont, Charles de Bourbon who, though he was Philip the Good's brother-in-law, having married Agnes of Burgundy, was by no means averse to a little private aggression into neighbouring territories in the name of Charles VII, whose lieutenant he was. It was at this dangerous moment in the affairs of the duchy of Burgundy that all available troops had to be sent to help the count of Vaudémont in his war against René of Anjou for possession of the duchy of Lorraine. But the Burgundian victory of 30 June, at Bulgnéville in Lorraine, did much to restore the situation, and in September 1431 the régime of truces protecting the duchy of Burgundy was restored by the conference of Bourg-en-Bresse.

The French military offensive of 1430–1 against the duchy of

---

[1] Du Fresne de Beaucourt, *Charles VII*, ii. 423 n. 1. For what follows, on affairs in the duchy of Burgundy until 1435, see Bazin, *MSHA Beaune* (1897), 202–52; Bossuat, *Gressart et Surienne*, 136–218 and *AB* xxiii (1951), 7–35; Déniau, *Commune de Lyon*, 557–89; the *Journal* of J. Denis, with accompanying texts, in *Documents pour servir à l'histoire de la Bourgogne*, i; and Leguai, *Ducs de Bourbon*, 133–44.

Burgundy comprised a succession of scattered, uncoordinated and sometimes ill-conceived raids, none of which were pressed home sufficiently. The fact is that Charles VII was in no position to wage a successful war of conquest on the boundaries of his kingdom, for his government was weak, disunited and engrossed in court intrigue or private warfare. The reigning favourite, George de la Trémoille, was far more interested in his personal disputes with court rivals, in plotting to assassinate his enemies among the French princes, and in augmenting his own power and opulence, than in prosecuting the war against Burgundy. But if the French themselves were incapable of waging successful war on Philip the Good, perhaps someone else could be persuaded to do so. And so it was that, just at the time when the affairs of Liège and Cassel were threatening Philip's northern territories, and French aggression was bringing war and devastation to the duchy of Burgundy in the south, King Charles VII's diplomats induced the duke of Austria, Frederick IV of the Tirol, to promise to attack the duke of Burgundy.

The Austrian affair of 1430–1, with its insignificant, if not ridiculous, little war, was never a real threat to Burgundian power.[1] Nevertheless, it represents an attempt by Charles VII to embroil Burgundy in a major war. After all, the ambassadors he sent out in April 1430 were instructed to visit Duke Louis of Bavaria and Albert V of Austria, as well as Frederick IV and the towns of Strasbourg, Bern, Basel and Zurich, to warn them of the dangers of Burgundian policies or ambitions and to invite them to join an alliance with France aimed specifically against Philip the Good. Duke Frederick of Austria alone took up the offer. Matters of dispute between him and Philip concerning their common frontier between the counties of Burgundy and Ferrette, and concerning the jewels and dowry of Catherine of Burgundy, who had died in 1426, were by no means lacking, though these seem mostly to have been settled at a conference at Montbéliard in 1427 held under the mediatory auspices of the duke of Savoy. In May and June 1428 the Burgundian accounts record the making at Mons of some war saddles to be presented by Philip to

[1] See, especially, Jouffroy, *Oratio*, 144–5; Plancher, iv. 123, 129 and nos. 69, 78, 82, 83, 86, 87, 88 and 100; and Toussaint, *BCRH* cvii (1942), nos. 1–15; du Fresne de Beaucourt, *Charles VII*, ii. 427–35; Valois, *Pape et concile*, i. 111–15 and 134–5; Leroux, *Nouvelles recherches*, 213–29; Toussaint, *Relations diplomatiques*, 27–41 and d'Herbomez, *RQH* xxxi (1882), 150–8.
[2] ADN B1938, f. 117.

'the duke of Austria',[2] and we hear of an Austro-Burgundian treaty at this time. What then induced Frederick of Austria to turn against Burgundy in 1431? Apparently the French offers of a marriage alliance between Charles VII's two-year-old daughter and his three-year-old son, coupled with the promise of Artois, if it could be conquered from Philip, were sufficient to persuade Frederick to promise to invade Burgundy.

A serious Austro-German invasion of the county of Burgundy, at a time when the duchy was under attack by the French, might have proved disastrous for Philip. But how serious were Frederick of Austria's military intentions against Burgundy? He delayed making the promised declaration of war till long after the agreed date. And even when it did come, reinforced on 20 July 1431 by 248 separate challenges addressed to Philip by the Austrian vassals and supporters, the warfare waged by Frederick was limited to a few border raids. There was no invasion whatsoever of Philip's territories. Instead, one of Philip's captains seized the Austrian castle of Belfort in Ferrette in a night attack. But Philip himself had no aggressive plans against Austria, though he had taken the precaution, in August–September 1431, of signing treaties with the archbishop of Cologne and the bishop of Strasbourg.[1] The second of these stipulated that the bishop was to declare war on Duke Frederick IV and to field a contingent of 600 troops, to be paid for by Philip at the rate of 19,000 Rhenish florins per annum. But these episcopal armaments were never called on and, when the Fathers of the Church then assembling at Basel for the Council found their diplomatic immunity compromised by some isolated acts of war, Philip did his best to further their pacificatory efforts. By October an Austro-Burgundian truce had been signed and in May 1432 this was reinforced by a six-year treaty.

The Franco-Burgundian truces of September 1431 were local and shortlived. The year 1432 saw the duchy of Burgundy still under military threat from France. War was waged in earnest in the countryside around Auxerre, where a peace conference opened and closed without effect. The French even resorted to conspiracy in their attempts to bring Philip to heel.[2] A plot to kidnap the Burgundian

[1] AGR CC132, fos. 35b–39. A copy of the Strasbourg treaty is noted by Laenen, *Archives à Vienne*, 95.
[2] For what follows in this and the next paragraph, see Fyot, *MCACO* xiv (1901–5), 103–12; BN Coll. de Bourg. 99, pp. 310–12 (mostly printed in Bazin, *MSHA Beaune* (1897), 234–9); A. Bossuat, *AB* xxiii (1951), 7–35;

chancellor, Nicolas Rolin, was apparently the work of George de la Trémoille, but the motive in his case seems to have been purely private, and mercenary: he hoped for a ransom of £50,000. However, the chancellor had a lucky escape at Semur-en-Auxois in autumn 1432, when he happened to leave the town in a hurry and by an unexpected route. Another attempt to seize him, in Dijon in January 1433, was foiled by the vigilance of the ducal government. By this time the wary chancellor had sought, and obtained from the duke, permission to have a personal bodyguard of twenty-four archers. A more serious conspiracy in 1432, in which several French captains participated, aimed at a clandestine attack on Dijon with scaling ladders. This was revealed by a French herald who was arrested and tortured by the civic authorities of Dijon early in October 1432.

More dangerous than these conspiracies themselves was the fact that a pro-French party existed in the duchy at this time. Several Burgundian nobles had made separate truces with Charles VII, covering their own estates. One of the most prominent, Jehan de la Trémoille, lord of Jonvelle, was a brother of George de la Trémoille, and a Knight of the Golden Fleece. At the third chapter of the Order, held at Dijon in 1433, Jehan de la Trémoille was accused of complicity in the conspiracies of the previous year and of spying for the French. He denied everything. Another influential Burgundian nobleman, Louis de Chalon, prince of Orange, went over to Charles VII in 1432, having first sent his Garter back to Philip's ally John, duke of Bedford. This change of allegiance may have been partly due to his exclusion from the Order of the Golden Fleece on the grounds that he had infringed the statutes of the Order at the battle of Anthon, by retreating after banners had been unfurled. In 1433 another Burgundian noble, Guillaume de Châteauvillain, made a treaty with Charles VII, declared war on Jehan de Vergy, lord of Fouvans, and attacked places in the duchy of Burgundy.

Thus the political and military situation in Philip's southern lands deteriorated. But the campaigns of 1433 and 1434, though they were the most serious and prolonged of all his wars in the south, were successful. That of 1433, led by Philip in person, lasted from July to November and resulted in the recapture of many places around Auxerre which had been lost in 1431. Its importance may be judged from the entries in the account of the receiver-general of all finances,

Armstrong, *PCEEBM* v (1963), 72–4; and Vienna, AOGV, Regest i. fos. 10–13b = de Reiffenberg, *Histoire de l'Ordre de la Toison d'Or*, 5–6, 14–15 and 17.

which show that it cost over 150,000 francs.[1] In 1434 several different campaigns had to be fought, for the defection of Guillaume de Châteauvillain was matched by the hostilities which Count Charles of Clermont renewed against Burgundy soon after he succeeded his father as duke of Bourbon. But these enemies were dealt with piece-meal. The castle of Grancey, not far from Langres, on the northern border of the duchy, which was Guillaume de Châteauvillain's principal stronghold, was forced to surrender at the end of the sum-mer. In September, after he had cleared the duke of Bourbon's troops from Charolais in a vigorous three-week campaign, Philip carried the war into his brother-in-law's territory of Beaujolais by besieging Belleville. In December 1434 Bourbon was forced to sue for peace; and in January 1435 treachery put Guillaume de Château-villain's last refuge, the castle of Châteauvillain itself, into Philip's hands. Thus, hostilities in and around the duchy of Burgundy con-tinued until almost the eve of the treaty of Arras in 1435 which, as we shall see later, by no means seriously interrupted them.

The winter of 1434–5 was long remembered as a particularly cold one, at a time when the winter climate of north-west Europe was much colder than it is now. Not only the Thames itself froze, but most of the Thames estuary also, and the wine-ships from Bordeaux had to be unloaded at Sandwich.[2] At Arras, the civic authorities drafted a special memoir to record the numerous snowmen which were set up in the streets and squares. They included the figure of Danger, the *Grand Veneur* with his dogs, the Seven Sleepers, the *Danse Macabre*, and Joan of Arc at the head of her men. But Philip the Good's councillors had more important matters to attend to at this time for, while the prolonged and bitter warfare of 1434 had devastated the borders of the duchy of Burgundy and depleted the ducal treasury, an old but hitherto ineffective enemy of Burgundy had appeared in a new and aggressive guise. This was Sigismund, the Holy Roman Emperor who, towards the end of the year 1434, declared imperial war, or the *Reichskrieg*, on Philip the Good. What was new about this imperial hostility was not its existence,

[1] ADN B1948, fos. 336 ff.
[2] *Brut*, 571 and, for the next sentences, Besnier, *RN* xl (1958), 193–4. For what follows, on Philip and Sigismund, see *Regesta Imperii*, xi. *Die Urkunden K. Sigmunds* and *DRA*, viii–xii and especially xi. 369–72; von Löher, *Münchner historisches Jahrbuch für 1866*, 305–419; Leroux, *Nouvelles re-cherches*, 182–94; Barbey, *Louis de Chalon*; *Geschiedenis van Vlaanderen*, iii. 157–71; and Toussaint, *Relations diplomatiques*, 106–24.

but its translation into an actual declaration of war. Sigismund had always been an enemy of Burgundy, but his military involvement with the Hussites, which continued throughout the 1420s, had forced him to remain a passive if indignant observer of the seizure of some of the wealthiest imperial territories of the west by Duke Philip of Burgundy. He had watched powerless while two usurpers, Philip and Jacqueline, fought for imperial Holland. He had seen Hainault slip from his grasp, Holland conquered, and Brabant occupied, while all he could do was to write letters. He wrote to Dordrecht and other Dutch towns in 1426;[1] he wrote to the Estates of Hainault in 1425; he cited Philip the Good and Duke John IV of Brabant to appear before his imperial court on a charge of usurping Brabant; he wrote to the imperial city of Frankfurt in October 1426 requesting a commercial boycott of Burgundy.

As in the north, so with Philip's southern territories, Sigismund was powerless. Here he had taken up an aggressive posture right from the start of Philip's reign, but to no purpose. In June 1421 he appointed Louis de Chalon imperial vicar in Burgundy, Dauphiny, Viennois and Provence, granting him the right to an imperial court of justice and mint at Jougne in the county of Burgundy. The Burgundian government retaliated by summoning Louis before the *Parlement* of the county at Dole for infringing Philip the Good's monetary and judicial rights. But Sigismund went further. He transferred the *garde* of Besançon, which had been ceded to Philip, to Louis de Chalon in December 1422,[2] and he even authorized Louis to take possession, on behalf of the Emperor, of all Burgundian territories which were imperial fiefs. But nothing came of these pinpricks, and we find Louis de Chalon campaigning loyally for Philip in Holland in 1426 and, later, receiving the duke and duchess of Burgundy at his ancestral castle of Nozeroy.

Not only was Sigismund involved with the Hussites in these years; he also needed Philip's help against them, and the two rulers were in touch on this subject in 1422, 1427 and 1428.[3] At first the suggestion was that Philip should lead or provide a contingent for the imperial army but, in 1428–30, a grandiose plan for a mainly Burgundian

[1] *Groot charterboek van Holland*, iv. 867–9 and de Dynter, *Chronique des ducs de Brabant*, iii. 473.
[2] Clerc, *Franche-Comté*, ii. 391 and Fohlen, *Besançon*, i. 436–7.
[3] Windecke, *Denkwürdigkeiten*, 160–1; *IAM*, iii. 45–8; *DRA*, ix. 88 and 175–6; and ADN B1938, fos. 107, 203 and 225b. For what follows, see G. de Lannoy, *Œuvres*, xx–xxi, 164–6, 201–2 and 227–53 (the quotation is from pp. 236–9) and Lacaze, *RH* ccxli (1969), 69–98.

expedition against the Hussites was proposed to Philip the Good and reported on at length by the well-known councillor and ambassador, Guillebert de Lannoy, who was sent to Germany in 1428-9 for this purpose. A preliminary paper explained that, at this time, Sigismund and Philip were the only available leaders for such an expedition: the king of Denmark was involved in warfare; Louis, count palatine of the Rhine, was critically ill; Frederick, elector of Saxony, had just died and his son was only sixteen; the margrave of Brandenburg was a sick man; and Duke Albert of Austria could not command the support of the other imperial princes. In another memorandum, Guillebert de Lannoy submitted a detailed plan of action. Philip would lead the expedition, accompanied by Henry Beaufort, 'cardinal of England', with 4-6,000 English archers, and papal blessings, bulls and finance. His army would include 3-4,000 gentlemen and 4,000 archers and crossbowmen from his own lands, perhaps 15,000 combatants in all. Nothing was omitted:

> The pope must be asked, in good time, to give his advice concerning the rightful owner of the lands to be conquered, God willing, from the heretics.
> The duke ought to send a notable embassy of people knowing the country, to Germany, to accomplish the following:

> 1. Ascertain from the princes, prelates and civic authorities what financial and military aid will be forthcoming from them.

> 2. Request lodgings, free passage and supplies from these people, and advice on whereabouts to enter enemy territory.

> 3. Discover the situation of the enemy, how they wage war, what numbers of mounted men they have, how they are armed, how many infantrymen they have, and how many archers and crossbowmen.

> 4. Find out what tactics are best suited to tackle the enemy and what should be done in the event of their avoiding a pitched battle and withdrawing into their fortresses and towns.

> 5. Get advice on what would be the most profitable gold and silver money for the ducal army to take with it.

> Besides this embassy, my lord the duke should send a few experienced and knowledgeable gentlemen to inspect two or three possible routes, as well as the rivers and passes. If there are rivers, the means of crossing them should be looked into by these people, who should not rely for this on the statements of the local inhabitants. . . .
> Another embassy must go to the Emperor Sigismund, to obtain his official authorization for the expedition.

The document then gives details of the composition of the proposed army, the wages of which would cost Philip 100,000 crowns per
month. The Burgundian contingent was to be accompanied by the
dukes of Brabant, Brittany, and Savoy, and the bishop of Liège. Lead
mallets, axes, lances, cannon, powder and other armaments would
have to be procured and, since the army was for the benefit of
Christendom, it was hoped that John, duke of Bedford, would provide a supply of the best bows and arrows from England. Finally the
thoughtful Guillebert advises the duke to appoint a council of ten or
twelve notable clerics and experienced knights to accompany him;
to provide himself with suitable clothes, horses, and arms for the
journey; not to omit to make provision for the administration of his
territories during his absence; and, lastly, to sign truces with all his
enemies before he leaves.

Philip's ambition to lead a victorious crusade against the Hussites
endured at least until the end of 1431, when we find him stipulating,
in the peace treaty with the bishop of Liège, that Jehan de Heinsberg
was to accompany him in person on this campaign, at two months'
notice, with 300 men for six months.[1] But the expedition, which
might perhaps have transformed Philip's relations with Sigismund,
never set out. Instead by 1433 the embattled Hussites had been
induced to make peace with the rest of Europe. Moreover, Sigismund
had found time at last to visit Italy and collect an imperial crown
from the hands of the pope. By 1434 his aggressive intentions were
diverted from Bohemia to Burgundy, and Philip's alert councillors
had already, in November 1433, sensed a repetition of the Franco-
imperial alliance against Burgundy which Sigismund had engineered
in 1414.[2]

First sign of a renewed imperial diplomatic offensive against Philip
was Sigismund's solemn judgment in favour of René of Anjou in his
dispute for the succession of Lorraine with Philip's partisan Anthony,
count of Vaudémont, which was pronounced at Basel in April 1434.[3]
At this time Philip was still involved with the Emperor over his
claims to Brabant. Within days of Philip's formal inauguration as
duke of Brabant, in October 1430, Sigismund had written to protest
in the strongest terms, and had warned Philip to leave the duchy

---

[1] *Cartulaire de Hainaut*, v. 127 and cf. Dex, *Metzer Chronik*, 379.
[2] Plancher, iv. no. 111 and Stouff, *Contribution à l'histoire de la Bourgogne au
concile de Bâle*, 116. See, too, Vaughan, *John the Fearless*, 252–4.
[3] Text in *Chronique de Lorraine*, xxix–xxx. See Lecoy de la Marche, *René*,
i. 107–9.

alone. Since then, Philip had circulated a lengthy and well-argued memorandum which presented his case in forty-eight separate articles;[1] and, of course, he had incorporated Brabant into the Burgundian state. Brabant, undoubtedly, was the chief bone of contention so far as Sigismund was concerned, and he now embarked on a series of efforts to regain this territory for the Empire. First, the expected treaty with Charles VII of France was signed on 8 May 1434. It was explicitly aimed against Philip, 'disobedient rebel, self-styled duke of Burgundy'. Charles promised to pursue his war against Burgundy more effectively than ever; Sigismund, somewhat disingenuously perhaps, promised to declare war on Philip within six months of his ratification of the treaty, and actually to wage war within two months of the declaration. The Emperor did his best to obtain the support of the duke of Savoy and others; he even tried to persuade Liège to renew its war against Philip. But the Council of Basel, which had been another cause of trouble between Sigismund and Philip, turned against its patron for stirring up animosity by this bellicose diplomacy. The English embassy at Basel sent the following letter to Sigismund, couched in elegant Latin, which I have pruned of some of its verbiage:[2]

Basel, 5 March 1435

Most serene and excellent prince, invincible Caesar. . . . We wrote in all humility not many days ago to your imperial highness, confident in your goodwill, pointing out that the letters of defiance your serenity then proposed to send to the most illustrious lord duke of Burgundy would, in our judgment, occasion scandal to the church, the dissolution of the Holy Council, and trouble and disturbance throughout Germany. . . . Now, we have learnt definitely that these letters of defiance from your highness have actually been communicated to the above-mentioned illustrious duke, not without aggravating him. So we, most humble orators and servants of your imperial highness, of the church, and of peace, and faithful ambassadors of our most christian prince . . . , not forgetting to promote most sincerely the honour and prosperity both of your august eminence and of your relative and vassal the aforesaid lord duke . . . offer ourselves as mediators, urging your imperial benignity and clemency to give up and desist from any further action in this matter. . . . We have written, to this effect to the aforesaid illustrious lord [duke], for surely, most serene prince, this world is already troubled by enough wars and battles, without starting any new ones.

[1] Text in Galesloot, *BCRH* (4) v (1878), 437–70 and *DRA* xi. 413–22.
[2] Plancher, iv. no. 119.

Sigismund's warlike projects and preparations were much in evidence in the winter of 1434–5.[1] He duly declared war on Philip, within the term of six months laid down by his treaty with France, in December 1434, but the imperial princes refused to supply him with an army. He had to be content with the circulation of anti-Burgundian manifestoes, to which the duke of Burgundy replied in kind. With deft diplomatic touch, Philip circulated a copy of the imperial declaration of war, with letters of his own attached, requesting an assurance as to the safety of Burgundian merchants. These letters, appealing to the material interests of the recipients, were distributed throughout the Empire, to everyone that mattered. One mounted messenger took copies to Stephen of Zweibrücken, the archbishop of Mainz, the municipal authorities of Strasbourg, Speyer, Frankfurt and Cologne; another visited the duke of Saxony, the margrave of Brandenburg, Constance, Nürnberg and other towns; a third was sent to the elector Louis, count palatine of the Rhine, the duke of Brunswick and the towns of Freiburg, Bern and Luzern. Nor were the more distant merchant cities of Hamburg and Lübeck forgotten.[2]

Of course, Sigismund's spring campaign against Philip never came off. The attitude of the imperial city of Frankfurt was typical.[3] To the Emperor's pressing request for war, its reply was cautious and unenthusiastic. War would damage its trade and cause loss of life and suffering. The city would prefer to avoid hostilities if possible. To Philip's pressing request for peace, couched in the form of a request for the protection of merchants, the reply was affirmative. Their safe conduct would be extended to Martinmas 1435 and, if the city was forced to relinquish this protection, it would notify Philip at once. Nürnberg and other cities wrote in the same vein, and in May 1435 Sigismund shelved his military plans with honour by gracefully accepting the pacificatory advances of the Fathers of the Church at Basel.

The peace of Arras, signed between Charles VII and Philip the Good in September 1435, deprived Sigismund of his French ally, but he still persevered in his hostility towards Philip. Instead of waging

[1] De Dynter, *Chronique des ducs de Brabant*, iii. 506–18 and *DRA* xi. 422–6 give the texts of several documents. See, too, du Fresne de Beaucourt, *Charles VII*, ii. 480–3 and Dex, *Metzer Chronik*, 442–6.
[2] ADN B1954, fos. 43a–b. Compare de Dynter, *Chronique des ducs de Brabant*, iii. 517.
[3] Documents in *Septendecim diplomata*, 476–94.

the *Reichskrieg*, he now conceived the plan of encouraging some of the imperial princes to attack Philip. After all, Duke Frederick of Austria had already tried to persuade Sigismund to allow him to conquer Brabant for himself.[1] In November 1436 Count Eberhard of Lupfen received an imperial authorization to attack any of Philip's subjects. In July 1437 Sigismund went further, and empowered the landgrave Louis of Hesse to recover for the Empire all the territories which Philip had usurped from it: Brabant, to which Louis had a claim, for he was descended from a thirteenth-century duke, Holland, Hainault, Zeeland, Antwerp, Friesland and Limbourg.[2]

Louis of Hesse was in earnest. He had hired a troop of French knights in July 1430, apparently having heard of the illness of the then duke, Philip of St. Pol. But Philip the Good forestalled him. In May 1431 he disguised himself as a pilgrim and travelled incognito through Brabant, and a similar piece of espionage was undertaken by his marshal in 1436. The excuse for these antics was a visit to the shrine of St. Josse, at Montreuil-sur-Mer in northern France. Louis lost no time in 1437 in exploiting the permission given him by Sigismund. At Aachen he summoned an assembly of urban representatives from Brabant and Hainault in order to persuade them to accept him as their rightful ruler. They were not enthusiastic. Steps were taken by the civic authorities at Mons to send the required deputy, but the landgrave's seditious letters were sent off to Philip at Brussels.[3] Louis resolved on force and sent a contingent of German knights into Limbourg on 17 September 1437. But the local inhabitants, who resented this intrusion, rallied and drove the German knights off their territory. Indeed, they went further than this, and pursued them into the city of Aachen. Louis went home a few days later, a disappointed man, and the Emperor Sigismund himself died in December, having seen all his anti-Burgundian schemes end in failure.

The imperial campaign against the duke of Burgundy, especially the attempt on Brabant, had been well timed. For not only was Philip involved in a war with England in 1436, but in 1437 he had to face

[1] Cartellieri, *AB* i (1929), 81–2.
[2] Latin text in de Dynter, *Chronique des ducs de Brabant*, iii. 519–21; German text in *DRA* xii. no. 96. For what follows see *Aachener Chronik*, 9–10; Windecke, *Denkwürdigkeiten*, 436–7; and Knetsch, *Des Hauses Hessen Ansprüche auf Brabant*.
[3] *Particularités curieuses*, ii. 180–1 and 181 n.

a revolt in Flanders which was much more serious than the Cassel affair. The English war was an interlude, rather than a turning-point, in Anglo-Burgundian affairs.[1] An interlude of hostility, that is, in a long history of peaceful alliance. It was precipitated by the peace of Arras, when Philip, abandoning the English alliance, made a settlement with Charles VII. From that moment, at four minutes past seven in the evening of 21 September 1435, according to an observant Welsh astrologer, Thomas Broun of Carmarthen, who predicted, not without malice, that the peace would prove 'unfortunate' for its signatories,[2] Anglo-Burgundian relations rapidly deteriorated. Some of the English ambassadors to Arras were insulted and roughly treated by the inhabitants of the Flemish town of Poperinge as they rode through it on their way home. A placatory embassy which Philip sent to London at the end of September was coolly received and, before the end of the year, the English government had begun a diplomatic offensive against Burgundy. The Dutch received letters inviting them to consider the commercial benefits of the traditional Anglo-Dutch friendship, and asking them to declare their intentions in the event of war.[3] Jacqueline of Bavaria, the Emperor Sigismund, Louis, count palatine of the Rhine, and Arnold, duke of Guelders were among those approached by the English with a view to an alliance against Burgundy. At the same time desultory acts of piracy on either side soon developed into a virtual war at sea, in which the unfortunate Portuguese, Genoese, Hansards and others suffered at

---

[1] For what follows, Kervyn, *Flandre*, iv. 265–87 is still useful, but see especially Thielemans, *Bourgogne et Angleterre*, 65–107 and the references given there. The most important chronicle sources for the siege of Calais and its aftermath are *Brut*, 571–82, on the English side; de Waurin, *Croniques*, iv. 132–5 and 147–206 and Monstrelet, *Chronique*, v. 238–60 on the Burgundian side; and O. van Dixmude, *Merkwaerdige gebeurtenissen*, 147–53, for the Flemish. Also important are *Livre des trahisons*, 211–12; *Kronyk van Vlaenderen*, ii. 36–42; J. van Dixmude, *Kronyk*, 48–51; *Cronycke van Hollandt*, fos. 284b–286; d'Oudegherst, *Chroniques et annales de Flandres*, 329–30; and, representing the London chronicles, *Chronicles of London*, 141–2. See, too, Fris, in *Mélanges Paul Frédéricq*, 245–58 and Blok, *MAWL* lviii (1924), 33–51. I am indebted to Professor R. Weiss for lending me his microfilm of Frulovisi's poem, entitled *Humfroidos*, which describes the events of 1435–6 in excruciating Latin verse; see Weiss, *Fritz Saxl memorial essays*, 218–27.
[2] Wickersheimer, *XIIe Congrès de l'Association bourguignonne*, (1937), 202–4.
[3] The English letters to Holland and Jacqueline are printed in *Documents pour servir à l'histoire des relations entre l'Angleterre et la Flandre*, 425–30.

the hands of both the English and Flemish; and angry letters were exchanged, to no purpose, between the two governments.[1]

The Burgundian decision to attack Calais was apparently made in January 1436. Certainly, discussions were in progress at Brussels·on this subject in February[2] and, early in March, Philip himself went to Ghent to begin the difficult task of persuading the Flemish to help him. A Burgundian chronicler has preserved for us what he claims to be the exact words spoken on this occasion by the sovereign bailiff of Flanders and the duke himself, but it has been left to an English spy to record for posterity the conditions which Ghent insisted on:

There ben certayn tydynges that we have by special frendes, and en special, how that on Fryday viii day of [March] the Duyk of Burgayne with his houne counsel was at Gaund, and ther was assembled togedre the Quatre Membris and al the Councel of the mene landis, desirynge of thaym to have a notable power of men and monaye to bisege the town of Calys. Wheruppon they aunsuerid agayn that, if he wolde graunte them fyve poyntes selid under his gret seal as they folwye herafter in articles, they wolde be redy to performe his desir.

The first article, that his mynte that now ys in the land of Flandres shal nat be chaungid wythinne the terme of xx yere, etc.

The seconde, that non Englishman shal be suffred to selle non English cloth at non market withinne the lordshipes of the seid Duyk.

The thridde, that the [people of] Cassel, the whiche risen ayens the Duyk iiij yer passid, that were distrussed by trete of the seid Duyk and his officers, shullen be restored ayen to alle here godes that they loste, and they to take it ayen of the persones that toke hit from thaym withoute sute of parties.

The fourth, that non maner of officers as capitaynes, baillifs, resseyvours, secretaries, ne other officer, shal be maad wythinne the lond, safe such as that natif born wythinne the same.

The fyfthe, that the townes of Flaundres have the wollys of Calys departid among them withoute letting of hym or his officers, yf they mowe gete thaym.

And so forthwyth the Duyk with his counseil grauntid hem the same articles after their entent.

Whereupon the town of Gaund have grauntid hym xv^m men, and other townes of Flaunderes xv^m, and beth redy at alle oures at his

[1] Letter of Philip to Henry of 19 February in Thielemans, *Bourgogne et Angleterre*, 437–8 and Henry's reply of 17 March in *Procs. and Ords. of the P.C.*, iv. 329–34. See, too, *Documents pour servir a' l'histoire des relations entre l'Angleterre et la Flandre*, 431–5.
[2] ADN B10401, f. 29. For what follows, see le Févre, *Chronique*, ii. 374–81 and *Report on mss. in various collections*, iv. 197–8 (whence the extract).

comaundement, wythoute Hollanders, Zelanders, Brabanders, Ghelders, Hanawders that ben apoyntid unto the same nombre, whyche amounteth in al lx^m men. And also there ys redy at ye Scluse, Barflete[1] and Roterdame iiij^c shippes of forstage wythoute other smal shipes stuffid with the most straunge ordnaunce and alle other abillemens of werre that ever any man herde tell of. And they ben fully concludid, apointid and acorded sodenly to come and bisege the town, the whyche is ryght feble arraied and ordeinyd, fore that God amende, help and preserve for His gret pitte.

In spite of the tinge of hyperbole in the last paragraph, this report was in essence accurate. Copies were promptly circulated by the English government, together with letters warning that 'he that calleth hym Duc of Burgeyne disposyth hym wythinne ryht hasti tyme on this side Easter nyxt to lay assege to oure toun of Caleys'. As a matter of fact, it took much longer than that to call up the Flemish militia and assemble the ducal artillery. The English had ample time to reinforce Calais, to improve its fortifications and to prepare for a siege.[2]

Sir John Radecliff, the Leotenaunt of the toune, Robert Clidrowe the Meyre, and Thomas Thirland, Leotenaunt of the staple of Caleis, with the sawdioures, marchaundes, and burgesses and comyners, kest up a faire brode dike on the south side of the toune, and made three strong bullwerkes of erthe and clay, one att the corner of the castell without the toun, another att Bulleyn gate, and another at the postern be the Princes Inne. And att Mylke gate was a fair bulwerk made of breke. . . . And thai fortifiet the walles, toures, and dikes on ich a side of the toune, within and without, and dresset theire lopes and theire gunnes to shote both hye and lawe. . . .

Both citizens and soldiers were kept on the *qui vive* by Sir John Radcliffe, whose activities on 23 April 1436 are described by the same chronicler as follows:

And on Saynt George day, Sir John Radcliff sent word prevely to the Daywach of the toune in the nonetyme to rynge out the larom bell, unwetyng to the sawdioures of the toune. And so ther was a grete Alarom, and saudioures were onon in thaire harneys, and comyners with hem. And wende that enemys hade comen to haue fechet the bestys that were pasteryng about the toun; but there was non; for Sir John Radclif did it for a sport, because it was Saint George day, and for that he wolde se howe saudioures wold bokkell and dresse hem to theire harneys.

---

[1] Biervliet.   [2] *Brut*, 573, and for the next extract, 574.

The English even had time to get in the first blows, for they made a series of pillaging expeditions into the country round Calais, first, towards Boulogne, then towards St. Omer; and finally, on 14 May, they set out through the countryside south of Gravelines, setting fire to villages and rounding up cattle, as far as Looberghe, where they burnt down the church with the local inhabitants in it. On the return they headed north to the coast between Dunkirk and Gravelines and then drove their stolen cattle back to Calais along the sands, crossing the harbour of Gravelines at low tide after a sharp skirmish on the beach with some hastily assembled Flemish forces. Their only casualty was an enthusiastic young gentleman who galloped into Gravelines by mistake, and found himself a prisoner. The leader of this expedition, Edmund Beaufort, later duke of Somerset, was rewarded by the king as soon as he had news of it by the despatch of a Garter to him at Calais.

In England, meanwhile, an old enemy of Philip had appeared on the scene. Indeed, one cannot dissociate the outbreak of war between England and Burgundy in 1436 from the death of John, duke of Bedford in September 1435, and the subsequent emergence of Humphrey, duke of Gloucester as the most powerful figure in the English government. In the past he had tried unsuccessfully to seize Hainault by force of arms; he now sought to exploit the situation to his own advantage by conquering Flanders from Philip the Good. Already in November 1435 he had himself appointed royal lieutenant in Calais, Picardy, Flanders and Artois; and, by the early spring of 1436, the decision had been made to launch an attack on Flanders. Early in August Humphrey, newly appointed lieutenant-general of the English army, set sail from Sandwich and Dover for Calais 'with all the sustaunce of lordys of this land'.[1] The immediate aim of this expedition was to break up the siege which Philip the Good had laid to Calais on 9 July; but the fact that Humphrey was granted the county of Flanders at this very moment by the English government shows that he entertained ambitions of personal territorial conquest.

By the time Duke Humphrey arrived on the scene on 2 August the Burgundian siege of Calais had already been raised. At first, Philip's plan had worked like clockwork. While the Flemish civic militia set out from home early in the second week of June and took up their posts around Calais early in July, artillery was assembled from all parts of the Burgundian state. Three large bombards were brought from Holland together with 275 stones for them. At Châtillon, in

[1] *Chronicles of London*, 142.

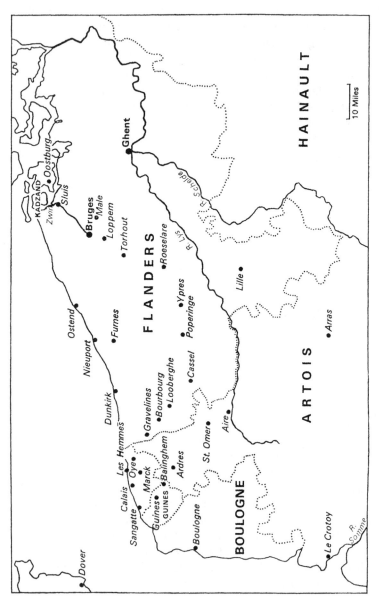

2. Flanders with Calais

THE CRITICAL DECADE 79

Burgundy, the passage of the ducal heavy artillery en route for Calais badly damaged the bridge on the main road.[1] Not only did the Flemish militia invest Calais closely by land but, one by one, the ring of English-held castles in the countryside around Calais were conquered by Philip's army. First, Oye and Marck fell, between Calais and Gravelines; then Balinghem, south of Calais near Ardres, surrendered to a force of Picard cavalry, while Sangatte, on the coast west of Calais, yielded to treachery. Guines alone, five miles south of Calais, held out, in spite of bombardment by a 'gret brasen gunne'. Thus Calais was rapidly and effectively blockaded by land. At sea, however, Philip's efforts proved in vain, and this failure was an important cause of the failure of the whole enterprise. The plan was to assemble a fleet at Sluis, sail it down the coast to Calais, and use it to deny the town reinforcements and supply ships from England. But the admiral of Flanders, Jan van Hoorn, had great difficulty in mustering the necessary ships, for the inhabitants of Nieuport, Ostend and various places near Bruges claimed that they had already made their military contribution on land, and in any case needed ships for their own defence.[2] When eventually the fleet did arrive off Calais on 25 July the Flemish besiegers had already been demoralized by its absence for, while they were told that their own navy had been delayed for want of a favourable wind, they had watched English vessels coming and going every day with no difficulty whatsoever. Flemish morale was dealt a further shattering blow when the long-awaited fleet sailed home again two days after its arrival. It had failed completely in its main purpose of blocking the mouth of the harbour. True, some old ships loaded with masonry were successfully scuttled there at high tide one day but, as soon as the tide receded, the inhabitants of Calais went out with axes and demolished the obstructions. The timber came in handy for firewood; the stones were given to the church of St. Mary to be used for building.

On the very day when this was going on, watched by the Flemings gathered on the neighbouring dunes, who had hoped that henceforth Calais would be deprived of help from outside and therefore effectively blockaded at last, a party of troops from Bruges was attacked and defeated by a surprise sortie from the Boulogne gate. Philip the Good himself had a narrow escape at this time when reconnoitring unarmed in the dunes, but was saved by his bodyguard. Two days

---

[1] *IACOB* ii. 62 and Garnier, *Artillerie des ducs de Bourgogne*, 150–7.
[2] Vlietinck, *ASEB* xl (1890), 94–5; and *Précis analytique*, (2) ii. 50. For the admiral and his fleet, see Degryse, *MAMB* xvii (1965), 151–2.

D

later, on 28 July, the English sallied out again, this time to attack and destroy a wooden tower which the men of Ghent had erected in the dunes to the east of the town. A wave of panic and defeatism swept through the Ghenters' camp, which was scarcely compensated for by the jubilation of the Brugeois, who had been suffering the jeers of the Ghenters ever since their defeat two days before. Accusations of treachery were made, and the lives of the ducal councillors who were thought to have been responsible for suggesting the campaign, were threatened. The Ghenters were ready to decamp at any moment.

All this time, Philip had been expecting the arrival of Duke Humphrey with the English army. But he was not prepared for it. Throughout July, as the entries in the accounts reveal,[1] frantic messages were being sent, to Holland and Flanders especially, to try to raise finance to pay the troops, both men-at-arms and archers, who did not form part of the civic militia, but whose participation in a pitched battle with Humphrey's army would be essential. For the Flemish civic militia, whose services were offered to Philip free of charge, could not be expected to fight the English army without help from these other salaried and better-armed soldiers. They had still not been assembled on 26 July, when Philip's urgent summonses for troops from Flanders, Artois and Picardy show that he had definite information about the imminent arrival of the English army. During the night of Saturday 28 July, immediately after the men of Ghent's tower had been captured by the English and its defenders killed, some English reinforcements disembarked at Calais. The English chronicler says they made so much noise that the men of Ghent mistook them for the main English army. On this hypothesis it was fear of the outcome of a battle the following morning before Philip's cavalry and other troops could have assembled which caused the Ghenters to pack their bags that night and flee. Philip went with them, or followed soon after, and the daily flow of correspondence from him, recorded in the accounts, ceases altogether until the following Thursday, 2 August, when the duke 'reappears' at Watten, between Gravelines and St. Omer.

Early next morning, on Sunday 29 July 1436, when the night watch was relieved, the Brugeois were awakened as usual by the four English trumpets who 'blewe up on hye uppon Milkgate toure'. They noticed at once that their compatriots had decamped, and they and the whole of the rest of the ducal army promptly followed suit. Provisions in quantity were abandoned. Cannon were left behind,

[1] ADN B1957, fos. 176b–178.

some of them hastily buried in the sand. Once again, as after the conquest of Ham in 1411, the Flemish had deserted their duke in the hour of need. But one at least of Philip's military advisers was not content to blame the failure of the siege of Calais on the Flemish retreat. The soldier-chronicler Jehan de Wavrin, who took part in the siege, observes that the whole enterprise was foolish, and doomed to failure, because of the impossibility of blockading Calais by sea. Ships, he pointed out, could not anchor there because of the dangerous currents, while the English could easily sail in and out. The duke himself found it convenient, in a letter written to his brother-in-law Charles, duke of Bourbon, a few days after the débacle, not only to blame the Flemish, but also to try to salvage his honour by the pretence that there had been no real siege. Nor does he mention that shortage of cash had resulted in the absence of part of his army at the crucial moment. His version of the affair runs in part as follows:[1]

Dearest and well-loved brother, you know how I called up and assembled my army, consisting of my people and subjects of the Four Members of Flanders, as well as some of my nobles, vassals, and loyal soldiers from Picardy, with the aim of laying siege to my town of Calais, which is part of my ancient patrimony and inheritance, in order to wrest it from the hands of the king of England, inveterate enemy of my lord the king and of us.

To carry out our plan, we arrived outside the said town with our army, and camped in two groups, the men of Ghent and its castellany with us in one place, and the men of Bruges, Ypres, the Franc of Bruges their followers and some of our nobles in another place. This was an encampment only, and not designed for a siege for, although our army was numerous and well-supplied with war materials and we were fully resolved to see the business through yet, because we discovered after our arrival certain things which weakened our faith in the determination and loyalty of our Flemish people, and especially of the men of Ghent, we had some doubts. . . . So we took up quarters in a camp, and not for a siege, and we neither fired artillery against the town nor did we make the customary preliminary summons to the defenders. After the arrival of the herald Pembroke, who came to challenge us to battle on the duke of Gloucester's behalf, we informed our Flemish people of his message and of our reply, telling them that, because of the enduring confidence

[1] Thielemans printed this letter in *BCRH* cxv (1950), 285–96, but thought it had been sent to Arthur, count of Richemont. Leguai, *Ducs de Bourbon* (1962), 151 and n. 4, correctly identifies the recipient as Charles, duke of Bourbon, but describes the letter as *inédite*. Keen, *Laws of war* (1965), 120 n. 4 and 132 likewise supposed it to be unprinted.

and hope we had in God's help, and in themselves and the promises they made to us, we were determined to await the enemy's arrival. . . .

Because the spot where we and our people of Ghent were lodged was unsuitable for fighting a pitched battle when the enemy came, we asked them to withdraw with us and the noblemen in our company to a certain place quite near their encampment . . . which was thought to be the best, most suitable and most advantageous position to await the enemy in battle order, and they agreed to do this. . . .

Nevertheless, on Saturday 28 July late at night, these people of Ghent, considering neither our honour nor their own, regardless of the promises which they had that very day renewed, and at a time when we were expecting the enemy to arrive on the following Monday or Tuesday, came to tell us that they had decided to decamp that night and to withdraw to a place near the town of Gravelines in Flanders, which is three leagues from Calais. There, they would await events, having put the river [Aa] at Gravelines between themselves and the enemy. And at once, without listening to our requests or waiting for our advice, they departed that night, together with the men from the castellany of Ghent, and withdrew to the above-mentioned position near Gravelines. Moreover, not content with this, they persuaded the men of Bruges, Ypres, and the Franc of Bruges, who would willingly have stayed to carry out our wishes, to withdraw likewise. Since the contingent of noblemen we had with us was too small to do battle with the enemy . . . we were forced to depart and withdraw to Gravelines with the Flemings, abandoning what we had begun with the utmost chagrin.

Since then, dearest and well-loved brother, we have discovered for certain . . . that the duke of Gloucester has arrived in Calais with an army, and that more English are due to arrive shortly. Therefore, we have published a general summons throughout our northern lands, with the intention of mounting the biggest possible force to resist the enemy's enterprises. We have written to you about this so that you know the whole truth of the affair and what happened, and we shall be very glad if . . . you would come here as quickly as possible with as many troops as you can, both men-at-arms and archers. We hope that, with God's help and us two united together, we shall achieve something very much to the honour and profit of my lord the king, and to the great damage and dishonour of his ancient enemies.

In the event, the English were much too quick for Philip. While he was at Aire and Arras, frantically despatching summonses for troops in all directions, including the duchy of Burgundy,[1] Humphrey duke of Gloucester launched a well-disciplined, swift-moving raid into

---

[1] ADN B1957, fos. 178b–181.

West Flanders. Bypassing defended places like Bourbourg and Gravelines, Humphrey's men were soon busy burning down villages in the countryside south of Dunkirk. Heading straight for Ypres, his point of furthest penetration was reached on 15 August, when he had himself proclaimed count of Flanders in Poperinge before he burnt the place to the ground. Meanwhile, Philip sent his duchess Isabel to try to rally the Flemish. At Ghent, her representative implored the citizens to 'defend the boundaries and frontiers of their own land, together with their own possessions and belongings, their privileges, rights and liberties, their lives, and the lives of their women and children, as well as the honour and good renown of their posterity'.[1] But the most that Ghent could manage for this purpose was a contingent of 100 archers, and Philip's planned reassembly of the Flemish army on 16 August was a complete failure.

The success of Humphrey's raid into West Flanders was not solely due to its lightning speed and the excellent discipline of his army, whose rearguard gave no opportunity to Jehan de Wavrin, the chronicler-captain of Gravelines, now shadowing them with a detachment of cavalry, and hoping to pick off stragglers. Much more important was Humphrey's skilful use of the fleet for this, though deprived of its fighting men, cruised menacingly along the Flemish coast, serving to divert the attentions of the Flemish from Humphrey's activities. Thus at Nieuport the magistrates were busy laying in a supply of cheeses against the possibility of an English blockade by sea, and at Ostend, which had no fortifications, the authorities were arranging for the temporary evacuation of jewels and charters to the relative safety of Bruges. But this was only a feint. After sailing as far as the estuary of the Zwin and devastating part of the island of Kadzand and some other coastal regions, the fleet returned early in September to Calais to pick up Duke Humphrey and his men, who had returned laden with plunder and with very few casualties.

To be fair to the Flemish, they had fitted out some warships and raised some local militia to defend themselves against the English fleet. But, unfortunately for them, their two main contingents, from different areas, came unexpectedly in sight of each other. Each mistook the other for an English naval detachment which had disembarked for purposes of plunder, but each decided that it was greatly outnumbered by the other. So both contingents hastily with-

[1] Fris, *Mélanges Paul Frédéricq*, 254. For the next paragraph, see Gottschalk, *Westelijk Zeeuws-Vlaanderen*, ii. 46–50; Vlietinck, *ASEB* xl (1890), 91–101 and van Werveke, *ASEB* lxxiv (1931), 183–8.

drew homewards![1] As to the Dutch, they had never been eager to involve themselves in a war with their principal partners in commerce, the English. They had delayed making their promised financial contribution; they had sent little more than a few cannon and possibly one or two ships, to the siege of Calais; and now they flatly refused to make any hostile move against the English fleet: they would defend their own shores, but they would on no account attack the English.

In England the relief of Calais and Humphrey's expedition into Flanders were celebrated in jubilant and chauvinistic ballads which demonstrated the superiority of the English to the Flemings and boasted of English military prowess.[2] Philip pondered on projects of revenge, but his efforts to implement these plans met with failure. At the end of 1437 he laid siege to the town of Le Crotoy, on the northern shore of the estuary of the Somme, which was at that time held by the English. But this further attempt at siege warfare on Philip's part was no more successful than his previous one. Although he constructed a bastille outside Le Crotoy and garrisoned it with nearly a thousand men, and though he fortified the northern shore of the Somme, nevertheless an English relieving force from Rouen, led by that great commander John Talbot, earl of Shrewsbury, easily forced a crossing at the ford of Blanche Taque and penetrated into Artois. The Burgundian besiegers of Le Crotoy melted away, abandoning their bastille, while Philip himself had insufficient troops, or courage, to advance out of Abbeville. All this happened in the first ten days of December 1437, and a chronicler observes that Philip's anger was increased by the fact that four of the defenders of his bastille, including the captain, Jehan de Croy, were Knights of the Golden Fleece.[3] We read of yet another anti-English scheme of Philip in 1438, aimed against Calais. The idea was to inundate the whole town by breaching one of the sea dykes. An army of pioneers and labourers was escorted by 1,600 men-at-arms, but the work was abandoned almost as soon as it was begun. Once again the duke had been badly advised, but this time the only casualty sustained was the loss by one of his knights, Simon de Lalaing, of the jewelled insignia

[1] J. van Dixmude, *Kronyk*, 52 and O. van Dixmude, *Merkwaerdige gebeurtenissen*, 152–3.
[2] *Historical Poems*, 78–89 and 289–94, with references.
[3] O. van Dixmude, *Merkwaerdige gebeurtenissen*, 160–1. See, too, Monstrelet, *Chronique*, v. 308–16; de Waurin, *Croniques*, iv. 227–39; ADN B1963, fos. 86a–b, 88, 90a–b, etc.; and, above all, Huguet, *Aspects de la Guerre de Cent Ans*, i. 230–99 and ii. 240–76.

of the Golden Fleece, which every knight was required to wear on his person. The mishap had to be formally reported at the next chapter of the Order.[1]

The withdrawal from Calais and Humphrey's expedition into West Flanders were not just military defeats for the duke of Burgundy in the war against England. They also involved the Flemish, and in a manner which had unfortunate, almost disastrous, results for Philip. As a direct result of these events, serious rebellions broke out in both Bruges and Ghent which brought on a new crisis in the Burgundian state, already shaken by war or threats of war.

The Flemish towns experienced just the same waves of social discontent that swept through many other European towns towards the close of the Middle Ages. Repeatedly, the people took up arms in revolt and tried to seize power; and, repeatedly, they failed. Moreover, the Flemish urban populations found ranged against them a formidable alliance consisting of the merchant patriciate, or upper classes, of their own cities, and the duke; while their own internal struggles were complicated by bitter intertown disputes. Nor was social unrest confined to the towns, as the revolt of Cassel in 1430 had shown. The essential social ingredients of urban revolt are well shown in the riots at Grammont in April 1430. Typically, we find 'the craft gilds and common people' (*mestiers et communaulte*) at daggers drawn with the civic authorities (*loi*) representing the urban patriciate and the bailiff representing the duke. The same combination, of urban upper class and ducal government, in the form of some echevins or councillors from Ghent together with some ducal councillors, was called in to 'arbitrate' this dispute at Grammont, which actually meant suppressing the revolt with some brutality.[2]

Other revolts followed the one at Grammont and, if the actual causes were different, the pattern was everywhere the same. At Grammont, the civic authorities had been accused of mismanaging the civic funds; at Ghent, on 12 August 1432, the common people or working classes, consisting mostly of weavers, rose up in arms in the first place because of the economic consequences of Philip the Good's monetary policy. They assembled in the market-place, killed some city councillors, threw open the prisons, and scared the personnel of

[1] De Reiffenberg, *Histoire de la Toison d'Or*, 26; and see Monstrelet, *Chronique*, v. 353–4, and de Waurin, *Croniques*, iv. 253.
[2] AGR CC21804, fos. 10b–11b, summaries of letters of Ghent council to Philip; *Kronyk van Vlaenderen*, ii. 33 (wrongly dated 1431); and J. van Dixmude, *Kronyk*, 42.

the duke's council of Flanders, which sat at Ghent, out of their wits. Fortunately for them, the leaders of the revolt had given orders that the duke's people were not to be harmed. Indeed, on 14 August a civic deputation came to the council of Flanders to insist that the revolt was the work of the common people and was for the good of the town, which remained loyal to its duke. On the same day, the ducal councillors sent an urgent letter to a prominent Flemish nobleman, Jehan, lord of Roubaix,

> describing at length the rebellion at Ghent and imploring him as a great lord, native of Flanders and with many lands there, and as someone who had looked after my lord the duke in his youth and knew him better than others, to go to the duke as soon as he received these letters and beg him . . . to extend his mercy over the town of Ghent and to pardon them their deeds and assemblies. Otherwise we and the other poor ducal officers living in Ghent will be on the way to total perdition of lives and goods, as the lord of Roubaix, who knows the world and has lived through critical times, must realise and can well imagine.[1]

Fortunately things did not go too far on this occasion and the duke did pardon the citizens of Ghent. But troubles continued there. More riots occurred in May 1433, and in 1434 or thereabouts the fullers planned to set fire to the city in several places at once in order to over-throw the city government. At the same time the animosity of Ghent towards Ypres and Bruges, which was inflamed by commercial rivalry, threatened to involve the Flemish towns in civil war as well as internal sedition. This was the background, these disturbances were the preliminaries, to the troubles of 1436 and 1437, which must now be briefly described.

These troubles originated in the traditional demands made by the civic militia on their return home from campaigns. The situation, and events, of 1411[2] were virtually repeated in 1436. At Ypres the civic authorities were able to persuade the returning troops to disarm and

---

[1] AGR CC21805, f. 20b; see, too, fos. 20 and 21, and, on this and subsequent Ghent disturbances in general, Fris, *Histoire de Gand*, 115–17 and *BSHAG* viii (1900), 163–73. The main chronicle sources are J. van Dixmude, *Kronyk*, 42–3 = *Kronyk van Vlaenderen*, ii. 33–4; O. van Dixmude, *Merkwaerdige gebeurtenissen*, 137–8; and *Memorieboek der stad Ghent*, 192–4. The last two wrongly place the revolt in 1431.

[2] Vaughan, *John the Fearless*, 165–9. For what follows, on the Flemish troubles of 1436–8, see Kervyn, *Flandre*, iv. 287–328; Fris, *Histoire de Gand*, 119–23 and *Mélanges Paul Frédéricq*, 245–58; and, among the chroniclers, especially O. van Dixmude, *Merkwaerdige gebeurtenissen*, 152–64; J. van Dixmude, *Kronyk*, 53–101 = *Kronyk van Vlaenderen*, ii. 42–101.

go home by promising to redress their grievances. At Ghent, too, the militia was demobilized without incident but, on 3 September, the populace rose in revolt and, disarming Philip's bodyguard, detained him under virtual arrest until he had agreed in writing to a long list of points which they had submitted to him. But the worst disturbances were at Bruges, where the returning militia refused to re-enter the town till their demands had been met. Eventually, on 12 August, the duchess Isabel persuaded them to station themselves at Oostburg, ready to resist the feared English landing. Two days later some of them went to Sluis and were involved in a dispute with the Burgundian captain there, Roland d'Uutkerke, who refused them entry. The old rivalry of Sluis and Bruges was excited by this incident, and punishment of Roland d'Uutkerke was now added to the Brugeois' demands. The militia returned to Bruges on 26 August, proclaimed a general strike, and occupied the market-place in battle array. They murdered a ducal official, the *écoutète*; they insulted Duchess Isabel when they discovered her trying to smuggle Roland d'Uutkerke's wife out of town in her baggage-train; and on 3 September, the very day when Philip was apprehended by the revolutionaries at Ghent, the popular and social nature of the troubles at Bruges was amply demonstrated by the arrest of all those who had held office as burgomaster, treasurer or town clerk during the previous thirty years.

Discontent seethed at Bruges throughout October but by the end of the year 1436 pacification seemed in sight, partly as a result of the mediation of the foreign merchants there. Philip spent Christmas in Bruges without any serious incident, though his seven-hundred-strong bodyguard had to be urgently assembled late one night when a report reached him that some of the craft gilds had taken up arms in the market-place. But enquiries showed that the deans of the gilds concerned were either in bed or dining at home, and the market-place was empty. Early in the new year, however, one of the burgomasters of Bruges, Morissis van Varsenare, reported to Philip that the common people were still in mutinous mood. He was right. In April he and his brother were murdered because 'he worked with the prince to keep down the common people of Bruges',[1] and many of the wealthy merchants and burgesses of Bruges fled. In Ghent more riots occurred in April 1437.

In this critical and deteriorating situation Philip now apparently resolved to intervene with a show of force. The plan was to march part of his army through or near Bruges on its way to Holland. It

[1] J. van Dixmude, *Kronyk*, 176.

does seem that Holland was the real destination of this expedition, and that a military demonstration, rather than conquest or occupation, was the aim at Bruges, for an entry in the ducal accounts records the payment for troops reviewed at Lille on 17 May 1437, to accompany the duke 'on the expedition which he planned at that time to make from the said town of Lille to his lands of Holland and Zeeland'.[1] But things went awry. Philip only escaped with his life by a hair's breadth and his most famous and trusted captain, Jehan de Villiers, lord of l'Isle-Adam, met a violent death in the streets of Bruges: an event which was subsequently celebrated in verse. Two detailed accounts in Flemish of this dramatic incident have come down to us, one by the author of the chronicle attributed to Jan van Dixmude, the other written by Philip himself, in a letter which only survives, in a Flemish version, among the records of the Hanseatic League. The reader may like to compare the two.[2] First, that of the Flemish chronicler.

On Wednesday 22 May the burgomaster Lodewic van den Walle went to the duke of Burgundy at Lille, and received a letter from the prince for the officers and deans of the craft gilds in Bruges, mentioning that the duke planned to go to Holland with 3,000 Picard soldiers who, following the shortest route to Sluis [for the passage to Holland], would go through Male,[3] rather than Bruges. But the duke himself would stay in Bruges for three or four days with his household retinue and up to 500 nobles, in order to see that justice was done for the deaths of the burgomaster Morissis van Varsenare and his brother Jacop. So it was agreed that the 3,000 Picards would go to . . . Male that day and have their meal there, [for which purpose] supplies of bread and butter, 4,000 eggs, eight tuns of beer and a vat of wine would be sent out from Bruges. But none of the Picards arrived at Male. Instead, they accompanied the prince to the Boeveriepoort[4] where, at about three o'clock in the afternoon, all the gilds and societies of Bruges were in procession to meet him. . . . He was held up there for a good two hours by the burgomaster Lodewic van den Walle, [during which time] he sent a knight, the bastard of Dampierre, with eleven companions, into the Boeveriepoort to jam the portcullis so that it could not be lowered before the prince and all his people had got into Bruges.

---

[1] ADN B1961, f. 179. The poem on l'Isle-Adam's death is printed in *Historischen Volkslieder*, ii. 352–5.

[2] J. van Dixmude, *Kronyk*, 76–80 and *Hanserecesse von 1431 bis 1476*, ii. 106–9.

[3] A place about three miles east of Bruges, on the Ghent road, where a comital castle was situated.

[4] The south-western gate of Bruges, leading to Loppem, Torhout and Lille.

The Brugeois noticed with considerable distrust and suspicion that the prince, who was armed, had six or seven battle pennons and some 4,000 people, some wearing battle tunics, with him. . . . At about 5.0 p.m., when at least 1,400 men had been allowed in, the prince entered and rode to the Fridaymarket, assuming that those who were still outside the Boeveriepoort would follow him into the town. But the magistrates and the deans managed with great difficulty to close the Boeveriepoort, so that some 2,500 armed men, mostly on horseback, remained outside. They went to the Smedenpoort, but this was shut in time to keep them out. If they had got in, Bruges would have been lost, for the Brugeois were unarmed, since in every gild they had been ordered that morning to turn out in the afternoon to meet the prince unarmed and in their best clothes.

When the prince reached the Fridaymarket with his people, he sent Sir Josse de Heule to the market-place to see if the town authorities had stationed any troops there. When he arrived there, Sir Josse turned to his companions and said:

'We can go straight back to my lord of Burgundy. The market-place is his and Bruges is won. We'll kill these rebel Brugeois!'

He rode towards the prince's palace past the mint, and came across the prince with his nobles in the Dweersstraat. As the prince still wasn't certain if the market-place was his, the bastard of St. Pol called out that they should return to the Fridaymarket, and, though this was [now] full of common people, unarmed, he shouted 'Haubourdin! Haubourdin! Draw your bows! Draw your bows!'[1] The archers shot at the people up the street, they shot at the houses, and they shot at the people who were looking, bareheaded, out of windows to welcome the prince. Numbers were wounded, and some 300 arrows remained stuck in the dormers, gables and tiles of the houses all along the Dweersstraat as far as the Zuidzandbrugge, on either side of the street. The prince stationed himself on the higher ground of the Fridaymarket, at the cattle market. There he was with his nobles, armed, holding a drawn sword in his hand, sitting up on his horse while his men either shot at the common people of Bruges or laid about them with their swords, and wounded many. A master baker, Race Yweyns, was shot dead as he stood in front of the prince doffing his hat in welcome. . . . Thus at the cattle market, the prince's people did battle . . . , and they yelled 'The town is won! Town won! kill them all!' so loud that their companions outside the Boeveriepoort heard them and some of them tried to swim on horseback across the moat into Bruges. . . .

When the common people of Bruges saw that people were being killed, and heard the cry 'Kill them all! Town won!', they rushed back to their houses to arm themselves, and some of the gilds brought small cannons to the Noordzandbrugge and Zuidzandbrugge, and fired

---

[1] The bastard of St. Pol was Jehan de Luxembourg, lord of Haubourdin.

wooden missiles at the Frenchmen and the prince's people, who turned and fled back towards the Boeveriepoort. But they found it closed. And at St. Julian's a horrible battle was fought. The bastard of St. Pol slew Jan van der Hoghe's son, and two Brugeois were killed by the moat. The other Brugeois saw this and spared no-one. Soon seventy-two Picards had been killed between St. Julian's and the fountain in Boeveriestraat, including the lord of l'Isle Adam, who was struck down dead in front of St. Julian's chapel. The prince, realizing that his people were being killed, rode with a good many of them through the Andghewercstraat towards the moat and the Boeveriepoort. Jacop van Hardoye, the head night watchman, had in his house a hammer, a pair of pincers and a chisel and, with these, the Boeveriepoort was broken open and, at about 7.0 p.m., the prince rode out of Bruges towards Lille, with his company. The burgomaster Lodewic van den Walle, Sir Roland d'Uutkerke, Sir Colard de Commynes the sovereign bailiff, and many burgesses . . . left with him.

The duke's version of what happened in Bruges on 22 May 1437 is less circumstantial and does not ring quite so true. It was written at Lille the day afterwards, and formed part of a letter which was sent to all 'archbishops, bishops, dukes, counts, knights, squires and good towns', to apprise them of the villainous conduct of the populace of Bruges.

On Wednesday last we arrived at our village of Roeselare *en route* for Holland and Zeeland, where we met some notable persons, both lay and ecclesiastic, from the authorities of Bruges . . . who told us that we could have entry to and submission of our town, as we had requested, and who assured us that the aforesaid town would remain in peace and in good order under us and our rule. So we left Roeselare for Bruges, with a certain number of men-at-arms and archers who were to accompany us to Holland and Zeeland. It is true that the ecclesiastics, magistrates, and other burgesses of Bruges came out in procession some distance to meet us, in order, as it seemed, to do us honour and reverence. . . . Yet, as we arrived at the gate, we noticed that it was manned and guarded by the Brugeois. After they had held us up for three or four hours in front of the gate, we rode in and found everyone in arms, ready to oppose and rebel against us and our companions, with cannons and guns and other weapons of war all prepared. Very soon after we entered they closed the barbican gate and raised the drawbridge . . . shutting out the greater part of our people without our realizing it, for we had already gone quite some distance into the town on the way to our own palace. When we discovered that the gate had been shut, and tried to return towards it in order to make our way out of the town, we were attacked on all sides by people intent on murdering us and our company, a fact which shows that all this had been treacherously planned long before-hand. Among our people who were there murdered was one particularly sad loss, our well loved and loyal knight, councillor, chamberlain and brother of our Order, the lord of l'Isle-Adam. . . .

Though Philip escaped from Bruges with his life on 22 May, the incident led rapidly to further troubles in Flanders. A state of open war now obtained between Philip and Bruges, where twenty-two Picard prisoners-of-war suffered public execution in the market-place. A determined effort was made to starve Bruges into submission by blockade and boycott.[1] The Zwin, which connected Bruges to the sea, was staked, and all the commercial privileges of Bruges were made over to Sluis. The inevitable riposte of Bruges was the siege of Sluis in July, which Philip managed to raise before the end of the month. Ghent tried to mediate but, in the autumn, fell victim to violent internal upheaval, and a war between Ghent and Bruges almost ensued. Thus throughout much of 1437, as in the second half of 1436, Flanders suffered from rebellion, warfare and civil chaos. In all this, three elements were present: the class struggle within the city walls; bitter inter-urban rivalries; and a clash of interests between Philip the Good and his subjects.

It was not until February 1438 that Flanders was pacified by an agreement reached at Arras. Bruges had to make her peace with Philip on terms which were bizarre in their elaboration and humili-ating in the extreme. The next time the duke visited Bruges, the civic authorities were to process out of the town to meet him and kneel in apology before him, bare-headed and bare-footed. The gate which had been closed against him, together with its bridges, barriers and fortifications, was to be demolished. In its place, a chapel was to be erected where a perpetual daily mass would be celebrated for the souls of those killed. On every anniversary of 22 May the civic authorities were obliged to celebrate divine service in the church of St. Donatian, supported by twenty-four men bearing burning torches, each of six pounds in weight. Bruges was to pay the duke a fine of 200,000 riders, and he reserved the right to demand further compensation on behalf of other victims of the Bruges revolt. Sluis was henceforth to be almost entirely freed from the jurisdiction of Bruges, nor would the Sluis contingent in future have to march behind that of Bruges when the Flemish militia were mobilized. There

[1] On this paragraph, besides the sources already mentioned on p. 86 above, see ADN B1963, fos. 66b, 67b, etc.; *IAM* iii. 63–4; and Monstrelet, *Chronique*, v. 282–9, 295–6 and 307–8.

were many other clauses and conditions,[1] and Bruges was only pardoned after forty victims had been nominated for execution. Although a good many of these contrived to escape, ten were beheaded on 30 April, sufficient to adorn each of the gates of Bruges with a grisly reminder of its rebellion against the duke.

In the wake of these Flemish revolutions and wars came rising prices, hunger and disease; phenomena which form a dismal backcloth to the history of Philip's northern territories in the late 1430s. The Flemish chroniclers placed the worst period in the second half of 1438; in Holland the famine reached its peak somewhat later. The disturbances at Rotterdam early in 1439 have been linked to the shortage of corn at this time.[2] In Holland things were aggravated by a war between Holland and the Hanseatic League which broke out in 1438. Admittedly, the decentralized structure of the Burgundian state, combined with the interests of the people themselves, enabled Philip to restrict this war to Holland, leaving Flanders neutral; just as Holland had not been involved in the Anglo-Flemish war of 1436. But on each occasion a general dislocation of commerce resulted.

The war of 1438–41, in which Holland attacked all Hanseatic shipping, though in actual fact only the so-called Wendish quarter of the Hanse, comprising Lübeck, Hamburg, Wismar, Rostock, Stralsund and Lüneburg, had declared war on Holland, was a direct result of commercial competition. It was partly a war of pirates and privateers; partly a struggle for control of the Sound in which the Dutch were at first allied with King Eric of Denmark against his nephew and rival Christopher of Bavaria, protégé of Lübeck; and partly a war of economic blockade. It was a war in which almost no actual fighting took place, in spite of the emphatic manner in which it was declared by the Dutch administration on 14 April 1438.[3]

[1] Full text in *IAB* v. 136–57.
[2] Jansma, *TG* liii (1938), 337–65. See too J. van Dixmude, *Kronyk*, 103 and O. van Dixmude, *Merkwaerdige gebeurtenissen*, 163.
[3] Printed, Van Marle, *Hollande sous Philippe le Bon*, xxv–xxix and *Hanse-recesse von 1431 bis 1476*, ii. 162–4. For this paragraph and what follows, see especially *Hanserecesse von 1431 bis 1476*, ii; *Hansisches Urkundenbuch*, vii; Daenell, *Blütezeit der Hanse*, i and *HG* xi (1903), 1–41; Stahr, *Die Hanse und Holland*; Vollbehr, *PHG* xxi (1930); Warnsinck, *Zeeorlog van Holland tegen de wendische steden*; and Jansma, *RN* xli (1960), 5–18 and the references given there.

To all those who see this letter or hear it read, the council of my gracious lord the duke of Burgundy and of Brabant charged by him with the government of Holland, of Zeeland, and of Friesland, offers its friendly greetings. We wish it to be known that for more than three years the people of Holland, Zeeland and Friesland have suffered unjust and unreasonable damage to lives and goods at the hands of the duke of Holstein and his subjects and the six Wendish towns, that is, Lübeck, Hamburg, Lüneburg, Rostock, Wismar and Stralsund. . . . The Four Members of Flanders, who trade a great deal with the Hansards, persuaded our gracious lord [the duke] to agree to hold a conference between his lands of Holland, Zeeland and Friesland and the above-mentioned duke of Holstein and the six Wendish towns, which took place in the town of Bruges and then at Ghent. At this conference a truce was arranged, which has been continued from time to time since, in the hopes that the complaints of either side might meanwhile be submitted in writing to arbitrators in order to achieve a settlement . . . but the deputies of the duke of Holstein and the Wendish towns refused to accept arbitrators . . . and planned to ally with the Prussians and other Hanseatic towns to retaliate for the damages they claimed to have suffered in Holland, Zeeland and Friesland. . . .

Consequently, the nobles and towns of Holland, Zeeland and Fries-land have asked us to allow and permit them, in the name of our gracious lord of Burgundy, count of Flanders, to recover the value of the damage they have suffered from those who caused it. And we, unable to deny this, have consented and agreed on behalf of our gracious lord of Burgundy, count of Holland, that the duke of Holstein's subjects and those of the six Wendish towns may be damaged, seized and injured in lives and goods wherever they can be found, and . . . that in future no-one shall take any merchandise eastwards by sea.

This declaration was followed in May by the mobilization or creation of a Dutch fleet. All suitably-sized ships were to be got ready to put to sea on a war footing within a fortnight, complete with tackle, guns and crews. Moreover, before the end of the month, a certain number of warships, seventy-nine in all, were to be constructed in every town or port of Holland. But the Dutch navy achieved little in 1438, apart from the seizure of some neutral shipping. For months on end, both in 1439 and again in 1440, the fleet cruised in the Sound, though it failed to penetrate into the Baltic. Thus the war dragged on inconclusively but with disastrous commercial consequences.

But Scandinavian affairs now impinged on the fortunes of the war for in 1440 King Eric was dislodged from the Danish throne by Christopher of Bavaria with the help of Lübeck and the Wendish towns. Though King Eric's Dutch allies were forced by these events to withdraw from the Sound in the summer of 1440, Christopher himself, once in power, was far from being averse to a *rapprochement* with the Dutch. He is said to have complained, in 1441, that the Wendish towns had more privileges in Denmark than his own subjects, and he was largely instrumental in bringing about the conference of Copenhagen in August–September 1441 at which ambassadors of Denmark, Lübeck, Prussia, Holstein, Holland and Duke Philip himself, thrashed out a settlement. The Dutch negotiated separate treaties with Denmark, the Wendish towns, and Prussia, obtaining respectively commercial privileges, a truce and access to the Baltic, and a settlement in return for reparations. They emerged from the war with commercial wounds that would take years to heal, but with an assured possibility of the further expansion of their Baltic trade.

In the very years 1436 to 1440, when Philip's northern territories experienced the warfare and revolts, and the economic troubles, which we have briefly touched on, his southern lands, the two Burgundies, were suffering from the attentions of the *écorcheurs*. These *écorcheurs*, or flayers, so-called because they were reputed to strip their victims of everything they had save their shirts, were a fifteenth-century version of the companies of demobilized soldiery which had ravaged parts of France in the 1360s. Just as those earlier wandering bands were a by-product of the peace of Brétigny, so these later ones resulted from the peace settlement of Arras. Burgundy became one of their principal victims and theatres of activity partly because of the encouragement given to them there by Charles VII, who preferred to see them ravaging territories other than his own and who was still in any case a determined enemy of Philip the Good.[1] Thus the cessation of hostilities envisaged and demanded by the treaty of Arras never came about. The captains who had up to then acted against Burgundy on behalf of France, now continued their operations of pillage and ransom on their own account. True, there were lulls in 1436 and 1437, but at the end of the latter year the *écorcheurs* were ensconced in the heart of the duchy, around Beaune and Nuits-St.-Georges to the south of Dijon, and at places like Is-sur-Tille to the north. On 16 December 1437 the civic authorities

[1] For what follows, see *Documents pour servir à l'histoire de Bourgogne*, i. 372–485 and Denis, *Journal, ibid.*, 267–96; Bazin, *MSBGH* vi (1890), 97–112; de Fréminville, *Les écorcheurs en Bourgogne*, and Tuetey, *Les écorcheurs sous Charles VII*.

4. Nicolas Rolin, chancellor of Burgundy.
Jan van Eyck (detail)

5. Jacqueline of Bavaria, countess of Hainault
and duchess of Brabant

closed three of Dijon's gates. The contingent of troops hastily levied by the governor of Burgundy, Jehan de Fribourg, to resist the écorcheurs, themselves constituted a menace to the local populace which, in many places in the winter of 1437-8, rose in what amounted to open revolt against the ducal government. The inhabitants of the citadel-town of Talant, near Dijon, refused to accept a ducal garrison and defied the governor and his men in January 1438. At about the same time a detachment of écorcheurs made as if to invade the county of Burgundy. To forestall them, Jehan de Fribourg had to lead a contingent of his men through Auxonne. Early one Sunday morning, one of his captains arrived to request urgent passage for these ducal troops, but the mayor and councillors calmly informed him that they would have to consult the citizens after mass. Asked if at least they would repair the bridges which the citizens had dismantled for fear of the écorcheurs, they replied that they did not know where the timbers and planks were! After mass, the mayor sent a messenger to tell Jehan de Fribourg that his troops could pass through the town, but only in groups of twenty. The distrust and hostility of the inhabitants was further demonstrated when these isolated detachments marched through the main street, for they found all the side-streets closed and barricaded against them. In view particularly of the extremely cold weather, some of the soldiers would have liked to stop for a bite of food, but the watchful citizens refused them this favour; nor would they even permit the governor himself to stop for a glass of wine and some fireside warmth in the local hostelry. Years later ducal justice caught up with the mutinous citizens of Auxonne, and their mayoral and civic institutions were abrogated. Their defiant attitude was by no means unique. Other places behaved in exactly the same way, as if a ducal garrison was just as much feared as a visit from the écorcheurs. In July 1438 the gates of Nuits-St.-Georges were firmly closed at midnight one night against the commander of the ducal garrison of neighbouring Argilly, though he only wanted to arrange a surprise attack on some écorcheurs, and only asked for a meal for himself and his troops. He went on his way, but received similar treatment at Beaune, where on another occasion a ducal embassy on its way to France was kept waiting outside the gates for four hours.

Every means was tried to rid the duchy of the écorcheurs. Aides were levied to purchase their withdrawal, armies were mustered and marched against them, the frontiers were patrolled, and towns which could be persuaded to admit ducal troops were garrisoned. These measures were carried out with patience and vigour but very limited success by the marshal and governor of Burgundy, and by the council and *chambre des comptes* at Dijon. In September 1438, at a time when much of the western half of the duchy was virtually under enemy occupation, the *écorcheurs* were tardily and, as we may suppose, insincerely, ordered out of the duchy by King Charles VII. In any case his orders were ignored, and the *écorcheurs* continued their ravages. Even if an expected attack or invasion did not materialize, elaborate precautions had to be taken against them. On 1 May 1439, for example, when the town council of Mâcon feared their attentions, the following preparations were resolved upon.[1]

1. The keys of the town gates to be handed over for safe keeping to certain burgesses.
2. The artillery to be set up on the walls and gates.
3. Watch to be kept at night by forty well-armed citizens.
4. Every night six people to do the rounds outside the walls.
5. Two of the gates to be walled up; the others to be permanently guarded.
6. A sentry to be stationed at St. Peter's belfry.
7. The artillery to be inspected.
8. An inventory to be made of the inhabitants' arms and artillery.
9. People to be designated to place hurdles and stones on the walls.
10. All the boats as far as Tournus to be collected and moored to the base of the bridge.
11. The sale of arms to people outside the town to be forbidden.

The *écorcheurs* continued to cause disruption and damage in the duchy and county of Burgundy until well into the 1440s, when their activities culminated in the dauphin's expedition of 1444 against the Swiss. It is not our purpose here to describe their ravages in detail, but rather to draw attention to the fact that these ravages, which contrasted with the successful local truces of the 1420s, continued intermittently throughout the late 1430s, forming a sort of unofficial, but extremely damaging, sequel to the Franco-Burgundian hostilities of the early 1430s in this area. The crises and difficulties in the north, diverse in origins and nature, and ranging from internal revolts, like those of Cassel in 1429 and Bruges in 1437, to external warfare, as with England in 1436 and the Hanse in 1438, must be seen against this background of repeated hostilities in the south. The perspective that emerges is one of turbulence and disorder, of danger and crisis, in the history of the Burgundian state.

[1] De Fréminville, *Les écorcheurs en Bourgogne*, 118–19.

One by one, even at last the *écorcheurs*, the trials and tribulations of the 1430s were surmounted but, before we turn to examine the inner workings of Philip the Good's state in its heyday, something must be said of the diplomatic relations of Burgundy, France and England in the years after the peace of Arras.

CHAPTER FOUR

Burgundy, France and England: 1435–49

Europe's first real peace congress opened at Arras, capital of Philip the Good's county of Artois, on 5 August 1435, in the Benedictine abbey of St. Vaast. Ever since May the quartermasters of the Burgundian court had been busy booking lodgings there for the duke and his entourage.[1] Everybody sent ambassadors or observers to attend the public sessions of the conference, which were presided over by two cardinals, one representing the pope, the other from the Council of Basel. Besides the deputations from the three principal negotiating powers, England, France and Burgundy, there were representatives of every important French prince and of many French or Burgundian towns and territories. An idea of the total number present may be derived from the report of a chronicler, that the personal retinue of a single one of the English ambassadors, Cardinal Henry Beaufort, bishop of Winchester, comprised 800 horse. On its return to England, we are told, every member of this numerous entourage was dressed in the cardinal's vermilion livery, with the word 'honour' embroidered on his sleeve. There must certainly have been 5,000 strangers in Arras that August, among them a fine display of heralds and poursuivants, for France had sent twenty-eight, including Mountjoy, Pierrepont, Feu Gregeois, Loyauté and Beauvais; England provided Garter and Suffolk; and Philip the Good sent Golden Fleece, Flanders, Hainault, Avant Garde, Franchecomté, Fusil, Vray Desir, Bonne Querelle and a host of others.

[1] ADN B1954, f. 44. For what follows, see especially Plancher, iv. 198–219; du Fresne de Beaucourt, *Charles VII*, ii. 505–59; Schneider, *Europäische Friedenskongress von Arras*; and Dickinson, *Congress of Arras*, and references given there. Among the chroniclers, de la Taverne, *Journal de la paix d'Arras*; Monstrelet, *Chronique*, v. 150–83; le Févre, *Chronique*, ii. 305–66; and Chartier, *Chronique de Charles VII*, i. 185–213, are of particular importance.

Philip's avowed aim, in convoking the Congress of Arras, was to negotiate a 'general peace', that is, to bring to an end all hostilities between England, France and Burgundy, and the 'particular peace', that is, the Franco-Burgundian peace, which was signed on 21 September, was largely the result of French initiative. The English and French deputations were so ill-disposed towards one another that they refused to meet together in the same room, either for purposes of negotiation, or even for divine service. Instead, they appeared alternately in front of the mediating cardinals to denounce each other; to critize each other's credentials; to protest against each other's infringements of diplomatic procedure; and to make the most extreme demands, or impossible conditions, that they could think of. As a matter of fact, the two countries were in the middle of a rather important war for control of Paris, which the English still held by a narrow margin, and a peace settlement between them was, at that juncture, unthinkable.

After the English deputation had left Arras in a huff on 6 September, the French lost no time in detaching Philip the Good from his English alliance. In earlier chapters we have watched Philip reacting with firmness and determination to the military situations created by the exigencies of aggression or internal revolt. But the hero of the conquest of Holland, the ruler who time and again faced and overcame internal crises in Flanders, was no diplomat. At Arras he was induced by the skilful tactics of the French king and government to abandon his ally and subscribe to a peace the terms of which were never intended to be honoured by Charles VII. Philip was duped in this way partly by the allure of the terms themselves. Cession, for example, of the territories which Philip possessed, but without the sanction of the French crown: Péronne, Montdidier, Roye, Auxerre, Bar-sur-Seine, Mâcon and the rest. Cession, in the form of a mortgage, of the coveted Somme towns of St. Quentin, Amiens and Abbeville, with the county of Ponthieu, against their redemption by the king for 400,000 gold crowns. Above all, full moral satisfaction promised for the crime of Montereau, including a formal apology from King Charles VII, and expiatory religious foundations.[1] But it was not only the terms of the treaty itself which persuaded Philip to play the French game at Arras. The personnel of the French embassy had been skilfully chosen: it was led by two of Philip's brothers-in-law, Charles, duke of Bourbon, and Arthur, count of Richemont. While they involved Philip in an unending round of social and

[1] The text of the treaty is in *Grands traités*, 116–51.

sporting festivities, well-calculated to win his sympathies for a 'particular peace' with France, the French government had bribed an influential section of the Burgundian council. The remarkable document which follows was unearthed and published by Dr. Thielemans.[1]

Amboise, 6 July 1435

Charles, by the grace of God, king of France, greetings to all those who see these letters. Be it known that we, having heard on good authority . . . of the good will and affection which Nicolas Rolin, knight, lord of Authumes and chancellor [of Burgundy], and the lords of Croy, Charny and Baucignies, councillors and chamberlains of our cousin of Burgundy, and other servants of his, cherish for the reconciliation and reunion of us and our cousin . . .; bearing in mind that this peace and reconciliation is more likely to be brought about by our cousin's leading confidential advisers, in whom he places his trust, than by others of his entourage; and having regard for the great benefits likely to accrue to us, our subjects and realm as a result of this peace and reconciliation, which we hope that the aforesaid chancellor and lords of Croy, Charny and Baucignies will do their best to bring about . . .; we grant and have granted by these present letters the sum of 60,000 gold saluts . . . to divide between them as follows:

To the said Nicolas Rolin,	10,000 saluts
To the said lord of Croy, likewise,	10,000 s.
To the said lord of Charny,	8,000 s.
To Philippe, lord of Ternant,	8,000 s.
To the lord of Baucignies,	8,000 s.

And to Jehan de Croy, brother of the said lord of Croy; Jaques, lord of Crèvecoeur; Jehan de Brimeu, lord of Humbercourt; and to Guy Guilbaut, all councillors of our aforesaid cousin, 10,000 saluts to share between the four of them. . . .

The men who permitted themselves to be bought over in this way by the king of France were, as this document implies, no ordinary councillors.[2] Anthoine, lord of Croy, was Philip's closest associate and favourite councillor throughout his long reign, a status which found formal and official expression in his office of first chamberlain. His brother Jehan was captain-general and bailiff of Hainault. Pierre de Bauffremont, lord of Charny, had been captain-general of the

[1] *Les Croÿ, conseillers des ducs de Bourgogne*, 71–3.
[2] See Richard, *MSHDB* xix (1957), 107 n. 3 and Bartier, *Légistes et gens de finances*, 257 (Bauffremont); Hulin, *BSHAG* xix (1911), 329–41 (Guilbaut); Perier, *Nicolas Rolin* and Valat, *MSE* (n.s.) xlii (1914), 53–148 (Rolin); and below, p. 337 for the Croy family.

duchy of Burgundy and was later privileged to become the husband of a ducal *bastarde*, Marie de Bourgogne. These three, as well as Philippe, lord of Ternant and Jaques, lord of Crèvecoeur, were all of them Knights of the Golden Fleece. The lord of Baucignies was Jan van Hoorn, admiral of Flanders, who was killed in 1436 by the angry Flemings after being accused of accepting English bribes.[1] Guy Guilbaut was second only to the chancellor Nicolas Rolin in the ducal administration for, as treasurer, he was in charge of Philip's finances. More remarkable, perhaps, than this wholesale perfidy among Philip's leading councillors and officials, was the fact that his wife, Isabel of Portugal, had also been won over. Here at Arras she displayed for the first time her undoubted gifts as a negotiator, but on behalf of France, not Burgundy. While the councillors received bribes beforehand, she accepted a reward afterwards: on 21 December 1435 Charles VII confirmed to her an annual rent of £4,000, which the counts of Hainault received from the French crown, and which Philip had agreed to make over to her. In the document, Charles VII explicitly states that this was because of her services in negotiating the Franco-Burgundian 'peace and reunion' at Arras.[2] Surely the historian of the Congress was mistaken in supposing that she was a mere spectator?

The peace of Arras, between Charles VII and Philip the Good, was only signed after a prolonged debate within the ducal council and entourage. Influential and determined men like Jehan de Luxembourg, count of Ligny, Jehan, lord of Roubaix, and Roland d'Uutkerke made a last-minute bid to prevent a settlement. Above all, Hue de Lannoy, lord of Santes and governor of Holland, councillor and writer of memoranda addressed to the duke on affairs of state, did his best to avoid a Franco-Burgundian treaty and to warn the duke of the likely consequences: a breach with England, leading to English attacks on Flanders which, by disrupting Flemish commerce, would arouse the Flemings to revolt. But, having failed to prevent what he saw as a catastrophe, the assiduous Hue submitted a memorandum in November 1435 outlining his suggestions for the conduct of the war which he thought must inevitably follow this diplomatic disaster.[3] The kings of Castile and Scotland were to be

[1] Thielemans, *Bourgogne et Angleterre*, 95, n. 177.
[2] *Cartulaire de Hainaut*, v. 338–40. For the next sentence, see Dickinson, *Congress of Arras*, 66, n. 4.
[3] Potvin, *BCRH* (4) vi (1879), 127–38.

induced to attack England simultaneously by sea and land; the defence of Picardy and Flanders was to be carefully organized to resist attacks from Le Crotoy and Calais, and by sea; and five or six salaried spies were to be employed in England. In the event, the English successfully raided Flanders after Philip's siege of Calais had ended in dishonourable withdrawal, and revolution broke out in Flanders immediately afterwards, just as Hue had predicted. By the early autumn of 1436 he was busy with yet another memorandum, in which, after a penetrating and somewhat pessimistic analysis of Philip the Good's general situation, he once again advocated the 'general peace' which he had hoped Arras would achieve.[1]

Written at Ghent, 10 September, 1436

Most redoubted lord, I, your obedient subject and servant, who has more loyalty and goodwill than wisdom and discretion, have been pondering and considering your present situation, day and night, with such wits as God has given me, to see what can be done, and to let you know what benefits may emerge for yourself and your lands. But, most redoubted lord, after considering this a great deal, I have come to the conclusion that you and your affairs are in a most dangerous situation.

In the first place, I see that you are at war with the king of England and his kingdom. He is powerful both on land and sea, and you are necessarily forced to maintain powerful garrisons against him on the frontiers of Flanders and Artois. After all, one can well imagine that he has two or three thousand combatants at Calais, Guines, Les Hemmes and Le Crotoy, who are quite capable of making effective war in your territories, thus compelling you to maintain a good many troops, or else lose towns, castles and other places or have your lands ravaged and pillaged. Nor can such garrisons be maintained without a great deal of expense, as is well known to you and all.

Moreover, wherever war is waged and the countryside is destroyed and plundered by friend and foe alike and the populace is restless, little or no money can be raised. Yet this war cannot be conducted without large sums of money for the above-mentioned garrisons and other armaments. You must have appreciated, during the siege of Calais, what harm was done by lack of finance,[2] and it is to be feared that the war has only just begun. If you need to raise finance in Brabant, Holland and other lands of yours, it can only be with the consent and good will of the people, especially when they see that you are at war [with England] and that the Flemish seem likely to rebel against you at any moment. If

---

[1] Printed, but wrongly dated, by Kervyn de Lettenhove, *BARB* (2) xiv (1862), 218–50, and partly by du Fresne de Beaucourt, *Charles VII*, iii. 81–2.
[2] See above, pp. 80–1.

the truth be told, you have no territory whose populace is not hard pressed financially; nor are your domains, which are mortgaged, sold or saddled with debts, able to help you.

Again, you have seen how agitated your Flemish subjects are; some of them, indeed, are in armed rebellion. Strange and bitter things have been said about yourself, your government, and your leading councillors; and it is very likely that, having got as far as talking in this way, they will soon go further than mere talk. Moreover, if you pacify them by kindness and by accepting their demands, other towns, which have similar aspirations, will rebel in the hopes of getting similar treatment. On the other hand, if you punish and repress them, it is to be feared that they will make disastrous alliances with your enemies. If by chance they start pillaging and robbing, it is possible that every wicked person will start plundering the rich, practising the profession of moving in one hour from poverty to wealth. Covetousness exists among the well-off; you can imagine how much worse it is among the populace. In this matter, there is much cause for anxiety.

I note that, according to report, the English are planning to keep a large number of ships at sea in order to effect a commercial blockade of your land of Flanders. This is a grave danger, for much harm would result if that country were deprived for any length of time of its cloth industry and commerce. And you can appreciate how much it would cost to send a fleet to sea to protect this commerce and resist the enemy. Moreover, if Holland and Zeeland continue their trade with the English, and they very probably will want to do this, the Flemish, finding themselves without commerce, without their cloth industry, and involved in war at sea and land, will probably make an alliance with the English, your enemies, which could be very much to your prejudice and dishonour.

I note, too, that the king of France can scarcely help you with finance and, if he sends troops, they will be the sort, which you know of, who are as good at destroying the country as defending it. Nor will they serve you at all without payment and, if not paid, they will pillage and plunder those very lands of yours which, as you know, are already devastated. As to the nobility of your lands in Picardy, their estates have already been ravaged and destroyed by the armies that have been assembled there, and are likely to be ravaged still more. Moreover, what is worse, hatreds and divisions will probably be stirred up because of this devastation, so that you will get little help from them. It is to be feared that this war will last such a long time that certain people, who secretly harbour feelings of hostility towards you but have hitherto not dared to reveal them, will come out into the open when they see you thus involved. As you know, your lands of Brabant, Holland, Namur and others have some very unfriendly neighbours.

Most redoubted lord, when I examine carefully these perils and dangers, your lack of funds, the divisions which exist among your people, and other matters which it would take too long to relate; and when, on the other hand, I consider ways and means of avoiding them, with my limited understanding I see only one way, in which you can escape once and for all from these difficulties, which would be in your own and the public interest. This is, to find some means of arranging a general peace settlement between the king and kingdom of France, on the one hand, and the king and kingdom of England, on the other. I do not see any way, considering past events and your relation to these two kings and kingdoms, in which you can maintain the lands, peoples and merchants along the seaboard, who are inclined towards rebellion and disturbance, in peace, justice and obedience towards yourself (as they ought to be), while the war continues between the two above-mentioned kings. For those who are rebelling or who do rebel in the future, not only in Flanders, but equally well in your other countries, will gladly ally with one of these two kings or kingdoms, whenever you set out to punish and subdue them as they deserve. I have heard it maintained by old people as a truth that, ever since the wars began between the king of France and king Edward of England for the crown of France, the Flemish have been less obedient to their ruler than they were before.

If anyone wants to argue and maintain that it is out of your power to negotiate a general peace between the two kings, and that, because of the particular peace you made at Arras, you no longer ought to try . . ., it seems to me, subject to correction, that you still can help a great deal towards a general peace, more than any christian prince, if you put your heart into it and follow the advice given here. . . .

To appreciate how such a general peace could be achieved, the internal state of these two kingdoms must be examined. To take France. You can appreciate what sort of prince the king is, who does not himself rule, but is ruled, the great poverty in his situation and throughout the kingdom because of the wars . . ., how little he is obeyed by his captains, the melancholy and displeasure he has suffered from being in such difficulties for so long, and also the longing to be rid of the war which is shared by a good part of the nobles, ecclesiastics and townsmen of France. The probability is, that if they can find a reasonable way to achieve this, they will heartily welcome it.

As regards the king and kingdom of England, the king is young, too young to rule; they have spent excessive sums of money on the French wars for the last twenty years; they have lost a considerable number of captains, nobility and others in France during these wars; and you, my most redoubted lord, have left their alliance, so that their own English people now have to sustain the whole war and pay for it. All these things are dangerous and difficult for them. Moreover, rumour has it that the common people of England are so tired of the war that they are more or less desperate. It is true that they have experienced important disputes among themselves, for the majority of the people blamed the royal council for not achieving a general peace at the Congress of Arras, and for refusing the offers made to them immediately after it. Besides, because of the wars in Scotland and Ireland; the damage sustained by the king and the merchants owing to the consequent interruption of commerce; and because, to help Calais, they had to denude the country of its nobility . . . , it is probable that, everything considered, they are tired of war and will gladly embrace a more reasonable policy, the more so now than ever before, since the king will be fifteen on St. Nicholas's day.

To come to the actual negotiation of this general peace. When you, most redoubted lord, decide to undertake it, you will easily find suitable means and persons to open negotiations with the two kings and their councils. . . . The first means in your power is my lord [René of Anjou], duke of Bar, your prisoner, brother of the queen of France and of Charles of Anjou, who has much influence with the king. In return for the release of my lord of Bar, you could have the help of his sister the queen of France, of his mother [Yolanda of Aragon] the queen of Naples, and of his brother Charles of Anjou, in negotiating the general peace with the king of France. The second means is that you hold the county of Ponthieu, Amiens and the Somme towns in mortgage for 400,000 crowns [from the king of France]. Now it is unlikely that a general peace can be achieved without the transference of the duchy of Normandy to the king of England. But the king of France would be very unwilling to part with it. . . . However, it is possible that, if you were prepared to quit him of this mortgage of 400,000 crowns, he might in return transfer the duchy of Normandy to the king of England. . . . The third means concerns my lord the duke of Orleans, a prisoner in England [since Agincourt], who as is natural, has been trying for a long time and by various means to effect his release. But this does not seem likely to come about, except by means of a general peace between the two kingdoms. Thus, if the king of France were to place difficulties in the way of a general peace, the bastard of Orleans and several captains who are close friends of my lord of Orleans, as well as his servants and officials in his French lands, could well persuade the king to change his mind in favour of [my lord of Orleans], thus facilitating the peace [negotiations]. On the other hand . . . , if the English freed my lord of Orleans, he could, in return for his release, considerably advance the peace [negotiations] by influencing the king and lords of France. And if his release had been effected by you, he would always be indebted, and grateful, to you.

Most redoubted lord, nothing ought to stand in the way of your pursuit of this general peace, and I would like to assure you, truthfully and without flattery, that, in case you think your honour has been tarnished by the withdrawal from Calais [in such a way as to require you to continue the war], those knights, squires and other people who know what honour is . . . would never blame you for this. Everyone knows how your civic troops, forming the main part of your army, shamefully abandoned you, and how you faced considerable personal danger, accompanied by very few men-at-arms, in resisting your enemy while they were pursuing your civic militia as they withdrew in disorder. Moreover, your intrusion into English territory to destroy four notable castles, burning them down and taking their garrisons prisoner, as is well known, must be taken into account. Whereas after this, when the English entered your territory to burn and pillage . . . , they failed to destroy a single one of your notable fortresses.

My most redoubted lord, if it seems to you that the abandonment of the above-mentioned mortgage of 400,000 crowns and the suggested release of my lord of Bar would mean too great a financial loss for you, it could be truthfully urged in reply that, if you took careful stock of your own situation and the government of your lands; if you took your affairs to heart in an effort to adjust your way of life and the duchess's, to moderate the liberality in which you have been somewhat excessive, to introduce order and some regulation in your court expenses and remove the superfluities and duplications that exist in many ways, but especially in the number of your financial councillors and other people, about which everyone is talking; [if you took care] to regulate and organize the judicial administration of your lands by appointing good, experienced and reliable judicial officers of your own choosing rather than as a result of bribery, petition or importunities . . . ; if you took all this to heart and followed the advice of good, loyal and experienced people, you would find that you would recover each year as much, or almost as much, revenue as the mortgage you hold from the king brings in to you.

You may rest assured that, if your subjects of every estate see that you are diligently trying to reorganize your administration in the light of reason by implementing the above-mentioned measures, and that you have made peace, so that commerce is unrestricted in your lands and lordships, they will make generous financial provision for you so that you can redeem your [alienated] domain. And, if you and your lands remain in peace with the two above-mentioned kings and kingdoms and your domain has been redeemed and relieved of debt, if you govern reasonably and spare your people excessive taxes . . . , undertaking no wars except by permission of the Estates of your lands, and taking advice from people who are experienced, rather than those inspired by flattery or greed . . . you will find yourself among the richest princes in the world, feared and loved by all your subjects. . . .

My most redoubted lord, to sum up my advice, you must arrange things so that your Flemish people are induced to lay aside their arms and banners and return to their work . . . , you must ensure that peace is made between the two kings and kingdoms as soon as you possibly can ..., and you must reform your government in matters of finance and justice so that you win more popularity than you currently enjoy.

The diplomatic history of Burgundy in the decade after Arras was largely concerned with the implementation of suggestions made in this interesting memorandum. A threefold Burgundian diplomatic initiative may be discerned. First, the negotiation of a 'particular peace' with England, to repair the damages of war and restore the commerce of Flanders. Second, a determined, but unsuccessful and shortlived, effort to achieve the 'general peace', through Burgundian mediation of an Anglo-French settlement. Thirdly, Burgundian diplomacy had to face constant aggression from France, linked to a refusal to implement the terms of the treaty of Arras. The easy success of the first of these aims; the failure of the second; and the continuance of French hostility just mentioned, all underline the fact that the Congress of Arras was by no means a turning-point in the diplomatic history of Western Europe.

The siege of Calais in July 1436 marked only a brief interruption in Anglo-Flemish commercial relations and inflicted only superficial damage on Anglo-Dutch trade. It fell to Hue de Lannoy himself, acting in his capacity of stadholder of Holland, to take the initiative in implementing his own proposals in May 1438, when he led a Burgundian embassy to England to settle the outstanding commercial differences between England and Holland. By August 1438 Flemish economic interests were likewise the subject of negotiations and, by the end of the year, their scope had been broadened, in a conference at Gravelines, to include the mediation by Burgundy of a general Anglo-French peace and the release of Charles, duke of Orleans. During the next two years the negotiations for a general peace remained intimately linked to those concerning the commercial relations of Flanders and Holland with England. On the English side, the principal negotiator was Henry Beaufort, bishop of Winchester and cardinal; on the Burgundian side, the negotiations seem to have been entirely entrusted to Duchess Isabel, whose English connections and sympathies were well known, and whose diplomatic skill had been demonstrated at Arras, at least to the satisfaction of Charles VII.[1]

[1] For this paragraph and what follows, see especially Thielemans, *Bourgogne et Angleterre*, 111–63 and the works cited there; and Allmand, *BIHR* xl (1967), 1–33.

The first conference of Gravelines, in December 1438, had been held on the frontiers of continental England and Flemish Burgundy, that is, in the fields between Marck and Oye-Plage, on the road from Calais to Gravelines. It successfully paved the way for the second, which opened on 6 July 1439. Henry Beaufort brought an assortment of bishops and noble lords; Isabel brought a group of pro-English

ENGLISH CONNECTIONS OF ISABEL OF PORTUGAL DUCHESS OF
BURGUNDY

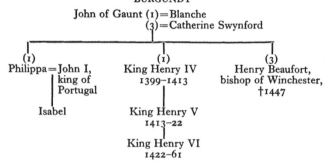

```
              John of Gaunt (1)=Blanche
                          (3)=Catherine Swynford

         (1)                    (1)                   (3)
   Philippa=John I,         King Henry IV        Henry Beaufort,
         │  king of          1399-1413          bishop of Winchester,
         │  Portugal                                  †1447
         │
       Isabel                 King Henry V
                               1413-22

                            King Henry VI
                             1422-61
```

Burgundian councillors, including Hue de Lannoy, as well as the Burgundian chancellor, Nicolas Rolin, or Rawlyn as Dr. Thomas Beckington, secretary to the English ambassadors, spelt it;[1] and the French sent a deputation as well. The proceedings took place under canvas and continued even when rain leaked through the hundred-foot-long pavilion in which the meetings were held. The English excelled themselves in the extravagance of their demands, which comprised the crown of France itself, the duchies of Normandy, Brittany, Anjou, Touraine and Aquitaine, and the counties of Flanders, Maine, Toulouse, Poitou, Ponthieu, besides Calais, Guines, etc. A deputation of clerics from the Council of Basel, offering to mediate, was rebuffed and after several adjournments the conference broke up in September. But the grandiose and unattainable notion of an Anglo-French peace settlement had not been alone on the agenda of Gravelines, for ambassadors had also been empowered to discuss Anglo-Flemish and Anglo-Dutch commercial relations. Anglo-Flemish negotiations continued in September at Calais, and resulted in the commercial treaty or *intercursus* of 29 September 1439, which was initially to remain in force for three years. It restored Anglo-Flemish relations to their normal friendly state; a state which had endured since the end of the previous century, and was to continue

---

[1] His Journal is printed in *Procs. and Ords. of the P.C.*, v. 334-407.

until the beginning of the next. Some of the clauses of this important treaty, which has only recently found its way into print, were as follows:[1]

1. Merchants of England, Ireland, Calais, Brabant, Flanders and Malines to enjoy unmolested passage to and fro between Calais and their destinations in Brabant, Flanders or Malines.
2. Similar free passage, at sea between English ports and ports in Brabant and Flanders, for English and Burgundian merchants, to apply to all sorts of merchandise except artillery, gunpowder and other war material.
3. Merchants of each country to pay the other's legitimate tolls and dues; and no merchant to travel armed, except for a knife, dagger or sword for self-defence.
4. Merchants of either country permitted to stay unmolested in the other.
5. Free passage through Flanders and Brabant for English pilgrims, and clerics on their way to pope or Council. But they must ask leave before entering a fortified town, and must not stay more than one night unless constrained to do so, in the case of a port, through illness or by the lack of a ship or suitable wind.
6. Fishing to be freely permitted on either side and fishing-boats to be allowed to take refuge in the other country's harbours.
7. Neither side to handle merchandise belonging to enemies of the other.
8. A fine wide road to be marked out through the dunes between Calais and Gravelines, passing north of the castles of Marck and Oye, for the use of merchants of either side. But they are not to take dogs with them, nor hunt for rabbits in the dunes.

Within a few months of its signature this treaty was prolonged for a further term of years, until 1447, and it continued in force thereafter. Infringements of its terms were settled by reparations, and disputes about them were arbitrated at Calais or elsewhere. Anglo-Flemish commercial relations, thus restored, were reinforced by a perpetual truce which Isabel negotiated in 1442–3 with Richard, duke of York. In particular, this protected the frontiers of Flanders, Artois and the Somme towns. Meanwhile, from December 1439 onwards Anglo-Dutch commercial negotiations were in progress, though it was not until 1445 that outstanding difficulties were settled, to the advantage of England, for the Dutch had to pay a substantial sum in reparations. By means of the Anglo-Flemish treaty, the truce and the Anglo-Dutch settlement, Philip the Good was able to recover, by diplomatic

[1] Thielemans, *Bourgogne et Angleterre*, 443–53.

initiative, the ground which he had lost by war with England in 1436, though Anglo-Burgundian relations were never again quite restored to their pre-1435 status of an outright alliance. In those days Philip had fought, when it suited him, on the side of England against France; now, after 1439, he remained strictly neutral, officially at peace with both combatants. Only once was this policy of non-belligerence towards England seriously endangered. This was in the summer of 1449, when some Flemish and Dutch merchantmen, laden with salt, fell victim to English pirates. In reprisal, Philip the Good ordered the arrest of English merchants in his lands and the confiscation of their belongings, and he kept the ducal fleet of four warships at sea off the coast of Normandy and Brittany all that summer in case serious hostilities broke out. But the affair came to nothing, and the only help Charles VII was able to extract from Philip, in his conquest of Normandy from the English, was permission to recruit volunteers in Burgundian territories.[1]

Historians of Scotland have not so far troubled themselves with the relations of Burgundy and Scotland in the fifteenth century. But these relations, which were carefully maintained and developed by Philip the Good, were by no means unimportant. For Burgundy they formed part of a system of protective alliances and of commercial connections, while their existence helped to display the status of Burgundy as a European power. As early as 1426 Philip and the Four Members of Flanders had jointly sent an embassy to Scotland to negotiate a settlement of commercial differences.[2] In 1431 Philip sent Guillebert de Lannoy, brother of Hue, on an embassy to the king of Scotland. Unfortunately, his instructions have not survived, and his own account of this embassy mentions only his itinerary. He left Sluis on 4 March to proceed by sea to Calais, whence he crossed to Sandwich. Passing through London, Huntingdon and Doncaster, he un-accountably turned aside from the direct route north, which would have taken him through Pontefract and Boroughbridge to Northallerton, and instead visited York, travelling thence into Scotland via Hull, Newcastle and Bamburgh. In Scotland he visited Dunbar, Stirling and Dumfries. After the completion of this diplomatic mission,

---

[1] *Brut*, 515; d'Escouchy, *Chronique*, i. 183; *Urkundenbuch der Stadt Lübeck*, viii. 663–5 (compare *Hanserecesse*, iii. 404–5); and Leclercq, *Politique navale*, 31.

[2] *IADNB* i (1), 376; *IAB* iv. 485; and *Précis analytique*, (2) ii. 29–30 and 40. Compare *Groet charterboek*, iv. 816–17. For what follows, see de Lannoy, *Oeuvres*, 166–73 and 205–7.

Guillebert undertook some private tourism of his own by crossing to Ireland on 27 May to visit St. Patrick's Isle in Lough Erne.

A more important mission to Scotland took place in 1449, when the daughter of the duke of Guelders was sent off from Sluis to marry King James II, then aged nineteen. The exact origins of this marriage alliance remain obscure, but the initiative may have come from the Scottish government, which approached Charles VII in 1447 about the matrimonial prospects of James II and his two sisters.[1] In 1446, a series of negotiations between Scotland and Burgundy had taken place, mainly at Bruges, as a result of which the 1427 commercial treaty was amplified and confirmed at the end of 1447. Then, on 6 May 1448, King James II empowered ambassadors to visit the Burgundian court to seek a wife for himself, to make an alliance with Philip the Good, and to find husbands, in Burgundy or Austria, for his sisters Joan and Eleanor. Philip had been blessed with an abundance of bastards, but these were of no value for marriage alliances with other powers. In contrast to his father, who had had seven legitimate daughters, Philip had not a single one. He therefore had to make use, for this purpose, of other people's daughters and, in particular, of the daughters of neighbouring rulers who were more or less in his pocket, and who were relatives of his, notably the dukes of Cleves and Guelders. Thus it was Philip who now arranged the marriage of James II and Mary of Guelders, who was actually Philip's great-niece.[2] It was Philip who provided a ship to take the bride to Scotland and a warship to escort her; it was Philip who paid her expenses; and it was Philip who exploited the transaction to sign a treaty of alliance with James II, which also comprised the dukes of Brittany and Guelders. Finally, it was Philip who paid his niece's dowry of 60,000 crowns.

The chronicler Mathieu d'Escouchy was given a detailed account of the journey to Scotland with Mary of Guelders by one of the participants. The small convoy left Sluis at 4.0 a.m. on Thursday 12 June, when the wind unexpectedly became favourable, and sailed direct to the Isle of May, taking exactly a week to complete the crossing. The wedding was celebrated at Edinburgh a few days later. Immediately after the ceremony, the queen was fitted out in violet

---

[1] *Letters and papers*, i. 194–8 and 221–3. For what follows, see *IAB* v. 297 and 299; Ruwet, *Archives et bibliothèques de Vienne*, 187; and *IADNB* i (1), 297.

[2] See the genealogical table on p. 291 below. For what follows, see ADN B2002, fos. 188a–b and *IADNB* i (1), 233 and 297–8.

E

robes lined with ermine, 'of a most unusual and peculiar style, judged by French standards', and was then brought back to the altar to be crowned. The wedding-feast followed.[1]

When [the king and queen] were seated, the first dish to be brought in and presented to them was a boar's head, which had been painted and stuffed, on a huge plate. Round the head were a good thirty-two banners, with the arms of the king and the other lords of the country. Then, the stuffing was set on fire, to the great joy of everyone in the room. Next, a fine and beautifully-made ship was brought in, which had a forecastle, masts with a top, and cords of silver. Then the earl of Orkney entered, with four knights, followed by the meat course, comprising various dishes. Each dish was brought in by some thirty to forty people, all carrying plates . . . and, as each plate was set down, the waiter knelt until the person served had started eating. . . . At another table, a patriarch, three bishops, an abbot and other clerics, were merrily celebrating their king's wedding. These five prelates were drinking heavily from a huge wooden goblet, without pouring anything back; for wine and other drinks seemed in as plentiful supply as sea-water. The same thing happened at the table of knights and squires of Scotland. This feast lasted four or five hours, during which time a very large number of dishes were served.

Connections between Scotland and Burgundy were maintained after this and on 12 October 1450 some Scottish knights and squires, accompanying William, earl of Douglas, had an opportunity, at Lille, of sampling the fare at the Burgundian court. They were treated to beef, mutton, pork, with mustard and brown and white bread; and they and their hosts, among them Philip himself, ate two hares, ten pheasants, one heron, four bitterns, 156 rabbits, seventy-two partridges, ten geese, twelve water birds, thirty-four dozen larks, 231 chickens and fifty-six brace of pigeons.

Philip the Good's diplomatic relations with England and Scotland have been briefly traced in the period after the treaty of Arras. His English diplomacy in these years was largely conditioned by the failure of de Lannoy's carefully argued project for a general Anglo-French peace. This general pacification had been seriously attempted, under Burgundian auspices, at Arras in 1435 and at Gravelines in 1439. Burgundian, and ecclesiastical, mediators continued to pay lip-service to the idea during the 1440s, summoning conferences and

[1] D'Escouchy, *Chronique*, i. 181–2. For what follows after the extract, see *IADNB* viii. 23–4.

despatching ambassadors in its name. Meanwhile the English and French were determined to fight it out, while Philip the Good had discovered, very soon after the treaty of Arras, that, so far as France was concerned, the protection of his own interests must have diplomatic priority over prestigious but idealistic schemes of general pacification.

It seems incredible that the Burgundian councillors who negotiated the treaty of Arras in September 1435 really believed that Charles VII, who had not scrupled to arrange or condone the murder of John the Fearless in 1419, intended to keep to its terms. But, as we have seen, they had been bribed. It is in fact abundantly clear that the French government had no intention of honouring the treaty, nor of relaxing for one moment its deep-felt hostility to Burgundy. Charles VII had only signed the treaty of Arras in order to detach Philip from the English alliance. But he achieved far more than this, for his action involved Philip in a war with England and with revolts in Flanders, while it bore immediate fruit, for him, in the reconquest of Paris from the English, with Burgundian help, in April 1436. Directly after the treaty Philip sent an embassy to Charles which obtained his ratification of it, and this was followed by his formal oath to abide by its terms.[1] Nevertheless, before the end of 1435 Philip had had occasion to complain to Charles that the towns of Chablis and Charlieu, belonging respectively to the counties of Auxerre and Mâcon, both of them ceded to Philip in the treaty, were still in royal possession. Thus began the so-called 'quarrel of the enclaves', which really consisted of a determined and prolonged attempt by the French crown to undermine ducal territorial and judicial rights in and around the duchy of Burgundy.

The exchange of gifts and letters between Charles and Philip which took place in February 1436 seemed a token of friendship, particularly as Philip then accepted the king's invitation to be godfather to his newly born son. But the letters show that Charles was dissatisfied both with Philip's exclusion of his prisoner, René of Anjou, duke of Bar and Lorraine, from the treaty of Arras, and with Philip's insistence that his councillor, Jehan Chevrot, must become the new bishop of Tournai, and not the royal nominee, Jehan d' Harcourt, whom he curtly requested Charles VII to have transferred

---

[1] In all that follows, to p. 118, I am deeply indebted to Mme Hillard's thesis *Relations diplomatiques entre Charles VII et Philippe le Bon*, which she kindly lent me. It is summarized in *PTSEC* (1963), 81–5. Otherwise, one must still rely on the narratives of du Fresne de Beaucourt, iii. and Plancher, iv.

elsewhere.[1] Within a few weeks of this correspondence Philip had to send an embassy to the king to complain about the activities of the Paris *Parlement*, and this seems to have resulted in the temporary suspension, by Charles VII, of all cases pending in which Philip was involved. This was in April, when Philip's help in the reconquest of Paris from the English was at stake. Later in the year, yet another Burgundian embassy complained to Charles VII about infringements of ducal prerogatives in the duchy by royal officials, especially through the issue of royal safe-conducts; and Charles gave him at any rate legal satisfaction, by issuing letters on 30 August forbidding this practice. Irritating, though minor, disputes of this kind continued in 1437, when, for example, royal officials claimed the fines imposed by the Paris *Parlement* in Flanders, in cases of unsuccessful appeals, though these had hitherto been levied by Philip.[2] But a rapprochement still seemed possible, particularly when, in July 1438, a Burgundian embassy requested Charles VII to give one of his daughters in marriage to Philip's only legitimate child, the six-year-old Charles, count of Charolais. Two daughters were apparently sent to Philip, who was allowed to choose between them, and in June 1439 the elder, Catherine of France, aged about ten, was duly wedded to Charles at St. Omer. The accounts disclose that each of the two wedded children was placed in the care of a governess.[3] Their marriage was ended by Catherine's death on 28 July 1446.

In spite of this marriage alliance the French attitude towards Philip the Good remained fundamentally hostile. Little was done by the French authorities to remove or deter the *écorcheurs*, who were universally, and not wholly inaptly, referred to throughout Philip's lands as *les gens du roi*, 'the king's people'. Nor were the activities of these roving bands of French soldiery limited to the duchy of Burgundy. They menaced Hainault in 1439 and some of them, subjects of Charles VII, were later arrested there by the bailiff of Avesnes.[4] Early in 1441 the diplomatic experience of Duchess Isabel was pressed into service. She was sent by Philip the Good to Laon, to

[1] Le Févre, *Chronique*, ii. 366–73; see too below, pp. 218–20.
[2] AGR CC21807, f. 10. For what follows, see ADN B1966, f. 130; Monstrelet, *Chronique*, v. 344 and 400–2; *IADNB* i (1), 294–5; du Fresne de Beaucourt, *Charles VII*, iii. 101–2; and Armstrong, *AB* xl (1968) 38–40. The text of the marriage treaty is printed in *Corps universel diplomatique*, iii (1), 58–60.
[3] ADN B1966, 74b and 75b.
[4] ADN B10405, fos. 36 and 39, and see Monstrelet, *Chronique*, v. 468–70 on what follows.

present a series of complaints to King Charles VII, accompanied by the above-mentioned French prisoners from Hainault, and a 500-page report on the points at issue between her husband and the king. But she was coolly received. Not a single one of her requests was granted, and she returned frustrated to report her failure to Philip. From this moment on, the chronicler Monstrelet hints, fears of a French attack on Burgundy were seldom absent from the thoughts of Philip and his councillors. There certainly was a group of French councillors which advocated war against Burgundy, and continued to advocate it during the rest of Charles VII's reign and afterwards, but the king himself, yielding to the persuasions of Arthur, count of Richemont, Regnault de Chartres, archbishop of Rheims and chancellor of France, and others, preferred a policy of consistent and determined hostility; of provocation, alliances, litigation, and even sedition, against Philip; but always stopping short of actual warfare.

The matters of dispute, between Charles VII and Philip the Good, in the early 1440s, were far too numerous to mention individually. They included rival claims to the county of Étampes, which Philip had given to his cousin Jehan de Bourgogne, later count of Nevers, though it was actually in the possession of Richard of Brittany and was confirmed to his son, later Francis II, duke of Brittany, by Charles VII in 1442.[1] They included the piratical activities of French fishermen from Dieppe against Flemish commerce, and the hostile behaviour of French troops in or near Hainault. Nor were Franco-Burgundian relations improved when Philip's alliances with French princes like the dukes of Orleans and Bourbon blossomed out into a formal conference of princes in January 1442 at Nevers. During 1443 and 1444, things went from bad to worse. To the continuing ravages of the *écorcheurs*, with whom Charles VII repeatedly but hypocritically disclaimed any connection, were now added hostile incursions by the dauphin's troops: in 1443 near Dieppe, and in 1444 around Montbéliard and elsewhere. The whole course of French foreign policy in 1444 seemed to threaten Burgundy, for, while Charles VII himself held court at Nancy in Lorraine and unsuccessfully besieged Metz, the dauphin Louis campaigned against the Swiss. Charles was supposedly acting on René of Anjou's behalf, and Louis had gone to the rescue of Frederick III of Habsburg, but the real aim of their expeditions seems to have been to extend French

[1] Champion, *Charles d'Orléans*, 453. For what follows, see *Précis analytique*, (2) ii. 58 and 59; ADN B10407, 24b and 27b; Tuetey, *Les écorcheurs sous Charles VII*; and de Fréminville, *Les écorcheurs en Bourgogne*.

influence over Metz, Toul, Verdun and Basel. This sudden French incursion into the Burgundian sphere of interest was made possible by the Anglo-French truce signed at Tours on 28 May 1444.

At the end of 1444 and early in 1445 Philip's officials were busy compiling a comprehensive list of complaints against the encroachments of French royal officers on ducal rights.[1] This diplomatic ammunition was fired off at the king in two important conferences, at Rheims in March 1445, and at Châlons, where Duchess Isabel represented Burgundy and Charles VII appeared in person, in May and June. Philip's instructions to his ambassadors going to Rheims, drawn up in thirty-two articles on 4 March, list the grievances to be presented. Among them, the following were prominent:

1. Occupation by royal troops of certain places in the duchy of Luxembourg.
2. Damages done by royal troops in garrison on the frontiers of the county of Burgundy.
3. Failure of the king to do justice to those responsible for John the Fearless's murder, in spite of his promise to this effect in the treaty of Arras.
4. Similar failure of the king to implement the clauses of the treaty of Arras obliging him to found certain religious houses in expiation for the murder of John the Fearless.
5. Debt of 35,000 crowns owed to the duke of Burgundy by the king.
6. Continued interference by royal officials in the county of Mâcon, including the fact that the royal bailiff of Lyons styled himself 'bailiff of Mâcon', though the cession of the county of Mâcon to Philip was stipulated in the treaty of Arras.
7. Infringements by royal officials of ducal rights in the counties of Burgundy and Auxerre, at Bar-sur-Seine, and in the duchy of Burgundy.[2]
8. Interference by royal officials in the ducal mints at Dijon, Mâcon, Auxerre, St. Quentin and Amiens.[3]
9. Royal appointment of a bailiff of Amiens.
10. Issue of royal letters referring to Philip as 'self-styled lord of Lille, Douai and Orchies'.

[1] See, for example, Plancher, iv. no. 138. For what follows, see Plancher, iv. no. 139. For the conferences of Rheims and Châlons, see especially d'Escouchy, *Chronique*, iii. 98–112; du Fresne de Beaucourt, *Charles VII*, iv. 112–41; Tuetey, *Les écorcheurs sous Charles VII*, i. 345–66 and ii. 184–91; Thibault, *Jeunesse de Louis XI*, 429–49; and Hillard, *Relations diplomatiques entre Charles VII et Philippe le Bon*, 136–97.
[2] See Richard, *AB* xx (1948), 89–113.
[3] On the last two, see Spufford, *Monetary problems and policies in the Burgundian Netherlands*.

As if the thirty-two articles of complaint thus presented to the royal representatives at Rheims in March were insufficient in number or of inadequate weight, a further series was submitted on 13 May 1445, to inaugurate discussions at Châlons. These demands, which were of a somewhat more mercenary nature, were in some cases ridiculously far-fetched. For instance, Philip now demanded half a million francs owed, but never paid, by the French crown to his grandfather Philip the Bold, as well as the sum of £345,591 *tournois* which Charles VI had admitted he owed to John the Fearless on 15 April 1407.[1] He asked, too, for payment of a sum of 10,000 florins owed to the dukes of Brabant by the kings of France as a result of a transaction of 1347. On no better pretext, Philip demanded 800,000 crowns in reparations for damages recently committed by royal troops in Artois, Picardy and Hainault. All this was hardly the way to lubricate the machinery of diplomacy, but the evidence shows that these additional Burgundian demands were merely an attempt to counter a systematic and purposeful onslaught on Philip by Charles VII and the dauphin Louis, which was being mounted to coincide with the conferences. The twenty-three-year-old dauphin, who later, as King Louis XI, was to become famous for his diplomatic contortions, was apparently only too glad to further this tortuous double-faced policy of his father towards Philip.

On 9 April 1445 the marshal of Burgundy, Thibaud de Neuchâtel, wrote to Duchess Isabel complaining bitterly of the depredations of the dauphin's troops around Montbéliard, and reporting that he had been told on good authority that 'the king and my lord the dauphin had secretly ordered these troops to live off Burgundian territory until the conference of Rheims . . . and to act in such a way as to ensure that complaints were made about them.'[2] There is little doubt that such orders were given, and extended, for acts of provocation or open hostility by royal troops or officials continued right through the spring and summer of 1445. They continued, too, after the conference of Châlons had closed at the beginning of July with a settlement of some outstanding points, showing the Charles VII had no intention whatsoever of achieving a genuine settlement with Philip. For example, in July a French captain ravaged parts of Mâcon and Charolais, and protests were made in the French council against Philip's use of the title 'by the Grace of God'.

It has been claimed that the conference of Châlons narrowly

[1] Vaughan, *John the Fearless*, 42–3. The document of 13 May 1445 is printed in d'Escouchy, *Chronique*, iii. 105–12.   [2] Plancher, iv. no. 141.

averted a Franco-Burgundian war.[1] But it seems more probable that the French government's policy was to go as far as it could, in hostility towards Philip, without provoking a war. In this it was completely successful. Philip the Good was forced into a defensive posture, and soon found himself making concessions to the French crown in the hopes of palliating or removing its hostility. The principal concession he made, in the summer of 1445, was the release of René of Anjou, titular king of Sicily and duke of Bar and Lorraine, from all his obligations. Captured by the Burgundians at the battle of Bulgnéville in 1431, René had become Philip's prisoner-of-war. Excluded from the treaty of Arras, he was eventually released in 1437 against payment to Philip of a ransom of 400,000 gold crowns and the cession of various lands and claims to lands in Flanders. But René found it impossible to raise the ransom money. He was burdened in 1445 with a massive debt to Philip, which was increasing at the rate of twenty crowns for every day that payments were in arrears. The treaty which finally cleared René of Anjou of these consequences of his military disaster fourteen years before, was negotiated by Isabel on Philip's behalf, and signed on 6 July. It was more of a surrender than a concession, to the French crown and, as we have seen, no pacification, or change of heart on Charles VII's part, accompanied it. The only concessions made to Philip in return were the evacuation of Montbéliard, which had been occupied by the dauphin during the course of his expedition against the Swiss in 1444, and the issue of royal letters, on 4 July 1445, withholding, or delaying for nine years, all appeals to the *Parlement* of Paris against judgments of the Four Members of Flanders.[2] But these royal letters had only been obtained by the duchess as a result of bribery, to the tune of 6,000 crowns, paid by her to royal officials, a sum which the Four Members refused to defray, but which Bruges eventually agreed to lend. As to Philip's demand that the dauphin and others should swear to, and Charles VII should implement, the treaty of Arras, it seems to have been completely ignored by them. The treaty was, however, ratified by René of Anjou, by his son John, duke of Calabria, and by some other less important persons.[3]

[1] E.g. by J. Maupoint, *Journal parisien*, 35–6 and Hillard, *Relations diplomatiques entre Charles VII et Philippe le Bon*, 197. For what follows, on Philip and René, see especially Lecoy, *Roi René*, i. 93–106, 110–11, 116–28 and 246–8. Plancher prints some of the documents, iv. nos. 97, 124, 145 and 148.

[2] *Ordonnances des rois*, xiii. 441–2 and, for the next sentence, *IAB* v. 279–81.

[3] *IAEG* 167–8.

René of Anjou's misfortune had been unscrupulously exploited by Philip. Instead of adopting Hue de Lannoy's advice, quoted at the beginning of this chapter, of treating René magnanimously and releasing him quickly from his gaol and his obligations, in order to gain his friendship, Philip tried to extract the last pound of flesh, in terms of ransom money and land. In the event, he failed to lay his hands on René's duchy of Bar, and he was forced to forego a substantial part of the ransom money. Instead of winning René's friendship, he earned his undying hatred.

At Gravelines and at Châlons, Isabel, duchess of Burgundy, had shown herself to be a diligent and skilful negotiator. The daughter of one of her Portuguese ladies-in-waiting, Alienor de Poitiers, recorded what her mother told her about the Burgundian court at this time, and her account of the duchess Isabel at Châlons, though it throws no light on diplomatic affairs, permits us to appreciate the minutiae of courtly politeness which accompanied the negotiations.[1]

My lady the duchess [of Burgundy], accompanied by my lord of Bourbon [Jehan, count of Clermont], her nephew, and several French princes, came with all her company on horseback and in carriages into the courtyard of the mansion where the king and queen were staying. The duchess dismounted, and her maid of honour held her train while my lord of Bourbon took her hand, and all the other knights and gentlemen preceded her. Arrived at the room where the queen was, the duchess stopped, and sent my lord of Créquy, her knight of honour, to ask the queen if it was her pleasure that the duchess should enter to do her reverence. When the lord of Créquy returned, the duchess, preceded by her knights and gentlemen, walked as far as the doorway of the queen's room, where she took her train from the lady who was holding it. As she entered the room, she let it fall behind her, and curtsied almost to the ground. Then, walking as far as the centre of the room, she curtsied again before approaching the queen, who was standing near the head of her bed. As the duchess knelt for the third time, the queen moved forward two or three paces and, placing her hand on the duchess's shoulder, embraced her and made her get up. The duchess curtsied again, very low, and went to my lady the dauphiness, who was five or six feet from the queen. Again, the duchess knelt, and the dauphiness kissed the duchess just as the queen had done, but, to judge from the way the dauphiness behaved, she tried to stop the duchess from kneeling right down to the floor. . . . Thence, madam went to salute the queen of Sicily [wife of René of Anjou], who was sitting two or three feet from the dauphiness, but this time she only performed a shallow curtsy:

---

[1] De Poitiers, *Les honneurs de la cour*, 196–201.

according to my mother neither of them were likely to damage their knee-caps in curtsying to each other. . . .

Of the duchess's ladies-in-waiting, the queen kissed my lady of Montagu, my mother, and my lady of Crèvecoeur, and no others, but she shook all the gentlewomen by the hand, and the dauphiness did the same. Then, the duchess kissed all the queen's and the dauphiness's ladies, but only as many of the queen of Sicily's ladies as the queen of Sicily had embraced of hers. On no account would my lady the duchess allow herself to be preceded by the queen of Sicily, for she maintained that my lord the duke [her husband] was more nearly related to the crown of France than the king of Sicily [René of Anjou]. Also, she was the daughter of a king of Portugal, who is much more important than the king of Sicily. . . . According to my lady of La Roche-Guyon, who was the queen's first lady-in-waiting, she had never seen anyone to whom the queen had done so much honour, as my lady the duchess [of Burgundy].

Alienor of Poitiers goes on to tell us that Isabel had taken the trouble to consult a reference work on court etiquette, since French practice differed somewhat from Portuguese. She also tells us how to lay the table for a prince or princess, but that is beyond the scope of the present narrative.

Franco-Burgundian relations showed no signs of improvement in the years 1445–7. The solemn assembly of the Order of the Golden Fleece in December 1445 was interrupted by the unexpected appearance of an usher from the *Parlement* of Paris, who had the effrontery there and then to summon the duke of Burgundy to appear before that court.[1] Philip began to lose patience with Charles VII's attitude to the treaty of Arras and appealed to the pope to arbitrate on the question of whether or not it had been properly implemented. His grievances came to a head again late in 1448, when important discussions took place in Paris. This time, sixty-seven separate articles of complaint were submitted to the royal representatives. They covered every conceivable issue, including disputed enclaves in the duchy of Burgundy; the frontiers of the county of Burgundy; continued hearing of appeals to the Paris *Parlement* against judgments of the Four Members of Flanders in spite of the royal letters of July 1445;[2] and Philip's use of the title 'by the grace of God'. Much has been made of the accommodating attitude of Charles VII on this occasion, and

---

[1] Chastellain, *Œuvres*, vi. 289. For the next sentence, see Plancher, iv. 263–4 and Gachard, *Rapport sur Dijon*, 76.
[2] See Philip's letters of 16 February 1447 on this in *Analectes historiques*, vii. 359–62.

it has been plausibly suggested that the numerous concessions he made in a series of letters-patent issued on 28 January 1449 were designed to ensure the friendly neutrality of Philip in the coming struggle with England: for the truce of Tours was about to be shattered by the closing campaigns of the Hundred Years War. But in fact the king either ignored or studiously evaded the great majority of Philip's points, and the few that were officially recognized in the letters of 28 January were mostly trifling. Thus Charles VII permitted Philip to use the title 'by the grace of God'; he ordered the royal bailiff of Sens to stop calling himself 'bailiff of Auxerre'; he formally ceded the county of Mâcon to Philip, admitting that this ought to have been done in 1435; he forbade his troops to make war on Burgundian territory; and he prohibited royal officials from exercising certain rights in the duchy of Burgundy. These and similar concessions were demonstrably hypocritical; without the king's goodwill and without some intention to implement them, they were so many scraps of parchment. According to the historian of Charles VII, du Fresne de Beaucourt, these royal acts attested Charles's 'firm desire to give his vassal every possible satisfaction compatible with the interests and dignity of the crown'. In actual fact, Charles only wanted to gain time, and these gestures of amity were hollow and meaningless. Behind them, and all the negotiations that led to them, lay the stark realization by the French king and government that Philip the Good, his state, his policies, his attitudes, his very existence, were in themselves against 'the interests and dignity of the crown'.[1] The Saxon ambassador who reported home from Bruges on 15 June 1447 that Philip was more hated and opposed at the French court than anyone, had touched the heart of the matter.

Charles VII's hostility to Philip the Good was by no means limited to the kind of domestic or juridical provocation we have so far described, for this French aggressiveness was projected onto the European stage by means of a system of alliances evidently aimed against Burgundy, which was put together in 1444 and 1445, and maintained thereafter as a standing threat to Philip. These French allies included Jacob von Sierck, archbishop of Trier, Dietrich von

[1] For the conference of Paris, see du Fresne de Beaucourt, *Charles VII*, iv. 375–84, who mentions some of the royal letters of 28 January 1449 on pp. 383–4. Others are referred to or printed in *IADNB* i (2), 8 and 274 and Faussemagne, *Apanage ducal*, 310–11; and still others are transcribed in BN Coll. de Bourg. 95, pp. 1030–1 and 99, pp. 476–7. For the following sentence, see Hansen, *Westfalen und Rheinland*, i. 279.

Mörs, archbishop of Cologne, William, duke of Saxony, Philip's rival for the possession of Luxembourg, and Frederick III of Habsburg.[1] In 1445 Charles VII was involved in negotiations with another of his allies, Girart de Looz, count of Blankenheim, concerning the possibility of French help in expelling the Burgundians from Luxembourg, and over a possible alliance of France with Liège. At the same time, Charles VII did his best to support Evrard de la Mark, owner of certain castles in the episcopal principality of Liège, who, 'though a young man, inexperienced, and with little money', as he described himself, had dared, on 6 June 1445, to declare war on the duke of Burgundy. In 1447 there seemed at one time to be a serious danger that the local conflict over the possession of Soest, between the archbishop of Cologne and Philip's ally and brother-in-law Adolf, duke of Cleves, would escalate into a general war as a result of the intervention of France on behalf of Cologne and that of Burgundy on behalf of Cleves. Thus was the personal enmity of Charles and Philip reflected in European affairs.

Although Philip the Good's defensive reactions to Charles VII's onslaught were, on the whole, weak and indecisive, he did make an attempt, which was not wholly unsuccessful, to consolidate and develop his system of connections and alliances with the French princes. Indeed, he initiated a minor diplomatic revolution by his close alliance with Charles, duke of Orleans, whose father had been assassinated in 1407 by John the Fearless. But Philip invariably shrank from direct confrontation with Charles VII, and this weakness on his part ensured that the princely combinations against Charles, which were mounted in the years 1437–40, were all of them failures.

Some of the French princes with whom Philip enjoyed friendly relations in the years 1435–49 were his traditional friends or close relatives. The two brothers, Charles, count of Nevers and of Rethel, and Jehan de Bourgogne, count of Étampes, were his cousins. The former was an ineffective ally of Philip; the latter, during a good part of the reign, was his loyal captain and trusted administrator. Of Philip's two brothers-in-law among the French princes, Arthur,

[1] Petit-Dutaillis, *Charles VII, Louis XI et les premières années de Charles VIII*, 307 and Hansen, *Westfalen und Rheinland*, i. 74, 77–8, etc. For what follows, besides these works, see du Fresne de Beaucourt, *Charles VII*, iv. 126–7, 138–9, etc.; d'Escouchy, *Chronique*, i. 72–4; d'Oudenbosch, *Chronique*, 23–5; and de Stavelot, *Chronique*, 547–59, 566–7 and 578.

count of Richemont, constable of France, exercised a staunchly pro-Burgundian influence at court, especially before the death of his wife Margaret of Burgundy in 1442. The other was Duke Charles of Bourbon, who had married Agnes of Burgundy in 1425. Though he had waged war on Philip in Charles VII's name in the years before the treaty of Arras, Charles was entirely reconciled to Philip by 1437, and the two dukes signed an alliance in January 1440. Thereafter the connection was assiduously maintained by Philip the Good, who brought up Charles's son Louis de Bourbon at his own court, and sent him to the University of Louvain, maintaining him there for some ten years, from 3 July 1445, on a generous allowance.[1]

Brittany had been a traditional ally of Burgundy during the reigns of Philip the Bold and John the Fearless, and this tradition was maintained by Duke John V of Brittany, who received the insignia of the Golden Fleece in 1440 and at the same time signed a commercial treaty with Philip. After his death in 1442 the new duke, Francis I, began by confirming the alliance of 1425, but he refused the offer of the Golden Fleece in 1445 and soon proved himself to be a consistent supporter of Charles VII. The loss of Brittany as a Burgundian ally was perhaps compensated for by the acquisition of Alençon, for Duke John II did not disdain the Golden Fleece offered him in 1440. Subsequently his loyalty to Burgundy seems to have been nurtured with bribes.[2] But much more important was Philip the Good's achievement, in the years after the treaty of Arras, in winning Charles, duke of Orleans, over to the Burgundian interest.

Ever since his capture by the English at Agincourt in 1415, Charles of Orleans had been wiling away his time in the Tower of London writing poetry, playing chess, and intriguing for his release. But nobody intervened on his behalf. The English had no objection to retaining the dukes of Bourbon and Orleans, and other French notables, in the Tower, against the day when their release could be usefully bargained for; the French king and council managed very well without these princes; and none of their relatives could afford to pay their ransoms. So it was that Charles of Orleans remained in the Tower until eventually released in 1440 through the good offices of

[1] ADN B1988, fos. 44b–45 and B2004, f. 86. See, in general, Cosneau, *Connétable de Richemont*, and Leguai, *Ducs de Bourbon* and, on what follows, Knowlson, *Jean V, duc de Bretagne* and Pocquet, *RCC* xxxvi (1) (1934–5), 651–5.
[2] See, for example, ADN B2002, fos. 169a–b.

Philip the Good, who needed allies in France. In this matter, at any rate, Philip took the advice of his councillor Hue de Lannoy, proffered in 1436 and quoted above.[1]

The negotiations for Charles's release were undertaken by the duchess of Burgundy, who visited him at Calais during the conference of Gravelines in July 1439. Charles was overjoyed, and encouraged these Burgundian efforts on his behalf in verse, by sending ballads to Philip the Good. The treaty arranging his release was eventually signed on 2 July 1440, after Duchess Isabel had passed the hat round the French princes for donations towards his ransom money of 240,000 crowns. Practically everybody in France contributed, except Charles VII; practically everyone in England seems to have favoured the release, except Duke Humphrey of Gloucester. Charles set sail for Calais on 5 November 1440, having promised to do his utmost to bring about a Franco-English peace, and leaving behind him in gaol his unfortunate younger brother Jehan, who had shared his twenty-five years of English imprisonment.

He was met outside Gravelines by Isabel herself, and the new-found Burgundian ally was then paraded round Flanders with all the extravagant pomp the Burgundian court could muster. At St. Omer Philip took Charles into the abbey of St. Bertin to hear the archdeacon of Brussels read out the treaty of Arras, in Latin and French, which Charles of Orleans then solemnly swore to adhere to. Next, he was married to a wife provided for him by Philip. This was Mary of Cleves, one of the numerous children of Philip's brother-in-law Duke Adolf I of Cleves.[2] Charles was aged forty-five, Mary was only fourteen; but the match was satisfactory at any rate from Philip's point of view, for Charles's financial indebtedness to him enabled Philip to dispose of Mary virtually without the need to pay her dowry. The wedding was followed by the annual St. Andrew's day celebrations of the Golden Fleece, when Charles, unanimously chosen to fill one of the vacancies, took his place as a member of the Order. Finally, he accompanied Philip on 11 December 1440, when that prince made his first entry into Bruges since his narrow escape there in May 1437. The two dukes rode together through streets decorated with coloured cloth, past pageants, tableaux, and the usual

[1] Page 105. For what follows, see Champion, *Charles d'Orléans*, 272 ff. For Charles's reception in 1440, see O. van Dixmude, *Merkwaerdige gebeurtenissen*, 171–4 and Monstrelet, *Chronique*, v. 433–44. The marriage treaty is printed by Plancher, iv. no. 134.

[2] See the genealogical table on p. 291 below.

ceremonial contrivances, such as the statue of a boy, pissing hippocras, which had been set up in front of the church of St. Donatian.

From the end of 1440 until his death in 1465 Duke Charles of Orleans was Philip's principal ally in France. He visited Philip at Hesdin in 1441 at Philip's expense; he sat on Philip's right at the annual feast of the Golden Fleece at Ghent in 1445; and he received an important financial contribution from Philip, as well as a contingent of Burgundian troops, to further his attempt to take possession of Asti, and possibly also the duchy of Milan, in 1447–8.

Philip the Good, then, had certainly made efforts to find allies in France, in order to counter Charles VII's systematic hostility to him. But he failed utterly to make effective use of these French connections, in spite of the opportunities offered by three princely plots or revolts against Charles, in 1437, 1440 and 1442.[1] In the first, which folded up almost before the king had time to field an army, Philip took no part at all. In the second, he intervened in the rather futile rôle of arbitrator; futile, because Charles VII's vigorous military action soon put the dauphin and his fellow conspirators to flight. In the third, which culminated in an assembly of French princes at Nevers early in 1442, Philip was an active participant, supported in particular by the newly elected French members of the Order of the Golden Fleece, the dukes of Orleans, Brittany and Alençon. But the dissident princes were skilfully outmanoeuvred by Charles VII, who contrived to disperse them without conceding their demands and without any military confrontation.

In spite of the efforts of Duchess Isabel, notably at Gravelines in 1439 and Châlons in 1445, and of other Burgundian diplomats, Philip the Good's relations with France, in the fifteen years after Arras, were fundamentally unsatisfactory. Charles VII enjoyed the initiative all along, and was constantly forcing Philip onto the defensive. He had no intention of implementing the treaty on which Philip had pinned his hopes of a settlement. In all this, Philip emerges as a poor statesman. The limited action he did take, in seeking allies among the French princes, was misguided, for he allied himself to the wrong princes. Neither Charles of Orleans nor Charles of Bourbon enjoyed any real influence with Charles VII; and Philip had turned René of Anjou, the one prince who did play a leading rôle in the French government in these years, into a bitter enemy. Moreover, he never seized the opportunity presented by the discontent of the princes in

[1] Du Fresne de Beaucourt, *Charles VII*, iii. 46–8, 115–42 and 194–231. See, too, Leguai, *Ducs de Bourbon*, 155–77.

1437–42 to exact concessions from the French king, or even to try to smash the power of the French crown once and for all. Perhaps a more determined and farsighted ruler, a man of the calibre of Philip's father or grandfather, would have entered into a firm alliance with England in these years, and seen to it that Burgundy shook herself free from the irksome shackles of French sovereignty. But Philip, throughout his long reign, was apparently incapable of appreciating the hostility, even hatred, which the French king and many of his councillors and advisers, entertained towards him. He failed to understand that there was no place at all for Valois Burgundy, as it was now constituted, in the eyes of the French government. For Charles VII, as later for Louis XI, it was almost a political axiom that somehow, sooner or later, Burgundy must be destroyed or dismembered.

The abandonment of the English alliance and the treaty of Arras with France in 1435 was a diplomatic blunder for Burgundy. The men who perpetrated it, Duke Philip the Good's trusted advisers, were, as we have seen, bribed by Charles VII. Two of them at least, the two most influential councillors and friends of Philip, remained indebted to the French king, if not in his pay or pocket, in the years that followed. These two were the Burgundian chancellor, Nicolas Rolin, and Anthoine, lord of Croy. On 21 December 1435 each received very substantial territorial concessions from the king of France.[1] Other favours followed, and Anthoine, lord of Croy, was heavily bribed by the king during the conference of Laon in 1441. The course of Franco-Burgundian relations, as outlined in this chapter, in the fifteen years after the treaty of Arras, can only be properly understood in the light of the continued treason, or divided loyalty, of these men.

[1] D'Arbaumont, *RNHB* (n.s.) i (1865), 10–14; du Fresne de Beaucourt, *Charles VII*, iii. 196 nn. 3 and 5, pp. 196–7; and *Les Croÿ, conseillers des ducs de Bourgogne*, 73–86.

CHAPTER FIVE

The Duke and his Court

In every way, the personality of the duke dominated the life of the court. What was Philip the Good actually like? Fortunately we possess a pen-portrait by George Chastellain, official court chronicler, the accuracy of which is confirmed by other contemporary accounts, as well as by paintings and manuscript illuminations. The description of Philip's person and habits which follows occurs in a work entitled 'Declaration of all the noble deeds and glorious adventures of Duke Philip of Burgundy'.[1]

> In stature he was a fairly tall man . . . , and his legs and arms were thin, though not excessively so. He had a handsome figure, upright, strong in the arm and back, and well-knit. His neck was well-proportioned to the body; he was lean of hand and foot, and bony rather than fleshy, with full-blooded veins that stood out. He had the rather long face of his father and grandfather, brown and weather-beaten. The nose was long but not aquiline, his forehead was high and large, but he was not bald. His hair was between blond and black. . . . He had large bushy eyebrows which stood out like horns when he was angry. His mouth was just the right size, with large well-coloured lips. His eyes varied considerably, sometimes looking fierce, at other times amiable. His face reflected his inner feelings. . . . Such looks, and such a figure, seemed more befitting an emperor or a king, than an ordinary man . . . , and he deserved a crown on the strength of his physical appearance alone. . . .
> He walked solemnly, carrying himself well and with nobility. He sat but little, stood for long periods, dressed smartly but in rich array, and was always changing his clothes. . . . He was skilful on horseback, liked

---

[1] Chastellain, Œuvres, vii. 213–36; the passage translated here is from pp. 219–21. The best recent discussion of Philip's personality is by Huizinga, Verzamelde werken, ii. 216–37. For the ducal court in general, see André, PTSEC (1886), 1–5; Huizinga, The waning of the middle ages; Cartellieri, The court of Burgundy; and Hexter, JMH xxii (1950), 11–13.

the bow and shot very well, and was excellent at tennis. Outside, his chief pastime was hunting, and he spared no expense over it. He lingered over his meals. Though the best-served man alive, he was a modest eater.

Guillaume Fillastre, bishop, and chancellor of the Golden Fleece, bears this out, though he concentrates on the duke's moral, rather than physical, attributes. He takes pains to defend Philip against the charge of idleness, claiming to have known him often turn in at two a.m. and yet be up at six.[1] But the good bishop is referring to Philip's declining years. Earlier, in 1435, when he was not yet forty, we learn from the local ecclesiastic who wrote a journal of the Congress of Arras, that Philip was in the habit of sleeping after his midday meal, and that, on at least one occasion, some morning visitors to him were turned away because he was still in bed. His habits as an old man were commented on in 1461 by the Parisian chronicler, Jehan Maupoint.

My lord Philip, duke of Burgundy, stayed at Paris during the whole of September, leaving his hôtel d'Artois, near the Halles, on the last day of the month. Every day people flocked to see him there, in the great hall hung with fine tapestry worked in gold thread, which depicted the story of Gideon. It is noteworthy that the duke heard mass every day between two and three o'clock in the afternoon. This was invariably his habit, for he stayed up at night almost till dawn, turning night into day to watch dances, entertainments and other amusements all night long. He maintained this way of life till his death, which amazed some good people, not without cause, though it was said that he had a dispensation to do this.

As a matter of fact, he did have a papal dispensation to hear mass in the afternoon,[2] but otherwise his religious practices seem to have been conventional in the extreme. His alms-giving was as liberal as it ought to have been and his pilgrimages were as frequent and as pious as everyone else's. For example, he visited Notre-Dame of Boulogne on some dozen occasions. Like every prince, he possessed a portable chapel. In 1457 he had a wooden one made at Lille, which was designed 'to be transported and brought after him by cart when

[1] Fillastre, *Toison d'Or*, f. 131b. For what follows, see de la Taverne, *Journal de la Paix d'Arras*, 29 and 30 and Maupoint, *Journal parisien*, 47–8.
[2] As did Louis XI, see Dubrulle, *Bullaire de Reims*, 273 and Chastellain, *Œuvres*, vii. 225. For the rest of this paragraph, see Benoit, *BSEPC* xxxvii (1937), 119–23; ADN B2026, f. 106; Fillastre, *Toison d'Or*, f. 131b; and, for the extract, Dupont, *Histoire de Cambrai*, ii. xvi–xxiv.

he took the field in arms against his enemies'. Guillaume Fillastre naturally emphasizes Philip's religious devotion, excusing his late appearance at mass on the grounds that he was often so busy that his time was not his own. He too notes Philip's moderation at table: 'he frequently left partridges on one side for a Mainz ham or a piece of salt beef'. And, like Chastellain, he mentions Philip's pleasure in archery, adding that he was fond of reading too.

Another ecclesiastic who came into close contact with Philip was the abbot of St. Aubert's, at Cambrai, who played host to the duke when he lodged there. He gives us a detailed account of Philip's visit in January 1449. On this occasion the abbot celebrated mass for the duke before dinner and, after it, Philip was invited to see and revere the local relics: he was even given a tooth of St. Géry to kiss. That evening, abbot and duke supped together. The abbot writes as follows, confirming in part Guillaume Fillastre's comments on Philip's eating habits.

He boasted that either he would get drunk, or I would. It had been agreed that we should provide three meat courses, to honour him and his nobles, and that he would provide one course, of whatever he chose. Our three courses were supplied from our own resources, under the supervision of his steward and cooks. They consisted of veal, mutton, six rabbits, nine capons, six partridges, six pheasants and two peacocks for the first two courses, and then cakes, pears cooked in wine with sugar and hippocras, . . . and several other things which I cannot remember. And I gave him a large piece of prime salted beef, of which he willingly ate a good deal, and enjoyed very much, and the others likewise. He was very happy and jovial, and drank to me three times, emptying his glass on the first two occasions, and I toasted him similarly. We drank the health of the lords of Étampes, Beaujeu, Cleves and Longueval; of Anthony, bastard of Burgundy; of the lord of Crèvecoeur, Baudoin de Noyelles, governor of Péronne, Charles de Rochefort and several others who were at supper in the Lady room. We continued till midnight. There were twelve of us at this supper, and my lord the duke was in excellent form and believed that I really was tipsy, for I made him laugh enough, and the others too.

The next day Philip heard mass and kissed the relics again; and dined by himself in the refectory, where the abbot was summoned afterwards to say grace. When the duke was about to take his leave, there was a delay, while some of his people got ready. However, he was entertained by a song, sung by two choir-boys, with one of the duke's gentlemen taking the tenor part. The abbot was obviously

impressed by Philip's civilities on leaving: the duke shook him by
the hand and then, after mounting his horse, turned back and took
his leave again, doffing his hat in so doing. He was followed by the
count of Étampes, who shook hands with the abbot after he had
mounted his horse, while carrying a sparrowhawk on the other hand.
The next occasion when Philip visited Cambrai was on 25 August
1457. This time mass was not celebrated till the early afternoon, but
still before dinner. Philip ate little and left the next day at three
o'clock in the afternoon, without having dined. He did find time to
inspect a painting of Our Lady, said to have been executed by the
hand of St. Luke, and he remembered his earlier visit, laughingly
apologizing to the abbot for the fact that he had no time on this
occasion to drink with him.

The Flemish lawyer, Philippe Wielant, who was born at Ghent in
1439 and had some firsthand personal knowledge of Philip, tells us
that he was not a great talker but, when he did say something, it was
to the point. He was invariably polite to women and maintained that,
by treating women well, one would necessarily be popular with their
menfolk since, Philip claimed, there was only one family in forty
which was not ruled by the lady of the house. He liked to read
romances and humorous farces and, in his youth, he enjoyed dancing,
feasting, jousting, falconry, tennis and archery. Later on, towards the
end of his life, he developed other interests. He had a special room,
which he took about with him, full of gadgets, in which he amused
himself threading needles, making clogs, soldering broken knives,
repairing broken glasses and so on. His son Charles laughed at this,
and destroyed the whole outfit after Philip's death.[1]

The catalogue of contemporaries who knew Philip the Good and
have left us their impressions of his personal habits and personality,
is soon exhausted. But what of the duke's own private correspondence? Scarcely a trace of this remains, yet Philip undoubtedly wrote a
large number of personal letters, a good many of them in his own
hand. No copies of these were made, to be preserved among the well-
kept and carefully inventoried files of the ducal government, and few
of their recipients seem to have treasured them. In 1925 the Belgian
scholar Armand Grunzweig printed the texts of four such autograph
letters, written by Philip to his nephew Duke John I of Cleves in the

[1] For this paragraph, see Wielant, *Antiquités de Flandre*, 56–7 and, for what
follows, Grunzweig, *RBPH* iv (1925), 431–7, where the letters translated
here are printed. I am indebted to my friend Dr. M. H. Tweedy for the
English rendering.

years 1451–2. These he had unearthed in the archives of North
Rhine-Westphalia at Düsseldorf. They were the only four private
letters of Philip the Good known to exist, and almost the only known
examples of his handwriting. They were rendered completely
illegible in 1945, after the boat they were in was sunk by bombs in
the Mittelandkanal. Two of these letters, written in a familiar,
bantering style, are noteworthy for the light they throw on Philip's
personality. We glimpse him here in friendly, flippant mood, and we
can sense his humour.

My lord Sharp-wits,
   I commend myself to your very bowels and am ready to pout like a
pigeon with the rest of them and otherwise to do nothing, and for good
reason. Since I wrote to you I have no further news. I beg you, tell me
about the fair lady, all that can be put into writing, and about your
doings, if such is your pleasure, fine sir. The Ghenters still have as
much love for me as for the Devil, and are as amiable as they are wont
to be. Farewell, turd, you shall have no more, for I am going to see if I
can puff myself up after your fashion, you know how, or whether I've
lost the knack! Heigh-ho!

Well now, my lord, I have already written you with news from here-
abouts, and of Luxembourg. I am back in Brussels, and God knows how
I am acquitting myself domestically, in as spirited a fashion as I am
accustomed and is appropriate to the case. I do nothing save go hunting,
but the wild boars are so thin they run like the wind. But we shall have
news of you in your own good time, and we shall expect you when we
see you. Farewell, turd, no more for the present; I am supping in the
town. Your uncle, Philip, whom I'll not call greybeard.

During most of his long reign, Philip was blessed with excellent
health. Apart from three quite serious, but brief, illnesses in the
1420s,[1] and an occasional bout of fever in the succeeding decades, he
seems to have kept out of the clutches of his doctors until Saturday
17 June 1458 at Brussels, when he was struck down with fever after
playing tennis. He lost consciousness for thirty-six hours, but recovered soon after. The duke suffered a more serious and prolonged

---

[1] *Extraits analytiques de Tournai, 1422–1430*, 14–15; AGR CC21802, f. 5b;
and Morosini, *Chronique*, iii. 56. For the rest of this paragraph, see ADN
B2017, fos. 279 and 284b and Pius II, *Orationes*, iii. 71; Chastellain, *Œuvres*,
iii. 441–4; *Paston Letters*, ii. 93; Kervyn, *Flandre*, v. 57 n. 1; ADN B2045,
fos. 182, 183b, 184 etc. and de Laborde, *Ducs de Bourgogne*, i. 477–9;
Dépêches des ambassadeurs milanais, i. 191–4; and de la Marche, *Mémoires*,
ii. 421–2.

illness in the early months of 1462, again at Brussels. Early in the year, some French sailors arrested at Sheringham reported that 'the duke of Burgoyn is poysened and not like to recovere'. On 29 January, writing to Louis XI, he explained that he was too ill to sign the letter. Charles, Philip's son and heir, had been summoned to his father's sick-bed on 20 January. Doctors came scurrying from all directions: from Le Quesnoy, from Malines, from Louvain, an Armenian and an Italian from Bruges, and even from Savoy. But it was Luca Alessandro, official doctor to the duke of Milan, who happened to be in Brussels with some Milanese ambassadors to Philip, who cured the duke and saved his life, by the simple means, according to one of the ambassadors, of reversing the treatment of his own doctors, which consisted in the main of an intensive programme of blood-letting! Olivier de la Marche says that Philip's doctors compelled him to have his hair shaved off and that the duke, not wishing to be alone in this, insisted that all his courtiers do likewise. Five hundred gentlemen are said to have complied, and others were in danger for a time of having their hair forcibly removed by zealous victims of the ducal edict.

Bishop Guillaume Fillastre's flattering portrait of Philip the Good is somewhat marred by his admission that the duke suffered from what the bishop called 'the weakness of the flesh'. But the bishop, who was himself a bastard, son of an abbot and a nun, makes two points in Philip's mitigation. First, that chastity, which is more of an angelic than a human quality, is in any case given only to a few; and second, that the duke never actually committed rape or violence.[1] It is Olivier de la Marche who tells us that Philip had 'a very fine company of bastards of both sexes—*de bastards et de bastardes une moult belle compaignie*'. But his wives were notably unsuccessful in bearing him children. The first two, both French princesses, bore him none. Michelle of France died in 1422 when Philip was only twenty-six. Bonne of Artois, whom Philip married in 1424, lived barely a year thereafter. His third wife, Isabel of Portugal, bore him three sons in 1431–3, but only the third, Charles, survived.

Though Philip the Good's sex life was vigorous and varied, he does not seem to have indulged in the perversions of a Charles VII, whose mistress, Antoinette de Maignelais, kept herself in the royal favour, not only by the exercise of her own charms, but also by procuring teenage girls for the king from among the French nobility.[2] Unlike

[1] Fillastre, *Toison d'Or*, f. 131b; see Du Teil, *Guillaume Fillastre*, 3. For the next sentence, see de la Marche, *Mémoires*, ii. 55.
[2] Du Fresne de Beaucourt, *Charles VII*, vi. 9 and Duclercq, *Mémoires*, 90–1.

many other rulers, Philip altogether excluded his mistresses from state affairs, though he made use of his bastards, in the service of politics and war, more successfully than most. His mistresses by no means followed the normal pattern, of a succession of favourites. Instead, he maintained a number at once, in different places. This was merely a matter of convenience and economy; it is reflected in the surnames given to three of the bastards by a chronicler: Baudouin of Lille, Jehan of Bruges, and Philippe of Brussels.[1] Other mistresses lived at Arras and Louvain. One cannot pretend that the subject of Philip's mistresses and their progeny has yet been illuminated by historical truth. Instead, their numbers have been exaggerated by the devious enthusiasm of genealogists, behind whose efforts may be discerned the aristocratic aspirations of a number of people alive today, who are proud to bear the surname Bourgogne. A recent genealogical work lists twenty-six bastards of Philip, and thirty-three mistresses;[2] one suspects that the severe pruning of historical scholarship might reduce the numbers to perhaps fifteen and twenty respectively. A near contemporary list, made by Philippe Wielant, gives eleven bastards in all, six boys and five girls. The portraits of two mistresses and several bastards appear in the famous sixteenth-century collection of pen and ink drawings in the Public Library at Arras.

One must not imagine that there was anything very exceptional in Philip's troop of bastards. On a rough calculation, about five per cent of the court personnel in his reign were illegitimate. His officials, who naturally found it easy to prevail on their duke to legitimize their bastards, vied with him in the numbers they produced. In 1420 the duke legitimized Jehanne, illegitimate daughter of his Flemish archivist and councillor Thierry Gherbode, and in 1424, after Thierry's death, the duke legitimized no less than five more of his bastard children.[3] When Philip took over the duchy of Brabant in 1430 he inherited with it five 'bastards of Brabant', illegitimate children of his predecessors. At court, besides the duke's own

[1] De But, *Chronique*, 238. For the next sentence, see below, p. 134.
[2] Bergé, *IG* lx (1955), 352-9. See too, de Reiffenberg, *BARB* xiii (1) (1846), 172-87 and xiv (1) (1847), 585-97 and, for what follows, Wielant, *Antiquités de Flandre*, 79-81, and Quarré-Reybourbon, *BCHDN* xxiii (1900).
[3] ADN B1602, f. 101 and B1603, f. 51b. See, too, B1602, fos. 152a-b, 116b, 122b-123 and B1604, fos. 129b, 130. For the next sentence, see AGR CC2409, f. 37 and Nelis, *RBPH* i (1922), 337-40. For Guyot and Philipotte see, for example, ADN B1604, f. 4 and de Laborde, *Ducs de Bourgogne*, i. 234, 286, 311, etc.; and, for Cornille's and Anthony's bastards, ADN B1607, fos. 176-7 and AGR CC25191, fos. 24-5.

bastards, there were other 'bastards of Burgundy', illegitimate children of John the Fearless; and these, among them Guyot and Philipotte de Bourgogne, have not always been distinguished from Philip's own children. Moreover, there were bastards of bastards too, for Philip's two oldest bastards, Cornille and Anthony, soon had illegitimate offspring of their own, and these were also 'bastards of Burgundy'. Besides these bastards of Burgundy and of Brabant, there were bastards of Luxembourg and of Bavaria, and probably others.

The Bohemian traveller Leo of Rozmital was surprised to find that bastards were not held in disrepute at the Burgundian court, but enjoyed the same food and drink as the duke's legitimate son.[1] As a matter of fact, their food and clothing was meticulously accounted for. In 1439 they were fitted out in a livery of grey; and in the household account of 1462–3, at the end of a list of courtiers receiving bread and meat come repeated mentions of 'the two little bastards of Burgundy'. But the duke's accounting officers were usually discreet in the extreme, and Philip's mistresses are seldom identified, or even mentioned as such. In one place the 'mother of Cornille, bastard of Burgundy', is mentioned but not named; elsewhere, a gift of cloth to the mothers of Philip's bastards, is recorded, again without naming them. Besides gifts of jewellery and the like, most of Philip's mistresses received favours of some kind from the duke. Nicole la Chastelaine, David's mother, was given money towards the repair of her Arras house and was provided with a husband by the duke. Similarly, Isabel de la Vigne received money towards the purchase of a house at Louvain; she also enjoyed a small pension, which the accounting officials were loth to pay, declaring that they had no idea why the duke had given this woman a pension. Jehannette de Presles, mother of Anthony, was married off by Philip in 1432 to a minor court official.

After their early education at court Philip the Good's bastards were usually provided with careers if they were male, and husbands if female. Yolande was married in 1456 to Jehan d'Ailly, lord of Picquigny in Picardy; Marie was married in 1447 to Pierre de Bauffremont, lord of Charny in Burgundy; Anne was married first to a Dutch nobleman, Adrian van Borselen, and then to Adolf of Cleves,

---

[1] Rozmital, *Travels*, 39. For what follows, see ADN B1966, fos. 110b and 118; ADN B2048, f. 60b, etc.; ADN B1951, f. 139b; de Laborde, *Ducs de Bourgogne*, i. 262; 'F.B.' *SFW* xiv (1874), 186–95 (Nicole); Bergé, *IG* lx (1955), 353 and n. 56, and AGR CC17, f. 56 (Isabel); de Laborde, *Ducs de Bourgogne*, i. 266 and 304 (Jehannette).

THE DUKE AND HIS COURT 135

lord of Ravenstein.[1] Some of the boys were sent to university, Louvain or Paris being favoured, and thence found ecclesiastical preferment. David's studies at Louvain were cut short by his promotion to the bishopric of Thérouanne, in spite of the canonical doubts raised by his illegitimacy; and in 1456 Philip placed him forcibly on the episcopal throne of Utrecht, at the head of an army. He was followed there, in 1517–24, by another bastard son, and namesake, of Philip the Good. Other ecclesiastical bastards were Raphael, abbot of St. Bavo's, Ghent, and Jehan, a papal notary.[2] Barbe de Steenbourg, abbess of Bourbourg, was exceptional among Philip's *bâtardes*. Some male bastards pursued a career at court and in the duke's wars. Cornille, whose name figures at the head of every list of ducal bastards till his death, and whose mother, Catherine Scaers, is described in a ducal document as 'our well-loved demoiselle', received a pension of 3,000 francs per annum after 1446, as well as his salary as governor of Luxembourg, a post he held from 1444 until he was killed in battle in 1452 during the Ghent war. Philip founded a perpetual mass for his soul, and ordered holy water to be sprinkled daily on his tomb at St. Gudule's in Brussels. Anthony, the so-called 'Grand Bastard of Burgundy', was being paid £3,840 per annum in 1462. He rose to prominence at court both as a patron of the arts and collector of illuminated manuscripts, and as a jouster. A Knight of the Golden Fleece in 1456, he was Philip's chosen crusading leader in 1464, though his expedition got no further than the south of France. He lived to serve Charles the Bold loyally, to fight for him at Nancy in 1477, and to see the first few years of the sixteenth century.

What were the material surroundings of Philip the Good's court? A study of the itineraries[3] shows that the court gradually became sedentary towards the end of the reign, when there was a pronounced tendency for Brussels to take pride of place. The court's first prolonged stay in one spot occurred in 1439, when Philip and Isabel were at St. Omer for the last seven months of the year. Then, in 1442–3,

---

[1] *IADNB* viii. 31, n. 1, 21, n. 4 and 36, n. 2. For what follows, see AGR CC2411, f. 95, *IADNB* iv. 173 and Zilverberg, *David van Bourgondië*.
[2] Nelis, *RBPH* i (1922), 341–2. For the next sentence, see Toussaert, *Sentiment religieux en Flandre*, 381. For what follows, see below, p. 321, ADN B1606, f. 168b and ADN B1991, f. 48 and *Table chronologique des chartes de Luxembourg* xxx (1875), 138 (Cornille); ADN B2045, f. 103b, Doutrepont, *Littérature*, 43–4 and Boinet, *BEC* lxvii (1906), 255–69 (Anthony).
[3] Vander Linden, *Itinéraires*, can usefully be supplemented, for the years 1427, 1428, 1441, 1462 and 1466, by the older but fuller itinerary in Gachard's *Collection des voyages des souverains des Pays-Bas*, i. 71–100.

they remained at Dijon for over a year. In the 1440s, Bruges was as popular as Brussels, and Philip was at Bruges for over three months in 1447 and again in 1449. His first long stay at Brussels was in 1450, and the court was there a good deal in 1451 and early 1452. But, throughout the period of the Ghent war Philip was based at Lille. In the late 'fifties the court alternated for the most part between Bruges and Brussels, after a stay at The Hague in 1455–6 while Philip‚was engrossed in the affairs of Utrecht. The pre-eminence of Brussels was finally established in 1459, for the court remained there throughout that year, and indeed from then till Philip's death in 1467 Brussels was his normal place of residence, though Hesdin, Lille and Bruges were all visited for at least one spell of two or three months.

The five principal ducal residences in Philip the Good's reign were at Brussels, Bruges, Lille, Dijon and Hesdin in Artois. The magnificent hôtel d'Artois in Paris, where the first two Valois dukes of Burgundy had spent a great part of their time, was given over to a caretaker and cobwebs, except for brief visits from Philip near the beginning and end of his reign. Although the duke was not an enthusiastic builder, he took care to ensure that his residences were commodious, and a certain amount of building was carried out during his reign on all of them. At Lille Philip spent money early in the reign renovating the ancient hôtel de la Salle; later, in 1452–63, he built an entirely new palace at what is now the Place Rihour.[1] At Dijon, between 1450 and 1455, the tower de la Terrasse, from which on a clear day Mont Blanc can just be made out over 100 miles away, the Salle des Gardes, and other important additions, were made to the ducal palace. At Bruges, the Cour des Princes, or Prinsenhof, which had been improved in 1429 with temporary structures, ready for Philip and Isabel's wedding festivities early in 1430, was rebuilt and enlarged in the years after 1446 and, at the same time, Philip acquired and restored another palace in Bruges, the hôtel Vert, which seems to have been conceived as a private residence for him to withdraw to from the busy life of the court. At Brussels, where, according to one learned writer, Philip spent a total 3,819 days, the ancient ducal palace of the Coudenberg was more or less rebuilt in the 1430s,

[1] Leman, *LFCL* xiii (1922–3), 293–306; and *Comptes généraux*, i. 280–1. For what follows, see Gras, *Palais des Ducs*, 10 (Dijon); Zuylen van Nyevelt, *Épisodes*, 263–86 (Bruges); and Saintenoy, *Les arts et les artistes à la cour de Bruxelles*, 12–122, and Bonenfant and others, *Bruxelles au xv*[me] *siècle*, 157–9 and 239–43.

and further augmented after 1450 with a great hall which Philip persuaded or compelled the townspeople to pay for.

These ducal building works cannot compare with the splendid efforts of civic authorities during Philip the Good's reign when, for example, the town halls of Brussels, Louvain and Middelburg were built.[1] At Dijon, the communal archives reveal no grandiose schemes of public building at this time, but they do illumine the varied initiatives taken by the municipality of the town which was the original capital of Philip's lands. Six new pieces of artillery were added to the twenty-six cannon already owned by the town; public conveniences were installed; new shooting butts were set up; a silver trumpet was bought to replace the horn hitherto used at proclamations, which had become a source of merriment for strangers; the rue des Forges was repaved; free medical attention was arranged for the poor; six dustbin-men, each with a horse and cart, were hired to collect refuse on Saturdays; and a house was bought for the civic brothel and baths. The archives tell us much else about fifteenth-century Dijon. We learn that police measures were taken against leprous strangers, blasphemers, and persons who made 'leurs grosses aisances' in the streets; and that some carriers were fined for playing tennis during a procession for ducal victory in the war with Ghent. Philip's sculptor, Juan de la Huerta, was punished in an ususual way for insulting the mayor. He was condemned to carve a statue of the Virgin Mary, together with the arms of the town supported by two monkeys, the whole to be set up over the main doorway of the town hall. It is curious to find that, apparently as a precaution against French spies, the Dijon hoteliers were required to report names of strangers to the authorities.

The ducal castle at Hesdin in Artois, though it was only visited by Philip from time to time, was maintained by him with care, and several thousand pounds were being spent annually on rebuilding there, in the 1440s and 1450s.[2] The local artist and ducal *valet de chambre*, Hue de Boulogne, looked after the duke's aviary there and its birds until, in 1445–6, he was too old to continue at work. In 1433 £1,000 was spent on refurbishing the famous mechanical contrivances,

---

[1] Bonenfant, *Philippe le Bon*, 27. For what follows, see *IACD* i. 30–40.
[2] See, for example, ADN B1972, f. 54b, 1978, f. 42, 2004, f. 82a–b, 2045, f. 100, and 2048, f. 102; and de Laborde, *Ducs de Bourgogne*, ii. 220. For what follows, see *IADNB* iv. 155 and 170, and Vaughan, *Philip the Bold*, 205. The extract is from *IADNB* iv. 123–4 = de Laborde, *Ducs de Bourgogne*, i. 268–71.

or practical jokes, which had originally been installed in the thirteenth
century, and in adding to their number. The clerk who wrote the
entry in the account recording this payment launches out with relish
into a detailed enumeration of these curiosities of medieval crafts-
manship and primitive humour.

Paid to Colard le Voleur, *valet de chambre* and painter of my lord the
duke, the sum of £1,000 . . . for the following work which he has carried
out at Hesdin castle.

For painting the gallery of the castle in exactly the same style as
before, ornately and with the best available materials. For making or
refurbishing the three figures which can be made to squirt water at
people and wet them, a contrivance at the entrance of the said gallery
for wetting the ladies as they walk over it, and a distorting mirror; and
for constructing a device over the entrance of the gallery which, when a
ring is pulled, showers soot or flour in the face of anyone below. Also, in
the same gallery, a fountain from which water spurts and is pumped
back again, and another contrivance, at the exit from the gallery, which
buffets anyone who passes through well and truly on the head and
shoulders.

[For the restoration of] the room before [you reach] the hermit, where
water can be made to spray down just like rain, also thunder, lightning
and snow, as if from the sky itself; and, next to this room, a wooden
hermit which can be made to speak to anyone who enters. Also, for
paving the half of this room which was not previously paved, including
the place where people go to avoid the rain, whence they are precipitated
into a sack full of feathers below.

To carry out these works, my lord duke has provided him with wood
and stone. . . . He has also had to restore most of the ceiling of the above-
mentioned room, and to reinforce the part of it which produced the rain,
which had become too weak. . . . He also made a bridge in this room,
constructed in such a way that it was possible to cause anyone walking
over it to fall into the water below. There are several devices in this
room which, when set off, spray large quantities of water onto the people
in it, as well as six figures, more than there had been before, which soak
people in different ways. In the entrance, there are eight conduits for
wetting women from below and three conduits which, when people stop
in front of them, cover them all over with flour. When someone tries to
open a certain window, a figure appears, sprays the person with water,
and shuts the window. A book of ballads lies on a desk but, when you
try to read it, you are squirted with soot, and, if you look inside it, you
can be sprayed with water. Then there is a mirror which people are
invited to look at, to see themselves all white with flour; but, when they
do so, they are covered with more flour. A wooden figure, which appears
above a bench in the middle of the gallery announces, at the sound of

trumpet, on behalf of the duke, that everyone must leave the gallery. Those who do so are beaten by large figures holding sticks . . . and those who don't want to leave get so wet that they don't know what to do to avoid the water. In one window a box is suspended, and above the box is a figure which makes faces at people and replies to their questions, and one can both hear and see the voice in this box.

He has decorated the room in front of the hermit, where it can be made to rain, in good quality oil colours of gold, azure, and so on . . . , and he has done the whole ceiling and panelling of this room in azure sewn with large stars picked out in gold. . . . After all this was completed, my lord [the duke] ordered him to make conduits and suitable contrivances low down and all along the wall of the gallery, to squirt water in so many places that nobody in the gallery could possibly save themselves from getting wet, and other conduits and devices everywhere under the pavement to wet the ladies from underneath.

Knowledge of the day-to-day working, and of the organization and administration, of Philip the Good's court, is somewhat limited by lack of evidence. Fortunately, nearly a quarter of the *escroes* or daily accounts, that is nearly 4,000 of a possible 18,000, have survived in the departmental archives at Lille. Others were used and destroyed by the French artillery in the nineteenth century, though the military authorities at Dunkirk were enlightened or enterprising enough to sell a bundle of them to a local historian.[1] But the vast majority of the monthly and annual accounts of Philip the Good's court have disappeared. On the other hand, we still possess a series of court *ordonnances* of Philip the Good, and these yield valuable information which supplements that found in the *escroes*. For example, the *escroes* record the size of the court on any particular day, but the *ordonnances* reveal the total number of courtiers and officials who were, so to speak, on the establishment of the court and available for service in it. Most of these people served annually, for either three or six months at a time. For example, there were four *maîtres d'hôtel* or stewards, one for each quarter; and two barbers, each serving for half the year. During the first half of his reign Philip's court grew in size, partly because of the expansion of the Burgundian state. In 1433 additional chamberlains from Brabant and Limbourg appear, and the document explains that this was so that the duke could have people from all his

[1] Derode, *ACFF* (1862–4), 283–302 and 383–400. See, *IADNB* viii. 5–46 and David, *AB* xxxvii (1965), 256. On *escroes*, see too Vaughan, *Philip the Bold*, 145. For what follows, I have leaned heavily on Schwarzkopf, *Studien zur Hoforganisation der Herzöge von Burgund*, partly summarized in *PCEEBM* v (1963), 91–104.

lands in his service. It is interesting to compare the numbers of personnel in the more important court departments, according to the first three *ordonnances* of the reign. A multitude of lesser people, including innumerable valets, the tailor, the ducal artists, the confessor, wardrobe aides, ushers, keepers of the duke's tapestry and jewels, the surgeon, physicians and so on, are here omitted.[1]

	1426	*1433*	*1438*
First chamberlain and knight-councillor-chamberlains	9	21	21
Other chamberlains	24	28	28
Stewards	5	5	5
Bread-pantry personnel	18	26	27
Cup-bearers and wine-pantry personnel	22	31	31
Trencher-squires	12	16	16
Kitchen staff	41	44	41
Equerries	39	c. 38	44
Mounted messengers	12	12	12
Quartermasters	5	7	8
Heralds and Kings-of-Arms	3	7	7
Trumpets and minstrels	9	10	10
Falconers and assistants	16	20	c. 13
Archers of the bodyguard	12	24	50
Secretaries	7	7	9
Councillors	—	13	29
Total	234	309	351

When Philip married Isabel in January 1430 a separate court or household was set up for her. It was just like the duke's, but on a smaller scale. Instead of chamberlains, she was allotted a *chevalier d'honneur* with six attendants. She had two *maîtres d'hôtel* serving alternately for six-month spells of duty; a single secretary, but with three horses and two valets; and a physician, a confessor and her own separate accounting office. No doubt this establishment too grew with the years.

The senior court official, who was responsible for the administration of the whole complex institution, was the first chamberlain of the duke. His office must be carefully distinguished from that of his

---

[1] For the *ordonnances* see *IADNB* vii. xc–xciii (summarized from ADN B1603, fos. 91–7, 1426); ADN B1605, fos. 181–90 (1433); and Vandeputte, *ASEB* xxviii (1876–7), 6–24 (printed from ADN B1605, fos. 212–25b, 1438). See too Lameere, *Grand conseil*, 39–49 and, for the duchess's court, *Mémoires*, ii. 249–57.

hereditary counterpart in the duchy of Burgundy. It was the rights of this 'first chamberlain of the duchy of Burgundy' which were in dispute in 1420, when Jehan de la Trémoille, lord of Jonvelle, solemnly claimed, before the assembled members of the Dijon council and *chambre des comptes*, that Philip the Bold had granted the following perquisites to his grandfather in 1381.[1]

1. He ought to be maintained continually in the ducal court with a suitable retinue.
2. If a knight, he is and ought to be *grand maître d'hôtel*.
3. Whenever a squire at court is dubbed a knight, his squire's robes should belong to him.
4. Whenever a baron, prince or banneret does homage to the duke for a duchy fief, he should receive a gold or silver mark.
5. He should be paid half a mark for every ducal letter sealed with a silk cord.
6. He should be given the covers of all the dishes served to the duke at banquets and the furnishings of his bridal suite whenever he marries.

The councillors not only rejected the majority of these claims, but they protested that the ducal letters of 1381, which were signed by the ducal secretary Jaques du Val, had probably been forged by him, for he was reputed to have annoyed Philip the Bold on several occasions by writing and signing ducal letters without his knowledge.

This hereditary chamberlain's office in the duchy of Burgundy was a mere relic of the past. By contrast, the first chamberlain of the duke was an influential person carrying out important duties. Throughout most of Philip the Good's reign the office was held by Anthoine de Croy. His duties included sleeping near the duke, carrying the ducal banner in battle, and supervising the purchase of cloth for the duke's person.[2] At court, he alone was permitted the luxury of taking his meals privately in his own lodgings or apartment. He was to be served twice a day, according to the *ordonnance* of 1438, with a plate of meat, two quarts of wine, and four small white and six small brown loaves.

A picture of the Burgundian court on the move was painted unwittingly by the clerk who kept the accounts of the receipt-general of all finances.[3] It had been in Burgundy throughout the winter, but in

[1] *Mémoires*, ii. 33–5, printed from ACO B15, fos. 145b–146. On the first chamberlain, see Huydts, *Mélanges Henri Pirenne*, 263–70, which should be read in conjunction with Bonenfant, *Meutre de Montereau*, 46, n. 1.
[2] De Lannoy, *Œuvres*, 51 and ADN B1605, f. 189.
[3] ADN B1954, fos. 198–202.

April 1435 it was transported from Dijon to Arras and Lille. The move took almost a month, and the hire of carts alone cost nearly 5,000 francs. No less than seventy-two carts were used, most of them drawn by five or six horses. The convoy was accompanied by two carpenters to make good breakages. Five carts were needed for the duke's jewels, four for his tapestry, one for spices, one for the chapel furnishings, one for the trumpets' and minstrels' gear and two for artillery. The kitchen required five, the bread-pantry and wine-pantry three each, and one was taken up with an enormous tent. The duchess's things occupied at least fifteen carts, including two for her tapestry, one for her spices, two for her jewels and three for her trunks. Even the one-year-old Charles, count of Charolais, required two carts for his toys and other belongings. On this occasion the whole move was administered by an equerry, specially deputed for this purpose by the duke.

The stewards, or *maîtres d'hôtel*, were responsible for the supply of food to the Burgundian court. Even in Lent, the menus were rich and varied, for there was generally somebody to be entertained. For example, on 27 March 1456 Philip invited some chaplains and canons of St. Peter's, Lille, to dine at court. Apart from wine, three pints of hippocras and a cask of beer, mustard had to be supplied, as well as one large pike and thirty smaller ones, eighty carps, sixteen eels, two breams, a salmon and other fresh fish, and twelve hundred salted herrings.[1] Outside Lent, and when more distinguished, or attractive, guests were at court, quantities of food were larger and delicacies more apparent. For instance, when Philip gave a supper for the ladies of Brussels on 11 November 1460, present also the duke of Cleves, Jaques de Bourbon, Eberhard of Württemberg, and other notables, the provisions included seventy-four dozen rolls, cress and lettuce, six joints of beef, forty-three pounds of lard, twenty-one shoulders of mutton, six-and-a-half dozen sausages, three pigs, tripe and calves' feet for making jellies, a bittern, three geese, twelve water-birds, four rabbits, twenty-two partridges, 159 chickens, sixteen pairs of pigeons, eighteen cheeses, 350 eggs, pastries, flour, cabbages, peas, parsley, onions, 100 quinces and 150 pears, cream, six pounds of butter, vinegar and oranges and lemons.

These were by no means special occasions. When the duke gave a banquet for a wedding or other event, the meal was even more elaborate, and the tables would be loaded with extravagant decorations

[1] *IADNB* viii. 30 and, for what follows, *IADNB* viii. 35–6. See too, David, *AB* xxxvii (1965), 245–53.

and even *tableaux vivants*, as well as food. The table decorations for a banquet at Lille in 1435, in honour of the duke of Bourbon, René of Anjou and Arthur, count of Richemont, were painted by Philip's artist and *valet de chambre*, Hue de Boulogne. On each of the two principal tables a hawthorn tree with flowers of gold and silver bore five banners, with the arms of France and those of the leading guests, painted in full colour. Eighteen smaller trees each carried the ducal arms. A live peacock on a dish was surrounded by ten gilt lions, each holding a banner with the arms of all Philip's lands. The ducal painter also had the task of painting fifty-six wooden plates in grey and black, adorned with the duke's favourite emblem, a flint and steel, with sparks and flames.[1]

Not that the Burgundian court was unusual in this sort of extravaganza: the chronicler-herald Jehan Lefèvre has described the wedding-festivities arranged by the duke of Savoy for his son, at Chambéry in February 1434, where Philip the Good was an honoured guest. At the supper before the wedding-day swans were brought in carrying the arms of the guests, followed by two of the duke of Savoy's heralds, who rode through the hall on horseback displaying the arms of Savoy on their costumes and on their horses' caparisons. They were followed by trumpets, and gentlemen with banners, likewise mounted, but not on real horses. After supper, twenty-six knights, squires and ladies all dressed in vermilion danced together in couples. At dinner next day a huge model ship complete with mast, sail and crow's nest with a man in it, was brought into the banqueting-hall between two rows of singing syrens. It discharged a cargo of fish for the high table. At supper, a horse got up like an elephant was led through the hall by two valets. In a wooden castle strapped on the animal's back a gentleman decked out in peacock's wings and feathers represented the god of love. From this vantage-point, he shot red and white roses among the guests with a bow. That night the dancers wore white. Other feasts followed. At one, an immense pie was brought in and opened in front of the high table, and a man dressed as an eagle, with a most realistic eagle's head and beak, emerged from its interior flapping his wings, releasing a flock of white doves which flew about and settled on the tables.

Best known, most bizarre and extravagant of all fifteenth-century court banquets was, by common accord, the Feast of the Pheasant, held by Philip the Good at Lille on 17 February 1454. Its object was

---

[1] De Laborde, *Ducs de Bourgogne*, i. 348–9. For what follows, see le Févre, *Chronique*, ii. 287–97.

F

to proclaim the crusade and encourage the duke's knights and courtiers to make their crusading vows. It was organized by a special committee of courtiers, which consulted the chancellor and other important officials. Not only did a numerous audience watch this banquet from the galleries of the hall where it was held, but a full official account of it was drawn up and distributed. No less than thirty-five artists were employed on the décor, representations and other paraphernalia for this feast, as well as a plumber, six joiners, a sculptor and a locksmith; and Colard le Voleur was specially summoned from Hesdin to help.[1] The following letter, sent to an unknown person, who evidently lived in Burgundy, by a minor figure attached to the ducal court, has not before been printed. It adds some points of detail not recorded in the official account which found its way into the chronicles of Olivier de la Marche and Mathieu d'Escouchy.

Lille, 22 February, 1454

Dearest and honoured sir . . . I recommend myself to you. Since you like to have news from here, may it please you to know that my lord the duke, my lady the duchess and my lord of Charolais are in good health . . . as I write this. Last Sunday my lord the duke gave a banquet in the hôtel de la Salle in this town. . . . The dishes were such that they had to be served with trolleys, and seemed infinite in number. There were so many side-dishes, and they were so curious, that it's difficult to describe them. There was even a chapel on the table, with a choir in it, a pasty full of flute-players, and a turret from which came the sound of an organ and other music. The figure of a girl, quite naked, stood against a pillar. Hippocras sprayed from her right breast and she was guarded by a live lion who sat near her on a round table in front of my lord the duke. The story of Jason was represented on a raised stage by actors who did not speak. My lord the duke was served at table by a two-headed horse ridden by two men sitting back to back, each holding a trumpet and sounding it as loud as he could, and then by a monster, consisting of a man riding on an elephant, with another man, whose feet were hidden, on his shoulders. Next came a white stag ridden by a young boy who sang marvellously, while the stag accompanied him with the tenor part. Next came an elephant . . . carrying a castle in which sat Holy Church, who made piteous complaint on behalf of the christians persecuted by the

---

[1] De Laborde, *Ducs de Bourgogne*, i. 422–9. The letter which follows is from BN MS. fr. 5044, fos. 30–1. See too Cartellieri, *HBKD* clxvii (1921), 65–80 and 141–58 and references given there; Doutrepont, *Littérature*, 106–17 and *NEBN* xli (1923), 1–28; and Cartellieri, *Court of Burgundy*, 135–52. See further, on the vows, below p. 297.

Turks, and begged for help. Then, two knights of the Order of the Golden Fleece brought in two damsels, together with a pheasant, which had a gold collar round its neck decorated with rubies and fine large pearls. These ladies asked my lord the duke to make his vow, which he handed in writing to Golden Fleece King-of-Arms to read out. It was understood that, if the king [of France] would go on crusade, the duke would follow him in person and with all his power. If the king did not go, but sent a royal prince instead, the duke would obey him; and if the king neither went, nor sent anyone, but other princes went, he would go with them provided his lands were at peace. If, when he was there, the Turk challenged him to single combat, my lord the duke would accept. Everyone was amazed at this, but Holy Church was overjoyed, and invited the other princes and knights to vow. Thereupon, my lord of Charolais, my lord of Cleves, my lord of St. Pol, my lord of Étampes and several others swore the oath. And it was announced that everyone who had sworn, or who wanted to swear, should hand in their vows in writing to Golden Fleece. . . .

All this I saw. I took the trouble to stay till nearly 4.0 a.m., and I believe that nothing so sublime and splendid has ever been done before. The knights wore robes of damask, half grey, half black; the squires wore satin in the same colours. . . . My lord the duke had so many diamonds, rubies and fine large pearls in his hat that there was no room for any more, and he was wearing a very fine necklace. It was said that his jewels were worth 100,000 nobles, more or less. You shall have no more for the moment.

J. DE PLEINE

Besides the provision of dinner and supper every day, and the occasional banquet for the duke and his entourage and guests, the court had to provide recreational and sporting facilities. In particular, it was the scene of jousts, and it included among its departments those of *fauconnerie* and *vénerie*, responsible for falconry and hunting respectively. Nor should the menagerie be forgotten, for Philip had wild pigs in the park at Brussels;[1] he kept a lion in the castle court-yard at Brussels which devoured half a sheep per day, and was supplied by contract with a local butcher; and at Ghent there were two monkeys and four lions. On one occasion a spectacle was provided by releasing these lions in a field with two bulls. Unidentifiable curiosities among animals included a 'dromedary from Poland' and an 'Indian rat'.

Philip the Good was himself an enthusiastic jouster and often took

[1] ADN B1966, f. 135. For what follows, see AGR CC17, fos. 58b, 59 and 168b; de Laborde, *Ducs de Bourgogne*, i. 216-17, 223 and 372.

part in person. The sport was extremely popular at the Burgundian court and among Philip's nobility, and the tournaments seem to have become more elaborate and grandiose as the reign progressed. Arras, in April 1423, was the scene of a tourney over which Philip presided and acted as judge. On the first day, the two contestants tilted on horseback, but a slight wound to one of them prevented them from breaking the agreed number of lances. On the next day they fought on foot with axes and one of them was accused of cheating for raising the other's visor during the combat, and then striking him in the face with a gauntlet.[1] In February 1430 Philip again judged a tournament at Arras. This time five French knights were matched against five Burgundians, and the proceedings continued for five days.

The joust which Philip presided over at Arras in the following year, on 20 June 1431, was more in the nature of a judicial duel. A Flemish chronicler describes the combatants arriving at the lists, each led in by two seconds. One held a banner with the Virgin Mary painted on it. When all was ready, the duke of Burgundy came forward with his secretary, who received the oath of each, sworn on a cross, that he was in the right. Then the herald cried 'Let them do their duty!' They fought for an hour, till Philip called out 'Hola!', and each then promised to make peace with the other and accept arbitration of their dispute by the duke and his council.

A similar contest was held at Arras in August 1435 during the Congress. The appellant was a Spanish or Portuguese knight, Juan de Merlo, who has the distinction of a mention by Cervantes in the immortal pages of *Don Quijote*. The chronicler explains that de Merlo had challenged his opponent, 'not because of a quarrel, but solely to acquire honour'. He entered the lists on the first day with a white plume on his helm and carrying a banner of vermilion with a white cross. After him four white lances were brought in by some of the twenty-four knights attending him. His opponent, Pierre de Bauffremont, lord of Charny, carried a banner depicting the Virgin Mary on one side and St. George on the other. His lances were blue, and it was found that they were not the same length as de Merlo's. However, the problem was solved by the contestants agreeing to tilt each time with lances belonging to one of them. After sixteen courses

---

[1] Monstrelet, *Chronique*, iv. 151–4 and de Fenin, *Mémoires*, 202–4. For what follows, see Monstrelet, *Chronique*, iv. 376–8 and Chastellain, *Œuvres*, ii. 18–26 (1430); Monstrelet, *Chronique*, iv. 434–9 and O. van Dixmude, *Merkwaerdige gebeurtenissen*, 135 (1431); Monstrelet, *Chronique*, v. 138–43 and le Févre, *Chronique*, ii. 321–4 (1435).

and only one lance broken, Duke Philip declared that they had done their duty, but they had some difficulty about leaving the lists, because neither wished to be the first to go. Next day, they returned at 8.0 a.m. to duel on foot with axes, and Juan de Merlo attracted considerable attention by fighting with his visor raised, a move which apparently disconcerted his opponent, and also by complaining loudly when the duke eventually stopped the combat that he had not had enough.

More elaborate and more fanciful were the passages of arms, which were undertaken by Philip the Good's courtiers at various places in his lands. Pierre de Bauffremont proclaimed one in March 1443. He and twelve companions were to defend a causeway on the road from Dijon to Auxonne at a point where a huge tree, called the Hermit's Tree, grew by the roadside. On this tree two shields would be hung, and all a challenger had to do was to send a herald or pursuivant to touch one of the shields: the black one for a mounted contest, the violet one if he wished to fight on foot with battle-axes or swords. Detailed regulations were drawn up by the defendants. The feats of arms on horseback were to be performed on Mondays, Tuesdays and Wednesdays, those on foot on Thursdays, Fridays and Saturdays. The passage of arms was to start on 1 July 1443 and to continue for forty days, excluding Sundays and feast-days. No nobleman would be permitted to pass within a quarter of a league of the Hermit's Tree without either entering the lists, or leaving his sword or spurs as a pledge. In the event, the place of combat was moved to the Tree of Charlemagne, a mile out of Dijon on the road to Nuits-St.-Georges, where Pierre de Bauffremont installed the lists, a large tent and a wooden pavilion, mounting-blocks, a stone crucifix and the black and violet shields. Within a mile or two of the spot, three of his mansions were well-stocked with food and drink: one for himself and his companions, one for the use of challengers and visitors, and the third in which to entertain participants after they had finished jousting. The tournament was a success. Challengers arrived from Dauphiny, Savoy, north Italy and Spain; and Duke Philip himself judged the contests on two occasions. The chronicler Olivier de la Marche gives a lengthy and elaborate account of the proceedings 'partly because this was the first tournament I had ever seen, and partly to inform my readers, if this is necessary, of the noble ceremonies attached to the exalted art of jousting'.[1]

[1] De la Marche, *Mémoires*, i. 300. For this paragraph, see Monstrelet, *Chronique*, vi. 68–73 and de la Marche, *Mémoires*, i. 282–6 and 290–334. For

One of the 'hardest-fought and most hazardous' feats of arms at the Burgundian court was the combat between Philippe, lord of Ternant, and the Milanese squire, Galeotto Balthazar, which was fought in the main square at Arras in April 1446. They duelled on foot first: seven thrusts with lances, eleven with swords, and fifteen blows with axes. The Milanese squire impressed everyone by leaping several times into the air after entering the lists for the first combat, fully armed and holding his lance. The lord of Ternant was seen to dig his foot firmly into the sand just as the lances found their targets. After the first encounter, each withdrew seven paces, which were carefully measured out with a knotted cord, and received a new lance. Then they advanced towards each other at a fast walk for the second encounter. After exchanging the agreed number of blows with swords, the contestants were furnished with special battle-axes for duelling which, lacking blades, were more like two-handed sledge-hammers. Even with this weighty equipment Galeotto managed a preliminary leap or two which may have been calculated to dismay his opponent, though some bystanders thought this manoeuvre might result in his being caught off balance. As a matter of fact, Galeotto did advance somewhat too rapidly towards his opponent, who neatly side-stepped and then landed a tremendous blow on Galeotto's helm as he lumbered past. A lesser man would have been felled to the ground, but Galeotto only staggered a little, then turned, and forced the lord of Ternant to give ground. A few days later Galeotto and Philippe entered the lists on horseback for their mounted combat, and Galeotto had to remove a number of steel spikes from his horse's trappings, which the marshal of the lists deemed to be against the rules. After they had fought for some time, Duke Philip, presiding as judge, stopped the jousts by throwing his white baton to the ground, preventing the combatants from exchanging the thirty-one blows they had agreed on beforehand. A similar thing happened during a combat at Ghent at the end of 1445, when Philip stopped the contestants after they had completed twenty-seven encounters with lances, out of thirty-one agreed to, on the grounds that it was nearly dark.

The hero of this contest, Jaques de Lalaing, set out for Scotland in 1448 with his uncle Simon de Lalaing and a companion, and the three of them held a tournament at Stirling with three Scots. On this occasion all six combatants entered the lists at once, armed with

the next paragraph, see de la Marche, *Mémoires*, ii. 64–79, d'Escouchy, *Chronique*, i. 91–5 and the *Livre des faits de Messire Jaques de Lalaing*, 82–9 and 164–79.

battle-axes, lances, swords and daggers, but the Burgundians discarded their lances in order to fight more effectively with their axes. In spite of all these weapons, Jaques de Lalaing, who was attacked by James Douglas (spelt du Glas by the chronicler d'Escouchy), was completely disarmed, but managed to avoid defeat by gripping Douglas's wrist so that he was unable to use his dagger. As was normally the case, the contest was stopped before any real damage was done.

Burgundian jousting in Philip the Good's reign reached its climax shortly before 1450 with two elaborate passages of arms: the *Belle Pèlerine*, held by Jehan de Luxembourg, bastard of St. Pol, between Calais and St. Omer, and the *Fontaine aux Pleurs*, which Jaques de Lalaing undertook at Chalon.[1] In spite of the fact that the former was advertised all over Europe by ducal heralds, who were sent in person to England, Scotland, Germany, Spain and France for this purpose, it was badly supported. Nor did Jaques de Lalaing, who installed his tilting-ground on an island in the Saône and defended the bridge there for an entire year, setting up his tent solemnly every Saturday, attract many comers. He closed the proceedings with a banquet, the distribution of prizes to his most valorous opponents, and the ceremonial removal by heralds of the figure of the Lady of the Fountain, the shields sprinkled with blue tears which the challengers had to touch, and other chivalric or romantic paraphernalia. With this and his other feats of arms, the youthful Jaques won European renown as a jouster and valiant knight; but a cannon-ball during the Ghent war brought his colourful career in the lists to an untimely close when he was only thirty-two. His exploits have been recorded for posterity in all their bizarre detail by an anonymous admirer, under the title *Livre des faits du bon chevalier Messire Jaques de Lalaing*: a work which reads more like romance than biography.

The everyday recreations of the duke of Burgundy and his courtiers were hunting and falconry, rather than jousting; for the elaborate equipment and décor needed for tournaments made them of necessity only occasional. Game was carefully preserved by the duke. When, in January 1458, a Dijon poacher received a ducal pardon, it was only on condition that he handed over his nets and traps, and that he put down six dozen live partridges near Rouvres, to replace those he had

---

[1] D'Escouchy, *Chronique*, i. 244–63 and de la Marche, *Mémoires*, ii. 118–29; d'Escouchy, *Chronique*, i. 264–73, de la Marche, *Mémoires*, ii. 142–204, and the *Livre des faits de Messire Jaques de Lalaing*, 188–246. For a joust at Valenciennes in 1455, see Cartellieri, *Festschrift für J. Hoops*, 169–76.

taken.[1] Philip bought three falcons in 1419, in 1442 he was hoping to acquire a goshawk, and in 1446-7 he bought ten gyrfalcons from Norway. His falconry establishment consisted in 1463 of a master-falconer, three falconers, three assistants to look after the sparrow-hawks, and valets. Only the master-falconer was employed on a whole-time basis; the others served Philip at court turn and turn about for some months at a time. These falconers sometimes lost a valuable bird, but Philip seems to have been lucky in recovering them. In November 1461 he lost his best saker (*le grant sacre*) in Luxembourg, but it was brought back to him in July 1462 at Brussels, having been recovered 'on the territory of the margrave of Branden-burg'.[2] An entry in the accounts of Luxembourg shows how such lost birds were identified:

> To Hans, falconer of my lord the margrave of Brandenburg, who, in the month of June, brought to Luxembourg a peregrine falcon carrying a bell and [other] fittings decorated with the name and arms of my lord the duke [of Burgundy], which had been found in Austria . . . 15/-.

While Philip the Good's falconers lived in his northern territories, the ducal huntsmen, with their assistants, pages, valets and clerk, were based in the duchy of Burgundy. In 1427 the master-huntsman, Jehan de Foissy, was allowed £2,000 per annum to cover all his expenses, which included the feeding, mainly with bread, of ninety-five hounds. It was the duty of the *vénerie* not only to provide Philip and his courtiers with sport, but also to supply him with venison, especially when he was visiting the duchy.

It would be foolish to attempt here more than the briefest survey of the varied and splendid artistic and cultural activity which flourished at Philip the Good's court. As a patron of music and painting, of jewellers and goldsmiths, of literature, and of many minor arts and crafts, he was far more munificent and enlightened than any other ruler of his day north of the Alps. The incomparable Jan van Eyck was his *valet de chambre*; Gille Binchois, the composer, was his chaplain; the poet Michault Taillevent was his *joueur de farces*; and he was the proud possessor of one of the finest libraries of illustrated books ever put together.

---

[1] *Correspondance de la mairie de Dijon*, i. 88-9. For what follows, see *Comptes généraux*, i. 484; ADN B1975, f. 77; *IADNB*, iv. 175; de Laborde, *Ducs de Bourgogne*, i. 481-92; and, in general, Picard, *MSE* (n. s.) ix (1880), 297-418.
[2] ADN B2045, f. 273. The extract which follows is from AGR CC2631, f. 19. For the next paragraph, see *Mémoires*, ii. 242-5.

At the Burgundian court, jewellery and plate, or goldsmith's work, served three different purposes. It was needed for the personal use and adornment of the duke and his relatives; for hoarding, against the need to raise cash in emergency by pawning it; and for exhibition. When the Czech traveller, Leo of Rozmital, visited the court at Brussels in the winter of 1465–6 he was astonished to be shown cabinet after cabinet of gold and silver vessels and ornaments. The keeper of the jewels told him that it would take three days to look over them all. Leo's German companion, Gabriel Tetzel, took the trouble to list and value the principal items, which included Philip's hat and the ostrich feather in it, together worth 110,000 crowns.[1] The chronicler Chastellain records an interesting example of the public display of these treasures for political reasons, in May 1456 in Holland. Some people, we are told, believed that Philip could not afford to pay for an army with which to conquer Utrecht. To prove the contrary, he organized a sumptuous display of jewels and plate in his palace at The Hague, and even placed on show, as well, two chests full of gold coins which were specially brought from Lille for this purpose. Earlier in the reign, an inventory of the ducal plate and jewels was drawn up, 'so as to know whereabouts they are'. At the head of the list is 'the gold goblet, with cover, with which my lord is served daily'. There follow silver plates and bowls; a gold bracelet studded with rubies; 'a vermilion robe made in 1424'; a quantity of rubies, pearls and other stones, some individually named; 'a clasp with King Richard's device of a stag, ornamented with twenty-two large pearls, two square balais, two saphires on one side and a ruby, with a large square diamond the size of a hazel-nut . . .'; and many jewelled crowns, crosses, clasps and other pieces, some of which had belonged to John the Fearless and were decorated with his favourite emblem, a plane. Precious few of these treasures have survived to the present day. One modest relic is an elegant silver bowl made in about 1450, which was carried away triumphantly by the Swiss from the battlefield of Nancy in 1477, and is now in the town hall of Liestal.

Near the beginning of Philip the Good's reign, in July 1420, a complete inventory was made of all his jewels, plate, tapestries, books and other precious belongings, which shows that the ducal treasury already possessed sixteen pieces of plate in solid gold, fifty-three of silver, and hundreds of jewels, not to mention swords, reliquaries,

[1] Rozmital, *Travels*, 28. For what follows, see Chastellain, *Œuvres*, iii. 90–2, and, for the next paragraph, *IADNB* viii. 161–4 and Deuchler, *Die Burgunderbeute*, 139–41.

necklaces and the like. Among the subjects of tapestries were the Twelve Peers of France, the Nine Worthies, male and female, the Seven Sages, the Apocalypse, the battle of Othée against Liège in 1408, Jason, William the Conqueror and the Norman conquest of England, stag-hunting, shepherds and shepherdesses, Renaud de Montauban, Bertrand du Guesclin, Charlemagne, and Godefroi de Bouillon. Also mentioned are 'nine large tapestries and two smaller ones, worked in gold, showing plovers, partridges and other birds, with the figures of the late Duke John and my lady the duchess his wife, both on foot and on horseback'. A separate list of tapestries with religious subjects, for the chapel, is given. Evidence that Philip took a personal interest in his tapestries is found in an entry in the accounts, which reads as follows:[1]

> To Robert Dary and Jehan de Lortye, tapestry merchants of Tournai, the sum of 500 gold crowns . . ., part of the 8,960 crowns which they are to be paid by my lord [the duke] in the four years ending 15 August 1453, for eight large pieces of tapestry . . . which the said merchants have contracted with Philippe, lord of Ternant, knight, councillor and chamberlain of my lord [the duke], and Jehan Aubry, *valet de chambre* and keeper of the duke's tapestry, to complete and deliver without any deception for the above sum and within the said four years wherever my lord [the duke] may please in his territories between the Somme and the sea. [They have also contracted] to have the patterns, with the figures and emblems decided on and explained to them by my lord [the duke], made by Baudouin de Bailleul or the best artist they can find, and [to see that] whatever is in yellow on the patterns is in the best gold thread of Venice in the tapestry; and whatever is shown white is in silver thread, except for the faces and flesh of the people.

A marginal note discloses the characteristically Burgundian subject-matter of these splendid tapestries: 'the History of Gideon and the Golden Fleece'. Perhaps the most famous of all Philip the Good's tapestries was made in Brussels in 1466 by Jehan le Haze. Two-thirds of it is preserved now in the Historical Museum at Bern; the remainder was at Fribourg, but has since been lost. On a blue-black background hundreds of finely worked and beautifully coloured plants are embroidered, surrounding the ducal arms in the centre. So carefully executed and so well preserved is this remarkable millefleurs tapestry, that thirty-five different species of flower have been identified by botanists. Its incompleteness is due to its division into two

---

[1] *IADNB* iv. 192. For what follows, see Schneebalg-Perelman, *JBHM* xxxix–xl (1959–60), 136–63 and Deuchler, *Die Burgunderbeute*, 172–8.

when the booty captured by the Swiss after the battle of Grandson was shared among the cantons.

As a builder and patron of sculpture Philip the Good cannot compare with his grandfather and namesake, who not only founded and built the Charterhouse of Champmol outside Dijon, but also employed the finest sculptor then to be found north of the Alps, Claus Sluter, to carve the monumental statuary for the convent, and his own tomb to place inside its church. Although John the Fearless had commissioned Sluter's nephew, Claus de Werve, to make a tomb for himself, like his father's but 'as cheaply as possible', the work was not continued under Philip the Good until 1436, when we hear of stone for it being sought in Dauphiny. Evidently Philip was in no hurry to complete the work. In 1439 Claus de Werve died, but nothing more was done till 1443, when a contract was signed for the tombs of John the Fearless and his wife, Margaret of Bavaria, with an Aragonese sculptor, Juan de la Huerta. He agreed to construct a tomb of the same size and quality as that of Duke Philip the Bold, with recumbent effigies of Duke John and his wife based on portraits provided for him. But Juan was a rascal. He insulted the mayor of Dijon, accepted private commissions, delayed, and clamoured for more money. Eventually, he absconded from Dijon, where the duke had given him a house, and disappeared without trace in 1462. A new contract for the tomb had to be signed, and a new artist was found in the person of Anthoine le Moiturier of Avignon, who submitted a model of his proposed tomb in 1466. When Philip died in the following year, Anthoine was thus just starting work on a tomb for his parents, and it was only in 1470 that the completed monument was finally installed in the Charterhouse of Champmol.[1]

Philip the Good's patronage of sculpture was in fact limited to the dutiful commissioning of a few necessary sepulchral monuments. At Ghent a sculptor was at work on a tomb for his first wife Michelle some twenty years after her death. In Paris, around 1440, Philip commissioned a tomb for Anne, duchess of Bedford. In 1453, he signed a contract, which was negotiated by his wife Isabel, for an elaborate monument at St. Peter's, Lille for his great-grandfather, Louis of Male, who had died in 1384, and two princesses, one of whom was surely Louis's wife Margaret. The other was probably his

---

[1] On this paragraph, see Chabeuf, *MAD* (4) ii (1890–1), 137–271 and Monget, *Chartreuse de Dijon*, ii. 113–36; and, on this and what follows, A. Humbert, *La sculpture sous les ducs de Bourgogne* and Kleinclausz, *Claus Sluter et la sculpture bourguignonne*. The extract is from *IADNB* vii. 364–5.

daughter, Margaret of Male, who was certainly buried there, though her effigy, next to that of her husband Philip the Bold, was already reclining on their tomb in the Charterhouse of Champmol. The contract is notable for its description of the tomb.

My lady the duchess has negotiated on behalf of my lord the duke with Jaques de Gerynes, called the Copper-smith, of Brussels, to have a tomb made in the following manner. First, he must provide a single, sound slab of Antoing stone, ringing true as sound stone ought to ring, twelve feet by nine, with a nicely carved moulding all round it, just as the drawings show, and it must be well and truly polished as smoothly as possible. This slab must be of a single piece, if such can be found; if not, of two pieces suitably joined together. It must be a foot thick, or thereabouts, and have four supports of the same stone, three feet high and likewise well polished. The bases of these supports should be carved with a fine moulding, as the drawing shows, and also be well polished. Moreover, the said Jaques is to make three effigies raised above this slab, one in the centre, of a prince armed, seven feet long, as shown in the drawing; and, on either side of the prince's effigy, a princess, likewise as shown in the drawing, each six-and-a-half feet long. At the heads of these effigies there are to be two kneeling angels, supporting a helm and crest over the prince's head, and each holding in its other hand a shield with the arms of the princess emblazoned in low relief, as with a seal. Around the slab, above the moulding, is to be an inscription in brass letters set in black cement, giving the titles of the prince and princesses and the dates of their deaths. Below the slab, and around the outside of the supports, there is to be an arcade made of brass, as the drawing shows. In each arch there is to be a brass figure of such height and width as the situation requires of a lord or lady descended from the above-mentioned prince and princesses, to a total of twenty-four. Each of these statuettes is to have a shield at its feet with the arms of the person represented, and the name is to be in brass letters set in black cement along the base of the arcade above-mentioned.

Philip the Good was more successful as a patron of painting than of sculpture, for he had the good fortune to employ at his court an artistic genius of the first rank, Jan van Eyck, though none of his surviving works is attributable to this ducal patronage. Born probably at Maaseik in the extreme east of present-day Belgium, Jan was employed in Holland by John of Bavaria until that ruler's death in 1425, when Philip the Good took over his territories and his artist. Indeed he persuaded Jan to move house to Lille in the summer of 1425, after appointing him official ducal painter and *valet de chambre* 'because of the excellence of his artistic work', at a salary of £100 of

Paris per annum. When, in 1428, Philip the Good sent ambassadors
to Portugal to investigate the possibility of marrying King John's
daughter Isabel, they took Jan with them to paint her portrait from
life.[1] By 1433 he was living at Bruges, and the duke on one occasion
visited his studio there to see him at work. In 1434 Pierre de Bauffremont held Jan's son at the font in Philip's name, and the duke sent
a gift of six silver cups. When court economies required the temporary withholding of salaries, Philip the Good insisted that Jan's
must be paid, 'for we should never find his equal in artistic skill'.
He remained in ducal service until his death at Bruges in the summer
of 1441, and subsequently his widow enjoyed a ducal pension.

The catalogue of the Burgundian ducal library which was made in
1420,[2] right at the start of Philip's reign, shows that he inherited
some 250 books, many of them illuminated. By the time of his death
he had nearly quadrupled the size of the library, adding, in particular,
a splendid series of superbly illuminated large-format volumes. While
the jewellery and plate, the tapestries, the paintings and even the
tombs and buildings of the Valois dukes have for the most part disappeared, about 350 of their books survive to this day. In spite of
depredations by the French in 1746 and 1792, 247 of these remain in
Brussels, where they were collected and housed by Philip the Good,
and where they now form part of the manuscript collection of the
Royal Library of Belgium, founded by Philip II in 1559.

Apart from scattered purchases and some intermittent rebinding,
Philip the Good seems to have done little to his library during the
first half of his reign. But in the years after 1445 a steady stream of
important commissions resulted in the formation of groups of scribes
and illuminators at Mons, Valenciennes, Hesdin, Lille, Oudenaarde,
Bruges, Brussels and Ghent; all of them engaged in producing
lavishly illuminated manuscripts for the Burgundian court. For the
duke himself was by no means the only bibliophile there: Anthony,
the Grand Bastard of Burgundy, put together a remarkable library of
his own, the principal treasure of which was the Breslau Froissart.
Other Burgundian courtiers who commissioned and collected illuminated books were Jehan de Bourgogne, count of Étampes, Jehan

[1] See below, pp. 178–84. For Philip the Good and Jan van Eyck, see the
documents in Weale, *Hubert and John van Eyck*, xxvii–xlvii.
[2] *Inventaire de la 'Librairie' de Philippe le Bon, 1420*. For what follows, see
especially Durrieu, *Miniature flamande*, Gaspar and Lyna, *Philippe le Bon et
ses beaux livres*, Delaissé, *Miniatures médiévales de la Librairie de Bourgogne*
and *La miniature flamande*, and Dogaer and Debae, *La Librairie de Philippe
le Bon*, and references given in these works.

de Wavrin the chronicler, Jehan, lord of Créquy, and Jehan de Croy.

Three men were above all responsible for providing Philip with the books he wanted and employing craftsmen to produce them: Jehan Wauquelin, at Mons in Hainault, Jehan Miélot at Lille, and David Aubert at Bruges and Brussels. Wauquelin seems to have been equally skilful as a translator, a scribe, and as an employer of artists and craftsmen. When, for instance, he undertook, in 1446 or soon after, to produce a French version of the *Chroniques de Hainaut* for Philip, he did the translation and some of the transcription himself, but employed at least three of the leading miniaturists of the day to illuminate these sumptuous volumes. We know the names of two of them, Guillaume Vrelant and Loyset Liédet. Conjecture has it that the famous illustration in volume one of these chronicles, showing the ducal councillor Simon Nockart presenting the book to Philip the Good in the presence of a group of courtiers,[1] is the work of Roger van der Weyden, but this is unlikely. Miélot was a canon of St. Peter's, Lille, and more of a translator than anything else, though he could act as scribe on occasion. He too employed others to decorate the books Philip commissioned from him, and in this matter he, too, showed admirable taste, for it was he who 'discovered' the exquisite illuminator Jehan le Tavernier of Oudenaarde. Aubert was a jack-of-all-trades too, but above all he was a scribe, though, like Wauquelin and Miélot, he was responsible for employing the illuminators of the books he contracted to produce for the duke.

Inextricably involved with the formation of this prestigious library are the literary interests and patronage of Philip the Good. For he was by no means just a picture-book man; he actually read a good deal, or had his books read to him, and he seems to have particularly enjoyed history and historical novels or, in the terminology of those days, chronicles and historical romances. Jehan Wauquelin, David Aubert, and others like them, not only supplied Philip with *de luxe* copies of existing texts, they were also required to make translations of Latin histories into French. The *Chroniques de Hainaut* already mentioned was translated from the Latin *Annales Hannoniae* of Jaques de Guise; another such work was the compilation from Latin historians, made at Philip's request by Jehan Mansel, called *Histoires romaines*. The mid-fifteenth-century translation into French of the fourteenth-century Latin chronicle of Holland and Utrecht, Johannes

[1] Reproduced here as Plate 2 .On Miélot, see Hautcoeur, *Église de Saint-Pierre de Lille*, ii. 151–8.

de Beka's *Chronographia*, was undertaken for Philip the Good.[1] Besides these translations, David Aubert and other book-suppliers were required by the duke to provide versions in prose of earlier medieval epic poems. A well-known example is the poem describing the adventures and quarrels with the king of France of the Burgundian hero Girart de Roussillon, a superb manuscript of which, produced for Philip by Wauquelin, is at Vienna. Other modernized prose versions of medieval poems produced for the Burgundian court or for Philip himself, were *La Belle Hélène de Constantinople, Perceforest, Renaud de Montauban, Olivier de Castille* and *Gilles de Chin*. This last describes the feats of arms of a legendary hero of Hainault, and is based on a thirteenth-century poem, but such was the influence, and popularity, of literature, at the Burgundian court, that Gilles de Chin was virtually reincarnated in Philip's courtier Jaques de Lalaing, who did his best to repeat Gilles's fictitious adventures in real life. Hence the quite remarkable similarity of the two works, which share a similar title: the *Chronique du bon chevalier Messire Gilles de Chin* and the *Livre des faits du bon chevalier Messire Jaques de Lalaing*. The former was a historical romance, the latter a biography.

Thus far we have mentioned a few among many works commissioned by Philip the Good. But his literary patronage extended also to the maintenance of writers and chroniclers at his court or in the administration of his state. For example, the two bishops who succeeded one another as chancellors of the Order of the Golden Fleece, Jehan Germain[2] and Guillaume Fillastre, were writers; so were Anthoine de la Sale, Bertrandon de la Broquière, and Michault Taillevent,[3] all of whom were attached, at one time or another, to the Burgundian court. As to chroniclers, Philip was one of the first European rulers to appoint an official court chronicler, in the shape of George Chastellain. Not that this can have been considered strictly necessary: after all, most of the leading French-speaking and some other chroniclers of the day were in Burgundian pay, or main-

---

[1] Noomen, ed., *La traduction française de la Chronographia Johannis de Beka*. On this and what follows, see especially Doutrepont, *Littérature* and *Mises en prose*; Rychner, *La littérature et les moeurs chevaleresques à la cour de Bourgogne*; Quicke, *Chroniqueurs des fastes bourguignons*; R. Bossuat, *Le moyen âge*; and Charlier and Hanse, *Histoire illustrée des lettres françaises de Belgique*, 81–129, and references given in these works.
[2] See Lacaze, *PTSEC* (1958), 67–75, *MSHAC* xxxix (1968), 1–24, and his thesis *Jean Germain*.
[3] See Champion, *Histoire poétique*, i. 285–338 and Duchein, *PTSEC* (1949), 49–52 on the last of these.

tained already at the court. Jehan Lefèvre and Jehan de Wavrin were ducal councillor-chamberlains, Edmond de Dynter was a ducal secretary, Jaques Duclerq at Arras was a ducal official, and Olivier de la Marche was the Burgundian courtier *par excellence*. He was everything except an official historian: page, equerry, steward and ambassador. The duke's own interest in history is attested over and over again, especially in the accounts, where we learn of a certain Hugues de Tolins, described as 'chronicler of the duke', who was sent in 1460 on a special mission to undertake historical research for Philip in the duchy of Burgundy.[1]

Of all the numerous and varied literary works which emanated from the Burgundian court under Philip the Good, the most original and the most entertaining is that museum of fifteenth-century obscenities, the *Cent nouvelles nouvelles* or *Hundred new stories*, which was perhaps composed in 1459 or soon after then.[2] A collection of salacious anecdotes exchanged between Philip the Good and his courtiers, the derivation from Bocaccio's *Decameron* is plain; especially when we find that the duke had already commissioned a lavishly illuminated French version of that work under the title *Cent nouvelles*.

The *Cent nouvelles nouvelles* is of much less literary distinction than the *Decameron*; but for all that the anonymous editor of these stories, who was invited by Philip to recount them, writes with a certain jovial vigour and directness of style which makes a refreshing change from the ornate vocabulary of other contemporary works. Moreover, besides this literary merit, the *Cent nouvelles nouvelles* has value as a historical source: well over half the tales, including some of the fourteen told by the duke, are true stories. Thus, for example, Philip is responsible for the tragic story of Clais Utenhove of Ghent, who fell into the hands of the Turks at the battle of Nicopolis in 1396 and was sold into slavery. His grief-stricken wife refused for years the

[1] On Burgundian chroniclers, besides the works referred to on p. 157, n. 1, see Vermaseren, *TG* lvi (1941), 258–73; Hommel, *Chastellain*, with references; and Stein, *Étude sur Olivier de la Marche* and *Nouveaux documents sur Olivier de la Marche*.

[2] Edited with introduction by P. Champion in 1928 and by Sweetser in 1966. My date 1459 is proposed on the basis of the statement in the *amman* of Brussels's story, no. 53, that a case before the bishop of Cambrai concerning two couples who were inadvertently muddled while being married by the priest was still unsettled, for Chastellain, who describes this mistake in the unpublished section of his chronicle (BM Add. MS. 54156, fos. 370b–372b, see below p. 350, n. 2) places it in the early morning darkness of the last Sunday on which marriages were possible before the beginning of Lent, 1459.

pressure of her relatives to remarry. Eventually, she succumbed; only to hear, six months later, that her former husband had contrived to escape, and was on his way home. She died of grief and shame shortly before he returned. The subject-matter of this particular tale is atypical. Usually we are told of wicked or lustful inn-keepers; of seductive chambermaids pursued by noblemen; of the erotic adventures of monks and priests; and, endlessly, of the hilarious gallery of cuckolds. The story-tellers are Philip's courtiers; but the setting of the stories is the world outside the court, of hotels and travellers, of merchants, of clerks and monks, and of the countryside. Over half of them take place in Philip's own territories, mostly in the Low Countries.

Few walks of life escape the ribald humour of the story-tellers of the *Cent nouvelles nouvelles*. The astute merchant and his faithless wife are characterized in the story told by a ducal squire, Philippe Vignier, of a London merchant who, after ten years abroad, returned to find his family augmented by a seven-year-old son. Pretending to accept his wife's explanation, that she had become pregnant shortly after eating a piece of frozen snow in the garden, having mistaken it for a laurel leaf, he set out again on his foreign travels some years later, taking his illegitimate son with him. At Alexandria, however, he sold him into slavery for 100 ducats. Returning home alone, he then explained to his wife, reminding her of her son's origins, that he had suddenly melted away one day when they disembarked in a very hot country. The clergy are not only pilloried for their gallantries. The subject of one story is an ignorant priest who forgets to announce the arrival of Lent to his parishioners till he sees palms for sale in the neighbouring town; of another, a bishop who devours two entire partridges one Friday, explaining to a critic that he had used the same powers which achieved transubstantiation at the mass, to transform the flesh of the partridge into fish.

One story is of particular interest for the historical details it gives about fifteenth-century Calais.[1] It concerns two English squires in the retinue of Henry Beaufort, cardinal-bishop of Winchester, who lodged at Calais in July 1439 while a diplomatic conference was held between Calais and Gravelines. We learn incidentally, in the course of an elaborate tale of how these two young Englishmen seduced their Dutch landlady, that the largest house in the town, where important visitors stayed, was owned by a Richard Fery; that the head of every household in Calais had to take his turn on guard duty on the walls

[1] Translated in Wyndham Lewis, *King Spider*, 346–52. See above, p. 108, for the diplomatic conference here mentioned.

for one night each week; that English girls enjoyed a reputation for generosity with their kisses; and that it was thought to be the custom, in England in those days, to repair after mass to a tavern to lunch and drink wine.

While Philip the Good and his courtiers exchanged these bawdy tales and other gossip after dinner at Genappe, Brussels, or elsewhere, they were entertained by the best musicians of the day. For music, like literature and the other arts already discussed, was an essential element of court life.[1] Was there any fifteenth-century ruler or nobleman who did not learn to play the harp in his youth? The instrumentalists who provided secular music on court occasions must be carefully distinguished from the ducal chaplains, who formed a choir which was used chiefly for liturgical purposes. Philip the Good's twelve trumpeters are said to have formed up and played a fanfare in front of his window to wake him in the mornings. Music was prominent during the Feast of the Pheasant: a shepherd stood on the table playing bagpipes, the sounds of a cornet, and a choir, emerged from within capacious pies, and there were organs and trumpets. Among his chaplains, whose voices, when they were recruited, were sometimes assessed by the duke himself, Philip could proudly number composers like Gille Binchois, fifty-four of whose *chansons* are reckoned to have survived.

There was little or no originality at the Burgundian court under Philip the Good. His patronage of the arts, his encouragement of literature, his music; all was taken over from Philip the Bold and John the Fearless. But Philip did succeed in something which his two predecessors had failed to do. He inaugurated a new, and specifically Burgundian, Order of chivalry, the Golden Fleece, which created and maintained an inner circle of privileged courtiers, councillors and captains.[2] They met regularly in solemn chapter to settle disputes and indulge in self-criticism, which was permitted to extend to com-

---

[1] See especially van Doorslaer, *RBAHA* iv (1934), 21–3; Marix, *Les musiciens de la cour de Bourgogne* and *Histoire de la musique de la cour de Bourgogne*; Van den Borren, *Geschiedenis van de muziek in de Nederlanden*, i.; and Bowles, *Galpin Society Journal*, vi (1953), 41–51.

[2] For what follows, see especially Vienna, AOGV, Regest i, summarized and partly printed in de Reiffenberg, *Histoire de l'Ordre de la Toison d'Or* and le Févre, *Chronique*, ii. 172–4. See too Doutrepont, *Littérature*, 147–70; Kervyn de Lettenhove, *Toison d'Or*; Hommel, *L'histoire de la Toison d'Or*; Tourneur, *BARBL* (5) xlii (1956), 300–23; Terlinden, Richard, Quarré, Dogaer and Armstrong in *PCEEBM* v (1963); and Armstrong, *Britain and the Netherlands*, ii. 25–7, and the references in these works.

plaints about the duke. At first the annual festivities of the Order were held in November and centred on St. Andrew's day, but in 1435 it was resolved to transfer them to the spring or early summer, because the days were too short in November. Nonetheless, the municipal authorities at Bruges continued, until the French Revolution, to fire off a salvo of artillery on the ramparts of the town, every year on 30 November, in honour of the Order. The Burgundian members of the Order, in Philip's reign, were predominantly French-speaking: Reinoud van Brederode probably caused mild astonishment by making a speech in Dutch at the 1456 chapter. The meeting-place of the Order varied. It was at Lille in 1431 for the first chapter, and at Bruges, Dijon, Brussels, Arras, St. Omer, Ghent, Mons and The Hague in subsequent years. But its seat was fixed by Philip, in January 1432, in the chapel of the ducal palace at Dijon, where the shields of its members were set up above the canons' stalls. It was given an elaborate set of statutes in November 1431, and a chancellor, treasurer, registrar or historiographer,[1] and herald.

The exact motives of the duke, in founding the Order, are far from clear. Chastellain hints that Philip needed an excuse for refusing Duke John of Bedford's offer of the Garter, and discovered one in his intention to found an Order of his own. However this may be, one of the main functions of the Order was to unite the nobility of the different Burgundian territories and bind them in close personal dependence on the duke. From soon after its foundation, it was made to play a similar rôle in consolidating Philip's alliances with neighbouring princes and other European rulers. Friedrich, count of Mörs, brother of the archbishop of Cologne, was elected in 1431. In 1440 four Burgundian allies among French princes were elected together: Charles, duke of Orleans, John V, duke of Brittany, John, duke of Alençon and the count of Comminges. The first reigning monarch to be elected was King Alfonso V of Naples and Aragon, who in 1445 reacted to the invitation to accept membership of the Burgundian Order by offering membership of his own Order to Philip.[2] He made difficulties, too, by requiring prior modification of the statutes because, he claimed, his royal dignity would not permit him to wear the insignia of the Order of the Golden Fleece every day, but only once a week, on Sundays. Philip the Good countered by insisting that he could not possibly wear the white band of Alfonso's Order of the

[1] Gorissen, *BGN* vi (1951–2). 218–24.
[2] For this and what follows, see Marinesco, *CRAIBL* (1956), 404–10 and Ruwet, *Archives et bibliothèques de Vienne*, 767–8.

Stola y Jarra, because this would 'displease his subjects by seeming to imitate the Armagnacs who had worn a similar band during the wars in France'. But the quarrel was amicably settled, and Alfonso's successor, John VI of Aragon, accepted membership of the Order of the Golden Fleece in 1461, by which time another ruler, the duke of Cleves, had been elected.

The Golden Fleece soon became an important motif in the art and literature of the Burgundian court. Jason, leader of the Argonauts, was the natural patron of the Order, and William Caxton mentions a room at Hesdin castle, which he had actually seen, 'wherein was craftily and curiously depeynted the conqueste of the golden flese by the sayd Iason'.[1] But Jason's desertion of Medea after his promise of eternal fidelity made him a less than perfect patron. The Burgundian bishops set to work on him. Guillaume Fillastre tried to improve his image with a spurious Christian ethos; Jehan Germain did away with him altogether, substituting, as patron of the Order, the impeccably biblical Gideon. In 1448 Philip ordered the tapestry mentioned above of the 'History of Gideon and the Golden Fleece', which was brought out thereafter on special occasions. As to the possible connection of the Golden Fleece with Philip's crusading projects, contemporary records bear little or no trace of this, nor do they support the legend that the Golden Fleece really represented the blonde hair of one of the ducal paramours.

Although the Order of the Golden Fleece helped in the process of making, or keeping, friends and allies among the aristocracy and ruling houses of Burgundy and Europe, the court itself played a far more important rôle in this respect. Not only was its membership much more numerous, amounting to well over a thousand persons in all, but it was drawn from other strata of society besides the upper ranks of the aristocracy, to which alone membership of the Golden Fleece was open. For instance, there was an important ecclesiastical and burgess element at court, comprising chaplains, legists, financial officials and the like, as well as numerous representatives of the lesser nobility. As for alliances with other rulers, here too, the court was far more effective in promoting and maintaining them than the Golden Fleece. Count Eberhard the younger of Württemberg was virtually brought up at the Burgundian court;[2] two sons of Adolf I, duke of

[1] Blades, *Life and Typography of William Caxton*, i. 139. See too above, p. 152, for what follows.
[2] Von Stälin, *Wirtembergische Geschichte*, iii. 555. For what follows, see Vander Linden, *Itinéraires* and *IADNB* viii. 5–46. See too, p. 123 above. For

Cleves, spent prolonged periods there; and the dukes of Cleves, Guelders and Savoy paid visits from time to time. Burgundian hospitality was extended, too, to French princes and princesses like Charles, duke of Orleans, and various members of the ducal family of Bourbon, some of whom stayed for protracted periods. Moreover, these and other client princes or relatives were paid handsome personal grants or pensions by Philip. In 1457–61, Adolf of Cleves, son of Duke Adolf I, received £3,200 per annum and £500 per month; Jaques de Bourbon was paid £2,400 annually; Count Eberhard had to be content with a mere £120 per month. Besides all this, the court was constantly entertaining foreign diplomats and visitors. Between May and September 1462, when Philip was holding court at Brussels, he was visited by ambassadors from Aragon, England, Brandenburg, Italy and distant Trebizond.[1] Other visitors in the same period were mere tourists. Two minstrels came from Brittany, sight-seeing. Various Byzantine refugees came to Brussels in the same period. It was the function of the court not only to entertain these people and many others like them, but also, by displaying to them the wealth and power of Burgundy, to enhance the prestige of the duke throughout Christendom.

The Burgundian court, then, fulfilled many rôles, from providing the duke with lodgings, food and sporting facilities, to linking his various territories in common dependence on a single central institution. Moreover, it was a medium for artistic patronage on a lavish scale and for projecting a resplendent ducal image far and wide through Europe. Above all, it was the actual seat of government, for it maintained permanently within itself the central council, or *grand conseil*, of Philip the Good.

---

the so-called pensions, see for example, ADN B2026, fos. 110b–112b and B2045, fos. 102b–104b.
[1] For this and what follows, see ADN B2045, fos. 265–78.

The Government at Work

It goes without saying that the mainspring of the machinery of
central government in the Burgundian state was the duke himself.
Aged twenty-three when he succeeded his father in 1419, having
already acted for some years as ruler of Flanders on John the Fearless's
behalf, he lived to be over seventy. Jouster, warrior, falconer, con-
noisseur of illuminated manuscripts, he shocked some contemporaries
by his penchant for nocturnal entertainments. Chastellain accuses
him of negligence in the affairs of state; suggesting that he only
presided over his own council when this was strictly necessary, and
that he entrusted the detailed administration of his territories and his
finances to others.[1] The Dutch historian Huizinga, taking this and
similar contemporary literary evidence at face value, claimed that
Philip as a rule did not concern himself with affairs of state. But these
judgments are wide of the mark. Philip may not have involved himself in trivial administrative matters; he may not have shared his son's
passion for work but, as Bonenfant has shown, he was a party to all
important decisions and was personally involved in every event of
significance throughout the greater part of his long reign. Only in the
last decade, when he was in his sixties, was his firm grip on affairs
significantly relaxed. It was perhaps this period of the reign which
was foremost in Chastellain's mind when, some time after Philip's
death, he accused him of neglecting his duties as a ruler. After all,
Chastellain only arrived at the Burgundian court in 1445, and did not
begin writing his chronicle till ten years later.

Evidence of Philip the Good's personal rôle in the government of
his state is scattered throughout the voluminous archival material still
to be found in Dijon, Lille, Brussels and elsewhere. In the accounts
of the receipt-general of all finances, for example, under the heading

---

[1] *Œuvres*, vii. 222–4. For what follows, see Huizinga, *Verzamelde werken*, ii.
230–1 and Bonenfant, *Philippe le Bon*, 28–32 and *BMHGU* lxxiv (1960), 12.

Menues messageries, where payments for the despatch of couriers with letters are recorded, we find, year after year, that the bulk of the outgoing correspondence of the Burgundian government emanated from the duke himself. Here, for example, is a list of the letters-close sent out by Philip from Hesdin, Houdain and Lille in the week 4–10 July 1425:[1]

4 July   To the *gens des comptes* at Lille

4 July   To certain persons in Paris, who had been sent there to collect Agnes of Burgundy's jewels, instructing them not to leave without a strong escort

7 July   To the receiver-general of Flanders, Gautier Poulain and other officials

7 July   To Jehan de Rynel, asking him to expedite certain letters which John, duke of Bedford, had promised the duke of Burgundy he would send to the archbishop of Cologne, and others, concerning the war they were waging against the duke of Cleves

8 July   To the duchess, the chancellor, and others, in Burgundy

9 July   To the ducal ambassadors with the archbishop of Cologne, at or near Cologne, about the war of the archbishop and his allies against the duke of Cleves

10 July   To the earl of Warwick and other English people then at Calais

10 July   To the count of St. Pol, in Brussels, concerning a conference to be held shortly between the dukes of Burgundy and Brabant.

The pattern remains similar right through to the end of the reign. The only change is the appearance of a verbal formula at the head of the section comprising payments for messages, which states that they were authorized by 'my lord the duke and my lords of his council'; and, later, by 'my lord the duke and my lords of his great council being with him'. This mention of the council should not be taken to mean that the correspondence was really handled by the councillors, acting in Philip's name. Other evidence shows that it was the duke himself who issued instructions and to whom his officials and courtiers, captains and ambassadors, turned when they were in doubt as to what to do. Surely we must take at face value the statement of the ducal councillor and ex-chancellor, Jehan de Thoisy, in a letter to Tournai written in August 1425, that he had discussed the town's affairs with the duke, who had decided to maintain the treaties with

[1] ADN B1931, fos. 158a–b.

it, while deploring the way it was conducting its affairs?[1] Nor can we ignore the failure of the attempts of Philip's leading councillors, in April 1426, to persuade him to sign the treaty with Tournai without a clause allowing him to revoke it in the event of English objections. Philip, anxious to defend his honour, overruled de Thoisy, Nicolas Rolin and other councillors. Elsewhere, we are told that the negotiations for a treaty with Tournai could not continue because the duke was absent.

If Philip the Good was personally involved in the negotiations with Tournai for a commercial treaty, the same goes for the negotiations with the Hansards in 1425 and 1429. In the summer of 1425 he spent several days in Bruges in order to negotiate personally with the Hansard ambassadors there: representatives of Lübeck, Cologne, Hamburg, Danzig, Stralsund and Riga.[2] In July 1429 Haarlem and Amsterdam wrote to the Bruges Hansards to explain that the duke had the matter in hand, but was absent from Holland; the negotiations would have to wait until his return. There is much other evidence to show that the duke himself directed negotiations of every kind. One of the Burgundian ambassadors to England in 1433 begins his report, addressed to Philip, with the significant words: 'As regards myself, Hue de Lannoy, I have kept to the terms you outlined to me in the garden of your house at Arras, as nearly as I can.' Later, in 1437, when Hue de Lannoy was stadholder of Holland, we find him sending to Philip at Arras to ask his advice as to what reply to make to some English proposals. Nor is this sort of thing limited to the early part of the reign. It is clear from a passage in the chronicle of Chastellain that, as late as 1457, Philip still had complete control of the very complicated negotiations then in progress with England, though this did not prevent him discussing the whole matter with his council.

Philip the Good's control of his own government can easily be demonstrated in military and administrative affairs, as well as diplomacy. The accounts of the receiver-general of Hainault, for example, show that the bailiff and councillors or officials of this relatively unimportant territory found it necessary, quite frequently, to

[1] For this and what follows, see Houtart, *Les Tournaisiens et le roi de Bourges*, 326–7, 331–2 and 262.

[2] *Hanserecesse, 1256–1430*, vii. no. 811 and *Hansisches Urkundenbuch*, vi. nos. 801 and 802. For what follows, see *Letters and papers*, ii (1), 218; *Bronnen van den handel met Engeland*, ii. 709; Chastellain, *Œuvres*, iii. 337–9.

consult the duke himself on administrative matters of a more or less routine nature. Sometimes, Philip was too busy to see them. In 1431 they were foolish enough to try to obtain an interview with him at the time of the St. Andrew's day festivities of the Order of the Golden Fleece. They waited patiently but had to defer their business when a French embassy arrived and took up the duke's attention. One cannot fail to be impressed by the number of minor matters which were dealt with by Philip the Good in person. For example, in November 1453 the bailiff of Hainault sent to him at Lille to enquire if he was prepared to pay for a certain bombard he had wanted at the rate of 2s a pound weight, ready cash. In Burgundy, in 1443, Philip took the trouble to receive in person, in his *chambre de retrait*, or private room, a civic deputation from Mâcon. He greeted them in a friendly manner, offered them hippocras, and sent someone to Mâcon to investigate their complaints. We must be careful not to assume that important official letters could be signed without ducal approval. In 1450 the town clerk of Malines, who had been sent to Philip at The Hague to expedite the despatch of promised ducal letters to the pope requesting a jubilee year indulgence for Malines, wrote back to Malines explaining that, because the letters were lengthy and the duke was entertaining every evening, he still had not succeeded in getting them sealed.[1]

Any examination of the mechanism of government in the Burgundian state must take into careful account the rôle of Philip the Good's third wife, Isabel of Portugal. Hitherto, this capable, energetic, even domineering personality has been ignored by historians.[2] Certainly, her part in affairs was limited chronologically, for Philip did not marry her until 1430, and she deserted him, and the court, in 1457. But within this period there can be no question of her importance in the central administration of the Burgundian state. Certain contemporaries, none of whom had any firsthand knowledge of the Burgundian court, were mistaken when they claimed that she was 'the master and governess of her husband the Duke Philip', or

[1] For this paragraph, see ADN B10396, fos. 37a–b and 10417, f. 34b; *Documents pour servir à l'histoire de la Bourgogne*, 429 n. 1; *Codex indulgentiarum neerlandicarum*, 79–80.
[2] See Drouot, *AB* xviii (1946), 142 and xix (1947), 234–5 and the unpublished thesis of Surjous, *Isabelle de Portugal*. Looten's superficial sketch in *RLC* xviii (1938), 5–22, reappears in Lagrange's useful itinerary of Isabel in *ACFF* xlii (1938). The quotations that follow are from de Stavelot, *Chronique*, 473; *Chroniken der deutschen Städte*, xiv, *Cöln*, iii. 183; and Pius II, *Orationes*, iii. 197.

that 'she was so powerful . . . that the duke had to give free rein to all her wishes'. Like them, Pope Pius II exaggerated her influence when he stated that 'this woman soon applied herself to increasing her power and, exploiting her husband's indulgence, she began to take everything in hand, ruling the towns, organizing armies, levying taxes on provinces and ruling everything in an arbitrary fashion'. Nevertheless, the documents show that Isabel was involved in all these matters, and others besides, though always as an auxiliary of the duke. Posted at Dijon in July 1443, she helped to assemble the army for the conquest of Luxembourg, and when this task was accomplished she moved to Namur in October to organize finance for the payment of the troops in Luxembourg.[1] In 1440 she visited all the more important Flemish towns requesting an *aide*, or subsidy, from Flanders of £350,000. When internal unrest broke out in the Dutch towns in 1444, it was Isabel who was sent by her husband, then at Brussels, to pacify them. At Haarlem she suffered the indignity of having her baggage searched by the angry citizens, who thought that the unpopular ducal stadholder might be concealed therein. Pius II could have mentioned many other governmental activities in which Isabel was involved. She handled the diplomatic negotiations with England in 1439–40 and with France in 1445; she even supervised the rebuilding operations at the ducal palace in Bruges in 1448–52. Not content with all this, she pursued her own private advancement with persistence and skill. Thus, in the midst of the important Franco-Burgundian negotiations of spring and summer 1445, we find her engrossed in the private purchase of some Burgundian lands and castles which happened at that moment to be for sale. Nor did her retirement from court bring to an end her interest in the administration of her own affairs. In 1459 she summoned an official to bring to her residence of La Motte, in the forest of Nieppe, some extracts from the accounts of her territory of Chaussin in Burgundy. It would be nice to know more about this remarkable woman.

Besides the duke himself and his wife Isabel there was a third person who played an active and important, though subsidiary, rôle in the central government of the Burgundian state: the chancellor, Nicolas Rolin. This burgess of Autun in Burgundy held office from

---

[1] ADN B1978, fos. 104, 113b–114, etc. For what follows, see ADN B1969, f. 155; *Cronycke van Hollandt*, fos. 289b–290b; above, pp. 107–8 and 116–17; Zuylen van Nyevelt, *Episodes*, 271–3; Hillard, *Relations diplomatiques entre Charles VII et Philippe-le-Bon*, 416 (letter of Philip to Isabel, of 22 May 1445, in ACO B11906), and *IACOB* ii. 87.

near the start of Philip's reign until he was gradually eased out of power in 1457–9.[1] He died in 1462 aged eighty-two, having amassed a fortune in the service of the duke, part of which he used to found and endow the celebrated hospital at Beaune called the Hôtel Dieu. How much truth is there in Chastellain's remark, that 'all the most important affairs of state were in the hands' of the chancellor? He is even more explicit when he comes to mention Rolin's fall from power, which he dates to 1457.

> This chancellor . . . had been ruling everything single-handed, making all important decisions of war and peace, and those concerning finance. The duke entrusted everything to him . . . and there was no office nor benefice, in town or country in all his lands, nor gift, nor loan, which was not in his disposition.

In a letter written in December 1444 the mayor of Dijon says as much. He was on embassy to the ducal court with a request from Dijon, and he wrote to his municipal colleagues at home to report the progress of his mission. Expressing fear that they will not obtain what they want, since Nicolas Rolin opposes them, he continues, '. . . and it is he who does and decides everything, and through whose hands everything passes'.

As with the duchess, so with the chancellor, certain biased or ill-informed contemporaries give a misleading impression. In fact, documents show that Rolin was the head of the Burgundian civil service, not the prime minister, and that he received his instructions from the duke or, on occasion, the duchess. Only in exceptional circumstances, when neither was available, did he act on his own authority. For example, in June 1431, when Philip and Isabel were in Brussels, Nicolas Rolin, with the help of the ducal council at Dijon, drew up instructions for the Burgundian negotiators going to a conference at Montbéliard with the Austrians.[2] On occasions like this, when duke and chancellor were apart, the correspondence between them illumines their relationship. On 13 October 1432 the duke sent a messenger from Sluis to Nicolas Rolin in Burgundy with written instructions. He was to tell the chancellor to make what arrangements he could with Perrinet Gressart about the truce, and to carry out the instructions concerning the conference of Auxerre which the duke had already sent him. Philip himself would be coming to

---

[1] Régibeau, *Rôle politique des Croÿ*, 47–50. For what follows, see Chastellain, *Œuvres*, iii. 30 and 330, and *Correspondance de la mairie de Dijon*, i. 42–5.
[2] Plancher, iv. no. 78 and, for what follows, no. 104.

Burgundy at the end of the year. Meanwhile, the chancellor was to see that ducal vassals in Burgundy did not make private truces with the enemy. He was not to call out any troops, but he could have the bodyguard of twenty-four archers he had asked for. The duke adds further instructions about minor matters, on some of which the chancellor had written requesting his advice. It was the duke then, not his chancellor, who made decisions and was in full control of affairs.

What part exactly, in the Burgundian state, was played by the central ducal council, the *grand conseil* or *groote raade*? How far did this council meet the requirements of Hue de Lannoy, who submitted a memorandum to the duke in 1439 suggesting, among other things, that any prince who wanted to rule an orderly and just state must have 'a council of eight, ten or twelve notable persons', and that he must 'conduct his affairs with their advice'?[1] By these standards Philip's council was on the large side. Indeed, it increased in size, between 1433 and 1438, from thirteen to twenty-three. On the other hand, councillors were often absent; so much so that, in 1446, when an *ordonnance* was published which was formerly thought to have set up the great council, though it did nothing of the kind, it was found necessary to insist on a quorum of four or five. The great council was not merely an advisory body, it was also a law court which, among other things, received appeals from the different ducal territories. It normally met under the presidency of the chancellor, but it had its own chief, who presided when he was absent. Philip's council certainly was composed of 'notable persons': one or two prelates, half-a-dozen nobles and a handful of legists, financial experts and secretaries would normally be present. But what of its actual relationship to the duke? This was theoretically defined in the 1446 *ordonnance* as follows:

[The councillors] shall take advice among themselves on the conduct of affairs, and on important matters which arise concerning us and our subjects, and discuss appointments to offices. . . . They shall report to us

---

[1] G. de Lannoy, *Œuvres*, 299. On the great council, Brabant, *BCRH* (4) v (1878), 145–60 and (5) i (1891), 90–101, Frederichs, *BCRH* (4) xvii (1890), 423–99 and (5) ii (1892), 124–8, and Gaillard, *BCRH* (5) vi (1896), 267–324, have been superseded by Lameere, *Grand conseil*. See too *Algemene geschiedenis*, iii. 260–6 and Lambrecht, *BGN* xx (1965–6), 98–106. The 1446 *ordonnance*, quoted here, is printed in *Mémoires*, ii. 172–7, *Analectes historiques*, xvi, 141–7, G. de Lannoy, *Œuvres*, 432–9, and van Marle, *Hollande sous Philippe le Bon*, no. 40 (pp. cxvi–cxxi).

and inform us in detail about the matters they have debated, whenever the case requires it, so that we can act, give orders, and decide as we think fit. And we declare that from now on in these matters we shall neither do nor order anything which has not first been discussed and debated by our council and on which we have not had their advice.

We do, as a matter of fact, possess a great deal of evidence to show that Philip's council, besides being kept very busy in its administrative and legal capacities, was also frequently consulted by the duke on important matters. Of necessity this evidence is indirect, for the registers of the council, in which the clerk transcribed its minutes, have not survived. The historian of the Congress of Arras, Joycelyne Dickinson, has shown that Philip consulted his councillors 'at each important stage of the Congress'.[1] A year later, in 1436, when war with England seemed imminent, Jehan de Wavrin tells us that Philip held 'many councils on this business, in order to . . . come to a conclusion on how this matter could best be handled . . . and many opinions were put forward and carefully examined and debated'. In the end, we are told, the war party won the day and it was resolved to attack Calais. Jehan de Wavrin even gives the names of the councillors who advised war, and complains that, the decision once made, the pro-English councillors, of whom he was one, were excluded from subsequent council meetings.

The composition of the occasional councils of regency, which were set up to govern some or even all of Philip's territories in his absence, underlines the importance of the duchess as his second-in-command, as well as the rôle of his leading councillors.[2] At first, when he left the northern territories to visit Burgundy, only Flanders and Artois were involved. The Duchess Michelle governed them for Philip in 1421–2, and letters were issued in her name. In 1424–5, when the duke visited Burgundy again, he left the council of Flanders at Ghent virtually in charge of the government. As soon as he returned, they asked him to relieve them of these additional duties, which had made them fall considerably behindhand in their legal business. In the 1430s the capable Isabel was on hand to help look after Philip's affairs, and she not infrequently acted for him in his absence. In August 1440, when

[1] Dickinson, *Congress of Arras*, 54–7 and, for what follows, de Waurin, *Croniques*, iv. 127–31.
[2] Lameere, *Grand conseil*, 71–1 and 91–8 needs correcting and supplementing from the accounts of the receipt-general of all finances. See, too, AGR CC21800, fos. 19b, etc. and 47b (1424–5); ADN B1606, fos. 50–1 (1441–2); and *Les Croÿ, conseillers des ducs de Bourgogne*, no. 19 (1442).

he left Hesdin on a visit to Cologne, she temporarily took over the administration, authorizing payments, sending letters and so on; and she was appointed to govern the northern territories on her husband's behalf when he visited Burgundy in winter 1441–2. Later in 1442, when Isabel joined Philip in Burgundy, Anthoine de Croy and Jehan Chevrot, president of the great council, were appointed in her place. By 1454, when Philip was away altogether in Germany for several months, his son Charles was old enough to act for him, though a powerful and numerous group of councillors was appointed by his father to assist him.

It must not be supposed that the Order of the Golden Fleece played any part in the government of the Burgundian state, though the incautious reader of Jehan Lefévre's chronicle might easily think otherwise, especially when the author, who was the official herald of the Order, names four of the councillors appointed in 1433 to govern the northern territories in Duke Philip's absence, and observes that they were all Knights of the Golden Fleece.[1] The Order as such met but once a year, and its members could not normally influence affairs except as members of the great council. Of the twenty-nine councillors enumerated in the 1438 household *ordonnance*, only ten were also Knights of the Golden Fleece, though some of the most influential were among them. In general, it is true to say that many of the courtiers in closest touch with the duke were also Knights of the Golden Fleece; but this is by no means the same as attributing power, or even influence, in the affairs of state to the Order as such. It had none. The letter signed by the Knights of the Golden Fleece and sent to King Charles VII in June 1456, on the subject of the crusade, was exceptional as well as ineffectual.

The central government of the Burgundian state comprised duke, duchess, chancellor and council. The exact interrelationship between the parts is well illustrated in the accounts of the bailiff of Hainault, which describe that official's visit to court in August 1438 in interesting detail.[2]

To the said bailiff who, on Tuesday 19 August 1437, on receipt of letters-missive from the duke summoning him, left Ecaussinnes to see the duke at Brussels, taking with him Godefroy Chauwet and Simon

---

[1] Le Févre, *Chronique*, ii. 372–3. For what follows, compare Lameere, *Grand conseil*, 48 with the list in *La Toison d'Or, Bruges 1962*. For the letter to Charles VII, see Plancher, iv. 288.
[2] ADN B10403, fos. 137a–b.

Nockart. When they arrived there, my lord the chancellor told them that their advice was required concerning a ducal *aide* in Hainault, and that they should speak to my lady the duchess when she was free to see them. The duke was not available the next day or the day after, nor was the duchess. On the Friday and Saturday, the above-mentioned bailiff, Godefroy and Simon were received, and it was decided and ordered by my lord the duke and my lady, present the bishop of Tournai, my lord the chancellor and my lord of Santes, that the three Estates of Hainault should meet in Hal on Monday, 1 September following.

Another useful source of exact information about the working of the Burgundian government is the report of Wilhelm von Rötteln, Austrian ambassador to Brussels in 1447.[1] He first contacted Anthoine de Croy and the chancellor Nicolas Rolin, and they obtained for him an audience with Philip and Isabel, who listened to his propositions and invited him to expound them to the council. In the morning, Isabel sent for him and spoke privately to him, giving him the impression that she would handle everything herself. Next, Wilhelm explained his business to Philip's leading councillors: Anthoine de Croy, Jehan Chevrot, bishop of Tournai, Jehan de Neuchâtel, lord of Montagu, and Nicolas Rolin, who promised to pass his requests on to the duke. After a week's delay, caused by the arrival at court of the duchesses of Guelders and Cleves, the chancellor gave Wilhelm a formal reply to these requests, speaking on behalf of Philip and in the presence of both Philip and Isabel. Wilhelm had further private conversations after this, with both the duke and duchess, and from his account of these discussions it is clear that Philip had an excellent knowledge of the intricacies of imperial politics at this time, and that he was in full control of Burgundian foreign policy. Isabel played an important but subsidiary rôle; the chancellor was an auxiliary; the council merely advised.

The financial administration of the Burgundian state had always been more or less centralized.[2] It had to be, for the luxuries of court life, not to mention warfare and diplomacy, could only be paid for if an effective means existed for collecting revenues from the increasing number of different territories that made up the Burgundian state, and disbursing them at the centre. At first, Philip maintained the administrative system of his father in being. The 'treasurer and

[1] Chmel, *Geschichte Kaiser Friedrichs IV*, ii. 744–6.
[2] What follows is largely based on Proost, *De financiele hoofdambtenaren van de Burgondische hertogen*. See, too, Lameere, *Grand conseil*, especially 58–70 and 85–90; and *Algemene geschiedenis*, iii. 266–9.

governor-general of all finances' remained in ultimate control of the whole financial administration, being particularly concerned with the supervision of expenditure; while the receiver-general of all finances was the principal accounting officer. The *maître de la chambre aux deniers* continued to keep account of court expenses, and the various provincial and local receipts continued in existence as before. The financial reforms that followed were partly the result of the addition of new territories to the Burgundian state, and partly an attempt to save money. Some of them were experimental, or ephemeral, in nature. Between 1426 and 1431 the *maître de la chambre aux deniers* disappeared, but his place was taken by a *gouverneur de la despense ordinaire et extraordinaire*. At the same time the treasurer/governor and receiver-general of all finances were relieved of their posts, apparently to avoid the expense of their salaries. Their work was supposed to have been done by the council, but both of them re-appeared in 1429–31, and the office of receiver-general of all finances continued in existence thereafter for the rest of Philip's reign, though a *contrôleur* was appointed from 1440 onwards to verify and enroll his outgoings.

In 1433, by which time Holland, Hainault and Brabant, each with its own receipt, or financial administration, had been taken over by Philip the Good, important financial duties were specifically attributed to the council: every ducal financial *mandement* was to be signed by a *secretaire signant en finance* in the presence of three councillors in-cluding, if possible, the treasurer. In 1437 the council's rôle in the administration of finances was further defined and extended, for a committee of the great council, consisting of the chancellor, ten named councillors and the central financial officers, was given full supervisory powers over the entire financial administration. But this experiment in direct conciliar control, or supervision, of the Bur-gundian financial administration, was not continued through the 1440s. Instead, in 1447, abolishing the treasurer/governor-general and reducing severely the rôle of the council, Philip appointed three *commis sur le fait des finances* to take over their combined duties. And, in spite of an *ordonnance* of 1449 which appears to have reconstituted the financial committee of the council on the basis of five named councillors, the *commis*, their numbers increased to six in 1457, seem to have remained in effective control until the end of Philip the Good's reign.

In spite of changes and evident experimentation, the central financial administration during Philip the Good's reign seems to have been reasonably efficient. One important institution, not so far mentioned, was added to it. This was a sort of private fund, into which certain defined revenues were diverted from the provincial receipts. The *épargne*, as it was called, was located at court, and seems to have had a twofold aim: to provide the duke with a supply of ready cash against emergencies, and to act as a savings-bank or treasure-chest. It seems likely that the immense treasure which Duke Philip is reputed to have stored in his castle at Lille represented the proceeds of the *épargne* hoarded there over a period of years, for its surviving accounts exhibit consistent, and sometimes quite substantial, surpluses.

There is no reason to suppose that there was anything original about Philip the Good's *épargne*. It could well have been modelled on that of the duke of Brittany whose 'treasurer of our *épargne*' is mentioned in 1407.[1] The Burgundian *épargne* seems to have come into existence in 1430, for Hue de Boulogne, who was keeper of Philip's jewels from 1420 onwards, was appointed in that year to receive certain revenues from Burgundy, Artois and elsewhere, with which to purchase plate for the ducal court. By 1433 revenues from Flanders had been added to these, though Hue de Boulogne is not actually referred to as 'keeper of jewels and of the *épargne*' until 1445. The particular revenues to be paid into the *épargne* were further defined and extended in ducal *ordonnances* of 1446 and 1447: they were to include the emoluments of the seals of the central ducal chancery and of the chancery of Brabant, as well as the proceeds of legitimations, ennoblements, ducal pardons and the like. At first the receipts of the *épargne* were limited to Flanders, Artois, Picardy and Burgundy, with the exception of the proceeds of the chancery of Brabant; but in 1463 they were extended to include all Burgundian territories. The organization of the *épargne* was not unlike a miniature version of the Burgundian financial administration. At Dijon, at Lille, and at Brussels, regional 'receivers of the revenues of the *épargne*' collected and accounted for its receipts. These moneys, and these accounts, were

---

[1] *Lettres et mandements de Jean V*, i. cxi. For what follows, on the *épargne*, see Kauch, *RBPH* ix (1932), 703–19; Renoz, *Chancellerie de Brabant*, 107–8 and 212–14; and *IADNB* vii. 362. Surviving *épargne* accounts are, AGR CC25191 (receipt-general, 1466–7); AGR CC25177 (receipts of Brabant, 1459–67); and ACO B1707, 1738 and 1744 (receipts of Burgundy, 1447–67). Ducal *ordonnances* concerning the *épargne* are in the *Registres des chartes* at Lille, e.g. ADN B1606, fos. 151–3b (1447); 1608, fos. 99–100 (1463) etc., and in the *Registres de Brabant*, e.g. AGR CC17, fos. 235–6b (1459).

G

to some extent centralized by the receiver-general of the *épargne*, who was normally also its keeper, though for a time in the 1460s there were two central *épargne* officials, a keeper and a receiver-general.

From time to time the administrative history of the Burgundian state was marked by the activities of special reforming commissions.[1] One was set up, for example, in the duchy and county of Burgundy in 1422. The motive for these 'reformations', as they were called, was primarily financial but, in the process of raising money, attempts were also made to improve the general efficiency of the administration. The commissions of reformation set up in November 1457 with powers in the duchy and county of Burgundy and in Brabant, were followed by others, in June 1458, with powers over Philip's northern territories in general. The task of these commissions was to investigate and do away with embezzlement and other abuses of ducal officers and to try to improve the administration in every possible way. They were to work in conjunction with the six *commis*, or sovereign-governors of finance, appointed on 21 September 1457 to supervise the administration of the duke's finances and domains, who were empowered to dismiss incompetent officials and provided with two secretaries to enroll their letters and documents. This activity stirred up a good deal of opposition, notably in Brabant and Flanders, where the powers of the commission of reformation had to be reduced. But it did result in an important financial *ordonnance* of 6 February 1458, which overhauled the entire machinery of financial administration; and it seems likely that the *ordonnance* of 8 May 1459, laying down a uniform financial year for all Philip's territories, to begin on 1 October, was an indirect result of this reformation. This last was by no means a new idea: long before, John the Fearless had tried to establish a uniform financial year starting on 1 January.

No discussion of the working of central government in Philip the Good's Burgundy would be complete without mention of the secretaries, some of whom exercised considerable influence in the administration.[2] These officials, though paid a daily wage and intermittently

---

[1] For what follows, see especially Bartier, *Hommage au Professeur P. Bonenfant*, 501–11 and Proost, *De financiele hoofdambtenaren van de Burgondische hertogen*, 106–9, and AGR CC133, fos. 45–51b, 74b–76, 93a–94, etc. For the 'reformations' of 1422 and 1435 in the two Burgundies, see below, p. 188.

[2] See Cockshaw, *Les secrétaires de Philippe-le-Bon*. The secretaries attached to the central government, who were maintained at court, must be carefully distinguished from those belonging to the chancery of Brabant (Renoz, *Chancellerie de Brabant*, 41–87) and to other regional or provincial administrations.

THE GOVERNMENT AT WORK 177

in receipt of gifts, received no annual salary. Attached to the court and, in particular, to the chancery, their primary responsibility was to draw up and sign the documents issued by the chancery in the name of the duke. But they were also employed on all kinds of ducal business. Inevitably they accompanied courtiers on foreign embassies, doubtless with the task of drawing up a report on the proceedings. Unlike the personnel of the great council and the central financial administration, which tended to be predominantly Burgundian, the secretaries were drawn in roughly equal numbers from Philip's northern and southern territories. But they were nearly all of them French-speaking; after all, the language of the Burgundian court, council and central administration was French.

In Burgundy, as in other medieval states, diplomacy was an intermittent, though important, activity, which was centrally organized and dependent on the court for its personnel. It made considerable inroads on the ducal finances, and served a multitude of purposes, from finding wives for the duke and making alliances and treaties, to obtaining information and advice.[1] Burgundian embassies usually consisted of a small group of ducal councillors and officials, seldom numbering more than a dozen people in all. The leading members of each embassy, to the number of two or three, were almost always councillors, and very often members of the great council; and they were accompanied by a secretary, sometimes a herald or pursuivant, and attendants. While some councillors were never sent on embassies, others, like Guillebert de Lannoy and Pierre de Bauffremont, were sent over and over again. There was some specialization. Early in the reign, Hue de Lannoy was the normal Burgundian ambassador to England; later, Jehan, lord of Croy, was invariably sent by Philip to Charles VII of France. Ambassadors were normally furnished with instructions drawn up in writing by the duke at a meeting of his council. They were handsomely paid, at a rate of four to eight francs per day, and we sometimes hear of funds being transferred to them at their destination. For example, on 25 July 1445, the clerk of the receiver-general of all finances was sent by Duchess Isabel from Mons to Bruges, to arrange with a merchant there for the payment to the ducal ambassadors then in London of the sum of 500 nobles.[2]

---

[1] For what follows, I have used Hillard, *Relations diplomatiques entre Charles VII et Philippe-le-Bon*, 205–73, and the accounts of the receipt-general of all finances, section *Ambassades*.

[2] ADN B1938, f. 121b. For what follows, see Stein, *BEC* xcviii (1937), 287–90 and ADN B2008, fos. 111–13.

A few of Philip the Good's officials were employed so frequently on diplomatic missions that they can almost be described as professional ambassadors. Anthoine Haneron, a cleric who began life as a university teacher at Louvain, was such a one. He was kept particularly busy, for example, in 1450. On 15 May he set out from Brussels on horseback with four attendants, sent by Philip to attend an assembly of French clergy in Chartres. Back on 26 June, he was off again three days later, this time to the city of Münster, where the death of Bishop Heinrich von Mörs on 2 June had precipitated a succession-struggle between rival candidates and their supporters. He returned to Philip at his 'castle and mansion' of Genappe on 21 July, and set off again, from Mons in Hainault, to see the bishop of Liège about the marriage of his niece. By the time he had accomplished this mission, still with four companions, all mounted, the duke was at Arras in Artois, where Anthoine arrived on 5 September. Finally, it was from Hesdin that he was sent off, on 21 September, to see the French royal ambassadors at Abbeville and Chancellor Nicolas Rolin at Antwerp; a trip which took him just over three weeks.

What was it like to go on embassy for Duke Philip of Burgundy? Fortunately, what seems to be the official report has survived on the important embassy which was sent to Portugal in 1428 to secure a third wife for the duke. This particular embassy travelled further, and lasted longer, than most; and its members had time and opportunity to indulge in some private tourism, during a period of enforced waiting.[1]

In the year 1428 the most noble, most high, and most powerful prince my lord Philip, duke of Burgundy, who had successively married two most noble ladies of exalted lineage, the first, Lady Michelle, daughter of the most christian, most excellent and most powerful prince King Charles VI of France; the second, Lady Bonne of Artois, both of whom had died leaving my lord the duke without issue, counselled and advised by courageous and loyal men, was moved by devout and commendable purpose to re-marry, in the hope that, with God's grace, he might have an heir to succeed to his important and noble lordships. So my said lord of Burgundy resolved to negotiate the marriage of himself and the most high and noble Lady Elizabeth,[2] infanta of the

[1] Text in *Collection de documents inédits*, ii. 63–91 and Weale, *Hubert and John van Eyck*, lv-lxxii; summarized by van Puyvelde in *VVATL* (1940), 20–6. Compare the chronicler's account of a Burgundian embassy to Scotland, above, pp. 111–12.
[2] But in Burgundy she was always known as Isabel.

most excellent, powerful and victorious prince King John of Portugal ...,
and, to do this, he sent his noble legation and embassy to Portugal. He
placed at its head his noble knight and loyal and intimate servant, Sir
Jehan, lord of Roubaix and Herzeele, councillor and first chamberlain,
and, with him, his loyal servants Sir Baudouin de Lannoy, called le
Beghe, knight, lord of Molenbaix and governor of Lille; Andrieu de
Toulongeon, squire and lord of Mornay, also his councillors and
chamberlains; and Master Gille d'Escornaix doctor of Canon Law and
provost of Harelbeke, likewise his councillor. . . . To these ambassadors
he gave his relevant instructions, letters, procuration and powers and . . .
the governor-general of his finances, Guy Guilbaut, gave them sufficient
finance for a large and honourable expenditure, to be under the care of
a gentleman named Baudouin d'Oignies, squire, who was appointed
steward of their expenses, with a clerk to make the payments.

These ambassadors and those of their company, which included
numerous gentlemen and others, thus furnished and provided, after
taking leave of my lord of Burgundy set out for Sluis in Flanders for the
start of their journey. They embarked in two Venetian galleys then
lying in the port and departed on 19 October 1428, arriving next day, 20
October, at the port of Sandwich in England. There they disembarked
and remained, waiting for two other Venetian galleys then at London,
until 13 November following, when they set out in these galleys. They
were driven by gales into various English ports, first the port of Camber,
second Plymouth, third Falmouth, where they arrived on 25 November
and left on 2 December. Sailing through the Bay of Biscay so as to
arrive and disembark on 11 December at Bayonne in Galicia, they left
there on the fourteenth of that month and on the sixteenth reached a
place called Cascais, six leagues from Lisbon in Portugal, where they
arrived on 18 December.

At that time the king of Portugal was in a town of his called Estremoz,
three or four days' journey from Lisbon, with his children, including
my lady the infanta above-mentioned, and a large gathering of lords,
knights, squires, ladies, and people of all estates, at a celebration which
was about to begin for the reception of Madam Leonor, infanta of
Aragon, wife of my lord the infante Duarte, eldest son of the said king
of Portugal. So the ambassadors immediately sent Flanders King-of-Arms
to the king of Portugal with letters explaining their arrival and its
cause. . . .

When the king of Portugal received the ambassadors' letters, he wrote
and invited them to come to see him and, as soon as they were able to
provide themselves with horses, they set out towards him. But, when
they were only three or four leagues from the place where he was, he
wrote asking them to delay their arrival till further notice, since he
wanted to have his children, who had recently departed, with him. So
they waited at a place called Reols until 12 January [1429], when the

king sent for them. On that day, the ambassadors left Reols and arrived at a town called Aviz, where the king was, being honourably met by some princes of the royal house and other gentlemen and notables in number, who gave them a magnificent and joyous reception.

Next morning, 13 January, after mass, the king sent for the ambassadors, who presented him with letters from my lord of Burgundy and made the customary reverences and salutations. The king received them kindly and joyfully and agreed to hear their credentials after dinner that day; at which time the said ambassadors appeared before the king in his council chamber in the presence of Dom Pedro, Dom Henry and Dom Fernando, his children, the count of Barcilas and other notables. The main reason why my lord [the duke] of Burgundy had sent them was then notably expounded, in Latin, by Master Gille d'Escornaix. This done, the king made known to them, in Latin, through a doctor, his councillor, that he was well pleased with their arrival and that he would take advice on what they had said and expounded on behalf of my lord of Burgundy and would then reply. At this point, the ambassadors withdrew to their lodgings.

On the same day, towards vespers, the king sent word to them that, since he was very busy and could not therefore easily attend to their business in person, he had asked my lord Duarte and his other sons to act for him in this matter. On the next day and the days following the affair was further discussed with them or some of them, and in conclusion, a document was drawn up in writing. At the same time, the ambassadors arranged for a *valet de chambre* of my lord of Burgundy named Jan van Eyck, who was an exquisite master of the art of painting, to paint my lady the infanta Elizabeth from life; and they also diligently informed themselves in various places through various people of the reputation, bearing, and health of that lady. . . . This done, on about 12 February [1429], the said ambassadors sent four messengers to my lord of Burgundy, two by sea and two by land. That is to say, by sea, Pierre de Vaudrey, squire and cup-bearer of my lord [the duke], and a pursuivant of arms called Renty and, by land, Jehan de Baissy, squire, and another pursuivant of arms called Portejoie. They wrote to my lord of Burgundy by each of these messengers explaining what had happened and what had so far been done concerning the marriage. They also sent to him the portrait of the said lady, painted as mentioned above.

While they were waiting to hear from my lord [the duke] of Burgundy in reply, some of the ambassadors, that is to say the lord of Roubaix, Sir Baudouin de Lannoy and Andrieu de Toulongeon, together with the above mentioned Baudouin d'Oignies, Albert, bastard of Bavaria . . . and other gentlemen and familiars, travelled to Santiago de Compostela in Galicia, and thence went to see the duke of Arjona, the king of Castile, the king of Granada and several other lords, countries and places. At the end of May following they returned from this tour and arrived at Lisbon just in time to see the magnificent first entry and joyous reception of my lady Leonor, wife of the infante Duarte, eldest son [of the king]. She was seated, side-saddle, on a richly adorned mule covered in cloth-of-gold, led by two of the brothers of the infante on foot, one on each side. . . . Above her, a large piece of cloth-of-gold, supported on poles carried by princes of the blood royal and others of the most notable knights and lords of the kingdom of Portugal, on foot, served as a canopy. My lords the brothers of the said lady had been waiting some time in the fields. As soon as they saw her they dismounted and, bowing, kissed her hand according to the custom of the country. Many well-mounted knights and squires also rode to meet her, together with the burgesses and notable merchants of Lisbon. The Jews and Saracens of the said place came separately, dressed in their own way, singing and dancing as was their custom. Thus was the lady led through the town to the infante's palace, with great joy and solemnity. There were many trumpets, musicians, and players of organs, harps and other instruments and the town was hung and decorated in many places with tapestries and other cloths and with branches of may.

On 4 June following the ambassadors . . . went to Cintra, five leagues from Lisbon, to see the king of Portugal who had summoned them to visit him in the very pleasant palace he was staying in there. Towards vespers, while they were in their lodgings, the above-mentioned Pierre de Vaudrey, who had gone back to my lord of Burgundy by sea, arrived at Cintra with letters and news from the duke. The ambassadors went to announce this to the king and to my lady the infanta his daughter, who were very glad; and there was much rejoicing at court in the arrival of the said Pierre and the good news he brought. After this, the ambassadors, knowing the duke's intentions, went ahead and negotiated the marriage-treaty with the king and some of his children. It was agreed to and concluded at Cintra on 11 June, and the contract was witnessed by a notary at Lisbon on 24 July 1429. The Sunday after this, at seven in the morning of 25 July in the royal palace at Lisbon, at the request of the king and his children, the lord of Roubaix, in the name of and acting as proctor for my lord of Burgundy, and having from him sufficient power and procuration, took and received my lady the infanta Elizabeth as wife and spouse of my lord of Burgundy, present the king, my lord Duarte, his eldest son, Dom Henry, Dom João and Dom Fernando, his children . . . and a large number of people of all estates. From this time on the ambassadors did their best to expedite the journey of my lady to Flanders, where the king was in honour bound, by the terms of the treaty, to transport her at his expense and deliver her to my lord of Burgundy. According to the promise of the king and my lord the infante his eldest son, my lady's departure would take place before the end of September, except if prevented by contrary winds, or by the death or illness of herself or the king.

When the date of her departure was approaching, my lord the infante Duarte, eldest son, organized festivities and a banquet for her and the king his father. On Monday 26 September and the two following days jousts and entertainments took place and a supper was given at Lisbon in the Hall of Galleys, which was cleared for the occasion and hung with tapestries high on the walls, with variously-coloured woollen cloths below them. The two rows of pillars in this hall were decorated likewise, and the floor was strewn with green rushes. Tables, magnificently adorned and covered with fine linen, were set up as follows. The king's, at the far end of the hall and taking up most of its width, was on a wooden dais several steps high. The king's place, in the centre of the table, was six inches higher than the rest and a canopy of cloth-of-gold was stretched over it. In front of this table, against a pillar, there was a platform for the Kings-of-Arms and heralds; at the other end, near the entrance to the hall, was another for trumpets and musicians. The other tables were arranged in three rows, down the centre of the hall and along either side. There were six sideboards richly decorated and loaded with gold and silver-gilt plate of various kinds, and the hall was so well lit with torches and candles that one could see very clearly everywhere. . . .

When it was time for supper the king seated himself in his place as above described with my lady the infanta Elizabeth his daughter on his right and the wives of the infantes Dom Pedro and Dom João on his left. My lady the wife of the infante Duarte, eldest son, since she was well-advanced in pregnancy and near delivery, was not seated at table, but watched the festivities from a well-decorated gallery high up on the right. The king caused the lord of Roubaix, leader of the embassy, to sit at the right-hand end of his table, and the other ambassadors were seated at a neighbouring table on the right. . . .

At this supper, which lasted a long time, certain entertainments took place which they call challenges. They happen like this. Knights and gentlemen, fully armed and equipped for jousting, enter on horseback accompanied as they please and approach the table where the lord or lady giving the feast is seated. Without dismounting, the knight bows and presents to his host a letter or piece of paper, fixed to a stick split at the end, in which it is stated that he is a knight or gentleman with such and such a name, which he had chosen, and that he comes from some strange land, such as 'the deserts of India', 'terrestrial paradise', 'the sea', or 'the land', to seek adventures. Because he has heard about this magnificent feast, he has come to court, and he now declares that he is ready to receive anyone present who wishes to perform a deed of arms with him. When the letter has been read out and the thing discussed, the host causes a herald to say to the gentleman, who is awaiting a reply in front of the table: 'Knight, or lord, you shall be delivered.' Then, bowing again as before, he leaves, armed and mounted as before. One came all covered in spines, both he and his horse, like a porcupine. Another came accompanied by the Seven Planets, each nicely portrayed according to its special characteristics. Several others came elegantly dressed and disguised, each as he chose. . . .

Next day, 27 September, after dinner, there was jousting in the Rua Nova in Lisbon, which was spread with a great deal of sand. There was a fence of stakes fixed into the ground at intervals, to joust along,[1] which was hung with blue and vermilion woollen cloths. Some of the jousters came with their horses adorned with cloth-of-gold, embroidered and fur-lined; others were decked out in cloth embroidered with silver, or silk cloth . . . and they jousted magnificently in front of the king and the lords and ladies who watched them from the windows of houses along the street. On the next day, 28 September, likewise, solemn and impressive jousts were held there.

On Thursday, 29th and penultimate day of the month, which was the day planned by the king for the embarkation of my lady the infanta Elizabeth on her journey to Flanders, he led her in the morning on horseback from his palace to the cathedral church of Lisbon . . . with the ambassadors and many lords, knights, gentlemen and others . . . , where mass was sung and divine service solemnly and magnificently accomplished. After which the king brought his daughter back to his palace. . . . He had planned to take her on board ship and dine there, but the weather was so bad, and the water so rough, that this could not be done. The next day, last day of September, after dinner, when the weather was better, the king, accompanied by all his children, their wives, the ambassadors and many lords, knights, squires, ladies and others, led my lady his daughter to the ship which he had got ready for her passage in the port of Lisbon. There she stayed, waiting for the other ships, and their crews, that were going with her, to be got ready, until Saturday, 8 October following. During this time she was frequently visited by her father the king, and by my lords her brothers and others.

On the said Saturday, 8 October, my lady, with her brother the infante Dom Fernando, the count of Orin her nephew, and several knights, squires, ladies and others of her company, to the number of 2,000 persons or thereabouts, in fourteen large ships well fitted-out, armed and provisioned, left Lisbon around vespers and moved some distance from where they had been berthed. The next day, they moved on to a place called Restel, where they remained until the Thursday following, 13 October, on which day she and her company arrived off Cascais around vespers. There they anchored and waited a little; but they weighed anchor that same day and left to continue their voyage, sailing a good way, night and day, till the Saturday 15 October, when

---

[1] The contestants galloped at one another along either side of a partition erected down the centre of the street, which prevented them from crashing into one another.

contrary winds forced them to return, and they arrived again off Cascais, anchoring there until Monday 17 October. They then departed and set sail, and continued on their way until once more, because of adverse winds, my lady had to abandon her voyage, and she entered the port of Vivero in Galicia on Saturday 22 October with only four sail of the fourteen she had set out with. Of the others, nothing was known for a long time, except for one of them, which made the port of Vivero four or five days later. My lady left this port on Sunday 6 November, but had to put into the port of Ribadeo, also in Galicia, on 9 November.

Now it happened that the lord of Roubaix, who had been ill for some days in my lady's ship, was so enfeebled and sick that he had to disembark at Ribadeo. There, my lady had him transferred to one of two Florentine galleys, en route for Flanders, which had arrived by chance.... He boarded this galley at Ribadeo on 25 November, together with Baudouin d'Oignies and some of his people, while others of his people, with others of the ambassadors, stayed in my lady's ship. And the five ships which they now had left Ribadeo on 25 November in company with the two galleys, sailing together through the Bay of Biscay until 28 November when, late in the night, the galleys mistakenly parted company from [my lady's] ships and hove to near Lizard[1] Point at the extremity of England, in grave danger of shipwreck and drowning. My lady, with her ships, went on her way and reached Plymouth in England on 29 November. The galleys left their anchorage near Lizard Point on 1 December and arrived at the port of Sluis in Flanders on 6 December. The lord of Roubaix disembarked and at once let my lord of Burgundy have news of my lady his bride, of whom my lord of Roubaix had made enquiries en route and ascertained that she and her company were safe and sound at Plymouth.... By the grace of God my lady and her company arrived safely at the port of Sluis on Christmas Day [1429], at about midday.

The fact that Burgundian ambassadors were almost invariably councillors is not without significance. One of their functions was to inform the duke; but sometimes they were also required to offer advice. Hue de Lannoy's numerous memoranda were mostly concerned with advising the duke on military, financial and administrative matters. Another ducal ambassador-councillor, the ecclesiastic Quentin Menart, wrote to Philip on 5 November 1433 advising him to get in touch with the Emperor Sigismund as soon as possible, to prevent him allying with Charles VII.[2] Indeed, it was almost cer-

[1] The printed versions have Caisart in error for Laisart of the MS., AGR CC132, f. 162.
[2] Plancher, iv. no. 111. For what follows, see Stouff, *Contribution à l'histoire de la Bourgogne au concile de Bâle*, 113–22.

tainly Quentin Menart who sent to Philip from the Council of Basel, where he was one of the ducal ambassadors in 1433, a regular programme of suggested diplomatic activity. Sigismund, 'who is much influenced by flattery', should be approached with a view to discovering his intentions. Was he planning an alliance with the duke of Burgundy's enemy, Charles VII? A stronger embassy should be sent to Basel, furnished with adequate funds for the distribution of gifts: the Council must be won over to the Burgundian interest. Moreover, if possible, alliances should be made with the duke of Milan and with the archbishops of Mainz, Cologne and Trier. The writer concludes by protesting that he would never have dared to offer this advice had he not been requested to do so.

The collection of information was by no means entrusted only to ambassadors. Philip the Good's administration employed spies, though not perhaps regularly enough, or in sufficient number, for us to talk of a Burgundian secret service. In the winter of 1425–6 several 'messengers' were sent on secret trips to England, from Bruges, 'to try to obtain information about the army which the duke of Gloucester is said to be assembling to attack my lord the duke in his land of Holland'.[1] Nor was Philip's government averse to using women as spies. In August 1421 four women were sent to Le Crotoy and Noyelles 'to find out about the duke's enemies there'. We hear, too, in the accounts, of counterespionage. In 1437 the executioner at Arras was called on to burn at the stake 'a woman called Maroye la Bourgoise, spy, who had contracted with the English to give them information concerning the fortifications and guard of Hesdin' and other places; and in 1441–2 an apostate friar who had been sent by the French to obtain details of Philip's military strength, was arrested at Chalon. The ultimate fate of another friar, the renegade Franciscan Estienne Charlot, is unknown. From his interrogation at Dijon in April 1424 it transpired that he had been captured after hurting himself badly when he tried to effect a nocturnal escape from a castle where he was staying. Hearing that he was about to be arrested, he tied his bed-clothes together and descended from his window; but his improvised rope broke, precipitating him into the moat. No torture was needed for him to confess that he had made several trips to the dauphin to inform him of matters of military importance, such as the whereabouts of the governor of Burgundy; the dispositions of the ducal garrisons in Burgundy; and the morale of the inhabitants.

[1] De Laborde, *Ducs de Bourgogne*, i. 228–9. For what follows, see *IADNB* iv. 108 and 139; *IACOB* ii. 10; and Lavirotte, *MAD* (2) ii (1852–3), 147–66.

Estienne had also been in touch with an ex-mistress of Charles VI, Odette de Champdivers, then living in retirement at Dijon, but she had resisted his efforts to turn her into a French spy.

In the distribution of news, or propaganda, the Burgundian government seems to have been active and skilful. Ducal messengers, each sporting a badge on his chest with the ducal arms,[1] were despatched in all directions whenever an important event occurred to ensure that an official Burgundian version of what happened was at once available. A week after Joan of Arc's capture at Compiègne by the Burgundians on 23 May 1430, ducal letters describing what happened were being circulated to Leiden, Delft, Dordrecht, Zevenbergen, Amsterdam and throughout Friesland. On 29 May 1437 mounted messengers were off to Cologne, Liège, Maastricht, Aachen, Frankfurt, Luxembourg, Basel and elsewhere, to distribute the official account of the revolt of Bruges a week before. When the duke of Lorraine received from Philip a letter describing the Burgundian victory over the English at Brouwershaven, he passed a copy on to the *chambre des comptes* at Dijon. He need not have troubled; they had already received one from the duke. Not that there was anything original about this Burgundian news service. Every fifteenth-century government did this sort of thing. Later, Louix XI turned it into a fine art.

The Burgundian state was put together from a number of different territories which, though by no means quite separate before the Valois dukes united them, for the most part possessed their own distinct governmental institutions. No conscious attempt was made by Philip the Good to centralize these various local or regional administrations but in the course of time they began to interlock to some extent one with another. Thus the two Burgundies tended to be ruled as a single unit, and Flanders and Artois were administratively closely linked. Each of these local administrations was directly dependent on the duke, his chancellor and the great council, and abundant documentary evidence survives to show that important affairs were often delayed while this central government was consulted. Yet the regional administrations were also perfectly capable of conducting their own affairs, and they carried out the routine business of administration, justice and finance without reference to the duke. These regional institutions, all of which were ultimately based on

[1] ADN B1931, f. 113. For what follows, see Jongkees, *Staat en Kerk in Holland en Zeeland*, 263 n. 2; AGR CC2410, f. 57b; and ACO B11942, nos. 48 and 49.

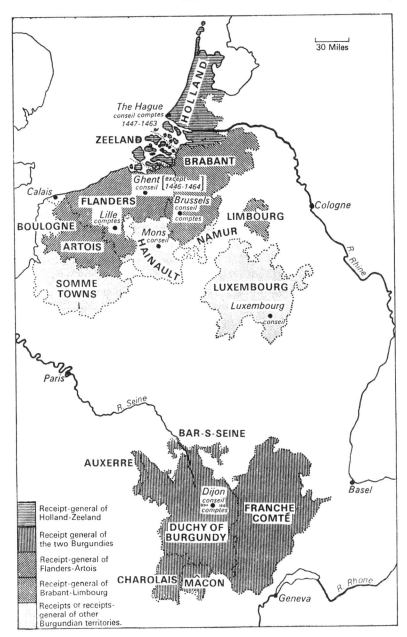

3. Administrative map of Burgundy, c. 1450

French models, were similar to each other in several important respects, and it was this essential uniformity, in the regional institutions of the Burgundian state which, above all, conferred political viability on it. The council and *comptes* at Dijon were duplicated by the Flemish council and *comptes* at Ghent and Lille respectively; by the Dutch council and *rekenkamer* at The Hague; by the council and *comptes* at Brussels. The governor of Luxembourg, the bailiff of Hainault, the stadholder of Holland, were dissimilar chiefly in name; while territories which had been longer in Burgundian hands, the Burgundies, Flanders, Brabant, were alike in doing without such an officer.

In the administrative history of the two Burgundies, the reign of Philip the Good presents a remarkable contrast to that of John the Fearless. No more radical reforming schemes were set on foot; few or no significant changes were made in existing institutions. True, the series of ducal *ordonnances* applying to both duchy and county continued; but even the most important of them, such as that of 1439 reforming judicial procedure and the administrative *ordonnance* of 1447, were conservative in nature. The only significant reform resulting from ducal initiative was the division in 1422 of one of the two county bailiwicks, that of Aval, into two parts, to be called Aval and Dole. Subsequently, the seat of the former was fixed at Poligny. The so-called 'reformations', which consisted of groups of ducal officials appointed in 1422 and 1435, ostensibly to investigate abuses in the administration of justice, were really only devices for raising funds. Throughout the long reign of Philip the Good the *chambres du conseil et des comptes* continued to act together at Dijon in much the same way as they had done before, and with much the same powers; though the importance of the *comptes* was somewhat diminished at the beginning of the reign, when the auditing of the central accounts of the Burgundian state, that is, those of the receiver-general of all finances and the *maître de la chambre aux deniers*, was transferred to their colleagues at Lille. Apart from this, the procedure, competence and general activity of the *comptes* remained unaltered. It enjoyed an astonishing degree of continuity in its personnel. Three of Philip the Bold's clerks there, who were promoted to the ranks of the *maîtres* in John the Fearless's reign, continued at work till around 1440. When one of them, Jehan Bonost, retired in 1443, he had been employed in the *chambre* continuously for fifty-five years, and had served as a *maître* for thirty-five. The *chambre des comptes* at Dijon continued right through Philip's reign in close contact with, and even in partial dependence on, the Paris *chambre*. In 1438 the Dijon *maîtres* resolved to cease working on Saturdays after dinner. Their excuse? The Paris *maîtres* did not do so. And in 1441 the Dijon *maîtres* submitted a query to, or sought advice from, the Paris *maîtres*, one of whom was the ex-Burgundian receiver-general of all finances, Robert de Bailleux. Like the *comptes*, the council at Dijon suffered no significant change in Philip's reign, for the *ordonnance* of 1422 purporting to set it up cannot be taken any more seriously than the 1446 *ordonnance* purporting to establish a central Burgundian council. In fact the 1422 *ordonnance*, far from introducing anything new, seems not even to have modified or extended the council's judicial competence.[1]

Although the council and *comptes* at Dijon, under their president, were perfectly capable of looking after the administration of the two Burgundies, a single person with wide powers and responsibilities, particularly in military affairs, normally acted as its head in the early part of Philip's reign. The dowager-duchess, Margaret of Bavaria, fulfilled this rôle till her death in 1424; the chancellor Nicolas Rolin, native of Autun, took it upon himself whenever he was in the duchy; otherwise, it was entrusted to a governor, or governor and captain-general, who, from 1425 on, was also the marshal. But the office of governor disappeared after 1440, and we can only assume that it was essentially a wartime post, abolished as soon as peace was more or less restored in Philip's southern territories. The defence of the duchy and county had been taken in hand by Margaret of Bavaria in the *ordonnance* of 26 July 1421, which made provision for the appointment of captains and garrisons, the organization of watches, and the demolition of undefended castles. Later, in 1427, two inspectors were appointed to see that the duke's own castles were properly defended. In 1426, and on other occasions, a special assembly of nobles was convened by the governor in the face of threatened hostilities. But, as in administration and justice, so in defence, no startling novelties or sweeping changes were made by Philip the Good.

The administration of Flanders also was characterized in Philip the Good's reign by the absence of significant reform, but a certain amount of makeshift modification did take place. There was no single official in control, for the sovereign bailiff's powers remained

---

[1] On this paragraph see *Ordonnances des ducs* and *Ordonnances franc-comtoises;* Andt, *Chambre des comptes*; Hozotte, *PTSEC* (1934), 71–81; Lot and Fawtier, *Histoire des institutions françaises*, i. 209–47; and ACO B15 and 16. On the next, see Richard, *MSHDB* xix (1957) 101–12 and xxii (1961), 125–33; and Plancher, iv. nos. 12 and 64.

strictly limited. An unsuccessful attempt was made in 1427, by certain ducal financial officials at Lille, with the support of the Four Members of Flanders, to revive the ancient office of chancellor of Flanders, which was traditionally assigned to the provost of St. Donatian's at Bruges. It seems that what was envisaged, or plotted, was Nicolas Rolin's dismissal and the appointment in his place of the ducal councillor Raoul le Maire, then provost of St. Donatian's.[1] As a matter of fact, in the early years of the reign and nearly until his death in 1433, the ex-chancellor Jehan de Thoisy, bishop of Tournai, was *de facto* head of the Flemish administration. The *chambre des comptes* at Lille continued much the same as before, with wide powers over the finances and domain. An *ordonnance* of 1429 reduced and limited the number of *maîtres* there to four. The financial administration of Flanders suffered one important, though temporary, change, in 1426, when the single receipt-general of Flanders and Artois was split into two. But the greater part of the separate receipt-general of Artois thus formed, which included Boulogne, Péronne, Montdidier and Roye, was apparently reunited with the receipt-general of Flanders not many years afterwards.

The council of Flanders was primarily a judicial institution. Its councillors claimed in 1433 that 'they had no commission from my lord [the duke] concerning the government of his land [of Flanders], but they were solely appointed to [administer] the sovereign justice of the land'.[2] They were a self-important and determined group of men. In November 1419 they warned three absentee members of their council, two of them nobles, that if they did not attend within eight days they would report them to the duke. In September 1420 they wrote to Simon de Fourmelles advising him to make up his mind whether or not he wished to continue as their president, and to let the duke know. In 1433 they sent word to the receiver-general of Flanders that, in spite of assurances and promises, they were experiencing great difficulty in getting their wages paid. They had decided that, if

[1] Bartier, *Légistes et gens de finances*, 54 and 433–4. For what follows, see *IAGRCC* i. 80–4; ADN B1603, fos. 89b–90a; and ADN B1961, f. 14, 1963, f. 16, 1966, f. 24, etc. For the Flemish bailiffs see van Rompaey, *Het grafelijk baljuwsambt in Vlaanderen*.

[2] AGR CC21806, f. 10b. For what follows, see AGR CC21797, fos. 35a–b and 38b, 21798, f. 26, 21806, f. 12, and ADN B1969, f. 141. See too *IAGRCC* iii. 379–81 (*ordonnance* of 4 June 1463); A. Matthieu, *AAAB* xxxv (1879), 207–26 and 436–8; Vandenpeereboom, *Le conseil de Flandre à Ypres*; *Geschiedenis van Vlaanderen*, iii. 243–6; Lot and Fawtier, *Histoire des institutions françaises*, i. 343–426 and Buntinx, *APAE* i (1950), 55–76.

6. Anthony, Grand Bastard of Burgundy

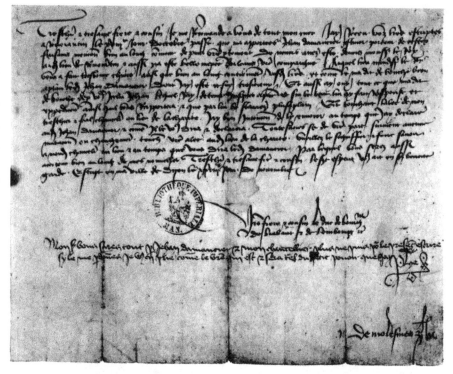

7. Letter of Philip the Good to Charles, duke of Orleans,
with autograph postscript.
Bibliothèque Nationale, ms.fr.5041, f.18.

they did not obtain immediate satisfaction, they would 'adjourn all the cases in progress in the council and cease to attend it'. One of their number, Master Jehan de Culsbrouc, provost of St. Pharahild's, Ghent, when ordered by the duke on 30 December 1419 to attend a diplomatic conference at Calais with the English, wrote protesting that he had no suitable clothes for the trip and knew nothing about the negotiations anyhow. Whether they liked it or not, these men were shifted from one place to another in Philip's reign, just as their predecessors had been under John the Fearless. It is not clear why they were moved temporarily to Courtrai at the end of 1439, but in July of that year the magistrates of Courtrai were negotiating with Philip in the hopes of effecting the transfer of the council to their town. It was back in Ghent in 1440, but was transferred temporarily to Termonde in 1446. In the years that followed, though the council was officially at Termonde, some of the councillors remained at Ghent till 1451, when, shortly before the outbreak of the Ghent war, the council was moved once more, this time to Ypres. It remained there until its return to Ghent in 1464. It was reorganized in 1463 by a ducal *ordonnance* which once again emphasized its function as a law court by referring to it as 'set up and established for the exercise, direction and conduct of the justice of our land and county of Flanders'.

Long before Philip the Good became duke of Brabant in 1430 the duchy had acquired institutions modelled on those of Burgundy and Flanders: a council and a *chambre des comptes*. But, unlike those territories, it retained a real chancery and chancellor of its own. The history of the council of Brabant is somewhat complex. Philip the Good put the finishing touches to a process that had begun around 1420, with the emergence of a *chambre du conseil* on the lines of those already existing at Dijon and Ghent. But the nobles of Brabant were strong enough to force on their weak or youthful rulers a council of government, and Philip found himself obliged, in 1430, to perpetuate this institution, as part of the price of obtaining the duchy, alongside the *chambre du conseil*, which he likewise kept in being. Thus we find his first chancellor of Brabant, Jehan Bont, presiding over a judicial-type council of legists, several of them ex-councillors of Duke John IV, which was instituted by Philip late in 1430. Alongside it, he appointed a commission of *heren van de regiment*, that is, a regency council of nobles to rule the duchy in his absence. But even before the end of 1430 it was clear that the *chambre du conseil* was destined to replace the council of government. The *chambre du conseil* was minutely organized in an *ordonnance* of 29 December 1430. While its councillors were paid a handsome annual salary, the members of the council of government received no regular remuneration; and from December 1430 onwards all official documents were issued by the *chambre du conseil*, not by the council of government. Small wonder that the latter disappeared entirely within a year or two. Henceforth there was a single council of Brabant: the *chambre du conseil*, which, primarily a law court, was closely modelled on the council of Flanders. It was presided over by the chancellor of Brabant.[1]

Little need be said of the Brussels *chambre des comptes* or *reken-kamer*, which had been set up by Duke Anthony in 1404. It was the subject of a number of *ordonnances* in the early part of the reign which fixed the wages of its *maîtres* and clerks, regulated its accounting procedures, and even exempted provisions destined for its staff from tolls. It experienced only one significant change when, in 1463, its jurisdiction was extended to include the county of Holland and the duchy of Luxembourg. Throughout Philip's reign it was closely linked to the rest of the financial administration and, especially, to the *comptes* at Lille. Indeed the two *chambres des comptes*, at Lille and Brussels, shared a single *premier maître* or *eerste meester* after 1436, in the person of Barthelemi a la Truye, who had begun his career at Lille in 1411 and been transferred to Brussels, as a *maître*, in 1430. Thus, continuity was maintained, and administrative practices were standardized.

It must not be thought that the duchy of Brabant was administered by the chancellor, council and *comptes* alone. In response to a ducal enquiry of 1451, seeking means of administrative economy, the *comptes* at Brussels submitted a full list of administrative personnel in the duchy and advised the duke on possible economies.[2] From this it emerges that the principal financial officer in Brabant was the receiver- or rentmaster-general. A staff of eight secretaries, one of whom was too old to work, was employed in drafting and issuing official documents, and the judicial officers comprised the *drossart*, seneschal, bailiffs, *amman* of Brussels and others. The council had its *greffier*; the *comptes* its *auditeur*; the secretaries their *audiencier*; and

[1] For this paragraph, see Gaillard, *Le conseil de Brabant*, i., Renoz, *Chancellerie de Brabant*, and Uyttebrouck, *RBPH* xxxvi (1958), 1135–72. The documents instituting Philip the Good's Brabant councils are in AGR CC132, fos. 11b–12 and 15 ff. For what follows, see especially *IAGRCC* i. 84–5, 93–6 and 97–105; Kauch, *BSAB* (1945), 15–22; and AGR CC132 and CC133 and the accounts of the Brabant receipt-general, AGR CC2409, etc.
[2] AGR CC17, fos. 1–80.

there were the *maîtres des œuvres*, ushers, caretakers, sergeants and so on. The *maîtres des comptes* pointed out that, though there were now seven salaried councillors, during the first ten years of Philip's ducal reign in Brabant there had only been four. They suggested that the number could well be reduced, but they did not presume to advise similar treatment for themselves, then four in number.

The influence of French culture and French institutions was already well marked in Holland before that county, and the closely linked county of Zeeland, succumbed to the expansionist ambitions of a French dynasty in the person of Philip the Good. The changes that he introduced in the pattern of government were hardly sweeping, though they were somewhat more radical in Holland–Zeeland than elsewhere.[1] Since he was bound to be a largely absentee ruler, Philip appointed a personal representative, the governor or stadholder. Stadholders had existed before this, under Count William VI, but the office was transformed, after 1432, from a temporary delegation of power, by the ruler to his lieutenant, to a permanent office which, in Philip's reign, was filled in unbroken succession except for the years 1445–8, when the experiment of a president of the council was tried. Philip the Good's first and most celebrated stadholder was Hue de Lannoy, lord of Santes, who held the post with distinction, though against his own wishes, between 1433 and 1440. In the half-century before Philip became count of Holland, a council had evolved on the lines of those of Flanders and elsewhere. Instead of a chancellor, a treasurer had emerged as the head of the comital administration, the presence of which had turned The Hague into the capital city of Holland. During Philip's reign the council, which comprised ten councillors in 1454 together with a recently acquired *procureur general* and registrar, developed a strongly collegiate nature. It continued to sit at The Hague and exercise extensive judicial and administrative powers, but the treasurer disappeared, transformed into a receiver-general, or *rentmeester-generaal*, on the Burgundian pattern.

Although the prestige and authority of the council of Holland remained high throughout Philip's reign, its control over the financial

[1] For what follows, see especially Jansma, *Raad- en Rekenkamer in Holland* and in *Algemene geschiedenis der Nederlanden*, iii. 313–33 and *TG* xlix (1934), 444–53 and li (1936), 401–19. See too, van Marle, *Hollande sous Philippe el Bon*; Blok, *NGWG* (1908), 608–36, and Meilink, *BVGO* (7) v (1935), 129–52 and (7) vi (1935), 49–66. See too, on the transference of the *rekenkamer* to Brussels in 1463, AGR CC133, fos. 155–6b.

administration had been abolished in 1432, when the title of treasurer disappeared. For more than a decade, from 1432 onwards, the accounts of the receiver-general of Holland and other Dutch accounts were audited by the indefatigable Barthelemi a la Truye with one or two assistants from the Lille or Brussels *comptes*. Thus the financial administration of Holland was brought thoroughly into line with that of Philip's other territories. Soon after Barthelemi's death in 1446 a *chambre des comptes* or *rekenkamer* was installed at The Hague, and from then on until 1463 the twin institutions of *raadkamer* and *rekenkamer* functioned there, just as they did in Brussels and, under the name of *conseil* and *comptes*, at Dijon. But in the summer of 1462 the *rekenkamer* at The Hague was abolished and its powers and duties transferred to the *rekenkamer* of Brabant at Brussels. The exact motive for this change remains obscure. Probably it was either concerned with economies, in part perhaps demanded by the Dutch Estates, or connected with the appointment of Charles, count of Charolais, as regent of Holland in 1462. The first is made probable by the fact that the size of the council at The Hague was severely pruned at the same time; the evidence for the second lies in the fact that Charles was thought by many, and accused by some, of attempting to supplant his ageing father as ruler of Holland. On this view, the *rekenkamer* would have been removed to Brussels to place some, at least, of the Dutch financial administration out of his control.[1] Whatever the reason for the abolition of the separate *rekenkamer* at The Hague, we may be sure that it had nothing to do with the so-called centralization which some historians have detected in Philip the Good's reign.

Force of circumstance had led to the evolution in Hainault of more or less autonomous governmental organs, for the counts of Holland had naturally tended to leave that county to its own devices. Philip the Good made few changes of significance to the existing institutions, which were settled at Mons by the fifteenth century. The sovereign court of justice there continued to function, providing, through fines, the financial resources for the administration of Hainault. These revenues came from murderers, men and women convicted of a dissolute way of life, thieves, kidnappers, abductors of widows and people who had insulted the duke or his officers. Other categories of offenders were added as the result of legislation: here is an example typical of the age.

[1] See below, p. 345.

Philip, by the grace of God duke of Burgundy, of Lotharingia, of Brabant, and of Limbourg; count of Flanders, of Artois, of Burgundy palatine; count of Namur, marquis of the Holy Empire, lord of Salins and of Malines, guardian, regent, governor and heir of the land and county of Hainault, to our grand bailiff of Hainault and to all the other bailiffs and judicial officers of the county and land of Hainault or their lieutenants, greetings.

For some time we have been told by our people, and we have actually noticed, that certain nobles and others in Hainault are giving liveries and causing them to be worn as often as they please, and to people other than their own officers, familiars, domestics and relatives; and they have been receiving gifts and other tokens of friendship in return. They have [also] been accepting unqualified persons, not their own people, and in greater numbers than permitted, to join their fraternities of crossbow-men or archers. Because of, and under cover of, these liveries, as well as otherwise, various musters of associates have taken place, bound together by oaths or alliances, from which all kind of trouble has arisen and will arise. . . . What is worse, some of these fellows, relying on the help of those whose liveries they wear, without any reasonable excuse, go around the land of Hainault flaunting hauberks, basinets, helmets, daggers, bodkins, swords, lances, spears, maces, mallets, falcon's beaks, axes and other prohibited and unnecessary armaments. . . .

Because of this, wishing always to keep our subjects in good justice, peace and union one with another, and to maintain our lordship and rights for the profit and advantage of the land of Hainault and of our subjects, we have decided and ordained and we do decide and ordain by these presents . . . , that from now on no one in the land and county of Hainault, of whatsoever condition or estate, shall make any kind of gift of livery, for confraternities or otherwise, and that no one shall wear liveries or accept them from any lord or other person, except for genuine relatives, officers, familiars and domestics; on pain of a fine of £10 each time they are apprehended.

Item, no one shall organize assemblies in the guise of dedications or weddings or otherwise, nor raise the cry of a lord of a town, on pain of a fine of £10 for the organizer of the assembly and 60s each for the participants.

Item, in future no one is to carry arms, that is to say: large knives, maces, leaded truncheons or other murderous and unnecessary weapons; offenders to be fined 60s and have their weapons confiscated. . . .

Given in our town of Ghent, on 13 March in the year of grace 1431, under our secret seal in the absence of the great seal.

At Mons, in Hainault, the council functioned on just the same lines as the other regional councils in Philip's territories, acting as a law court and controlling the administration. Its president, and the effective head of the administration, was the 'captain-general and bailiff of Hainault', who was also called the *grand bailli de Hainaut*. From 1434 until 1463 Jehan de Croy, lord of Chimay, and his son Philippe de Croy, lord of Sempy, succeeded one another in this office, and their accounts show that they were both actively engaged at Mons, on the minutiae of local administration, when not employed elsewhere by the duke in wars or embassies. These accounts were at first audited at Mons but from about 1435 on they were submitted to the *chambre des comptes* at Lille. The integration of Hainault into the rest of the Burgundian financial administration was completed by the appointment of a receiver-general. Finally, Hainault kept its own archives, which were under the care of a *garde des chartes*, in just the same way as every other territory; for there were muniments at Dijon, Poligny, Luxembourg, Lille, Brussels and The Hague, as well as at Mons.[1]

Although historians have been more interested in the history of the acquisition of Luxembourg by Philip the Good in 1443, than in the details of how it was governed after then, enough is known for us to be sure that its administrative institutions needed little or no change to bring them into line with those of Philip's other territories.[2] The government of the duchy was entrusted to a single lieutenant and captain-general, or governor, as he was variously called, with wide powers and the princely salary of 1,000 Rhenish florins *per annum*. Philip's bastard son Cornille was succeeded in this post on his death in 1452 by Anthoine, lord of Renty and of Croy, brother of the grand bailiff of Hainault. The governor of Luxembourg was assisted by a typically Burgundian council, fixed at Luxembourg, with a *greffier* or registrar, a president after 1452 and a *procureur general* in 1461. This council was 'appointed for the administration of justice and the affairs of the duchy of Luxembourg'. Inevitably, Luxembourg was provided with a receiver-general. His accounts were at first audited by a *maître des comptes* from Lille until, in and after 1462, they were sent for this purpose to Brussels. Thus, in almost every respect, Luxembourg followed the pattern of Hainault and the other Burgundian territories. In all of them, similar institutions had evolved, and Philip the Good completed a natural process which everywhere favoured administra-

[1] Richard, *BEC* cv (1944), 123–69. For this paragraph I have used the accounts of Hainault, ADN B10390–10431; *Cartulaire des comtes de Hainaut*, iv and v (the extract is from v. 137–9); Bruwier, *MA* liv (1948), 133–59; Gondry, *MPSALH* (4) x (1888), 1–9 and 96–111; and Pinchart, *Conseil souverain de Hainaut*.

[2] For what follows, see the accounts of the receipt-general of Luxembourg, AGR CC2630–2631 and N. van Werveke, *PSHIL* xl (1889), 253–92.

tive uniformity. The element of cohesion, or administrative integration, in Philip the Good's Burgundian state, was provided, not by centralization, but by this repetition everywhere of the same administrative patterns, and the standardization of administrative practices which went with it. Only in the sphere of jurisdiction is there real evidence of centralization under Philip the Good, for an effort was certainly made to extend the judicial powers of the regional councils at the expense of local jurisdictions, and to extend the appellate jurisdiction of the *grand conseil* over the regional councils.[1] But even here, progress was limited, and it is not until the next reign that words like 'reform' and 'centralization' take on significance. Meanwhile, it is as well to remember that the Valois duke who ruled for three times as long as any other made fewer governmental innovations than any other. His central chancellor, his great council, his financial administration, and almost all the regional institutions just reviewed, were already in existence when he became duke. The founder of the Burgundian state was Philip the Bold, not Philip the Good.

Within the constituent territories of the Burgundian state representative institutions abounded. Some of these Estates, like those of Charolais and Namur,[2] were local institutions of little significance, others, like the Four Members of Flanders, were influential and important. In general, the Estates of the more southerly territories were the least powerful in political terms. But, even in Holland and Flanders, where representative institutions were most powerful, their rôle was administrative and financial, rather than political, and they were able to wield effective political power only in crises. Normally, they were summoned to vote taxes, to discuss monetary matters or, especially in the northern territories, to deal with commercial affairs of all kinds.

Little is known of the Estates of the county of Burgundy in Philip's reign, beyond the fact that they voted taxes, or *aides*, at irregular but frequent intervals, that they consisted of two orders only, clergy and towns, and that they were usually convoked by the marshal or Dijon council. Before Philip's reign, the Estates of each of the two county bailiwicks had normally met separately; from about 1420 onwards

[1] Lambrecht, *BGN* xx (1965–6), 83–109.
[2] Laroche, *MSHDB* vi (1939), 145–94 and Brouwers, *Les aides dans le comté de Namur*, xi–xiv. For the Estates in Philip's northern territories see Lousse and others, *Assemblées d'États*, which contains articles on the Estates of Brabant (Lousse), Flanders (Prevenier), Hainault (Piérard), Luxembourg (Petit) and Limbourg (van Hommerich).

they usually met in a single assembly.[1] More influential, though still limited to a mainly passive rôle, were the Estates of the duchy of Burgundy, which met about twice a year throughout Philip's reign to vote an annual average sum, in *aides*, of £21,000 of Tours in the years before 1436, and about £10,000 after then. Exceptionally, they raised objections to the ducal demands for finance: in 1448 they only voted 5,000 francs instead of the 12,000 requested by the duke for the purchase of Châteauvillain. Exceptionally, as in 1435, they granted money only on conditions. More frequently, especially towards the end of the reign but still only occasionally, they submitted complaints and sent embassies to the duke. In 1428 they discussed in vain a plan to send him a deputation 'to beg and request him to be pleased to consider getting married, so that he could have an heir'. In 1431 they actually succeeded in obtaining the temporary abolition of the ducal *chambre du conseil* at Dijon, after sending an embassy to Philip to complain of its activities. But the councillors apparently refused to disband themselves and, the required *aide* once voted, Philip revoked his *ordonnance* and formally reinstated them. In 1459 the Estates established their own archive repository, in a chest in the church of Notre Dame, Dijon. Their reforming zeal or political ambition perhaps reached its peak in 1460, when they presented to Philip a whole series of grievances and suggestions. But, while points were conceded here and there by the duke, in general the influence of the Estates was confined to administrative matters of little importance. In essence, the Estates of the duchy of Burgundy were merely a mechanism for raising taxes.

Moving northwards, from Burgundy, the next territory is Luxembourg. Here, the Estates were less of an administrative instrument, and perhaps wielded more political power than in Burgundy. They did not meet frequently to vote taxes; they met occasionally to be wooed by rival claimants to the ducal throne and, very occasionally, to vote taxes. They played an important, and political, rôle in the complex process of negotiation and war which led eventually to the incorporation of Luxembourg into the Burgundian state. They were convoked, consulted, and cajoled in 1442–3, by Philip and Elizabeth of Görlitz on the one hand, and by the duke of Saxony's councillors

---

[1] Raffalli, *MAB* clxxii (1947–57), 380–93 adds nothing to Clerc, *États-généraux en Franche-Comté*, i. 77–128 and Prost, *PTSEC* (1905), 115–22, on the Estates of the county. For what follows on the duchy, see Billioud, *États de Bourgogne*, a comment on the 1448 assembly by Lewis, in *Past and Present* xxiii (1962), 23–4, and Richard, *APAE* xxxv (1966), 299–324.

on the other. After Philip the Good's military conquest in 1443, the Estates were called on to give his usurpation the stamp of legality and, on more than one occasion, to confirm their acceptance of him as ruler. In the case of Luxembourg in particular, not too much significance need be attached to the representative aspect of the Estates: in 1451, for example, they comprised deputies from thirteen towns, five abbots and some sixty nobles.[1] In character, therefore, they were essentially an assembly of nobles, quite different from the Estates of some of Philip's northern territories, which were dominated by urban representatives.

One of the more southerly of Philip the Good's northern territories was Artois, with its capital of Arras, where the Estates almost invariably met in the fifteenth century. Artois was similar in its representative institutions to Burgundy, though its Estates met more frequently, for they were convened on some 150 occasions during Philip the Good's forty-eight-year reign.[2] Their tax-voting functions were at times interrupted by consultations on monetary or other administrative affairs, and occasionally they were courageous enough to send a deputation to Philip seeking truces, a reduction of the vote, or merely expressing their impoverishment. They did at times vote less than the sum required, or adopt delaying tactics in the face of reiterated ducal demands. On occasions, too, they attached strings to their vote: they would contribute to Duke Philip's projected crusade only if he led it in person. In spite of their opposition, towards the end of the reign they found themselves in the position of voting an *aide* for more than a single year at a time, but, though this happened in 1451, when they voted an annual *aide* for three years, they managed to avoid it during the rest of Philip the Good's reign, though they were asked in 1462 for two *aides* each year for the next ten years.

The Estates of Hainault were not greatly different from those of Artois, but they succumbed more easily to Philip the Good's pressure for the vote of an *aide* over a period of years. This explains why they met a good deal less frequently after 1450. They voted a six-year *aide* in 1451, one for five years in 1457 and a ten-year *aide* in 1462. In their case, unlike that of Artois, where the *aide* had long been established as a fixed sum of £14,000 of Tours, voted annually, the

[1] *ICL* iv. 316–19. See too, on this paragraph, Richter, *Der Luxemburger Erbfolgestreit* and N. van Werveke *Definitive Erwerbung*, and the documents in *Table chronologique des chartes de Luxembourg* and *Choix de documents luxembourgeois*.

[2] On this paragraph, see Hirschauer, *États d'Artois*.

amount had always varied considerably, and had never been annual. The Estates of Hainault took part in the complex politics which accompanied the struggle for possession of that county between Philip, Jacqueline of Bavaria and Humphrey, duke of Gloucester, and Margaret of Hainault, in the years before 1433. But, the crisis once passed, they relapsed into relative insignificance, though they have been rescued from obscurity in modern times by the publication of a protestation they addressed to the duke in 1450. In this curious document they describe in a tone of colourful hyperbole the frightful destruction to their country caused by men-at-arms quartered in it, and ask the duke for redress.[1] But the poverty and destruction thus caused did not deter them from voting a substantial subsidy later that year.

In the duchy of Brabant the Estates, at least from 1436, normally voted *aides* in the form of a single large sum to be paid over a six-year period. The assemblies which resulted in these votes were not attended by the clergy, which made its own separate contribution. In 1451 the *aide* was only granted in return for a written guarantee of no further demands during the six-year period and a promise to limit the number of ducal officers in Brabant. In 1459 an *aide* was made conditional on the duke's withdrawal of his reforming commission, or 'reformation', from the duchy. But these little bargains were a far cry from the state of affairs before 1430, when internal crises had from time to time bestowed significant political power on the Estates of Brabant. Now, they existed to serve the administrative and financial convenience of a powerful ruler, though they did maintain virtual control of the coinage of the duchy.[2]

In the county of Flanders two representative institutions existed side by side, the Estates and the so-called Four Members. But the Estates were really only the Four Members reinforced, as it were, with a handful of nobles and perhaps some clergy, and they met so seldom that they can only be regarded as insignificant. On the other hand, *parlementen* or assemblies of the Four Members (Ghent, Bruges, Ypres and the Franc of Bruges) met frequently, voted taxes on behalf of the whole county, and wielded a measure of political power, even though, in Philip the Good's reign, they were consider-

[1] Matthieu, *BSBB* i (2) (1909), 38–45. See, on this paragraph, *IAEH* ii. lxxxii–xci and Arnould, *Dénombrements de foyers dans Hainaut.*
[2] For this paragraph, see Cuvelier, *Les dénombrements en Brabant* and *IAGRCC* iii. 3–5. For what follows see, on the period up to 1427, Stabel-Stasino, *Standenvertegenwoordiging in Vlaanderen.*

ably less influential than they had been under his two predecessors.[1] Among medieval representative institutions, the *parlementen* of the Four Members were quite exceptional in their frequency. In the first eight years of Philip's reign, 280 *parlementen* were held, that is, three each month. Matters discussed ranged from *aides* requested by the duke to requests by the Four Members that the duke should reside in Flanders. They included the defence of the land, disputes between different Members, disputes with Hansards, Spaniards and other groups of foreign merchants, the coinage and monetary policy and many other economic and administrative matters. In contrast to the Burgundian Estates, which discussed but did not implement a plan of petitioning the duke to marry, the Four Members sent a firm request to this effect in 1428.[2]

But, though in many respects they were the most active and influential of the Burgundian Estates, the Four Members had one serious weakness. They were divided among themselves: Bruges against the Franc of Bruges; Bruges against Ghent; Bruges and Ghent against Ypres. These internal divisions were due to civic particularism and commercial rivalry; they even extended on occasions to open warfare, as for instance between Bruges and the Franc of Bruges, headed by Sluis, towards the end of 1436. This internal tension, coupled with the fact that, under Philip the Good, Flanders was only one among several ducal territories in the Low Countries, prevented the Four Members from continuing to exercise that political influence which they had developed under Philip the Bold and John the Fearless. Moreover, it should be borne in mind that it was the ruling merchant oligarchies of Ghent and Bruges that were represented in the *parlementen* of the Four Members. The Flemish troubles in Philip the Good's reign, including the Ghent war, were in essence social disturbances, and the urban oligarchs were able to involve the duke, in these internal struggles, as their ally. In this respect there was no profound divergence of interest between the duke and many members of the *parlementen*: they fought on the same side against the unrepresented but politically or socially ambitious artisan populace of the Flemish cities.

Although the Estates of Zeeland have been admirably studied by Lemmink, the history of those of Holland remains to be written. In each county there were normally two orders only, nobles and towns, and the Estates of both assembled together when matters of general

[1] Vaughan, *Philip the Bold*, 177 and *John the Fearless*, 163, 169, etc.
[2] See above, p. 55.

interest were under consideration. Their functions comprised the voting of taxes and the discussion of administrative and monetary affairs, but they were also consulted on a wide range of economic and commercial problems, including some which might now be described as 'foreign policy'. On 10 March 1437, for example, they were convened at The Hague by the stadholder and asked in the strongest possible terms to make war on the English, or at least to prepare to defend themselves against a possible English attack.[1] They refused. Later that year they took part in discussions which led to the publication of an *ordonnance* regulating the price, and forbidding the export, of corn. During the war between Holland and the Wendish towns of the Hanse, the Estates helped in the organization of convoys and fleets, and their deputies took part in the peace negotiations. In 1441 the Estates of Holland and Zeeland signed a treaty between Holland and Castile, together with the king of Castile, the duke of Burgundy, and the council of Holland at The Hague; and in 1462 they forced the duke to promulgate a series of administrative and judicial reforms in Holland, mostly affecting the council. In spite of all this activity and influence, the Dutch Estates had long lost the right to vote taxes every year. Instead they voted an *aide* to be paid over a period of six or ten years, and the same was true of Zeeland. On the whole, however, the Estates of Holland and Zeeland were more powerful than the Estates of Philip the Good's southern territories; they certainly intervened in a far wider range of governmental activities.

It would be foolish here to enter the lists in the quarrel over the date of the first meeting of the States General of the Burgundian Netherlands. Though the Acts concerning this body have been printed from 1427 onwards, its origins can be traced earlier.[2] For example, to meetings of representatives of the towns of Brabant and Flanders at Malines in 1424, and to an assembly of the Estates of

[1] The full text of Hue de Lannoy's speech is in van Marle, *Hollande sous Philippe de Bòn*, no. 9 (pp. x–xiv) and B. de Lannoy, *Hugues de Lannoy*, 246–9. For this paragraph see Lemmink, *De Staten van Zeeland, Boergoensche Charters*, and, on Dutch finances, Blok, *BVGO* (3) iii (1886), 36–130, summarized by Terdenge, *VSW* xviii (1925), 95–167.

[2] *Actes des États généraux*; Meilink, *BGN* v (1950), 198–212; Van den Nieuwenhuizen, *TG* lxxii (1959), 245–50; Van de Kieft, *500 Jaren Staten-Generaal in de Nederlanden*, 1–27; and Gilissen, *APAE*, xxxiii (1965), 268–74. See too, on the Burgundian States General, Heimpel, *Festschrift Gerhard Ritter*, 155–60, Helbig, *RV* xxix (1964), 56–8, and Blockmans, *APAE* xlvii (1968), 57–112. For the next sentence see ADN B4095, f. 110 ff. and ADN B1931, fos. 67a and 70b.

Brabant, Holland and Zeeland in 1425. On the other hand, most recent writers have preferred to withhold the title of States General from all assemblies prior to that held at Bruges in January 1464. Be this as it may, there were at least twenty assemblies of representatives of more than one of Philip's territories in the Netherlands between 1427 and 1464, and the incompleteness of some of these was not due to the duke, for on at least two occasions particular Estates refused a ducal summons to attend a 'general assembly' of his lands.[1] Naturally, the evolution of the States General was a slow and complex process. There was no such thing as a first meeting.

What was the purpose of the States General in Philip the Good's reign? It was called into being, in gradual stages, by a ruler who found it convenient to consult representatives from several of his territories at once. That is, when matters arose which affected the Estates of several territories, he summoned them together. An early example was the attempt in 1433 to enforce an embargo on the import of English textiles throughout the Burgundian Netherlands,[2] and it has been shown that the unification of the coinage of these territories after 1433 made further meetings of the States General an urgent necessity: the meetings held between 1437 and 1461 were summoned primarily for the purpose of dealing with monetary problems. Other matters soon arose which could most conveniently be dealt with in this way: in 1463–4, the arrangements to be made for the government of Burgundy in the duke's absence on crusade; and in 1465 the request for a special tax or *aide* to finance the coming war in France. Like every other medieval parliament, the Burgundian States General exploited internal crises to enhance its own prestige. For example, in the winter of 1463–4 it took the initiative in reconciling Philip with his son Charles. An important limitation to the influence and status of the States General was the absence of representatives from the two Burgundies. Nor, it seems, was there any prospect of a comparable institution for the southern territories, for in 1465, when an attempt was made to hold a joint assembly of duchy and county Estates, the representatives of the county insisted on a

---

[1] Hirschauer, *États d'Artois*, ii. 36 (Artois, 1462) and E. Matthieu, *BSBB* i (2) (1909), 41 (Hainault, 1449).
[2] Van Marle, *Hollande sous Philippe le Bon*, no. 7 (pp. viii–ix); *Memorialen van het Hof*, no. 163; AGR CC21806, f. 17b; and Thielemans, *Bourgogne et Angleterre*, 60–1. For what follows, see Spufford, *APAE* xl (1966), 61–88 and references given there; on the composition of the Burgundian States General in 1464 see Blockmans, *APAE* xlvii (1968), 57–112.

quite separate meeting.[1] Nevertheless, by the end of Philip the Good's reign, a new and significant representative institution had evolved sufficiently to have begun to exercise a unifying influence over a large part of the Netherlands, including Artois and Picardy.

[1] Billioud, *États de Bourgogne*, 366.

CHAPTER SEVEN

Philip the Good and the Church

Burgundy had been put together in the first place by permission of the pope, for the marriage of Margaret of Male and Philip the Bold in 1369, which brought Flanders, Artois and the two Burgundies under a single ruler, was made possible only with a papal dispensation, issued by Urban V. Throughout the reign of Philip the Good a close alliance was carefully maintained between himself and successive popes, which was based on a system of mutual advantages. Philip obtained bishoprics and benefices for his councillors, his civil servants, his friends and his bastards of both sexes; while the popes in return welcomed first his support against the Council of Basel, and then his crusading enthusiasm. This papal alliance was also of political value to the duke of Burgundy, for example, in his struggle with Jacqueline of Bavaria for possession of the county of Holland. But the papacy was never subservient to him, and was sometimes even defiant. In 1459–60 Pius II insisted, against the wishes of Philip and his nephew John, duke of Cleves, that Soest and Xanten were under the jurisdiction of the archbishop of Cologne;[1] and at the same time he rejected Philip's request that his bastard son, Bishop David of Utrecht, become also bishop of Tournai. At the papal court in Rome a permanent Burgundian envoy, the *procureur de monseigneur le duc en cour de Rome*, was posted to further the interests of the duke, and he was aided by people in the entourage of the pope ranging from

[1] Hansen, *Westfalen und Rheinland*, i. 137–8. For the rest of the sentence, see BM Add. MS. 54156, fos. 363 and 365a–b (see below, p. 350 n. 2). For what follows, see de Laborde, *Ducs de Bourgogne*, i. 261; Nelis, *RBPH* x (1931), 599–600; ADN B1972, f. 83; and Hansen, *Westfalen und Rheinland*, i. no. 125 and ii. no. 385. For this chapter in general, Jongkees, *Staat en Kerk in Holland en Zeeland*, is indispensable; see too Frédéricq, *Rôle politique*, 97–109; Mazeran, *PTSEC* (1910), 147–51; Lenain, *RDT* (1953), 46–52; *Algemene geschiedenis der Nederlanden*, iii. 411–35; and de Moreau, *Église en Belgique*, iv.

cardinals to lesser officials, who either enjoyed the title of ducal councillor and were doubtless remunerated in some way, or who were relatives of the duke.

Right at the start of Philip the Good's reign an embassy from Martin V had visited him in October 1419 at Arras and, in November, the dowager duchess of Burgundy, Margaret of Bavaria, was in touch with the pope.[1] Though he was thought to have been displeased with the treaty of Troyes, and though he wrote in 1425 urging Philip to make peace in France, Martin V consistently supported Philip's territorial expansion in the Low Countries and his interventions in Utrecht. Furthermore, in 1424 and 1426 he issued dispensations for the marriages of Philip the Good and Bonne of Artois, and of Charles of Bourbon and Agnes of Burgundy. The relationship was by no means wholly one-sided. In 1422–3 a merchant of Lucca established at Bruges called Giovanni Arnolfini, later immortalized in paint by Jan van Eyck, supplied Philip with six tapestries figuring scenes from the life of the Virgin Mary, which were sent to Rome to the pope 'so that his holiness would maintain the duke in his favour, as well as his friends and servants and all his lands'.

When, in March 1431, Eugenius IV succeeded Martin V as pope, a sword of Damocles, in the shape of a general council of the Church, hung over him.[2] For the Council of Constance, before it had ended the schism in 1417 by causing Martin V to be elected pope, had passed the decree *Sacrosancta*, which proclaimed the superiority of a council over the pope and provided for its summons by the pope, or automatic meeting if he failed to do this, at regular intervals ever after. The first of these assemblies had been held by Martin at Pavia and Siena in 1423–4, and Philip had sent an envoy. Helped by a visitation of the plague and by the unwillingness of many northern prelates to travel so far, the pope had succeeded in dispersing the Council of Siena before it had time to do any damage to papal prestige. But another council was due to be convened in 1431, and it fell to Eugenius IV to summon it and, if possible, to circumvent and dismiss it expeditiously. Basel was the chosen venue and already in

[1] *Comptes généraux*, i. 484 and du Fresne de Beaucourt, *Charles VII*, i. 327 n. 4. For what follows, see du Fresne de Beaucourt, *Charles VII*, i. 330; Plancher, iv. nos. 38, 39, 43 and 52; and *IADNB* iv. 96.

[2] For what follows, see Valois, *Pape et concile* and Fliche and Martin, *Histoire de l'Église*, xiv and, on the Council of Basel, Toussaint, *BCRH* cvii (1942), 1–126 and *Relations diplomatiques*, with references. The two last must be used in conjunction with Jongkees, *TG* lviii (1943), 198–215. The rôle of Jehan Germain at Basel is analysed by Lacaze, *Jean Germain*.

March 1431 a solitary but enthusiastic Burgundian prelate had arrived there and, in a sermon in Basel cathedral, claimed that the Council ought to have already begun. Even when it was officially proclaimed open on 31 July, by a papal emissary, the abbot of Vézelay had only been joined by a handful of French clerics. Meanwhile, Eugenius IV had lost no time in cultivating the Burgundian alliance. He wrote to Philip recognizing him as legitimate ruler of his territories and promised to arbitrate the differences between him and Sigismund over his imperial lands in the Low Countries.[1] Nevertheless, Philip did nothing at first to interfere with the Council. Indeed he took steps to bring to an end the warfare which broke out in the neighbourhood of Basel in 1431 as a result of the duke of Austria's declaration of war against him. By the end of 1431 pope and Council were at loggerheads. In December, at the very moment when Eugenius published bulls dissolving the Council, the Fathers assembled at Basel loftily declared that they would not quit the place until they had restored peace to Christendom, extirpated heresy and reformed the Church. Still Philip did nothing, resisting throughout 1432 repeated requests from the Council for a deputation of senior Burgundian clerics to be sent to Basel.

It must not be imagined that the Burgundian policy of neutrality in the growing dispute between pope and Council was seriously altered by Philip's tardy despatch, early in 1433, of a Burgundian embassy to Basel, led by Bishop Jehan Germain, chancellor of the Order of the Golden Fleece, who had recently been promoted by Eugenius to the bishopric of Nevers. In his opening speech, on 16 March 1433, Jehan Germain spoke virtually in favour of the pope. He urged conciliation on the Council, and voiced his regrets, on behalf of the duke, that there should be any disputes between the head and members of the Church. This ducal policy of neutrality and arbitration continued during the ensuing years. Philip was not prepared to incur the hostility of a Council which was supported by most of Europe; nor was he willing to abandon an alliance with the pope which had proved invaluable in the past.

It can scarcely be said that the Burgundian ambassadors at Basel contributed to expediting the proceedings of the Council. As soon as they arrived they provoked a controversy over the seating arrangements of the delegates or, as the Germans have it more succinctly, a *Sitzstreit*. This quarrel over precedence threatened to undermine

[1] Plancher, iv. no. 96, Gachard, *Rapport sur Dijon*, 60-1, and Faussemagne *Apanage ducal*, 276.

H

the Council altogether and seriously delayed its deliberations. Philip's envoys insisted that their rightful place, on the wooden benches which had been specially erected for the Council in the nave of the cathedral, was immediately next to the royal ambassadors, and they appealed to the precedent of the Council of Constance. The ambassadors of the imperial electors were furious; they, too, appealed to Constance, and a great deal of time was spent in May 1433 interrogating the thirty-three prelates present at Basel who had been at Constance some eighteen years before about the seating arrangements then. Many could not remember exactly where the Burgundians had been seated, but a majority were sure that the ambassadors of the electors were below them.[1] However, the electoral ambassadors advanced other reasons for their priority over the Burgundians. They argued that just as the cardinals, because they elected the pope, were superior to all other prelates so the imperial electors, who elected the Emperor, ought to have precedence over all other princes, apart from kings. Jehan Germain held forth on 26 May 1433 in defence of Burgundian superiority. He pointed out that Duke Philip's ancestors included such rulers as Francus, the Trojan prince, Gundulph, the Burgundian king, Charles Martel, Pepin, Charlemagne and Louis the Pious. He was related to the royal dynasties of France, England, Castile, Portugal, Navarre and Cyprus, and his possessions comprised four duchies, fifteen counties, and numerous other territories and towns. Naturally, each side to this dispute threatened to leave the Council and go home if it was not given satisfaction.

The affair was in no sense settled by a provisional decision in June which gave the advantage to the Burgundians. In August, the duke of Savoy's ambassadors made out a case for their precedence. The Emperor Sigismund, whose anti-Burgundian policies were then gaining momentum, lent his whole-hearted support to the electoral delegates. Indeed he went so far, on Christmas Eve 1433, as to order the removal from the cathedral of the Burgundian ambassadors' stalls, observing angrily that the aim of the Council was peace and reform, not the inflation of the duke of Burgundy's ego. No wonder that the Christmas midnight mass was disturbed by Burgundian protests. The turmoil was such that the disputants had to be banned from attending divine service in the cathedral; and the situation was hardly improved by the arrival in March 1434, just a year after Jehan Germain and his colleagues had begun the quarrel, of the ambassadors of Duke John V

[1] Stouff, *Contribution à l'histoire de la Bourgogne au Concile de Bâle*, prints these depositions and other documents.

of Brittany. Not only were they forcefully told, on the very day of their arrival, that their duke was inferior to the duke of Burgundy, but their presence introduced Franco-Burgundian rivalries into the Council alongside the imperial anti-Burgundian sentiments which Sigismund had introduced there. The French protested vigorously when both Burgundian and Breton partisans, vying with each other for superiority, denied their duke's vassalage to the French crown.

A scheme to rearrange all the deputations on an equal basis met with an impassioned defence of royal prerogatives by a French ecclesiastic, and when Sigismund returned to Basel in May 1434 he again took up the electors' cause, accusing the duke of Burgundy of excessive ambition, and the Council of negligence in failing to seat the electors' deputies in the proper place. At last, in July 1434, a committee of arbitration, after hearing witnesses and taking depositions from all concerned, hit on an ingenious compromise. The electors' people were to be seated immediately below the imperial throne. On the right, the Burgundians were to sit next to the ambassadors of the king of Scotland; on the left, the Bretons were placed next to the king of Denmark's embassy. The quarrel was over. Or was it? The Bretons protested, and only accepted the settlement on receipt of a promise that they would be given a bull guaranteeing its provisional nature; the duke of Orleans's proctor demanded a written statement that the decision would in no way prejudice his master's rights in the matter; and the ambassadors of the kings of France, Cyprus, Scotland, Aragon, Sicily, Denmark and others beside insisted that the Burgundians would have to give way to delegates of their eldest sons.

Other matters besides the seating arrangements occupied the attention of the Council of Basel in the years 1433–5. The Hundred Years War had its repercussions there and the Fathers of the Church made a determined but unsuccessful effort to bring it to an end. They did have the satisfaction of seeing the Congress of Arras bring to fruition their repeated attempts at a Franco-Burgundian entente; and the treaty of Arras was celebrated at Basel with processions, solemn masses, and illuminations paid for jointly by the French and the Burgundians. Again, their mediatory influence was felt on Philip the Good's behalf in 1434–5, when Sigismund's hostility to him culminated in a declaration of war which threatened to involve Basel and its neighbourhood in fighting and plunder. But above all, in these years, the Fathers were involved in a protracted and complex struggle with the pope. Diplomatically, Eugenius IV was clumsy and intemperate; but he was stubborn; and he was consistently sustained throughout the dispute by Philip the Good, whose initial neutrality, as between pope and Council, soon developed into overt support for the pope.

Eugenius IV had officially dissolved the Council of Basel before the end of 1431, but the only effect of this papal onslaught was to increase the number of ecclesiastics assembled there and provoke their anger and ambition. In the spring of 1431 the Council formally resolved that it would not and could not be dissolved by the pope, since its power came directly from Jesus Christ, and on 29 April 1432 it cited Eugenius and the cardinals to appear before it within three months. If there was a lull in this papal-conciliar conflict after 1433, this was at least partly due to Philip the Good, who accredited a new and much larger embassy to Basel in September 1433. Its instructions, which were drawn up at Ravières 'by my lord the duke in his council', ran in part as follows:[1]

> They are to explain that, on 17 August last, news came to the duke of a session of the Council at which certain letters of the king our lord [Henry VI of England] were read out. Because [King Henry] had styled himself 'king of France', the archbishops of Bourges and of Tours impugned these letters on behalf of the dauphin their master . . . and said several things which amounted to reproaching the duke. The duke's ambassadors replied by declaring the truth of the matter and explaining that the duke was not to blame. But while they were doing this, or immediately afterwards, several persons cried out at the tops of their voices in an outrageous and insulting manner, 'Burgundian traitors!'; words which are extremely injurious and quite intolerable. . . . The duke is extremely annoyed at this and the ambassadors are to demand that reparation be made forthwith. . . .
>
> Item, as to the Council itself, they are to explain that the duke, as he previously affirmed, has been and is ready to support the Council in the business for which it was assembled: that is, the reform of the church, the extirpation of heresies and the pacification of christendom. But as regards the dispute between our holy father the pope and the Council, the duke has been and is very displeased about this and wishes to help appease it, fearing that if this is not done . . . a schism might be caused in the church, which is something to be feared and avoided for various reasons . . . which the speaker may advance as necessary.
>
> Item, the duke instructs his ambassadors, together with those of my lord of Savoy . . . and those of other princes who agree to join them, to try to persuade the Council . . . to adjourn or suspend its recent decree

---

[1] Stouff, *Contribution à l'histoire de la Bourgogne au concile de Bâle*, 97–107.

[against the pope] for three months. . . . If the Fathers of the Council refuse the ambassadors' request and do not accept this delay of three months, then the duke instructs his ambassadors to leave the Council. . . .

Item, concerning the place assigned by the Council to [the ambassadors of] my lord the duke, which has been in dispute, the ambassadors are to protest and defend the duke's rights to the place his ambassadors enjoyed at Constance. They are to explain that the arrangements so far made by the Council have wronged the duke more than the electors.

Whether or not Burgundian diplomacy at Basel was decisive in patching up the quarrel between pope and Council at the end of 1433, Eugenius expressed his gratitude to Philip by promising to promote Jehan Germain from Nevers to the more lucrative see of Chalon and by sending to Philip a host which had been pierced by a Jew and thereafter become miraculously blood-stained; it remained an object of devotion at Dijon until it was publicly burnt during the French Revolution. Eugenius also transferred Jehan d'Harcourt to Narbonne in 1436 so that Philip's councillor, Jehan Chevrot, could have the see of Tournai,[1] and ducal secretaries were promised ecclesiastical preferment at Utrecht and Chartres. Meanwhile, the Council supported anti-Burgundian candidates to disputed sees: at Trier, at Tournai, and at Utrecht. Council and pope drifted further apart. While the Council appointed a commission of enquiry to investigate the pope's infringements of its rights and decrees, and prided itself on having brought the heretical Hussite church back into the fold, Eugenius once more proclaimed its dissolution, and even summoned a council of his own, or anti-council, to meet at Ferrara, to discuss with Byzantine delegates the union of the Western and Eastern Churches. The standing of the Council of Basel began to decline; moderate elements left it. There were few secular princes who did not share Philip's fears of a schism in the Church, and the Council began to take on the character of a rump of frustrated radicals, especially after its suspension of Eugenius in January 1438.

Towards the end of 1437 Philip the Good assembled his clergy to discuss the dispute between Council and pope. A preliminary meeting of Flemish clerics on 21 October was followed on 8 January 1438 by an assembly at Arras, 'to come to a conclusion in the affair of the pope and the Council', of the clergy of Picardy, Flanders, Hainault and Brabant.[2] Already, the duke had taken steps to prevent the sale of

---

[1] See below, pp. 219–20.
[2] ADN B1963, fos. 92b–93 and AGR CC21808, f. 5. The 8 January assembly is wrongly placed in 1439 by Toussaint, *Relations diplomatiques*, 163 and de

indulgences issued by the Council. Now, in 1438, he further publicized his support for Eugenius by despatching an embassy to the Council of Ferrara which included Jehan Germain and others who had been representing him at Basel, thus lending credence to Eugenius IV's pretence, or claim, that the Council had been transferred from Basel to Ferrara. Jehan Germain and his colleagues were formally welcomed at Ferrara on 27 November 1438, but they infuriated the Byzantine Emperor by omitting to bow or salute him as they passed his throne on their way to greet the pope. He angrily resolved to boycott the Council, and the Burgundians had to make full public apology, and to present forged letters from Philip the Good in which he was made to express his 'burning desire for the union of the Greeks' with the Western Church, before the Emperor would change his mind. The union was only achieved on 6 July 1439, after the Council had been transferred to Florence because of an outbreak of plague, and after Eugenius had promised to do his best to bring military help to Byzantium in the form of a Western crusade against the Turks.

Soon after this papal triumph, bizarre events occurred at Basel. With the help of the single cardinal left among them, the Fathers of the Church formed an unofficial conclave of thirty-two electors and, on 5 November 1439, they chose as pope to succeed or supplant Eugenius, the retired duke of Savoy, Amadeus VIII, who had handed the cares of administration over to his son so that he could enjoy a quiet though eccentric old age in the castle-hermitage of Ripaille, half-way along the southern shore of the lake of Geneva, which he had specially designed for this purpose. Here he had installed himself in 1434 at the age of fifty, along with six elderly companions, forming with them the seven-strong Order of St. Maurice.[1] In the castle, each Knight of St. Maurice lived in a separate suite of rooms with its own tower and its own garden. They dressed as hermits and grew white beards and long hair, but Amadeus was compelled to sacrifice his beard on the altar of ecclesiastical ambition when he accepted the Council of Basel's invitation to become pope. He received the name of Felix V, but he was only taken seriously in out-of-the-way places like Aragon, Brittany, Scotland, Poland, Hungary, and, naturally, his own duchy of Savoy, now ceded fully to his son.

Moreau, *Église en Belgique*, iv. 51. On Philip and the Council of Ferrara-Florence, Perrault-Dabot, *MCACO* xiii (1895–1900), 199–214 and Gill, *Council of Florence*, are of limited value.

[1] José, *Amédée VIII*, ii. 103–175, describes Amadeus at Ripaille.

Philip the Good had long since withdrawn his embassy from the Council, nor did the election of his uncle Amadeus to a papal throne of dubious validity alter his growing hostility to the clerical diehards at Basel. He forbade appeals to the Council; he prohibited the circulation of indulgences, dispensations, pardons or letters emanating from Basel. Burgundian churchmen and diplomats were despatched into Germany on Eugenius's behalf in 1441 and, in 1443, when he met Frederick III at Besançon, Philip was assisted by a papal legate, Giovanni Capistrano,[1] in rebuffing Frederick's plans for yet another Council to arbitrate between the two popes. His loyal support for Eugenius in these years extended also to the creation of a Burgundian fleet to help implement the planned crusade against the Turks.[2] He was amply rewarded. After the decree of union with the Greeks had been signed, the grateful pope sent Philip a richly illuminated copy of it decorated with the ducal arms. He issued the dispensations necessary for the marriage of Charles of Orleans and Mary of Cleves and he granted to Duchess Isabel the right to appoint to twelve Burgundian benefices. Moreover, he made it possible in 1439 for Philip's bastard brother Jehan de Bourgogne, then a student at Louvain University, to become bishop of Cambrai; and on 6 November 1441 and 23 April 1442 Eugenius signed concordats with Philip for his territories outside the kingdom of France which limited or defined papal powers in appointments to benefices, and restricted appeals to Rome, along lines similar to those already laid down in 1438 for his French territories by the Pragmatic Sanction of Bourges.[3]

The advantages derived by duke and pope from their collaboration are well illustrated, and somewhat exaggerated, by Jehan de Stavelot, a monk of Liège, who transcribed into his chronicle the text of a papal bull of 19 February 1441 permitting Philip to levy one tenth of clerical incomes in all his lands. He comments as follows:

> You should understand the reason why our holy father the pope granted this favour to the duke of Burgundy. The foregoing bull states that it was because he had made peace in France and had helped to win over the Greeks. . . . But the main reason, which is not mentioned in the bull, was to encourage him to help and support Pope Eugenius against the Council of Basel and its partisans. For the same reason Pope Eugenius permitted the duke, during his lifetime, to collate to all benefices

---

[1] Lippens, *AFH* xxxv (1942), 113–32 and 254–95.
[2] See below, pp. 270–1.
[3] Valois, *Pragmatique sanction de Bourges*; Jongkees *Postillen aangeboden aan Prof. R. R. Post*, 139–53 and *AB* xxxviii (1966), 161–71.

throughout his lands. The pope was much criticized for gifts of this kind.[1]

Eugenius's generosity towards Duke Philip the Good reached its climax during 1446. In an ill-judged and clumsy attempt to disperse the supporters of Felix V, he deposed the archbishops of Cologne and Trier, Dietrich von Mörs and Jacob von Sierck. Each of these prelates was, in a certain sense, an opponent of Philip the Good, for the archbishop of Cologne was involved in a war against Philip's brother-in-law the duke of Cleves, while the archbishop of Trier had intervened against Philip in Luxembourg. In their place, Eugenius appointed two relatives of the duke of Burgundy: to Cologne, his nephew Adolf of Cleves; to Trier, his bastard brother Jehan de Bourgogne. Reaction in Germany to this aggressive and unprecedented move on the part of the pope was immediate and unfavourable. To avoid further serious defections to Felix V Eugenius found it necessary to reverse his decision and took steps to reinstate the two archbishops. Philip himself had played a passive rôle well suited to his diplomacy, which was somewhat more subtle than the pope's. Though he was clearly not averse to extending Burgundian influence in the Rhine valley, he could not afford to alienate the electors. Nor did he wish to offend Frederick III, from whom he hoped, with papal help, to obtain a crown. He was therefore quite willing to accept the cancellation of his relatives' promotion, provided of course that they were adequately compensated by the pope.

Eugenius's death on 23 February 1447 transformed the whole situation of the Church, though it did not affect Burgundian relations with the papacy. By maladroit diplomacy and precipitate legislation Eugenius had kept the Council of Basel in being when he could have dissolved it; provoked it into violent opposition when he could have conciliated it; and, finally, goaded it into the ultimate protest against his own misused authority, the election of an anti-pope. This irresponsible and imprudent pope, whose ambitions as a statesman were in no way matched by his political talents, was succeeded by Nicolas V, who was more interested in the Vatican Library than in affairs of church and state. Under him, the difficulties which had seemed insurmountable under Eugenius were quickly resolved. Admittedly, an outbreak of plague at Basel helped him to disperse the last remnants of the Council. The Fathers, or what remained of them,

---

[1] De Stavelot, *Chronique*, 469–70. For what follows, see Hansen, *Westfalen und Rheinland*, i. 71–82, etc. and Toussaint, *Relations diplomatiques*, 180–202.

regrouped at Lausanne and surrendered, yet with a last spark of defiance. Declaring their assembly dissolved, they had the solemn effrontery to elect Nicolas V as pope! As to Felix, he received a cardinal's hat and became papal legate for life in his own territory of Savoy.

It was in the troubled decade of Eugenius's pontificate that Philip the Good acquired his reputation for zealous loyalty to the Holy See. No doubt his ecclesiastical spokesmen, men like Jehan Germain, Jehan Jouffroy and Gillaume Fillastre, liked to think of their duke as a defender of the faith, inspired by a passionate and devout desire for the peace and unity of the Church. But Philip the Good's religious policy was dictated by his own interests, and he had been just as ready to request or accept favours from Basel, as from the pope. In 1431 the Council helped to pacify his quarrel with Austria; in 1435 it sought to reconcile Sigismund to him. And if Philip found it unhelpful in the matter of certain vacant or disputed episcopal thrones, this was not for want of initiative on his part. Nor had he taken more than minimal steps against his uncle the anti-pope Felix. His religious policy in Eugenius's pontificate, which was broadly similar to that of other rulers, had been to exploit the papal-conciliar confrontation to his own advantage, by gaining the maximum possible control over appointments to ecclesiastical benefices in his territories. His support for the pope went far enough to secure this, and no further. The fruits of this prudent, self-interested diplomacy continued to ripen in the decade following Eugenius's death. In 1447–9 Nicolas V firmly demonstrated his intention of maintaining the Burgundian connection. Eugenius's bulls recognizing Philip as legitimate ruler of all his lands, and excepting them from taxes levied on clerical incomes in France, were confirmed or repeated. On 15 March 1448 Philip was empowered to appoint to a further 112 benefices, and Isabel was granted another dozen three days later. In July 1448 Nicolas reserved a canonry and prebend at Utrecht for the eight-year-old son of Isabel's secretary, Paul Deschamps. In December he gave a cardinal's hat to Jehan Rolin, son of Philip's chancellor, and granted indulgences to benefactors of St. Julian's hospital in Rome 'where poor people and pilgrims from Burgundy and Brabant are made welcome and cared for'.[1] In 1450 a plenary indulgence was granted to any of Philip's subjects who, having failed to visit Rome in the jubilee year 1450,

[1] Brom, *Archivalia in Italië*, i (1) no. 93; see too, nos. 78, 79, 87, 88, 91 and 112. For the next sentence, see *Codex indulgentiarum Neerlandicarum*, nos. 71, 74–6, 91, 93, 94 and 106 and Remy, *Grandes indulgences pontificales*, 40–52.

visited instead the seven churches of Malines. Philip himself, and his wife and son, qualified for this indulgence in 1451, and it was such a success that it was later prolonged for a ten-year period at the request of the enthusiastic civic authorities of Malines.

These favours continued through the 1450s, when their number was increased by the needs of papal crusading ambitions, for it was the crusade which formed the pivot of papal-Burgundian relations in the second half of Philip the Good's reign. Both Calixtus III and Pius II, whose pontificates extended from 1455 to 1464, were dedicated crusaders, and Philip responded to this papal initiative with more enthusiasm and sincerity than any other contemporary ruler. From time to time he even hovered on the brink of personal participation. After all, his father had led a Burgundian crusade to the disastrous battlefield of Nicopolis in 1396, and he himself was well aware of the value of the crusading posture, both in terms of prestige, and in connection with his special relationship to the papacy. He must have appreciated the reference to himself, in a papal bull of Calixtus III, as *christiane fidei fortissimus athleta et intrepidus pugil*.[1] Papal-Burgundian relations were never closer, or more advantageous to Philip, than under Pius II. Their anatomy is nicely displayed in the instructions of a Burgundian diplomat, Anthoine Haneron. This hard-worked ambassador had been a member, in 1459, of Philip's embassy to Pius II's crusading Congress of Mantua and, on his return thence in the autumn, he had been sent to the imperial court of Frederick III at Vienna. Now, in 1460, he set out on the same travels in reverse. First to Vienna, but via Milan because of disorders in southern Germany, and afterwards back to Pope Pius in Italy. His business at the papal court was thus defined at Brussels on 1 May 1460.

> When the aforesaid Master Anthoine has finished his business with the Emperor he is to proceed to our holy father the pope and report to him on his negotiations concerning help against the Turks and the other points and articles, thanking our holy father for the special favour he has shown towards my lord the duke in the conduct of these affairs and recommending the duke's business, concerning which the said Master Anthoine is fully informed, to him.
>
> Item, Master Anthoine will try to ascertain from the pope what his

---

[1] Cited by Jongkees, *Staat en Kerk in Holland en Zeeland*, 37 and n. For the crusade, see below, pp. 268–74 and 358–72. For Anthoine Haneron, see too above, p. 178. The extract that follows is from Cartellieri, *MIOG* xxviii (1907), 462–4.

intentions are concerning the expedition against the Turks, and also concerning the settlement of disputes in France and elsewhere; and he is to bring back a full report to my lord the duke.

Item, if it is true that our said holy father plans to levy a tenth from the clergy of my lord the duke's lands and a thirtieth from the laity, the proceeds to be sent outside the duke's lands and spent wherever the pope wishes, the said Master Anthoine is to point out that my lord the duke's lands contain many persons of privileged status . . . and that troubles and difficulties are very likely to occur if my lord the duke attempts to levy this tenth and thirtieth in his lands and lordships. . . .

Item, the said Master Anthoine is to ask my lord the bishop of Arras and Master Pierre Bogaert, *procureur* of my lord the duke at the papal court, to do their utmost to support, help and advise him in obtaining satisfaction on the following points.

That is to say, may it please our said holy father to promote my lord [the bishop] of Arras to the status and dignity of cardinal. The duke has already written about this to the pope, explaining the reasons (which Master Anthoine is fully informed about) that can and should influence him. [Master Anthoine is also to explain] what my lord the duke told him verbally when he took his leave, and he is to approach the cardinals on this subject when opportunity arises and tell them that my lord [the duke] has heard that the holy father has recently created four or five cardinals, yet has not promoted my lord of Arras to this dignity, a fact which amazes the duke, taking into account what he has written on this matter, and considering that the appointment of my said lord of Arras to the cardinalate is essential for the duke's own needs and affairs and likewise for the good of his lands and subjects.

Item, since our said holy father has already issued his bulls in favour of reverend father in God the bishop of Toul, president of my lord the duke's council in the chancellor's absence, prohibiting the chapter of Chalon from proceeding to the election of a new bishop when the bishopric next becomes vacant, and since it is said that the bishop of Chalon is at present indisposed, may it please the holy father to bear in mind what is referred to above concerning the bishop of Toul and, as soon as he hears about the above-mentioned vacancy, to promote the bishop of Toul to the said bishopric before anyone else.

Item, may it please our said holy father to look after the interests of Master Anthoine de Neuchâtel, son of my lord of Neuchâtel, marshal of Burgundy, who is a protonotary of the papal court, and to be as favourably disposed as possible to the requests which he will be submitting to his holiness for his own advancement and promotion.

Item, may it please the holy father to look after the interests of Ernoul and François de Lalaing, legitimate sons of Sir Simon de Lalaing, as regards their promotion and advancement in the church.

Item, may it please our holy father to bear in mind the recommendation made by my lord [the duke] on another occasion by his two previous ambassadors on behalf of the said Master Anthoine, to the effect that he should be provided for with benefices reserved for the disposition of the pope in the churches of Utrecht and Deventer. . . .

Item, may it please our said holy father to issue his apostolic bulls prohibiting the Benedictine abbey of St. Peter at Chalon from electing an abbot when a vacancy occurs through the death of the present abbot, considering that the said abbey is directly subject to the holy see.

Item, may it please the holy father, at the request of my lord the duke, to accept as specially commended Master Pierre Milet, the duke's secretary signing in financial affairs, who is provost of St. Peter's Aire, and to treat the requests which he will be making to his holiness as favourably as possible. . . .

Throughout his pontificate until his death at Ancona on 14 August 1464, while he was waiting to set out on a crusade which never materialized, Pius II cajoled and exhorted Philip the Good to undertake the long-promised Burgundian crusade.[1] But the vows that had been made at the Feast of the Pheasant in 1454 and the papal favours that had been bestowed so liberally on Philip before and since then, only produced a limited expedition in 1464, led by the duke's bastard Anthony, which came to an end in Marseilles at about the time when Pius II's crusade failed to take shape at Ancona.

Philip the Good's special relationship with the papacy was a means to two related ends. In the first place, it enabled him to place his protégés on numerous episcopal thrones, some of which were of especial political importance, such as Tournai, Liège and Utrecht, and to a lesser extent, Cambrai, Thérouanne and Besançon. Secondly, it enabled him to reward, directly or indirectly, and at no cost to himself, a large proportion of his servants, officials and courtiers.

The city of Tournai, situated on the river Schelde, formed an enclave of French territory between Philip the Good's counties of Artois, Flanders and Hainault. Apart from its political significance as a French outpost, it harboured a numerous and turbulent class of artisans whose periodic rebellions could scarcely be disregarded by a duke who faced constant trouble of the same kind in his own territories, notably at Ghent and Bruges, both of which were in the diocese of Tournai. Philip the Bold had engineered the appointment of his councillor Louis de la Trémoille as bishop of Tournai in 1388, and John the Fearless had seen to it that his successor, in 1410, was

[1] See, for example, Pius II, *Opera*, 848 and 855–8.

a leading Burgundian civil servant, subsequently chancellor, Jehan de Thoisy. Thus a measure of Burgundian influence was exercised at Tournai until Jehan de Thoisy's death on 2 June 1433. This event marked the beginning of a hard-fought struggle for the succession, in which the principal protagonists were King Charles VII of France and Philip the Good, though other parties, including Pope Eugenius and the Council of Basel, infused their quarrels into this one. The dispute continued for five years, for the peace of Arras, which was supposed to represent a Franco-Burgundian peace-settlement, neither mollified nor affected it in the least.

A week after Jehan de Thoisy's death on 9 June 1433, letters from Philip were read out at Tournai inviting the civic authorities to accept Jehan Chevrot, the recently appointed president of the duke's great council; and on 17 June ducal letters were issued placing the regalia of the vacant see under the control of Philibert de Jaucourt, on behalf of the duke.[1] But Charles VII acted with equal speed and greater success. As early as 15 July Eugenius wrote to Philip to inform him that he had transferred the bishop of Amiens, Jehan d'Harcourt, to Tournai. This was the result of a French royal request to the pope. Philip responded by instructing his officials and subjects to refuse obedience to Jehan d'Harcourt, and he sent an embassy to Eugenius requesting the appointment of Jehan Chevrot. Both parties sought support from Ghent and other Flemish cities. Jehan d'Harcourt actually took up residence in Tournai in September 1435, but Philip had kept control of the greater part of the revenues of the see and eventually persuaded Eugenius to take action on his behalf. On 5 November 1436 Jehan d'Harcourt was promoted to the archbishopric of Narbonne, and Jehan Chevrot was appointed bishop of Tournai. But Charles VII, the Council of Basel and the people of Tournai continued to support Jehan d'Harcourt, who himself refused to accept Eugenius's decision.

In 1437 the consuls of Tournai were ordered by Charles VII to disobey the pope and to accept no other bishop but d'Harcourt, and at the same time they were invited by Philip the Good to publish Eugenius's bull appointing Chevrot. When they refused, Philip in November 1437 ordered a commercial boycott of Tournai, and it was this measure, rather than the spiritual artillery which had been fired

[1] *Extraits analytiques de Tournai, 1431–76*, 17–18 and *IAB* v. 49–51. On what follows, besides these two, see AGR CC21806, f. 13a–b, etc.; Monstrelet, *Chronique*, v. 58–62; Toussaint, *Relations diplomatiques*, 154–7, with references; and Bartier, *Légistes et gens de finances*, 312–15.

at them on Eugenius's behalf by the provost of Cassel, Pierre de Rosay, which persuaded the civic authorities to seek a negotiated settlement in 1438. With the help of Duchess Isabel and the duke of Bourbon, who intervened to arbitrate, the dispute was eventually settled in favour of Jehan Chevrot and Philip the Good shortly before the end of 1438. Burgundian influence at Tournai was thereafter reinforced by a visit from Philip himself, with his duchess and youthful heir, on 14 May 1439.

The five-year succession struggle at Tournai in the 1430s was a direct result of Franco-Burgundian rivalry, and it was Charles VII's continued hostility to Burgundy that led him to support an opposition candidate at Tournai once again when, in 1460, Philip tried to avoid a disputed succession by arranging an exchange. Guillaume Fillastre, bishop of Toul, accepted the see of Tournai, while Jehan Chevrot, who actually died before the end of the year, resigned from Tournai and accepted Toul instead.[1] Royal ambassadors were sent to Tournai to protest at the way Fillastre had been insinuated there; a royal candidate, Charles de Bourbon, archbishop of Lyons, was put forward; and Guillaume Fillastre was arraigned before the Paris *Parlement*. But, once more, Charles VII's intervention was ineffective. Once again the pope went out of his way to make things easy for Philip the Good. After all, this was the year of the Congress of Mantua, and a favourable Burgundian response to Pius II's crusading enthusiasm was essential.

Among episcopal sees in the Burgundian sphere of influence, Liège was exceptional. The extensive territories which formed its temporality were situated along the Meuse between Brabant and Limbourg. They included towns like Tongres and Dinant as well as the city of Liège itself, where thirty-two craft gilds infused a certain element of popular democracy into the tumultuous civic politics. The bishop's secular power was limited, imperial influence had long since disappeared, and Burgundian intervention had already occurred on a massive scale in 1408, when John the Fearless fought and defeated the Liégeois on the field of Othée. The brief but devastating war which flared up in 1430 between Philip the Good and Liège has

[1] For this paragraph, see BM Add. MS. 54156, fos. 393–7b (see below, p. 350 n. 2); *Extraits analytiques de Tournai, 1431–76*, 250–1; Duclerq, *Mémoires*, 151; Bartier, *Légistes et gens de finances*, 320–1; and Jongkees, *AB* xxxviii (1966), 167–8. For Chevrot, see de Morembert, *MAM* cxlv (1963–4), 171–220.

already been recorded in these pages.[1] At that time the bishop, Jehan de Heinsberg, had reluctantly declared war on the duke of Burgundy. Throughout his long episcopate (1419–55), he managed to keep Philip more or less at arm's length, and yet to exercise an effective, if uneasy, authority over the city of Liège. He was no hireling of the duke of Burgundy. Forced to subscribe in 1431 to a humiliating treaty of peace, he was bullied in June 1434 by Philip the Good into a singularly one-sided treaty of alliance, which marks his nearest approach to total surrender to Burgundian pressure. The main clauses of this treaty were as follows:

1. Duke and bishop agree to help each other in the event of either being involved in a war against the city of Liège.
2. The bishop promises to see that the articles of the 1431 treaty are properly implemented.
3. If the duke finds it necessary to make war on Liège, the bishop will declare war against the city within six weeks and do all in his power to help the duke.
4. Until the terms of the 1431 treaty have been carried out, the bishop may not make war on Liège without the duke's consent.
5. If, as a result of a war started by Philip, the bishop is driven out of Liège, Philip will pay him 10,000 francs in compensation. But if this happens as a result of a war started by the bishop, he will receive nothing.
6. The bishop promises to help the duke with all his available forces, though at the duke's expense, in any war in which the duke of Burgundy becomes involved against his own subjects.

In the years that followed, in spite of repeated disputes with his subjects, Jehan de Heinsberg managed to maintain his authority both over the city of Liège and throughout his territories. In the early summer of 1436, when Philip the Good was preoccupied with preparations for the siege of Calais, de Heinsberg organized a punitive expedition into the south-western corner of the principality and destroyed a group of castles which had been used by certain freelance captains, or brigands, to devastate and terrorize the surrounding countryside. One of them, Beauraing, had only recently been rebuilt

[1] Above, pp. 58–62. For what follows in general, Dabin, *BIAL* xliii (1913), 99–190 adds little to Daris, *Liège pendant le xve siècle* and Kurth, *Cité de Liège*, iii. The main chroniclers are d'Oudenbosch, de Stavelot and Zantfliet; relevant documents are calendared or printed in *Régestes de Liège*, iii (see pp. 293–300 for the treaty discussed below) and iv, and *Cartulaire de Saint-Lambert de Liège*, v and vi. Pirenne, *Histoire de Belgique*, ii. 282–99 and *Algemene geschiedenis*, iii. 303–5 with references, are valuable.

by its owner, who had named its four massive corner-towers 'Hain-ault', 'Namur', 'Brabant' and 'Rethel', since he claimed that each had been financed by plunder from one of these territories. Beauraing and several others were now demolished by the Liègeois, who were only deterred from advancing into French territory and attacking Hirson and other places belonging to Philip's captain Jehan de Luxembourg by a warning letter from Philip and an offer from Jehan to discuss matters of dispute at the conference table.[1]

The forces of rebellion and plunder gained the upper hand in the same area in 1445, when Evrard de la Mark found himself involved in a war with Philip the Good, who sent Anthoine de Croy and the bastard Cornille to attack him. But Jehan de Heinsberg, who was evidently not prepared to stand by and watch Burgundian troops invading and possibly occupying parts of his principality, himself raised an army and reduced Evrard de la Mark to obedience after his castles of Agimont and Rochefort, in the extreme south-west of the principality, had surrendered. At this very time, Philip the Good was complaining bitterly that the bishop and city of Liège had not imple-mented the terms of the peace treaty of 1431: the tower of Montor-gueil had still not been demolished,[2] the seventeen villages the Liègeois unjustly occupied in Namur, the surrender of which to Philip had been stipulated in the treaty, had not yet been handed over, and no expiatory chapel had been founded. Moreover, the authorities of Brabant, Namur and Hainault were involved, early in 1445, in disputes with Liège, whose territories bordered on all of them.[3] It was only towards the end of 1446, after a whole series of conferences, that Jehan de Heinsberg and the representatives of the chapter and Estates of Liège yielded to Philip the Good's demands concerning the 1431 treaty. The ducal accounts tell the story of these events.

The said bailiff, receiver and *procureur* of Namur, on receipt of the bishop of Liège's letters of 18 October 1446 agreeing on behalf of himself, his chapter and city to send deputies on the Tuesday following to negotiate the surrender of the seventeen villages with my lord the duke's deputies, wrote back in reply to the said bishop stating that they were ready for the conference. They assembled together on the Tuesday at Namur and spent that day and the whole of the next day

[1] Monstrelet, *Chronique*, v. 225–8.
[2] See above, pp. 59–62.
[3] AGR CC2413, f. 52b. The extract which follows is from ADN B1991, f. 80.

8.   Philip the Good and Charles the Rash. Recueil d'Arras

9. King Charles VII of France. Jehan Fouquet (detail)

discussing their powers and what they were to do. Then they visited each of the seventeen villages in turn to take possession according to the duke's authority. This journey, including two days which they spent inspecting the chapel which the Liègeois had to found in the church at Bossière and in visiting the tower of Montorgueil to make sure that it had been demolished according to the terms of the peace treaty, took ten days.

That Jehan de Heinsberg was no Burgundian lackey is shown by his attitude in these and other disputes; by the fact that Girart de Looz, count of Blankenheim, ally, chamberlain and pensioner of the king of France, was his relative; by his attempted arbitration in 1452 of Philip's quarrel with Ghent;[1] and above all by his deliberate failure, in 1452 and again in 1454, to see that Louis de Bourbon, nephew and protégé of Philip, obtained the prebend or canonry in the cathedral church of St. Lambert, Liège, which Philip had hoped for and demanded on his behalf. Why then did Jehan de Heinsberg resign his bishopric while on a visit to the Burgundian court in Holland towards the end of 1455? Unfortunately this event has not yet been elucidated by historical research. It is clear that Jehan de Heinsberg was at this time at loggerheads with Philip over numerous matters. In particular, he was supporting Gijsbrecht van Brederode, bishop-elect of Utrecht, possibly even to the extent of offering him military aid, against Philip the Good and the Burgundian candidate for the episcopal succession there, David of Burgundy.[2] But the exact motives and the actual pressures which induced Jehan de Heinsberg to resign are so far unidentified. On the other hand, no mystery surrounds the mechanism of Louis de Bourbon's promotion in his place. In return for yet another assurance that he would do all in his power to promote the crusade, Philip persuaded Pope Calixtus III to appoint the eighteen-year-old Louis de Bourbon to the vacant bishopric of Liège.

It is often assumed, quite wrongly, that Burgundian influence at Liège was somehow strengthened after Louis de Bourbon's installation there as bishop in 1456. As a matter of fact, Philip's choice of candidate for this important see was unwise and ill-considered. Far from being made on a basis of calculated political ambition, or specifically to further Burgundian expansion, the choice of Louis was

[1] *Chronique des Pays-Bas et de Tournai*, 488.
[2] *Cronycke van Hollandt*, fos. 297b–298; Zantfliet, *Chronicon*, cols. 488–9; d'Escouchy, *Chronique*, ii. 314–15; and see Lacaze, *AB* xxxvi (1964), 99–100.

an example of mere favouritism, for he was a weak-willed pleasure-loving youth, quite devoid of experience in administrative and ecclesiastical affairs. Unlike his predecessor, he failed to find a *modus vivendi* with the turbulent citizenry of Liège, whom he soon provoked into riot and rebellion. Indeed, within a year of his arrival at Liège the danger of open war between him and his subjects was so great that Philip the Good ordered the mobilization of Burgundian vassals in Hainault, Flanders and elsewhere; and on 27 August 1457 a cleric at Cambrai in close touch with the duke recorded that he was about to set out on 'an expedition against the Liègeois who were in revolt'.[1]

The crisis blew over, but Burgundian influence at Liège was now brought into question and undermined. In the first place, relations between Louis and the citizens rapidly deteriorated. When he was forced into exile, he retaliated by excommunicating his flock; but the episcopal messenger who brought the document proclaiming the excommunication was forced to eat it, and the houses of Louis de Bourbon's friends and officials were burnt down. Secondly, the people of Liège, who had traditionally regarded the king of France as a potential friend and protector in the face of Burgundian aggression, now entered into close contact first with Charles VII, who made an alliance with them in 1458 and took their city under his protection and safeguard in 1460, and, after 1461, with Louis XI, whose agents were active at Liège from 1461 onwards. Thus the installation of a Burgundian puppet on the episcopal throne of Liège by no means led to the extension of Burgundian power there. This was only achieved after a series of devastating military campaigns which began in 1465, and continued after Philip the Good's death.

The territories of the see of Utrecht, collectively known as *het Sticht*, which were as extensive as those of Liège, were divided by the Zuiderzee, for they lay partly to the south of it, around Utrecht itself and Amersfoort, and partly on the eastern shore in Friesland. As with Liège, so with Utrecht, careful distinction must be made between the lands over which the bishop ruled as a temporal prince, and his ecclesiastical diocese, which in this case included much of Philip's county of Holland. Actually, Philip the Good intervened in the affairs of Utrecht before he became count of Holland.[2] After the

[1] Dupont, *Histoire de Cambrai* ii, xxiii. For the mobilization, see AGR CC21825, f. 96 and ADN B10422, f. 62b.
[2] For what follows on Utrecht, see *Utrechtsche jaarboeken*, i and ii; Hansen, *Westfalen und Rheinland*, i and ii; de Hullu, *Utrechtsche schisma*; Post,

death of Bishop Friedrich von Blankenheim on 9 October 1423 the canons elected Rudolf von Diepholz, who was rejected by Pope Martin V in favour of a candidate supported by John of Bavaria and Philip the Good, Zweder van Culemborg. It was on Zweder's behalf that Philip campaigned in 1427 when he was repulsed from before the walls of Amersfoort. But Zweder failed to establish himself and, after he had definitively obtained control of Holland through the treaty of Delft in July 1428, Philip the Good lent his support instead to Zweder's successful opponent Rudolf von Diepholz. Zweder, abandoned by Philip, rejected by Pope Eugenius, Martin V's successor, and expelled from the bishopric, sought refuge and support at the Council of Basel, which promptly recognized him as bishop of Utrecht. Moreover when, after his death in 1433, a group of canons perpetuated the schism at Utrecht by electing a successor to Zweder in the shape of Walram von Mörs, the Council of Basel and the Emperor Sigismund, who dreamt of restoring imperial influence at Utrecht, supported him.

Much of the political significance of Utrecht lay in its connections with the secular states and the other ecclesiastical principalities of north-west Germany. Walram von Mörs's candidature was part of an attempt by a single family to gain control over a wide and politically complex area. This ecclesiastical dynasticism was initiated by Walram's brother the ambitious archbishop-elector of Cologne, Dietrich von Mörs, who was also duke of Westphalia. He ruled his extensive territories from 1414 until his death in 1463. Pius II described him as 'easily the foremost German of his time'.[1] Besides Cologne, he administered the bishopric of Paderborn and, in 1424, he placed his brother Heinrich on the episcopal throne of Münster. To the lands belonging to this bishopric, which bordered on those of the bishop of Utrecht, Heinrich von Mörs in 1441 added control of the see of Osnabrück. Nor were the territorial ambitions of Dietrich and his brothers limited to ecclesiastical principalities, for they hoped to swallow up the duchies of Cleves and Berg, and the county of Mark, and doubtless other territories as well. It was thus hardly surprising that Philip's brother-in-law Duke Adolf of Cleves found himself involved, in 1444-8, in a war against Dietrich von

---

Utrechtsche bisschopsverkiezingen; Jongkees, *Staat en kerk in Holland en Zeeland*, especially 133–45; Zilverberg, *David van Bourgondië*; *Algemene geschiedenis*, iii, especially 357–60; and, in general, Petri, *Gemeinsame probleme*, 92–126 and Lacaze, *AB* xxxvi (1964), 93–8.

[1] *Commentaries*, 748.

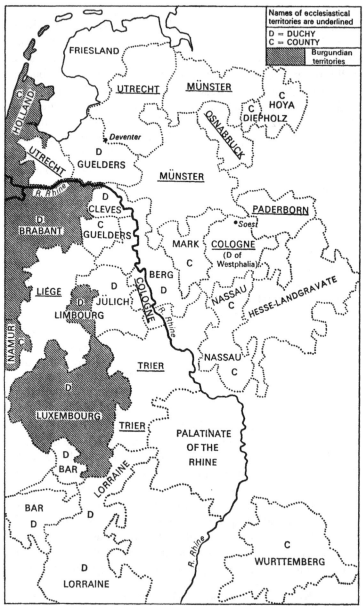

4. Eastern neighbours of Burgundy

Mörs over the possession of the town of Soest, to which both Cologne and Cleves laid claim. Naturally, Philip supported Adolf. At first, Rudolf von Diepholz, opposed as he was in Utrecht by Walram von Mörs, was an ally of Cleves and Burgundy, but by 1448 he had contrived to purchase the withdrawal of his rival, and when the bishop of Münster, Heinrich von Mörs, died in 1450, and Walram von Mörs was one of the two rival candidates for his brother's succession there, Rudolf supported him. Subsequently, in 1451, he took over Walram's claims to Münster on behalf of his nephew Conrad von Diepholz, but was militarily opposed by the town of Münster, a rival episcopal candidate, Erich von Hoya, and by Cleves and Burgundy. In Utrecht his war for Münster was unpopular and, by the time of his death in March 1455, Rudolf had been virtually expelled from the bishopric.

Thus, quite apart from internal tensions in Utrecht itself, especially that between nobles and gilds, external pressures were extremely important in 1455. It was hardly likely that the powers whose interconnected territorial ambitions have just been outlined, would respect the choice of the canons of the five churches of Utrecht. Everybody had their own interests and their own candidates, and the future of Utrecht would certainly not be decided in the chapter-house. Philip the Good put forward his bastard son David, bishop of Thérouanne; John, duke of Cleves, who had succeeded his father Adolf in 1448, wished to promote his fifteen-year-old nephew Heinrich von Schwarzburg; while Dietrich von Mörs, archbishop of Cologne, supported the candidate of Duke Arnold of Guelders, Stephen of Bavaria. On 7 April 1455 all but two of the seventy electors, canons and officials of the Utrecht churches, voted for a member of a powerful noble family which had in the past represented opposition to Philip in Holland, the provost of the cathedral, Gijsbrecht van Brederode. Since the day when the rallying-cry of Dutch rioters had been 'Brederode!', Gijsbrecht himself had become a ducal councillor, and his brother Reinoud had been admitted to the Order of the Golden Fleece. Nevertheless the van Brederodes had a claim to the county of Holland and the canons' choice was certainly consciously anti-Burgundian. It was reinforced in September 1455, when the Estates of Utrecht elected Gijsbrecht their 'guardian, defender and protector'.

Meanwhile at Rome the promotion of the Burgundian candidate was never in doubt. On 12 September 1455 Calixtus III transferred David from Thérouanne to Utrecht. Duke John of Cleves abandoned his candidate and lent his aid instead to his powerful uncle, and Philip himself moved to The Hague in October 1455 for the first time in ten years. Nonetheless, a whole year elapsed before David was firmly established as bishop of Utrecht and, during most of this time, the Burgundian court was fixed at The Hague. It was Philip's longest stay in Holland since the late 1420s. But the promotion of David to Utrecht was not the only motive for this expedition to Holland, for the duke hoped to persuade the Dutch Estates to vote an *aide* for his crusade, and the personal advancement of his bastard son was accompanied by territorial ambition, for Philip evidently planned to extend Burgundian influence throughout the northern Netherlands. Chastellain talks of him wanting to conquer 'his kingdom of Frisia', and the duchy of Guelders was certainly not outside the scope of his expansionist projects in this area.

It was only in July 1456, after Gijsbrecht had rejected both the duke of Cleves's attempts at mediation and the duke of Burgundy's bribes, that Philip resolved on a show of force. An army was hastily collected, partly in Picardy and partly in Holland, where there was some support for a war against Utrecht, especially among the towns, each of which sent a contingent. An entry in the civic accounts of Haarlem tells its own tale:[1]

> Item, on the eve of the feast of St. Peter's Chains, [31 July] 1456, Claes van Ruven, at that time burgomaster of the town of Haarlem, set out from Haarlem with the town banner which it was his duty to carry, together with Aelbrecht van Raephorst the sheriff, Claes van Yperen, burgomaster, and Garbrant Claessoen, magistrate of Haarlem, with their servants and followers, and with the crossbowmen and men-at-arms, to take the field with my lord [the duke] wherever he might lead them, and they were out for seven weeks and three days. . . .

While these troops were assembling, Philip the Good spent his sixtieth birthday, 30 July 1456, at Ijsselstein on the frontiers of Holland and the *Sticht*. Here, on 2 August, a peace delegation arrived from Utrecht announcing Gijsbrecht's submission and resignation in return for 50,000 gold lions in compensation for the expenses of his 'episcopate'; an annual income from the revenues of the *Sticht* of 4,200 Rhenish florins; and the provostship of St. Donatian's, Bruges,

---

[1] Jongkees, *Staat en Kerk in Holland en Zeeland*, 141 n. 6. For what follows, besides the works cited on p. 224 n. 2 above, see Chastellain, *Œuvres*, iii. 69–80 and 98–196; de Waurin, *Croniques*, v. 370–2; *Cronycke van Hollandt*, fos. 297a–299a; van Veen, *WG* xiv (1920); Alberts, *GBM* l (1950), 1–22; and Struick, *Postillen aangeboden aan Prof. R. R. Post*, 85–115.

which Chastellain reckoned was worth 2,000 Rhenish florins per annum. Moreover, he was to be made a ducal councillor in Holland. Philip accepted these conditions and made his triumphal entry into Utrecht on 5 August. The civic troops from Holland entered first, followed by the captains of the archers leading their men, all mounted, in two columns, with helmets on and bows and arrows ready. Next followed the archers of the ducal bodyguard, then the heralds and, finally, the men-at-arms, among whom Philippe Pot was particularly worthy of note, for he was wearing a gold-embroidered robe of violet velvet which was so long and wide that he had to have pages following him on either side, some distance from his horse, to hold up its ends. Last of all, behind his son Charles, rode Philip the Good, with six pages and trumpets sounding before him. 'That evening,' says Chastellain, 'you could see a fantastic number of lanterns hung at the windows, with people going and coming throughout the city, jostling each other like a swarm of ants.' David made his separate and more modest entry on the following day. Security measures were strictly enforced during the duke's week-long stay in Utrecht. The night watch consisted of a small army of 800 archers and 200 men-at-arms, who moved round the streets during the night carrying torches. But, though the Nedersticht, that is the part of the *Sticht* immediately surrounding Utrecht, had submitted and accepted David as its bishop, the Oversticht, that is, the episcopal territories beyond the river Ijssel, still held out for Gijsbrecht. The ducal army had to advance further and, between 9.30 and 10.0 a.m. on 10 August, while Chastellain and others served Philip his breakfast, he watched from the window of his lodgings while his troops filed out of Utrecht on their way to the siege of Deventer.

At Deventer, even more than at Utrecht, Philip entered the arena of north-west German power politics. To reach Deventer and the Oversticht from Utrecht, he had to march across the Veluwe, through the duchy of Guelders. Duke Arnold, whose episcopal candidate at Utrecht had been brushed aside, and who was fighting with Conrad von Diepholz against Cleves and, indirectly, Burgundy, in the Münster war, was anti-Burgundian. He would probably have liked to intercept the Burgundian army on its way across Guelders; he apparently hoped to trap and defeat it at Deventer, whose citizens received an offer of military help from his German ally, Conrad von Diepholz. But his authority inside Guelders was insecure and he was vigorously and successfully opposed there by towns like Nijmegen and Arnhem, as well as by his wife Catherine of Cleves and his son

Adolf who had been quarrelling with him for years. Philip the Good encouraged these dissident elements, but his military failure at Deventer, where Chastellain thought it a shame to see the valiant Burgundian knights up to their knees in mud, as well as the un-expected arrival at Brussels of Louis, the dauphin of France, caused his withdrawal. Thus Burgundian designs on Friesland and Guelders failed to materialize, though Philip continued his intrigues against Duke Arnold in the following years. On the other hand, within a short time David was recognized throughout the *Sticht*. At last, the bishop whose diocese extended over Holland was a Burgundian.

The episcopal sees of Tournai, Liège and Utrecht were of the first importance politically. Moreover, from the ecclesiastical point of view the diocesan territories of all three extended over Philip's lands, covering between them most of Flanders, Namur, Holland and Zeeland, and a large part of Brabant. But there were other bishoprics over which it was important or useful for Burgundian influence to be extended. Thérouanne, in Artois, was occupied until 1436 by a Burgundian supporter, Louis de Luxembourg and, in 1451, Philip persuaded the dean and chapter to elect his bastard son David. At Cambrai in 1439 he introduced his bastard brother Jehan, and thereafter was able to intervene to some extent in the administration of his episcopal territories, which formed an enclave between Artois and Hainault. Jehan de Bourgogne, however, was said to have visited Cambrai only once during an episcopate of forty years. At Arras, a succession of Burgundian bishops occupied the see at Philip's request, though not without certain complications. For example, Quentin Menart, ducal councillor and provost of St. Omer, who was appointed by Pope Eugenius IV in January 1439, was transferred to Besançon later in the year because Philip preferred to install his first chaplain and councillor Forteguerra da Piacenza, at Arras. And in 1453, when Philip's first candidate, Duchess Isabel's nephew Dom Jaime, was transferred instead to the archbishopric of Lisbon, he had some difficulty in establishing his second choice, Jehan Jouffroy, abbot of Luxeuil, his almoner and councillor, as bishop of Arras, against the claims of one of the canons, who sought and obtained the support of King Charles VII of France.

In the southern territories, Quentin Menart occupied Besançon between 1439 and his death in 1462, when Charles de Neuchâtel, brother of Philip's marshal Thibaud, succeeded him and continued to represent Burgundian interests there. Every bishop at Chalon, in

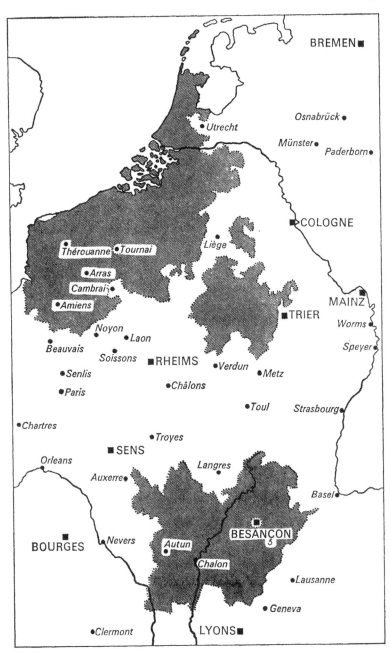

5. Archbishoprics and bishoprics in and near Burgundian Territories

Philip's reign, was a Burgundian protégé or nominee: Hughes d'Orges (1417-31), Jehan Rolin (1431-6), Jehan Germain (1436-61) and Jehan de Poupet (1461-80). At Auxerre, Pierre de Longeuil was a ducal councillor and Laurent Pignon was Philip's confessor. At Mâcon, Autun, Nevers and the other bishoprics of Philip's southern territories the picture is the same. Nor did Philip limit himself to his own bishoprics. He used his friendly relationship with the popes to place his officials or partisans on the episcopal or archiepiscopal thrones of Soissons (Jehan Milet), Lyons (Charles de Bourbon), and Toul (Guillaume Fillastre and the twelve-year-old Anthoine de Neuchâtel, son of Thibaud). Failures in the extension and maintenance of this Burgundian episcopate were rare. Perhaps the most notable Burgundian rebuffs in this respect were at Paris in 1420, at Bayeux and Trier in 1432, and at Cologne in 1463.[1]

It must not be supposed that Philip the Good in any sense incorporated sees like Tournai, Cambrai, Liège and Utrecht into the Burgundian state, and it would be utterly misleading to produce a map showing them as among his possessions. Nor did the establishment there of his councillors, relatives and supporters serve to avoid the perennial disputes between secular and spiritual powers which wasted the revenues and undermined the authority of every medieval state. The historian of Church and State in Holland in Philip the Good's reign could detect little difference, in this respect, before and after David's appointment to Utrecht.[2] Indeed if anything the situation deteriorated, for after 1456 the bishop's officials no longer considered themselves bound by the terms of the concordat which Rudolf von Diepholz had accepted in 1434, as part of the price for Philip's support. Town after town was placed under interdict. In December 1460, when representatives from Amsterdam were summoned to The Hague concerning an *aide*, the bishop of Utrecht had first to be asked to raise a ban proclaimed by his officials, who had imposed an

---

[1] For Burgundian bishops see ADN B2008, f. 207 (Thérouanne, 1451); ADN B10404, f. 50b, Dubrulle, *Cambrai à la fin du moyen âge*, and Toussaint, *Relations diplomatiques*, 175 (Cambrai); Lestocquoy, *Évêques d'Arras, Quelques documents inédits*, and Fierville, *Jean Jouffroy* (Arras); Dunod, *Histoire de Besançon*, i, Piquard, *PTSEC* (1929) and *BHPTH* (1932-3), 35-46 (Besançon); Bazin, *MSHAC* xv (1918) (Chalon); and see too Jongkees, *Staat en Kerk in Holland en Zeeland*, 38-9 and Bartier, *Légistes et gens de finances*, 125-7. For Philip's setbacks, see Wylie and Waugh, *Henry V*, iii. 233 (Paris); Toussaint, *Relations diplomatiques*, 17-19 (Bayeux and Trier); and Pius II, *Commentaries*, 748-9 (Cologne).

[2] Jongkees, *Staat en Kerk in Holland en Zeeland*, 168-86.

interdict over Amsterdam and any place visited by its citizens. One can only feel sorry for Leiden, which incurred this same interdict much as one might contract a disease, when Amsterdam's deputies attended a conference of Dutch and Wendish towns there in 1461. Even when the 1434 concordat was republished in 1462 disputes continued unabated.

The accounts of the grand bailiff of Hainault, which lay mostly in the diocese of Cambrai, show that the installation of Jehan de Bourgogne in 1440 made no difference whatsoever to the constant disputes between the ducal government there and the episcopal authorities. Indeed the situation deteriorated so much that in 1449 the duke issued letters prohibiting the Hainaulters from obeying their bishop except in certain specified instances, 'because the said bishop of Cambrai has infringed the duke's prerogatives so much that my lord the duke is not prepared to put up with this any longer'.[1] Early in 1451, when the *gens des comptes* of Brabant at Brussels were asked to advise the duke on his administration in the duchy, they took care to make specific recommendations concerning the juridical abuses of the local bishops:

> Although in the past an effort has been made to induce reverend father in God my lord the bishop of Liège and the officials of his spiritual court, and likewise my lord the bishop of Cambrai and his officers, to desist from the abuses, outrages and violations which they daily perpetrate in various ways by their summonses, citations, prohibitions, excommunications, nullifications and otherwise against the good people and subjects of my lord the duke and against his officers and jurisdiction, in taking cognisance of all sorts of cases both real and personal, including amends and forfeitures, also those involving Lombards and usurers, and other things, nevertheless little has been achieved towards making them see reason. . . . Subject to correction, it seems that my lord would be justified in making statutes and ordinances in his lands to maintain his dignity and prerogatives and to ensure that his good people and subjects cannot infringe the statutes and ordinances of our mother holy church in such a way that the ecclesiastical judge has reason to punish them.

Quite apart from the political significance of Burgundian bishops in sees like Liège and Utrecht, and the general extension of Burgundian influence which was inevitably brought about by Philip's numerous episcopal appointments, the conferment of benefices, large and

---

[1] ADN B10413, f. 45 and see Thelliez, *RN* xl (1958), 375–80 and 428. The extract which follows is from AGR CC17, fos. 77b–79.

small, was an admirable and indeed essential means of rewarding Burgundian servants and officials and advancing ducal friends and relatives, not to mention the dependants of both these groups. A document drawn up early in the reign shows that this process had already at that time been reduced to a regular system.[1]

> This is the arrangement made in October 1428, which my lord the duke wishes to be observed in the distribution of benefices in his collation, in order to provide chiefly for the clerics of his court, but also for other servants and friends, and for his principal officials. My lord the duke does not mean by this to bind himself to such an extent that he cannot dispose of these benefices in some other way than set out here, according to his pleasure, at the request of any lords or ladies of his lineage, or others.
>
> For a chaplain of my lord [bishop] of Tournai, the first vacant prebend at Lens.
>
> For my lord the chancellor, for his two sons, the first prebend at Courtrai and the first at Mons in Hainault in the gift of my lord the duke.
>
> For my lord of Roubaix, for his chaplain, the first chaplaincy at Aalst.
>
> For my lord of Croy, for his chaplain, the second prebend at Béthune.
>
> For Sir Lourdin [de Saligny], for his chaplain, the first prebend at Dole.
>
> For my lord [the bishop] of Bethlehem, for his clerk, the first prebend at Roye.
>
> For my lord the marshal of Burgundy, for his chaplain. . . .
>
> For Master Guy Serrurier, the second prebend of the [ducal] chapel.
>
> For Master Christian Hautain, for his nephew, the second prebend at Roye.
>
> For Master Jehan Germain, the first curacy vacant at Poligny or elsewhere in Burgundy.
>
> For Guy Guilbaut, the second vacancy at the Bruges Béguinage. . . .

Duke Philip the Good was able to appoint to ecclesiastical benefices throughout his territories, either by prescriptive or hereditary right, or by special leave of the pope. For example, in Holland and Zeeland he appointed to about one-third of the parochial churches and half the canonries, simply as count. As to papally conceded appointments to benefices, these were literally showered on Philip the Good. In 1436 the provost of St. Omer was permitted to dispose of benefices to 100 persons named by the duke, and Duchess Isabel was granted the collation to twelve benefices in 1442. Between 1458 and 1462 some forty benefices were individually conferred by Pope Pius II on coun-

[1] Cockshaw, *Les secrétaires de Philippe le Bon*, 176–8, from ADN B1283/ 15588.

cillors, chaplains, doctors and other dependants of the duke.[1] Besides
the collegiate churches, with their provostships and canonries, the
abbeys of the Low Countries provided an admirable means of rewarding or financing ducal clerics and others. In the chronicle of the
abbey of Liessies in Hainault the characteristic entry occurs under
the year 1461: 'Anselme du Sars, twenty-ninth abbot of Liessies. This
man was forcibly intruded into the administration of the house by
Duke Philip of Burgundy, in spite of the fact that the monks had
chosen Thomas Bouquemiau.'[2] In 1447–8 Philip took endless trouble,
ending with a personal visit to St. Omer, to make sure that his
councillor Guillaume Fillastre became abbot of the wealthy monastery
of St. Bertin in place of the person actually elected by the monks.
Sometimes Philip and his wife were in competition for the same
abbacy. In 1442, Philip wanted to make Guillaume Fillastre abbot of
Les Dunes at Koksijde, while Isabel tried to obtain the abbey for her
Portuguese nephew Dom Jaime.

The abuse of granting abbacies *in commendam* appeared in the
Low Countries at this time. This was an arrangement whereby the
recipient of an abbacy enjoyed the revenues normally accruing to
the abbot but was expected neither to reside there nor to administer
the convent. Fillastre's appointment to St. Bertin's in 1447 was the
first important Burgundian grant *in commendam* by the pope. Many
others followed, nearly all in favour of Philip's candidates. Abbacies,
in commendam or otherwise, like other benefices, were granted to the
duke in groups and in advance of vacancies. For example, in 1442
Eugenius IV reserved for the duke the appointment of ten abbots,
including those of important houses like St. Vaast's at Arras and
St. Peter's and St. Bavo's at Ghent, at the same time prohibiting the
monks of these houses from proceeding to an election when a vacancy
occurred. Naturally the system facilitated the worst sort of clerical
pluralism: Guillaume Fillastre was abbot of St. Bertin's at St. Omer
and of St. Vaast's at Arras, but this did not preclude him from
serving as bishop successively of Verdun, Toul and Tournai.[3]

The collegiate church of St. Peter, Lille, may be taken as an

[1] Dubrulle, *Bullaire de Reims*. For this paragraph as a whole, see especially
de Moreau, *Église en Belgique*, iv. 69–92.
[2] *Chronique de l'abbaye de Liessies*, 430. For the next sentence, see Quenson
de la Hennerie, *RN* xii (1926), 159–60, and, for abbacies *in commendam*,
Berlière, *La commende aux Pays-Bas*.
[3] Du Teil, *Guillaume Fillastre*. For the next paragraph, see Hautcoeur,
Histoire de Saint-Pierre de Lille, ii. 443–9, etc. and *Cartulaire de Saint-Pierre
de Lille*, ii. 1022–9.

example of the effect of ducal control of appointments to benefices on a single church, though it was perhaps peculiarly exposed to pressure. The provosts were invariably appointed by the duke and most of them were Burgundian courtiers or clerics of some note. Henri Goethals (1419–33), ducal councillor and dean of St. Lambert's, Liège, was succeeded by Jehan Lavantage, *premier médecin* and councillor of Philip, who became bishop of Amiens in 1437. Philip's bastard brother, Jehan de Bourgogne, was provost of St. Peter's and of St. Donatian's at Bruges in the years before his appointment as bishop of Cambrai in 1439, and his successor as provost of St. Peter's, Forteguerra da Piacenza, likewise held office before promotion to the episcopate, in his case at Arras. Another ducal physician, Eustache Cailleu, was provost between 1440 and 1451, and he was succeeded by Duchess Isabel's nephew Dom Jaime and Louis de Bourbon in rapid succession. Philip the Good's last appointment to the provostship at Lille was Adrien de Poitiers, ducal councillor and *maître des requêtes*, who held the post from 1456 until 1508. Many of the canons were ducal people too, though they absolutely refused to accept among their number in 1457 the illegitimate son whom Nicolas Rolin, Philip the Good's chancellor, tried to thrust upon them. Appealing to a privilege, or statute, that no bastard could be a canon of St. Peter's, they complained to Philip and to King Charles VII of France, but pressure from both of these, as well as from others, was needed before Anthoine Rolin's claims were eventually withdrawn some years later.

The wholesale intrusion of Philip the Good's courtiers, officials, relatives and followers into the bishoprics, abbeys and churches of his territories and neighbouring lands worked significantly towards the creation of a specifically Burgundian church, and indirectly helped to unify the Burgundian state. At the same time, like every other prince, Philip exploited the Church and resisted its encroachments. He taxed the clergy by means of papally-conceded crusading tithes and through particular votes in each territory. He legislated against the acquisition of lands by religious houses, though this anti-mortmain legislation was not strictly enforced for, like the ducal *ordonnances* prohibiting the sale of indulgences, it was, especially in Holland and Hainault, a response to demands from the towns rather than a result of ducal initiative. In the foundation of new religious houses, which was proceeding apace in the northern territories in his reign, Philip the Good played little part, though he was liberal in his donations towards the building and rebuilding of churches and their

provision with stained glass and statuary. Nor can the duke's encouragement of the Observants, his constant demand for processions
to celebrate a victory or intercede for success, and the privileges he
granted to religious houses, be taken to imply that he particularly
encouraged the *Devotio moderna*, the pietistic movement which
reached its peak in his ducal reign and in his northern territories.
In all these respects, he acted, or rather reacted, towards religious
affairs in just the same way as any other ruler.

Philip the Good also played a typically passive rôle in connection
with certain rather sinister and particularly nasty events which occurred at Arras in 1459–60. They were described in all their unsavoury
detail by history's first specialist crime-reporter, the chronicler
Jaques Duclerq, who lived, conveniently, on the spot. The so-called
vauderie, or witch-hunt, of Arras, though it claimed only a dozen
victims, burnt at the stake, was a harbinger of far worse horrors to come.
This outbreak of clerical superstition was due to the incredulity or
fanaticism of a handful of ecclesiastical officials in Arras, including
the inquisitor there and the dean of the chapter, acting in the absence
at Rome of the bishop, who censured their proceedings on his
return. One of the first suspects was a sixty-year-old man, who
tried to cut off his tongue to avoid having confessions wrung out of
him on the rack. He and a group of prostitutes were accused of kissing
the devil's posterior, and even of sexual intercourse with the devil,
who was said to have appeared to them sometimes as a man, sometimes as a woman, and sometimes as an animal. Handed over to the
civic authorities for execution by burning, they recanted, accusing
their lawyer and judges of extorting confessions from them by
deceitfully promising that they could go free if only they admitted
their witchcraft. Other victims followed, but public opinion was
outraged and horrified. To his eternal credit, the bishop of neighbouring Amiens declared that if anyone accused of witchcraft was
brought before him, 'he would let them go free, for he did not believe
that these people had done or could do what they were accused of
doing'.[1] When Philip the Good consulted a group of senior Burgundian clerics in August 1460, opinion was divided; but the witch-hunt
subsided quickly, claiming its last victim on 22 October 1460.
Meanwhile appeal had been made to the Paris *Parlement* which, after
characteristically protracted legal proceedings, finally revoked and

[1] Duclerq, *Mémoires*, 144. Besides Duclerq, and Duverger, *Le premier
grand procès de sorcellerie aux Pays-Bas*, see Cartellieri, *The court of Burgundy*,
191–206, and references on pp. 268–9.

annulled the judgments of the inquisition in 1491. All documents were to be destroyed; all victims rehabilitated. So far as one can tell, Philip the Good's only interest in this whole bizarre affair was the confiscation of the landed property of its unfortunate victims; for the estates of convicted heretics traditionally fell to the duke.[1]

[1] Duverger, *BCRH* (4) vi (1879), 139–46.

CHAPTER EIGHT

Economic Affairs

There can be no question here of attempting to write the economic
history of the Burgundian state. This chapter has the more modest
purpose of briefly sketching the broad lines of economic activity in
Philip the Good's principal territories; of examining, albeit cursorily,
ducal economic legislation and governmental initiatives in economic
affairs; and finally, of presenting some scattered observations on the
financial resources available to the duke. Nor must the reader expect
here more than a very incomplete guide to the extensive literature
relating to the economic history of fifteenth-century Burgundy.

The economic life of Philip the Good's southern territories was
characteristic of most of medieval Europe. It was predominantly
rural, rather than urban, and the cultivated areas were interspersed
with forests which were far more extensive than they are now. The
towns were small and scattered. The population of the largest, Dijon,
was around 10,000: about one-tenth of what it is now. Auxonne and
Beaune probably each had between two and three thousand persons
in the fifteenth century. What industry there was produced mainly
for the local, or at best, regional market; just as the agricultural
produce of the surrounding countryside found its chief outlet in the
towns. The buying and selling of these local products, as well as
imports and exports, tended to be concentrated at the fairs, the most
famous of which was that held twice a year at Chalon. In the towns,
a thriving corporate life catered for the social, economic and religious
needs of the various crafts. At Dijon there were gilds of goldsmiths,
painters and glaziers, weavers, fullers, saddlers, joiners, locksmiths,
cutlers and others, as well as the gilds concerned with provisioning:
butchers, fishmongers, bakers and, inevitably at Dijon, mustard-
makers. All these economic activities were minutely regulated by the
mayor and corporation or the gilds themselves. The weight of the
different loaves of bread was exactly fixed and adjusted according to

the price of corn; each goldsmith had to stamp his products with his individual mark; a foot measure for measuring glass for windows was set up in the town hall to serve as a guide and model; surgeons had to obtain the mayor's permission before making an incision.[1]

By Philip the Good's reign, in the larger towns of the two Burgundies, a few wealthy burgess families had begun to produce individual merchants of real note. Thus at Dijon, Odot Molain, son of a tinker, numbered the duke among his clients and became an official ducal salt merchant or distributor in 1424. He must have made a great deal of money from this lucrative business before he was dismissed in 1447 by the *chambre des comptes*, who accused him of selling some of the duke's salt for his own profit. He held various minor posts, lent large sums to the duke, and acquired lands. At Auxonne, the wealthiest citizen in the early part of Philip's reign was probably Amiot le Chisseret. Founder of a veritable dynasty of burgesses, his money was made in the ducal mints of Auxonne and Dijon, and he too was accused of swindling the duke. In 1433 he paid one-twentieth part of the town's contribution to an *aide* of 700 francs. He was by no means only a moneyer; he sold cloth, wool, cheese, herrings, cattle and wine. Conveniently enough for himself and the town, he produced lime from a recently constructed kiln at the very moment when Auxonne was extending or rebuilding its ramparts.

Only two commodities were produced on a large enough scale in Burgundy to be exported in any quantity: salt and wine. There were two salt-works at Salins in the county of Burgundy, where the brine from several springs or wells was boiled. One of them was more or less owned by the duke for, though he had to share the profits with his co-owners, they were his vassals for their shares, and he alone appointed the officials. The duke also enjoyed a monopoly of the sale of salt within the duchy of Burgundy. A recent study has suggested that the total annual production of salt at Salins in the fifteenth century was between seven and eight thousand metric tons, which would make it one of the major European salt-producing centres in the later Middle Ages. Every day fifty wagons lumbered in and out of the ducal salt-works alone, carrying firewood on their way in and salt on their outward journey.[2]

[1] *IACD* i. B. 33 and ii. G. 1–2. For what follows, see Bartier *AB* xv (1943), 185–206; Camp, *Histoire d'Auxonne*, 174 and Bartier *Légistes et gens de finances*, 148 n. 1; and Geoffroy, *AB* xxv (1953), 161–81.
[2] Dubois, *MA* lxx (1964), 419–71. For the next paragraph, see especially Tournier, *AB* xxii (1950), 7–32 and 161–86; Renouard, *RBG* i (1952),

More important than salt, which was found only at Salins, was the production and export of wine, which extended over a large part of Philip the Good's southern territories. 'It is well enough known', said the mayor and corporation of Dijon in 1452, 'that this town is based on the culture of vines, and that wine, through which the greater part of its inhabitants earn their living, is its chief merchandise.' The duke too, was proudly conscious of the merits and economic significance of Burgundian wine. A document of his claimed in 1460 'that wines of unsurpassed excellence are produced in the territory of Beaune, because of which merchants have long been accustomed to buy their wines at Beaune and transport them to various different countries. Because of the excellence of these wines we are reputed to be lord of the finest wines in christendom.' Much of this Burgundian wine was exported westwards and northwards to France and the Burgundian Low Countries; above all, it travelled to Paris and, via Paris, to Artois and Flanders. Much of it was consumed in Burgundy, where, apart from water, there was nothing else to drink in those days, for beer was only just beginning to spread from the Low Countries. Wine, in fact, was a bulk, not a luxury product. At Auxonne the mean annual consumption per head in the fifteenth century has been calculated (incredibly) as approaching 300 litres. Even in towns like Ghent, the average inhabitant apparently consumed upwards of a litre of wine every week.[1]

The present state of our knowledge of the economic life of fifteenth-century Burgundy does not permit generalizations about population changes, nor about the prosperity of the area as a whole. At Dijon, the population seems to have peaked in the 1390s at about 11,000, declined suddenly to 8,000 as a result of the plague of 1399, remained at or slightly below this figure until 1430, and then increased to 12,000 or more by 1450. In the bailiwick of Dijon, which covered a considerable area of countryside around the town, the peak of 32,000 in 1380 was not surpassed until the early 1430s, after a decline around 1420 to about 25,000. Whereas in Dijon itself the population declined

---

5-18; and Craeybeckx, *Vins de France aux anciens Pays-Bas*. The quotations are from F. Humbert, *Finances municipales de Dijon*, 246 and *Chartes de communes*, i. 278.

[1] Camp, *Histoire d'Auxonne*, 161, and Craeybeckx, *Vins de France aux anciens Pays-Bas*, 5–8, and, in general, Dion, *Histoire de la vigne*. For the next paragraph, see Garnier, *Recherche des feux en Bourgogne*, and F. Humbert, *Finances municipales de Dijon*, 20–3 and table 1.

somewhat between 1450 and 1465, a fact attributed by the mayor to emigration, the population of the bailiwick continued to rise. We may assume that the general prosperity of the region was at a low ebb during the period of warfare in the first third of the fifteenth century and that the years of peace that followed had a beneficial effect on economic life, but there is insufficient quantitative evidence to prove the point. The town accounts of Dijon do not help us much. They are neatly balanced throughout this period, and the average annual receipt of the first five years of Philip's reign, at 540 francs, is only marginally exceeded by that for the last five surviving accounts, those for 1451–6, which is 543 francs.

It is quite impossible, in a few pages, to do justice to the thriving and diverse economic activity of Philip the Good's northern territories, which were more urbanized than any other part of Europe, save perhaps north Italy. Seat of the ducal financial administration of Flanders, Artois and Burgundian Picardy, and an important transit centre for merchandise of all kinds, Lille was the capital of *Flandre gallicante* or French-speaking Flanders. Unlike Bruges and Ghent, it did not suffer from internal revolts, perhaps because its artisans were not sufficiently numerous. Its economic life was in many respects similar to that of Dijon and was likewise the subject of minute regulation. Every craft or occupation had its inspectors, or *eswardeurs*, appointed annually by the echevins. In 1421, the civic authorities passed a decree containing eighty separate clauses laying down a complete code of conduct for the sale of sea fish in their town. In the following year sixty-two different regulations were drawn up for the benefit of the cordwainers and tanners.

At Lille the textile industry by no means suffered the decline which was so apparent elsewhere in Flanders during Philip the Good's reign. Indeed at the very time when other towns were complaining bitterly of the impoverished state of their cloth manufacture, a Lille document of 1458 observes that 'for some time since, cloth-making in this town has increased so much that the craft gilds occupied with it have multiplied both in the number of households and in the wealth of their members'. At Lille too, a flourishing tapestry industry developed in the fifteenth century with international connections. In 1466, six tapestries of the Knights of the Round Table were exported from Lille to England; and in 1453 Giovanni de' Medici ordered several tapestries from an unnamed craftsman in Lille, described as 'the finest master there was', through the branch of the Medici bank at Bruges. The cartoons for these tapestries were sent from Florence and the work took almost a year.[1]

Just as Dijon depended on wine, so Bruges and with it the whole of Flanders depended in Philip the Good's reign on foreign trade. As a ducal document of 1459 puts it, 'this land has from old depended on the arrival of merchants and captains of ships and sailors coming by sea from all Christian kingdoms and, as everyone knows, more trade is carried on [in Flanders] than in any other area whatsoever'.[2] Around 1455, when Philip the Good was making serious preparations for a crusade, a list was made, with a view to possible requisitioning, of 'ships lying at present in the harbour of Sluis'. They were as follows: three Venetian galleys; a Portuguese hulk of 150 tons; a small carvel of 40 tons; a Scottish barge, belonging to the bishop of St. Andrews, of 500 tons, 'a very fine ship'; another Scottish barge of 350 tons; a carvel belonging to the bishop of Aberdeen, of 140 tons; a Scottish barge of 150 tons; a small Scottish carvel of 28 tons; a small Scottish balinger of 20 tons; a small Spanish carvel of 50 tons; 41 carvels from Brittany, from 130 to 30 tons; two barges from Normandy of 100 and 50 tons; a small carvel of 25 tons and four small balingers of 30 to 36 tons from Normandy; 12 heavy sailing-ships from Hamburg 'which are lying on the mud, without masters or sailors; also on the mud, 36 to 40 fishing-boats, useless for any other purpose'.

It is only the hindsight of the historian which has surrounded Philip the Good's Bruges with an aura of decadence and decline. Contemporaries thought otherwise. Leo of Rozmital's companion Schaseck described it at the end of the reign in glowing terms.[3]

> This is a large and beautiful city rich in merchandise, for there is access to it by land and sea from all countries of the christian world. The merchants have their own stately houses there in which are many vaulted rooms. They lie close to marshes which extend through the town as far as these houses. There are many canals in the town and some 525 bridges over them. At least it is so reported, but I did not count them.

The Spanish traveller Pero Tafur was likewise favourably impressed, even though he visited Bruges in the famine year 1438.

[1] *Correspondance de la filiale de Bruges des Medici*, i. nos. 14, 15 and 17. On this paragraph, see Marquant, *Vie économique à Lille*; the quotation is from p. 291.

[2] *Coutume de Bruges*, ii. 36. For what follows, see *IADNB* viii. 291.

[3] Rozmital, *Travels*, 41. The extract which follows is from Tafur, *Travels and Adventures*, 198–200, with minor changes. On Bruges in general, see van Houtte, *Bruges*.

This city of Bruges is a large and very wealthy city, and one of the greatest markets of the world. It is said that two cities compete with each other for commercial supremacy, Bruges in Flanders in the West, and Venice in the East. It seems to me, however, and many agree with my opinion, that there is much more commercial activity in Bruges than in Venice. The reason is as follows. In the whole of the West there is no other great mercantile centre except Bruges, although England does some trade, and thither repair all the nations of the world, and they say that at times the number of ships sailing from the harbour of Bruges exceeds seven hundred a day. In Venice, on the contrary, however rich it may be, the only persons engaged in trade are the inhabitants.

The city of Bruges is in the territory of the count of Flanders, and is the chief city. It is well peopled, with fine houses and streets, which are all inhabited by work people, very beautiful churches and monasteries, and excellent inns. It is very strictly governed, both in respect of justice as in other matters. Goods are brought there from England, Germany, Brabant, Holland, Zeeland, Burgundy, Picardy, and the greater part of France, and it appears to be the port for all these countries, and the market to which they bring their goods in order to sell them to others, as if they had plenty at home.

The inhabitants are extraordinarily industrious, possibly on account of the barrenness of the soil, since very little corn is grown, and no wine, nor is there water fit for drinking, nor any fruit. On this account the products of the whole world are brought here, so that they have everything in abundance, in exchange for the work of their hands. From this place is sent forth the merchandise of the world, woollen cloths and Arras cloths, all kinds of carpets, and many other things necessary to mankind, of which there is here a great abundance. There is a large building above a great tract of water which comes from the sea at Sluis, which is called the Waterhalle. Here all goods are unloaded in the following manner. In these parts of the West the sea rises and falls greatly, and between Bruges and Sluis, a distance of two and a half leagues, there is a great canal, as great and as deep as a river, and at different places sluice-gates, as of water mills, are set up, which when opened admit the water, and on being closed the water cannot escape. When the tide rises the ships are laden and travel with their cargoes from Sluis on the tide. When the water has reached its highest point they lock it up, and those ships which have been unloaded and filled with fresh cargoes return with the same water which carried them up-stream, travelling down again with the falling tide. Thus the people by their industry make use of the water, carrying great quantities of goods to and fro, the transport of which, if they had to use beasts, would be exceedingly costly and troublesome.

This city of Bruges has a very large revenue, and the inhabitants are very wealthy. . . . Anyone who has money, and wishes to spend it, will find in this town alone everything which the whole world produces. I saw there oranges and lemons from Castile, which seemed only just to have been gathered from the trees, fruits and wine from Greece, as abundant as in that country. I saw also confections and spices from Alexandria, and all the Levant, just as if one were there; furs from the Black Sea, as if they had been produced in the district. Here was all Italy with its brocades, silks and armour, and everything which is made there; and, indeed, there is no part of the world whose products are not found here at their best.

Actually, the finances of Bruges were in a most unhealthy state, but this was due to a combination of accumulated debts and ducal pressure. In 1430–1, for example, Bruges paid more than one-third of its revenues to Philip and this was before the revolt of 1437 saddled the unfortunate town with a fine of 200,000 gold riders.[1] Financial mismanagement by the civic authorities and financial exploitation by the duke must not be mistaken for poverty. More than ever before, or since, Bruges in the mid-fifteenth-century was a cosmopolitan city. In December 1440, when Philip made a ceremonial entry into the town, the procession which welcomed him included 136 Hansards on horseback, dressed in scarlet with black hoods, 48 Spaniards, 40 Milanese and 40 Venetians, 12 citizens of Lucca, 36 Genoese, 22 Florentines, and others. Antwerp and Amsterdam may have been expanding rapidly at this time, the Zwin may have been silting up, the English may have been sailing to Antwerp and Middelburg, but Bruges still maintained her commercial and financial supremacy among the cities of the Burgundian Netherlands until the end of Philip the Good's reign.

This continuing importance of Bruges is reflected in the presence there of one of the subsidiary companies, or branches, of the Medici bank, which was probably fifteenth-century Europe's largest firm. It engaged in every kind of financial and commercial transaction: importing wool from England to Bruges and re-exporting it to Italy; sending Flemish tapestries to Florence; importing alum from the Mediterranean to the Low Countries; supplying silks and other luxury goods to the Burgundian court; and providing financial and credit facilities for the duke of Burgundy, such as, for example, a loan of £10,000 to Tours from the branch at Geneva in 1462.[2] The

---

[1] *IAB* iv. 532 and v. 169–70 and, for what follows, Daenell, *Blütezeit der Hanse*, i. 394–5.
[2] *IACOB* i. 171. See, in general, de Roover, *Money, Banking and Credit in Medieval Bruges*, *MKVAL* xv (1953), and *The Medici Bank*; and *Corre-*

contract which was signed in 1455 to renew the Medici partnership at Bruges for a further term of years shows how such a branch company was set up and organized in the fifteenth century.

Be it known that a commercial and financial company has been set up at Bruges by Piero, Giovanni, and Piero Francesco de' Medici, Gierozzo de' Pigli and Agnolo Tani, for a term of four years, from 25 March 1456 to 24 March 1460, with Tani as manager, according to the following arrangements.

1. The firm is to be called 'Piero di Cosimo dei Medici and Gierozzo dei Pigli and Company' and its trade-mark is ⚓.

2. Its capital will be £3,000 groat, of which the three Medici will subscribe £1,900 gr., Pigli £600 gr., and Tani £500 gr. Furthermore, Tani is to serve the company in person at Bruges.

3. The profits or losses (may God forbid them) will be shared as follows: 12s in the pound to the three Medici; 4s in the pound to Pigli; and 4s in the pound to Tani, who is also allowed £20 per annum for his living expenses.

4. Tani may not lend money to, nor provide exchange or credit facilities for, any spiritual or temporal lord or priest or functionary or anyone save a merchant or manufacturer, without the written permission of one of his associates.

5. Tani may not undertake any business on his own account, or on behalf of anyone except for other Medici branches, on pain of a fine of £50 gr.

6. He promises not to play at games of dice or cards, on pain of a fine of £100 gr. for each time, all his gains to be confiscated by the company but his losses to remain his alone. He will also be expelled from the company and his shares in it confiscated. Under the same penalty, he is prohibited from keeping a mistress in his house.

7. He is to send the company's profits, books and balance sheet to Florence every 24 March, and more often if required.

8. When the company is wound up, the house and warehouse at Bruges and all the records there will remain the property of the Medici and Pigli, but Tani will be allowed to consult them. All the firm's creditors will be paid by the Medici and Pigli.

9. Tani is not allowed to employ an office boy or factor without the written leave of one of his associates.

spondance de la filiale de Bruges des Medici, i. The summary that follows is from Correspondance de la filiale de Bruges des Medici, i. 53–63; compare de Roover, The Medici Bank, 87–9.

10. The business may be closed down before the four years if the Medici and Pigli so desire. Tani must remain at Bruges for six months after the liquidation to wind up the company's affairs.

11. Tani may not leave Bruges except on the company's business, such as when visiting the fairs of Antwerp and Bergen-op-Zoom or going to Middelburg, Calais or London, without the written permission of one of his associates.

12. He may not purchase wool or cloth in England or Flanders in excess of a total value of £600 without permission.

13. He must insure everything he sends by sea, except that he may risk up to £60 on any one Florentine or Venetian galley. Losses caused by infringements of this rule to be made good by him. He may use his judgment about insuring goods sent by land, up to a maximum of £300 worth.

14. Tani is to hand over to the company any present which he receives of over £1 in value. Otherwise such gifts will be debited to his account.

15. He promises not to break the laws of Flanders.

Bruges was by no means the only important commercial centre in Philip the Good's northern territories. Antwerp was described as follows by Tafur:[1]

I departed from Ghent and came to the city of Antwerp, which is in Brabant and belongs to the duke of Burgundy. It is large, and has about 6,000 burghers. There is also an excellent wall with a rampart and a moat. The houses and streets are very fine and it has a good harbour. The ships enter by a river so that the galleys can be fastened to the city walls. The fair which is held here is the largest in the whole world, and anyone desiring to see all christendom, or the greater part of it, assembled in one place can do so here. The duke of Burgundy comes always to the fair, which is the reason why so much splendour is to be seen at his court. For here come many and divers people, the Germans, who are near neighbours, likewise the English. The French attend also in great numbers, for they take much away and bring much. Hungarians and Prussians enrich the fair with their horses. The Italians are here also. I saw there ships as well as galleys from Venice, Florence and Genoa. As for the Spaniards they are as numerous, or more numerous, at Antwerp as anywhere else. . . .

As a market Antwerp is quite unmatched. Here are riches and the best entertainment, and the order which is preserved in matters of traffic is remarkable. Pictures of all kinds are sold in the monastery of St. Francis; in the church of St. John they sell the cloths of Arras; in a

[1] *Travels and adventures*, 203–4.

Dominican monastery all kinds of goldsmith's work, and thus the various articles are distributed among the monasteries and churches, and the rest is sold in the streets. Outside the city at one of the gates is a great street with large stables and other buildings on either side of it. Here they sell hackneys, trotters and other horses, a most remarkable sight, and, indeed, there is nothing which one could desire which is not found here in abundance. I do not know how to describe so great a fair as this. I have seen other fairs, at Geneva in Savoy, at Frankfurt in Germany, and at Medina in Castile, but all these together are not to be compared with Antwerp.

The principal industry of Flanders in the late Middle Ages was the manufacture of cloth. This was at first concentrated within the cities, especially at Ghent and Ypres, but the rural cloth industry developed rapidly during Philip the Good's reign, indirectly as a result of competition from England and Holland; directly as a result of the restrictive practices of the urban craft gilds. At Ypres, especially after the siege of 1383, the surrounding villages competed so successfully that the urban textile industry suffered a rapid decline in the first half of the fifteenth century. The same thing happened at Dixmude, Comines and elsewhere, but we have no means of knowing if an overall decline in cloth production resulted. Nor do we know how true the claim of the author of *The Libelle of Englyshe Polycye*,[1] that 'the wolle of Englonde susteyneth the comons Flemynges', remained in the second half of Philip's reign, for it seems clear that the growing rural cloth industry was drawing more and more of its raw material from neighbouring parts of continental Europe, and from Spain. On the other hand, in Holland the urban cloth industry was flourishing at this time and the Dutch were still importing quantities of English wool. A case which came before the Exchequer court at Westminster in May 1449 shows that some of it was smuggled past the English customs.[2]

A certain Gerard Dutchman of Dordrecht in Holland on 18 March last after sunset at the town of Kingston-upon-Hull, that is, at a certain staithe of William Hedon's, caused eight pokes of wool, containing about eight sacks, and nine bundles of woolfells, each containing about 100 woolfells, on which customs duty had not been paid, belonging to the said Gerard, to be placed and loaded in a certain barge capable of

[1] Ed. Warner, 5–6. The Flemish cloth industry is documented in *Recueil de documents relatifs à l'industrie drapière en Flandre*, ii. *Le sud-ouest de la Flandre depuis l'époque bourguignonne*.
[2] *Bronnen van den handel met Engeland*, ii. 866–7.

carrying about ten tons of cargo owned by William Horne, and of which a certain William Robinson of Kingston-upon-Hull was the master, [to take them] thence to a certain ship, called the Maryknyght, of Dordrecht in Holland, which was lying at anchor off Pauleclife, a place on the shore about four miles seawards from Kingston-upon-Hull, waiting for the abovementioned wool and woolfells. On 18 March, in the dead of night, the said William Robinson transported the said wool and woolfells in the said barge to the abovementioned ship and loaded the wool and woolfells into the ship with a view to despatching them to foreign parts without having paid customs duty on them.

On a basis of the scantiest quantitative information, some economic historians have advanced the hypothesis that the fourteenth and fifteenth centuries were an age of contraction, regression, crisis or decline, to use their own conveniently vague terms. If this theory were true of the Low Countries, the history of the Burgundian state would be inconceivable. As a matter of fact, so far as Philip the Good's reign and territories are concerned, the reverse is the case. The volume of trade in the duke of Burgundy's northern territories, which of course included expanding Antwerp and Amsterdam as well as supposedly stagnating Bruges and declining Malines, seems to have doubled during the fifteenth century, and it certainly increased considerably in Philip the Good's reign.[1] In Flanders and Brabant, while a still vigorous cloth industry was invading the countryside, the manufacture of linen and leather goods, tapestry-making and, especially at Brussels, jewellery, metal work and arms was expanding. Along the coasts of Flanders and Holland the herring fishery enjoyed a remarkable boom. At Ostend a new harbour for the fishing fleet was built in 1445-6, and production more than doubled between 1450 and 1469.[2] At Dunkirk a foreign observer stated in 1466 that 'more than a hundred fishing-boats are sent out when the wind is favourable'. In

[1] On this and the following paragraph see especially the following, with the works referred to in them: Geschiedenis van Vlaanderen, iii. 301–20; Jansma, Het vraagstuk van Hollands welvaren; van Uytven, RN xliii (1961), 281–317; Alberts and Jansen, Welvaart in Wording; and Thielemans, Bourgogne et Angleterre. See too Pirenne, Histoire de Belgique, ii. 412–48; Prims, Geschiedenis van Antwerpen, vi and van der Wee, Growth of the Antwerp market; Laenen, Geschiedenis van Mechelen and Trouvé, HKOM lvi (1952), 46–67; and Bonenfant, Bruxelles au xve siècle.
[2] Degryse, ASEB lxxxviii (1951), 122–5. The quotation which follows is from Rozmital, Travels, 41–2. For Dutch commerce, see especially Kerling, Commercial relations of Holland and Zeeland with England and Ketner, Handel en scheepvaart van Amsterdam.

Holland, the cloth industry made rapid strides, as did the brewing of beer; and the need for the raw materials of these activities, which came from far afield, corn from the Baltic and wool from England, stimulated the shipping and commerce of Amsterdam in particular, and of Holland in general.

Statistical information is naturally lacking, but it seems that the population of the Low Countries in general increased, certainly it did not decline, during the fifteenth century, in spite of severe temporary setbacks like that caused by the famine and epidemic of 1438. Too much emphasis has perhaps been placed on figures from individual towns or areas, and some of these are in any case of doubtful significance. For example, Pirenne long ago supposed late medieval Ypres to have been in fast demographic decline. Yet in fact nothing definite is known of its population in the fourteenth century and the only certain conclusion from the figures published by Pirenne is that during much of the fifteenth century its population fluctuated at around 10,000.[1] Throughout Philip the Good's reign, wages and prices remained relatively steady, and there is no sign of a general crisis or depression in agriculture. Moreover, apart from interruptions following the warfare of 1436 and 1452–3, new land was being won from the sea in north-eastern Flanders and southern Zeeland.[2] The hypothesis of economic wellbeing is borne out by the ducal revenues from the northern territories, which show no signs of diminution. With reservations about some areas, including perhaps Holland, whose commerce suffered considerably from the wars of Burgundian conquest as well as from those between Holland and the Wendish towns of the Hanse, and between Dordrecht and the Rhine towns of Cologne, Wesel, Arnhem and Nijmegen in 1438–45,[3] and with the qualification that, if the number of poor was increasing, wealth was probably being concentrated in fewer hands, the general conclusion seems inescapable, that the Low Countries as a whole under Philip the Good were prosperous, and that their prosperity was increasing.

Every medieval ruler was perfectly well aware that the general welfare of himself and his family, his pleasures and comforts, and his power and prestige, all depended on his subjects' prosperity. Every-

[1] Pirenne, *VSW* i (1903), 1–32. The figures are: 10,736 in 1412; 10,523 in 1431; 9,390 in 1437; 7,626 in 1491; and 9,563 in 1506.
[2] Gottschalk, *Westelijk Zeeuws-Vlaanderen*, ii.
[3] Jansma, *TG* liii (1938), 337–65; Warnsinck, *Zeeorlog van Holland*; Jansma, *RN* xlii (1960), 5–18; and Niermeyer, *BMHGU* lxvi (1948), 1–59.

where, economic legislation was designed to protect or increase this prosperity. Philip the Good was no exception, though many of his economic initiatives originated from merchants and other groups, working through representative institutions like the Four Members of Flanders and the States General, or through individual municipalities. Inevitably, a large majority of ducal interventions in economic affairs were only of limited, or purely local, significance. For instance, in July 1455 Philip authorized the echevins of Lille to impose a duty for one year on merchandise in transit through their town, to pay for the upkeep of the roads.[1] If we confine ourselves here to topics like the coinage, incentives for foreign merchants, commercial treaties, the protection of industries and the regulation of corn supplies, this is because these were matters of more general interest, not because they were representative of the duke's economic legislation as a whole.

Although John the Fearless had drawn handsome profits from the mints of his southern territories by manipulating the coinage, it was soon stabilized under Philip the Good. Moreover, production declined rapidly in the first years of the reign and remained so meagre thereafter that the mints at Auxerre, Chalon and Mâcon were closed for long periods, and that at Dijon seems to have been kept in being merely as a matter of principle. These mints were technically royal, though Philip's emblem of a flint and steel replaced the royal fleur-de-lis on the coins struck by them which until 1435 were issued in the name and with the title of King Henry VI of England and France. At Auxonne the mint was not on French territory, and it struck Burgundian coins which in 1439 were brought into line with those of the duke's northern territories.

The coinage of the Burgundian Low Countries was much more important than that of the two Burgundies. It was to a great extent unified by Philip the Good in 1433-4, when he introduced a common gold and silver currency for Flanders, Brabant, Holland, Zeeland and Hainault. This reform was undertaken as soon as possible after Philip had acquired these territories, and it was accompanied by a promise, which was kept, that monetary stability would be maintained for the next twenty years. Thus the duke deliberately renounced the practice of devaluation or debasement as a source of revenue for himself, even though it had been used with considerable effect by many other rulers, including in particular John the Fearless and Louis of Male. Naturally, the motives of his government are presented in the most altruistic

[1] Marquant, *Vie économique à Lille*, 288-90.

252 PHILIP THE GOOD

and enlightened form possible in the preamble of the monetary *ordonnance* of 12 October 1433:[1]

> We, considering that one of the principal needs of all good polities, on which the public welfare of both prince and people is based, is to have a sound and stable gold and silver coinage; having a genuine desire to provide for the welfare and profit of our said lord [the duke] and his lands; and wishing to do all in our power to increase trade, attract and retain merchants and defend and preserve the common people from grief and harm. . . .

The renunciation of debasement was brought about because of repeated demands by the Estates of the different territories, and a request by the Estates of Brabant in 1428 for monetary unity with Flanders[2] makes it probable that the same was true of the unification of the coinage of the Burgundian Netherlands as a whole. Another activity in which ducal legislation was mainly a response to requests from interested parties and representative institutions was the encouragement of foreign merchants, which usually consisted in the grant or confirmation of privileges by the duke. For example, in 1422 and 1434 Philip the Good confirmed and modified the privileges which John the Fearless had granted in 1414 to Genoese merchants at Bruges. He had charged them a lump sum of 800 gold crowns for this favour; Philip, in 1434, sold them the same privileges, slightly altered, in return for a levy of £2 groat on every Genoese ship entering Sluis harbour. Some of the more important of these privileges, which were typical of many issued to other merchants, may be summarized as follows.[3]

1. No Genoese subject, or sailor belonging to a Genoese ship, shall be accused or hindered by any of our officers, or by anyone else from Flanders, on account of a crime committed outside Flanders.
2. The owners, masters and officers of Genoese ships in Flemish waters or harbours may punish their own people without inter-

---

[1] ADN B639/15625, cited by Spufford, *Monetary Problems and Policies*, 240. Besides this unpublished thesis see on this paragraph Barthélemy, *Essai sur les monnaies des ducs de Bourgogne*, 63–77, Lièvre, *Monnaie et change en Bourgogne*, Bailhache, *RNum* (5) i (1937), 235–44, Dubourg, *PTSEC* (1957), 57–64 and *AB* xxxiv (1962), 5–45 (southern territories); Deschamps de Pas, *RNum* (n.s.) vi (1861), 458–78 and vii (1862), 117–43 and xi (1866), 172–219, H. van Werveke, *ASEB* lxxiv (1931), 1–15, van Gelder, *RBN* xvii (1961), 150–3 and Spufford, *APAE* xl (1966), 61–87 (northern territories).
[2] *ICL* iv. 204.
[3] Finot, *ACFF* xxviii (1906–7), 300–17 and see de Roover, *Money, Banking and Credit in medieval Bruges*, 14–15.

ference provided they do not wound or mutilate them. Conversely, our officers will not intervene in quarrels and riots on Genoese ships except if someone is wounded.

3. If a Genoese subject dies in Flanders, our officers shall inventory his belongings and look after them for a year and a day in case anyone claims them.

4. The cargoes of Genoese ships may be freely sold in the port of Sluis or elsewhere in Flanders, provided our maritime bailiff at Sluis, or his lieutenant, is informed about them within three days of the ship's arrival.

5. Any Genoese subject, or person belonging to a Genoese ship, may go to and fro freely at any hour of the day or night on land or water between his ship and his lodgings and through the streets of Sluis, carrying a sword or knife until the last bell rings.

6. The personnel of Genoese ships at Sluis or elsewhere in Flanders may carry corn and flour and bake their own bread provided they pay the customary dues.

7. A Genoese ship that is ready to set sail in favourable weather and is moored with one anchor only shall not be prevented from leaving, except for known debt or for a crime concerning which judgment has been passed.

8. The Genoese may salvage any of their ships, with their cargoes, which are shipwrecked in Flemish waters. If anyone else salvages them, they must hand them over to the owners, on payment of the usual salvage dues.

9. If any goods belonging to the Genoese are thrown overboard in a storm to save the ship, and those goods are washed ashore, they are to be returned to their owners on payment of the usual salvage dues.

10. If any Genoese vessel leaves any Flemish port without its anchors and cables, its crew is free to recover those anchors and cables without seeking permission.

11. The Genoese may repair their ships and scrape their bottoms in any of the accustomed places in Flanders without paying dues or seeking permission.

Among numerous other grants of privileges by Philip the Good were those to Castilian, Portuguese and Scottish merchants at Bruges and elsewhere in Flanders, and to English merchants visiting Antwerp.[1] The Castilians and Portuguese were permitted, in 1428 and

---

[1] *IAB* iv. 496–500 and v. 299–300; *Cartulaire de l'Estaple de Bruges*, i. 615–17 and 647; Schanz, *Englische Handelspolitik*, ii. 162–70 and Prims, *Geschiedenis van Antwerpen*, vi (2), 146–64. For what follows, see Martens,

1438 respectively, to set up consulates at Bruges; the English did the same at Antwerp in 1446. Sometimes, instead of the issue of privileges for a whole group of merchants, the duke issued safeguards for individuals: several Milanese subjects received them, at the request of Francesco Sforza, duke of Milan, in the late 1450s. Sometimes privileges were issued to all foreign merchants resorting to a particular place: in 1454 all those visiting Flanders were granted a safe-conduct for ten years. Closely connected with these grants of privileges were the commercial treaties which Philip the Good either negotiated and signed himself, or confirmed. In June 1438 he confirmed a treaty made between the Dutch towns of Haarlem, Leiden, Amsterdam, Hoorn, Enkhuizen, Medemblik, Monnikendam, Edam, Naarden, Muiden and Weesp on the one hand, and Deventer, Kampen and that part of the *Sticht* of Utrecht which lay beyond the river Ijssel, on the other. In 1441 he and his council at The Hague confirmed a commercial treaty between Holland and Castile which settled disputes and established freedom of access for merchants of the two countries.[1]

Of commercial treaties negotiated by Philip with neighbouring towns and territories, those with Tournai and England at least, deserve mention. The treaty with Tournai was renewed periodically between 1421 and 1434. It provided for mutual free access for trading purposes between Flanders and Tournai and prohibited the molestation of each other's merchants. While Philip's subjects were permitted to import what goods they pleased from Tournai, 'provided that the town of Tournai was not thereby deprived of food and other necessary provisions', the Tournaisiens were not allowed to import meat and cheese from Flanders.[2] More important was the commercial truce, or *intercursus* with England, which Philip inherited from his predecessors and maintained throughout his reign except between 1436 and 1439. This treaty applied only to Flanders and Brabant; a separate one was negotiated for Holland in 1445 which stipulated, among other things, that the Dutch were to pay the

---

BIHBR xxvii (1952), 221–34 and *IAB* v. 372 and 397–8; compare ADN B1607, fos. 164b–165 (1456). See too Finot, *ACFF* xxiv (1898), 1–353 and Verlinden, *Hispania* x (1950), 681–715 on Spanish merchants and de Roover, *Money, Banking and Credit in Medieval Bruges*, especially pp. 9–23, on Italian merchants.

[1] *Boergoensche charters*, 44–5 (compare p. 63) and van Marle, *Hollande sous Philippe le Bon*, no. 27, pp. lvi–lxiii.

[2] Houtart, *Les Tournaisiens et le roi de Bourges*, 260–1. For what follows, see above, pp. 198–9, and *Bronnen van den handel met Engeland*, ii. 832–8.

English 7,000 nobles in reparation for damages, and that seven solemn masses, with suitable prayers, were to be performed in St. Stephen's, Westminster, and the ducal chapel at The Hague, for the souls of those killed on either side during the recent quarrels.

Perhaps the most all-embracing intervention of the duke in the economic affairs of his lands was his protectionist legislation in favour of established industries and, above all, on behalf of the urban cloth industry of Flanders. Regulation after regulation was drawn up in a desperate but wholly unsuccessful effort to prevent this industry from leaving the towns and establishing itself in the surrounding country-side. At Ypres the ducal *ordonnance* of 10 March 1428 prohibiting the manufacture of cloth in the villages and towns of the castellanies of Ypres, Warneton, Bailleul and Cassel, that is, in the countryside around Ypres, nearly provoked a serious riot.[1] From 1428 onwards this ducal protectionism included an embargo on imports of English cloth, which was imposed first in Holland, but which was extended in 1434, after consultations with deputies from the towns of Brabant, Holland, Zeeland and Flanders in December 1433, to cover all Philip the Good's northern territories. It was reimposed in 1436, 1447 and 1464, but seems to have been seriously and consistently applied only in Flanders, though elsewhere it was frequently reinforced by local prohibitions, for example at Leiden. But other Dutch towns depended for their livelihood on imports of English cloth. At Middelburg the civic officials were fitted out in English scarlet, and the town messengers of Veere were dressed in English cloth. In general, the embargo was evidently ineffective. In 1451 the duke's officials at Brussels claimed that it had done nothing to improve the cloth industry of the towns of Brabant and Flanders, but had considerably decreased the transit trade of English cloth through Antwerp to Germany and north Italy. They suggested that the duke should impose a toll instead of an embargo.[2]

Some further examples of ducal economic activity may be cited to give an idea of its scope and variety. The herring fishery was closely regulated by a series of *ordonnances* which fixed the opening of the season on 24 August and laid down the quality of salt to be used for

---

[1] Diegerick, *ASEB* xiv (1855–6), 285–310; and *Recueil de documents relatifs à l'industrie drapière en Flandre*, ii: *Le sud-ouest de la Flandre depuis l'époque bourguignonne*, i. 3–7.

[2] AGR CC17, fos. 72b and 256. On the embargo, see Thielemans, *Bourgogne et Angleterre*, 203–12, with references, and AGR CC21806, f. 17b (December 1433 assembly).

barrelling the fish.[1] Many *ordonnances* referred to the cloth industry, including one prohibiting certain materials from being used as dyes, which applied to all the duke's territories. On 12 October 1445 Philip the Good, learning that the new Rhenish wine was being sold at a higher price than in the previous year, which would be very much to the disadvantage of his subjects, fixed a maximum price. A month later, an *ordonnance* laid down rules to ensure that the wine-sellers at The Hague gave full measure. In 1443, the ducal councillors at Dijon wrote to the civic authorities of Besançon pointing out that Dijon's prosperity depended on wine, and that the vineyard workers were demanding higher and higher wages. Could the governors of Besançon send them a copy of their recent statutes regulating the wages of their vineyard workers?

A detailed study of the economic history of the duchy of Limbourg in Philip the Good's reign has shown that the ducal authorities took an interest in the exploitation of its mineral resources, among which calamine was the most important. In place of the old communal and seigneurial organization, Philip introduced capitalist entrepreneurs, granting them funds and privileges in return for a share in the proceeds.[2] In the two Burgundies, in 1449, he hopefully conceded mining rights in gold, silver, lead and other metals to the Aragonese sculptor Juan de la Huerta, who was at work on his parents' tomb, reserving 10 per cent of the profits for himself. But Juan was a good-for-nothing, and in any case there was no gold and silver. The main motive for this over-optimistic mining venture seems to have been the shortage of these metals at this time, which led also to a ducal embargo on the export of bullion.

Like other rulers, the duke of Burgundy engaged from time to time on commercial ventures of his own. His Mediterranean fleet, though designed primarily to combat the infidel, was used to trade on his behalf. The ships left Sluis in 1441 with cargoes of cloth, and they took merchandise from Provence to Constantinople in 1444. In the Black Sea they preyed successfully on Turkish merchant shipping and sold their booty, which included female slaves, furs of fox, ermine, beaver and otter, bales of silk, wool and cotton, in Constantinople or

[1] Degryse, *ASEB* lxxxviii (1951), 120 and *Boergoensche charters*, 82. For what follows, see Marquant, *Vie économique à Lille*, 158, *Boergoensche charters*, 83 and *Correspondance de la mairie de Dijon*, i. no. 21, pp. 32–3.
[2] Yans, *Histoire économique de Limbourg*, 115–232. For what follows, see ACO B16, fos. 32b and 42–44b, Leclercq, *Politique navale*, and Finot, *MSSL* (4) xxi (1895), 163.

elsewhere. They also seized two boatloads of salt fish from near Trebizond, but later paid compensation to the owner.

Another aspect of ducal economic activity was governmental intervention in times of dearth or famine. Two means were employed to counter crises of this kind: an embargo on corn exports and the control of prices. Right at the start of Philip's reign it was thought that the troubles in France might cause a scarcity of corn in Flanders, but the ducal letters of 24 September 1419 prohibiting exports were partly revoked before the end of the year,[1] and the prohibitions of corn exports from Flanders which followed in 1422 and 1423 do not seem to have reflected a very serious famine there. On the other hand, a widespread famine in 1437–9, linked with an epidemic, provoked a whole series of measures which, however, were limited in the main to Holland and Zeeland. On 11 September 1437 the ducal authorities at The Hague banned the export of corn and authorized that of beer only if sufficient corn to brew it was imported. On 22 October a new *ordonnance* laid down the maximum prices of corn imported from the Baltic and established control of its distribution by setting up official corn-buyers in the principal Dutch towns. The effects of the scarcity were soon felt elsewhere. In November the authorities in Hainault passed on to the duke complaints that all available corn had been bought up so quickly in August that very little remained, and the price had tripled. The outbreak of war between Holland and the Wendish towns of the Hanse in the spring of 1438 only made things worse, and it was not until 1439 that the cessation of the repetition and modification of these ducal measures shows that the famine was over, though there was a further prohibition of exports of corn from Flanders in February 1440. There is little trace of further legislation of this kind after then, and we may assume that there were no further serious famines in the Burgundian Low Countries under Philip the Good.

The impact of the duke's government on economic affairs was felt in at least one other significant way. Scattered throughout his territories were numerous tolls and, though the great majority of these were levied by individual noblemen and towns, some of the most important were owned or imposed by the duke. Their purpose was

[1] AGR CC21797, fos. 32a–b and 36b; and, for the rest of the sentence, see *Hanserecesse von 1256 bis 1430*, vii. 260–5, *IAG* i. 185, *IAM* ii. 34–5. For the rest of the paragraph, see *Boergoensche charters*, 37–52; van Marle, *Hollande sous Philippe le Bon*, nos. 10, 11, 17 and 19, pp. xiv–xli; *Memorialen van het Hof*, 261–2; ADN B10403, f. 35b and *IAB* v. 228–9.

normally fiscal, though in some cases they may have partly served a protectionist purpose. One of the most important and lucrative was established at Gravelines by Philip the Good between 1438 and 1440 and from 1446 onwards.[1] It comprised a special duty on English wool imported from the Calais staple, and a tax on all merchandise passing through Gravelines on its way to and from Calais. The aim may partly have been to discourage the Flemish from depending too much on English wool and to undermine the Calais staple, but the fiscal motive was surely uppermost. After all, the Gravelines toll brought in 10,000 francs in its first year of operation; it was farmed out to Giovanni Arnolfini in 1456 for a second six-year term, for 15,000 francs per annum; and, after Arnolfini had made his fortune from it, the Florentine merchant Tommaso Portinari took it over for a five-year period in 1465 for 16,000 francs per annum.

We have already had occasion to mention the purely fiscal toll which Philip applied to Genoese ships entering the port of Sluis when he confirmed their privileges in 1434.[2] The 10 per cent customs duty he levied on all imports from Scotland, which King James I confirmed to him in 1420, was probably similar in origins. Other ducal tolls were those on Dutch beer imported into Flanders and on wine exported from the two Burgundies. The philosophy, such as it was, behind tolls like these is well set out in the preamble of a ducal *ordonnance* imposing a duty on salted herrings exported from the northern territories.

> Philip, by the grace of God duke of Burgundy . . . greetings to all who see these letters. We have been informed and assured that day by day and every year large quantities of herrings barrelled in salt and red herrings are produced in our lands of Flanders, Holland, Zeeland, Boulonnais and elsewhere in this area and exported to supply and nourish foreign countries. Since it is certain and well known that in many other regions and countries heavy imposts, subsidies and duties are levied for the profit of their rulers on these and similar goods and provisions exported from them, and since it would be convenient and proper for us, who have the care and expense of being in charge of the government of the lands from which these herrings come, to draw some profit and emolument from them . . . we . . . considering these matters

---

[1] Thielemans, *Bourgogne et Angleterre*, 175–8. I have not seen Roffin, *Le tonlieu du port de Gravelines*. For what follows, see ADN B1963, fos. 31–2, Bigwood, *Régime juridique et économique du commerce de l'argent*, i. 662–3, and AGR CC25191, f. 1.

[2] Above, p. 252. For what follows, see ADN B1603, f. 38; AGR CC2705, f. 98; ACO B16, fos. 28b–29; and ADN B1606, f. 182a–b, whence the extract.

and in order to help us to bear the costs of affairs of state which press daily upon us in many ways . . . have ordained and do now ordain . . . that a duty of two Flemish groats be levied on each barrel of salted herrings exported from our lands of Brabant, Flanders, Hainault, Holland, Zeeland, Boulonnais and others in this area . . . , and two groats likewise on every thousand red herrings. . . . Given in our castle of Hesdin, 2 September, 1448.

This is not the place for a systematic and detailed analysis of Philip the Good's revenues and expenditure. His finances were basically sound. Accounts were neatly kept and carefully balanced; credit was usually raised without much difficulty; taxes, or *aides* were voted more or less as required; and Philip the Good even managed to hoard treasure, both in the form of specie in his castle at Lille, and in the form of plate and jewellery. The financial administration was partly centralized, but the accounts of the receipt-general of all finances,[1] which were balanced during Philip the Good's reign with remarkable consistency at about £350,000 of Tours, included only a selection, so to speak, of the duke's revenues and expenditure. They neither centralized the surpluses from the individual territories, nor included all the revenues from the *aides* levied in them. But, in spite of the apparently healthy state of Philip the Good's finances, his councillor Hue de Lannoy submitted at least two memoranda outlining suggestions for improving them. In one, he concentrated on expenditure. Given substantial economies, he estimated the ducal revenues, all necessary expenses paid, at 160,000 crowns. This sum, he suggested, might be apportioned as follows:

1. Personal expenses of the duke, and those of Anthony, the bastard of Burgundy, Adolf of Cleves and Pierre de Bourbon	£62,680 of 40 groats
2. Expenses of the duchess, the countess of Charolais, and my ladies of Bourbon, Guelders and Étampes	£31,600
3. Extra expenses of the duke, 'if he can be content, at least for a time, with less than he has had'	30,000 crowns
That is to say:	
His armour, weapons, horses and clothes	12,000 cr.
His gifts	12,000 cr.
Hunting with dogs and birds	6,000 cr.

---

[1] Analysed by Mollat, *RH* ccxix (1958), 285–321. For Hue de Lannoy's scheme, see G. de Lannoy, *Œuvres*, 308–9; the crowns were of 40 groats.

4. Extra expenses of the duchess and the count
   and countess of Charolais   10,000 cr.
5. Ambassadors and messages, 'though this is
   difficult to estimate'   8,000 cr.
6. Pensions for the duke's relatives, the chancellor, my lord of Croy and others   17,000 cr.
   These six parts total   159,300 cr.

These figures are, of course, quite fanciful. If Hue de Lannoy had taken the trouble to inspect the accounts of the receiver-general of all finances, which were audited and filed in the *chambre des comptes* at Lille, he would surely have had to revise them upwards. It has been calculated that Philip the Good's average annual expenditure on gifts alone, recorded in these accounts, was £36,523 of Tours; and pensions, including wages, amounted to £32,703 *t.* p.a.[1] The cost of ambassadors, too, was a great deal more than what Hue allowed for. In his other financial memorandum he drew up an equally fanciful scheme, this time for improving the duke's revenues.

It appears that the kingdom of France has 1,700,000 towns with bell-towers, from which 500,000 must be subtracted because of their destruction by war or otherwise, so that 1,200,000 remain. If twenty francs, which is not a large sum, was levied from each of them, the larger helping to pay for the smaller, the total would be twenty-four million. Now it seems that my lord the duke of Burgundy has in all about half as much territory as there is in the kingdom of France, and his lands are as populous or more so. It may therefore be supposed that he could well have in all 600,000 towns with bell-towers, which is half [the total in France]. But, to be more certain, let us take it as one-third of those in the kingdom, that is 400,000 towns. If twenty francs were levied from each in the way described, this would total eight million. If need be only taking half of this, a sum of four million is produced, which would be a fine thing to advance the affairs of my lord the duke.

To discover the actual number of such towns in all the duke's lands, as well as the number of hearths and persons, the duke would have to write to all his governors, bailiffs, provosts, seneschals, receivers and other officers in each duchy, county and lordship asking them to let him know as quickly as they could the true number of towns with bell-towers in their administrative districts, together with the number of hearths, without divulging the reason for doing this. Thus the duke

[1] Dancoine, *Évolution des finances bourguignonnes.* The extract which follows is from BN MS. fr. 1278, f. 66a–b, partly printed in G. de Lannoy, *Œuvres,* 488.

would ascertain the true basis on which to levy this tax. Now if this can be done in this way it would be convenient and advantageous for my lord the duke to appoint two notable and worthy knights in each country, natives of it, who could put the request for the levy of the above-mentioned tax to the three Estates, and who could be authorized to collect the revenues . . ., rendering a true and accurate account of them to my lord the duke or to his deputies.

The way in which *aides* were actually levied in Philip the Good's territories, and the revenues they produced, were in practice quite different from this. The Estates of each territory or, in the case of Flanders, the Four Members, were asked to vote a lump sum, which they then apportioned among the different townships and, ulti-mately, hearths. Sometimes the Estates persuaded the duke to reduce the sum requested. In some territories the *aide* was voted for a single year, in others for a term of years. The *aide* was known as an 'extra-ordinary' tax because it was originally levied only occasionally as a contribution over and above the customary rents and dues or 'ordinary' revenues. But by the fifteenth century it had become a regular and important feature of public finance in much of western Europe. For reasons which are mainly technical, the size and incidence of *aides* probably more accurately reflect the relative contribution of the different territories to the ducal finances than even the most thorough analysis of the accounts of the receiver-general of all finances. Moreover, since these contributions may to some extent reflect the relative prosperity of the individual territories at different times, it has seemed worth while to try to set out here the *aides* voted during Philip the Good's reign by the representative institutions of his more important territories. Because these figures are incomplete and will need modification in the light of further research, they have neither been totalled nor reduced to a single currency.[1]

Although nobody disputes that Philip the Good was a relatively wealthy ruler, his dependants and officials lived under almost per-manent threat of cuts in their allowances and salaries, and the administration as a whole was the subject of intermittent economy drives. The reason for these measures was more often than not the

[1] The figures are partly from Pirenne, *Histoire de Belgique*, ii. 404–5, cor-rected and supplemented in the case of Flanders from ADN B1923–2061 (accounts of the receipt-general of all finances). I have also used Billioud, *États de Bourgogne*, 384–405 and F. Humbert, *Finances municipales de Dijon*, 218–25; Cuvelier, *Dénombrements en Brabant*, and *IAGRCC* iii. 3–5; Hir-schauer, *États d'Artois*, ii. 18–37; *IAEH* i. lxxxiii–xci and Arnould, *Dénombre-ments de Hainaut*; Blok, *BVGO* (3) iii (1886), 36–130.

AIDES levied by Philip the Good in his principal territories

	Duchy of BURGUNDY	BRABANT	FLANDERS	ARTOIS	HAINAULT	HOLLAND
1420				14,000		
1421				14,000		
1422	36,000		100,000 crowns			
1423	20,000			14,000		
1424	20,000			14,000		
1425	20,000			14,000		
1426			100,000 crowns	14,000		
1427				14,000		
1428			40,000 crowns		60,000	50,000 cr.
1429						50,000 cr.
1430	30,000		150,000 nobles	28,000		50,000 cr.
1431	25,000				10,000	50,000 cr.
1432						50,000 cr.
1433	40,000			14,000		50,000 cr.
1434	17,000			28,000	49,200	50,000 cr.
1435	34,000			21,000		50,000 cr.
1436	8,000	50,000	150,000 nobles		46,000	50,000 cr.
1437	7,500	50,000				50,000 cr.
1438	2,750	50,000		14,000	30,000	
1439		50,000	150,000 nobles	14,000		36,000 r.
1440	3,000	50,000	350,000	14,000	40,000	36,000 r.
1441	10,400	50,000		17,500	6,240	36,000 r.
1442	22,000			28,000	6,000	36,000 r.
1443	12,000	24,000			13,000	36,000 r.
1444	12,700	25,143		28,000	52,500	
1445	6,000	25,143	25,000	28,000	10,000	40,000 r.
1446		25,143	25,000	28,000		40,000 r.
1447	6,000	25,143	25,000	28,000		40,000 r.
1448	5,000	25,143	25,000	28,000	43,000	40,000 r.
1449	8,000	25,143	25,000	28,000		40,000 r.
1450		25,143	25,000	14,000		40,000 r.
1451	30,000	25,000	25,000	14,000	20,000	
1452		25,000	25,000	14,000	20,000	40,000 r.
1453		25,000		25,000	25,000	40,000 r.
1454		25,000	50,000	28,000	20,000	40,000 r.
1455	60,000	25,000	50,000	28,000	20,000	40,000 r.
1456		25,000	50,000	28,000	20,000	40,000 r.
1457		25,000	50,000	21,000		40,000 r.
1458	12,000	25,000	50,000	21,000	18,000	40,000 r.
1459		25,000	46,000	21,000	18,000	40,000 r.
1460	10,000	25,000		28,000	18,000	40,000 r.
1461		25,000		28,000	18,000	40,000 r.
1462	12,000	25,000	25,000	28,000	16,000	54,000 r.
1463	14,000	25,000			24,000	54,000 r.
1464		25,000		17,500	24,000	54,000 r.
1465	14,000	25,000	36,000	14,000	24,000	54,000 r.
1466		25,000	40,000		24,000	54,000 r.
	pounds tournois of 32 Flemish groats	riders of 48 Flemish groats	riders unless otherwise stated	pounds tournois	pounds of 20 Flemish groats	riders, or crowns of 40 Flemish groats

short-term one, of raising money quickly for some urgent specific purpose. This applied in particular to the periodic withholding of pensions or allowances, paid to ducal relatives and others, and of annual salaries paid to officials. Daily wages, paid to councillors, secretaries and others when on ducal business, were not normally affected. An *ordonnance* of 12 February 1425 stopped pensions altogether for the entire calendar year 1425, and halved salaries; and a similar one of 15 July 1430 did the same for the year beginning 1 June 1430.[1]

Of a different, and longer-term character, was the reduction in the salaries of local Burgundian officials, ordered in 1422. It was these lesser, local officials, like the unfortunate castellan of Beaune, whose salary was reduced from £80 of Tours per annum to £50 in 1422, and still further, to £40 p.a. in 1454, who suffered the brunt of these economies in the ducal wages bill. Some higher-placed people, like the secretary Thomas Bouesseau, threatened with redundancy in 1439 when Philip planned to abolish his office of keeper of the ducal archives at Dijon, were able to use their influence to escape the axe. But others, like Hue de Lannoy, lord of Santes, who was Philip the Good's stadholder in Holland between 1433 and 1440, were not only affected, but also infuriated. It is a matter of no surprise that the man who habitually pestered the duke with reforming memoranda on military, financial, political and administrative affairs, many of which have been quoted in the foregoing pages, should have something forceful to say to Philip and his advisers about this niggardly policy of reducing salaries. He sent off a messenger on 2 March 1438, to protest, furnishing him with the following written instructions.[2]

Instructions concerning what is to be said to my lord the duke of Burgundy, to his great council, and to the superintendents of his finances.

Firstly, they must be told that the lord of Santes, who some time ago was appointed by the duke head of his council in Holland, wishes, in order to carry out the oath he has made to the duke, to make it clear to him above and beyond what the council [at The Hague] has written to him and what was made known to him through the secretary Andrieu de la Croix . . . that he, the lord of Santes, finds in truth that all the

[1] ADN B1603, f. 49b and B1931, f. 92; Champion, *de Flavy*, 172–3 and Proost, *Financiele hoofdambtenaren*, 72. For what follows, see Bartier, *Légistes et gens de finances*,168–9 and nn. and 422–6.
[2] I have used van Marle, *Hollande sous Philippe le Bon*, no. 12, pp. xxii–xxv and the text he printed from, BN MS. fr. 1278, fos. 124–125b. See, too, B. de Lannoy, *H. de Lannoy*, 141–2.

duke's councillors in Holland and others of his people there, who love him loyally and cordially, are astonished at the extraordinary way in which my lord the duke and his great council treat them, although they are his faithful subjects and servants, and it seems to them that they are serving him as well and loyally according to their lights as if they were actually with him. And if there is going to be any question about it, it seems, considering the present state of affairs in the duke's lands, that those who serve him loyally and well in his absence are just as much to be commended and borne in mind by the duke as the others. Nor should any distinction be made between those who are retained on a daily, monthly or annual basis; but rather the duties they carry out should be taken into consideration. Nevertheless, regardless of what services they performed, last year those who served on a daily basis are said to have been paid, while those serving on an annual basis suffered a reduction in their salary by half, at least in the lands round here.

It seems to the councillors and other officials here that they have been strangely treated, more so than those in other lands, for three reasons. First, when the duke issued new coins, the [old] clinkarts then current at 40 groats each became worth only 28 groats, losing a third of their value, while elsewhere the duke's officers and servants are paid in the new money. Second, last year their salaries were reduced by half; and third, the duke has recently issued an order withholding all salaries, the proceeds to be put to his own profit.[1] The said councillors understand from this that there is no intention to pay them at all. When the receiver of Holland saw this order he frankly said that he daren't pay anything, and that he did not intend to do so until he received ducal letters patent about this. Now consider the state of affairs down here. None of the councillors is willing to travel abroad on official business, and God knows with what danger and difficulty the land has been maintained in peace in the duke's absence. Nevertheless, confident that the duke will recognize their services, they will continue diligently with the duke's affairs as they have done hitherto, notwithstanding everything, until Mid-Lent next, awaiting a statement from the duke on these matters.

As for me, Hue de Lannoy, I could not be more astonished at the way I've been treated, when I consider that I originally agreed to stay in this land of Holland against my wishes and only by command of the duke, as my lord [the bishop] of Tournai, my lords of Croy and Roubaix, Sir Roland [d'Uutkerke], the duke's treasurer Guy Guilbaut and other notable persons who were with him then, can verify. Since then, about eighteen months ago, both because I have been very ill with gravel and for other reasons . . . I pressed my lord the duke to release me from the

---

[1] Ducal *ordonnances* of 1 February 1437 halving salaries and of 12 January 1438 withholding all pensions, ADN B1605, fos. 178b–180b and 198a–b, both applying to all lands.

governorship of Holland. He agreed to this, and in expectation of it I sent my wife home. Yet notwithstanding this and all my efforts, I have constantly been asked to stay on until the duke's affairs were in a better state. . . . Last year the salary which I receive for governing this territory in the duke's absence was reduced by half; by the present order I am to be deprived of all of it, a fact which I find incredible, for I have served by constraint and only to please the duke. If my lord the duke wants to make economies, he should certainly not apply them to me, who has no desire to serve and who ought to be discharged because of illness. . . . I have been a knight for thirty-two years, and chamberlain of my lord the duke's father John, God rest his soul, and of the present duke, and I have been their councillor for twenty-eight years. It seems to me a peculiar result of such service, that the salary should be taken away from people who have been employed by the duke against their will and who have never received from him any life pension or gift of land. God knows what dangers and perils I have been through on their behalf. I ask my lord the duke and my lords of his great council to consider these matters and let me know their intention and good pleasure, so that I may decide what to do.

A great deal of Philip the Good's governmental activity, which comprised investigations like those into the administration of Brabant and Burgundy in 1451 and 1462;[1] periodic 'reformations' like that of 1457; and reforming *ordonnances*, was aimed simply at saving money. Take, for instance, the ducal *ordonnance* of 5 May 1447 applying to Holland, which among other things abolished a number of financial offices, reduced the wages of several Dutch receivers, and economized on the staff of the ducal hôtel at The Hague, to the extent, for example, of reducing the watchman's wages there from £38 to £12 p.a. The purpose of this *ordonnance*, we are told, was to 'diminish and lessen the unnecessary expenses which we have to bear in various ways', and the preamble stated that investigations into such unnecessary expenses were being made in all the duke's lands. Similarly, the general administrative *ordonnance* of February 1437 was wholly concerned with economies. Besides the reduction of wages resented by Hue de Lannoy, it reduced the number of secretaries maintained at court at the duke's expense from seventeen or eighteen to seven, and ordered the use of foot messengers instead of mounted ones whenever the matter was not urgent. Its immediate purpose seems to have been to restore the duke's finances after their depletion by the recent war with England.

[1] ACO B341 and AGR CC17, fos. 1–80 and fos. 121 ff. For what follows, see ARH AR1, fos. 11b–14b.

The most striking and far-reaching of all Philip the Good's economy drives was ordered on 22 March 1454, not long after the Feast of the Pheasant, when the duke had vowed to go on crusade. Indeed the aim was explicitly stated to be to help raise money for this expedition. Six separate *ordonnances* were published on this occasion, one dealing with court economies, one ordering economies in the administration of the domain in all territories, and four regional *ordonnances*, one for Flanders, Artois, Picardy and Hainault; one for the two Burgundies; one for Brabant and Limbourg; and another for Holland and Zeeland. The preamble to the first of these gives an interesting review of the duke's expenses since the start of his reign:[1]

Philip, by the grace of God duke of Burgundy . . . greetings to all who see these letters. Since the death of our very dear lord and father, whom God forgive, which happened in the year 1419, at which time we were accepted in his lordships as his true heir, because of the wars which we have fought since then against several princes and lords; the armies we have mounted and maintained at sea against the infidels for the aid and advancement of the christian faith, together with the construction and purchase of ships and artillery and other equipment for them; the sumptuous marriage-gifts we have provided for several members of our family and others, whom we have married and allied to important and noble houses; the generous and excessive gifts we have made of various towns, castles and other parts of our domain . . .; the great increase in the ordinary costs of our households and those of our dearest and well-loved companion the duchess and our nephews and nieces . . .; also because of the costly and lavish pensions we have granted to several people . . .; the extravagant gifts made by us of cloth of gold, of silk and . . . of jewellery, at high and excessive prices; not to mention . . . the great expenses . . . of the war we have waged to reduce the town of Ghent to our obedience, as well as several places and castles which rebelled against us in Luxembourg. . . .

The *ordonnance* then proclaims the complete abolition of 'the ordinary expenses of our court and the wages which the court officials and servants are paid daily, as from today until 1 January 1455, from then on for a further year, and thereafter until such time as we return from crusade. . . .' There follows a long list of pension and salary reductions. The duke of Cleves's pension of 7,250 francs p.a. was suppressed altogether; the count of Étampes, in receipt of a pension

[1] ADN B1607, f. 97 and *DRA* xix. 156-7. For these *ordonnances*, see ADN B1607, fos. 97-106 and 111-12b; Gachard, *Rapport sur Dijon*, 91-2 and 156; and *DRA* xix. 156-8.

of 8,000 francs p.a. plus 2,000 as captain of Picardy, 750 for silk robes and 1,460 for his commons, lost these allowances but kept the pension. The senior officials of the Burgundian civil service suffered too. The bishop of Tournai, president of the great council, lost his annual pension of 1,000 francs but kept his daily wage of 4 francs, amounting to 1,460 f. p.a. The chancellor Nicolas Rolin also lost his pension of 2,000 f. p.a. but kept his daily wages of 8 francs. The receiver-general of all finances, whose total annual emoluments of 2,380 f. comprised various allowances besides daily wages and a pension, suffered a loss of 700 f. p.a. Similar cuts were made by the other *ordonnances* of 22 March 1454 in every single one of the duke's territories, and they were accompanied by a variety of administrative measures, all designed to economize. Two days later, at 5.0 a.m. on 24 March 1454, the duke of Burgundy set out from Lille incognito, with thirty companions,[1] to travel to Germany to settle the final details of the crusade which in fact was never launched.

In spite of recurrent and often quite desperate shortages of ready funds, notably during the campaigns of 1436, 1453 and 1465, but with the help of the savage economies and administrative reforms just mentioned, Philip the good was able to surround himself with lavishly illuminated books, superb tapestries and jewellery and plate which was the admiration of Europe. His court was sumptuous, his tastes were extravagant, he involved himself in expensive wars. Yet he managed, towards the end of his reign, through the mechanism of his *épargne*, to put by a substantial sum of money in his castle at Lille. The immense financial resources which made all this possible were provided, in the main, by the commercial and industrial activities of the towns of his northern territories; activities which the duke and his government did their best to promote by conferring privileges on foreign merchants, by protectionist legislation, by industrial regulations of all kinds, and by means of a stable gold coinage. Surely these various initiatives, taken together, amount to something that can legitimately be described as an 'economic policy'?

[1] D'Escouchy, *Chronique*, ii. 243.
[2] See above, pp. 80–1 and below, pp. 328 and 384–5.

CHAPTER NINE

The Mediterranean, Luxembourg and the Empire: 1440–54

In the second half of Philip the Good's reign external ambition began to replace internal consolidation as the mainspring of ducal policy, for it was only after Brabant and Holland had been incorporated into the Burgundian state and the wars in France and against England had been brought to a conclusion, that any more distant schemes could be seriously entertained. Philip the Good's projects and achievements in the Mediterranean and the Empire, which form the subject of this chapter, are linked in a single theme: the enhancement of Burgundian prestige and the duke's renown in the eyes of Europe. Naturally, the duke looked eastwards and towards Germany to extend his fortunes and try his luck. Westwards the way was blocked by France, where any furtherance of the Burgundian interest was prevented by a combination of sustained hostility and renewed vigour on the part of a monarchy restored at last by victory against England in the ultimate campaigns of the Hundred Years War.

Born in the very year of the crusade of Nicopolis, which was organized by his grandfather and led by his father, Philip the Good was brought up in the best crusading tradition. We are told that, as a five-year-old, he played in the park at Hesdin dressed up as a Turk. This interest or passion was maintained throughout his long life, being attested by the presence in his library of copies of contemporary works describing the eastern Mediterranean by Guillebert de Lannoy, Emmanuele Piloti, Bertrandon de la Broquière and John Torzelo. Some time before he fancied himself at the head of a victorious

expedition against the Hussites,[1] Philip had sent the first of these
to the east on a kind of strategic reconnaissance both on his own
behalf and for King Henry V of England. Guillebert left Sluis on 4
May 1421 and visited during the next two years Prussia, Russia, the
Crimea, Constantinople, Rhodes, Jerusalem, Cairo and Crete, returning via Venice to write a lengthy report of his travels which he took
to London in person. The professional, military nature of this tour
of inspection is revealed in Guillebert's description of places of
potential crusading significance like Gallipoli:[2]

Gallipoli is situated on the Greek side of the straits of Romania. It
is a large, unfortified town with a square castle near the sea which has
eight small towers surrounded by deep ditches. On the landward side,
these ditches are deep but apparently dry; those nearer the sea are
shallower and hold water. On the shore immediately below this castle is
an excellent little harbour for galleys and all sorts of small boats, with a
fine large square tower low down on the shore near the castle to defend
it. On the other side is a mole in the sea which, together with some tall
stakes, encloses the port so that there is only a small entrance, without a
chain, for the galleys to enter. When I was there, there were four galleys
in this port and a very large number of smaller craft. The Turks usually
keep more galleys and other ships here than elsewhere. Directly opposite
Gallipoli, beyond the sea known as the straits of Romania, is a very fine
tower whence the Turks usually pass over from one country to the other.
The straits are about three or four miles wide here and whoever had
possession of the castle and harbour above-mentioned could make it
impossible for the Turks to cross over, so that their conquests in Greece
would be rendered untenable. It is 150 miles from Constantinople to
Gallipoli. Off Gallipoli there is a suitable place for big ships to anchor
even though there is no enclosed port for them.

In 1425, not long after Guillebert de Lannoy's return from the east,
Duke Philip the Good sent his bastard brother Guyot, together with
the lord of Roubaix and four others, to the Holy Sepulchre at

[1] See above pp. 68–70. For the preceding sentence see Doutrepont, *Littérature*, 237–65, Piloti, *Traité sur le passage de Terre Sainte* and Dogaer,
Spiegel historiael ii (1967), 457–65.
[2] G. de Lannoy, *Œuvres*, 160–1, and see pp. 196–7. On G. de Lannoy, see
too Halecki, *BPIAA* ii (1943–4), 314–31 and Maschke, *Syntagma Friburgense*,
147–72. On what follows in general, see especially Jorga, *Notes et extraits*,
Hintzen, *Kruistochtplannen van Philips den Goede*, Atiya, *Crusade in the Later
Middle Ages* and Marinesco, *Actes du VIᵉ Congrès des études byzantines*,
149–68 and references in these works, and the unpublished thesis of Leclerq,
Politique navale.

Jerusalem.[1] On 8 May 1432 another group of Burgundian nobles, including Andrieu de Toulongeon, Bertrandon de la Broquière and Geoffroy de Thoisy set out from Venice for Jerusalem. They were encouraged and rewarded, if not actually sent, by the duke. Bertrandon must have created quite a stir when he arrived back in July 1433 at Pothières in Burgundy, where the duke then was, dressed in 'Saracen' clothes. He proudly presented his outfit to the duke, as well as the horse he had ridden all the way from Damascus, and a copy of the Koran. Years later he wrote an account of his travels for the duke. In 1437, Philip paid for a stained-glass window with his coat-of-arms to be installed in the church of Our Lady at Mount Sion near Jerusalem, and in 1435 and 1440 he was visited by ambassadors from Egypt.[2] There is some evidence that he was planning to attack the Turks as early as 1436, but it was not until 1438 that the formation of a Burgundian fleet was begun, and even then the purpose of the carvel, *grand nave* and other ships, which were constructed at Sluis, Brussels and Antwerp, is far from clear. It seems possible that they were originally laid down by Duchess Isabel for use in a projected Portuguese crusade against Tangier; they were certainly built under the supervision of Portuguese technicians.

The appearance of a Burgundian fleet in the Mediterranean was due in a general way to the duke's crusading aspirations. But, in particular, it was a response to the appeal of the Hospitallers of Rhodes for help against the Egyptians. Geoffroy de Thoisy, former companion of Bertrandon de la Broquière, was appointed captain of the ducal army 'going to Rhodes' on 25 March 1441, and on 8 May the duke went in person to Sluis to see off his *nave* and three other large ships.[3] He was concerned enough about their welfare to send off a small carvel a few weeks later as far as the Bay of Biscay, to discover how the expedition was faring. Geoffroy de Thoisy sailed via Lisbon, Ceuta and Barcelona to the port of Villefranche near Nice, and thence to Rhodes, where his fleet was based throughout the first half of 1442. Thereafter he returned to Villefranche to refit.

[1] De Laborde, *Ducs de Bourgogne*, i. 234. For what follows, see ADN B1948, f. 162b and de la Broquière, *Voyage d'Outremer*.

[2] *IADNB* iv. 137; ADN B1954, fos. 133b–134; ADN B1969, f. 244. For the next two sentences, see Perret, *France et Venise*, i. 324, n. 2; Leclercq, *Politique navale*, 16–18 and ADN B1966, f. 253; *Chroniken der deutschen städte*, xiii. *Cöln*, ii. 183–4; and above all, Degryse, *MAMB* xvii (1965), pp. 161–2 and 227–52.

[3] Nelis, *Catalogue des chartes du sceau de l'Audience*, 11 and *IADNB* viii. 17. For what follows, see ADN B1972, f. 92 and *IADNB* viii. 18.

For some time before Geoffroy de Thoisy set out in aid of Rhodes Pope Eugenius IV had been doing his best to fulfil the promise he had made to the Byzantine Emperor, during the negotiations at Ferrara and Florence that led to the so-called Act of Union of the Greek and Latin Churches, to provide a fleet to help in the defence of Constantinople against the Ottoman Turks. Philip and other princes had been granted a crusading tithe, or tenth from clerical incomes, for this purpose in 1441, and Philip's decision to create a Burgundian fleet may have been partly a result of this papal initiative.[1] While Geoffroy de Thoisy was cruising in the eastern Mediterranean, a Byzantine embassy arrived at Chalon in March 1442 and appealed for the duke's help. The chronicler Jehan de Wavrin claims that it was his nephew Waleran who suggested to Philip that suitable galleys could most conveniently be hired at Venice. By the spring of 1444 Geoffroy de Thoisy had repaired and rearmed his ships and renewed their sails, in part with materials sent to Villefranche from Genoa, sailors and 'vagabonds' had been recruited to serve in them, and more Burgundian ships had been built at Nice. When Waleran de Wavrin, who had been appointed captain and governor of the four ducal galleys at Venice, put in at Dubrovnik on 22 July 1444 on his way to the East, his colleague Geoffroy de Thoisy had already left Provence long before, cruised off the African coast, visited Corfu, and was at that moment at Rhodes helping the Knights of St. John to defend their island fortress against the Mamluks of Egypt.

Waleran landed at Tenedos and again in the Dardanelles to look for the site of Troy, but he reached Gallipoli in time to join forces with some other Venetian galleys sent by the pope under the command of his nephew Antonio Condulmaro. At Constantinople council of war was held with the authorities and, while two of the Burgundian galleys remained at Gallipoli, Waleran took the others into the Bosporus to try to prevent the Turkish army from crossing the straits and attacking the crusading army under John Hunyadi, King Ladislas of Poland and Hungary, and a papal legate. But Waleran's

---

[1] *IADNB* i (1), 170–1. For what follows, besides the works cited in the notes on pp. 269 and 270 above, see de Waurin, *Croniques*, v. 32–119 etc.; Jorga, *Aventures 'sarrazines'*, especially pp. 26–31; and, for the recruitment of crews in 1443, *IACOB* i. 256 and *Documents pour servir à l'histoire de la Bourgogne*, 435. De Waurin, *Croniques*, v. 20, describes the Byzantine embassy visiting Philip when the duke was at Chalon 'with the dukes of Bourbon and Savoy and the count of Nevers'. This can only refer to March 1442 and not, as some writers claim, July 1443; see Vander Linden, *Itinéraires*, 209–10 and 219.

K

crews found it impossible to row their galleys in the Bosporus current and a storm, not to mention the Turkish artillery, made matters worse. The Turkish army brushed aside the Burgundian fleet, crossed into Europe, and inflicted a catastrophic defeat on the Christian army at Varna on 10 November 1444.

Soon after these events Geoffroy de Thoisy and the rest of the Burgundian fleet arrived from Rhodes and, after a winter spent at Pera and Constantinople, the fleet sailed into the Black Sea in the spring of 1445, once more splitting into two contingents. Waleran took two galleys to cruise along the north shore of the Black Sea, past the mouth of the Danube to Kaffa in the Crimea, while Geoffroy de Thoisy sailed along the southern shore towards mythical Colchis, land of the Golden Fleece.[1] The piratical activities of this Burgundian Jason led to his ambush and arrest at Poti on the Georgian coast, but the emperor of Trebizond subsequently secured his release. After this humiliating episode Geoffroy de Thoisy returned to Constantinople, passing through in July 1445 on his way to Italy, while Waleran, having assembled a mixed force of eight galleys, arranged a joint campaign along the Danube with John Hunyadi, to be financed by a Hungarian loan of 3,000 florins.[2] In spite of a serious illness, he reached the rendezvous at Nicopolis on 12 September before the Hungarians, having attacked several Turkish strongholds en route. He was well enough to be shown the battlefield of Nicopolis from his cabin window, and to receive John Hunyadi a few days later, though the Hungarian had to remove his armour before he could squeeze through Waleran's cabin door.

After military consultations between the captains, the Burgundian galleys sailed up the Danube, accompanied on the north bank by the Hungarian army, while an army of Turks followed them on the south bank. But there was no engagement, nor did the subsequent withdrawal of the Turks entice Hunyadi into a rash pursuit. Indeed he now advised Waleran to sail back down the Danube, which would soon be frozen, and the Burgundian fleet arrived back at Constantinople on 2 November. Waleran himself was at Venice on 15 January 1446, visited the pope at Rome, and eventually reported to Philip the Good at Lille in March or April. His fleet returned in a more leisurely and roundabout way, only reaching Marseilles to disarm after a piratical cruise along the coast of north Africa, from Egypt to Tunis.

[1] Marinesco, Le Flambeau xxxix (1956), 382–4.
[2] IADNB iv. 173 and ADN B1991, f. 106.

The Turks were not the only ones to suffer from the activities of Burgundian ships in the Black Sea. Their allies the Genoese resented this disruption of their lucrative trade with the infidel, based on the ports of Pera and Kaffa. Before he set out on his Danubian expedition, Waleran de Wavrin had fitted out and armed a galliot, which he placed under the command of a certain Jaques de Ville. But, when Jaques sailed triumphantly into Pera with a Turkish prize, the Genoese authorities there disarmed his galliot, tore up his ducal pennon, and confiscated his booty. He complained of this treatment, but was told that 'they lived by trading with both Turks and Christians, and their port was just as open to the Turks as to Christians'. Jaques, undeterred, sailed on, seized more booty and took it to the port of Kaffa in the Crimea. But he was treated worse there than at Pera. His written protest was torn up and, to prevent him complaining to his captain, he was held in prison until news reached Kaffa that Waleran was safely back in Constantinople. Jaques de Ville and Waleran de Wavrin complained to the duke. After a court of enquiry, Philip wrote to Genoa in June 1448 demanding restitution. Complaints and counter-complaints dragged on. Eventually, in 1458, Philip issued letters of marque for Waleran and Jaques against the Genoese and the affair was still in dispute at the time of the duke's death in June 1467.

Burgundian ships in the Mediterranean and the Black Sea continued their activities, which can only be described as piratical, during several years, and the Genoese authorities complained to Philip about them in May 1447, August 1448 and June 1449. Meanwhile, we hear of one of the Burgundian galleys based in Provence and captained by Jaquot de Thoisy, nephew of Geoffroy, being attacked and robbed by Venetian galleys off the Sardinian coast near Alghero, in the summer of 1448.[1] Some time after his return from the East, Geoffroy de Thoisy was sent to Antwerp to supervise the construction of four more galleys, which were completed by the end of April 1449, and in February 1449 the bailiff of Hainault was instructed to find 'a certain number of crewmen for these galleys, that is to say gamblers, thugs, good-for-nothings and such-like ruffians'. But they were destined to be used against the town of Ghent rather than against the Turks.

---

[1] Lacaze, *PH* lvii (1964), 221–42. For this paragraph, see *Documenti ed estratti*, i. 421, 423 and 424; *Codice diplomatico*, i. 840–8; and Finot, *Flandre et Gênes*, 132–6 and 174–84. For what follows, see Leclercq, *Politique navale*, 29–30 and ADN B10413, f. 42.

Philip the Good's crusading projects of the 1440s not only involved him in closer diplomatic contacts with the Byzantine Empire, Genoa and Venice. They were also accompanied by the emergence of Italian ambitions and the development of relations with other Italian powers. A scheme was mooted in 1445 for the cession of Genoa by Filippo Maria Visconti, ruler of Milan, to Philip the Good.[1] Apparently Philip hoped to use it as a naval and crusading base, while his wife Isabel dreamed of granting it as an apanage to her son Charles. But though Filippo Maria proudly styled himself *Dominus Janue*, the Milanese had been expelled thence ten years before. Moreover, Charles VII had his eye on the republic. When Filippo Maria died in August 1447 interested parties advanced from all sides to quarrel over, or seize parts of, the Visconti inheritance. Among them was Charles, duke of Orleans, who claimed Asti in particular and the whole duchy of Milan in general. He got nowhere, in spite of a contingent of Burgundian troops and a sum of Burgundian money, provided by his ally Philip with motives which can scarcely have been purely altruistic.

While Philip thus failed to extend Burgundian influence in north Italy, he cemented a close alliance with the King of Aragon and Naples, Alfonso V. Embassies began their journeys to and fro between Naples and Dijon or Brussels in 1442, and these comings and goings continued throughout the decade. Orders of chivalry, as well as ambassadors, were exchanged by the two rulers whose motives for this parade of friendship were avowedly crusading, for they vied with each other in offering themselves in the service of Christendom against the infidel. Their alliance was such, by the end of the decade, that the famous Burgundian knight-errant and hero of the lists, Jaques de Lalaing, was unable to find an opponent in the kingdom of Naples: Alfonso, because of his affection for Philip the Good, had forbidden his subjects to challenge Jaques.

According to the chronicler Jehan de Wavrin, Philip the Good's plans to send a naval expedition to the East were delayed in 1443 by the duke of Saxony's attempts to drive Philip's aunt, Elizabeth of Görlitz, out of her duchy of Luxembourg. Not that Philip was in the

---

[1] Grunzweig, *MA* xlii (1932), 81–110. For what follows, see du Fresne de Beaucourt, *Charles VII*, v. 149–50 and Champion, *Charles d'Orléans*, 358–79 and, on Philip and Alfonso V, Marinesco, *Actes du VIᵉ Congrès des études byzantines*, 156–8 and 164–5, above, pp. 161–2, de la Marche, *Mémoires*, ii. 89 and 203–4 and *Livre des faits de Messire Jaques de Lalaing*,

least interested in going to the rescue of his aunt; he wanted Luxembourg for himself. The Valois dukes of Burgundy had for long cast acquisitive glances at this imperial territory, which, though rural and feudal in character, and by no means wealthy, was situated very much within their natural or geographical sphere of influence. Philip the Bold had actually acquired control of the duchy for a brief period in 1401–2, and John the Fearless had arranged in 1409 for his brother,

THE SUCCESSION TO LUXEMBOURG

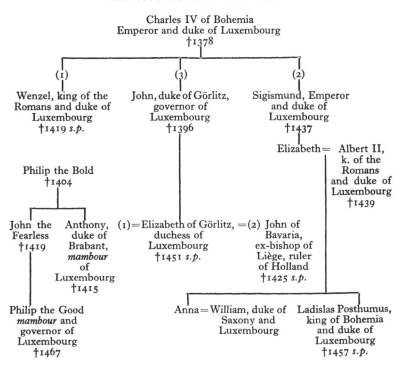

s.p. = sine prole, without issue

Duke Anthony of Brabant, to marry Elizabeth of Görlitz. By a treaty negotiated with Wenzel, king of Bohemia and hereditary duke of Luxembourg, the duchy was ceded to Elizabeth in lieu of a dowry. She would use the title duchess, rule the duchy, and enjoy its revenues in her lifetime, and her husband was to act as her governor or *mambour*. Wenzel remained the hereditary lord and kept the right to redeem or buy back the duchy from Elizabeth for 120,000 Rhenish florins. But Wenzel's brother Sigismund also used the title duke of

Luxembourg, and he refused to recognize the rights of Anthony and Elizabeth as mortgagee rulers, doing his best to act as ruler himself.

The battle of Agincourt removed Anthony from the scene and Wenzel died not long after, in 1419. Elizabeth married again, this time with Sigismund's support, for her new husband John of Bavaria was regarded by him as a potential check to Burgundian expansion in the Empire. After John of Bavaria's death early in 1425 Elizabeth of Görlitz continued as sole mortgagee ruler of a duchy which was moderately peaceful and where she was widely accepted, though complaints about her inadequacy as a ruler were made to Sigismund from time to time. He, for his part, could not possibly afford to redeem the mortgage, and therefore left Luxembourg in her hands.[1]

There was no prospect of a successful Burgundian intervention in Luxembourg during John of Bavaria's lifetime but, once he was dead, Philip set negotiations on foot which were designed to lead to his acquisition of the duchy. In 1427 he persuaded Anthony's second son Philip of St. Pol, who had recently succeeded his brother, John IV, as duke of Brabant, to cede him his claims to Luxembourg, and he negotiated the treaty of Dordrecht with Elizabeth of Görlitz, according to the terms of which she was to hand over a good part of the administration of Luxembourg to him and cede all her rights on her death, in return for revenues from Holland and Zeeland worth 3,000 crowns per annum. The Estates of Luxembourg refused to accept the treaty of Dordrecht and protested to Sigismund. But Philip was undeterred. In 1431 he signed a treaty with Duke Adolf of Jülich and Berg, who promised to help him obtain Luxembourg, and in 1435 he negotiated the treaty of Malines with Elizabeth of Görlitz who was always in debt, partly because of Philip's confiscation of certain Dutch revenues which had been assigned to her as part of her dowry by John of Bavaria. She was to cede all her Luxembourg rights to Philip for 80,000 florins and an annual payment of 4,000 florins. For some reason she did not do this but, in 1436, she appointed Ruprecht, count of Virneburg, a partisan and protégé of Philip among the local nobility, as captain or governor of Luxembourg. The Emperor Sigismund, whose increasing hostility to Philip had already

---

[1] For this and what follows on Luxembourg, see *Table chronologique des chartes de Luxembourg*, *Choix de documents luxembourgeois*, ICL iv and *DRA*, especially vols. xvi and xvii, for the documentary material. Gade, *Luxembourg in the Middle Ages* adds nothing to Schötter, *Geschichte des Luxemburger Landes* and du Fresne de Beaucourt, *Charles VII*, iii. 306–17. For the period up to 1443, Richter, *Luxemburger Erbfolgestreit* needs to be supplemented by von Dietze's thesis, *Luxemburg zwischen Deutschland und Burgund*.

led to a declaration of war against him in December 1434, was actively encouraging the anti-Burgundian elements in Luxembourg at the time of his death at the end of 1437.

Sigismund was the last male member of the once flourishing Luxembourg dynasty. His title and status of hereditary duke of Luxembourg now passed to his only child Elizabeth, wife of Duke Albert of Austria, who succeeded him in 1438 as king of the Romans. Albert acted promptly and decisively. He made contact with the town of Luxembourg and had the citadel handed over to his partisans, and he made arrangements to redeem the mortgage from Elizabeth of Görlitz by paying her the sum of 120,000 florins. But Albert died on 27 October 1439, before these arrangements bore fruit and his widow, Queen Elizabeth, was in no position to prosecute her claims to Luxembourg. She found a husband for her elder daughter Anna, then aged seven, in the person of the fifteen-year-old Duke William of Saxony, and ceded Luxembourg to him on condition that he re-deemed it from Elizabeth of Görlitz and that, if her unborn child proved to be a son, he would have the right to redeem it from Duke William. Thus Ladislas Posthumus, born on 22 February 1440, became hereditary duke of Luxembourg, while Duke William of Saxony maintained his right to redeem the duchy from Elizabeth of Görlitz who seemed on the point of surrendering her rights as mort-gagee to Philip the Good. Nor were things simplified by the appear-ance on the scene of a shrewd ecclesiastical politician, the archbishop of Trier, Jacob von Sierck, who, though he contrived to play the part of a disinterested arbitrator, was actually intent on his own aggrand-izement. These three princes hoped to exploit the weaknesses of Elizabeth of Görlitz, widowed, elderly and in debt, to obtain control of her rights in Luxembourg. Already in 1439 one of them, Jacob von Sierck, had cajoled her into ceding him some of her castles by paying some of her debts. Another, Philip the Good, had negotiated two treaties with her for the transference of her rights, but neither had been implemented. The third, Duke William of Saxony, promised in March 1440 to redeem the mortgage but, when he could not pay the requisite 120,000 florins, Elizabeth of Görlitz turned to Jacob von Sierck and made over Luxembourg to him in a document of 1 May 1441.

It was soon after this that Philip began the negotiations which led to a third, and this time definitive, treaty between himself and Elizabeth. This was the treaty of Hesdin, of 4 October 1441, by which she ceded virtually everything she had to her nephew and made him her universal heir in return for 7,000 florins per annum. This time she handed over the duchy to him as her *mambour* or guardian and in February 1442 her representatives asked the Estates to accept him as their new ruler. But Philip was not yet prepared to annex Luxembourg, where armed opposition to any attempt on his part to do this would have been led by a newly appointed Saxon captain of Luxembourg, Ernst, count of Gleichen. He hoped instead to negotiate a settlement with the new king of the Romans, Frederick III, whereby he could not only obtain peaceful possession of the mortgage of Luxembourg, but also enfeoffment with his other imperial territories. The years 1442 and 1443 were thus occupied in constant negotiation, over the question of Luxembourg, between Philip the Good, Elizabeth of Görlitz, Duke William of Saxony, Frederick III and finally, Jacob von Sierck, who fancied himself as a beneficiary as well as a mediator of any Luxembourg settlement.

Meanwhile in Luxembourg the count of Gleichen, after sending letters of defiance to the count of Virneburg and Elizabeth of Görlitz in March 1442, began slowly to extend his power in a duchy which was by no means well disposed towards him and his tiny Saxon army. While Elizabeth adjured the inhabitants to be loyal to her nephew, Frederick III wrote to them on 13 April 1442 announcing that William duke of Saxony and his wife Anna (aged eighteen and eleven respectively) had now consummated their marriage and requesting all the inhabitants of the duchy to do homage to Duke William. Through much of 1442 and 1443 a régime of ill-kept truces kept the counts of Gleichen and Virneburg from open war but, during the summer and autumn of 1443 after the breakdown of negotiations at Trier in June, the situation deteriorated rapidly. Philip resolved at last on military action, and some of his Picard contingents were at St. Quentin on their way south by mid-July. The duke himself had been at Dijon since December 1441. He ended the only prolonged stay he ever made in his southern territories by marching out of Dijon in battle array towards the end of August 1443. The scene was described by Olivier de la Marche, then a ducal page.[1]

The duke mounted his horse at about 4.0 p.m. It was raining hard, and it was a pity that it was not a fine clear day, for this was a splendid

---

[1] De la Marche, *Mémoires*, ii. 11–12. On the Luxembourg campaign, the main chronicle sources are de la Marche, *Mémoires*, ii. 5–50; Monstrelet, *Chronique*, vi. 83–93; Jouffroy, *Oratio*, 167–84 and O. van Dixmude, *Merkwaerdige gebeurtenissen*, 176–9.

occasion. The nobility was in superb array, especially the duke, who was a courteous and amiable prince. He liked clothes and adornments, and the way he wore them suited him so well and agreeably that he had no equals in this. With him were eighteen horses identically caparisoned with black velvet embroidered with his emblems, which were steels with flints causing sparks, and over the velvet were large studs of gold enamelled with steels, which cost a great deal to make. His pages were richly decked out and wore various head-armours decorated with pearls, diamonds and balais, marvellously ornate. One sallet alone was estimated to be worth 100,000 gold crowns. The duke himself was armed richly and nobly, with vambraces and leg-harness, and these, together with his horse's chanfron, were decorated all over with large jewels which were worth a fortune. I speak of this as one who was then a page of the duke. . . .

In brief, the departure from Dijon was extremely splendid, but the weather was dull and full of rain and all this finery was very much spoilt.

The Luxembourg campaign was brief, bloodless and successful. After marching north through Champagne as far as Mézières, and collecting en route further Picard contingents, the duke, whose leading captains were his cousin Jehan, count of Étampes and his bastard Cornille, struck east to Arlon and Yvois, which, like most other places in Luxembourg, surrendered without a blow. Apart from the castle of Villy, which had to be taken by siege, and a skirmish or two with Saxon soldiers, no fighting hindered the triumphant progress of the duke, who carried with him his gouty old aunt Elizabeth. At Flörchingen near Thionville the ducal army halted. Virtually the whole of the duchy was in Burgundian hands except for the towns of Luxembourg and Thionville, but these, garrisoned with contingents of Count Ernst of Gleichen's Saxons, prepared to resist till the rigours of winter compelled the invader to withdraw. Peace talks were initiated at Flörchingen, and the usual invitations or challenges to a pitched battle were exchanged. The official text of a pompous and hypocritical speech made to the Saxon ambassadors on 26 October by Philip himself has survived.[1]

You have heard what my chancellor has said concerning the rights of my aunt, and myself as her *mambour*. Adam, please repeat to them in German what I say in French, because I cannot speak German, and they cannot understand the Flemish which I speak. In any case, French comes easier to me than Flemish.

---

[1] *Analectes historiques*, vi. 202–4. The document in which it is incorporated is also printed in *Table chronologique des chartes de Luxembourg*, xxviii (1873), 135–61.

It is true that my aunt, who has been prevented from enjoying what is her own, prayed and requested me to help maintain her rights and, in particular, asked me to undertake the guardianship of herself and her lands and subjects. Considering that she is my aunt, having married two of my uncles, one paternal and the other maternal, and that we are otherwise related, I agreed to this, nor could I honourably have refused, for no noble prince . . . ought to want to ruin a widow or take away her property without reasonable cause, and to do so would be against reason, justice and all honour, for all princes, nobles and others ought to place themselves at the service of widows and help to defend their rights. I have come here for this reason, with no intention at all of harming anyone . . . , but to employ myself on behalf of my said aunt in the maintenance of her rights, which are clear enough, and to offer my body and my resources to the utmost extent with the help of God and of her good and just quarrel. . . . And I am amazed at the way Duke William has behaved towards my aunt, whom he wrongly and unreasonably wishes to expel from her own property which she has peacefully enjoyed for thirty years or more, and to which he has no right.

As to the offer of battle you made on the said duke's behalf, though apparently without having been so empowered by him, I have never heard that when one gentleman, however poor, wants to challenge another to do battle, he should do it otherwise than with sealed letters or in some other proper way. However, if Duke William of Saxony wishes to challenge me to fight and lets me know a convenient date and place in the country under dispute, by means of sealed letters or in some other proper manner, I shall certainly reply to him at once, maintaining my aunt's rights, in such a way as a prince ought honourably to reply and, God willing, there shall be no defaulting on my side. I have heard that the said Duke William of Saxony is a powerful lord and prince, and I suppose he will bring with him other princes, with abundant nobility and chivalry as well as other people and I would do the same, bringing with me those whom I could. But, since every good christian prince should try to prevent the shedding of human blood, and especially defend and protect their own subjects, it would be much better, in my opinion, if the thing were decided by the two of us, man against man, without the shedding of so much noble christian blood.

The picturesque but dubious solution of a single combat between Philip and William was rejected by the Saxons, who pointed out to Philip that their duke was only eighteen or nineteen years old; nor did they take seriously Philip's counter-proposal that he should take on instead William's older brother Frederick. However, negotiations were continued while Burgundian escaladers made a close inspection of the walls of Luxembourg and Thionville. The latter was thought too strong, but the former offered the possibility of a successful surprise attack. The escalader who was sent to investigate the defences of Luxembourg contrived, after several failures because of the vigilance of the watch, to scale the wall by fixing his silk scaling-ladder, which had iron hooks on one end, to a contraption of sticks fitting into each other end to end. With this the hooks were lodged on the top of the wall and he was able to enter the town to ascertain the movements of the watch and to inspect the defences thoroughly. He discovered a place where there was a postern used by the in-habitants in time of peace for going out into the moat to spread their washing out to dry, and where a stone drain, to carry off surplus water from the streets into the moat, pierced the wall. It was barred up with iron, but would be invaluable for observing the movements of the watch.

A plan was drawn up and approved by Philip and, on the darkest night of the year, 21–22 November, some hundred chosen men assembled in the moat. The scaling-party, shoeless and armed only with daggers and breastplates, took with them an enormous pair of pincers, with handles twelve feet long, to break open the locks and bars of the postern. Everything went like clockwork and, at two o'clock in the night the cry 'Long live Burgundy!' startled the inhabitants and the Saxon garrison from their beds, and was even heard a mile outside the town. The Burgundians rushed for the market-place, smashing open doors and windows as they went, and seized it with scarcely a casualty. While some of the citizens fled, the count of Gleichen and his Saxons withdrew into the citadel. Philip took the news of this remarkable military success calmly; much too calmly for some of his people, as de la Marche explains:[1]

> As soon as the escaladers had scaled the walls messages were sent to the duke of Burgundy, who was in the town of Arlon, five leagues from Luxembourg. Once they were inside the town, another message was sent, so that the duke knew, by one message after another, that Luxem-bourg had been won. This was about two hours before dawn. The trumpet was sounded for saddling, and everyone got himself armed and ready. The duke armed himself fully and went to mass, and he heard mass and said his hours and ordinary as coolly as usual. And then, every-thing heard and finished, he said certain thanksgivings in his oratory, which took quite a long time. And I recall that we, his pages, who were on horseback, overheard his troops talking and murmuring that the duke was taking his time and that he could well make up lost paternosters

---

[1] *Mémoires*, ii. 40.

on some other occasion. So much so that Jehan de Chaumergy, who was first squire of the stables, reported this to the duke, who replied to him: 'If God has given me victory, he will keep it for me. . . . My cousin and my bastard are with the conquerors, together with such a number of my subjects and servants that, with God's help, they will manage very well until I arrive.'

The nocturnal escalade of the walls of Luxembourg was one of the more decisive victories in Burgundian history. A few weeks later, after Ernst, count of Gleichen had escaped, the citadel surrendered. The horses of its Saxon garrison had been fed on woodshavings. Philip now installed himself there for a festive Christmas in the company of Duchess Isabel. Negotiations soon led to a treaty which was favourable to Philip. Thionville was to be evacuated by its Saxon garrison, and Duke William of Saxony and his wife Anna promised to renounce their claims to the duchy of Luxembourg in return for the payment to them by Philip of a sum of 120,000 Hungarian florins. They agreed to try to persuade King Frederick III to ratify the treaty, which explicitly allowed for the eventual transference of the duchy to Ladislas, once he had repaid Philip his 120,000 florins. In fact, Frederick refused to sign and Philip refused to pay. But Luxembourg now became a Burgundian province. Its revenues, its coinage and its administration were taken over by Philip who, on the death of Ruprecht, count of Virneburg in 1444, appointed his bastard son Cornille to succeed him as governor. While both William and Ladislas continued to use the title duke of Luxembourg, Philip was content to describe himself to his dying day only as its *mambour* or guardian, but to enjoy actual control and possession of it.

For a decade after its conquest, Philip enjoyed peaceable possession of Luxembourg, though troops had to be maintained there, and reinforcements sent, especially in 1445 and 1447, when Duke William of Saxony seemed about to attempt to reassert his claims by force of arms.[1] In the summer of 1447 he fielded an army on behalf of Dietrich von Mörs, archbishop of Cologne, in his war against Soest and the duke of Cleves, and planned in the event of victory against Soest to use the army in the conquest of Luxembourg. Both Jacob von Sierck and Frederick III were parties to this plan, news of which caused

[1] ADN B1991, f. 256 and Plancher, iv. no. 150. For the next sentences, see Hansen, *Westfalen und Rheinland*, i. 105–15, etc. and nos. 136, 267, 300 and *DRA* xvii. no. 349. For what follows, besides the works cited above p. 276 n. 1, see Lippert, *MSE* (n.s.) xxv (1897), 1–44.

Philip to send a body of eighty-five men-at-arms, in July 1447, to reinforce his Luxembourg garrisons, and to prepare a contingent to take part in the Soest war against Dietrich von Mörs and his Saxon ally. But the citizen-army of Soest repulsed the Saxons with their Bohemian mercenaries, and nothing came of Duke William's plan.

In August 1451, when Elizabeth of Görlitz died at Trier, Saxon aspirations revived again, and a Saxon partisan in Luxembourg wrote to tell Duke William that the whole country would go over to him at once if only he would appear there in person. William did write to the Estates of Luxembourg on 30 August asking them to support his rights, but further action on his part was forestalled by Philip the Good who, warned of the dangers, promptly embarked on a round of negotiations, proposing the marriage of Charles, count of Charolais and Anna, daughter of the elector Frederick of Saxony, Duke William's elder brother, and the cession to Charles of the Saxon claims to Luxembourg. At the same time, in October 1451, he went in person to Luxembourg with his chancellor Nicolas Rolin to receive confirmation from the Estates that they recognized him as their rightful ruler, 'saving the rights of the hereditary lords of Luxembourg'.[1] But the negotiations, which were not facilitated by the ambush and imprisonment of the entire Burgundian embasssy by rebellious Saxon vassals when it was on its way from Erfurt to Naumburg, came to nothing.

In 1452 a new treaty, which gave Charles Anna in marriage together with the titles and rights of the duke of Luxembourg in return for certain payments, was drawn up and agreed on, but neither Frederick III nor King Ladislas of Bohemia would ratify it. Indeed, the second of these now inaugurated a new phase in the history of the Luxembourg succession question by entering the arena himself, having apparently taken over his kingdom of Bohemia from the guardianship of Frederick III, though he was only twelve. In December 1452 he wrote to the Estates of Luxembourg asking them to recognize him; he appointed deputies to take possession in his name and in spring 1453 his partisans seized Thionville and raised the standard of revolt against Philip the Good.

Ladislas had chosen his moment well, for Philip was ensconced at Lille throughout the winter of 1452–3, directing the confused and

---

[1] De la Marche, *Mémoires*, ii. 206–7. For the next sentence, see ADN B2008, f. 219 and B2017, f. 122, etc. For what follows, *DRA* xix. 346–415 covers events in detail, with references and a wealth of new material, between July 1452 and June 1454. See too Lacaze, *AB* xxxvi (1964), 82–92.

284 PHILIP THE GOOD

difficult winter fighting around Ghent, which was in open revolt
against him. But Ladislas lacked the resources to conquer Luxembourg, which was firmly under the control of its Burgundian governor
Anthoine, lord of Croy. The herald Hungary, who was instructed to
summon the Estates of Luxembourg in February 1453 on Ladislas's
behalf, was arrested by Anthoine and thrown into prison, and in May
Ladislas approached Philip with a request for negotiations. Desultory
fighting continued in Luxembourg through the early summer but by
September, after reinforcements had been sent, the Burgundians had
expelled or subdued the last remnants of Ladislas's partisans.[1]
    The negotiations which followed these events were protracted,
acrimonious and barren. Under the protection of a truce and under
the presidency of that seasoned intriguer and arbitrator Jacob von
Sierck, the deputies of Philip and Ladislas met at Mainz in March
1454 to discuss the relative merits of the Burgundian and Bohemian
claims to Luxembourg. The conference was augmented but not
expedited by the arrival of the count palatine of the Rhine and by
deputies from the archbishop of Cologne, the margrave of Brandenburg, Duke Louis of Bavaria and several towns, including Frankfurt and Nürnberg. The leaders of the Burgundian delegation,
Guillaume Fillastre, bishop of Toul, and John, count of Nassau, had
been furnished with detailed instructions, divided into ninety-five
separate articles, setting out their duke's claims to Luxembourg, and
these were expounded in Latin to the assembled company by Guillaume Fillastre. But, because 'everyone in the audience had not
understood this so well as they would have done had it been said in
German', a German summary had to be made and read out at the
next session of the conference. The Bohemian spokesman who
replied managed things better, for he followed up a speech in elegant
German with the same speech in Latin. The Burgundian's trump
card was the document of 25 October 1451 which set out the decision
of the Estates of Luxembourg, made in Philip the Good's presence,
to accept him as their ruler. But these letters were impugned by the
Bohemians, who claimed that the Estates had only accepted Philip
if he was the rightful heir; that some of those listed as signatories of
the letters were not in fact present; that they did not represent truth-

---

[1] De la Marche, *Mémoires*, ii. 301–2 and 332–3 and d'Escouchy, *Chronique*,
ii. 43–9. Two of the most important records of the Mainz conference, quoted
in what follows, are printed in *Table chronologique des chartes de Luxembourg*,
xxx (1875), 74–82 = *Analectes historiques*, vii. 372–86 and *Choix de documents luxembourgeois*, 229–35.

fully the decision of the Estates; and that in any case the decision had been made under pressure 'because the duke had people around him holding axes, gisarmes, swords and other weapons. Nor were they allowed time to deliberate at their leisure, for they were told to hurry up because the duke wanted to go and dine.' Guillaume Fillastre angrily protested against this direct attack on his duke's honour.

My lord of Toul continued thus, addressing his words to Gerhard von Wiltz. 'You, Gerart de Weltz, have you not said that the document produced by us in the duke's name is false?' To which the said Gerhard replied in the affirmative. Then my lord of Toul said, 'You are lying in your teeth because, whatever you say, this document will be proved sound and valid and, if I wasn't a churchman, I would address you in more forceful terms than this.' To which this Gerhard replied, that my lord of Toul had lied and that he would be talking through his hat every time he repeated what he had said.

This was not the way to settle disputes, and the conference of Mainz was followed by others, notably at Speyer in October 1455 under the presidency of Duke Louis of Bavaria, whom both parties had accepted as arbitrator.[1] But all were equally without result. Philip remained effective ruler of Luxembourg, protected by truces though threatened by the possibility of renewed intervention on the part of Duke William of Saxony or King Ladislas. But the subsequent history of this affair, which involved the king of France, must be left for a later chapter.

Philip the Good was an imperial prince; indeed, he was the leading imperial prince of his day. This was why he sent his deputies to the *Reichstage* or imperial diets. This was why his ambassadors disputed their seats at the Council of Basel with those of the imperial electors. And this explains Philip's close and constant involvement in imperial affairs.[2] Under Sigismund, he was regarded as an usurper. Not only did the Emperor refuse to recognize him as rightful ruler

[1] See especially *Urkunden, Briefe und Actenstücke*, 13–18, 62, 68, 69, 74 and 77–8; *Urkundliche Beiträge*, 92–3; *Speierische Chronik*, 404–5; and AGR CC2417, account for 1455, fos. 67b–68, etc.
[2] Rachfahl, *WZGK* xix (1900), 81–4. For what follows on Philip and Frederick in 1442 see *Analectes historiques*, vi. 167–216 = *Table chronologique des chartes de Luxembourg*, xxviii (1873), 135–61, and *DRA* xvi, especially 157 and 634–5; and, for the Besançon meeting, de la Marche, *Mémoires*, i. 270–82, Dunod, *Histoire de Besançon*, i. 265–8, O. van Dixmude, *Merkwaerdige gebeurtenissen*, 175–6, *DRA* xvii. 6–7, 40 and 46 and Lippens, *AFH* xxv (1942), 257–9.

of Brabant and Holland, he also supported rival claimants to these territories and even declared war on Philip the Good in 1434. But the attitude of Frederick III of Habsburg, who was crowned king of the Romans at Aachen on 17 June 1442 after the brief reign of Albert II, was different. Though he was firmly hostile to Philip's plans of further territorial aggrandizement at imperial expense, notably in Luxembourg, he apparently hoped for a settlement on the basis of recognition of Philip as ruler of Brabant and Holland. At Aachen, when Philip's ambassadors offered homage on their duke's behalf for these imperial territories, Frederick III deferred the matter. Philip later complained that before he would invest him with his imperial fiefs, thus recognizing him as their rightful ruler, Frederick had insisted on the settlement of the Luxembourg question, demanded the renunciation of all Burgundian claims to the county of Ferrette, and declared that the duke of Burgundy must serve him with an army for a year wherever he pleased. Philip told the ambassadors who expounded these imperial conditions to him that fulfilling them 'would constitute an excessive ransom if he were a prisoner'. But this apparent impasse did not prevent the two rulers meeting in November 1442 in the imperial city of Besançon, an enclave in Philip's Franche-Comté, as it was now beginning to be called. Olivier de la Marche, then a page in the duke's retinue, set down his recollection of this occasion many years afterwards.[1]

> It was on a Tuesday that the duke rode out into the fields with a numerous company. He had gone a good half league before he met the king of the Romans, who arrived well accompanied by the princes and nobility of Germany and all his own people, of whom he had a great many, riding in excellent order, carrying lances, shields, crossbows and [wearing] armour. They rode some distance from him, escorting a huge standard with a large eagle on it. They kept excellent order, and it certainly was very strange to see this vast number of variously emblazoned shields, and the blond hair of these Bohemians and Germans gleaming in the sun. The king's trumpeters announced his arrival, but the duke of Burgundy's ceased to sound once they saw the ensigns of the king of the Romans. . . .
> The king of the Romans was dressed in a large-collared doublet after the Bohemian fashion, with a blue-grey robe. Round his neck he wore a hood, the liripipe of which, edged with tabs, reached to his saddle. On his head was a small grey fur hat on top of which he wore a tight-fitting crown. This was his first crown, with which he had been crowned at

---

[1] *Mémoires*, i. 273–9.

Aachen in Germany. He had a well-proportioned figure and was a handsome lord, and he must have been about twenty-six years old. . . . As to the duke, he was dressed in a black robe and wore the collar of his Order round his neck. He certainly looked as fine a prince and lord as any I have seen since. He was mounted on a bay horse and acknowledged the honours which the king did to him in so courteous and polite a way that everyone found his manner pleasant and agreeable. . . .

This noble company rode on till it arrived at the entrance to the city. There, the citizens brought a canopy of cloth-of-gold, supported by the most notable burgesses of the city, under which the king of the Romans went; and in truth he tried hard to persuade the duke of Burgundy to join him under it. But the duke would on no account do so. Instead, he rode on the left of the king, keeping his horse's head just in front of the king's thigh. All the nobility, both of the Empire and of Burgundy, rode in good order. The worthy archbishop of Besançon was there, on foot in the procession, with all the prelates and churchmen of the city carrying relics and pious objects in front of the king. So they rode till they reached the palace, where the king dismounted, and the duke with him. . . .

Each day the duke of Burgundy visited the king, and, on the following Sunday, the duke gave a magnificent dinner for the king and the lords of his company. I well remember that the duke wore that day a sash decorated with balais and pearls which was estimated to be worth more than 100,000 crowns. No one dined at the king's table except his host the duke, who received him most gladly and courteously . . . and served him at this dinner like an expert. After dinner the king withdrew to a room with his principal courtiers and the duke joined him there with his chancellor and others of his council, and there they began to discuss the business in hand.

Historians may be forgiven for having ascertained very little about the 'business in hand' at Besançon, and still less about what was decided. The usually well-informed Ypres chronicler, Oliver van Dixmude, says that king and duke 'had many discussions, and I heard from a messenger who was sent on behalf of the town of Ypres to my lord the duke [at Besançon], and who saw and heard everything, that nobody discovered what was decided'. Probably, nothing was decided, but friendly talks took place on a wide variety of topics, including the future of Luxembourg, the investment of the duke of Burgundy with Brabant, Holland and his other imperial territories, the possibility of Burgundian help for the house of Habsburg against the Swiss, the payment of certain debts which Philip claimed were still owing to him as a result of the marriage of his aunt Catherine to Duke Leopold of Austria, and the difficult question of the dispute between Pope Eugenius IV and the Council of Basel.[1] Henceforward, the relations of Burgundy with the Empire were on the whole good, but the pattern of Besançon was repeated in subsequent negotiations: nothing was settled.

Philip the Good can hardly have taken seriously schemes like that proposed to him in 1444 by a councillor of Frederick III, Conrad von Weinsberg, who suggested the cession to him of various imperial mints, taxes and castles and even hinted that he might secure Philip's election and coronation as king of the Romans, once Frederick had been crowned Emperor.[2] He was far more interested in his formal recognition as ruler of Brabant, Holland and Luxembourg and his investment with these imperial fiefs, and in arranging a marriage between his nephew John of Cleves and Frederick's sister Catherine, which he had already proposed at Besançon. Although diplomatic contacts between Philip and Frederick continued in the years after their meeting at Besançon, on 7 April 1446 Frederick authorized his brother Albert, duke of Austria, to negotiate with Philip on his behalf and to invest him with his imperial lands, excluding Luxembourg. These negotiations, between Philip and Albert, which had really begun in 1445, continued in 1446 and 1447, but without result, apart from a treaty of alliance between the two princes. Parallel negotiations were conducted in 1447 and 1448 between Philip and Frederick, but none of the schemes and projects discussed at this time was implemented. The marriage alliance between Cleves and Austria was dropped, and other proposed marriages, between Albert and Mary of Guelders and between Charles, count of Charolais, and Elizabeth, second daughter of King Albert II, were likewise relinquished.

At the same time various schemes for the conferment of a royal crown on Duke Philip the Good were put forward, only to be rejected. The original suggestion of creating a kingdom of Frisia or Brabant for Philip probably came from one of the envoys, the herald Heinrich von Heessel, or from the imperial chancellor Caspar Schlick, but Philip took the matter up with enthusiasm, proposing that all

---

[1] On this last, see above, p. 213.

[2] *DRA* xvii. 235 and 311–14. For what follows see *Materialen zur österreichischen Geschichte*, i.; Chmel, *Geschichte Kaiser Friedrichs IV*, ii. 742–51; *Actenstücke Herzog Philipps Gesandtschaft*; von Kraus and Kaser, *Deutsche Geschichte im Ausgange des Mittelalters*, i. 278–86; A. M. and P. Bonenfant, *MA* xlv (1935), 10–23; Grunzweig, *RBPH* (1946–7), 343; Jongkees, *Het Koninkrijk Friesland*, 7–11; P. Bonenfant, *BARBL* xli (1955), 270–5; and von Dietze, *Luxemburg zwischen Deutschland und Burgund*, 86–103.

his imperial lands should form part of the new kingdom, 'that the duchies of Guelders, Jülich and Berg and other duchies, counties and lordships in lower Germany' should become its fiefs, and that it should owe no homage to the Empire. In subsequent negotiations the Burgundian envoy specifically defined the 'other duchies, counties and lordships in lower Germany' as the duchies of Cleves, Bar and Lorraine and the counties of Mark, Mörs and Vaudémont. Frederick III was by no means prepared to set up Philip the Good as a powerful independent sovereign, and went no further than offering him a kingdom of Brabant, of which his other imperial lands would form fiefs, and which itself would be an imperial fief. These negotiations for the enhancement of Burgundy's status in the Empire, and Europe, either by means of a marriage-alliance or by its erection into a kingdom, eventually terminated in stalemate in 1448. They were not resumed seriously until 1459, though a matrimonial link was established in 1452, when Frederick III married Eleanor of Portugal, daughter of King Edward and niece of Duchess Isabel of Burgundy.

Philip the Good's imperial policies were by no means limited to negotiations with the Emperor himself, whether these aimed at legitimizing his rule over those of his lands which were technically imperial fiefs, or at increasing his influence in the Empire in some other important respect. He was also concerned to improve his status there by means of alliances and diplomatic contacts with the imperial princes and vassals. A sort of Burgundian system came into being within the Empire, and was particularly apparent in the years between the conquest of Luxembourg in 1443, which marked the end of the first series of Burgundian imperial conquests, and 1456, when Philip managed to place Burgundian bishops at Liège and Utrecht. This system was based on three groups of connections, one, in north-west Germany, where Cleves and Guelders in particular were, or looked like becoming, Burgundian client states; another, along the entire border between the French and German speaking worlds, where many a nobleman or petty ruler was persuaded to be a Burgundian partisan; and a third consisting of a series of alliances between Philip and the imperial princes.

Ever since the marriage of Duke Adolf of Cleves and Philip the Good's sister Mary in 1406, Cleves had become more and more subject to Burgundian influences of all kinds, cultural, administrative and political. In the wars and disputes in which Duke Adolf was constantly involved, Philip had intervened repeatedly on his behalf, arbitrating settlements of the quarrels between Adolf and the arch-

bishop of Cologne in 1425–6, and between Adolf on the one side and
Duke Arnold of Guelders and the bishop of Münster on the other
in 1437–9.[1] Throughout the war which Duke Adolf fought in defence
of Soest against the archbishop of Cologne, Philip's diplomacy was at
the service of Cleves, and in 1447 he prepared a military expedition
in support of his brother-in-law. Philip was on the most intimate
terms with Adolf's eldest son, John, who succeeded his father as
duke of Cleves in 1448, and in 1450 he was largely instrumental in
arbitrating a settlement and partition of family territories between
Duke John and his younger brother Adolf, lord of Ravenstein.[2] These
two older sons of Adolf and Mary were brought up at the Burgundian
court and were provided with Burgundian wives, for John married
Isabel, daughter of Jehan de Bourgogne, count of Étampes, and
Adolf was married successively to a niece of Duchess Isabel and a
bâtarde of Philip the Good.

As a matter of fact, the marriages of nearly all Philip's nephews
and nieces of Cleves were arranged by him to suit his needs, and in
this respect they helped to make good his own lack of legitimate
children. To extend his connections with the princely houses of the
Iberian peninsula, Philip married Agnes of Cleves to King Charles of
Navarre's grandson Charles, prince of Viana, as well as Adolf of
Ravenstein to Duchess Isabel of Burgundy's niece Beatrice, daughter
of the duke of Coimbra. A special section, totalling over £16,000, was
entered in the accounts of Philip's receiver-general of all finances for
the expenses of sending Agnes of Cleves to Navarre.[3] At first it was
planned to send her by land, and a ducal coachman was sent 'to see
and inspect the roads between here and the land of Navarre' to
ascertain their condition and suitability. But in the event she travelled
by sea via England in ships requisitioned at Sluis, taking with her
gold necklaces studded with pearls and rubies, jewelled gold clasps,
rings, robes, six hats, plates and cutlery, serviettes, tapestries depicting
stag-hunting and a *plaidoyerie d'amours* or court of love, silver

[1] ADN B1933, f. 77b and B1935, f. 45b and *Gedenkwaardigheden*, iv.
143–56 and 167, nos. 165 and 177. For the next sentence, see Hansen,
Westfalen und Rheinland, i. For what follows in general on Burgundy and
Cleves, see Gachard, *BCRH* (4) ix (1881), 292–3 and Petri, *Gemeinsame
Probleme*, 99–101, with references. For the whole of what follows, see the
map on p. 226 above.
[2] See above, pp. 130–1 and *Urkundenbuch des Niederrheins*, iv. 359–62. For
what follows, see Armstrong, *AB* xl (1968) 19–22.
[3] ADN B1966, fos. 312–321b, and, for what follows, B1966, f. 123b, 132b,
138b, 141b, etc. and *IADNB* i (1), 295–6.

MARRIAGE ALLIANCES OF CLEVES AND GUELDERS

Adolf I, duke of Cleves=Mary of Burgundy, sister of Philip the Good

Margaret=(1) William III, duke of Bavaria (1433) (2) Ulrich V, count of Württemberg (1441)

John, = Isabel d'Étampes duke of (1456) Cleves

Agnes=Charles, prince of Viana (1439)

Adolf=(1) Beatrice of of Coimbra Raven- (1453) stein (2) Anne de Bourgogne (1470)

two others

Mary=Charles, duke of Orleans (1440)

Catherine=Arnold, duke of Guelders (1430)

Isabel=Henry, count of Schwarzburg–Blankenburg (1434)

Helen=Henry, duke of Brunswick (1436)

Adolf of Egmont=Catherine duke of Guelders de Bourbon (1463)

Catherine

Mary=James II, king of Scotland (1449)

Margaret=Frederick I, count palatine of Simmern

chandeliers, velvet cushions embroidered with gold, and other personal belongings, some or all of which were provided by her uncle.

To enlist the alliance and help of princes nearer at hand whose friendship was required by Philip, Margaret of Cleves was married successively to the houses of Bavaria and Württemberg, Catherine of Cleves was married in 1430 to Duke Arnold of Guelders, Helen of Cleves married Duke Henry of Brunswick, and Mary married Charles, duke of Orleans. No wonder that Duke John and Adolf of Ravenstein were honoured, in 1451 and 1456 respectively, with election to the Order of the Golden Fleece; no wonder Duke John turned out in 1452 with a company of 100 men-at-arms to help his uncle in the war against Ghent.[1] Cleves had become a client state of Burgundy, its duke was a Burgundian puppet. But the ducal house of Cleves did obtain some financial compensation for this subservience. In 1449 Adolf of Ravenstein was receiving 1,200 francs per annum from his uncle, while his mother was being paid 2,000 crowns per annum as part of her dowry. Later, Adolf's pension was raised to 4,000 francs, and Duke John was enjoying a subsidy of 500 francs per month in 1461.

While Arnold of Egmont was duke of Guelders, Burgundian penetration of that duchy was limited by his firm resistance to it.[2] Nevertheless, the Cleves pattern was in part repeated. Philip and Arnold were allies against Jacqueline of Bavaria and Rudolf von Diepholz in 1426–7; Philip negotiated a settlement of the war between Arnold and Duke Adolf of Jülich and Berg in 1436; and, above all, Guelders was linked to Burgundy by the marriage alliance of 1430. Moreover, in 1448, when serious internal disputes broke out in Guelders between the duke and his eldest son Adolf, Philip intervened as an arbitrator and used the opportunity to support those elements in Guelders which were dissatisfied with Duke Arnold. These included Adolf, Philip's niece Duchess Catherine of Guelders, and certain nobles and towns, Nijmegen especially. In 1456 a Burgundian army marched across Guelders with impunity to

[1] Hansen, *Westfalen und Rheinland*, ii. 250–4. For what follows, see ADN B2000, f. 24a–b, Gachard, *BCRH* (4) ix (1881), 292–3, and ADN B2045, fos. 102b-103.
[2] For what follows on Guelders and Jülich-Berg, see Alberts, *De Staten van Gelre en Zutphen*, i. and *GBM* 1 (1950), 1–22; Petri, *Gemeinsame Probleme*, 102–3 with references; and Gail, *Festschrift G. Kallen*, 145–53. For the next sentences, see *Groot charterboek*, iv. 862–3, *Historia Gelriae*, 109 and above, pp. 229–30, *Gedenkwaardigheden*, iv. 126–9, no. 155 and ADN B1957, fos. 122b-123 and 126b.

besiege Deventer in the bishopric of Utrecht, and in the following year Philip made a determined diplomatic effort to persuade the Guelders towns to appoint Adolf governor of Guelders in place of his father. Meanwhile, Duke Arnold's anti-Burgundian policies and attitudes further aroused his wife's hostility, especially when he opposed the duke of Cleves's candidates for the bishoprics of Münster and Utrecht, which fell vacant in 1450 and 1455. Thus, in spite of his efforts, the duchy of Guelders remained open to Burgundian intervention, enjoying an independence which was both precarious and limited.

The dukes of Jülich–Berg, Adolf and Gerhard, were only slightly less exposed to Burgundian ambitions than their neighbours of Cleves and Guelders. In 1431 Philip signed a treaty of mutual defence and security with Adolf, in which Adolf was very much the junior partner;[1] in 1445 his successor Gerhard founded the Order of St. Hubert in imitation of the Golden Fleece. Thus Burgundian influence made itself felt throughout the area of the lower Rhine. After all, there was some justification, and some reality, behind Philip's ambitious suggestion, in 1447, that Cleves, Guelders and Jülich should all form part of a new Burgundian kingdom.

Taken together, the territories ruled by the duke of Burgundy and the king of France, stretching from Holland in the north to the county of Burgundy in the south, formed an area of relatively stable well-organized government; of straightforward political alignments and more or less undivided loyalties. Luxembourg and the county of Burgundy were only partial exceptions. But to the east of this area extended a kind of Franco-German no-man's-land where towns, bishops and feudal barons jostled for pockets of power and where the Emperor, the king of France and the duke of Burgundy were rivals in the slow and intricate extension of their political influence. In this western march of the Empire Philip the Good maintained and extended the system of connections with the local aristocracy that his father and grandfather had put together. Many of the nobles who became Burgundian partisans possessed lands both inside and outside the ducal territories; their loyalty was sometimes sufficiently sustained by this fact alone. John, count of Nassau, for example, owned extensive lands in Brabant and Holland as well as the county of Nassau. But the Burgundian sympathies of these men were also nourished by gifts of money, plate or land; by participation in the life of the Burgundian court; by military, diplomatic or other service on

[1] *Urkundenbuch Niederrheins*, iv. 233–5, no. 204.

Philip's behalf, handsomely paid for; by an annual grant or pension or the conferment of a fief-rent; by admission to the ranks of the Golden Fleece; or by the arrangement of marriage alliances favourable or flattering to them.

These allies and partisans played a vital part in the extension of Burgundian power in the Empire. Luxembourg could never have been annexed without the assistance of Ruprecht, count of Virneburg, and other members of his family. In 1425 he sent Philip two 'fine large horses, to help him in the duel he was to fight with the duke of Gloucester'.[1] He was elected a knight of the Golden Fleece in 1433. Two years later Philip gave him £18,000, apparently for helping to negotiate the treaty of Malines, and in 1436 his power and Philip's was much extended in Luxembourg by his appointment as governor of the duchy. To the north, Count Friedrich of Mörs, though his brother was the somewhat anti-Burgundian archbishop of Cologne, devoted himself to the service of Burgundy in a similar way. Elected to the Golden Fleece on 4 December 1431, having conveniently arrived in Lille the evening before, he performed several diplomatic missions for Philip, helping, for example, to mediate the quarrel with Liège in 1431.[2] After his death in 1448 his son Vincenz permitted a daughter of his to marry Philippe de Croy, lord of Sempy and, in 1456, he received from Philip the grant of an annual rent from the toll at Gorinchem. To the south the margraves of Hochberg, Wilhelm and Rudolf, played a similar rôle, the former receiving a Burgundian pension in return for diplomatic and other services; and their relative Thibaud de Neuchâtel, who became marshal of Burgundy in 1443, helped to extend Burgundian influence in Lorraine. The ranks of this Burgundian clientele were strengthened by the Burgundian bishops whom Philip placed on the episcopal thrones of Utrecht, Liège, Toul, Verdun and Besançon; and the system was reinforced by his friendly and often commercial connections with such towns as Cologne, Frankfurt and Basel, and by his rights as protector of the cities of Besançon and Verdun.

Of more potential political importance, perhaps, then either Burgundian expansion in north-west Germany or the system of con-

[1] ADN B1931, f. 113 and, for what follows, ADN B1957, f. 230. On this paragraph see, in general, Gruneisen, *RV* xxvi (1961), 27–30 with references and, in particular, Bauer, *Négotiations et campagnes de Rodolphe de Hochberg* and Marot, *AE* xliv (1930), 21–36 (Neuchâtel).

[2] Vienna, AOGV Regest i. f. 3b and de Stavelot, *Chronique*, 271–2. For the next sentence, see *Les Croÿ, conseillers des ducs de Bourgogne*, 88–95, no. 20 and Busken Huet, *Verslag*, i. 120.

nections which Philip developed along the imperial borderlands, was his policy of friendly contact and alliance with the imperial electors and other princes. Among them Philip was careful to have few or no outright enemies. Jacob von Sierck, archbishop of Trier, may have been his rival for influence in Luxembourg, but Philip had helped to place him on his archiepiscopal throne[1] and his position was that of competitor rather than enemy, of Burgundy. Nor must the anti-Burgundian posture of the archbishop and elector of Cologne, Dietrich von Mörs, be exaggerated. In 1431 he visited Philip and signed an alliance with him; in 1440 Philip visited Cologne; and there never was a Burgundian declaration of war against Cologne in the years when Cleves and Soest opposed the archbishop in arms. Moreover, Philip had taken good care to win over to his interest certain councillors and employees of these ecclesiastical princes. Thus in 1425 individual councillors of the archbishops of Mainz, Trier and Cologne were granted Burgundian pensions, and in 1444-8 'a squire of the archbishop of Cologne' was receiving £100 *per annum* from Philip's receiver-general of all finances.[2]

It is true that Frederick, elector palatine of the Rhine, was an enemy of Philip and an ally of France, but Philip found an ally in his relative and rival for possession of the Palatinate, Louis of Zweibrücken, even lending him military aid, though without success, in 1455. Saxony, in the form of the brothers William and Frederick, ruling different territories with the same title 'duke of Saxony', was hostile because of Luxembourg, but Burgundian relations with them were usually diplomatic rather than military. Elsewhere among the princes of the Empire Philip had nothing but friends. The strained relations with Austria, which had accompanied Duke Frederick's declaration of war against Philip in 1431, were not prolonged, in spite of Burgundian claims to Ferrette, and in May 1447 Philip signed a treaty of alliance with Duke Albert of Austria which was subsequently ratified by his cousin Duke Sigismund. With Duke Louis VIII of Bavaria–Ingolstadt, Philip was on excellent terms, and he signed a treaty with him in October 1444 shortly before his death.[3] Ten years later he accepted Louis the Rich, duke of Bavaria–Landshut, as

---

[1] *Choix de documents luxembourgeois*, 197. For what follows, see in general du Fresne de Beaucourt, *Charles VII*, iv. 333–71; Gruneisen, *RV* xxvi (1961), 22–77; and Lacaze, *AB* xxxvi (1964), 81–121; and, for the next two sentences, de Laborde, *Ducs de Bourgogne*, i. 285, 289, 295 and 325–6, AGR CC132, fos. 37–9 and de Stavelot, *Chronique*, 444 and above, pp. 53 and 65.
[2] *IADNB* iv. 102 and ADN B1991, f. 62 and B1998, f. 27b.
[3] Plancher, iv. no. 137 = *DRA* xvii. 709.

mediator in the Luxembourg dispute. Above all, Philip maintained his contacts and alliance with the two brothers, Counts Louis and Ulrich of Württemberg, who visited Brussels together in 1446 to do homage for certain lands in the county of Burgundy which they had acquired by inheritance.[1] These connections with the imperial princes were not only of importance in helping to extend Burgundian influence in the Empire, they were significant too, in terms of Franco-Burgundian relations, for King Charles VII was doing his utmost, in the 1440s, to construct an anti-Burgundian system of alliances in Germany.

The culmination of Philip the Good's political influence in Germany came in 1454, when his journey to Regensburg nicely combined Burgundian penetration of the Empire with preparations for a crusade. It seems that rumours of Mohammed II's plans for an assault on Constantinople reached Philip in the first week of May 1451 at Mons, where the knights of the Golden Fleece were gathered for their annual celebrations and chapter.[2] This news aroused Philip's yearnings to organize and lead a crusade; yearnings which were encouraged by the chancellor of the Order of the Golden Fleece and bishop of Chalon, Jehan Germain, who had just recently preached on the subject of the crusade to the assembled knights. Ambassadors proposing a coalition of European powers to this end were at once despatched from Mons to France, England, Austria, Hungary and Italy. But Philip's prestigious and romantic dreams of eastern adventure and crusading renown were soon forcibly dispelled by the hard facts of Flemish politics.

Ghent was in turmoil; in 1452 it was in open revolt; and, during the months that preceded the fall of Constantinople in May 1453 Philip the Good was fully occupied preparing for the siege of the rebellious city. Thus, the only western prince who might have been foolhardy enough to send an army to help defend Constantinople was busy with the defence of his own authority in his own lands. The verbose appeal which the Franciscan crusading propagandist Giovanni Capistrano sent him from Breslau in March 1453 was of no avail, and it was only after the peace with Ghent in July, the pacifica-

[1] Von Stälin, *Wirtembergische Geschichte*, iii. 460-1, etc. See too ADN B1991, f. 193 and *IADNB* viii. 20.
[2] D'Escouchy, *Chronique*, i. 346-55 and Germain, *Liber de virtutibus*, 75-96. See too, on this and what follows, Devillers, *BCRH* (4) vi (1879), 344-8; Grunzweig, *Byzantion* xxiv (1954), 49 n. 3 (references); and *DRA* xix. 143-4.

tion of Luxembourg in August–September, and the receipt of the news of the fall of Constantinople at the Burgundian court at about the same time, that Philip applied himself once more to the crusade.[1]

At the Feast of the Pheasant, the sumptuous public banquet held at Lille on 17 February 1454, the duke announced with a flourish to his courtiers and to Europe his imminent departure on crusade. He went further. He swore a solemn crusading vow suitably hedged with conditions which, though they exhibited an unfortunate subservience to the king of France, at least had the merit of being unlikely to be fulfilled.

> I vow to God my creator and to the most glorious Virgin his mother and to the ladies, and I swear on the pheasant, that if the most christian and victorious prince my lord the king [of France] takes the cross and exposes his body in defence of the christian faith and in resisting the damnable enterprises of the Grand Turk and the infidels, and if I am not physically incapacitated, I shall serve him on the crusade in person and with an army. . . . And if the affairs of my lord the king are such that he cannot go in person and he appoints a prince of the blood or other lord head of his army, I shall obey and serve him on the crusade as best I can, as if the king himself were there in person. If because of pressing affairs the king is neither disposed to go nor to send someone, and other sufficiently powerful christian princes undertake the crusade, I shall accompany them and employ myself with them to the best of my power in the defence of the christian faith, provided that this is with the agreement and permission of my lord the king and that the lands which God has entrusted to me to rule are in peace and security. . . . If during the crusade I by any means discover that the said Grand Turk would be willing to do battle with me in single combat, I shall fight him with the aid of God and the Virgin mother . . . in order to sustain the christian faith.
>
> Made at Lille, 17 February . . . , signed with my hand, Philippe.

Philip's crusading vow was followed by some hundred others, sworn by his courtiers, which were either recorded then and there during the banquet or submitted next day to the ducal herald, Golden Fleece, and the texts of all of them were incorporated in the official account of the banquet.[2] Many of the authors were flushed with wine and this, rather than genuine crusading enthusiasm, no doubt

---

[1] Du Fresne de Beaucourt, *ABSHF* (1864) (2), 160–6 prints Capistrano's letter. For the vow which follows, see *DRA* xix. 150 (text with references).

[2] For this and what follows see in particular d'Escouchy, *Chronique*, ii. 116–237 and Doutrepont, *NEBN* xli (1923), 1–28 and, in general, above, pp. 143–5 and references given there.

accounts for the extravagant or even bizarre clauses of some of the vows. One nobleman promised not to sleep on Saturday nights till he had fought a single combat with a Saracen; another promised not to drink wine from the day of his departure until he had drawn an infidel's blood. When Philippe Pot vowed not to wear armour on his right arm till he met the Saracens in battle, the duke intervened with a solemn statement that 'it was not his wish that Sir Philippe Pot accompany him on crusade with his arm unprotected'. Even the seventy-year-old Hue de Lannoy vowed to accompany the duke for a year, unless prevented by 'old age and bodily weakness'. Far different in tone were the vows extracted as it were in cold blood in the days and weeks that followed, from the nobles of Philip's territories. Thierry de Pottes, a squire of Hainault, stated less than enthusiastically at Mons on 25 April 1454 that

> ... he was by no means a person of such means and substance that he could undertake so distant a journey in the company of his most redoubted lord at his own expense. . . . It would be madness for him, and he would not be able to look after his wife and family as he should. But the said Thierry would be very willing to serve his prince and rightful lord . . . or other lords of his company . . . at their expense.

The chronicler Jehan, lord of Haynin, declared his willingness to serve the duke, but claimed that he was prevented from doing so by the meagreness of his rents and revenues, and 'also my body is by no means large and powerful enough to endure the pain and hardship'. Charles de Lombize would not take the vow until he had consulted his father, who claimed that he was old and sick and could not help him financially. He too was ready to serve the duke only if his expenses were paid.

The fact that the ducal authorities took the trouble to collect these vows and declarations after the Feast of the Pheasant points to the seriousness of Philip's crusading intent early in 1454. This impression is borne out by the ducal *ordonnance* of 22 March, which provided for the possibility of a period of two or more years elapsing before the duke returned 'from the said crusade and campaign which we have vowed to undertake against the Turks and infidels'.[1] As a matter of fact, soon after the Feast of the Pheasant, letters had arrived from Frederick III summoning Philip, as a prince of the Empire, to attend

---

[1] *DRA* xix. 157 and above, p. 266. For what follows, see *DRA* xix, especially 141–93, 282–305 and 339–415, with full references, and Lacaze, *AB* xxxvi (1964), 88–9.

an imperial diet and general congress of princes to be held'at Regensburg on 23 April to organize the crusade. The opportunity of a personal visit to the Emperor and other German princes was eagerly seized by the duke, who evidently hoped that the crusade would follow directly after the congress. His progress through Germany is chronicled in every trivial detail in the accounts, where we learn, for example, that Philip made small financial grants to the innkeepers where he stayed to enable them to erect the ducal arms over their doors. But the description sent home by a clerk of the ducal secretary Jehan Scoenhove to his friends and colleagues at Dijon brings the duke's imperial travels to life in a more vivid manner.[1]

Lauingen,
6 June 1454

Most honourable sirs and masters, I humbly commend myself to you, and . . . since I know you like to have news of the condition of my most redoubted lord my lord the duke and of those of his company, may it please you to know that since I last wrote to you the said lord has arrived in the town of Ulm in Swabia, where he was most notably received and entertained at his entry by the lords and governors of the place, who gave him various presents of wine, oats and so on, as is the custom here. And besides, the townspeople assembled the ladies, gentlewomen and other damsels in a suitable hôtel on a certain day, in the duke's honour, and there entertained him exceedingly well. After this, on the Sunday following, the young burgesses of the town jousted most wonderfully for, on their flat German saddles, they never once tilted without bringing down horse and rider or the rider alone.

In this town, while we were there, Count Ulrich of Württemberg came to see my lord [the duke], presenting him with ten or twelve casks of wine, ten or twelve cart-loads of venison, oats and more venison daily. And in truth he acquitted himself most generously towards my lord [the duke], and so did the people of Ulm. When the said count realized that my lord was on his way to the assembly at Regensburg, he invited my lord to revisit his lands and lordships on his return, and pressed him so hard that, as I understand it, he agreed to do so.

Leaving Ulm, we made for another town, belonging to the duke of Austria, called Günzburg, and we were escorted by some people from Ulm as far as their jurisdiction extended. There we found the duke of Austria, who came to meet my lord [the duke] along the road well accompanied with a notable and numerous chivalry. He received the duke honourably and took him that evening to Günzburg where he entertained him very well and kept him the whole of the next day.

---

[1] *DRA* xix. 175–6 and 185–6.

After leaving Günzburg we met Duke Louis of Bavaria a great German league outside the town. He was on the road coming towards my lord [the duke of Burgundy] accompanied by Cardinal Peter [bishop] of Augsburg and a large company of chivalry. He received my lord the duke there and took him to his town of Lauingen that evening, where he detained him for two days and entertained him and all his people on a lavish scale. When we left, he met all our expenses so that no-one had to produce a single penny for the cost of wine, horses, forage for the horses or anything else whatever. The duke of Austria had done just the same. When [my lord the duke] wished to leave, the duke of Bavaria offered to facilitate his journey by escorting him as far as Regensburg through his own lands and lordships and, though the duke would not suffer this, nevertheless the said Duke Louis conducted him and those of his company for six whole days to the town of Regensburg. During the journey he paid for everything. When we were at Lauingen and wanted some necessary things, such as linen, cloth, shoes, hose or such like, the good people and tradesmen let us have them for a very reasonable price and, when we wanted to pay them, they would not take the money, saying that their good prince, the said duke, had paid for everything. And when some people refused, for reasons of honour, to take these things without paying for them, and consequently left them behind, they followed them at a distance to their inns and, once they had discovered the inn, they delivered the things there. Some of our company were constrained by necessity to do this and, as they said, received their things [free] whether they liked it or not.

Ever since we first met the said Duke Louis he has accompanied my lord [the duke] all the time, both going to Regensburg, during the conference, and since then. After the conference he was by no means content to have entertained my lord [the duke] in this way, but managed to persuade the duke to return via his town of Landshut where, after my lord [duke's] arrival, the duchess of Bavaria, wife of the said duke, came with a large company of ladies, and also the margrave Albert of Brandenburg with a large company of people. He was at the conference at Regensburg together with the other princes, lords and ambassadors. Several other lords and gentlemen came to Landshut to see my lord [the duke]. We stayed there ten whole days, and not a day passed without the said Duke Louis maintaining at his own expense and in honour of the duke [of Burgundy] some 1,800 to 2,000 men and as many horses. Every day during the visit to Landshut we were most nobly and honourably entertained with dances, hunts and jousts. To tell you the truth, for four or five days there was jousting with blunted lances and neither duke nor margrave by any means lacked courage, for they were always in the front rank. There you would have seen the good duke, margrave and others, who tilted time after time, topple down from their horses. It was amazing that they did not break their necks at every encounter. It was really terrifying to watch them, and quite often the horse fell too. They all jousted on these small German saddles. In truth I cannot describe to you all the good cheer and entertainments arranged for my lord [the duke] and those of his company. When the time came for the duke to set out on his return journey the ladies presented him with a beautiful gold clasp richly ornamented with precious stones which was said to be worth a fortune. Besides this, each of the knights and gentlemen of his court [was given] a gold clasp decorated with diamonds, rubies and sapphires, and I believe our company received in all some forty clasps. My master had a gold ring which is particularly fine. Besides all this, it is said that they also gave to my lord the duke and others of his company hats decorated with fine large pearls, which were worth a great deal, especially my lord the duke's; but that my lord the duke of Burgundy, on his part, gave in return to the duchess of Bavaria a present which was finer and worth more than the cost of all the gifts and expenses which the duke and his company had received. . . . When we left they cried 'Villainy'! when we tried to pay for wine or sausage.

We have now left Landshut, and the said duke [of Bavaria] escorted my lord [the duke of Burgundy] to a town of his called Ingolstadt two days' journey from Landshut, where my lord the duke would on no account permit him to proceed further, though the duke [of Bavaria] begged [the duke of Burgundy] to let him continue in his company. But when he saw that my lord the duke wanted him to return and come no further, he took his leave, asking [the duke of Burgundy] in all humility to excuse the poor reception [he had had]; explaining that manners among the Germans were coarse and rude; and offering all his lands and places to my lord [the duke of Burgundy]. . . .

We arrived in this town two days after leaving Ingolstadt and, on the way through [Duke Louis's] lands, all our expenses have been paid. It seems that they will also be defrayed while we are here. It is said that we won't be leaving till after Whitsun. When we set out, we shall go to Stuttgart which belongs to the count of Württemberg, whom my lord [the duke] wishes to visit according to the promise he made on leaving Ulm. From Stuttgart we go to Neuchâtel, from Neuchâtel to my lord the prince [of Orange] at Nozeroy and thence, God willing, to you at Dijon. Judging by our present rate of progress, it will be near the end of this month before we reach Burgundy.

As to the condition of my lord [duke], it is true that he was ill for four or five days at Regensburg with fever and a cold, and he was ill-disposed for a day or two at Landshut. Since we arrived here, he is said to have become ill with piles and he has found it impossible to leave. . . . But, thanks be to God, he is now in fairly good health; the worst is over and it's hoped he'll be quite cured by Whitsun.

In addition, most honourable sirs and masters, because I know that you also want to hear about the business done at the Regensburg conference, I am sending you enclosed with this a schedule containing the propositions made there on behalf of the Emperor, and another containing in effect the reply of my lord [the duke] to the Emperor's letters. . . .

There is nothing else to write about for the present. I shall send you more news, if there is any, by the next messenger. My very honourable sirs and masters, always make your wishes known to me and I will accomplish them willingly to the best of my power, as indeed I must and am bound to do. Please excuse my inexpertness. . . .

Your humble servant and clerk Jehan Meurin, clerk of Master Jehan Scoenhove, secretary.

[P.S.] Thank you, my lord the audiencer and Master Nicolas, for what you have written to me concerning the state of affairs over there, and that there are some good wines. Those of this area are so sour that they hurt your throat.

Apart from trips to Paris in the 1420s and again in 1461, Philip the Good's visit to Regensburg in 1454 was the only important journey he ever made outside his own territories. So far as the crusade was concerned, it was without immediate result: Frederick III himself was prevented by Hungarian affairs from attending in person at Regensburg, and consideration of the proposed expedition was deferred to a subsequent meeting at Frankfurt. As for imperial affairs, we can safely assume that Philip would have liked to discuss with Frederick the succession to Luxembourg and his investment by the Emperor with his imperial lands. Indeed we know that the stadholder and council of Holland sent word to Philip at Regensburg asking him to do his utmost to persuade Frederick III to raise the imperial ban which had lain over Holland for many years.[1] But, in the absence of Frederick, no settlement of these problems, no official recognition of Philip as ruler of his imperial territories, was forthcoming. However, Chastellain tells us that the duke 'made a long and perilous journey of little result, but full of merit nonetheless and of glory as far as his person was concerned'; and we can scarcely doubt that Burgundian prestige was considerably enhanced by this triumphant progress through Swabia and Bavaria. Moreover, if the elusive Frederick shrugged off in 1459 a further attempt of Philip to achieve a settlement, Burgundian alliances among the German princes were maintained and extended in the last ten years of Philip's life as a direct result of the personal contacts and friendships, especially with Duke Louis of Bavaria, made in 1454.

[1] AGR AR vi. 24, f. 118. The quotation from Chastellain that follows is from Œuvres, iii. 6.

CHAPTER TEN

The Ghent War:
1449–53

The fires of social discontent smouldered in every late medieval town
which was large enough to support an artisan population. Intermittently this discontent was fanned into open revolution as a result
either of the oppressive measures of some princely government, or of
the policies and activities of the ruling urban oligarchies. Or else it
was the brute force of dire economic circumstance, even stark poverty,
which drove the *communes* or populace into desperate armed uprising.
The power of the Valois dukes of Burgundy had been established in
Flanders in the 1380s over the dead bodies of thousands of Ghenters,
slain on the field of Roosebeke, and Ghent remained a trouble-spot
for every one of Philip the Bold's successors. In Bruges, too, revolt
flared up from time to time, notably in 1437, when Philip the Good
only just escaped with his life. In 1439 and 1445 it was the Dutch
towns, Rotterdam, Amsterdam and Leiden in particular, which were
convulsed by civic commotion and revolt, though here the situation
was complicated by party struggles.

At Besançon, where the dukes of Burgundy had gradually extended
their influence by exploiting a series of disputes between archbishop
and town, communal revolt flared up in 1451.[1] Certain popular
elements refused to contribute to a civic tax and a plot was set on foot
to seize control of the government. Chains were thrown across the
streets, fires were lit at night, houses were fortified and cannon were
set up at street corners. Attempts were made to extract secret information about the government of the city from its secretary, who
was thrown into a ditch and threatened. The marshal of Burgundy,

---

[1] Plancher, iv. no. 163, *IADB* i. 135, *IACB* i. 29–44, *Correspondance de la
mairie de Dijon*, i. no. 37 and BN Coll. de Bourg. 99, 494–500. See too Clerc,
Franche-Comté, ii. 476–86 and Fohlen, *Histoire de Besançon*, i. 508–12.

Thibaud de Neuchâtel, was sent by Philip to mediate with a group of councillors. He barely escaped with his life after being hit on the shoulder by a boulder thrown from one of the city gates as he made a hurried and clandestine departure. The duke was in Flanders, but Thibaud wrote to him requesting wider powers, and received instructions to take the city by force of arms if necessary. He reappeared at Besançon early in September 1451 at the head of 1,600 men, but found the gates open to him and the city in the grip of a plague. The ringleaders of the revolt were quickly caught and executed, and the affair ended with the drawing up of a treaty between Philip the Good and the civic authorities of Besançon which significantly extended Burgundian power over their city. The duke was to receive half the profits of justice and half the proceeds of certain civic taxes, and he was to be permitted to appoint a captain of Besançon and a judicial officer there.

At Amsterdam and Leiden, Bruges and Besançon, this social discontent was on a relatively limited scale and was suppressed without serious difficulty by an alliance of duke and merchant oligarchs, or by the duke alone. But the troubles at Ghent exploded into a prolonged and disastrous war which involved the ducal government and the entire Burgundian state in a veritable struggle for survival. The flourishing commerce, the institutions, the internal security and the general wellbeing of what was in so many ways the most important single Burgundian territory, Flanders, were jeopardized and undermined. Ducal finances were exhausted, ducal favourites and bastards were killed in battle, ducal policies of aggrandizement elsewhere had to be modified or abandoned. This protracted crisis began in 1447 with a clash between ducal authority and civic pretensions. It was soon complicated by the activities of the artisan populace of Ghent, who took advantage of the situation to seize control of their town, precipitating a bitter military struggle between their own revolutionary government and the ducal army which was only terminated on the battlefield of Gavere in July 1453.

Ghent was unusual in many respects. It was 'the most powerful town in the duke's territories, extremely wealthy in all respects, incredibly large, and with an exceptionally numerous population'.[1] It enjoyed judicial rights and even political power over a wide area of the surrounding countryside, and this control was reinforced by the system of non-resident burgesses or *hagepoorters*. By the mid-fifteenth

[1] D'Escouchy, *Chronique*, i. 368–9. For the rest of this paragraph, see *Dagboek van Gent*, i. 1–45 and Fris, *BSHAG* xi (1903), 78–82.

century all the leading citizens of Ninove and a large proportion of
the better-off inhabitants of the castellany of Ghent were burgesses
of Ghent, enjoying the full privileges of the resident burgesses,
among which was virtual immunity from comital justice. Ghent also
enjoyed a greater degree of autonomy than other Flemish towns, for
half of the eight electors who were appointed annually on 12 August
to choose the echevins for the coming year, beginning on 15 August,
were appointed by the outgoing echevins. The other four electors
were appointed by the duke, but if this electoral college was divided
equally on any particular nomination, one of the ducally appointed
electors had to give way. Thus, even though municipal elections were
conducted under the supervision of a ducal four-man commission of
councillors and officials, which was specially set up each year in
August 'to renew the municipality (loi) at Ghent', the duke often
found it impossible to place his supporters and partisans on either of
the two benches of echevins. The distribution of the echevins among
the three 'Members' or sections of the town populace was fixed: the
burgesses had six echevins, three on each bench, and each of the
other 'Members', the weavers and the other fifty-two craft gilds, had
ten, five on each bench. Every gild had its dean and, by the mid-
fifteenth century, the two head deans or *hoofdekens*, one the dean of
the weavers, the other chosen from the deans of the other craft
gilds, had acquired so much power that Philip the Good accused
them of becoming virtual heads of state and appointing all the other
town officials. The common will of the people of fifteenth-century
Ghent was supposed to be expressed, in times of crisis and decision,
by the *collatie* or grand council, which comprised single representatives from each of the craft gilds, twenty-three representatives from
the weavers, and ten burgesses. Supreme power rested with this body
which was in fact by no means representative of the common people
of Ghent, for it was dominated by the better-off merchants and craftsmen or *goede lieden*, who alone were permitted to take office in gild
or municipality.

One of the most fascinating aspects of the Ghent war is the
abundant documentation which has survived from both sides.[1] Within

[1] For this paragraph, see Fris, *BSHAG* viii (1900), 212–43. For the Ghent
war as a whole, besides the sources mentioned here, i.e. *Dagboek van Gent*,
i and ii, *Kronyk van Vlaanderen*, ii, *Chronique des Pays-Bas et de Tournai*,
Chastellain's chronicle in *Œuvres*, ii., de la Marche, *Mémoires*, ii., Duclercq,
Mémoires, and d'Escouchy, *Chronique*; de Waurin, *Croniques*, v and Jouffroy,
Oratio, 186–204 are sometimes useful. See too van Werveke, *Gent*, Fris,

the walls of the beleagured and rebellious city two diligent diarists recorded the course of events in considerable detail. One, a civic official, author of the *Dagboek van Gent*, wrote his work up day by day and transcribed into it the texts of all the significant documents he could lay hands on in the town hall or elsewhere. The other, whose text was subsequently incorporated into the *Kronyk van Vlaanderen*, was probably a native of Ghent and certainly lived there during the war: he tells us in July 1453 that he heard, from the Fishmarket, the ducal cannon firing at the castle of Gavere some nine miles to the south. These two authors were well informed and are remarkably unbiased, unlike the Burgundian chroniclers, who are open partisans of the duke. Fortunately, the two groups of writers cover different aspects of the war. The Ghenters were civilians who concentrated on affairs inside Ghent, while Chastellain and de la Marche were soldiers who campaigned with the duke and were thus extremely well informed on military affairs. Their narratives are usefully supplemented by those of Duclerq at Arras and d'Escouchy at Péronne, who obtained information at secondhand but were well placed to do so. Finally, we have a contemporary account of the Ghent war from a reliable and more or less disinterested observer at Tournai, who describes, among other things, how he saw the glow in the sky from the burning suburbs of Oudenaarde in April 1452. Besides these chroniclers the historian is able to make use of a wealth of documentary evidence for the Ghent war, including some ducal letters.

All the Burgundian chroniclers trace the beginning of the Ghent war to a request by Philip the Good, which was actually made in January 1447, for a new tax on salt on the lines of the French *gabelle*: he promised to abolish all *aides* in return for 24 Flemish groats on every sack of salt sold in Flanders. Duclerq explains that a sack was 'as much as a sturdy well-built man of thirty could carry on his shoulders from one place to another'[1] and he, as well as d'Escouchy and others, imply that the refusal of Ghent, which prompted the refusal of the other Members of Flanders too, angered the duke and led to a rapid deterioration in his relations with Ghent. Thomas Basin, writing twenty years after events which in any case he knew nothing about, argues that it could not have been the proposed *gabelle* which started the war because, in the first place, if it had been

---

Histoire de Gand, Oorkonden betreffende den opstand van Gent, Nieuwe oorkonden and *Documents concernant la révolte de Gand.*
[1] *Mémoires*, 40. For what follows, see Basin, *Charles VII*, ii. 204–6.

the rest of Flanders would have fought beside Ghent. Secondly, he points out that Philip, after winning the war decisively, never imposed the salt tax nor even attempted to do so. Nevertheless, both the Flemish chroniclers of the Ghent war open their narrative with an account of this episode. One of them, the author of the *Dagboek*, fortunately transcribes the text of the speech delivered on Philip's behalf and in his presence to the *collatie* of Ghent in which the request was made. This confirms beyond all doubt the significance of the proposed salt tax, for Philip evidently hoped, by enlisting the cooperation of Ghent, to establish the tax in Flanders and, by invoking the example of Flanders, to impose it throughout his other territories. No wonder he took the trouble to preface the request with an extended, though hypocritical and tendentious, review and justification of his policies and prospects. No wonder he took care to entertain some of the deans of the Ghent craft gilds at his Bruges hôtel before the request was put to the *collatie*, with a view to purchasing their support.[1] The speech in question, which was also submitted in writing to the three 'Members' of Ghent, ran in part as follows.

My good people and true friends, you all know that I was nourished and brought up as a child and young man in this good town of mine, for which reason I have entertained more favour, love and friendship for this town and all of you, than for any of my other towns. I have often made this clear by gladly and willingly conceding everything you have sought and requested from me. At the same time I have always relied particularly on you to stand by me in my need and not to abandon me, which you have not done and I trust will not do.

Doubtless you all know perfectly well how and in what state my lord and father left me at his death. I, who was then a young prince, found myself heavily in debt, my domains were mostly alienated, and all the offices and jewels had been mortgaged or pawned, so that nothing more could be raised, which made things very difficult for me. As everyone knows, I found it necessary to undertake a prolonged and perilous war, with God and right on my side, to avenge my father, who was your prince and lord. In the conduct of this war, which lasted for many years, I incurred such expenses in paying my numerous troops, defending the castles and towns along my frontiers against the enemy . . . and maintaining my estate, that they could never be totalled or estimated. You also well know how, during a lull in the war in France, I had to wage a burdensome and murderous war against the English in my lands of Holland, Zeeland and Friesland in order to protect Flanders and for

[1] Fris, *BSHAG* xi (1903), 87. The extract which follows is from *Dagboek van Gent*, i. 57–68.

other reasons. This war, which was fought with God and right on my side, lasted as you know a long time and, before I brought it to a successful conclusion (for which thanks be to God) it had cost me, besides all the heavy expenses that I incurred throughout this period in the French war, over a million gold saluts, which at first I was extremely ill-prepared to find.

Again, as you all know, to protect my unfortunate land and subjects of Namur, I had to wage war against the people of Liège, who hoped, while I was preoccupied in France, to devastate and conquer my land of Namur, which originated in the bosom of Flanders. But, with God's help they failed and were defeated, which also cost me a great deal. All this does not include the heavy expenses I have sustained over a long period and still sustain every day in the service of God, in support of the christian faith and of the chapel of the Holy Sepulchre of our beloved lord at Jerusalem and of other holy places thereabouts, against the heathen and pagans. To these ends I have expended a good deal of money and I am still doing so willingly, for the atonement and honour of God and for the salvation of myself and my subjects. You can find out about this from people who have been to those lands, and also I hope that subjects of mine are well received by the christians living there.

Now it is true that some years ago, at the request of our holy father the pope and of the holy Council [of Basel] then in session, also to please God, to avoid the shedding of christian blood and to bring to an end all kinds of evils and wrongs caused by the war, I forgave my father's death and made peace with the king, as you must all know. After this treaty, considering that although I had maintained my lands and subjects so far as I could in peace, security and prosperity during the war, nevertheless I had levied numerous *aides* and taxes which were willingly granted me time and again; and considering that the offices of state were mortgaged or in debt to a dangerous extent and my rents and domains alienated or sold, I resolved with God's help to remain in peace and quiet and, with my people's help, to bring my lands, domains and offices into a satisfactory state and to maintain and uphold good government. But, in spite of the peace, I was treated shortly afterwards as if there was still open war and no peace had been made, and am still at the moment [being so treated], both on the frontiers of my lands and with reference to my rule as a whole, all of which, quite apart from the expenses I have incurred for a long time and am still incurring, has troubled and does trouble me very much. On top of all this came difficulty after difficulty, and I had to protect and defend the numerous rights which my aunt the duchess of Luxembourg and I possess in the lands of Luxembourg and Chiny, on behalf of which I have had a costly war which looks like continuing . . . , so that I must now send a considerable army there at great expense. I trust with God's help to defend my honour there, for my land of Luxembourg is well-situated to protect all my other lands, especially Flanders and Brabant. . . .

Considering all this, the fear and uncertainty in which I stand because of wars on all sides when my treasury is empty . . .; considering also the poverty of my good towns, the condition of which daily deteriorates rather than improves, and the pitiful circumstances of my poor country people, who are suffering because of the *aide* now being levied; considering also that I myself am firmly resolved that no one, whoever he may be, shall invade or attack my lands and subjects, especially Flanders, which some would certainly like to do, without my opposing them in person with God's help as long as possible . . .; considering all this, my good people and true friends, I announce to you all and tell you truthfully that I am more than ever in need of your help, for the wellbeing of myself, of you all and of my land of Flanders, which I would gladly see more prosperous.

To this end, so that I can be helped to improve my situation as is very necessary, for I am at the end of my tether, and also to prevent my good towns suffering any more, as they have done up to now, and to help them to strengthen and improve themselves, and especially to help sustain the poor country people who have suffered a long time from the above-mentioned taxes and *aides*, in the interests of everyone, I have decided, on good counsel and advice, to help you in the following way. That is to say, to assist my affairs the better, since my lands are emptied of gold, which is most grievous to me, and also in order to harm my people as little as possible, [I have decided to levy] a special tax for a term of years in Flanders and in all my lands and lordships, on every measure of salt, whether it be by the *hoed* or on each sack or otherwise according to the appropriate towns and measures. This tax on salt will be paid by foreign merchants and others coming from abroad and by my own subjects, and it should harm no one, least of all ordinary people and the poor; nor will they have to continue paying out money daily, as they do now, for the above-mentioned *aide*, which is most burdensome to them.

So I ask you in all friendship, considering the above, to help me without fail. And although I have asked for three shillings groat on every *hoed* of salt, measure of the Zwin at Sluis, which is equivalent to twenty-seven groats on a sack of salt at Ghent, nevertheless, since it was claimed that this was a heavy and burdensome duty, I have reduced it as much as I possibly can, that is to say, to two shillings on each *hoed* of salt measure of the Zwin at Sluis, which is eighteen Flemish groats or thereabouts per sack at Ghent. This and nothing less I pray and request you in as friendly and urgent a manner as possible, to agree to in good faith. . . .

My good people and true friends, you will understand that I ask this because of my urgent need, and for the protection of yourselves, myself, and my lands. And although it is true that it may bring in a little more than I receive annually in *aides*, you must appreciate that this will help me in minor routine expenses. Above all, these payments on salt will ruin nobody, but everyone will pay without difficulty and perhaps without even knowing it. The most notable people will pay the most, and in particular foreigners, monks and clerks, noblemen and burgesses and others will pay more, each according to his estate, and poor people the least. . . .

Moreover . . . because of the revenues from the above-mentioned salt tax, I propose to abolish and do away with all the remaining instalments owed by my land of Flanders on account of the *aide* mentioned above and now in course of being levied . . . except only what is due this Christmas Eve . . . , and although during the next twelve years I had fully intended to request some substantial *aides* from my land of Flanders, on account of certain important affairs, over and above the afore-mentioned payments due from the present *aide* . . . , nevertheless, since I particularly desire the welfare, security and prosperity of my lands and you all . . . , I intend to assure and promise you that, during this period of twelve years, provided the salt tax is levied in the above-mentioned way, I shall not request, desire or demand . . . any *aide* or subvention. I shall also see that my son promises not to seek any *aides* or subventions in Flanders during the said twelve-year period . . . for it is my resolve and intention to improve my land, strengthen my good towns and enrich my impoverished country-people . . . by ensuring, by means of the salt tax, that for twelve years you and my land remain quit and free of all other taxes and *aides*. . . . Finally, I propose to seek the agreement of all my lands round here to this tax, but I shall not impose it in Flanders alone if it is accepted there but refused elsewhere, for I have no wish to tax my good land of Flanders more than any other.

All the trouble Philip the Good had taken in presenting this request to Ghent was in vain. He met with a direct refusal, and left the town in anger. He seems now to have resolved on a policy of intervention there which was evidently designed, by gaining control of the municipality for his supporters in Ghent, to reduce the extent to which the town might again thwart his plans or undermine his power. He tried to influence the municipal elections in August 1447 to prevent one of the leaders of the anti-ducal faction, Daneel Sersanders, from being chosen head dean of the craft gilds. But this plan was foiled. He tried again in August 1449, including among his deputies to supervise the elections a firm supporter and secretary of his, the Ghent legist Pieter Baudins. This time, though Philip's opponents Lievin Sneevoet, Daneel Sersanders and Lieven de Pottere were successful, a pretext was found for rejecting the election on grounds of irregularity, and a new one was ordered. A prolonged dispute followed. While Ghent appealed to the other three Members of Flanders, Philip put pressure on the town by withdrawing his bailiff and other officials. He convoked the three Estates of Flanders at Malines on 26 January 1450 to remonstrate in person, though with the help of an interpreter, 'about the aggressions which the Ghenters have committed and are still committing against the duke and his government'.[1] Eventually, after the three Estates had met again in Ghent early in March, the town gave way and agreed to hold elections, the new echevins to sit until August 1450 while duke and town settled other points of dispute which had arisen meanwhile.

Besides this attempt to gain control of the municipality of Ghent, Philip tried at the same time to undermine the privileged status of the city and its burgesses. During the negotiations in 1450 he submitted demands, or made conditions, which revealed his aims: suppression of non-resident burgesses, extension of the authority of the bailiff, and reduction of the power of the craft gilds. Moreover, in August 1450 and thereafter he progressed from negotiation to legislation, ordering his officers to recognize the privileged status of Ghent burgesses only as defined in a document of 1297 and, in particular, he insisted that the non-resident burgesses were justiciable in his courts. This offensive against Ghent was intensified in the summer of 1451, after the failure of a plot to seize power on Philip's behalf organized by the ducal secretaries Pieter Baudins and Jooris de Bul. On 4 June 1451 Philip sent letters to Ghent complaining bitterly of the activities of Daneel Sersanders, Lievin de Pottere and Lievin Sneevoet, whom he accused, among other things, of encouraging opposition to his proposal for a tax on salt even though they had previously promised him they would accept it. The echevins were now bluntly ordered to dismiss the three offenders. When they refused, as if to emphasize the element of personal confrontation and involvement which had already been apparent in January 1447, Philip summoned them to appear before him at Termonde. The echevins drew up a solemn notarial act of protest against this ducal summons which, they claimed, infringed their civic privileges, and sent along one of their number only. But, after they had been assured of a full pardon if only they would apologize for their misdeeds, they duly turned up at Termonde on 5 August to submit to the duke. Significantly enough, they attributed their reluctance to appear before him to 'fear of the common people of Ghent'. The three ring-leaders were exiled from Flanders for vary-

[1] ADN B2008, f. 114. See too ADN B2004, fos. 122b–123.

ing terms of years, but the uproar and general strike at Ghent on 9 August had no immediate sequel. It looked as though the duke had won a bloodless victory.

Nevertheless, events occurred towards the close of 1451 which altered the whole character of the dispute. Hitherto, it had been partly between two rival factions inside Ghent and partly between the duke and the town. Now the common people began to assert their power and, during the winter of 1451–2 they took control of their town, raising the standard of revolt against their own echevins, the civic aristocracy of Ghent, the duke and his officials and indeed against anyone who chose to oppose them. The manner in which the civic constitution was subverted and the revolutionary government set up was, briefly, as follows.

In October 1451 several partisans of the duke, notably Pieter Tijncke and Lodewijk d'Hamere, both of whom were under the protection of ducal safe-conducts, were accused of complicity in the unsuccessful conspiracy which had been organized on Philip's behalf by Pieter Baudins and Jooris de Bul during the previous summer. They were arrested and interrogated, and executed on 11 November in spite of protests from Philip, who had retaliated by withdrawing his bailiff and other officials from Ghent on 26 October when a general strike had been proclaimed. A more revolutionary step was taken on the afternoon of 16 November when, during a mass meeting in the market-place, a *rechter ende justicier* was elected to take over the bailiff's judicial duties until such time as the duke chose to allow his return. This justiciar, the civic authorities hastened to explain in a letter sent to the duke that same day, 'will swear to look after your rights, prerogatives and privileges, to receive your fines and dues and keep account of them in good time, just as your bailiff has been doing'.[1] Both sides still hoped to achieve a settlement. The echevins of Ghent sent a deputation to the duke on 20 November which included several local ecclesiastics and other mediators, and Philip permitted Sersanders, de Pottere and Sneevoet to return to Ghent for six weeks.

But the common people were now thoroughly aroused. Complaining that the recent embassy to the duke had been sent without their knowledge and consent, they insisted on replacing the justiciar with another more in sympathy with themselves, even though he had to be released from prison to take up office, and they set up a special commission to investigate the alleged misdeeds and embezzlement of the echevins. Armed gatherings in the market-place succeeded one

[1] *Dagboek van Gent*, i. 161.

another in the first two days of December, and on 3 December the civic constitution and existing government of Ghent were overturned in favour of rule by three elected *hoofdmannen* or captains. Their régime was inaugurated in true revolutionary manner. Several ducal partisans were beheaded in the market-place, though the ex-bailiff of Ghent, Bauduin de Vos, received a last-minute reprieve; a list of 'enemies of the town' was published; 200 armed men were despatched to occupy Biervliet; and letters were sent to Bruges, Liège and even to the king of France, appealing for help, and to Brussels and elsewhere asking for the extradition of fugitives, for people now began to leave Ghent in increasing numbers. Even the most representative of the existing civic organs, the *collatie*, was abandoned or abolished by the three captains, who preferred instead to arouse the dubious passions of direct democracy by appealing to the votes of the people assembled in the market-place.

In spite of these illegal proceedings there was as yet no armed confrontation with the duke. In January and February 1452, while the other three Members of Flanders, the count of Étampes and others tried to mediate between Ghent and the duke, the internal revolution in Ghent continued, with more executions and the compilation of a lengthy dossier on the crimes, misrule and peculation of those who had ruled the town during the last fifteen or sixteen years, many of whom were accused of being supporters of the duke. In March the situation deteriorated still further, especially when the Ghenters discovered that the duke had prohibited the supply of corn to Ghent, ordered the arrest of all natives of the town who could be apprehended, and inaugurated a veritable blockade of their town. In the last days of March they appealed for help to Termonde, Aalst, Ninove, Oudenaarde, Courtrai, Bruges and elsewhere. Bruges refused; Tournai, actually a French city, promised to do what it could but offered no actual help; Ninove, alone of the smaller places normally dependent on Ghent, firmly committed itself in her cause. But Flanders as a whole stood firm for the duke, who now published a manifesto which set out his version of events, denying the significance of the rejected salt tax in causing the troubles and justifying the policy of military intervention on which he had resolved.[1]

Brussels, 31 March 1452

Philip by the grace of God duke of Burgundy, of Lotharingia, of Brabant, of Limbourg, count of Flanders, of Artois, of Burgundy

---

[1] *Collection de documents inédits*, ii. 96–111.

palatine, of Hainault, of Holland, of Zeeland and of Namur, margrave
of the Holy Roman Empire, lord of Frisia, of Salins and of Malines
wishes to inform all prelates and other churchmen, nobles, knights,
squires, officers, municipalities, burgesses, urban communities and other
subjects of his and all merchants and foreigners in his lands and lordships and each one of them that the inhabitants of our town of Ghent,
subjects of ours, persevering from bad to worse in their provocations,
rebellions and acts of disobedience towards and against us, their natural
lord and prince, above and beyond and not content with the shocking
and detestable misdeeds perpetrated by them against us and our prerogatives, all of which are well known and some of which will be mentioned
below, have, by lies and false advice, tried to suborn and seduce our
good people of Flanders and incite them to rebellion with them and on
their behalf against us, by spreading word among the people that we are
malcontent and annoyed with them because they would not consent to
the salt tax which we some time ago requested in our land of Flanders
and in others of our lands and lordships. . . . However, this is wrong,
false and contrary to the truth, and we feel constrained, for our honour
and defence, and in order to refute the evil reports and sinister exhorta-
tions of the Ghenters, to demonstrate and explain the true causes of the
indignation which we entertain towards them. This did not originate in
their rejection of the salt tax, but it stems from the affronts, excesses and
abuses which the Ghenters have notoriously for a long time perpetrated
and still are perpetrating against us to the prejudice of us and our
prerogatives and also in general to the prejudice of our Flemish subjects,
both by the usurpation of the jurisdiction of others, and by exactions,
acts of violence and oppressions directly contrary to their privileges,
which they have infringed, especially in the following cases.

According to one of the privileges of Ghent concerning the [annual]
renewal of the municipality, the eight electors, four appointed by our
deputies and four by the echevins of Ghent, after being appropriately
sworn in, ought to meet in a certain place, just the eight of them, to
choose twenty-six notable burgesses of our town of Ghent as echevins of
the said town, which twenty-six, chosen in this way, ought to be received
and sworn in by our bailiff without any vote, authorization or intervention by the two head deans or anyone else in Ghent and in such a
way that the said twenty-six echevins-elect are not drawn more from one
'Member' or craft than another. Nevertheless, the contrary has been
done, for it is a fact that the head dean of the craft gilds and the head
dean of the weavers, each time the municipality is renewed, have arro-
gated to themselves powers over the proceedings in such a way as to
nominate twenty of the twenty-six echevins-elect, ten each, according
to their pleasure, commanding the electors to accept them and making
them swear to do so. That is to say, the dean of the crafts appoints ten
from the crafts under his jurisdiction, and the dean of the weavers ten

from his craft of weavers, that is, twenty persons in all from their side, and on our side there are only six, which is by no means a comparable or equal number. Thus the said two deans have exercised power, and those echevins nominated and promoted by them, that is, the majority, have conducted the affairs of the town, both as regards legal judgments and in other wicked and rebellious ways, without regard for right, justice, equity or conscience. . . .

Besides, the Ghenters have committed and are still daily committing serious abuses in the system of non-resident burgesses, for they regard as burgesses people who have neither lived nor kept house in Ghent for a long time and are still not doing so, but have lived and still live elsewhere, doing nothing that burgesses do. This is directly contrary to the privilege which permits those living out of Ghent to be burgesses only if they reside in Ghent for a year and a day and undertake the duties of a burgess. These non-residents, on the pretext that they are burgesses, have committed and continue to commit serious outrages, excesses, violences and oppressions against the common people who endure them, though reluctantly, because they dare not complain for fear of Ghent. And, if they do complain, they cannot obtain justice or a reasonable hearing, because when a non-burgess quarrels with a burgess for whatever reason, the non-burgess has to go to Ghent before the echevins, where the non-resident burgesses receive many favours through corruption, delays and otherwise . . . and the non-burgesses, in disputes with burgesses of Ghent, are usually severely treated and often serious injustices, exactions and oppressions are meted out to them. . . .

Then besides this the Ghenters have exiled people without the consent or knowledge of our bailiff, who is there in our name. This is an infringement of their privileges, which expressly state that the echevins of Ghent cannot banish a man or woman without the authority and consent of our bailiff of Ghent. Moreover, they have been asserting jurisdiction over our officers in matters which concern no one but ourselves, to whom these officers have sworn their oath of office and before whom in all cases of malpractice in that office they are answerable and justiciable and not otherwise, to be punished by us, when they do wrong, according to the seriousness of the case. Also, they have been claiming jurisdiction over places outside their boundaries to an extent not supported by their privileges, in an effort to dominate our land of Flanders, and they have committed various other misdeeds and outrages and are still committing them, directly against our dignity and rule, against the majority of the people of Flanders, and against their own privileges, infringing them in diverse ways which it would take too long to recite here. . . .

These things, and no others, are the cause and motive for our just indignation and anger against the Ghenters . . . who have persevered and continued from bad to worse both in the [annual] renewals of the

316 PHILIP THE GOOD

municipality, in the matter of non-resident burgesses, and otherwise in various ways hereinafter declared. At the renewal of the municipality which took place last August they were secretly in arms in their guild-halls and elsewhere, terrorizing the four electors appointed on our behalf so much that, to avoid the inconvenience which these electors were told would otherwise ensue, they had to agree, with the other four electors on behalf of the town, because of this fear, to elect as echevins the twenty persons nominated by the two head deans. . . . Soon after these elections . . . the Ghenters, discovering that we had left Flanders and were in our land of Luxembourg, assembled in arms in the market-place and have since continued their armed assemblies on several occasions. Moreover, not content with this, piling evil on evil, demonstrating more and more ill-will, obstinacy, pertinacity, rebellion and disobedience towards us, and to better implement their evil, damnable and detestable plans, and as it must be assumed, with the intention of stirring up the whole country against us and our well-wishers, they have created and set up three captains who have constituted themselves rulers of the town. They administer justice, ordain and publish edicts, levy fines and are obeyed throughout the town as princes and lords. . . . As everyone knows, [these captains] have, under the pretext of justice, on their own authority and against the privileges of the town, piteously and murder-ously tortured good and notable burgesses and people of substantial means. Some they have put to death, others they have shamefully branded with hot irons without any justification. They have put people to death summarily as soon as they were arrested without law, judgment or justice and without even explaining the cause, which is a most inhuman, cruel and horrible thing to relate. By these methods they hold the people of the town in such a grip that nobody dares do or say anything against the wishes of these captains and their satellites, accomplices and supporters. And because some of the burgesses of the town, wishing neither to accept them nor to countenance their wicked plans and acts of violence, have fled, they have banished them and placed rewards on their heads . . . declaring their belongings forfeited and confiscated. In fact they have seized and sold or otherwise disposed of the goods of several of these fugitives which they managed to lay their hands on both inside and outside the town, which is quite illegal. They have also caused forts to be constructed in the countryside and roads and passages to be fortified; they have appointed and established captains, constables and head men in the villages; and they have sent into the countryside to arrest and take to Ghent as prisoners our officers and other good people who have done nothing wrong. They even arrested our bailiff of the Pays de Waas while he was in the middle of judging and holding court in our name . . ., administering law, reason and justice to all parties. Nonetheless, they took him prisoner to Ghent and, after holding him for some days, put him to death, in defiance of

God and reason. In their letters, at the top of which they inscribe their names like princes, they send commands and prohibitions to our officers and to the authorities of our towns and others of our subjects in Flanders, just as they please, even prohibiting people from obeying our letters and written commands, though we are the prince and ruler of them and of the country. . . .

What then ought one to say and pronounce concerning the doings of these Ghenters, who conduct themselves in this way? They are still trying, like conspirators, by false cunning and evil tricks, to get control of our good towns. . . . They hope, by the lies and false rumours which they spread, to undermine the truth, to stir up our good people and raise the country in revolt against us. Certainly, they behave like people who recognize neither God in heaven nor prince on earth, but desire and attempt by themselves and for themselves to rule and govern at their pleasure. No wonder these things are grievous, painful, displeasing and intolerable to us, who are their prince and lord. . . .

Considering the obstinacy and continuing wickedness of the Ghenters . . . . we have summoned some of our noble vassals and loyal subjects from around here . . . to bring back and reduce them to obedience and humility towards us with God's help . . . and we pray and request all our good and loyal subjects . . . to take our cause and quarrel . . . to their hearts and to help us . . . against them as good and loyal subjects ought to do.

To this declaration of war the captains of Ghent reacted on 4 April by organizing a general procession, and on the same day they sent an embassy to Philip the Good which was reinforced with a selection of respectable prelates drawn from the neighbouring abbeys. On Good Friday, 7 April, while this embassy was still at Brussels aided, in its pacificatory initiatives, by a deputation from the other three Members of Flanders, a contingent of Ghenters occupied the duke's castle of Gavere. A week later, on 13–14 April, the Brussels embassy was recalled and one of the captains of Ghent, Lievin Boone, led the civic militia to attack and besiege the town of Oudenaarde. This place, some sixteen miles south-south-west of Ghent, on the Schelde, had apparently been garrisoned by Philip before Easter, when one of his leading captains, Simon de Lalaing, had been posted there to help strangle Ghent's river-borne trade and cut off her supplies of provisions from Tournai and elsewhere.[1] It may have been this move,

[1] Philip later claimed (ducal letters of 28 April 1452 referred to below, p. 323 n. 3), against Chastellain, Œuvres, ii. 225–6 and Duclercq, Mémoires, 42 that de Lalaing was in Oudenaarde merely by chance, with five companions only. This seems just as unlikely as the subsequent claim of Ghent (Dag-

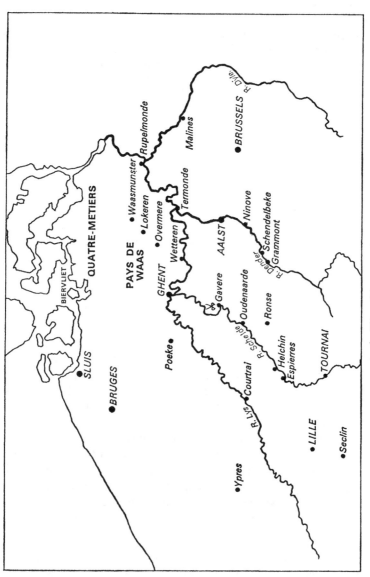

6. The Ghent war

following up the proclamation of a general blockade on 15 March, which forced the hand of the Ghenters and induced them to undertake military operations. Their strategy was to seize and fortify outlying places like Oudenaarde and Grammont in order to set up a first line of defence against the duke and to protect their supply-lines. Philip's strategy was the seizure and garrisoning of these same places in order to contain the Ghenters, to cut off their supplies and to be in a position to raid and pillage the countryside and the villages around Ghent. In this context the town of Courtrai, between Ghent and Lille, might well have been of crucial importance had not Philip taken the trouble during the previous autumn to secure its loyalty with a series of letters, supported by a strong garrison.[1] There remained Oudenaarde. While the Ghenters laid siege to this place on 14 April and Simon de Lalaing prepared to resist them by burning down the suburbs, they also established themselves firmly at Espierres, south-east of Courtrai on the Schelde, tried to seize Aalst,[2] and on Sunday, 16 April, unsuccessfully attacked Grammont, which was thereafter strongly garrisoned by Philip.

Inside beleagured Oudenaarde, where a substantial element of the population sympathized with Ghent, Simon de Lalaing faced close investment by the besieging Ghenters, whose artillery began a systematic bombardment. At night, incendiary missiles were fired into the town and de Lalaing had to place tanks of water at the street corners and organize fire-watching parties with the help of the women to watch where the missiles fell and put out the fires. The besiegers were by no means lacking in ingenuity in devising other less conventional methods of undermining the town's resistance. They used crossbows to shoot messages into Oudenaarde in French and Flemish which were aimed at weakening confidence in de Lalaing, for they 'requested and urged the said Sir Simon to surrender and deliver up the town on the day he had fixed with them and stated that the money they had promised him was all ready'.[3] When this ruse failed, they paraded two small children outside the walls of Oudenaarde, claiming that they were de Lalaing's two boys, whom they had seized during a raid into Hainault, and that they would put them to death unless

---

boek van Gent, ii. 141 and 171–2) that the siege of Oudenaarde had been initiated by country people and others, 'without the consent of the people of Ghent'.

[1] Analectes historiques, v. 103–8 and d'Escouchy, Chronique, iii. 409–12.
[2] Livre des trahisons, 221–2.
[3] De la Marche, Mémoires, ii. 232.

Oudenaarde surrendered. De Lalaing's reply was a cannonade. Unbeknown to the Ghenters, he himself narrowly escaped death by drowning when he fell into the Schelde one day while returning from inspecting the watch. He did not have to suffer the rigours of a siege for long. While Jehan de Bourgogne, count of Étampes, assembled an army at Seclin, south of Lille, Philip mustered another at Grammont. The aim of both was to raise the siege of Oudenaarde. At the end of April, while suspicion and turmoil in Ghent led to the dismissal and decapitation of the three captains and their replacement by five new ones, the duke was able to announce the successful conclusion of these military operations to his loyal town of Malines.[1]

> Grammont,
> 27 April 1452
>
> Dearest and well-loved, because we know that you want to hear news and be assured of our good estate and the state of our affairs we now let you know that, at the time of writing this, we are in excellent health and prosperity as to our person, praise be to our blessed creator. Moreover it is a fact that, last Friday, 21 April, those who held the bridge at Espierres on the Schelde on behalf of the town of Ghent, our enemies, rebels and disobedient to us, were defeated by our cousin the count of Étampes and those of our troops in his company, and the passage of the said river Schelde was cleared and opened, and Helchin, which they likewise held, was recovered. The Monday following, 24 April, my said cousin and his men raised the siege of Oudenaarde on the far side of the Schelde, and defeated the besiegers, and my cousin entered the town with his men. As to the Ghenters encamped on this side of the Schelde, as soon as they heard the news of the defeat of their people on the other bank, they evacuated the place and fled towards Ghent, abandoning their baggage and artillery. As soon as we received this news in our town of Grammont, we went after them in pursuit with all the troops we had with us. During this pursuit, which continued right up to our town of Ghent, a large number of the fleeing Ghenters were intercepted and struck down. We let you know these things, my good friends, for your information and so that from now on you have no communication with our enemies the Ghenters, rebels and disobedient to us, in matters of trade or otherwise in any manner whatsoever. Dearest and well-loved, may Our Lord be your guard.

By early May the ducal army was firmly established in Termonde, Aalst and Oudenaarde, and throughout the month a series of punitive raids was organized from these places to demolish the fortifications

---

[1] *IAM* iii. 94–6. Also printed in *Collection de documents inédits*, ii. 112–13.

hastily thrown up by the Ghenters. Ghent itself was attacked on 1 and 15 May and a knight in the count of Étampes's army was able to strike one of the town gates with his lance. Lokeren to the east of Ghent was raided on 18 May and Overmere was attacked on 24 May. These raids culminated in a veritable invasion of the Pays de Waas, which was led by Philip in person accompanied by his legitimate son Charles and his senior bastard Cornille. Near Rupelmonde on 16 June the Ghenters were tempted out of their fortified lines by the feigned flight of a ducal scouting party and then attacked and dispersed by the duke's van which had been concealed in a wood. Some of them escaped with their lives by using their long pikes to leap the dikes, but 1,500 were killed. Philip's entire army is said to have sustained but a single casualty, the bastard Cornille, who died shortly after being wounded in the neck or face with a pike by one of the Ghenters. He had raised his visor or removed his gorget because of the heat.[1] By early July, much of the country east of Ghent had been overrun and Philip was apparently making preparations for a close investment of Ghent itself. The organization of his army in the summer of 1452 is described by George Chastellain in reference to a raid on the fort at Overmere, in which the duke did not personally take part.

And there it was decided, after several discussions and debates, that they would attack a strong fort which the Ghenters were holding about half-way between Ghent and Termonde near a village called Overmere. It was resolved and commanded that the lord of Croy should go, and that he should guard the duke's standard and take with him the people of the court. This would constitute the advance-guard, and Sir Jaques de Lalaing would command the scouts, accompanied by Sir Anthoine de Vaudrey, Sir Guillaume his brother, the lord of Aumont and Sir François l'Aragonais. This Sir Jaques had with him twenty-five lances and eighty archers. A gentleman of Burgundy named Anthoine de Láviron had command of the advance scouts with seven or eight lances, and he went ahead of Sir Jaques de Lalaing. After Sir Jaques went Sir Daviot de Poix, governor and master of the ducal artillery. He led the pioneers and infantrymen, who carried axes, bill-hooks, saws and drills for demolishing barricades, filling in ditches and re-making roads wherever necessary. After Sir Daviot de Poix went the lord of Lannoy and the lord of Baucignies at the head of about a hundred combatants to support and

---

[1] Besides the Burgundian chroniclers cited above, p. 306 see on this de But, *Chronique*, 334. The extract which follows is from Chastellain, *Œuvres*, ii. 260–2.

reinforce the said Jaques as necessary. After the lord of Lannoy went the lord of Créquy and with him the lord of Contay and Morelet de Renty who led the archers of the ducal guard. The lord of Croy followed the lord of Créquy with the duke's standard and with him accompanying the standard were Adolf, my lord of Cleves, my lord the bastard of Burgundy . . . and a large number of other knights and squires. After the lord of Croy went the count of St. Pol and Jaques de St. Pol, the lord of Fiennes, brother of the said count of St. Pol, and numerous other knights and squires. The said count of St. Pol had command of this contingent and he was followed by Sir Jehan de Croy who was very magnificently accompanied with knights, squires and bowmen, and he commanded the rearguard. And it is true that on Wednesday 24 May all these contingents set out from Termonde to go and assault the fort at Overmere.

Long before the outbreak of hostilities both sides had been searching for allies or sympathizers. Philip the Good was reproached by his enthusiastic nephew of Cleves, Duke John, for not summoning him at once to his aid when the war began. But, in a letter to the duke of Cleves of 11 May 1452, Philip explained that the trouble had started so quickly that there would not in any case have been time for Duke John to arrive on the scene. He went on to assure him that he had plenty of troops. He had dismissed a third of them and did not know where to station the rest, and the Ghenters were already demoralized.[1] In spite of this Duke John rode out of Cleves with his friends on 11 June, forming a party of 100 horse in all, and took part in the later stages of the campaign. His brother Adolf apparently had been present throughout it.

Philip the Good had taken considerable trouble to ensure the loyalty of Courtrai, Bruges and other Flemish towns, and on 14 April special instructions were issued prohibiting his troops from molesting the inhabitants of Bruges, Courtrai, Ypres and Oudenaarde. He also made full use of his good relations with Malines which, for example, was urgently asked on 12 June to send all available boats and the town's 'two fine tents' as well as six pavilions, to the toll at Rupelmonde before 'tomorrow evening at the latest'. For troops, Philip relied at first almost exclusively on his Picard forces, and in Ghent all his troops were referred to as Picards. But when the need to invest Ghent on all sides necessitated the invasion of the Pays de Waas and the Quatre-Métiers, Dutch military aid was invoked,

---

[1] Grunzweig, *RBPH* iv (1925), 435–6. For what follows, see Hansen, *Westfalen und Rheinland*, ii. 250–4, *IAC* i. 214 and *IAM* ii. 101–3.

and some 3,000 men from the towns of Holland played a significant part in the summer fighting to the east of Ghent.[1]

The Ghenters also applied to Holland for help, but in vain. They appealed more hopefully to Bruges, but the ruling elements there were terrified that their city might contract the contagion of popular revolt from Ghent, and they stood firmly by the duke. When, on 27 May, a body of Ghenters several thousand strong arrived at Bruges with the apparent intention of 'having discussions with the people of the town to attract them to their side', the gates were closed against them and the authorities of Bruges reported the incident to the duke.[2] The only assistance forthcoming from Bruges was the pacificatory initiative of the foreign merchants there, who tried to persuade the Ghenters to seek a truce from Philip in the first week of June, at a time when neither side was prepared to cease hostilities. The only military aid the Ghenters succeeded in obtaining outside East Flanders was from the English, about fifty of whom had arrived in the beleagured town by early June, perhaps from Calais.

There was one person who was particularly well placed to intervene authoritatively and perhaps decisively in the quarrel between Ghent and her duke. This was the king of France, whose right to intervene was indisputable; after all, Ghent was a French town and Philip was a vassal of the French crown. Irksome as this must have been to Philip, he could not deny that the king of France was an interested party. On 29 July 1451 he wrote to the king complaining that Ghent had asked or was about to ask the king for 'certain letters and documents against me and to the prejudice of my prerogatives and lordship'. In January 1452 Philip's ambassadors sought an assurance from Charles VII that the king would in no way help or encourage the rebellious city, and on 28 April 1452 Philip found it necessary to write to Charles explaining how hostilities had started and reporting in detail his early military successes at Espierres and Oudenaarde, 'which things, most redoubted lord, I willingly inform you of because I know for certain that they will please you . . .'. On their side, the Ghenters were thoroughly outspoken in their appeal to the king. On 24 May 1452 they addressed him in the following terms.[3]

[1] Jongkees, *Handelingen van het zeventiende Vlaamse Filologen-Congress*, 63–7.
[2] Chastellain, *Œuvres*, ii. 283–7. The quotation is from p. 284.
[3] Text in Plancher, iv. no. 156; Kervyn, *Flandre*, iv. 408–12; partly in Chastellain, *Œuvres*, ii. 270–2; and in *Dagboek van Gent*, ii. 23–7. The

Most excellent and puissant prince, our most dear sire and sovereign lord, we commend ourselves to your royal majesty . . . and we wish to inform you how we and the other inhabitants of this land of Flanders have for a long time been burdened and charged in various ways, that is to say by the sale of bailliwicks and other offices which have been placed in the hands of the highest bidders without any regard to their personal suitability, nor to the benefit of justice; next, by the increase of existing tolls and the institution of new ones and also by taxes which were at first obtained through kindness, then by subtlety, fraud and malice, and lastly by force and violence; also, by bad echevins in this town pursuing their own interests with hate and greed, selling the minor civic offices, taking money often from both parties to litigation before them, using their authority to ransack whatever they stood in need of from among the possessions of the town and otherwise, shamelessly and without sparing anything, so that those who entered the municipality poor men suddenly enriched themselves. . . . [Moreover,] it has pleased our most redoubted lord and prince to show us his indignation by withdrawing his bailiffs and other officers, abandoning us without justice for seven months or so. . . . What is worse, besides all this, these wicked echevins and their supporters, enjoying great credit with our most redoubted lord and prince, sent four malefactors into our town to organize a nocturnal conspiracy with the object of killing their adversaries, and they have tried day and night to arouse the people and if possible to destroy this town. Two of the four were taken and beheaded and the said bailiff and officers have since been continually absent . . . and we are still without justice, though since then we have sent notable embassies of the three Estates of Flanders, and others to him, to try to restore his favour and the administration of justice. Meanwhile, to avoid riots, robberies and pillaging and other wicked things which could easily arise and multiply in this town, and since a multitude of people cannot be governed without any laws or fear of laws, we have been compelled to appoint captains to administer justice as effectively as possible according to their consciences. . . .

Finally, our said most redoubted lord and prince, in an effort to destroy us completely, has been pleased to publish his declaration of war, assemble troops against us, garrison several towns of his in Flanders, and blockade the waterways by means of which we are supplied with

documents referred to earlier in this paragraph are printed in *Analectes historiques*, vii. 362–4, Kervyn, *Flandre*, iv. 516–17 wrongly dated 1452, and d'Escouchy, *Chronique*, iii. 407–9 (29 July 1451); Plancher, iv. no. 155 and d'Escouchy, *Chronique*, iii. 413–15 (January 1452); and Kervyn, *Flandre*, iv. 506–10, Chastellain, *Œuvres*, ii. 237–41 and d'Escouchy, *Chronique*, iii. 415–21 (28 April 1452). On Charles VII and the Ghent war, see in general du Fresne de Beaucourt, *Charles VII*, v. 229–60.

corn and other provisions. Thus we are at war with our said lord and prince ... and, though it is most hard, difficult and unpleasant for us ... we intend, with the help and grace of God, to wage this war to the best of our ability and with all our power since, out of necessity and for the above reasons, we must conserve our rights, privileges, freedoms, liberties, customs and usages of which you, as our sovereign lord, are guardian and protector. . . . And we beseech you, most excellent and puissant prince, to remedy this state of affairs, about which we have informed you.

Early in June 1452 King Charles VII instructed ambassadors to proceed to Flanders and to negotiate a settlement between Philip and Ghent.[1] At the same time they were to invite Philip to return the Somme towns to the crown of France. At the French town of Tournai, where they stopped en route, the risks run by the king of France if he appeared to favour rebellious Ghent must have become clear to these royal ambassadors. They were told that the common people wanted to seize power in Tournai too; that people in Tournai would welcome the defeat of the duke of Burgundy by the Ghenters and might try to emulate them; and that contacts between the two towns were numerous. At first Philip refused to see the royal ambassadors, sending them off to Brussels to his chancellor and council. But they insisted on speaking to him personally and, when they did see him, at Waasmunster on 20 and 21 June, they insisted on negotiating a settlement with Ghent, though Philip and his councillors did their best to dissuade them. Philip himself told them that 'the Ghenters were the instigators of all rebellion, that they had committed the worst possible outrages, and that it was necessary to punish them in such a way as to be an example for all time'.

At first he would only permit the royal ambassadors to act as mediators alongside the foreign merchants of Bruges, Charles, count of Charolais, and Jehan, count of Étampes; but he was persuaded eventually to allow them to go by themselves to Ghent, which they did on 24 June. No more was said for the moment of the Somme towns, but Philip was compelled to sign a six-week truce with Ghent on 19 July and on 22 July he withdrew from his headquarters at Wetteren on the Schelde and disbanded his army, having first garrisoned and secured the towns of Oudenaarde, Courtrai, Aalst, Termonde and Biervliet. Though he may have been annoyed and

---

[1] This and other documents used in this paragraph are printed in Kervyn, *Flandre*, iv. 510–16, Plancher, iv. nos. 157–60 (the quotation is from no. 157) and *Collection de documents inédits*, ii. 118–25.

frustrated by the king's interference with what promised to be a successful siege of Ghent, he now bribed or persuaded the royal ambassadors to draw up a treaty favourable to himself. This document, which was published at Lille on 4 September 1452 after much debate and recrimination during which the Ghenters were accused of describing their duke as 'Philip Long-legs', stipulated an elaborate public apology by 2,000 bare-headed and penitent citizens; the closing of the three gates used by the Ghenters when setting out for the siege of Oudenaarde and the battle of Rupelmonde; the locking up in a coffer secured with five keys of the banners of all the craft gilds; reforms to the constitution to give the duke more influence in the election of echevins; various limitations on the jurisdiction and power of the civic authorities; and a fine of 250,000 gold crowns.

Not surprisingly, the Ghenters rejected this treaty and on 21 September they complained to the king in the strongest possible terms about the 'very rigorous and wicked agreement against us and our rights and privileges' which his majesty's ambassadors had signed.[1] They complained that, during the whole period of the truce, the duke had never once relaxed his blockade of their town, and they appealed to the king to punish his ambassadors for acting in flagrant breach of the royal intentions. The war continued. Philip's marshal of Burgundy, Thibaud de Neuchâtel, and others, saw to it that the towns were garrisoned and, during the autumn and winter, every village around Ghent was burnt down, every prisoner was hanged and the goods of every Ghenter they could lay their hands on were confiscated. At the same time, the Ghenters 'burnt and pillaged the lands of Flanders and Hainault on all sides all the long winter through, for the prince had dismissed his men for the winter except for the garrisons in Aalst, Termonde, Oudenaarde and Courtrai and these were not powerful enough to withstand the Ghenters'.[2] They hanged every 'Picard prisoner who fell into their power, including one with a long black beard, and their foragers brought in cart after cart of salt, corn and other stolen provisions, not to mention herds of cattle. Plundering raids were undertaken to Aalst at the end of September, through the Quatre-Métiers on 11 October, to Aalst again on 20 November, but this time heavy snow foiled them. In

[1] Plancher, iv. no. 161.
[2] *Kronyk van Vlaanderen*, ii. 173. For executions of prisoners and seizure of goods see especially *Collection de documents inédits*, ii. 133–42 and *IAGRCC* iii. 251–2. For what follows, see, besides the sources mentioned on p. 306, de But, *Chronique*, 335–6.

February they attacked Courtrai and burnt its suburbs, on 5 March they tried to intercept the duchess Isabel, on her way from Lille to Bruges. She evaded them by taking a devious route, but they ambushed instead a force under Simon de Lalaing which was on its way to meet and escort her. Two days later they returned triumphantly to Ghent with nine prisoners, captured horses and three cartloads of armour. They launched fierce attacks on Termonde and Aalst in April and May, but without success; and they also failed, though by a hair's breadth, to blow up the duke's artillery and ammunition which was in store at Lille ready for a renewed campaign against them in summer 1453.

Throughout the winter of 1452–3, and indeed well into the spring of 1453, peace efforts were intermittently but unsuccessfully continued. The foreign merchants of Bruges, their trade endangered and diminished by this catastrophic war, renewed their attempts, supported now by the other three Members of Flanders; the king of France continued his efforts in the hopes apparently of undermining Philip the Good's prestige by himself putting the duke's affairs to right; and Philip on his side appointed mediators and took intermittent initiatives, apparently to forestall the king. A royal embassy, ignored by a suspicious Philip and shrugged off by Ghent, remained fruitlessly at Tournai until the end of May, and the duke's final peace offers were rejected at Lille early in June.[1] On 18 June 1453 Philip the Good set out from Lille on the road to Courtrai and Ghent at the head of his army. His fleet had already been mobilized, under the command of the experienced captain Geoffroy de Thoisy, at Sluis and Antwerp, where the ducal galleys and other vessels which were to blockade Ghent by sea were stationed.[2] Those at Antwerp were manned in the second half of April with criminals specially released for this purpose from the town gaol of Malines.

The duke's plan of campaign was straightforward enough. First, conquer the few outlying castles which were held by the Ghenters: Schendelbeke to the south of Ghent near Grammont, Gavere on the Schelde between Ghent and Oudenaarde, and Poeke, about twelve miles west of Ghent. Next, invest Ghent closely and starve her into submission. While these operations were in progress, every possible means would be employed to tempt the Ghenters into committing

[1] Besides Chastellain's account, see Philip's letter to Malines of 11 June 1453 in *IAM* iii. 113–16. For the royal embassy, see especially the documents in Kervyn, *Flandre*, iv. 522–38 and *Analectes historiques*, vii. 364–8.
[2] ADN B2012, f. 207b, *Mémoires*, ii. 205 n. *b*. and *IAM* iii. 112.

themselves to a pitched battle. At first, things went smoothly and according to plan. Schendelbeke fell on 27 June after being invested in the first place at dawn on 25 June by the bailiff of Hainault, Jehan de Croy, and then attacked later that day by the entire ducal army, advancing from Ronse. The 104 members of the garrison were hanged.[1] Philip led his army back to Courtrai on 1 July and on 2 July he encamped at Poeke. It was here that the famous jouster and knight-errant Jaques de Lalaing was killed by a cannon-ball while he was observing the damage done to the walls of the castle by one of the ducal bombards. As a matter of fact, artillery played a vital part in the conquest of Schendelbeke and Poeke, both of which were battered and breached to such an extent that further defence was impossible. Poeke surrendered on 5 July and the garrison were hanged or strangled.

It was at this point in the campaign that Philip found himself incapable of paying his troops, and his whole army was in consequence immobilized for a week at Courtrai while the chancellor and others made frantic and ultimately successful attempts to raise the necessary funds by selling privileges to the Brabant towns and pawning quantities of ducal plate.[2] At last, on 16 July, the ducal army set out once again from Courtrai. Its objective this time was the last remaining stronghold still held by Ghent, the castle of Gavere, which stood on low-lying ground near the river Schelde, some ten miles from Ghent.

Curiously enough, one of the most interesting contemporary accounts of the battle of Gavere, which decided the Ghent war in Philip the Good's favour, has remained hitherto unknown to historians. It is contained in a statement drawn up by Jehan de Cerisy, secretary of the count of Étampes, Jehan de Bourgogne, who was one of the leading Burgundian captains. De Cerisy describes the events which took place between the breakdown of negotiations in May and the peace treaty at the end of July. In part, he was an eyewitness of them; in part, he relied on information from the count and others. His description of what happened at Gavere may usefully be quoted in full.[3]

---

[1] On these events see, besides the chroniclers, ADN B10417, f. 34 and *IAM* iii. 117–19 and, for the whole of what follows, Fris, *BSHAG* xviii (1910), 185–233.

[2] ADN B2012, fos. 89b–104. See too Philip's letters of 13 July 1453 to Anthoine de Croy, printed in *Collection de documents inédits*, ii. 131–3 and *Choix de documents luxembourgeois*, 226–7.

[3] BN MS. fr. 1278, fos. 161b–163b.

Thence [the duke] set out to besiege the castle of Gavere, two-and-a-half leagues from Ghent, which belonged to the lord of Laval. It too, was held by the Ghenters. The duke arrived there on Wednesday 18 July. After he had heavily cannonaded this place, in the night of Sunday 22 July the captain and some others with him to the number of fifteen, both English and others, escaped from the said castle secretly over the draw-bridge and slipped through the [besieging] army wearing St. Andrew's crosses and using the password 'Burgundy'. They crossed the river Schelde in a boat which was moored near the castle for the duke's foragers to cross over in to get forage for the horses, and in doing this they wounded some of the duke's men. These people went to Ghent, where they arrived about 5.0 a.m., and worked on the Ghenters to such an extent that that morning, which was Monday 23 July, they set out from the town of Ghent in force, with 30,000 men or more, to bring help to those defending the castle of Gavere by raising the duke's siege.

It so happened that, before these Ghenters had left their town to bring this help, those inside the castle of Gavere surrendered themselves unconditionally to the count of Étampes at about 8.0 a.m. Soon afterwards, the duke ordered them to be hanged and strangled on a gibbet, constructed on two forked trees, which had been set up in the camp in front of and quite near the castle while they were still inside it. They numbered twenty-eight to thirty persons, of whom some were English. While they were being executed, at about 11.0 a.m., definite news came to my lord the duke from one of his scouts that the Ghenters had set out and were approaching in great force. He had seen them and they were coming along the river Schelde, which was the most surreptitious route. The scout left the duke and announced his news from one encampment to another throughout the army, and at once everyone armed himself carefully and was ready. Soon my lord the duke sent out some patrols to skirmish with and inspect the enemy. Among them were my lords of Wavrin, of Haubourdin and of Saveuse, Sir Simon de Lalaing, my lord of Rochefort, Sir Hue de Longueval lord of Vaulx and other lords and knights with a certain number of archers. Soon afterwards, my lord the duke had his van drawn up in excellent order in front. The van remained for some time in the area of the camp, while advancing towards a wood, where there was also a church near the river Schelde on the Ghent road. The Ghenters assembled inside and in front of this wood and drew themselves up in battle order in great number, and there were many troops in their rearguard which one could not really see. As soon as the Ghenters saw the duke's van and the above-mentioned patrols they opened fire with the ribaudequins and culverins which they had brought with them, and also with crossbows and longbows, without leaving the wood. Likewise the said patrols, which comprised valiant knights, experienced in deeds of arms and battles, engaged the Ghenters hotly, firing veuglaires, ribaudequins,

330 PHILIP THE GOOD

culverins and longbows at them. Several culverins belonging to the town of Valenciennes, and some others, did excellent work.

When the Ghenters saw that they were being fiercely engaged, that the duke's people were conducting themselves well and that the duke's van was beginning to approach them, they began to be demoralized and discouraged and they broke rank, making for the further part of the wood. The duke's patrols, seeing this and realizing that they had broken rank and were in disarray, yelled loudly and fiercely at them to demoralize them the more, and the van advanced and charged at them furiously, killing them on all sides. Then my lord the duke and the people in his section of the army likewise began to yell at the Ghenters and advanced, together with the van, to attack them as they fled on all sides inside the wood and along the hedges, in the hopes of saving themselves. But they were so closely pressed that they were forced to leap into the river Schelde, in which ten or twelve thousand men were drowned. Only a few saved themselves by swimming across.

While my lord the duke and his contingent advanced through the wood some sixteen to eighteen hundred Ghenters assembled in a small field enclosed with dikes near the river Schelde, and organized themselves in a strong defensive position so that the duke and his people, who advanced [into this enclosure] on horse-back, found themselves restricted in such a way that they could not easily fight side by side in each other's aid. Some of them therefore withdrew until archers on foot could be brought into action against the defenders to disperse them. The fighting was so fierce that some of the Ghenters approached near the duke's person, so much so that he was wounded with a pole by a Ghenter whom he soon struck to the ground. There he broke his lance; and he conducted himself in this affair with great courage, as did those with him, in such a way that almost every defender was either killed or drowned. And the duke's people pursued and killed them to within a league of Ghent. Their dead were estimated at seventeen or eighteen thousand men, both killed and drowned. Among others, several of their captains and deans were killed, including a good ten or eleven of their echevins. Besides this, a number of prisoners were taken.

The substantial accuracy of this account is corroborated by others, which confirm that the fifty-seven-year-old duke's foolhardy display of personal valour was nearly disastrous. It was matched by his stupidity directly afterwards in allowing a patriotic local guide, who was asked to lead him and his men onwards to Ghent, to take him back by a circuitous route to his camp at Gavere, thus saving the town itself from conquest and plunder immediately after the battle. Some important gaps in Jehan de Cerisy's knowledge of the battle of Gavere can readily be filled, but others remain. Is it possible that the

captain of Gavere and those who escaped with him, including the
Englishman John Fox, were actually allowed to escape on condition
they betrayed the Ghenters by persuading them to take the field
against the duke? Or was their escape genuine, and did they persuade
the Ghenters to attack in good faith, in the hopes of securing a victory for Ghent and safety for their colleagues left within the castle?
Yet the rest of the garrison seem to have been under the impression
that their captain and his accomplices were mere fugitives, who had
fled to save their own skins. Why else should they have surrendered
so soon the next morning? In any event it is likely that John Fox acted
the part of a traitor, intent, as he must surely have been, only on
saving his own life. Of one thing we can be quite sure. All the
sources agree that it was the urgent entreaties of the captain of
Gavere and his companions which brought out the army of Ghent to
fight a pitched battle with the duke.

Jehan de Cerisy's failure to explain exactly why the Ghenters
broke ranks and fled at the beginning of the battle is easily explicable.
He was not to know that they had a perfectly good excuse for defaulting in this way, as their own chronicler explains. One of their
cannoneers inadvertently let a spark fly into an open sack of gunpowder and, as it burst into flames, he yelled to his companions to
keep clear. But those nearest him panicked, and those further away
panicked too, so that a large part of the army was suddenly in
disorder. It was this incident which gave victory to the duke. The same
chronicler describes the frightful scenes in Ghent later that same
day.[1]

> When the news reached Ghent that all her people were dead, slain or
> drowned, the pitiful wailing, wringing of hands and grief was indescrib-
> able. And when people saw how they came in, six and eight and ten
> together, all dripping, some barefoot and bloody-headed, some in their
> shirts, some in their jackets, just as they had swum through the water,
> so all this misery and grief was renewed among the women and the
> children who gathered in the streets moaning and groaning with dreadful
> anxiety, each for their own. This misery, which the disconsolate widows,
> who had been robbed so unexpectedly and in so short a time of their
> beloved companions, must have suffered in their hearts, every man
> experienced in himself. This misery, grief and wringing of hands lasted
> all the night through, so that even a heart of stone must suffer, and thus
> folk were waiting all night at the gates, each for his friend, for they came
> in all night long, four or six at a time.

---

[1] *Kronyk van Vlaanderen*, ii. 194.

When advised to destroy the town of Ghent after his victory at Gavere, Philip the Good was later said to have replied by asking who would replace this important part of his patrimony for him if he ruined it.[1] The city was neither occupied nor plundered by the ducal army, and the peace treaty imposed on it was similar to those which Ghent had previously rejected at Lille in May 1453 and September 1452. Reparations totalling 350,000 riders had to be paid. The two gates through which the Ghenters had passed on their way to besiege Oudenaarde on Thursday, 13 April 1452, were to be closed every Thursday in perpetuity; and the gate through which they had departed on the expedition to Rupelmonde which resulted in the death of Cornille, bastard of Burgundy, was to be permanently walled up. Certain important changes were made to the civic constitution. The two head deans were excluded from the annual municipal elections; the bailiff was given more control over the urban administration; the rights of non-resident burgesses were curtailed; and the jurisdiction of Ghent over the surrounding countryside was significantly restricted. Henceforth Ghent was to be deprived of her special position of power and privilege; she was to be relegated to the status of an ordinary Flemish town; and her echevins were to be chosen if possible from among ducal supporters belonging to the same class of merchant oligarchs which had ruled, or misruled, the town in the years before the popular revolt of 1451.

The Ghent war was only one of a series of urban struggles, of clashes between the towns of Flanders and their count, which were fought out in the fourteenth, fifteenth and sixteenth centuries. In a sense, Gavere was a sequel to Roosebeke, but it was a sequel which was by no means inevitable. The first two Valois dukes, notably John the Fearless, had progressed towards a *modus vivendi* with the turbulent Flemish cities. But, during the reign of Philip the Good, first Bruges and then Ghent were provoked into taking up arms against their ruler. In failing to devise a political solution to the problems her cities posed, Philip made it probable that Flanders would never provide that firm foundation for Burgundian power which its wealth, its early acquisition by the Valois dukes, and its culture might have led one to expect. Though the Ghent war ended with military

---

[1] Gachard, *Études et notices historiques*, ii. 407. The main documents concerning the peace of Gavere and its aftermath are mentioned or printed in *Collection de documents inédits*, ii. 142–61; de Barante, *Histoire des ducs*, ii. 701–2; Gauthier, *RSS* (7) vi (1882), 209–13; *Oorkonden betreffende den opstand van Gent*, 97–146; *Nieuwe oorkonden*, 190–219; and *DRA* xix. 367–8.

success, the whole episode was an unnecessary and costly blunder which did considerable harm to the economy of Flanders. But in one important respect it was a landmark in Burgundian history, for it was the first occasion on which all Philip the Good's territories joined to wage war together against a common foe. Warfare, in fact, which hitherto had been Dutch against the Hanse, Flemish against the English, or confined to the two Burgundies and Artois against France, now for the first time in the history of the Valois dukes became, in a real sense, Burgundian.

CHAPTER ELEVEN

Burgundy, France and the Crusade: 1454–64

The subject of this chapter is the decade which roughly extends from Duke Philip's return from Germany in 1454 until his son Charles, count of Charolais, began to exercise an influence on affairs in the autumn of 1464. At the beginning of this period, Philip was perhaps at the height of his power and prestige. He had defeated rebellious Ghent, he had made a triumphal tour through the Empire, and he was about to extend his influence over Liège and Utrecht by placing relatives of his on the episcopal thrones there. He enjoyed a rapturous reception wherever he went. For example, the chronicler Jaques Duclerq records the visit he paid to Arras on 24 February 1455, in the following words.[1]

> The duke entered the said town of Arras by St. Michael's gate, where there were tableaux vivants on raised platforms. There too several companies of girls came to meet him, all dressed in white and carrying lighted torches. As soon as they saw the duke they cried Noel! And there were many very lovely girls there. After he had entered the town he found, all along the tile-works and in the Petit Marché on platforms, scenes from the life of Gideon represented by live persons, superbly dressed, who said nothing, but went through the gestures and actions of the mystery. It was the most elaborate thing that had been seen for a long time and extremely well done and lifelike. People said it had cost more than a thousand gold crowns. In sum, if God had descended from above, I doubt if more would have been done, for it would be impossible to do more honour than was done to the duke. And in truth he was very much loved in all his lands . . . and, because of his valour, he was feared by all his neighbours and enemies.

The same enthusiasm and respect was evinced on the same occasion, that is, the duke's return from his travels in Germany, by

[1] Duclercq, *Mémoires*, 90.

the civic authorities of Mons in Hainault, who drew up their plans for welcoming the duke on 14 May as early as 30 March.[1]

For the arrival of our most redoubted lord and prince in his town of Mons, on his return from Burgundy and Germany, it was advised and agreed to act as follows.

First, five or six echevins with some members of the council, the *massart*, and Ponchiel, councillor of the town, together with as many mounted people as possible, to be sent out to meet him. They will be instructed to welcome our said most redoubted lord and do him reverence.

Next, the *massart* will have twenty-four four-pound candles made, to be carried by men wearing green jackets, twelve to go outside the town to accompany the duke into it when reverence has been done to him, and the other twelve to be all ready, at the entrance to the Havré gate, to walk in front of the duke, together with the first twelve, as far as his hôtel de Naast. Afterwards they are to take the said candles back to the *massart*'s house.

Item, from the Havré fort to the gate, and also extending into the town as far as the hôtel de Naast, lanterns are to be placed on each side of the street and with them some candles, in such a way as to provide adequate illumination. . . .

Moreover, between the two arches of the gateway and at the entry to it, in each of these places, up to ten or twelve notable and venerable men are to be stationed in their best clothes, to welcome our said most redoubted lord at his entry. They shall be accompanied by archers fully dressed . . . but without their bows, some of whom are to be at the sides of the gate, to make sure that the way is clear when the duke arrives.

Item, all the streets from the said gate to the entrance to the street in which the hôtel de Naast is situated are to be hung on both sides with tapestry. . . .

Item, it was agreed to erect a platform outside the said Havré gate on which there will be a lady holding a tablet on which will be written *Sancta Trinitas unus Deus, miserere nobis* or something else approved by the council concerning the faith. This lady will be named Catholic Faith. . . . She will be standing upright, and on her left side there will be a prince called Heresy with some of his accomplices. He will be menacing the lady with gestures, and raising an axe or other weapon. On the other side of her will be another prince, with his people, called Friend or Helper of the Faith. He will be armed, and with him and his friends will be angels, while with the others will be devils, appropriately dressed, without masks or fur but wearing black hoods with little horns attached to them. They will not have bells or anything else noisy.

---

[1] Devillers, *BCRH* (4) vi (1879), 349–53.

M

Item, on another platform . . . in front of the 'Pewter Pot', the conquest and capture of Constantinople in the year 1204 by Baldwin, count of Flanders and Hainault, will be represented by a tableau vivant.

Item, on another platform next to Colart Pietin's house, near the fountain in the market-place, the coronation of the said Baldwin as emperor of Constantinople will be represented as near to the history of this as possible.

Item . . . the craftsman who made the fountain, Jehan le Tourneur, will arrange something pleasant by way of a figure squirting water, or otherwise.

Another platform, extending from Huart de Biaumetiau's house to the hôtel which belonged to Bruyant de Sars, at the entry to the rue de Naast, will represent paradise, with the Assumption of Our Lady . . . with children dressed as angels singing her praises with holy songs and, next to God, some apostles and martyrs who were knights, such as St. George, St. Maurice, St. Victor, St. Eustace, St. Adrian and others, to please the chivalry who will see them, and, on the side near Our Lady, some virgin martyrs and confessors. . . .

Item, on each of these platforms there must be an eloquent man with a billet to explain to my lord as he goes past what the representation is. . . .

Item, the road between the Havré fort and the barriers, where there are some large puddles, must be put right . . . and the streets must be cleaned.

To take care of the accomplishment of all this, certain people were appointed by the town council, together with some of the echevins and the *massart*: Colart Crohin, Estievene de Gemblues, Bruyant Poullet and Jakes Coispiel.

But there were other matters of a less reassuring nature for Philip the Good than the serene and splendid façade of pomp and pageantry which chroniclers loved to describe and to which civic authorities so proudly contributed. In particular, the Burgundian court became the scene, from 1456, of disputes between jealous cliques of aristocrats, whose personal animosities and petty rivalries emerged at the very time when advancing age seems to have begun to weaken the duke's grip on affairs. Moreover, these factions partly caused and partly exacerbated a series of violent quarrels between Philip and his only legitimate son Charles, which broke out early in 1457. A root cause of these disturbances, which threatened the Burgundian state with disintegration from within, was the dominant situation enjoyed at court by a family from Crouy in Picardy, which had created a seigneurial empire for itself as a result of judicious marriage alliances and princely gifts. The swift rise to power of Jehan, lord of Croy, under John the Fearless, was perhaps partly due to the fact that he

THE CROY FAMILY

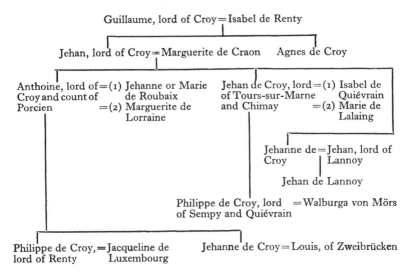

Guillaume, lord of Croy = Isabel de Renty

Jehan, lord of Croy ⚭ Marguerite de Craon   Agnes de Croy

Anthoine, lord of = (1) Jehanne or Marie   Jehan de Croy, lord = (1) Isabel de
Croy and count of   de Roubaix   of Tours-sur-Marne   Quiévrain
Porcien   = (2) Marguerite de   and Chimay   = (2) Marie de
             Lorraine   Lalaing

Jehanne de = Jehan, lord of
Croy   Lannoy

Jehan de Lannoy

Philippe de Croy, lord   = Walburga von Mörs
of Sempy and Quiévrain

Philippe de Croy, = Jacqueline de   Jehanne de Croy = Louis, of Zweibrücken
lord of Renty   Luxembourg

was the brother of one of the duke's mistresses, Agnes de Croy. Although he was killed at Agincourt in 1415, Jehan laid the foundations of his family's favour so firmly at the Burgundian court that his son Anthoine was already an active member of the great council in the 1420s. Indeed his name figures prominently in the very first of the accounts of Philip the Good's receipt-general of finances, as the recipient of the unusually generous gift of 1,000 francs.[1] Ten years later he and his brother Jehan de Croy were among the original twenty-five Knights of the Golden Fleece. In 1435 they figured among the small group of influential Burgundian councillors who accepted sums of money from the king of France in return for their help in arranging the treaty of Arras. At that time Anthoine, lord of Croy, evidently enjoyed a status and influence at court equal to that of Nicolas Rolin the chancellor. In 1442 he and Jehan Chevrot, bishop of Tournai and president of the great council, appear as the two principal governors of the Burgundian Netherlands in Philip's absence. His will, made in 1450, shows that he had amassed an astonishing fortune in the duke's service. By 1456 he was governor of

---

[1] *Comptes généraux*, i. 384–5. For this paragraph, see especially Gachard, *Études et notices historiques*, iii. 467–610, *Les Croÿ, conseillers des ducs de Bourgogne*, Régibeau, *Rôle politique des Croÿ*, Bartier, *Légistes et gens de finances*, 267, etc., and above p. 100. For the whole of the first part of this chapter, see Bartier, *Charles le Téméraire*, 17–39.

Luxembourg, of Namur and of Boulogne, and captain of St. Omer. His son Philippe was appointed a ducal chamberlain in 1458; his brother Jehan was succeeded as bailiff and captain-general of Hainault in 1458 by his nephew Philippe, Lord of Sempy. No wonder these people behaved like rulers in their own right. In 1455 Anthoine sent 4,000 Picard mercenaries to the help of his son-in-law Louis of Zweibrücken, involved in a war against the elector palatine; and in 1454 he side-tracked the ducal administration by writing direct from Luxembourg to his brother at Mons, asking him to raise some troops and send them in haste to Luxembourg to help him put down a baronial revolt there.[1] Such was the power of the Croy family towards the close of Philip the Good's reign; a power which was not finally broken until 1465.

The excessive influence of the Croy family at court was bound to provoke reactions, especially when it was used to obtain the duke's help in pursuing the family advancement. Louis de Luxembourg, count of St. Pol, whose eldest daughter was demanded in marriage by Anthoine for his son Philippe de Croy, found his land of Enghien in Hainault confiscated by the duke when he resisted an alliance with what to him was a low-born family, descended from a mere banneret.[2] He suffered the humiliation of having to agree to his daughter being brought up by the Croy till she was of marriageable age, and having to look on powerless while Anthoine, lord of Croy, insisted on the consummation of the marriage. On 16 September 1457 he saw the duke in Brussels and was interviewed by the council, but he still could not obtain the restoration of his confiscated lands. Much more serious in its eventual consequences was the dispute, which arose in 1456 over the succession of Jehanne d'Harcourt, widow of William II, count of Namur, between Anthoine and Charles, count of Charolais: Anthoine seized a good part of her possessions in spite of Charles's claim that his father had made them over to him. This incident aroused feelings of envy and hatred in the youthful Charles, whose influence at court and in affairs of state was much less at this time than that of the lord of Croy. His anger exploded in a violent outburst in front of the duke on 17 January 1457, when Charles refused to do as his father wished and appoint Philippe de Croy,

[1] Grunzweig, *Études F. Courtoy*, 550–1 and ADN B10418, f. 51.
[2] On this affair, see de la Marche, *Mémoires*, ii. 394–5, Duclercq, *Mémoires*, 103–4 and d'Escouchy, *Chronique*, ii. 306–10. For what follows, see Grunzweig, *Études F. Courtoy*, 533 n. 1, Chastellain, *Œuvres*, iii. 230–94 and de la Marche, *Mémoires*, ii. 414–21.

lord of Sempy, to a post in his household which he had reserved for Anthoine Rolin, son of the chancellor. The scene took place in the oratory of the ducal palace at Brussels, after mass, and Charles retired hurriedly, hustled out by his mother, leaving Philip in a towering rage.

This was the first serious clash between father and son. Its immediate result was a solitary nocturnal escapade of the furious old duke who, inviting the Croy brothers to meet him at Hal, left Brussels alone on horseback on that foggy wet winter's night in a fit of pique. He promptly got lost in the forest of Soignes and only with some difficulty found his way to Alsemberg and a mean lodging. The court chronicler Chastellain devotes pages to this bizarre affair, which provided him with all the best elements for a romantic story: the weeping duchess, search parties scouring the countryside, one of the world's greatest princes wandering alone in the dark forest without a coat, and the charcoal-burner's cottage where the duke sought shelter and where he had to break the bread 'with his own good hands and without a trencher-squire'. Although a reconciliation between father and son was effected, their estrangement was by no means terminated, and the affair had other serious consequences, particularly with reference to the duchess Isabel. According to Olivier de la Marche:

> The duke complained about his wife the duchess, who had abandoned him to follow her son. And I was present when the marshal [Thibaud de Neuchâtel] expressed to my lady the regret which the duke felt in this respect. To which she replied that she knew my lord her husband was a redoubtable knight, and she feared that, in his fury, he might attack her son. It was because of this that she got him out of the oratory and left after him. And she prayed that my lord would forgive her, for she was a stranger in these parts and had no one to support her save her son.[1]

Not long afterwards, Isabel withdrew from court altogether, though she still maintained her interest in Spanish and Portuguese affairs. Her retirement was attributed 'to the discord that had arisen between her son and her husband. The duke thought that this had been caused by her, therefore he would no longer speak to her.' But it was also perhaps due to a genuine desire on Isabel's part to lead a more devout and peaceful life, a desire which had already become evident in 1456.

[1] *Mémoires*, ii. 418–19. For the next paragraph see Calmette, *RB* xviii (1908), 138–96 and *AB* xviii (1946), 1–5; Duclercq, *Mémoires*, 100 (whence the quotation); *IADNB* iv. 202; Bartier, *Hommage au Professeur P. Bonenfant*, 501–11 and Régibeau, *Rôle politique des Croÿ*, 46–50.

She was not the only important person to withdraw from court at this time, for the chancellor followed suit. Nicolas Rolin's fall from power, which involved neither dismissal nor even complete disgrace, was not entirely disconnected with the quarrel of duke and count. It was engineered by Anthoine, lord of Croy, and a personal enemy of Rolin, the marshal of Burgundy Thibaud de Neuchâtel, aided by a great deal of envy, at court, of the power and fortune of the Rolin family, and by a family scandal. At the same time the gouty president of the great council, Bishop Jehan Chevrot of Tournai, retired.

The ageing duke, deprived of the assistance of wife and chancellor in handling the affairs of state, an assistance which had been of profound importance through the greater part of his long reign, was now virtually placed in the hands of the lord of Croy and his brother Jehan, the marshal Thibaud de Neuchâtel, and a respectable but politically ineffective ecclesiastic Guillaume Fillastre, who succeeded Chevot as bishop of Tournai in 1460 and Jehan Germain as chancellor of the Golden Fleece in 1461. Like Germain he was an enthusiastic crusader; but he was also a creature of Anthoine, lord of Croy. Although this change of government is rightly attributed by the chroniclers to faction, old age certainly played its part: Rolin and Chevrot were both well over seventy in 1457.

Philip the Good's heir Charles, count of Charolais, born on 11 November 1433, exercised little influence on affairs in the decade 1454–64. He seems to have been effectively excluded from power as a result of the influence and animosity of the Croy family, the withdrawal of the chancellor and the duchess and, above all, because of his quarrels with his father. He had been granted the title of count of Charolais on the day of his birth, though he never enjoyed its possession, nor even its ordinary revenues, in his father's lifetime. Instead, he was given scattered lands in Flanders, Artois and Namur, or grants of *aides*, by his father, which together brought him in some £15,000 in 1457. As a boy he developed a precocious and somewhat aggressive authoritarianism. For example, at the age of fifteen, he had the following letter sent to the mayor and echevins of Dijon:

Bruges, 3 September 1449

Dearest and good friends, because we have been told that several people have been hunting and taking hares and partridges around Dijon with nets, which is neither honest nor reasonable, for the countryside might be quite despoiled of hares and partridges, so that there would be none for us to hunt if we came down there, we expressly require you, on account of the pleasure we have in hunting, to see that no one attempts

from now on to net any hares or partridges around Dijon, nor anywhere
in the bailiwick, so that, when we are down there, as we hope to be soon
if it is our lord [the duke]'s pleasure, we shall find the countryside well
provided and furnished with the said partridges and hares, so that we
can enjoy ourselves and pass the time.[1]

When he was barely seventeen Charles graduated from hunting
to jousting, and the court gathered in the ducal park at Brussels to
watch him engage in a practice joust against Sir Jaques de Lalaing,
then at the height of his fame, in preparation for his first public
tournament. After the first tilt, the duke accused Sir Jaques of
letting his son off lightly and threatened to leave if things went on
like this. When, in the second tilt, both lances were broken, the duke
applauded, but the duchess was now fearful for her son's safety and
the proceedings were halted. At the tournament a few days later
Charles broke sixteen or eighteen lances and won the prize. De la
Marche, who was brought up with him, gives us this portrait of
Charles as a young man.

He was hot-blooded, active and irritable and, as a child, wanted his
own way and disliked rebuke. Nevertheless, he had such good sense and
understanding that he resisted his natural tendencies and, as a youth,
there was no one more polite and well-tempered. He swore neither by
God nor by the saints. He held God in great fear and reverence. He
learnt very well at school and retained what he learnt, and from early
on he applied himself to reading and having read to him the enjoyable
stories of the deeds of Lancelot and Gawain; and he retained what he
learnt better than anyone of his own age. More than anything, he had a
natural love of the sea and ships. His pastime was falconry with merlins,
and he hunted most willingly whenever he had time. He played chess
better than anyone. He drew the bow more powerfully than any of those
who were brought up with him. He played at quarterstaffs in the Picard
fashion.

Shortly before the battle of Gavere in the Ghent war, for fear of
'the total destruction of all the lands of the duke of Burgundy' if
both Philip and Charles were killed, an attempt was made to decoy
Charles out of danger by informing him that his mother was critically
ill at Lille. He dutifully went to see her, but found her well, and she
encouraged him to return to the army to fight with his father.[2] A

---

[1] *Correspondance de la mairie de Dijon*, i. 58–9. For the next paragraph and
the quotation that follows, see de la Marche, *Mémoires*, ii. 214–17.
[2] Chastellain, *Œuvres*, ii. 276–9 and Duclercq, *Mémoires*, 69. For the next
sentence, see *IAB* v. 373 and below, p. 359. For what follows, see some

year later, in 1454, the twenty-year-old Charles became 'governor and lieutenant-general, in the absence of my most redoubted lord and father, of his lands and lordships in the Netherlands' and it is probable that, had Philip then departed on crusade, Charles would have assumed the regency of all his territories. It was in this same year that Charles, who had been married when he was five to Catherine of France, and widowed at thirteen, was married a second time. His new wife was his cousin Isabel of Bourbon, who had been brought up at the Burgundian court. Though the marriage was subsequently said to have been a happy one, it seems that it was insisted on by Philip very much against the wishes of Charles himself and of Duchess Isabel, both of whom would have preferred an alliance with a daughter of Richard, duke of York. As a matter of fact, the duchess was negotiating with the English in the summer of 1454 while her husband was absent in Germany, probably on this very matter.[1] But

MARRIAGE ALLIANCES OF BURGUNDY AND BOURBON

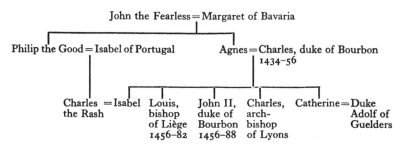

Philip had already sent to Rome for the dispensations necessary for the Bourbon alliance in March, before his departure for Germany, and soon after their arrival and his return, while he was still in Burgundy, he sent Philippe Pot off to Lille to see that the marriage was celebrated and consummated without delay. It was, on 30 October 1454. Isabel must have been annoyed and frustrated, but King Charles VII of France was surely gratified by this demonstration of Philip's respect for the French connection. Duke Charles of Bourbon, whose formal consent to the match had apparently not

---

of the relevant documents in *Corps universel diplomatique*, iii (1), 210, Plancher, iv. no. 165 and du Fresne de Beaucourt, *Charles VII*, v. 469–70. See too Chastellain, *Œuvres*, iii. 7–10 and 19–22, Duclercq, *Mémoires*, 88–9, d'Escouchy, *Chronique*, ii. 241–2 and 270–1, de la Marche, *Mémoires*, ii. 400–1, and du Fresne de Beaucourt, *Charles VII*, v. 399–404.
[1] ADN B10418, f. 39b.

been given, found himself compelled to cede the lordship of Château-Chinon to Philip as part of his daughter's dowry, but was probably flattered by the match.

The one surviving account of Charles's receiver-general of all finances of this period, meticulously kept by Roland Pipe, who went mad in 1461 and drowned himself, at the second attempt, by plunging head-first into a well, opens a window on Charles's interests, occupations, clothes and other matters mostly trivial, in the year 1457.[1] He has a jewelled gold clasp on a gold chain made by a Bruges jeweller for a New Year's gift to his wife. The earl of Warwick sends him an Irish pony. A poor Scottish clerk brings him some music. In March he went on a pilgrimage to Notre-Dame of Boulogne; in April he took his father Duke Philip and the dauphin Louis of France for an excursion in his brigantine, which he kept moored at Sluis. In August he took on the archers of Béthune and lost some wine to them. His continued enjoyment of falconry is well attested: he receives a goshawk from Burgundy, buys a dozen merlins at the Malines fair and sparrowhawks at Brussels and Louvain.

Excluded from a real share in the government of the Burgundian state in the years after his second marriage, Charles remained at court with his father until the first half of 1457. Thereafter, he divided his time between Bruges, Lille, Brussels, Mons and elsewhere in the Burgundian Netherlands, visiting his father at Brussels briefly once or twice a year. He visited Holland–Zeeland in 1458, 1459 and 1460 and paid his first visit to Burgundy late in 1461. He began to acquire important lands in Holland in 1457, and by 1461 he was well established there, possessing the lordships of Putten and Strijen, Arkel, Naarden and, above all, the strategically important town of Gorinchem, and having made close contacts with leading members of the Dutch administration, notably Anthonis Michiels the ex-receiver-general of Holland.[2] All this further strained his relations with the Croy, for their nephew, Jehan de Lannoy, was stadholder of Holland. Not only was de Lannoy's authority there eroded by these activities of Charles, but lands which had been promised to him, such as Arkel, now went to Charles.[3]

[1] *IADNB* viii. 407–17. For Roland Pipe, see Chastellain, *Œuvres*, iv. 203–4.
[2] *Boergoensche charters*, 118, 120, 121, etc. and, for Charles and Holland in general, Meilink, *BVGO* (7) v (1935), 129–52 and (7) vi (1935), 49–66.
[3] Pauwels, *Alia narratio*, 272–3. For de Lannoy, see de Lannoy, B. and Dansaert, *Jean de Lannoy le Bâtisseur*. For what follows, see Chastellain, *Œuvres*, iv. 234–69, Duclercq, *Mémoires*, 196–8 and *Cronycke van Hollandt*,

In July 1462 a strange and sinister incident occurred which increased Charles's insecurity at court. An intimate household servant of the duke, Jehan Coustain, *premier valet de chambre*, was accused of attempting to poison the count of Charolais. He was arrested at court in Brussels at the request of Charles, who took him to Rupelmonde castle and had him and his accomplice summarily executed. A chronicler tells us that it was Anthoine, lord of Croy, who had secured the promotion of Jehan Coustain at court, to such an extent that he shared all the duke's secrets and had clearly become an important part of the mechanism of Croy influence in the Burgundian government. We are left uncertain whether, as seems unlikely but as Chastellain believed, a genuine attempt on Charles's life was being made; or whether the poisoning charge was invented by Charles or his supporters to provide an excuse for eliminating Jehan Coustain, which seems equally improbable. More likely is the third alternative: Coustain was accused by a private enemy for personal reasons of a crime he never dreamt of committing. Whatever the true explanation of this odd affair, it clearly must have occasioned hatred, distrust and fear in all quarters. The duke is perplexed and shocked; Charles allows himself to be convinced that the Croy are planning his murder; while they, for their part, now come to the belief that Charles will stop at nothing to get rid of them.

Although Charles's appointment by Philip as his representative in Holland on 22 July 1462 was probably connected with the Coustain affair, and though Charles was in Holland in August and September of that year and issued documents on Philip's behalf, he by no means went into permanent retirement in Holland. Indeed, he did not go there again until September 1463, just after Philip had arrested, but he had released, his favourite Dutch official, Anthonis Michiels. On the other hand it is clear that Charles was genuinely worried by the fear that his father might either depart on crusade leaving his lands in the care of persons other than himself, or even that he might disinherit him. Charles therefore negotiated with the Dutch in 1463 for their recognition of himself as Philip's rightful heir, thus arousing

---

fos. 303a–304. From these accounts it emerges that Coustain was arrested and taken to Rupelmonde on 25 July 1462, and Vander Linden, *Itinéraires*, 443, shows that Charles went there on the same day and stayed at Rupelmonde castle until the Saturday following. Yet, of recent historians, Meilink, *BVGO* (7) v (1935), 149–50, dates the affair to July 1463, while Bonenfant, *Philippe le Bon*, 105, places it early in 1463. For Coustain, see Chastellain, *Œuvres*, iv. 235 n. 1 and references in Bartier, *Légistes et gens de finance*.

his father's worst suspicions. The Saxon diplomat Peter Knorre, reporting in late October 1463 on developments at the Burgundian court, even supposed that Charles had approached his father about the possibility of his making Holland over to him.[1]

> Item, a good friend tells me that the lord of Charolais asked his father recently at Bruges[2] if he might not be permitted to make do with the land of Holland instead of the annual rents his father allowed him. The duke denied him this, and said that he would remain ruler as long as he lived and was most unwilling to share with anyone. Since then Charolais has fled with his wife to Holland, where the towns have received him with much honour.

By the end of 1463 the quarrel between father and son, exacerbated by Philip's cession of the Somme towns to King Louis XI of France, had reached the proportions of a major crisis. It was only resolved by the intervention of the States General of the Burgundian Netherlands in January and February 1464.[3] A speech the chronicler Jaques Duclerq attributes to Charles, which was said to have been made to the deputies assembled at Ghent, apparently on 5 February 1464, illumines his attitude, which was singularly emotional, and shows how his quarrel with his father was connected with his grudge against the Croy.

> And first, he said that after he had returned from his recent visit to the king, the lord of Croy had told his wife the countess of Charolais who was then ill, that if he hadn't been afraid of angering others, he would have taken the count of Charolais prisoner and placed him somewhere where he could harm neither him nor anyone else.
> Item, he said that the lord of Croy had claimed that no one, however notable, was comparable to him, and he cared nothing for the count [of Charolais], for he had 900 knights and squires who had promised and sworn to serve him till death.
> The count also said that when the lord of Croy saw him approaching he exclaimed 'Look! Here comes that great devil! While he lives, we'll have no peace at court.'
> Item, he said that the lord of Croy had claimed, after he Charles had withdrawn to Holland, that he had done this for fear of the lord of Croy. . . .
> Item, he said that the lord of Croy had boasted that, if it came to a

---

[1] *Urkundliche Nachträge*, 24–5.
[2] They were together at Bruges throughout May 1463.
[3] See especially *Actes des États généraux*, 58–101, Chastellain, *Œuvres*, iv. 471–92 and Duclercq, *Mémoires*, 228–32 (the quotation is from 230–1).

show-down, he was sure of the support of Artois, and that all that country was in his pocket, continuing: 'What does my lord of Charolais hope to achieve and who does he think will help him? The Flemings and Brabanters, perhaps? He's hopeful! When it comes to the point they'll abandon him, as they have done others.' The count continued that he reputed the people of Flanders and Brabant his loyal friends and that the lord of Croy's words were wickedly spoken. Nor had he any fears or worries about the loyalty of the people of Artois, Picardy and thereabouts.

Item, he said he wanted everyone to know that the lord of Croy had sent details of his birth to the provost of Warneton so that he could cast his horoscope . . . which predicted the worst possible fortune and the biggest mischiefs in the world for him.

Item, the count continued, the said lord of Croy had sent again to the same provost to get him, by sorcery or otherwise, to arrange for the lord of Croy to keep my lord [the duke] his father in perpetual hatred of him. . . .

A settlement was achieved after this, and Philip and Charles were fully reconciled early in June, when they met one another at Lille. But the Croy were still in power and it was not until September 1464 that Charles began at last to gain ascendancy with his father and at court, and a further six months elapsed before he could finally get rid of the Croy.

During the whole decade 1454–64, when Charles was excluded from power, from the ducal council and even from court, Burgundian relations with France had been consistently unfavourable to Burgundy, and we must turn now to consider them in the light of the domestic developments at the Burgundian court just outlined. There is something almost pathetic about Philip the Good's naïve and constant assumption that Charles VII and Louis XI were men of good faith and that, because he, Philip, liked to think of himself as a loyal Frenchman at heart, they too would necessarily think of him in this way. Their historian, and enemy, Thomas Basin, bishop of Lisieux, saw things, and rightly too, in a very different light. He employs a striking metaphor to describe the policy and attitudes of Charles VII towards Burgundy.[1]

When someone wants to remove the massive bulk of an ancient tree with its huge trunk and extensive roots buried far in the earth, he starts by digging a deep trench right round it so that, after bringing up some

[1] *Charles VII*, ii. 246.

men and yoked oxen, he can drag it down with ropes when it has been entrenched round in such a way that it has very few roots still in the ground. In the same way, to bring down and humiliate the house of Burgundy, which at that time was the most flourishing and the most prosperous in France or Germany, Charles, king of France as it were undermined it all round, uncovering and severing its longest roots wherever he could, and doing his best to obtain the cooperation [in this work] of different princes and peoples.

With reference to this last-mentioned diplomatic offensive against Duke Philip, Basin mentions in particular Charles VII's alliance with the king of Denmark, of 27 May 1456; his negotiations with Liège in 1457–61; his conference with the duke of Savoy in 1452; his alliance with the Swiss in 1453; his connections with the Lancastrian England of Henry VI and Margaret of Anjou; and finally his alliances with 'various imperial princes and electors'.[1] Alongside this general policy of isolating Burgundy and undermining her prestige, Charles made a determined effort to deprive Philip of the duchy of Luxembourg which he had obtained, mostly by force of arms, at the end of 1443. Since then he had remained in more or less peaceable possession in spite of the well-founded claims of the youthful King Ladislas of Bohemia. Having failed to conquer Luxembourg from Philip at the time of the Ghent war, Ladislas had tried in the following years, but equally without success, to obtain it by negotiation. In 1457 he reacted to Charles VII's request to him for an alliance, originally made in 1454, by seeking his assistance in obtaining Luxembourg from Philip; at the same time he asked for Charles's daughter Madeleine of France in marriage. On 8 December 1457 an imposing Bohemian embassy, comprising 700 horse and twenty-six wagons, entered Tours. But Charles VII lay dangerously ill, and the ambassadors, whose out- landish names were too difficult for the Burgundian court chronicler, George Chastellain to record, had to wait. On 22 December they were feasted in truly Burgundian style by the count of Foix. Four of the entremets are described by Jaques Duclerq:[2]

---

[1] Basin, *Charles VII*, ii. 246–9, with references, to which should be added du Fresne de Beaucourt, *Charles VII*, v and vi and Gruneisen, *RV* xxvi (1961), 31–2; Dabin, *BIAL* xliii (1913), 99–190, Boutaric, *AMSL* (2) ii (1865), 295, *Régestes de Liège*, iv. 29–35 and Chastellain, *Œuvres*, iii. 367–8 (Liège); Liebenau, *Beziehungen der Eidgenossenschaft zum Auslande*, 27–36 and de Mandrot, *JSG* v (1880) 59–182 (the Swiss).

[2] *Mémoires*, 106. On this and what follows in general, see Duclercq, *Mémoires*, 105–7 and 109, Chastellain, *Œuvres*, iii. 388–95, Schötter, *Geschichte des Luxemburger Landes*, 141–3, du Fresne de Beaucourt, *Charles VII*, vi.

The first was a castle with four corner towers and a large central tower with four windows, in each of which appeared a girl's face, the hair brushed back. Only their faces were visible. Up above, there was a banner with King Ladislas's arms and, on the four towers, the shields of the principal ambassadors. Inside the [central] tower six children sang beautifully in such a way that it seemed to be the girls who were singing.

The second entremets was a terrible beast called tiger with a short thick body, horrible head and two short pointed horns. Inside the head was a man who made it move in a lifelike way, and he caused flames to shoot out of its mouth in a hideous manner. It was carried by four gentlemen dressed in the fashion of Béarn and they danced in the style of that country.

The third entremets was a large rock with a fountain in it, and pheasants, and rabbits both white and otherwise. And there were five little savage children, who came out of the rock and danced in moorish fashion.

The fourth entremets was a clever squire who appeared to be on horseback. . . . And he and his horse were well got up and he made his horse leap about.

But these festivities were rudely and sadly interrupted on Christmas Eve, when news arrived of the sudden death, by poisoning it was naturally though probably erroneously supposed, of the seventeen-year-old King Ladislas who had sent the embassy. Before they left for home, the ambassadors persuaded King Charles to take Luxembourg under his protection, and he infuriated and thoroughly alarmed Duke Philip in the early months of 1458 when he attempted to take possession of various places in the duchy by hoisting the royal standard on their battlements and by despatching a small force to the town of Luxembourg with a summons to open its gates in the name of the king. He also sent Philip a letter which Chastellain described as 'sinister, threatening and written in an equivocal style'.

When, later that year, Duke William of Saxony revived his claims to the duchy of Luxembourg, Charles VII persuaded him to sell them to himself for 50,000 gold crowns. He even paid the first instalment of this sum and added himself to the growing number of fifteenth-century princes who used the title 'duke of Luxembourg'. The indignant Philip sent troops to the disputed duchy, grants of privileges to Luxembourg and other towns, and ambassadors to France. But it seems to have been his discovery that King George Podiebrad of

153–78, etc., N. van Werveke, *Definitive Erwerbung*, Plancher, iv. nos. 176 and 177 and *Table chronologique des chartes de Luxembourg*, xxxi (1876), 1-134.

Bohemia was also entitling himself 'duke of Luxembourg' which caused Charles VII to withhold further instalments of the 50,000 crowns. Negotiations between the king of France and the duke of Saxony dragged on but, when a hopeful Saxon embassy arrived as arranged at Koblenz on 15 June 1461, to collect the money, it was confronted with an equivocal statement by a solitary French emissary, whose invitation to the Saxons to continue their journey into France was declined on the grounds that they had come by boat and were not equipped to travel overland. Duke William himself, who was not particularly interested in the money, nor even in ruling his own lands had characteristically set out from Venice on a pilgrimage to Jerusalem on the very day fixed for the meeting at Koblenz. Thus Philip the Good, though he was made anxious and indignant by these hostile moves of Charles VII, remained firmly in possession of Luxembourg.

The hostility to Philip the Good which was demonstrated by Charles VII in the affair of Luxembourg was equally apparent in all kinds of other ways. The king was evidently determined to regain possession of the Somme towns, which he had ceded to Philip in 1435 on a basis he regarded as purely temporary. He tried to exploit Philip's difficulties with Ghent to get them back in 1452.[1] According to the chronicler Mathieu d'Escouchy, he tried to exploit Philip's crusading ardour in 1455 by refusing to guarantee the safety of his lands during his expedition, unless he handed over the Somme towns, together with his son Charles as a hostage. On the same occasion, though perhaps without the same degree of spite, he refused to lend Philip the royal banner of France on the grounds that he might need it against the English.

Moreover, petty harassments of every possible kind were systematically organized against Philip. The king issued letters of safeguard for the collegiate church of St. Peter's, Lille and intervened in the election of a canon;[2] his officials continued to dispute possession of the so-called enclaves in and around the duchy of Burgundy; French

[1] Above, p. 325. For the next sentence, see d'Escouchy, *Chronique*, ii. 313.
[2] *Cartulaire de Saint-Pierre de Lille*, ii. 1021–3 and 1027. For the rest of the sentence, see ACO B1747, fos. 96 and 113b–114, Richard, *BHPTH* (1964), 113–32 and *MSHDB* xxvi (1965), 217–27; *Précis analytique*, (2) ii. 73–5 and *Cartulaire de l'Estaple de Bruges*, ii. 38–9; ADN B1607, f. 132 and ADN B2034, f. 103b. For what follows, see *Ordonnances des rois*, xiii. 441–2 and xiv. 41–3, Wielant, *Antiquités de Flandre*, 169–72, and *Précis analytique*, (1) i. 96 and especially *Les arrêts et jugés du Parlement de Paris sur appels flamands*.

pirates operated off the coast of Flanders; in spite of the fact that royal duties were not payable on wine in transit for consumption at the Burgundian court, Charles's officials impounded it. The nuisance value of the Paris *Parlement* was as persistent as ever, especially in Flanders, and even though appeals from the jurisdiction of the Four Members to the Paris *Parlement* were officially prohibited by Charles in 1445 and 1455 at Philip's request, they continued. In 1449 and 1459, for example, the *Parlement* judged disputes between the barbers of Sluis and Bruges. In 1448 the town of Sluis appealed to Paris, thus infringing 'the prerogatives and rights' of the duke; in 1451 Oudenaarde obtained a judgment from Paris against the duke's *procureur général* of Flanders which the ducal authorities tried to persuade the town to disregard.[1]

Not that these interventions were necessarily annoying for the duke. When in 1454 Ypres appealed to Paris against a judgment of the council of Flanders, the appeal was disallowed; and when, in 1455, French pirates were active off the Zwin, the duke and the Four Members together invited the Paris *Parlement* to set up a court of enquiry at Bruges. But, by and large, the activities of the Paris *Parlement* were aggravating and unwelcome, especially in cases concerning ducal officials. In 1447, for example, there was a case pending at Paris between Philip's *gens des comptes* at Dijon and the civic authorities there, over the liability of these ducal officials to pay rates. In 1459 Philip complained that the *Parlement*'s justice was invariably against, rather than for, him, and that he had not been allowed to appoint a single one of the twelve councillors of the *Parlement* which the king had promised him in 1442. It was in 1459, according to George Chastellain, that Philip's emissary and nephew, Duke John of Cleves, demanded a seat in the *Parlement* on the duke of Burgundy's behalf.[2]

In Hainault too, French royal aggression made itself felt; indeed the French crown seemed almost prepared to claim this county as part of the kingdom of France. But when in 1457 the bailiff suggested to Philip that he arrest French merchants in Hainault carrying royal money on them, in retaliation for the arrest by royal sergeants in or

---

[1] AGR CC21815, f. 7 (compare f. 3b etc.) and ADN B2008, f. 167. For what follows, see *IAY* iii. 224–5, *IAB* v. 380, ACO B16, f. 21, Wielant, *Antiquités de Flandre*, 171–2 and Delachenal, *BSHP* xviii (1891), 76–83.

[2] BM Add. MS. 54156, f. 373b. This manuscript, containing the unpublished section of Chastellain's chronicle from 1458 to 1461, is discussed by Armstrong, *PCEEBM* x (1968), 73–8.

near Hainault of merchants carrying Burgundian coins, the duke refused.[1] However, in 1456 ducal letters were issued disallowing appointments to benefices in Hainault which had been made by the cardinal of Avignon, improperly because he had never been appointed papal legate in imperial territory. In 1454 the curate of Hornu appealed to the University of Paris, which responded by summoning the bailiff of Hainault to appear before its tribunal in Paris. He naturally refused, 'because the said land, which is part of the Empire, is in no way subject to the kingdom of France', and found himself threatened with excommunication. Appeal was made to Duke Philip and his great council and the duke wrote to the University, which graciously permitted him to settle matters with the curate out of court. But the curate was not prepared to do this, and a notice was duly pinned to the doors of Tournai cathedral, solemnly excommunicating Jehan de Croy, bailiff of Hainault. All this is recorded in detail in the accounts of the receiver-general of Hainault, who spent over 500 francs on the case in 1455 alone, though his clerks could not spell the word excommunication. Eventually, Duke Philip appealed to Rome. No wonder opprobrium was heaped on the curate, Gilles Gillicque, by the clerks who kept the accounts:

> Notwithstanding that he was born a subject of my lord the duke, he has done him every conceivable harm and damage on the pretext that he is a cleric studying in the University of Paris. Although the said land of Hainault has never in any way been subject to nor required to answer to the said University nor to the kingdom of France, this Sir Gilles has come forward like a fool, inspired by perverse and outrageous effrontery, to bring various citations into Hainault.

From 1455 on there was a constant exchange of embassies, complaints and recriminations between the courts of France and Burgundy.[2] In August 1455, the king's replies to twenty-six separate articles of complaint involving the duchy enclaves, ducal rights in the sale and distribution of salt, the jurisdiction of the Paris *Parlement* and all kinds of other matters, showed that the most Charles VII was prepared to do was to allow investigations to be made. Relations were particularly strained in the spring of 1458 when, on top of the Luxembourg affair, a summons came from the Paris *Parlement* for Philip to

---

[1] ADN B10422, f. 64. For what follows, see ADN B10420, f. 57b, B10418, fos. 41–3, B10419, and B10420, fos. 53–54, 65b (whence the quotation) etc.
[2] See du Fresne de Beaucourt, *Charles VII*, vi. For the next sentence, see Plancher, iv. no. 171 and, for what follows, Chastellain, *Œuvres*, iii. 417–27.

appear in person at the trial of the duke of Alençon at Montargis. It was on this occasion, at a meeting of the great council presided over by Philip in person, that Charles gave vent to his pent-up indignation against the king of France, accusing him of repeatedly insulting his father, and offering there and then to lead an army into France right up to the walls of Paris. But this outburst was received with laughter by some of those present, and Burgundian policy towards France remained conciliatory. After all, it was partly inspired by Anthoine, lord of Croy and his relatives and, until recently, it had been guided by the chancellor Nicolas Rolin, who had maintained secret contacts with and enjoyed favours from the French king at least until the mid-'fifties.[1] Moreover, Duke Philip himself obstinately refused to believe that Charles VII was seriously trying to encompass his destruction; he preferred to attribute French aggression to the king's councillors.

A sort of diplomatic climax was reached at Montbazon in February–March 1459, when the full text of the king's replies to the duke's points was perhaps circulated by the French government in the form of an official news-bulletin. The duke's grievances, which were rejected outright by Charles VII, who submitted in reply a statement on the duke's own misdemeanours against his royal majesty which the king's *procureur général* claimed would take a fortnight to enumerate in full, were prefaced with an elaborate protestation of Burgundian friendliness and good will towards France. Had not the duke signed the treaty of Arras, made war against the English thereafter, and even helped Charles VII to recover Paris and Normandy? Had he not firmly resolved, from 1435 onwards, 'to cherish, love, serve, honour and obey the king'? Yet in return, the duke went on to complain, the king had 'sought alliances and confederations against him' with Denmark, Bern, Liège, King Ladislas, the Emperor and other imperial princes, and shown hostility to him in all kinds of ways, not least through the aggressive juridical activities of his supreme court, the Paris *Parlement*.

Beside these verbal exchanges ran the threat of warfare, which became more and more real as Charles VII's reign drew to its close. In 1453 it was suggested to Philip that, had it not been for the necessity to reconquer Bordeaux from the English, the French army would

---

[1] See his letter of 16 April 1455 to Charles VII in BN MS. fr. 5044, f. 32. For what follows, see BM Add. MS. 54156, fos. 338b–361 (Chastellain), d'Escouchy, *Chronique*, ii. 395–416, *Chronique de Tournai*, 537–53, de Reilhac, *de Reilhac*, 42–59 and Plancher, iv. no. 179.

have been turned against Burgundy.[1] There were rumours of French military plans against Burgundy in 1457, and Philip's conciliation of Ghent in 1458, when he made a ceremonial entry after the inhabitants had removed the town gates from their hinges and laid them down in the fields outside the town, was attributed to his desire to ensure that city's loyalty in the event of a war with France. These Burgundian fears were by no means ungrounded. On 28 July 1460 the royal council, 'meeting at Villefranche in Berry in the hôtel of my lord the count of Maine', resolved to recommend to the king that 'there is sufficient and just cause to proceed by force of arms to ensure obedience, in all my lord of Burgundy's lands in the kingdom of France, to the king's letters, *mandements* and *ordonnances* and to the judgments of his court of *Parlement*'.[2] By the summer of 1461 war between France and Burgundy seemed certain. On 27 May the bailiff of Hainault sent a spy to Laon 'to get news of the French, because there were rumours every day that the king had decided to make war on my lord the duke', and Jehan Maupoint in Paris had it on good authority that, in July 1461, at the time of his death, Charles VII had already given orders for the attack.

Philip the Good's relations with the dauphin Louis, who had been a fugitive in Brabant since 1456, did nothing to reduce Charles VII's hostility to Burgundy. In 1446 the king had banished Louis to Dauphiny for four months as a punishment for his court intrigues, but Louis remained there permanently, spying on his father, continuing his intrigues, and governing Dauphiny with energy and skill. He married Charlotte of Savoy in 1451 without his father's permission and relations between father and son deteriorated still further. Neither trusted the other, and in the summer of 1456 Louis, terrified of being arrested and imprisoned by his father, took flight from Dauphiny and made his way to Brussels to seek the mediation or protection of his 'bel oncle de Bourgogne', as he invariably referred to him in his correspondence.

Philip's attitude to Louis was one of obsequious servility. He made over the ducal residence at Genappe near Brussels for the dauphin's

---

[1] Kervyn *Flandre*, iv. 525. For the next sentence, see Duclercq, *Mémoires*, 102 and 111, and Chastellain, *Œuvres*, iii. 396–406. An 'official' account of the entry into Ghent found its way into the chronicle of Jehan Chartier, iii. 80–9; compare Chastellain, *Œuvres*, iii. 412–16.

[2] Plancher, iv. no. 181. For the rest of the paragraph, see ADN B10426, fos. 49b and 50, Maupoint, *Journal*, 48, and BM Add. MS. 54156, fos. 411b–412.

use, he gave him a handsome annual allowance, sent for his wife from Savoy, attended to his every whim, and resolutely refused to restore him to his father, in spite of Charles VII's repeated requests and threats. This deference to Louis took on ludicrous proportions from the start. According to Chastellain, when they first met in the palace courtyard at Brussels, Philip remained kneeling in front of Louis for so long that he eventually exclaimed, "Pon my faith, good uncle, if you don't get up I shall go away and leave you.'[1] On a subsequent occasion, when the dauphin doffed his hat to the duke, Philip went down on one knee and remained there until Louis replaced his hat. While at Genappe, Louis never concealed his longing to inherit the crown of France; indeed his constant and hopeful enquiries of the astrologers, especially when his father was ill, concerning the exact hour of his probable death, caused some comment. Chastellain says that Louis was not only happy to hear of his father's death—he had prayed for it.

Philip the Good was certainly happy too, on 14 August 1461, when he saw Louis crowned king of France in Rheims cathedral. Indeed it was probably the proudest moment of his life and, as he rode into Paris with Louis on 31 August he may well have speculated hopefully on the possibility of a restoration of Burgundian influence in France, or at least of a settlement of the many outstanding disputes between France and Burgundy.[2] If so, he was soon disillusioned. The son who had rebelled against his father undertook now in deadly earnest to pursue his father's policies to their logical conclusion. In the long term, Louis's aim was no less than the total demolition of the Burgundian state. In the short term, his plans were the same as those of Charles VII: to maintain and encourage a group of pro-French councillors at the Burgundian court, to develop an anti-Burgundian system of alliances and, above all, to regain possession of the Somme towns. Moreover, Louis took care to see to it that royal officials continued their aggressive attitudes and activities, especially in the duchy

[1] Œuvres, iii. 210. For the next sentence, see Duclercq, Mémoires, 132. On the dauphin at Genappe, see in general besides the chroniclers, de Poitiers, Les honneurs de la cour, 212–13, de Reiffenberg, MARB v (1829), Lettres de Louis XI, i. 177 ff. and Champion, Louis XI, i. On his relations with Charles VII, see du Fresne de Beaucourt, Charles VII, vi.
[2] This was certainly Chastellain's attitude to the new reign, see for example Œuvres, iv. 118–19. For an official Burgundian account of Louis XI's coronation at Rheims, see Collection de documents inédits, ii. 162–75 (compare Chastellain, Œuvres, iv. 50–62, Fragment d'une chronique du règne de Louis XI, 114–25 and Duclercq, Mémoires, 177–80).

of Burgundy.[1] Though he seemed, early in his reign, to be trying to win the confidence and even alliance of Charles, count of Charolais, he evidently despised him. On Christmas Day 1463 the Milanese ambassador Alberico Malleta had a long and confidential chat with Louis, during the course of which the king told him 'that this son of the duke of Burgundy was of very little worth and had little good sense. He was proud, irascible and somewhat bestial. And [the king] spoke of him most maliciously, making maniacal gestures which he claimed [the count of Charolais] was in the habit of making.' The king went on to tell the Milanese ambassador that the Burgundian state (*questo stato del duca di Borgogna*) was in worse shape even than Savoy.

At the time of this conversation Louis XI had just achieved what his father had failed to achieve and what some contemporary observers thought never could be achieved without warfare:[2] the recovery of the Somme towns. By the treaty of Arras, of 1435, the towns and castellanies of St. Quentin, Corbie, Amiens, Abbeville, Doullens, St. Riquier, Crèvecoeur, Arleux and Mortagne, together with the county of Ponthieu, comprising 'all the towns, castles, lands and lordships belonging to the crown of France on either bank of the river Somme', were ceded to Philip the Good and his heirs in mortgage, that is, against their redemption by the king of France for 400,000 gold crowns. It seems that Charles VII's financial circumstances had not at any time permitted him to offer Philip the Good this sum, or that he hoped to recover the Somme towns without paying it. But Louis XI was quite able and prepared to find the money. 'Don't you agree', he said to Malleta on a visit to Amiens in June 1464, 'that this city alone is worth much more than the 400,000 crowns I paid to my lord of Burgundy?'[3] With the recovery of the Somme towns in mind, he saw to it from the start of his reign that Philip's most trusted councillors the Croy would act in his interest, and he bought over or rewarded others who might be of service, or who were

[1] BN MS. Coll. de Bourg. 99, pp. 520–5, instructions for ducal ambassadors going to the king, dated 8 August 1462, etc, and see Plancher, iv. no. 188. For what follows, see *Dépêches des ambassadeurs milanais*, i. 357–64.
[2] See for example *Dépêches des ambassadeurs milanais*, i. 310–14. For what follows, see *Grands traités* 138–41 and the map overleaf.
[3] *Dépêches des ambassadeurs milanais*, ii. 181. For what follows, see especially *Les Croÿ, conseillers des ducs de Bourgogne*, nos. 27–31 and Duclercq, *Mémoires*, 223–4 (Croy); de Mandrot, *RH* xciii (1907), especially 9–12 (Étampes); de Mandrot, *JSG* v (1880), 114–15 (Neuchâtel); Bonenfant, *Philippe le Bon*, 106 (Coustain).

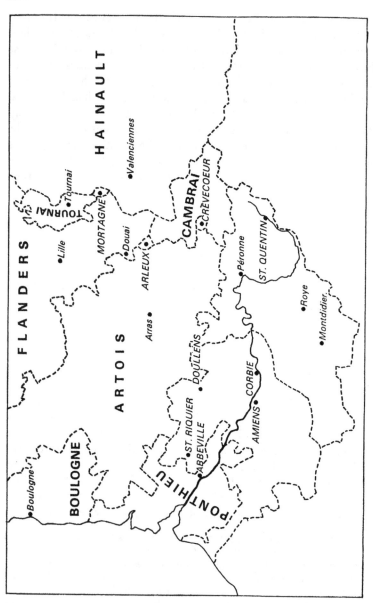

7. The Somme towns

known adherents of the Croy, such as Jehan, count of Étampes, the marshal of Burgundy, Thibaud de Neuchâtel, and even Jehan Coustain. Thus it was that, in the early autumn of 1463, against the wishes of Charles, count of Charolais, and with the help in particular of Jehan, count of Étampes and Anthoine, lord of Croy, Louis XI was able to recover possession of the Somme towns for the French crown.[1] The only concession he can be said to have made in return was the surrender of French claims to Luxembourg. This took the form of royal letters purporting to cede the territory to Philip, though in fact it was not Louis's to give, which were actually issued at the end of 1462, soon after Philip had agreed to purchase the duke of Saxony's claims to the duchy. So far as Louis XI was concerned, they were probably intended to pave the way for his acquisition of the Somme towns.

During the early years of Louis XI's reign the Burgundian alliance was an essential part of the king's diplomatic plans, which envisaged far more than the destruction of Burgundian power. Quite apart from his early involvement in Spanish affairs, Louis's political ambitions extended over Savoy, which he apparently hoped to annexe to the crown of France. To achieve this, he needed alliances elsewhere, notably with Savoy's powerful neighbours, Milan and Burgundy.[2] Hence his care to avoid, as far as possible, an open breach with Philip, and hence his signature of the treaty of Abbeville at the end of 1463 with Francesco Sforza. His negotiations and alliance with the Swiss, in 1463–4, must be seen in the light of this French expansionism rather than as an immediate threat to Burgundy. Curiously enough, the implementation of these French diplomatic plans depended in large measure on Burgundian help, for it was the marshal of Burgundy, Thibaud de Neuchâtel, who was mainly responsible for the alliances with Milan and the Swiss. Moreover, Philip the Good himself laboured on Louis's behalf through much of 1463, though in vain, to bring about a rapprochement and alliance between Louis and Burgundy's ally King Edward IV of England.[3]

[1] Documents in de Commines, *Mémoires*, ed. Godefroy and Lenglet du Fresnoy, ii. 392–407 and see Duclercq, *Mémoires*, 224–6 and Chastellain, iv. 341–3, 399–401, etc. For Luxembourg, see N. van Werveke, *Definitive Erwerbung*, 36–41.
[2] For this paragraph, see Bittmann, *RBPH* xxvi (1948), 1059–83 and *AMA* (1952).
[3] On Burgundy and England at this time, Thielemans, *Bourgogne et Angleterre*, 367–410, has full references, but see now too Brown and Webster, *EHR* lxxxi (1966), 80–2, with reference to 1464.

Thus Burgundy appears, early in Louis XI's reign, as an instrument of French foreign policy, while its duke does all in his power to further the interests of France and promote French advantage, even to the extent of ceding the strategically important Somme towns. This state of affairs was in part due to Philip's confidence in French intentions, especially to his touching faith in Louis's friendship and integrity; in part it was due to the fact that lifelong associates of his like Anthoine, lord of Croy, friends and relatives like Jehan, count of Étampes, and leading captains like Thibaud de Neuchâtel, were all of them in Louis XI's pocket.

But there was another element in Burgundian policy towards France at this time which was perhaps of overriding importance. Philip the Good had always been a dedicated crusader and, towards the end of his life, this crusading ambition was transformed into a veritable obsession which came to dictate his attitude to France. A Belgian historian has said of him that the 'great dream of his life was to play the leading rôle in French politics'.[1] Others may have supposed that imperial ambitions or even plans of centralization and independence were of paramount importance in Philip's personal political vision. But these suggestions are wide of the mark. Philip was neither interested in French power nor in imperial power; nor would he have understood the meaning of words like independence and centralization. What really absorbed his political interest and attention more than anything, especially towards the end of his life, when it grew to such proportions in his own mind that it even took precedence over the overriding urge of all rulers to augment their territories, was the crusade.

The famous Feast of the Pheasant, during which Philip and his courtiers vowed to go on crusade, followed not long after the news of the fall of Constantinople had reached the Burgundian court.[2] The Ghent war had been won by Philip in July 1453 and there is every reason to suppose that his visit to Germany in the spring and summer of 1454 was fully expected to be a prelude to the crusade. In the autumn of 1454 a general crusade for the following year was resolved on at the imperial Diet of Frankfurt, present ambassadors of Philip the Good and another 'crusading' monarch, King Alfonso V of Aragon

[1] Bonenfant, *Philippe le Bon*, 117. For this and what follows, compare Richard, *PCEEBM* x (1968), 41–4.
[2] Above, pp. 296–7.

and Naples.[1] Throughout these years, Philip participated in every western crusading initiative and kept in close touch with Alfonso V. A Burgundian crusade was so imminent in February 1455 that the bailiff of Hainault, Jehan de Croy, thought it necessary to send to Philip to explain that he was quite unable to go because of his bad leg.[2] In fact, at the end of 1454 Charles, count of Charolais, wrote to the authorities in each of his father's territories announcing a crusade for the following summer.

Bruges, 20 December 1454

Charles of Burgundy, count of Charolais, lord of Chastelbelin, governor and lieutenant-general, in the absence of my most redoubted lord and father, of his lands and lordships in the Netherlands. To the sovereign-bailiff of Namur or to his lieutenant, greetings.

After the fall of the city of Constantinople and the conquest by the Turk—enemy of the holy christian faith and of the name of the blessed saviour and redeemer—of several lands and regions near it, he has begun to assemble a powerful army with the intention of subjugating all the kingdoms and principalities of christendom, especially the neighbouring realm of Hungary and other countries near it, and of making them his tributaries, in order to continue and persevere with his damnable, disloyal and detestable plans for the complete destruction of our christian faith and the detraction of the name of our lord Jesus Christ. To resist and avoid this, and to assist those christian princes and their realms situated near the Turks which are likely to be lost as a result of the tyranny and power of the Turk unless immediate help is available, a meeting was held at Frankfurt by the ambassadors of our holy father the pope, of the Emperor, of my most redoubted lord and father and of several other princes, at which meeting it was agreed that all the christian princes who had sent to or who were present at the meeting should field a certain number of troops to make an army which would be ready next summer. My said lord in particular caused it to be declared by his ambassadors at that meeting that it was his intention to join the said army in person with as many men as he could raise, according to the vow he had made. . . .

My lord [the duke] has written to me about this and informs me that, in accordance with the decision of the congress of Frankfurt and to accomplish his vow, he for his part has resolved, determined and

---

[1] D'Escouchy, *Chronique*, ii. 272–3. For all of what follows, see especially Hintzen, *Kruistochtplannen van Philips den Goede* and Marinesco, *BEP* (n.s.) xiii (1949), 3–28.

[2] ADN B10419, f. 46 and, for the next sentence, B10418, f. 52 and B2020, f. 212b. The letters which follow are from *Analectes historiques*, iii. 141–3.

decided, with the help of our blessed creator . . . to undertake and carry out what is said above by recruiting as many troops as he can find, both from among those who have made a vow for the aid and defence of our said christian faith, and from among others who are resolved to go. And he himself intends to set out next spring in person on this journey, and requests us to publish and circulate this through all his lands and lordships in the Netherlands.

In the winter of 1454-5 *aides* for the crusade were being requested throughout Philip the Good's territories, and the ducal painter Jehan de Boulogne was kept busy decorating damask standards with Philip's device of flints and steels, and flames and sparks, in gold, not to mention numerous banners, pennons and coats of arms, all for the *voyage de Turquie*. The seriousness of the duke's crusading intentions at this time or a little later is abundantly demonstrated by the following detailed plan of campaign which may have been drawn up on 19 January 1456 at The Hague.[1]

Here follows advice concerning what is necessary for my lord the duke's crusade.

First, those who have taken the vow must hold themselves ready. My lord the duke will let them know as soon as possible but, in view of the news from the king of Aragon and the Emperor, the duke still does not know when he will set out. Everyone ought to be prepared from now on, so that he is not taken unawares. . . .

Item, as to the numbers of men-at-arms and archers that the duke will be employing, no decision can be made until he knows what *aides* will be forthcoming from his territories, so this must be left to him. However, it would be best if he could make a statement about this as soon as possible, so that everyone can get ready in good time to furnish and provide what is asked of him, and especially if he could inform the people and captains on whom he will be relying.

Concerning my lord the duke's lieutenant-general, the duke must appoint him soon so that he can muster suitable men to take with him. And it seems to those who have been [conferring] together that, if my lord the duke is determined to take my lord [the count] of Étampes, he would be the best choice.

Item, since there will be people of various languages in the army it will be expedient to see what leaders need be appointed for the different

---

[1] Printed by Finot, *Projet d'expédition contre les Turcs*, 191-200, but see *DRA* xix. 159. *Aides* were granted in the two Burgundies in December 1454 and January 1455 and in Artois in February; see Gachard, *Rapport sur Dijon*, 156-7 and Hirschauer, *États d'Artois*, ii. 34. For the banners, see de Laborde, *Ducs de Bourgogne*, i. 431-2.

languages. But no conclusion can be reached until it is known what troops will be available and which lords, and then the duke can appoint one or more to lead them.

Item, concerning finance, it appears that the duke should appoint one reliable and notable person to levy and collect the moneys which have been or will be granted him from his different lands, as well as whatever he wants to contribute from his coffers. All the proceeds should be given to the duke and those appointed by him but, to distribute and disburse them, it would seem expedient to have the advice of the *gens des comptes* and the financial officials, so that they can make arrangements for this expenditure, both as regards receipts and otherwise.

As regards the artillery, it seems that the duke ought to send at once for the master of his artillery so that he can ascertain what condition it is in and provide for more if there is insufficient. When he has done this, the duke should select what he needs and leave the rest behind. Then he can appoint a master of the artillery to go with him and he can leave behind a lieutenant who can keep a copy of the inventory, and the said master, who will be with the duke, can also have a copy. Then, if anything is needed subsequently, the lieutenant will be able to send it. The master of the artillery will have charge of twenty lances, to be included in the cost of the troops which are detailed to help and transport the artillery.

Five or six hundred gunners, carpenters, masons, smiths, pioneers, miners and workmen will be needed with their tools, armed and equipped with pikes, ready to fight if necessary, to have the same wages as archers. They should be distributed, while the army is on the march and otherwise, between the vanguard, the main division and the rearguard as convenient, under the command of the master of the artillery and of that person or those persons appointed by him. But some think that the pioneers should be under some other captain than the master of the artillery.

There ought to be three marshals, one for the duke's household, one for the German language, and the third for the rest of the army. The following would seem to be suitable: My lord of Moreuil, my lord of Humieres, Monsieur Baude de Noyelles, Sir François l'Aragonais, my lord of Contay, Sir François de Menthon, my lord of Espierres, my lord of Bergues and my lord Le Liegeoiz de Humieres. Three provosts of the marshals will be needed; and the following are suitable: Jehan de Bonem, Evrard de Brimeu, Guillaume de Cuinsy, Maillart de Ricamez, Digne Ste Paule, Chenevre and Anthoine de Laviron, or others, as my lord pleases. To lead the baggage-train: Sir Loys de Masingues, the bastard of Rosin, Sir Frederic de Meynynsrent.

Item, for the ordinary council to be with the duke every day, the duke should name as many as he pleases, but it seems that there cannot be fewer than eight noblemen and four clerics, and it is desirable that some should know German, both for interpreting and, if necessary, for embassies.

Item, four secretaries will be needed, two knowing Latin and German and the others Latin, French and Dutch. As regards the chapel, the duke ought to name now those he wishes to take with him so that they can get ready and they and their servants can be fitted out with brigandines or otherwise, according to their means.

Item, it seems that the duke should assemble his stewards and other household officers as soon as possible to decide what household to take. Above all they should put their advice in writing and choose people for each office who are sound in body and able to defend themselves or fight if this is necessary, without having any superfluous or useless people.

Item, when the duke decides to leave, he should send some notable members of his council two or three weeks beforehand to the lords and towns en route, to arrange for the passage of the army, to find lodgings and to make provision for victuals and other necessaries so that there is no confusion or quarrelling. But it would be best if, once the duke has fixed the route, he wrote to the said princes and lords along the route two or three months in advance, to warn them of his coming. Also, the marshals ought to arrange for some notable people to stay behind with one of the marshal's provosts till the army has gone by so that they can make good any complaints which are made.

Advice for my lord's route.

First, if my lord is disposed to go via Italy, all his army should assemble at Chalon and thereabouts on the Saône. Up to that point, 200 carts need to be provided for 4,000 archers. At Chalon these 200 carts . . . will be sent back, and boats will be provided to take the infantry, both archers and others, with some of the Picard men-at-arms to escort them and to accompany the artillery and the rest of the baggage as far as Aigues-Mortes. These boats will have to be bought, for they cannot return against the Rhone [current], so they will be sold, if possible at a profit, at Aigues-Mortes. A notable captain will be needed to lead them whom everyone will obey. The carts belonging to the ducal stable and the artillery which will not fit on the boats, such as those for the bombards and ribaudequins, will have to be dismantled.

At Aigues-Mortes, Nice and Marseilles or elsewhere ten or twelve large *naves* will have to be provided . . . which the duke will have to pay for, to take his men and baggage to the enemy's country . . . and the cost of this shipping is not likely to exceed the cost of the other transport.

Meanwhile, the Picard men-at-arms will go by land with the duke, taking with them the horses of those of their companions who travel by boat with the archers. All the men-at-arms from Burgundy and all other mounted troops will likewise travel overland with my lord duke, by companies and in accordance with an order of march to be drawn up.

After the carts have been left behind, the duke and the mounted troops with him will need mules and other beasts to carry the baggage they want to take with them, which has not been put on the boats, since carts cannot pass through the mountains. Each person will have to arrange this for himself and at his own expense. The pioneers, carpenters, masons and miners, or some of them, will have to go with these mounted troops to help provide roads and lodgings. The whole of the mounted contingent will have to continue thus to the embarcation port in the kingdom of Naples.

It seems that my lord [the duke] should divide his mounted force into two sections, one to travel over the Mont Cenis pass and the other over the St. Bernard pass, so as to have an easier passage and to better find provisions. These two groups should reassemble at Milan and take the direct route thence to Rome. . . .

Advice for Germany.

If my lord the duke prefers this route, then the entire army should assemble at Regensburg and thereabouts, so as to travel thence by the river Danube. Since the army will come from several different regions, those from Burgundy should cross the Rhine by the bridges at Basel or at Breisach and assemble around Ulm; those from Picardy, Hainault, Namur, Brabant, Flanders and Luxembourg could travel through Lorraine, over the bridge at Strasbourg, and thence to Ulm in Swabia to join the Burgundians; and the Dutch and Zeelanders and others from that side of the Rhine could go to Cologne, thence on the Rhine against the current as far as Speyer, and from there to Ulm through Swabia. From Ulm they would [all] proceed to Regensburg through Bavaria, along rivers, provided with the necessary boats, which flow into the Danube.

If the duke decides on this route, up to 300 boats will have to be found to transport the men and horses with their baggage as well as the carts, taken to pieces, needed for the entire army. Each boat, taking twenty-four to thirty horses and 100 men, two carts in pieces and provisions and baggage for the said 100 men, will cost fifty Rhenish florins. To provide these boats, five or six months' notice will be necessary but, if there is insufficient time to obtain them all, 100 might be enough. These would carry the infantry, the dismantled carts, the baggage and the best horses, while the other horses . . . could be led on foot. . . .

It takes at least a month to travel by water from Regensburg to Belgrade and, if part of the army goes by land and the rest by water, at least six weeks will be needed, for the boats will have to wait for the overland section. If the entire army, both infantry and cavalry and baggage-train, goes overland, it will manage well enough, but it will take two months or more.

Item, because Belgrade is the last place under Hungarian control, and thereafter one enters the lands of the despot of Russia and Serbia, no advice is offered here, for it will be necessary thereafter to be guided and advised by the inhabitants. It should be noted that the armies from Germany, Bohemia and Hungary are supposed to assemble at Belgrade and thereafter the river Danube will be left and an overland route taken to attack the enemy.

Advice on raising troops and what they will cost.

First, in Picardy and thereabouts 400 lances, three horses per lance, that is the man-at-arms, his valet armed in a corselet or brigandine and carrying a spear (*langue de boeuf*) or other appropriate weapon, and a sturdy page. At fifteen crowns per month, 6,000 crowns.

Next, 4,000 archers on foot at three patards per day, which is 15,000 crowns per month. They will need 200 carts for their baggage, for they can carry nothing on foot. Each cart will cost at least twelve patards per day, which is 3,000 crowns per month. . . . It will take these carts about a month to reach the rivers Saône or Danube from Flanders, Brabant, Picardy and Hainault, so the 4,000 archers on foot at three patards per day will cost, for this first month, including the carts, the sum of 18,000 crowns. Counting the above-mentioned 400 lances at 6,000 crowns, this makes 24,000 crowns in all for the troops from Picardy, Flanders, Brabant, Hainault and that area. . . .

Item, in Burgundy 300 lances, both from the country and from those of the [ducal] household and others who will not be included on the *escroes*[1], at four horses per lance, each comprising a man-at-arms, his page, a valet armed and equipped as above-mentioned, and a crossbow-man (*cranequinier*), at twenty crowns per lance, comes to 6,000 crowns. It should be noted that the Burgundians are paid twenty crowns per lance of four horses while the Picards get fifteen crowns for a three-horse lance, because, whereas the Picards can recruit archers and there will be ten archers with each of their lances, this is not so easy for the Burgundians, who cannot so easily find archers and captains for them. . . .

Item, 100 cannoneers and culverineers will be needed, 100 masons and smiths, 100 gunners, bowyers, fletchers and crossbow-makers, 300 miners and pioneers, making 600 men on foot, each carrying a defensive weapon and paid archers' wages of three patards per day . . . comes to 2,250 crowns for a month.

The total of the two armies of Picardy and Burgundy is 700 lances, 400 from Picardy making 800 combatants, and 300 from Burgundy making 900 combatants, plus 4,000 archers and 600 culverineers, pioneers, workmen etc. making 4,600 combatants; in all 6,300 combatants which will cost, without the cost of boats, 32,250 crowns. The cost of the duke's household and the transport of artillery is not included

---

[1] The daily accounts of the ducal household.

in this, nor is what needs to be bought for the artillery, which will have to be estimated with the advice of the masters of the artillery and other experts.

Item, some think that up to twenty moneyers will be needed for minting coins en route.

Advice on the shipping which will be needed if the route is via Italy.

First, if it is decided to hire shipping at Marseilles for 5,000 men and the baggage of the whole army, this could be provided by ten *naves* of about 700 tons (*bottes*) each on average, which . . . at 500 crowns per month each, makes 5,000 crowns. And it seems that they will be needed for at least three months, which will cost 15,000 crowns.

Item, if it is decided to make use of the duke's balinger and to buy outright twelve carvels in Portugal, which will cost 12,000 crowns, they will be able to carry 200 to 300 men each; and if besides them the duke buys two *naves* of 600 tons, costing at least 2,500 crowns each, these would suffice for the passage of those going by sea. And the said carvels and *naves* would cost 17,000 crowns in all. From the time they are ready, they will cost about 2,000 crowns per month, counting sailors and provisions, and they will have to be maintained at this cost for three months to complete the crossing, making 6,000 crowns for the three months. But, once these three months are over, these ships will soon recoup what they cost, because they will be the duke's and he will be able to use them either for warfare or for transporting victuals and other supplies, which will be extremely useful and helpful for the army. . . .

Item, if it is decided that everyone shall go by land on horseback, this is feasible, but it will be necessary to send all the artillery, which will not be needed between here and Naples, in the duke's balinger, likewise the tents. . . . And if there is a danger from the English, the balinger could be sent to Aigues-Mortes empty and the artillery and everything else by the Saône. The balinger could cost 2,000 crowns per month, including the sailors' wages and food.

Item, if the route through Germany is chosen, 300 boats will be needed on the Danube which will cost, at four Rhenish florins each, 15,000 florins of the Rhine. . . .

May it please my lord duke to take advice on all this and come to a decision as soon as possible. This is necessary so that what needs to be done can be attended to.

The reason for the deferment of Philip the Good's crusade from 1455 till 1456 and later was not primarily due to the equivocal and scarcely encouraging attitude of King Charles VII, who did eventually on 5 March 1455 authorize Philip to recruit troops in France.[1] The

---

[1] Plancher, iv. no. 166.

real explanation of this delay originated, curiously enough, in the deaths of two prelates on 24 March 1455. One was Pope Nicolas V, the other was Bishop Rudolf von Diepholz of Utrecht. The death of the former, though it led to the election of a dedicated crusader Calixtus III, as the next pope, inevitably delayed the complex negotiations that were the essential preliminary of an 'international' expedition of this kind; negotiations which were traditionally, and almost inevitably, largely in the hands of the pope. Thus the best Calixtus III could do was to announce a crusade for summer 1456. Rudolf von Diepholz's death had a far more deleterious effect on Burgundian crusading plans, for its gave Philip the long-awaited opportunity of extending Burgundian influence into the *Sticht* of Utrecht. From April 1455 onwards this important affair thrust itself more and more on his attention, so much so that he found it necessary to be at The Hague in person from November 1455 until July 1456, and he did not return to Brussels until October 1456, after his unsuccessful campaign to Deventer. Chastellain implies that the abandonment of the siege of Deventer was due to the unforeseen and somewhat embarrassing arrival of the dauphin of France at the Burgundian court, as a fugitive and supplicant for political asylum.[1] This event in its turn delayed the crusade, for Philip's attitude to the dauphin caused such a deterioration in Franco-Burgundian relations that neither a Burgundian crusade, nor even a joint crusade of the duke of Burgundy and the dauphin, which Philip suggested in November 1456, were serious possibilities while Charles VII lived.

But, if Burgundian crusading plans were shelved, crusading ardour was repeatedly stimulated at the Burgundian court in these years, and the duke still persisted in regarding himself as hovering on the very brink of a triumphant expedition to the East. In May 1455 some Turkish prisoners were exhibited at Lille.[2] In August and November 1455, help or participation in the crusade was sought from Brabant and Holland. In September 1455 the Grand Turk, signing himself as 'true heir of King Alexander and Hector of Troy, sultan of Babylon, king of Troy', made his own contribution to the arousing of crusading enthusiasm by addressing a challenging letter to Philip, in which he promised to treat his army just as Bajazet had treated his father's

---

[1] *Œuvres*, iii. 195–6.
[2] D'Escouchy, *Chronique*, ii. 305 and *IADNB* viii. 30. For the next sentence, see AGR CC2417, account for 1455, f. 63 and Jongkees, *Staat en Kerk*, 137. The Grand Turk's letter is in *Chroniken der deutschen Städte*, x. *Nürnberg*, iv. 212–13.

crusade at Nicopolis. The king of Aragon kept writing letters and sending ambassadors; Calixtus was in touch with everybody, and in July 1456 he sent a crusading banner to Philip at The Hague; and on 21 June 1456 the Knights of the Golden Fleece took the unparalleled step of addressing a letter to the king of France jointly with the duke himself, on the subject of the crusade.[1] There was a veritable craze, among European princes, for the crusading posture. Alfonso V of Aragon took the cross; the Emperor Frederick III took the cross; Alfonso V of Portugal promised to go in person provided the king of Aragon went too.

Crusading interest was likewise stimulated at this time by the occasional arrival of Byzantine fugitives and other colourful and outlandish people from eastern parts. At Tournai, in January 1459, a certain George Palaeologus was given six crowns by the tight-fisted municipality as a contribution towards his ransom money of 30,000 ducats and for 'the honour of the holy christian faith'.[2] In the years 1459–61 the Burgundian court was visited by a chancellor of the Byzantine emperor, by a Greek archbishop, and by Isaac Palaeologus. The last-named, with his son Alexander, accompanied Philip the Good to Louis XI's coronation at Rheims. It was in the summer of 1461 that representatives of a group of eastern potentates toured the West in a vain attempt to organize an effective alliance against the Turks. These ambassadors aroused much curiosity, especially in Ghent, where they stopped for a time while making arrangements to visit the duke. The local diarist says they were 'the most strange and wonderful ambassadors you ever saw' and he enumerates them as follows:[3]

1. The patriarch of Antioch, a Franciscan.
2. Nicolas, a knight, ambassador of the king of Persia, 'an old man, tall and handsome'.
3. Michael, likewise a knight, the emperor of Trebizond's ambassador. He spoke Italian well.
4. Castoniden, ambassador of the king of Georgia and Mesopotamia, who was a 'great gruff person of marvellously strange appearance,

---

[1] One of the king of Aragon's letters to Philip is in Plancher, iv. no. 172, dated 5 November 1455; others are printed by Marinesco, BEP (n.s.) xiii (1949), 26–8. For the rest of this sentence, see Chastellain, Œuvres, iii. 117–20 and Plancher, iv. 288.
[2] Extraits analytiques de Tournai, 1431–1476, 246. For the next sentence, see IADNB iv. 207 and 214 and, for this and what follows, Marinesco, AIPHOS x (1950), 419–28 and Grunzweig, MA lxii (1956), 121–4.
[3] Dagboek van Gent, ii. 190–3. See too BM Add MS. 54156, fos. 405–8b.

N

with two crowns on top of his head, rings in his ears, and a face and beard like a monkey'.
5. Maurat, ambassador of Armenia.
6. Mahon, ambassador of the 'lesser Turk, who was son-in-law of the Greater Turk'.
7. Hanse, a knight, ambassador of Prester John.

Though the Ghent diarist had them somewhat muddled, these ambassadors, apart from the two last at any rate, were perfectly genuine, and they carried papal credentials with them.[1] One of them, the emperor of Trebizond's ambassador Michael, visited the Burgundian court again a year later, but the Armenian who was brought from Bruges to Brussels on 30 May 1462 was a physician, not an ambassador, and his visit to court was occasioned by the duke's desire to investigate his medical skill. In the late summer of 1462 and doubtless on many other occasions, the duke gave limited financial assistance to Byzantine refugees who visited him: for example, on 1 August 1462 three brothers from Constantinople, who, like so many others, bore or claimed to bear the name Palaeologus, received a niggardly £9 12s.

No fifteenth-century pope tried harder to launch a crusade than Pius II, elected on 19 August 1458.[2] He summoned a congress of European powers to meet under his presidency at Mantua on 1 June 1459. For months nobody came and, when ambassadors did eventually arrive in September from Philip and still later from other rulers, none showed any real enthusiasm for the crusade. Philip, involved in worsening relations with France, could only offer to contribute a contingent and hope to receive papal favours in return for not abandoning the crusade altogether. He was angling at this time for a crown or, at least, for enhanced status in the Empire by way of a Rhenish vicariate or something of the kind.[3] Perhaps Pius could help him in his negotiations with Frederick III? In return, the crusade would not be forgotten. The congress ended early in 1460 with a grandiloquent but meaningless papal declaration of war against the Turks. This was supposedly reciprocated some time later by Moham-

[1] See the letters printed in Pius II, *Opera*, 848–55. For what follows, see ADN B2045, fos. 278, 267 and 274b.
[2] See especially his *Commentaries* and the references given there, pp. 865–8. I have found Voigt, *Enea Silvio de Piccolomini* and Mitchell, *The Laurels and the Tiara*, particularly useful. For the embassy of Duke John of Cleves to Mantua on Philip's behalf, see now Chastellain in BM Add. MS. 54156, fos. 381–3.
[3] Cartellieri, *MIOG* xxviii (1907), 448–64.

med II, who threatened to treat Rome like Constantinople and decapitate the duke of Burgundy.[1] In 1462 and 1463 the king of Bohemia, George Podiebrad, and Pope Pius II both tried to organize a kind of Grand Alliance against the Turk and their efforts resulted, in the autumn of 1463, in a coalition between Pius II, Philip the Good, Venice and the king of Hungary, Matthias Corvinus, all of whom had promised to go in person.

It was at this time, in the autumn of 1463 and the winter of 1463–4, that the sixty-seven-year-old duke of Burgundy came nearer than ever before to setting out on crusade. Why else was he prepared to accept now the long-resisted redemption of the Somme towns by the king of France? 'It seems', wrote the Milanese ambassador to the court of France on 17 September 1463, quoting an informant, 'that the duke is by no means unwilling to restore these lands [to the king of France] and to accept the money to spend it against the Turks.'[2] In October, the Saxon ambassador at the Burgundian court and in November the town clerk of Malines when at Bruges with the duke both wrote home to say that Philip was determined to go on crusade in the following summer. On Christmas Day 1463 when the Milanese ambassador asked Louis XI if he thought Philip would go, the king replied in the affirmative, explaining 'that he was a prince who had always had his own way, never having had to share power with a companion or equal, and that he was not of great intellect'.[3] At this time there was talk of the lord of Croy acting as regent of the Burgundian territories while the duke and his son both went on crusade or, if Philip's quarrel with Charles was still unresolved, while he remained, more or less in exile, in Holland. But early in February a settlement of the quarrel was effected by the States General. The lord of Croy departed at once for the French court and it was at this juncture that Louis XI, fearful of what Charles might do if his father appointed him regent, took the trouble to seek a personal interview with Philip at Lille, on 23 February 1464, to persuade him to delay his departure.

The reasons advanced by Louis XI in favour of the deferment of the Burgundian crusade are set out in detail in a remarkable

[1] *Chants historiques*, 48 ff. For the next sentence, see Odlozilik, *The Hussite King*, 154–5 and Vaněček, *The Universal Peace Organisation of King George of Bohemia*. See too, Perret, *France et Venise*, ii. 391–407.

[2] *Dépêches des ambassadeurs milanais*, i. 299. For the next sentence, see *Urkundliche Nachträge*, 23 and *IAM* iii. 138–9.

[3] *Dépêches des ambassadeurs milanais*, i. 361. For what follows, see especially *Actes des États Généraux*, 58–95 with references.

document which has only recently come to light.[1] The king relies on Philip to negotiate an Anglo-French peace but equally, if it comes to war between England and France, then as the king of France's leading vassal, Philip's help will be essential. Moreover, it would be scarcely honourable for him to help the 'emperor of Greece' and others to recover their kingdoms from the Turks while leaving the kingdom of France open to an attack from the English 'who have done more harm here than the Turks have in the lands they have conquered'. Then Louis gives vent to his habitual distrust and dislike of the Venetians. They are only interested in conquering Morea for themselves and, once they have done this, they will make a separate peace with the Turks, leaving the duke of Burgundy in the lurch. If only the duke will wait until peace has been made with the English he will be able to count on a French contingent of 10,000 men.

Whether or not these tendentious assurances had any effect on Philip, he could scarcely disregard his suzerain's wishes especially if, as a Milanese ambassador hinted, they coincided with some of his own private feelings: for the duke was said to feel too old, to dislike travel by sea, to be too engrossed in his women, to be short of money and to be worried about leaving Charles in charge of his lands.[2] He now resolved to send his bastard son Anthony on crusade and his explanations and apologies to the disappointed pope. Pius II was, in fact, grief-stricken by the depressing news of Philip's change of heart, but he did not lose faith in Philip's intentions. Instead, he blamed those who had dissuaded him. Not only were 'kings who had dared to put any obstacle whatever in the way of the crusade against the Turks' included in the customary anathema pronounced on Holy Thursday, but Pius took the trouble to state, in his *Commentaries*, 'that this applied to those who had diverted Philip, duke of Burgundy, from his holy purpose'.

The Ghent diarist proudly names individually the eighty-two volunteers who marched out of Ghent on 20 April and 4 May 1464, clothed in black with crusaders' crosses on their chests and silver Gs, for Ghent, on their backs, in order to embark at Sluis on 21 May with the bastard Anthony.[3] The ducal secretariat devoted hours of work

[1] Thielemans, *Bourgogne et Angleterre*, 465–9.
[2] *Dépêches des ambassadeurs milanais*, ii. 108–11. On this paragraph as a whole, Pius II, *Commentaries*, 852–7 (the quotation is from p. 856) is of great importance. See too Duclercq, *Mémoires*, 234–5 and Chastellain, *Œuvres*, iv. 440–4, 460–2 and v. 60–4.
[3] *Dagboek van Gent*, ii. 196–7. For what follows, see *IADNB* viii. 290–7 and AGR CC25191, f. 10b and Degryse, *MAMB* xvii (1965), 242–5 with

to drawing up inventories of the necessary supplies, from the complete equipment in every detail, including artillery, 426 oars, five large sails of cotton and canvas, swords and weapons, chains for the rowers and crockery, of the duke's galleys at Sluis, to a long list of medical supplies, including vinegar, ointments, plasters and powders of all kinds. The shipping needed, the artillery needed, the provisions needed, all were assessed and listed. A contract was drawn up for the hire from Louis XI of additional galleys at Marseilles, while other galleys were made ready at Sluis and still others were built for the duke at Pisa. At the time of the bastard's departure, Philip himself had once again decided to go as soon as he was in a position to do so, witness a letter sent by Guillaume Fillastre to his friend and colleague in the Burgundian government, Jehan Jouard, president of Burgundy.

> Lille, 6 June 1464
> Dearest and special lord and friend, I recommend myself to you. I have received your letter and I must reply to you on the business of the crusade. My lord the duke has ordered me to write to ask you to preach it and to place a chest or box in important churches everywhere, in which the contributions that the good people want to make can be placed. Each is to have three keys, one to be held by the bishop's official or the parish priest, another by a person appointed by the duke, and a third . . . by the local authorities. . . . As to preaching the crusade, you'll have to take advice on this. According to the pope, the duke will be going with him and will be setting out at the beginning of June, which is the present month. Since our holy father is reported to have already set out, while my lord the duke has stayed behind, it will be necessary to explain that this was on the advice of the king, so that he could negotiate a peace or truces with the English in order to obtain more help [for the crusade] from the two kingdoms [of France and England], that my lord the duke has already sent part of his army under my lord the bastard of Burgundy and that, the peace or truces once made, he intends . . . to follow with the rest of his army. . . .
> Here, I have acted as follows. To encourage the people I have caused every parish priest to be given a copy of the crusading bull, in French in French-speaking areas and in Flemish elsewhere, to read to the people every Sunday, so that it will come to everyone's notice. . . . As to news, our people have set out, a fine company some 3,000 strong, and, thanks be to God, have had a very favourable wind since then. . . . My lord of Charolais is in this town, joyously, praise be to our creator, with my

---

references. The letter which follows is from Gachard, *Rapport sur Dijon*, 157–9.

lord his father. I know of nothing else worth writing about for the present. Excuse my bad writing, but yours is no better. . . .

Your perfect friend,
G. bishop of Tournai

Yet Philip the Good never did set out on his crusade, and even the bastard's expedition, the departure of which is mentioned in this letter, was an utter failure, for it was held up at Marseilles by the news of Pope Pius II's death at Ancona, and then cancelled on the advice of Anthoine, lord of Croy and others.[1] A series of events now intervened which caused the displacement, in Burgundian policies, of the crusading obsession of the old man by the military ardour and anti-French ambitions of his son Charles. The crusade was forgotten while Burgundian troops marched into France in 1465 and against Dinant in 1466, but the duke maintained his interest to the end, though there is no means of knowing whether he ever read the lengthy report which the last of his many ambassadors to the East, Anthoine du Payage, sent him from Rhodes on 9 February 1467,[2] a bare four months before his death.

[1] Chastellain, *Œuvres*, v. 55–6.   [2] BN MS. fr. 1278, fos. 244–6.

CHAPTER TWELVE

The Close of the Reign: 1465–7

March will be somewhat unsettled and for the most part windy and rainy, the wind from west or south, mainly after the fourteenth. . . .

April will be quite reasonable. Sometimes, indeed often, there will be changeable periods of damp, cold, and wind sometimes from the north but mostly from the west. After the eleventh the weather will be mixed, sometimes fine, but with some cold periods or frosts, windy sometimes from the north and often from the west. . . .

May will be reasonably fine at first with some hot days and a south or west wind. But it is possible that thunderstorms and gales will follow this warm weather in some places, especially about the eighth. . . .

These cautiously worded long-range weather forecasts were among the prognostications for 1465 drawn up by a Flemish astrologer and copied for the duke of Burgundy.[1] After his meteorological predictions, the author deals in detail with the prospects for the principal items of food, corn, wine, honey and the like, and with the health or medical outlook for 1465, which is to be a bad year for head-aches and stomach-aches, but with no disastrous pestilence. Finally, he deals with human affairs.

According to Abumazar, because Mercury is in the Ram, important people such as kings, princes and lords will be unusually aggressive and ambitious for fame, honour, and renown. Moreover certain people, some of them great, will be more than usually ready to take up arms and it is possible that in some places there will be disputes, wars and arson . . . but, as far as warfare is concerned, more may be achieved by crafty tricks than by notable battles. . . . Notwithstanding that the discordant attitudes of several planets will bring divisions, disputes and dissensions among various people and assemblies of troops

---

[1] BN MS. fr. 1278, fos. 253a–257a.

374 PHILIP THE GOOD

and artillery and the like, and some minor skirmishes are possible, nevertheless one can hope that, with God's help, there will be no notable battle or war. . . .

One may perhaps forgive the astrologer his failure to predict the outbreak of a serious war in France in 1465, a war which has ever afterwards gone under the name of the war of the Public Weal, or, more fully, of the League of the Public Weal. On the other hand, if he had paid more attention to terrestrial matters and less to the movements and influences of Mercury and Venus, he could hardly have failed to notice the rapid deterioration in Franco-Burgundian relations in the second half of 1464 which was closely linked with the rise to power, at the Burgundian court, of Charles, count of Charolais. In particular, the affair of the bastard of Rubempré and its aftermath might have led him to expect a war between Burgundy and France in the not too distant future.

It was some time in September 1464 that the bastard brother of the lord of Rubempré was sent to Dutch waters by King Louis XI with an armed galley.[1] The real aim of this mission was the arrest of an emissary of the duke of Brittany, the vice-chancellor Jehan de Rouville. The king, who was profoundly suspicious both of Duke Francis II of Brittany and of Charles, count of Charolais, had learnt from his spies that Jehan de Rouville was under instructions to arrange an alliance with England on behalf of his duke, and then to cross to Holland to inform Charles and perhaps involve him in a coalition aimed against the French crown. Louis hoped, by intercepting de Rouville on his way from England to Gorinchem, where Charles was residing, to discover the truth about these treasonable projects of the duke of Brittany, and at the same time to prevent the plot spreading to include Charles.

This was at the very moment when, if we may believe Chastellain, Louis XI was waiting hopefully at Rouen for Philip the Good to suffer the very nasty (dur et perilleux) accident which the royal astrologers had predicted for the duke of Burgundy in September. Rumour had it that the king planned in this eventuality to seize the castle of Hesdin and some of Philip the Good's territories before

[1] For what follows see above all Chastellain, Œuvres, v. 75-7 and 81-92, Duclercq, Mémoires, 240-4, and Dépêches des ambassadeurs milanais, ii. 267-70 and 303-4. De la Marche, Mémoires, iii. 3-4, de Commynes, Mémoires ed. Calmette and Durville, i. 4-9, Basin, Louis XI, i. 140-50, and Livre des trahisons, 235-6 are also useful. See too Pocquet, RCC xxxvi (2) (1934-5), 182 and Bonenfant, Philippe le Bon, 109-11.

Charles had time to arrive on the scene from Gorinchem.[1] The discovery that the bastard of Rubempré, a relative of the lord of Croy, who was arrested after being found lurking in Gorinchem making polite enquiries about the health and habits of Charles, was under orders from Louis XI, added fuel to the flames of popular alarm, and Charles made no effort to quash the rumour or withdraw the accusation, now freely made, that the bastard of Rubempré had been sent by the king to arrest him. Thomas Basin goes further than this by suggesting that the bastard was instructed, if he failed to capture Charles alive, to bring back his head to the king.

These rumours and suspicions embarrassed Louis XI, who found it necessary to send ambassadors to present a detailed explanation of the bastard's presence at Gorinchem, not only to the Burgundian court, but also to the civic authorities of Tournai, Amiens and probably elsewhere, carefully exculpating himself from any question of an attempt on the person of the count of Charolais, and seeking the punishment of those spreading malicious rumours about the royal intentions.[2] These rumours evidently frightened the old duke, who began himself to entertain such serious apprehensions about Louis XI's intentions that he decamped suddenly from Hesdin on Sunday, 7 October, with only a handful of companions, when Louis was about to visit him.

It seems that Charles had exploited the Rubempré affair to arouse his father's fears, for the duke's departure from Hesdin followed shortly after his receipt of a letter from Charles in Holland,[3] and from now on Charles enjoyed a rapidly increasing influence with his father. At Lille in November they received the French royal embassy together and Chastellain describes their friendly, even intimate, meetings and conversations there later in the month. Thus the year that had begun with open dissension between father and son, occasioned in large measure by the son's dislike of the Croy and their pro-French policies, which had culminated in autumn 1463 in Philip's return of the Somme towns to Louis, closed with their complete reconciliation. Philip, as a result very largely of the Rubempré affair, had virtually

[1] Chastellain, Œuvres, v. 26.
[2] Documents in Extraits analytiques de Tournai, 1431–76, 275–80 and de Commynes, Mémoires, ed. Dupont, iii. 206–10.
[3] Dépêches des ambassadeurs milanais, ii. 303–4 confirms Duclercq, Mémoires, 241. For the next sentence see, besides the chroniclers already cited, the document in Chastellain, Œuvres, v. 118–122 and de Commines, Mémoires, ed. Lenglet du Fresnoy, ii. 417–20 and, for the reconciliation of father and son at Lille, Chastellain, Œuvres, v. 194–201.

come round to his son's point of view and Charles at last, from autumn 1464 onwards, began to command that credit and authority at his father's court which, as Philip's son and heir, he might reasonably have expected long before. This domestic revolution at the Burgundian court naturally brought with it an important diplomatic change. From now on Burgundian policy, inspired no longer by the Croy but influenced instead by the count of Charolais, became increasingly hostile to King Louis XI.

How far were the vigorous, even aggressive, policies of the closing years of Philip the Good's reign due to this new-found influence of Charles, count of Charolais? Against those who have argued that, from the spring of 1465, Philip handed over power entirely to his son, even appointing him his lieutenant in all matters, it has recently been convincingly shown that the Burgundian state continued until the day of his death to be ruled by Duke Philip, assisted by his council.[1] The lieutenancy of Charles, even though he described himself in official letters without any qualification as his father's lieutenant-general, extended in practice only over military affairs. His subordination to his father is made abundantly clear in a letter he wrote to Malines, on 25 November 1465, in which he announces his intention of proceeding to Namur 'to do whatever it pleases my most redoubted lord and father to command and ordain'. But this subordination by no means precluded Charles from playing a vital part in the formulation of policy and in making a positive contribution to the government of Burgundy, and his situation in 1465 and 1466 was thus utterly different from his status in the years before, when he was virtually excluded altogether from public affairs. We see him now permitted, and even encouraged, to implement his policy towards France which evidently aimed at the restoration of the Somme towns; we see him intervening in administrative matters and advising his father on the appointment of officers; and we may note that, from the autumn of 1464 onwards, he began to take his own initiatives in foreign affairs. His intrigues with the French princes were apparently initiated in the summer of 1463 by a clandestine alliance with Duke Francis II of Brittany, and this was followed on 10 December 1464 by a treaty with John of Anjou, duke of Calabria.[2]

[1] See Bonenfant and Stengers, AB xxv (1953), 7–29 and 118–33. For what follows, see BN MS. fr. 5044, f. 44 and de Commines, Mémoires, ed. Lenglet du Fresnoy, ii. 460–1; Collection de documents inédits, ii. 256–7.
[2] Pocquet, RCC xxxvi (2) (1934–5), 180–1 and de Commines, Mémoires, ed. Lenglet du Fresnoy, ii. 422–3. For what follows, see the documents in

Quite apart from these contacts in France, which formed a prelude
to the war of the Public Weal, Charles took care in these years to
establish himself on a European footing by means of a series of
personal connections with other powers. On 9 September 1464 the
duke of Cleves promised to be loyal to him and to serve him 'against
anyone'; in May 1465 he appointed ambassadors 'to contract and
make a firm alliance between the king of Scotland and my said lord
of Charolais and the lands of my lord the duke his father'; on 4 June
Louis, duke of Bavaria, signed a treaty of alliance with Charles, and
Frederick, the elector palatine, did the same on 15 June; and in
October 1466 King Edward IV of England declared that he would
'from this day on be a loyal friend' of Charles and bound himself not
to help any of Charles's enemies against him. Some of these alliances
were subsequently confirmed or reinforced by Philip; all of them help
to demonstrate Charles's new-found power and influence.

Although in terms of Charles's relationship with his father, the
affair of the bastard of Rubempré and its aftermath, in autumn 1464,
seems to have been the crucial turning-point, in terms of his relationship with the Croy and others the critical period for Charles was in
spring 1465, shortly before the outbreak in France of the war of the
Public Weal. He had established himself fully in his father's sympathy and esteem nearly six months before Philip placed him in
command of military operations in France by appointing him his
lieutenant-general in April 1465, but he still had not eliminated the
Croy. Late in 1464 he tried to negotiate a settlement with Anthoine,
lord of Croy, but, when this failed, he determined on a carefully
planned *coup d'état*. In February 1465 he moved to Brussels, where
he was soon after joined by his loyal bastard brother, Anthony, who
had just returned from his abortive crusade. Early in March, while
his father was undergoing a serious illness, Charles seized without
difficulty the places under the control of the Croy, which they
regarded as their own, including Namur, Boulogne and Luxembourg,
arrested several of their partisans, and tried to arrest their cousin
Jehan de Lannoy. By the time he published his manifesto against
them on 12 March, the Croy and de Lannoy had fled, abandoning

Analectes historiques, xii. 273–4 (Cleves), *Actes concernant les rapports entre
les Pays-Bas et la Grande-Bretagne*, nos. 8 and 9, and de Commines,
Mémoires, ed. Lenglet du Fresnoy, ii. 460–3 and 468–73, and see too Krause,
Beziehungen zwischen Habsburg und Burgund, 17–18, Bonenfant and Stengers,
AB xxv (1953), 27–9, Grunzweig, *Études F. Courtoy*, 552, and Gruneisen,
RV xxvi (1961), 40–2.

their extensive Burgundian lands and every vestige of power within the Burgundian state. It was not till after Charles had become duke that they were pardoned and reinstated.[1]

The count of Charolais had one other serious rival or enemy, as it were within the Burgundian state. Jehan de Bourgogne, count of Étampes, had served Philip loyally and well during the whole of the early part of his ducal reign, but in 1462 or 1463 he was accused of making wax images of Charles, count of Charolais and others, with intentions that were hostile and sinister, at any rate as regards the count of Charolais. He decamped to France and subsequently took service with Louis XI. In 1464, when his brother Charles died, he inherited the counties of Nevers and Rethel, not to mention a claim to the duchy of Brabant. Indeed, his threat to Charles was potentially a serious one. He was in possession of important pieces of Burgundian territory which Philip the Good had ceded to him, notably Auxerre, Péronne, Roye and Montdidier; and he was of course a Burgundian prince, son of a younger brother of John the Fearless, and therefore first cousin of Philip the Good.[2] In the war of the Public Weal he acted as captain of Picardy for Louis XI; after it, he was compelled to restore Péronne, Roye and Montdidier and to renounce his claim to Brabant. He too was thus successfully eliminated by Charles from any further possibility of challenging his position in Burgundy.

But the count of Charolais by no means rested content with the mere elimination of his rivals. He took important positive measures to reinforce his power. In particular he saw to it that the States General of the Burgundian Netherlands made a solemn declaration on 27 April 1465, that he was the 'sole and undisputed heir of his father Philip', and he issued a series of documents in which he was granted recognition as the next duke in return for a promise to confirm existing privileges.[3] For instance on 4 September 1464 he promised to maintain the privileges of the Dutch so long as they accepted him after his father's death; in May 1465 the Estates of Hainault

[1] For this paragraph see Grunzweig, *Études F. Courtoy*, 531–64 and Bonenfant, *Philippe le Bon*, 111–12. Charles's manifesto is in *Collection de documents inédits*, i. 132–42. For the next paragraph, see de Mandrot, *RH* xciii (1907), 1–45; de Beauvillé, *Montdidier*, i; and the documents in de Commines, *Mémoires*, ed. Lenglet du Fresnoy, ii. 392 and 577–95.
[2] See the genealogical table on p. xviii.
[3] *Actes des États Généraux*, 113–15 = de Commines, *Mémoires*, ed. Lenglet du Fresnoy, ii. 455–7; *Boergoensche charters*, 132; Matthieu, *BCRH* (4) xiii (1886), 225–42; and de Commines, *Mémoires*, ed. Lenglet du Fresnoy, ii. 479–81.

recognized him; and, in July he promised to confirm the privileges of
the towns of Brabant in return for their acceptance of him as the next
duke of Brabant. Thus Charles, by means of certain vigorous and not
unskilful manipulations, contrived to restore unity to a divided court
and to secure a position of uncontested power for himself under the
supreme authority of Philip the Good and the great council. The
sympathy which his estrangement from his father seems to have
widely invoked had already earned him a measure of popularity. Now,
the war of the Public Weal was to provide him with his first real
opportunity of acquiring prestige.

The war of the League of the Public Weal was an episode in the
history of France rather than Burgundy. It was the most serious, the
most prolonged, and the most nearly successful of a series of princely
revolts against the crown which had begun in 1437. A chronicler
enumerates the participants tersely in Latin: 'seven dukes, twelve
counts, two lords, one marshal, 51,000 men-at-arms—all against
King Louis and the city of Paris'.[1] Another describes the grievances
which had provoked this formidable combination against the king.
Louis had appointed unworthy people as bishops and abbots, he had
prevented his brother Charles from having peaceful possession of the
duchy of Berry, he had annoyed the count of Charolais by redeeming
the Somme towns from his father and sending the bastard of
Rubempré to Holland, he had stopped the duke of Bourbon's pension, he had unjustly seized the lands of Crèvecoeur from Anthony,
bastard of Burgundy, when he was on crusade, he had wronged the
duke of Nemours, and he had banned hunting throughout France.

[1] Maupoint, *Journal parisien*, 52. For what follows, see de Haynin, *Mémoires*,
i. 6–11, and *Dépêches des ambassadeurs milanais*, ii. 236–7. For the war of the
Public Weal in general, besides the three important sources just cited, see
de Roye, *Chronique scandaleuse*, i. 36–136; Duclercq, *Mémoires*, 243–88; de
Commynes, *Mémoires*, ed. Calmette and Durville, i. 9–88 and Bittmann,
Ludwig XI und Karl der Kühne, i. 23–192; *Lettres, mémoires et autres documents relatifs à la guerre du Bien Public*; and the documents printed in de
Commines, *Mémoires*, ed. Lenglet du Fresnoy, ii. 438–604. Less important
are Basin, *Louis XI*, i. 150–228, de la Marche, *Mémoires*, iii. 8–30, *Livre des
trahisons*, 238–50 and de But, *Chronique*, 464–8. The war still awaits its
historian. The narratives in Petit-Dutaillis, *Charles VII, Louis XI et les
premières années de Charles VIII*, 343–50, Champion, *Louis XI*, ii. 61–82 and
Bartier, *Charles le Téméraire* are useful but brief; Franz, *Die Schlacht bei
Montlhéry* is superficial; Plancher, iv. 325–41, de Barante, *Histoire des ducs*
ii. 227–53 and Foster Kirk, *Charles the Bold*, i. 211–85 are archaic; and
Stein, *Charles de France*, 45–127 and Finot, *MSSL* (5) v (1896), are valuable
but limited. A recent contribution is Grunzweig, *MA* lxxii (1966), 511–30.

Louis himself seems to have long remained blissfully unaware of the gathering storm, though the Milanese ambassador at his court, Alberico Malleta, surmised as early as December 1464 that a league of princes, embracing Burgundy, Brittany, Orleans, Bourbon and Armagnac had already been formed in defence of their rights against the king. It is generally assumed, though on flimsy evidence, that the events of March 1465 which inaugurated the revolt were carefully concerted. But it is equally possible that it was mere chance that Anthoine de Chabannes, count of Dammartin and a political prisoner of Louis, escaped through a hole in the wall of the Bastille six days after Charles, duke of Berry, Louis's disaffected younger brother, fled to the court of Francis II, duke of Brittany and two days before Charles, count of Charolais, published his denunciation of the Croy which set the seal on his rise to power at the Burgundian court. Indeed subsequent events appear to give the lie to any theory that the opening stages of the war of the Public Weal were prearranged and co-ordinated, for a period of sporadic negotiation intervened before the confederates began military operations and, even when they did so, they were so disorganized that Louis was able to attack them piecemeal, beginning with Bourbon.

What motives impelled Charles, count of Charolais, to persuade his father to respond to the duke of Berry's appeal of 16 March for military help against his royal brother with a declaration of war against Louis? His grievances against the king, which included the non-payment of an annual grant or pension of 36,000 francs Louis had promised him, were hardly serious enough to justify war. Nor was it sympathy for the French princes or personal antipathy to Louis XI that caused Charles to field an army against his suzerain. Rather, it was his profound determination to seize the first opportunity of recovering for the Burgundian ducal house certain territories, forming part of his inheritance, of which he believed he had been unjustly deprived. These were Péronne, Roye and Montdidier, which Philip the Good had ceded to Jehan, count of Étampes and Nevers, who had taken service with the French crown, and the so-called Somme towns,[1] ceded to Burgundy by the treaty of Arras in 1435, but which Louis had bought back from Philip in autumn 1463. Charles's strategy in the war of the Public Weal was dictated by these territorial ambitions.

It was not until the meeting of the States General on 25 April that formal announcement was made of the count of Charolais's impend-

[1] See the map, above, p. 356.

ing campaign in France.[1] Military preparations were well in hand by the first week of May, when Charles wrote to the civic authorities of Malines requesting the loan of two tents and two pavilions and the gift of a horse. At the same time three of the Somme towns, Arleux, Crèvecoeur and Mortagne were seized, while Jehan, count of Étampes and Nevers, alarmed at the prospect of an attack on his town of Péronne by the Burgundians, was doing his best to come to terms with Charles. When he failed, he contrived to enter Péronne with reinforcements on 15 May, just in time to prevent it falling into the hands of the vanguard of Charles's army under the command of Louis, count of St. Pol, who had already summoned it to surrender. Soon after the middle of May Charles himself set out with his main army from Le Quesnoy in Hainault. At Honnecourt, between Crève-coeur and St. Quentin, he waited a few days to hold council of war with Louis, count of St. Pol while his artillery was assembled, 'for 236 carts loaded with bombards, mortars, veuglaires, serpentines and other cannon had passed through the town of Arras, having been brought from the castle at Lille; and a great deal of artillery from Brussels and Namur was said to have passed through Cambrai, and it was all assembled in the count's army at Honnecourt'.[2]

But Charles was in no hurry to march on Paris, indeed his campaign seems to have been directed at first not against France, but against the count of Nevers. Early in June, bypassing Péronne, he seized the passage of the Somme at Bray. When St. Pol advanced thence into Santerre, the count of Nevers and the marshal of France had no option but to evacuate Péronne which did not however surrender, though Nesle, Roye and Montdidier capitulated on 6 and 7 June. Still, Charles made no move towards Paris. He even tried to initiate negotiations with the chancellor of France, and he made several attempts to persuade the citizens of Amiens to declare for him, explaining in a letter of 23 June that neither he nor his father had any intention 'of undertaking anything against the king's person, his crown or the welfare of his kingdom'. He and the other princes had allied together to see to the good order and government of the realm, and it was the duty of every loyal subject to support them. But the civic authorities of Amiens, unwilling to expose their citizens to these blandishments, confiscated Charles's letters and sent them on to the

---

[1] *Actes des États Généraux*, 108–28. For the next sentence, see *Collection de documents inédits*, ii. 191–4 = *IAM* iii. 147–9, and *Analectes historiques* x. 325.
[2] Duclercq, *Mémoires*, 263.

8. The War of the League of the Public Weal

king. Louis, who had been occupied since early May alternately campaigning against and negotiating with the duke of Bourbon and his princely allies some 200 miles south of Paris in Auvergne, seems to have convinced himself that he had nothing to fear in the north and that Charles would not enter the war against him. He was soon disillusioned.

After a fortnight's inactivity in the neighbourhood of Roye, Charles set out for St. Denis, where the confederates had agreed to assemble in arms. His advance parties crossed the Oise and took possession, probably through treachery, of Pont Ste. Maxence, thirty miles south of Roye, on 24 June. By the time the count reached there on 29 June part of his van was under the walls of Senlis, which however held firmly for the king. On the same day Jehan, lord of Haynin, and other soldiers in Charles's army found time to visit the castle at Dammartin from which, according to Sir Jehan, there was a very fine view, though not as fine as that from the top of the windmill at Boussu, near Mons in Hainault. It must have been a day or two later that, at Lagny-sur-Marne, Charles's troops made a gesture towards the much-vaunted Public Weal for which they were supposed to be campaigning. They burnt all the papers they could find concerning the *aides* or taxes; ordered that no more be levied; and organized a duty-free distribution of salt from the royal warehouse at Lagny for the benefit of the local inhabitants. By 5 July Charles's army was lodged at St. Denis, but not before the gates of Paris had been walled up and the marshal of France had installed himself in the capital with a numerous garrison. According to the chronicler Jehan de Roye, this was quite unnecessary, as the Parisians were perfectly able to defend themselves. Certainly Charles's attempts to persuade or frighten them into surrender, or even to take the city by assault, on 7 and 8 July, failed completely.

Instead of using the non-appearance of his allies the dukes of Berry and Brittany as a pretext for withdrawing from what could easily have become a dangerously exposed strategic situation, Charles now resolved to cross the Seine. He accordingly sent his van by boat across the river at Argenteuil on 9 July and, on 10 July, after attacking St. Cloud simultaneously from both banks, his troops seized the bridge there. His plans and situation a few days later are described in a letter he himself wrote to his father Philip the Good.[1]

[1] *Lettres, mémoires et autres documents relatifs à la guerre du Bien Public,* 346–8 = *Analectes historiques,* iv. 84–6. The last paragraph is said to be Charles's autograph.

At the bridge of St. Cloud,
Sunday, 14 July

My most redoubted lord and father, I recommend myself to you as humbly as possible. May it please you to know, redoubted lord and father, that since my last letter which I sent you by a knight of your stable, I have been at Boulogne-la-Petite,[1] on the other side of the Seine, until yesterday, when I moved here to St. Cloud and crossed the river by the bridge which I won as described in my letter. And to apprise you of further news, it is true, my most redoubted lord and father, that since I arrived here I have had three messages, one after the other, from my lord [the duke] of Berry, by which he has informed me that he is indeed near Chartres with [my] fair cousins of Brittany and Dunois and a large army, and that the king has left Bourbonnais to withdraw up here and is at the moment at Beaugency, where he has assembled his troops to do what they can against us. My lord of Berry has pressed me hard to march out towards him so that we can join together, and thus be more powerful and better able to deal with the king and his army before he has time to assemble it. For which reason, my most redoubted lord and father, and for the benefit and advantage of our affairs, I intend, if it pleases God, to leave here tomorrow for Étampes in order to join up with my lord of Berry. . . .

Redoubted lord, I recently wrote to you to say that I would not proceed beyond St. Cloud until I heard from you about the minimum sum of 100,000 crowns for the maintenance and payment of your troops while they are here, about which I have written to you several times in the hope that you would take pity on us all and that you would not wish, through lack of money, to delay or ruin our enterprise, nor to endanger me, your most humble and obedient son, your said army, nor the fine chivalry of your lands assembled here. To this end, my most redoubted lord and father, I shall leave sufficient troops here to defend the crossing so that the said money can be securely brought over as soon as you send it and also so that the troops from Burgundy, which I have summoned, can join me without danger. I beg you in all humility, redoubted lord and father, that I may have good and certain news from you of the said money as soon as possible. I shall let you know and write to you constantly and diligently about what happens to me, if it pleases God, to whom I pray, my most redoubted lord and father, that through his holy grace he will give you a good life and a long one and the accomplishment of your noble wishes.

My most redoubted lord and father, if it pleases God we shall assemble this week without fail with my lord of Berry and fair cousin of Brittany. Apart from the danger which might ensue, you can imagine what a

---

[1] In the area of the Bois de Boulogne.

dishonour, disgrace and shame it would be for you and for us all if, when in their company, we were still unable to pay our troops.

Your most humble and obedient son Charles

In accordance with this strategically somewhat rash plan of action, Charles set out from St. Cloud on 15 July and that night, while he lodged with the main army at Longjumeau, his van under the count of St. Pol reached the village of Montlhéry. But St. Pol's patrols, instead of contacting the forward troops of the duke of Brittany's army, soon discovered that the royal van was not far off and that some hundred royal troops were lodged at Arpajon, only a few miles south of Montlhéry. The Burgundian army was in fact moving head-on towards the advancing royal army while the dukes of Berry and Brittany, with their forces, were still 'in the neighbourhood of Chartres'. Louis XI had spent Monday, 15 July, in the very town that Charles was marching towards—Étampes. An Italian report describes him there, somewhat jittery on the eve of a battle which he had resolved to fight, celebrating nine sung masses 'at which his majesty stayed kneeling throughout on his bare knees . . . enough for a saint'.[1]

The battle of Montlhéry, fought in the hot, dusty afternoon of 16 July 1465, was bloody but indecisive. Charles remained in possession of the field and was able, a few days later, to join his allies at Étampes. The king was not prevented from reaching safety in Paris. Each side claimed the victory, but even contemporaries found it hard to decide who had won. A group of Burgundian fugitives were picked up at Pont Ste. Maxence, some fifty miles north-north-east of the battlefield as the crow flies, while Olivier de la Marche and others credit one of the French captains with a non-stop flight to Châtellerault, well over 150 miles to the south-west, and stories circulated of other French combatants fleeing to Parthenay and Lusignan in Poitou. An overwhelming mass of evidence survives to inform or confuse the historian of the battle: eye-witness accounts, reports at second and third hand, chroniclers, songs, one of them banned at Dijon,[2] which remained loyal to Charles in spite of Louis XI's agents, not to mention the accounts of the Burgundian artillery, in which practically every arrow and cannon-ball used in the battle is enumerated. Outstanding in this wealth of material is the classic account of

---

[1] *Dépêches des ambassadeurs milanais*, ii. 254–5.
[2] *IACD* i. 41. Several songs are printed or referred to in *Chants historiques*, 80–104; compare the Latin poem, *Liber Karoleidos*. For the attitude of Dijon, see Leguai, *AB* xvii (1945), 33–5.

386 PHILIP THE GOOD

de Commynes and the fascinating and detailed description of the battle by another Burgundian participant, Jehan, lord of Haynin. Naturally these are infinitely more informative than the brief and partly mendacious letter which King Louis sent to his loyal town of Lyons.[1]

From the king.   Corbeil, 17 July 1465
    Dear and well-beloved, yesterday at about two p.m., when the counts of Charolais and St. Pol, Adolf of Cleves, the bastard of Burgundy and all their people were drawn up in battle order near Montlhéry, defended by their transport, by trenches and by ribaudequins and much other artillery, we were advised to attack and engage them. And this was done. Thanks be to God, we had the better of them and victory was ours. The count of Charolais and most of his forces withdrew two or three times, together with the count of St. Pol. Since the battle a good 2,000 fugitives have been eliminated, either taken or killed, among others the lord of Aymeries and the lord of Haplincourt have been taken. Some of those who fled are still being pursued and several have already been brought into this town of Corbeil. As to the main result of the battle, it has been found that ten of theirs were killed for every one of ours. They lost 1,400 to 1,500 dead and 200 or 300 prisoners, among them some notable people. We have heard that the bastard of Burgundy was killed and the counts of Charolais and St. Pol badly wounded. We stayed on the battlefield till sundown and about then, being still in possession of the field, we withdrew to this town of Corbeil with all our army except for a few who, thinking things had gone otherwise for us, had retreated to

---

[1] *Lettres de Louis XI*, ii. 327–8; compare 329–30 and 334–5. Anthony, bastard of Burgundy, was not killed. Among the most important accounts of the battle are the letter of the lord of Créquy and the bastard of St. Pol to Philip the Good, printed in *Lettres et negotiations de Philippe de Commines*, i. 50–3, *IAM* iii. 153–7 and de Commines, *Mémoires*, ed. Lenglet du Fresnoy, ii. 484–6; the verbal report of Guillaume de Torcy, translated hereafter, in de Commines, *Mémoires*, ed. Lenglet du Fresnoy, ii. 486–8; and the letters printed by de Mandrot in *Dépêches des ambassadeurs milanais*, iii. 237–64 and 403–22. The main chronicle accounts are de Haynin, *Mémoires*, i. 54–80, de Commynes, *Mémoires*, i. 19–37, critically examined in Bittmann, *Ludwig XI und Karl der Kühne*, 43–107 and de la Marche, *Mémoires*, iii. 10–18 (Burgundian participants); Maupoint, *Journal parisien*, 57–8, de Roye, *Chronique scandaleuse*, i. 64–8, with a narrative by the editor, ii. 401–12 and de But, *Chronique*, 464–5 (living in Paris at the time); and Basin, *Louis XI*, i. 192–8, Duclercq, *Mémoires*, 268–70 and *Livre des trahisons*, 240–4. For the Burgundian artillery accounts, see *IADNB* viii. 244–8. For modern accounts of the battle, see above p. 379 n. 1. To them should be added Perroy, *RH* cxlix (1925), 187–9. Brusten, *L'armée bourguignonne*, 160–1 is brief and uncritical.

various places. We let you know of these matters so that you can give thanks to Our Lord.

Loys   Toustain

On 20 July 1465 Charles sent Guillaume de Torcy to present his version of the battle and its aftermath to his mother, the duchess Isabel.

First, he said that at 10.0 a.m. on 16 July the king arrived in force near Montlhéry where my lord of Charolais was with his troops drawn up on horseback, having made careful preparations. As to the actual meeting of the two armies, a little before the archers were engaged my lord of Charolais caused his artillery to open fire on the enemy, with great effect, so that they ceased to advance and 1,200 or 1,400 of the king's people were killed, with a large number of horses. Then the king reinforced the van and ordered it to advance against our people, and they made a fierce assault which wreaked havoc among the archers of our van.

When my lord of Charolais and those with him saw this they rushed forward to help their people, and in this encounter many were killed and taken on either side. On our side 300 or 400 men were killed, including notable people like Sir Philippe de Lalaing, . . . and some of my lord· of Charolais's squires. As to prisoners on our side, we have lost my lords of Crèvecoeur, and of Haplincourt, and the lord of Aymeries who was the cause of the first retreat of our people because he fled. . . . Concerning the number of French dead, the truth has not yet been ascertained, but there are said to be many, and innumerable wounded.

During the engagement my lord the bastard killed the horse the king was riding, and he would have finished him off had it not been for his archers, who rallied round and remounted him. And thereafter the king departed suddenly with a handful of people, so that his troops did not know which way he had gone, for they were looking for him here and there. My lord of Charolais followed him a good five or six leagues to a well defended place where he was said to have taken refuge. He was not there, but had taken to the woods to escape. If he had been at that place, it would have been besieged. In the battle, my lord of St. Pol and Monsieur Jaques his brother fought so bravely that no herald could recite all their deeds. Also my lord of Charolais fought in person. He was only mounted on a small horse so that his people could see that he had no intention of fleeing. He himself encouraged his archers.

After this, my lord returned to the battlefield where the dead were and remained there the rest of that day and night and the next day, while he had the dead buried. Then he caused proclamation to be made to the sound of trumpets, at various points on the battlefield, that if anyone wished to challenge him, he was ready for them. After this he went to lodge at Chastres[1] below Montlhéry, and the next day at Étampes. As to the king, his whereabouts was unknown till he arrived in Paris on Thursday evening with about 100 men in all, and it is said there that most of his people are either dead or wounded and that they have suffered incredible losses of horses and artillery. The king tried to persuade the Parisians to attack my lord of Charolais, but they replied that he was too powerful, that if they sallied out not a man would escape, and that they would do nothing. After the king had reached Paris with his small company, he tried to persuade the Parisians that he had been victorious, but they feared the contrary, especially when they saw so many of his people on the following day, wounded, having spent the night in the woods.

Finally, [Guillaume de Torcy] said that while my lord of Charolais was at Étampes . . . the quartermasters of my lords of Berry and Brittany arrived, reporting that they would be coming the next day and that they had captured en route the remnant of the royal artillery, which had escaped my lord of Charolais. He added that all my lord of Charolais's people had enriched themselves and had provisions enough. They asked nothing of their subjects, except to be prayed for. As to their power, it was sufficient, with God's grace, to resist all their adversaries.

Charles's account of events at Montlhéry is as much open to question as Louis's. Naturally he did not tell his mother that he had been wounded in the neck and very nearly taken prisoner. Naturally he minimized the loss of life and material in his own army, which other accounts show to have been nearly disastrous. It is noteworthy, too, that he remains blissfully unaware of the failures of his own generalship, for his pursuit of certain French fugitives, among them, as he thought, the king, which he describes in this report, would have certainly led to his defeat if that veteran captain, the lord of Contay, had not managed to restrain him. Even then, by the time he got back to his main army, much of it had ceased to exist. It is only by a hair's breadth that victory can be conceded to him. Nevertheless, the battle of Montlhéry enormously enhanced his prestige. After all, he had successfully faced the royal army without any assistance from his princely allies. A week later, on 27 July, he proudly set out his artillery at Étampes and fired it all off twice for the benefit of the dukes of Berry and Brittany.[2] He had created an image of invincible military power which was to impress his allies and overawe the king in the months to come.

The battle of Montlhéry was fought before Louis had received the reinforcements which his ally Francesco Sforza, duke of Milan, had

---

[1] Now Arpajon.   [2] *IADNB* viii. 245.

promised to send him, and before Charles had either united with the
duke of Brittany's army or even been joined by his troops from the
two Burgundies under the marshal of Burgundy, Thibaud de Neuchâtel. Instead of setting out directly for their prime objective, Paris,
the allies marched westwards from Étampes and crossed the Seine on
a pontoon bridge at Moret, between Melun and Montereau. The
passage was disputed by royal forces, but resistance crumbled after
the Burgundian artillery had bombarded the defenders from across
the river for some hours. The entire army passed over on 7 August
and joined up with the marshal of Burgundy and his 'fine company
of Burgundians, all wearing red bands and white St. Andrew's
crosses, with red pennons on their lances'. Here too they found
another member of the League of the Public Weal, King René of
Anjou's son, John, duke of Calabria. With Nemours, Nangis,
Provins and Brie-Comte-Robert in their hands, and their force
finally assembled in a single army, the Leaguers now marched on
Paris.

When on 22 August the six heralds of the six allied princes arrived
at the Porte Ste. Antoine and requested a general peace conference,
the strategic and political situation was extremely favourable to
them. Strategically, because they had protected their lines of communication by the seizure of Nogent-sur-Seine and Lagny-sur-
Marne, and had secured a base outside the walls of Paris by the
conquest of the bridge and castle of Charenton on 19 August.
Politically, because Louis had left Paris on 10 August, apparently to
collect reinforcements in Normandy rather than through fright, and a
section of Paris opinion was sympathetic to the princes. But the city
held out against their requests for the entry of themselves and some
of their forces and its morale was restored by the king's energetic
defensive measures after his return on 28 August.

The allies could not hope to invest a city as large as Paris. Their
encampments were limited to the eastern side, from St. Denis in
the north to Conflans in the south, where Charles himself stayed in
his own hôtel. Their troops could hunt for hares and deer with
impunity in the grounds of the royal castle of Vincennes, but they
were forced on several occasions to move their lodgings out of range
of the royal artillery. As to Paris, abundant supplies were brought
into the city from Normandy and the west. A chronicler thinks it
worth recording that, on 30 August, two horses arrived from Mantes
loaded with eel pasties which were sold in front of the Châtelet. The
first three weeks of September passed without any change in this

situation of stalemate. Desultory trench-warfare took place at Conflans, where Louis installed archers and artillery to fire on the Burgundian positions across the Seine, but truces were arranged at intervals from 3 September onwards. During them, in spite of a royal prohibition, people flocked out of the city to see the allied army, and some of them even had their names taken for hobnobbing with the Burgundians. On 9 September the allied troops began harvesting the grapes and making wine, and though these were by no means ripe, the Parisians were forced to follow suit. The wine was poor; 1465 was the worst vintage for years, and became known as the 'year of the Burgundians'.

Throughout the so-called siege of Paris false alarms and suspected treasons had kept the highly-strung king in a state of nerves. The last straw came towards the end of September, when Pontoise and Rouen went over to the rebel princes. Whether or not it is true, as Jehan de Haynin reports, that the king was so infuriated by this news that he threw his hat into the fire, it is quite certain that the settlement he now made with the princes was a product of these events. By the end of the month he had decided to buy off the individual princes by conceding their own personal demands, thus forestalling the implementation of their programme of constitutional reform. At the same time he did his best to ingratiate himself with the count of Charolais, whom he rightly saw as the military nucleus of the coalition, and whom he wrongly believed could be transformed into a loyal ally of the crown. Thus the duke of Brittany was given the county of Étampes and allowed to mint gold coins in his duchy; Charles of France, duke of Berry, was given Normandy instead of Berry; other princes were given money and lands; and Charles obtained the territorial concessions for which he had been fighting all along: restoration of the Somme towns, and the towns and castellanies of Péronne, Roye and Montdidier. He was also given the counties of Guines and Boulogne which were in his father's possession. When asked why he had signed treaties so disastrous for the French crown Louis, whose actions afterwards showed that he had no intention whatever of respecting their terms, replied that it was 'on account of the youth of my brother of Berry, the prudence of fair cousin of Calabria, the good sense of brother-in-law of Bourbon, the malice of the count of Armagnac, the excessive pride of good cousin of Brittany and the invincible power of brother-in-law of Charolais'.[1]

[1] De Commines, *Mémoires*, ed. Lenglet du Fresnoy, ii. 500.

The treaties with the individual princes were signed by Louis in the first week of October, though the general settlement was only completed at the end of the month. Royal favours were showered on Charles and the Burgundians. Louis himself visited Charles in person on at least two occasions, once to review the Burgundian army; on 4 October the Burgundians were allowed into Paris. The count of St. Pol was made constable of France; the castle of Vincennes was temporarily ceded to Charles; and the king even held out to Charles the possibility of replacing his recently deceased second wife, Isabel of Bourbon, with his eldest daughter Anne of France. Louis offered him Champagne as her dowry and invited him to accept the county of Ponthieu in compensation for the necessary delay in the consummation of the marriage, for she was only four years old.

The royal generosity towards Charles did not stop at this. Louis issued letters on 13 October making additional grants to Charles in the area of the Somme towns, and he made no attempt whatsoever to persuade Charles to make a settlement either with the Croy or with the count of Nevers, who were abandoned by the king they had loyally served. Jehan de Bourgogne, count of Étampes and Nevers, actually fell into Burgundian hands on 3 October 1465 when his town of Péronne was captured by a nocturnal escalade. Charles had begun the war of the Public Weal by attacking the count of Nevers's towns of Péronne, Roye and Montdidier. The two last had surrendered in the first week of June 1465; the fall of Péronne, four months later, was the last military engagement of the war. Louis's final act of ingratiation towards Charles was to accompany him on his departure from Conflans as far as Villiers-le-Bel. They parted on 3 November, but Charles was by no means returning home to Brussels; he was heading for Liège with what was left of his army, having proclaimed a further mobilization for 16 November 1465, at Mézières.

Philip the Good's difficulties with Liège had only been exacerbated by the appointment of his eighteen-year-old undergraduate nephew, Louis de Bourbon, as bishop in 1456, for the people of Liège, supported by Dinant and other towns of the principality, were soon in open revolt against their new bishop, who found himself exiled to Maastricht. Naturally, Louis appealed for help to Philip and excommunicated his rebellious subjects. They in their turn appealed to the king of France. Thus, in the winter of 1461–2, Philip the Good tried to arbitrate between the bishop and his flock and, a year later, ambassadors of Louis XI arrived on the same mission or pretext. In 1463 it was the turn of a papal legate, and he had nearly achieved a settlement when, in the municipal elections of July 1463, a certain Raes de Rivière, lord of Heers, was chosen as one of the burgo-masters of Liège. He was an extremist, and from now on he encouraged and pursued a policy of open defiance of the bishop, with the support of the populace of Liège. The ecclesiastics and wealthy burgesses were forced to accept Raes's revolutionary measures, which culminated in the early months of 1465 with the installation of a popular judicial administration to replace that dependent upon the bishop, and on 25 March with the election of a governor or *mambour* to rule Liège in the bishop's place. This governor, who perhaps hoped to become bishop himself after Louis de Bourbon had been deposed or transferred elsewhere, was Marc von Baden, brother of the margrave of Baden, Karl. He belonged to a family which, like others in the area of the Rhine, was trying to extend its power by collecting bishoprics. Thus another brother of Marc, Georg, was bishop of Metz, while the third, Jacob, was archbishop of Trier. Charles, count of Charolais, had tried to dissuade the Liègeois from taking the revolutionary step of electing a governor and his father Philip did his best to persuade Marc to decline the invitation. Neither wished to risk any deterioration of relations with Liège at a time when war was brewing in France and, in mid-May, while Charles was assembling his army for the invasion of France, the Brabant towns made a pacificatory approach to Liège on behalf of the Burgundian government.

These events at Liège played into the hands of Louis XI. As early as 16 May it was rumoured that Liège was about to attack Burgundy on behalf of the king.[1] Actually, the Liègeois were loth to provoke Philip the Good into a military confrontation even in the absence of a large part of his available forces, and it was not until 17 June 1465

[1] *Lettres, mémoires et autres documents relatifs à la guerre du Bien Public*, 263–4. For the whole of what follows, see especially *Collection de documents inédits*, ii., *Recueil de documents relatifs aux conflits*, *Régestes de Liège*, iv. and *Cartulaire de Dinant*, ii.; de Commynes, *Mémoires*, ed. Calmette and Durville, i., Basin, *Louis XI*, i., d'Oudenbosch, *Chronique*, de Haynin, *Mémoires*, i. de Merica, *De cladibus Leodensium*, de Los, *Chronique*, and Pauwels, *Historia*; and Daris, *Liège pendant la xve siècle*, Kurth, *Cité de Liège*, iii., Dabin, *BIAL* xliii (1913), 112–36, and *Algemene geschiedenis*, iii. 306–9 with references. The text of the treaty of 17 June 1465 is in *Corps universel diplomatique*, iii (1), 328–9 and *Collection de documents inédits*, ii. 197–205.

that they signed a treaty with the ambassadors Louis had empowered on 21 April. The terms were as follows:

1. Liège promises to make war against the dukes of Burgundy and Bourbon and the count of Charolais.
2. The king promises to help Liège against them and all her other enemies.
3. The king will provide 200 lances, each comprising three men and three horses. Wages at the rate of £15 per month to be paid by the king, and a captain to be appointed by Liège.
4. The king promises to do all he can to persuade the pope to confirm Marc von Baden's appointment as governor of Liège.
5. Each party promises not to make a separate peace with Charles, count of Charolais, and the other princes of the League.
6. The king will supply Liège with saltpetre, other things necessary for artillery, and two good *maîtres d'artillerie*.
7. While the king invades Hainault, Liège will invade Brabant, but the Liègeois need not march more than thirty leagues from their city.

It was not Liège, but the second town of the principality, Dinant, which opened hostilities at the end of June, as Charles's army was about to cross the Oise at Pont Ste. Maxence, by attacking her rival Bouvignes in Philip the Good's duchy of Namur.[1] Not until 1 August did the margrave of Baden arrive in Liège with three German counts, 400 knights in red uniforms, and an enormous bombard. Even then the governor and the civic authorities refused to take the field, and it was left to the craft gilds of the vine-growers and the drapers to take up arms on their own account. They set off to invade Limbourg on 28 August and at last, on the following morning at 8.0 a.m., a messenger left Liège carrying the following belated but official declaration of war.[2]

28 August 1465

Resplendent prince, Lord Philip, duke of Burgundy, of Brabant and of Limbourg, count of Flanders, of Artois, of Burgundy, of Hainault, of Holland, of Zeeland and of Namur and Charles of Burgundy, count of Charolais, lord of Chastelbelin and of Béthune, lieutenant etc., we Marc, by the grace of God margrave of Baden, administrator-postulate of the church of Liège, governor and regent of the lands of Liège, of Bouillon, of Loz, of Clermont, of Franchemont etc., we . . . make it known to you that we are reliably informed of various injuries and oppressions perpetrated by you and yours . . . to the very great harm, prejudice and damage of our said lands. These we can no longer suffer

---

[1] See above, pp. 58–60.   [2] D'Oudenbosch, *Chronique*, 273–4.

nor tolerate since we, by the pleasure of almighty God, have been elected governor and regent as mentioned above, and since we and our said lands have an obligation towards the most excellent prince and lord, Lord Louis, most christian king of France, our very dear and beloved lord, against whom you are waging open war. So much so that, for the above-mentioned reasons and others, we prefer a royal master to you. Because of this we, with our lands and subjects, wish to be your enemies and the enemies of your lands and subjects. . . . And in this matter we wish to maintain our honour, and if any further defence of it is necessary, we hope to have preserved it fully through these letters-patent of ours. In sign of their authenticity we have fixed our secret seal to these letters.

Although Marc von Baden and his German allies and troops joined the Liègeois in the field on 29 August, their participation in the invasion of Philip the Good's duchy of Limbourg was short-lived. Pretending that they were horrified by the belligerent ardour of the citizens of Liège, who began by despoiling the church of Herve and burning down the surrounding villages, Marc and his people decamped early in September and returned, not to Liège, but all the way home to Germany. The Liègeois, though abandoned in this way by their governor, who had evidently had no intention of waging war against the duke of Burgundy, continued hostilities in a desultory manner through September, encouraged by Louis XI's emissaries. But it was now the turn of the king to leave Liège in the lurch, to the extent even of omitting them altogether from the peace of Conflans, which he negotiated with Charles and the French princes in October, though he did his best to conceal this treachery by a straight lie, in the following letter, which reached Liège on 31 October.[1]

Paris, 21 October [1465]
Louis, by the grace of God king of France.
Dearest and special friends, following what we recently wrote to you we have sent our beloved and loyal equerry Jannot de Ste. Camelle so that you can learn from [him] . . . about the state of affairs here and about the treaty and final peace made between us and those who were mobilized and assembled against us. We are well content with the way you have conducted yourselves in this matter, by employing yourselves in our favour against those who opposed us. We are eternally obliged to you and we thank you most warmly. Nevertheless, because of the

---

[1] *Lettres de Louis XI*, iii. 1–2.

treaty between us and the above-mentioned [princes], especially in so far as fair uncle of Burgundy and brother-in-law of Charolais are concerned, and because you are comprised in the said treaty as our special good friends, we ask you, just as we have asked all our other allies and supporters, to desist from and stop waging the war you have begun in the lands of our said uncle and brother-in-law. If you do not do this, since hostilities here have now ceased and treaties have been made between us and the above-mentioned [princes], it is likely that a large and powerful army will fall on your lands, perhaps with dire consequences, for it would be difficult for you to resist and for us to help you. Therefore you should take good advice about this and, for your part, accept the said treaty. We have empowered the lord of Ste. Camelle to explain this more fully to you.

Loys

To our old and particular friends, the masters, jurors and council of the city and land of Liège.

Inevitably, ambassadors went off from Liège to Brussels to seek first a truce, then peace. They were told first, that Louis de Bourbon must be recognized as bishop of Liège and then that Philip the Good must be accepted as *advocatus* or protector of Liège. Meanwhile the 'large and powerful army' mentioned by Louis XI was assembling under the count of Charolais, who had written to Malines as early as 26 October announcing his intention of attacking Liège. Charles himself set out from Mézières on 26 November, but an attempt to take Dinant by surprise after dark on 28 November was foiled by the town's excellent defences. After this, military operations were interrupted, but diplomacy continued, with constant interchanges between Charles's headquarters, Liège and Brussels. A delicate situation soon developed. Overawed by the military power of Burgundy now deployed against them, many of the Liègeois were prepared to submit to an unfavourable, even disastrous, peace. On the other hand, by haggling over the terms and delaying the negotiations, they might hope to force Charles to disband his forces. After all, a medieval army normally supplied itself by living off the land but, because negotiations were in progress, Charles's troops were unable to forage and pillage. They were short of provisions; their pay was in arrears; and, perhaps worst of all, they were soon suffering the rigours of mid-winter. New Year's Eve was celebrated at St. Trond, where 'the trumpets, bugles and tambourines of the princes and lords lodged there never ceased to be sounded from street to street from midnight to dawn'.[1] But these apparent high spirits did not last and soon afterwards, at Heers, some fifteen miles north-west of Liège, the army was on the verge of mutiny. Meanwhile, the Liègeois had succeeded in re-negotiating the treaties originally signed at St. Trond on 22 December.

In the last week of January Charles disbanded his forces and withdrew, evidently in the belief that a favourable settlement had been achieved. But Raes de Rivière and his supporters prevented the implementation of the treaty and popular disturbances continued in Liège during the early months of 1466. By the time the peace of St. Trond was at last officially published at Liège, one of the leading citizens had been executed for his part in negotiating it. Moreover, Dinant had been excluded from the settlement. Indeed both towns, which were dominated internally by popular, or radical elements, continued to defy the duke of Burgundy and to reject their bishop. It was to quell this continued revolt that Charles prepared once more, in August 1466, for military action.

Legend has it that the town of Dinant had incurred Charles's especial displeasure, not to mention the anger of his mother Duchess Isabel, during the war of the Public Weal. A group of citizens, encouraged by news, which later turned out to be false, of Charles's defeat at Montlhéry, had hanged him in effigy in full view of his father's town of Bouvignes and proclaimed at the same time that Charles was not the son of their duke at all, but the illegitimate child of the previous bishop of Liège, Jehan de Heinsberg, and Duchess Isabel. As regards Jehan de Heinsberg, they may have been readily forgiven: other sources credit him with up to sixty bastards. But this was the only slur on the otherwise impeccable reputation of Duchess Isabel. Nevertheless, although in consequence Dinant found herself excluded from the peace of St. Trond, the Burgundian government did attempt to negotiate a separate peace with her in the spring of 1466. But the situation was exacerbated by the perennial rivalry of Dinant and Bouvignes. The truce between these two hostile cities was even infringed during Holy Week, when some citizens of Bouvignes amused themselves by throwing stones across the river Meuse at some anglers from Dinant. It was incidents like these, and trivial but bitter local squabbles, reinforced by the activities of extremists within Dinant, which prevented a settlement with Burgundy. By mid-June, Philip the Good had resolved to besiege the town. This

[1] De Haynin, *Mémoires*, i. 134–5. For what follows on the treaties of St. Trond, see Stengers, *Annales du XXXIII⁰ Congrès*, iii. 741–8.

time a combination of the summer season, a better equipped and organized army, and the panic or lethargy of Liège, permitted Charles to lay siege to Dinant and compel it to surrender. He entered it on 25 August, and his troops sacked and burnt it on the succeeding days. Thus fell the town which proudly boasted that it had resisted seventeen sieges, victim of a week-long bombardment by the finest artillery in Europe, and abandoned, partly owing to a muddle over who was to carry the civic standard, by its powerful ally and neighbour Liège.

After the virtual destruction of Dinant, Charles prepared to march once again on Liège, still dominated by popular elements which were hostile to Louis de Bourbon, to Burgundy, and to most of the better-off citizens, and which supported the radical policies of Raes de Rivière and his friends. Yet another peace treaty was imposed, named after the village of Oleye where Charles camped, a treaty which was similar to that of St. Trond but somewhat harsher. But Liège continued in revolt against its bishop and in partial defiance of the duke of Burgundy. News of Philip the Good's death in June 1467 was greeted there with festivities and satirical songs, and the history of the final, and forceful, annexation of Liège to Burgundy must be related in the next and last volume of this history.

In spite of quite serious illnesses in 1465 and 1466, Philip the Good remained in full possession of his faculties until very shortly before his death on 15 June 1467 at the age of seventy-one. The circumstances of this were recorded in macabre detail by one of his servants, in a letter to the mayor and echevins of Lille, in such a way as to lead at least one expert to believe that the duke succumbed to a sudden bout of pneumonia.[1]

Most honoured sirs, I recommend myself to you as warmly as I possibly can. May it please you to know, my most honoured sirs, that today, date of these letters, I received your letters of the same date asking me for news of our most redoubted prince. May God, in his grace, receive his soul. I can by no means send you word of his recovery but write only to report our grievous loss and the manner of his illness. That is to say that he made good cheer and was as happy as ever throughout last week, often chatting and joking with others, myself among them. Last Friday, because [on Fridays] he customarily ate nothing which had been killed, he ate scarcely anything at dinner. After dinner

[1] Lemaire, RN i (1910), 321–6 who prints the letter already printed in de Commines, Mémoires, ed. Lenglet du Fresnoy, ii. 607–8.

he spent a long time watching his workmen, and went to sleep from four o'clock until six. He then got up perfectly well and happy and, at about seven o'clock, my lord the chancellor came to speak with him for an hour. After the chancellor had left, my lord [the duke] drank twice from a cup of almond-milk and ate an omelet. Afterwards when he went to bed he chatted happily to those with him. Everyone thought he was perfectly well when he went to bed.

At two o'clock after midnight a quantity of phlegm gathered in his throat and he was so troubled by this that it seemed he would die then. By frequent insertion of a finger in his throat much of this was ejected, but he was in great difficulty and soon afterwards developed a high temperature which continued from 6.0 a.m. on Saturday until Monday evening at nine, when he gave his soul to God. And I certify you that the good prince died because of the phlegm which descended from his brain to his throat and blocked the passages so that he could only breathe with great effort. He was in this pain for twelve hours, on the brink of death. The grief of my lord his son when he entered the room and saw him struggling thus in the utmost agony was indescribable. My lord of Tournai arrived soon after his death and renewed the grief of all of us with his lamentations.

Today my lord [the duke], whom God pardon, has been placed on his bed between two sheets as if he were alive and the public has been permitted to come and see him. He looked as if he was asleep, with half-smiling face, but he was deadly pale and no one had the heart to look at him for long. As the public filed past, the lamentations and moaning which the wretched people made, large and small alike, has continued from the hour of his death till the day following, date of writing these, at 3.0 p.m., at which time the autopsy was carried out, his heart removed, also the intestines, liver, lungs and spleen, and the body embalmed and made ready to be taken wherever it pleases my lord his son. And to let you know the true state of his body, his liver was healthy and clean; the spleen was all decomposed and in pieces together with the part of the lung touching it; and the heart was the most perfect ever seen, small and in good condition. When my lord was opened he was found to have two fingers' thickness of fat on his ribs. His head was opened to see the brain because some doctors maintained that he had a tumour on the brain, but this was by no means the case, for it was found clean and as perfect as has ever been seen.

Now sirs, I tell you of these things because I well know that you will by no means obtain so much information as I can give you, who has been present throughout the above-mentioned events. . . . Now, to make an end of it, I have lost my master and you have lost our good prince. . . . Written at Bruges, 16 June 1467, by the hand of your humble servant, who is utterly desolate and disconsolate,

Poly Bulland

When the long, prosperous and mainly peaceful reign of Philip the Good came to an end at last in June 1467, people may be forgiven for mourning the loss of a prince who seemed to them pre-eminently fortunate, popular, famous and successful. It is true that he was responsible for generating at the Burgundian court a unique and splendid burgeoning of cultural and artistic life. It is true that he conquered and collected territories with zeal, determination and even with skill. It is true that by the end of his reign he had amassed a treasure in the castle at Lille. But if, leaving aside the music and manuscript illumination, the territorial acquisitions and the wealth of Philip the Good, we turn the cold and searching light of history on this apparently resplendent and powerful ruler, serious doubts arise as to the validity of the rôle in which generations of admirers have cast him; a rôle which has been variously described as founder of the Burgundian state or 'the great duke of the West';[1] a rôle which invariably implies that Philip the Good was the most distinguished, or at least the most important, of the Valois dukes of Burgundy. Furthermore, the contrast between this supposedly peace-loving and cautious statesman and his foolhardy and belligerent son has been intensified by sober historians into high drama and in Philip's favour, for Charles has been accused of wrecking a superb structure which his father is supposed to have meticulously erected during his long reign.

The fact is that Philip the Good was by no means a successful dynast. Until 1430 he had no heir at all and his life alone separated Burgundy from disintegration. Though he fathered a bevy of bastards, he contrived to provide his house with but a single male heir. The fact is, too, that Philip the Good did little or nothing to consciously develop, or centralize, the administrative machinery of his territories, in contrast to his father and his son, both of whom made serious attempts at rationalization and reform. Moreover, his internal policies had the effect of provoking damaging revolts against him in Ghent, Bruges and elsewhere. Nor in the field of diplomacy, in his relations with other powers, can Philip be described as successful. He failed to secure a crown or even an improved status of some kind in the Empire. He allowed himself to be duped and bullied by the French until, towards the end, Louis XI had not only recovered the strategically vital Somme towns but also nearly divided the Burgundian state from within. While Philip quarrelled irascibly with his son, he permitted the Croy to construct a private empire for themselves

[1] See Grunzweig, *MA* lxii (1956), 119–65.

o

within the framework of the Burgundian state. It was his grandiose and romantic concept of himself as a Valois prince of France and as the leader of a great European crusade which seems to have undermined his powers of practical statesmanship, especially towards the end of his reign. The failings of this self-assured and flamboyant ruler became more and more apparent as he grew older; his final fault, perhaps, was that he lived too long. It would be going too far to say that he left the Burgundian state in ruins when he died; after all, Charles had begun to take matters in hand two years before the end; but besides the hoard of gold at Lille and his numerous territories, he bequeathed to his son a clumsy administration, a legacy of hatred and distrust in towns like Liège and Ghent and, above all, the problem of French hostility, unresolved in spite of the vigorous counter-measures which Charles had taken in 1465. In the pursuit of pleasure and renown Philip the Good had enjoyed a measure of success given to few rulers of his time but, in spite of his early territorial successes, he had done little to consolidate his dynasty's precarious power. It was left to his son Charles to try, and to fail, to weld the scattered territories that constituted Burgundy into a more coherent and contiguous whole.

Bibliography

Full titles of works referred to in the notes. For abbreviations used see pp. xi–xiv

Aachener Chronik. Ed. A. Loersch. *Annalen des historischer Vereins für den Niederrhein,* xvii (1866), 1–29.

Actenstücke Herzog Philipps Gesandtschaft an den Hof des römischen Königs Friedrich IV in den Jahren 1447 und 1448 betreffend. Ed. E. Birk. *Der österreichische Geschichtsforscher* i (2) (1838), 231–71. French translation under the title *Documents relatifs à l'ambassade envoyée par Philippe, duc de Bourgogne, à la cour de Fréderic IV en 1447 et 1448. MSHB* (1842), 422–72.

Actes concernant les rapports entre les Pays-Bas et la Grande Bretagne de 1293 à 1468 conservés au château de Mariemont. Ed. P. Bonenfant. *BCRH* cix (1944), 53–125.

Actes des États Généraux des anciens Pays-Bas, i. Ed. J. Cuvelier and others. CRH. Brussels, 1948.

Alberts, W. Jappe. 'De anti-Bourgondische politiek van Hertog Arnold van Gelre in de jaren 1452–1456.' *GBM* l (1950), 1–22.

——. *De Staten van Gelre en Zutphen.* 2 vols. *BIMGU* xxii and xxix. Groningen, 1950, 1956.

——. and H. P. H. Jansen. *Welvaart in Wording.* The Hague, 1964.

Algemene geschiedenis der Nederlanden. Ed. J. A. van Houtte and others. 13 vols. Utrecht, 1949–58.

Allmand, C. T. 'The Anglo-French negotiations, 1439.' *BIHR* xl (1967), 1–33.

Analectes historiques, iii. Ed. L. P. Gachard. *BCRH* (2) vii (1855), 25–220.

——, iv. Ed. L. P. Gachard. *BCRH* (2) viii (1856), 67–268.

——, v. Ed. L. P. Gachard. *BCRH* (2) ix (1857), 103–256.

——, vi. Ed. L. P. Gachard. *BCRH* (2) xi (1858), 167–418.

Analectes historiques, vii. Ed. L. P. Gachard. *BCRH* (2) xii (1859), 359–516.

——, x. Ed. L. P. Gachard. *BCRH* (3) iv (1863), 323–566.

——, xii. Ed. L. P. Gachard. *BCRH* (3) viii (1866), 273–506.

——, xvi. Ed. L. P. Gachard. *BCRH* (3) xii (1871), 141–316.

André, E. 'Recherches sur la cour ducale de Bourgogne sous Philippe le Bon.' *PTSEC* (1886), 1–5.

Andt, E. *La chambre des comptes de Dijon à l'époque des ducs Valois*, i. Paris, 1924.

Arbaumont, J. d'. 'Nicolas Rolin, chancelier de Bourgogne.' *RNHB* (n.s.) i (1865), 4–14, 77–89, 110–18 and 165–76.

Armstrong, C. A. J. 'La Toison d'Or et la loi des armes.' *PCEEBM* v (1963), 71–7.

——. 'Had the Burgundian government a policy for the nobility?' *Britain and the Netherlands*, ii. 9–32. Ed. J. S. Bromley and E. H. Kossmann. Groningen, 1964.

——. 'La double monarchie France–Angleterre et la Maison de Bourgogne, 1420–1435. Le déclin d'une alliance.' *AB* xxxvii (1965), 81–112.

——. 'Le texte de la chronique de Chastellain pour les années 1458–1461 retrouvé dans un manuscrit jusqu'ici inconnu.' *PCEEBM* x (1968), 73–8.

——. 'La politique matrimoniale des ducs de Bourgogne de la Maison de Valois.' *AB* xl (1968), 5–58 and 89–139.

Arnould, M. A. *Les dénombrements de foyers dans le comté de Hainaut, xive–xvie siècle*. CRH. Brussels, 1956.

Arrêts et jugés du Parlement de Paris sur appels flamands, Les. Ed. R. C. van Caenegem. Recueil de l'ancienne jurisprudence de la Belgique. Première série. 3 vols. Brussels, 1966– .

Atiya, A. S. *The crusade in the later middle ages*. London, 1938.

Avout, J. d'. *La querelle des Armagnacs et des Bourguignons*. Paris, 1943.

B., F. 'La fin d'une maîtresse de Philippe de Bon. Nicolle la Chastellaine, dite du Bosquel.' *SFW* xiv (1874), 186–95.

Bailhache, J. 'Le monnayage de Philippe le Bon au nom de Charles VII.' *RNum* (5) i (1937), 235–44.

Barante, A. de. *Histoire des ducs de Bourgogne de la Maison de Valois*. Ed. L. P. Gachard. 2 vols. Brussels, 1838.

Barbey, F. *Louis de Chalon*. Mémoires et documents publiés par la Société d'histoire de la Suisse romande, 2e série, xiii. Lausanne, 1926.

Barthélemy, A. de. *Essai sur les monnaies des ducs de Bourgogne*. 2nd edn., Dijon, no date. Reprinted from *MCACO* (1849).

Bartier, J. 'L'ascension d'un marchand bourguignon au xve siècle. Odot Molain.' *AB* xv (1943), 185-206.

——. *Charles le Téméraire*. Brussels, 1944.

——. *Légistes et gens de finances au xve siècle. Les conseillers des ducs de Bourgogne*. MARBL l (2). Brussels, 1952.

——. 'Une crise de l'État bourguignon: la réformation de 1457.' *Hommage au Professeur P. Bonenfant*, 501-11. Brussels, 1965.

Basin, T. *Histoire de Charles VII*. Ed. C. Samaran. CHF. 2 vols. Paris, 1933, 1944.

——. *Histoire de Louis XI*, i. Ed. C. Samaran. CHF. Paris, 1963.

Baudot. 'Complainte inédite de Guillaume Vaudrey sur la mort de Bonne d'Artois.' *MAD* (1827), 194-6.

Bauer, E. *Négotiations et campagnes de Rodolphe de Hochberg, 1427-87*. Recueil de travaux publiés par la Faculté des Lettres de l'Université de Neuchâtel. Neuchâtel, 1928.

Bazin, J. L. 'Un épisode du passage des écorcheurs en Chalonnais, 1438.' *MSBGH* vi (1890), 97-112.

——. 'La Bourgogne de la mort du duc Philippe le Hardi au traité d'Arras, 1404-1435.' *MSHA Beaune* (1897), 51-269.

——. 'Histoire des évêques de Chalon-sur-Saône.' 2 vols. *MSHAC* xiv (1914) and *MSHAC* xv (1918).

Beauvillé, V. de. *Histoire de la ville de Montdidier*. 2nd edn. 3 vols. Paris, 1857.

Benoit, A. 'Les pèlerinages de Philippe le Bon à Notre-Dame de Boulogne.' *BSEPC* xxxvii (1937), 119-23.

Bergé, M. 'Les bâtards de la Maison de Bourgogne, leur descendance.' *IG* lx (1955), 316-408.

Berlière, U. 'La commende aux Pays-Bas.' *Mélanges Godefroid Kurth*, i. 185-201. Liège, 1908.

Besnier, G. 'Quelques notes sur Arras et Jeanne d'Arc.' *RN* xl (1958), 183-94.

Bigwood, G. *Le régime juridique et économique du commerce de l'argent dans la Belgique au moyen âge*. 2 vols. MARBL xiv (1921) and (1922).

Billioud, J. *Les États de Bourgogne aux xive et xve siècles. MAD* (5) iv (1922), extra number.

Bittmann, K. 'La campagne lancastrienne de 1463.' *RBPH* xxvi (1948), 1059-83.

——. 'Die Ursprünge der französisch-mailändischen Allianz von 1463.' *AMA* (1952).

Bittmann, K. *Ludwig XI und Karl der Kühne. Die Memoiren des Philippe de Commynes als historische Quelle*, i. Göttingen, 1964.

Blades, W. *The life and typography of William Caxton*. Reprint, 2 vols. New York, no date.

Blockmans, W. 'De samenstelling van de Staten van de Bourgondische landsheerlijkheden omstreeks 1464.' *APAE* xlvii (1968), 57–112.

Blok, P. J. 'De eerste jaren der bourgondische heerschappij van Holland.' *BVGO* (3) ii (1885), 319–48.

——. 'De financien van het graafschap Holland.' *BVGO* (3) iii (1886), 36–130.

——. 'Holland und das Reich vor der Burgunderzeit.' *NGWG* (1908), 608–36.

——. 'Philips de Goede en de hollandsche steden in 1436.' *MAWL* lviii (B2) (1924), 33–51.

Blondeau, G. 'Guy Armenier, chef du conseil ducal, président des Parlements des comté et duché de Bourgogne.' *MSED* (10) viii (1938), 56–76 and (10) x (1940–2), 38–66.

Boergoensche Charters, 1428–82. Ed. P. A. S. van Limburg Brouwer. Amsterdam, 1869.

Boinet, A. 'Un bibliophile du xve siècle. Le grand bâtard de Bourgogne.' *BEC* lxvii (1906), 255–69.

Bonenfant, A. M. and P. 'Le projet d'érection des États bourguignons en royaume en 1447.' *MA* xlv (1935), 10–23.

Bonenfant, P. *Philippe le Bon*. Brussels, 1955.

——. 'État bourguignon et Lotharingie.' *BARBL* xli (1955), 266–82.

——. *Du meutre de Montereau au traité de Troyes*. MARBL lii. Brussels, 1958.

——. 'Les traits essentiels du règne de Philippe le Bon.' *BMHGU* lxxiv (1960), 10–29.

——. and others. *Bruxelles au xvme siècle*. Brussels, 1953.

Bonenfant, P. and J. Stengers. 'Le rôle de Charles le Téméraire dans le gouvernement de l'État bourguignon en 1465–1467.' *AB* xxv (1953), 7–29 and 118–33.

Bossuat, A. *Perrinet Gressart et François de Surienne*. Paris, 1936.

——. 'Une clause du traité d'Arras: Philippe le Bon et l'abbaye de Luxeuil.' *AB* ix (1937), 7–23.

——. 'Les prisonniers de guerre au xve siècle.' *AB* xxiii (1951), 7–35.

——. 'Le Parlement de Paris pendant l'occupation anglaise.' *RH* ccxxix (1963), 19–40.

Bossuat, R. *Le moyen âge*. Volume i of *Histoire de la littérature française*. Ed. J. Calvet. Paris, 1955.

Boutaric, E. 'Rapport sur une mission en Belgique à l'effet de rechercher les documents inédits relatifs à l'histoire de France au moyen âge.' *AMSL* (2) ii (1865), 231–319.

Boutiot, T. *Histoire de la ville de Troyes*. 5 vols. Troyes, 1870–80.

Bowles, E. A. 'Instruments at the court of Burgundy.' *Galpin Society Journal* vi (1953), 41–51.

Brabant, F. 'Note sur le Grand Conseil de Philippe le Bon.' *BCRH* (4) v (1878), 145–60.

——. 'Étude sur les conseils des ducs de Bourgogne.' *BCRH* (5) i (1891), 90–101.

Brom, G. *Archivalia in Italië belangrijk voor de geschiedenis van Nederland*. 3 vols. The Hague, 1908–14.

Bronnen tot de geschiedenis van den handel met Engeland, Schotland en Ierland, 1150—1485. Ed. H. J. Smit. 2 vols. Rijks Geschiedkundige publicatiën lxv and lxvi. The Hague, 1928.

Brouwers, D. D. *Les aides dans le comté de Namur au xvᵉ siècle*. Namur, 1929.

Brown, A. L. and B. Webster. 'The movements of the earl of Warwick in the summer of 1464—a correction.' *EHR* lxxxi (1966), 80–2.

Brusten, C. *L'armée bourguignonne de 1465 à 1468*. Brussels, no date.

Brut, The, or the chronicles of England. Ed. F. W. D. Brie. Early English Text Society. 2 parts. London, 1906, 1908.

Bruwier, M. 'Notes sur les finances hennuyères à l'époque bourguignonne. Le domaine de Mons de 1438 à 1477.' *MA* liv (1948), 133–59.

Buntinx, J. 'De raad van Vlaanderen (1386–1795) en zijn archief.' *APAE* i (1950), 56–76.

Busken Huet, G. and J. S. van Veen. *Verslag van onderzoekingen naar archivalia te Parijs belangrijk voor de geschiedenis van Nederland*. 3 vols. The Hague, 1899–1901.

But, A. de. *Chronique*. Ed. Kervyn de Lettenhove. *Chroniques relatives à l'histoire de la Belgique sous la domination des ducs de Bourgogne. Textes latins. Chroniques des religieux des Dunes*, 211–717. CRH. Brussels, 1870.

Calmette, J. 'Contribution à l'histoire des relations de la cour de Bourgogne avec la cour d'Aragon au xvᵉ siècle.' *RB* xviii (1908), 138–96.

——. 'Dom Pedro, roi des Catalans, et la cour de Bourgogne.' *AB* xviii (1946), 1–15.

—— and E. Déprez. *La France et l'Angleterre en conflit. Histoire générale. Moyen âge*, vii (1). Ed. G. Glotz. Paris, 1937.

Camp, P. *Histoire d'Auxonne au moyen âge*. Dijon, 1961.

Cartellieri, O. 'Über eine burgundische Gesandtschaft an dem kaiserlichen und päpstlichen Hof im Jahre 1460.' *MIOG* xxviii (1907), 448–64.

——. 'Das Fasanenfest. Am Hofe der Herzöge von Burgund, 1454.' *HBKD* clxvii (1921), 65–80 and 141–58.

——. 'Ein Zweikamp in Valenciennes im Jahre 1455.' *Probleme der Englischen Sprache und Kultur. Festschrift für Johannes Hoops zum 60. Geburtstage*, 169–76. Germanische Bibliothek, xx. Heidelberg, 1925.

——. 'Philippe le Bon et le roi de France en 1430 et 1431.' *AB* i (1929), 78–83.

——. *The court of Burgundy*. London, 1929. Translated from *Am Hofe der Herzöge von Burgund*. Basel, 1926.

Cartulaire de la commune de Dinant. Ed. S. Bormans and others. 8 vols. Namur, 1880–1908.

Cartulaire de l'ancienne Estaple de Bruges. Ed. L. Gilliodts van Severen. 4 vols. Bruges, 1904–6.

Cartulaire de l'église St. Lambert de Liége. Ed. S. Bormans and E. Schoolmeesters. CRH. 6 vols. Brussels, 1893–1913.

Cartulaire de l'église collégiale de Saint-Pierre de Lille. Ed. E. Hautcoeur. 2 vols. Paris, 1894.

Cartulaire des comtes de Hainaut. Ed. L. Devillers. 6 vols. Brussels, 1881–1896.

Cent nouvelles nouvelles, Les. Ed. P. Champion. 2 vols. Paris, 1928.

——. Ed. F. P. Sweetser. Geneva, 1966.

Chabeuf, H. 'Jean de la Huerta, Antoine le Moiturier et le tombeau de Jean sans Peur.' *MAD* (4) ii (1890–1), 137–271.

Champion, P. *Louis XI*. 2 vols. Paris, 1902.

——. *Guillaume de Flavy*. Paris, 1906.

——. *Vie de Charles d'Orléans, 1394–1465*. Bibliothèque du xve siècle, xiii. Paris, 1911.

——. *Histoire poétique du xve siècle*. 2 vols. Paris, 1923.

—— and P. de Thoisy. *Bourgogne—France—Angleterre au traité de Troyes. Jean de Thoisy, évêque de Tournai*. Paris, 1943.

Chants historiques et populaires du temps de Charles VII et de Louis XI. Ed. Le Roux de Lincy. Paris, 1857.

Charlier, G. and J. Hanse. *Histoire illustrée des lettres françaises de Belgique*. Encyclopédie artistique belge. Les lettres. Brussels, 1958.

Chartes de communes et d'affranchissements en Bourgogne. Ed. J. Garnier. 3 vols. Dijon, 1867–77.

Chartes et documents de l'abbaye de Saint-Pierre au Mont Blandin à Gand. Ed. A. van Lokeren. 2 vols. Ghent, 1868, 1871.

Chartier, J. *Chronique de Charles VII.* Ed. A. Vallet de Viriville. 3 vols. Paris, 1858.

Chartularium universitatis Parisiensis. Ed. H. Denifle and A. Châtelain. 4 vols. Paris, 1897.

Chastellain, G. *Œuvres.* Ed. Kervyn de Lettenhove. Académie royale de Belgique. 8 vols. Brussels, 1863–6.

Chmel, J. *Geschichte Kaiser Friedrichs IV und seines Sohnes Maximilian I.* 2 vols. Hamburg, 1840, 1843.

Choix de documents luxembourgeois inédits tirés des Archives de l'État à Bruxelles. Ed. N. van Werveke. PSHIL xl (1889), 149–252.

Chronicles of London. Ed. C. L. Kingsford. Oxford, 1905.

Chroniken der deutschen Städte, Die. Ed. Historische Kommission bei der bayerischen Akademie der Wissenschaften. 37 vols. Leipsig etc., 1862–1931.

Chronique de l'abbaye de Floreffe. Ed. F. A. T. de Reiffenberg. *Monuments pour servir à l'histoire des provinces de Namur, de Hainaut et de Luxembourg,* viii. 63–188. Brussels, 1848.

Chronique de l'abbaye de Liessies. Ed. F. A. T. de Reiffenberg. *Monuments pour servir à l'histoire des provinces de Namur, de Hainaut et de Luxembourg,* vii. 385–436. Brussels, 1847.

Chronique de Lorraine, 1350–1544. Ed. A. Calmet, *Histoire de Lorraine,* vii. cols. v–cl. Nancy, 1757.

Chronique des cordeliers. Ed. L. Douët d'Arcq. E. de Monstrelet, *Chronique,* vi. 191–327. SHF. Paris, 1862.

Chronique des Pays-Bas, de France, d'Angleterre et de Tournai. Ed. J. J. de Smet. *Recueil des chroniques de Flandre,* iii. 115–569. CRH. Brussels, 1856.

Clerc, E. *Essai sur l'histoire de la Franche-Comté,* ii. Besançon, 1846.

——. *Histoire des États Généraux et des libertés publiques en Franche-Comté.* 2 vols. Besançon, 1882.

Cockshaw, P. *Les secrétaires de la chancellerie de Flandre-Bourgogne sous Philippe le Bon.* Unpublished thesis. University of Brussels, 1964.

Codex documentorum sacratissimarum indulgentiarum neerlandicarum. Ed. P. Fredericq. Rijks Geschiedkundige publicatiën, xxi. The Hague, 1922.

Codice diplomatico delle colonie tauro-ligure durante la signoria dell'Ufficio de S. Giorgio, 1453–1475, i. Ed. P. A. Vigna. Atti della Società ligure di storia patria, vi. Genoa, 1868.

Cognasso, F. *Amedeo VIII, 1383–1451.* 2 vols. Turin, 1930.

Collection de documents inédits concernant l'histoire de la Belgique. Ed. L. P. Gachard. 3 vols. Brussels, 1833–5.

Collection des voyages des souverains des Pays-Bas, i. Ed. L. P. Gachard. CRH. Brussels, 1876.

Commines, P. de. *Mémoires*. Ed. D. Godefroy and Lenglet du Fresnoy. 4 vols. Paris, 1747.

Commynes, P. de. *Mémoires*. Ed. Dupont. SHF. 3 vols. Paris, 1840–7.

——. ——. Ed. J. Calmette and G. Durville. CHF. 3 vols. Paris, 1924–5.

Comptes généraux de l'État bourguignon entre 1416 et 1420. Ed. M. Mollat and R. Faureau. Recueil des historiens de la France. Documents financiers, v. 2 vols. Paris, 1965, 1966.

Corps universel diplomatique. Ed. J. Dumont. 8 vols. in 16 parts. Amsterdam and The Hague, 1726–31.

Correspondance de la filiale de Bruges des Medici, i. Ed. A. Grunzweig. CRH. Brussels, 1931.

Correspondance de la mairie de Dijon. Ed. J. Garnier. 3 vols. Dijon, 1868–70.

Cosneau, E. *Le connétable de Richemont, Artur de Bretagne. 1393–1458.* Paris, 1886.

Coutumes de Namur. Ed. J. Grandgagnage and others. Recueil des anciennes coutumes de la Belgique. 3 vols. Brussels, 1869–1955.

Coutumes des pays et comté de Flandre. Coutume de la ville de Bruges. Ed. L. Gilliodts van Severen. Recueil des anciennes coutumes de la Belgique. 2 vols. Brussels, 1874, 1875.

Craeybeckx, J. *Les vins de France aux anciens Pays-Bas.* Paris, 1958.

Cronycke van Hollandt, Zeelandt ende Vrieslant, Die. Leiden, 1517.

Croÿ, Les, conseillers des ducs de Bourgogne. Documents extraits de leurs archives familiales, 1357–1487. Ed. M. R. Thielemans. BCRH cxxiv (1959), 1–141.

Cuvelier, J. *Les dénombrements de foyers en Brabant, xive–xvie siècle.* CRH. 2 vols. Brussels, 1912, 1913.

Dabin, J. 'La politique française à Liège au xve siècle.' BIAL xliii (1913), 99–190.

Daenell, E. 'Holland und die Hanse im 15. Jahrhundert.' HG xi (1903), 1–41.

——. *Die Blütezeit der deutschen Hanse.* 2 vols. Berlin, 1905, 1906.

Dagboek van Gent van 1447 tot 1470. Ed. V. Fris. MVP. 2 vols. Ghent, 1901, 1904.

Dancoine, P. *L'évolution des finances bourguignonnes.* Unpublished thesis, University of Lille, 1957.

Daris, J. *Histoire du diocèse et de la principauté de Liège pendant le xve siècle.* Liège, 1887.

David, H. 'L'hôtel ducal sous Philippe le Bon.' *AB* xxxvii (1965), 241–55.

Degryse, R. 'De Vlaamse haringvisserij in de xve eeuw.' *ASEB* lxxxviii (1951), 116–33.

——. 'De admiraals en de eigen marine van de Bourgondische hertogen, 1384–1488.' *MAMB* xvii (1965), 139–225.

——. 'De Bourgondische expedities naar Rhodos, Constantinopel en Ceuta.' *MAMB* xvii (1965), 227–52.

Delachenal, R. 'Une clause de la paix d'Arras. Les conseillers bourguignons dans le Parlement de Charles VII.' *BSHP* xviii (1891), 76–83.

Delaissé, L. M. J. *Miniatures médiévales de la Librairie de Bourgogne au Cabinet des Manuscrits de la Bibliothèque Royale de Belgique.* Brussels, 1959.

——. *La miniature flamande. Le mécénat de Philippe le Bon.* Brussels, 1959.

Déniau, J. *La commune de Lyon et la guerre bourguignonne, 1417–1435.* Lyons, 1934.

Denis, J. *Journal.* Ed. M. Canat de Chizy. *Documents pour servir à l'histoire de la Bourgogne,* i. Chalon, 1863.

Dépêches des ambassadeurs milanais en France sous Louis XI et François Sforza. Ed. B. de Mandrot and C. Samaran. SHF. 4 vols. Paris, 1916–23.

Derode, V. 'Rôles des dépenses de la Maison de Bourgogne.' *ACFF* vii (1862–4), 283–302 and 383–400.

Deschamps de Pas, L. 'Essai sur l'histoire monétaire des comtes de Flandre de la Maison de Bourgogne. Philippe le Bon.' *RNum* (n.s.) vi (1861), 458–78 and (n.s.) vii (1862), 117–43. See too the 'Supplément à l'essai', *RNum* (n.s.) xi (1866), 172–219.

Desplanque, A. 'Troubles de la châtellenie de Cassel sous Philippe le Bon, 1427–1431.' *ACFF* viii (1864–5), 218–81.

Deuchler, F. *Die Burgunderbeute.* Bern, 1963.

Deutsche Reichstagsakten. Ed. J. Weizsäcker and others. In progress. Munich etc., 1867 onwards.

Devillers, L. 'Les séjours des ducs de Bourgogne en Hainaut, 1427–1482.' *BCRH* (4) vi (1879), 323–468.

Dex, J. *Die Metzer Chronik.* Ed. G. Wolfram. Quellen zur lothringischen Geschichte, iv. Metz, 1906.

Dickinson, J. G. *The Congress of Arras, 1435.* Oxford, 1955.

Diegerick, I. 'Les drapiers Yprois et la conspiration manquée. Épisode de l'histoire d'Ypres, 1428–1429.' *ASEB* xiv (1855–6), 285–310.

Dietze, U. von. *Luxemburg zwischen Deutschland und Burgund, 1383–1443.* Unpublished thesis. University of Göttingen, 1955.

Dion, R. *Histoire de la vigne et du vin en France.* Paris, 1959.

Dixmude, J. van. *Laetste deel der kronyk.* Ed. J. J. de Smet. *Recueil des chroniques de Flandre,* iii. 30–109. CRH. Brussels, 1856.

Dixmude, O. van. *Merkwaerdige gebeurtenissen vooral in Vlaenderen en Brabant van 1377 tot 1443.* Ed. J. J. Lambin. Ypres, 1835.

Documenti ed estratti . . . riguardanti la storia del commercio e della marina ligure, i. *Brabante, Fiandra e Borgogna.* Ed. C. Desimoni and L. T. Belgrano. Atti della Società ligure di storia patria, v. 355–547. Genoa, 1867.

Documents concernant la révolte de Gand contre Philippe le Bon en 1451–1454. Ed. V. Fris. *BSHAG* xxii (1914), 333–452.

Documents pour servir à l'histoire de la Bourgogne, i. Ed. M. Canat de Chizy. Chalon, 1863.

Documents pour servir à l'histoire des relations entre l'Angleterre et la Flandre. Ed. E. Scott and L. Gilliodts van Severen. CRH. Brussels, 1896.

Dogaer, G. 'Des anciens livres des status manuscrits de l'Ordre de la Toison d'Or.' *PCEEBM* v (1963), 65–70.

——. 'Handschriften over de kruistochten in de librije der hertogen van Bourgondië.' *Spiegel historiael* ii (1967), 457–65.

——. and M. Debae. *La Librairie de Philippe le Bon.* Brussels, 1967.

Dognon, P. 'Les Armagnacs et les Bourguignons en Languedoc.' *AM* i (1889), 433–509.

Doorslaer, F. van. 'La chapelle musicale de Philippe le Beau.' *RBAHA* iv (1934), 21–58 and 139–66.

Doutrepont, G. *La littérature française à la cour des ducs de Bourgogne.* Bibliothèque du xve siècle, viii. Paris, 1909.

——. 'La croisade projetée par Philippe le Bon.' *NEBN* xli (1923), 1–28.

——. *Les mises en prose des épopées et des romans chevaleresques du xive au xvie siècle.* MARBL xl. Brussels, 1939.

Drouot, H. 'La personnalité d'Isabelle de Portugal.' *AB* xviii (1946), 142 and xix (1947), 234–5.

Dubois, H. 'L'activité de la saunerie de Salins au xve siècle d'après le compte de 1459.' *MA* lxx (1964), 419–71.

Dubourg, F. 'Le monnoyage des ducs de Bourgogne, 1363–1477.' *PTSEC* (1957), 57–64.

——. 'À propos de l'atelier royal de Dijon.' *AB* xxxiv (1962), 5–45.

Dubrulle, H. *Cambrai à la fin du moyen âge.* Lille, 1904.

Dubrulle, H. *Bullaire de la province de Reims sous le pontificat de Pie II.* Lille, 1905.

Duchein, M. 'Le poète Michault de Caron dit Taillevent.' *PTSEC* (1949), 49–52.

Duclercq, J. *Mémoires.* Ed. J. A. C. Buchon. *Choix de chroniques et mémoires relatifs à l'histoire de France. Jacques du Clercq, Mémoires,* etc., 1–318. Paris, 1875.

Du Fresne de Beaucourt, G. *Histoire de Charles VII.* 6 vols. Paris, 1881–91.

——. 'Lettre de Saint Jean de Capistran au duc de Bourgogne.' *ABSHF* (1864) (2), 160–6.

Dunod, F. *Histoire de l'église, ville et diocèse de Besançon.* 2 vols. Besançon, 1750.

Dupont. *Histoire ecclésiastique et civile de la ville de Cambrai.* 3 vols. Cambrai, 1759–67.

Durrieu, P. *La miniature flamande au temps de la cour de Bourgogne.* Paris, 1931.

Du Teil, P. M. J. *Guillaume Fillastre.* Paris, 1920.

Duverger, A. 'Une page de l'histoire des franchises communales sous Philippe le Bon.' *BCRH* (4) vi (1879), 139–46.

——. *Le premier grand procès de sorcellerie aux Pays-Bas. La vauderie dans les États de Philippe le Bon.* Arras, 1885.

Dynter, E. de. *Chronique des ducs de Brabant.* Ed. P. de Ram. CRH. 3 vols. Brussels, 1854–7.

English chronicle of the reigns of Richard II, Henry IV, Henry V and Henry VI, An. Ed. J. S. Davies. Camden Society. London, 1856.

Escouchy, M. de. *Chronique.* Ed. G. du Fresne de Beaucourt. SHF. 3 vols. Paris, 1863–4.

Extraits analytiques des anciens registres des consaux de la ville de Tournai. 1385–1422. Ed. H. Vandenbroek. Tournai, 1861.

——. *1422–1430.* Ed. H. Vandenbroek. Tournai, 1863.

——. *1431–1476.* Ed. A. de la Grange. Mémoires de la Société historique et littéraire de Tournai, xxiii. Tournai, 1893.

Fauquembergue, C. de. *Journal.* Ed. A. Tuetey. SHF. 3 vols. Paris, 1903–15.

Faussemagne, J. *L'apanage ducal de Bourgogne dans ses rapports avec la monarchie française, 1363–1477.* Lyon, 1937.

Fenin, P. de. *Mémoires.* Ed. L. M. E. Dupont. SHF. Paris, 1837.

Fierville, C. *Le cardinal Jean Jouffroy et son temps. 1412–1473.* Paris, 1874.

Fillastre, G. *Histoire de la Toison d'Or.* Paris, 1517.

Finot, J. *Projet d'expédition contre les Turcs préparée par les conseillers du duc de Bourgogne Philippe le Bon. MSSL* (4) xxi (1895), 161–206.

——. *L'artillerie bourguignonne à la bataille de Montlhéry. MSSL* (5) v. Lille, 1896.

——. 'Relations commerciales et maritimes entre la Flandre et l'Espagne au moyen âge.' *ACFF* xxiv (1898), 1–353. Reprinted as *Étude historique sur les relations commerciales entre la Flandre et l'Espagne au moyen âge.* Paris, 1899.

——. 'Étude historique sur les relations commerciales entre la Flandre et la république de Gênes au moyen âge.' *ACFF* xxviii (1906–7). Reprinted, Paris, 1906.

Flamare, H. de. *Le Nivernais pendant la Guerre de Cent Ans.* Paris, 1913.

Fliche, A. and V. Martin. *Histoire de l'Église*, xiv. *L'Église au temps du Grand Schisme et de la crise conciliaire.* Paris, 1962.

Foedera, conventiones, etc. Ed. T. Rymer. 20 vols. London, 1704–35.

Fohlen, C. *Histoire de Besançon.* 2 vols. Paris, 1964, 1965.

Foster Kirk, J. *History of Charles the Bold.* 3 vols. London, 1863–8.

Fragment d'une chronique du règne de Louis XI. Ed. A. Coulon. *Mélanges d'archéologie et d'histoire. École française de Rome*, xv (1895), 103–40.

Franz, F. *Die Schlacht bei Montlhéry.* Berlin, 1893.

Frederichs, J. 'Le Grand Conseil ambulatoire des ducs de Bourgogne et des archiducs d'Autriche, 1446–1504.' *BCRH* (4) xvii (1890), 423–99.

——. 'Seconde suite à ma notice sur le Grand Conseil des ducs de Bourgogne.' *BCRH* (5) ii (1892), 124–8.

Frédéricq, P. *Essai sur le rôle politique et social des ducs de Bourgogne dans les Pays-Bas.* Ghent, 1875.

Frederiks, J. G. 'Het geheim huwelijk van Gravin Jacoba.' *BVGO* (3) viii (1894), 47–70.

Fréminville, J. de. *Les écorcheurs en Bourgogne, 1435–1445. MAD* (3) x (1887).

Fris, V. 'Onderzoek der bronnen van den opstand der Gentenaars tegen Philip den Goede, 1449–53.' *BSHAG* viii (1900), 212–43.

——. 'De onlusten te Gent in 1432–1435.' *BSHAG* viii (1900), 163–73.

——. 'Een strijd om het dekenschap te Gent in 1447.' *BSHAG* xi (1903), 74–89.

——. 'Documents gantois concernant la levée du siège de Calais en 1436.' *Mélanges Paul Frédéricq*, 245–58. Brussels, 1904.

——. 'La bataille de Gavre, 23 juillet 1453.' *BSHAG* xviii (1910), 185–233.

——. *Histoire de Gand.* Brussels, 1913.

Fyot, E. 'Complot de la Trémoille contre le chancelier Rolin.' *MCACO* xiv (1901-5), 103-12.

Gachard, L. P. *Rapport sur les archives à Lille*. Brussels, 1841.

——. *Rapport sur les archives de Dijon*. Brussels, 1843.

——. 'Les archives royales de Düsseldorf; notice des documents qui concement l'histoire de Belgique'. *BCRM* (4) ix (1881), 267-366.

——. *Études et notices historiques concernant l'histoire des Pays Bas*. 3 vols. Brussels, 1890.

Gade, J. A. *Luxembourg in the Middle Ages*. Leiden, 1951.

Gail, A. 'Die burgundische Ausdehnungspolitik und das Herzogtum Jülich im 14. und 15. Jahrhundert.' *Aus Mittelalter und Neuzeit. Festschrift für Gerhard Kallen*, 145-53. Bonn, 1947.

Gaillard, A. 'L'origine du Grand Conseil et du Conseil Privé.' *BCRH* (5) vi (1896), 267-324.

——. *Le conseil de Brabant*. 3 vols. Brussels, 1898-1902.

Galesloot, L. 'Revendication du duché de Brabant par l'Empereur Sigismund, 1414-1437.' *BCRH* (4) v (1878), 437-70.

Garnier, J. *La recherche des feux en Bourgogne au xive et xve siècles*. Dijon, 1876.

——. *L'artillerie des ducs de Bourgogne*. Paris, 1895.

Gaspar, C. and F. Lyna. *Philippe le Bon et ses beaux livres*. Brussels, 1944.

Gauthier, J. 'Documents inédits sur la bataille de Gavre et la capitulation de Gand, 22-23 juillet 1453.' *RSS* (7) vi (1882), 209-13.

Gedenkwaardigheden uit de geschiedenis van Gelderland. Ed. J. A. Nijhoff. 6 vols. Arnhem and The Hague, 1830-75.

Gelder, H. E. van. 'Aantekeningen bij de Vlaamse muntslag, 1384-1434.' *RBN* cvii (1961), 137-56.

Geoffroy, P. 'Commerce et marchands à Dijon au xve siècle.' *AB* xxv (1953), 161-81.

Germain, J. *Liber de virtutibus Philippi, Burgundiae et Brabantiae ducis*. Ed. Kervyn de Lettenhove. *Chroniques relatives à l'histoire de la Belgique sous la domination des ducs de Bourgogne. Textes latins*, 1-115. CRH. Brussels, 1876.

Geschiedenis van Vlaanderen. Ed. R. van Roosbroeck and others. 6 vols. Amsterdam, 1936-49.

Geste des nobles françoys. Ed. Vallet de Viriville. *Chronique de la Pucelle*, 87-204. Paris, 1864.

Gilissen, J. 'Les États Généraux des pays de par deça, 1464-1632.' *APAE* xxxiii (1965), 261-321.

Gill, J. *The Council of Florence*. Cambridge, 1959.

Gondry, G. H. *Mémoire historique sur les grands baillis de Hainaut.* *MPSALH* (4) x (1888), 1–247.

Gorissen, P. 'De historiographie van het Gulden Vlies.' *BGN* vi (1951–2), 218–24.

Gottschalk, K. E. *Historische Geografie van westelijk Zeeuws-Vlaanderen*, ii. Assen, 1958.

Grands traités de la guerre de Cent Ans, Les. Ed. E. Cosneau. Paris, 1889.

Gras, P. *Palais des Ducs et Palais des États de Bourgogne*. Dijon, 1956.

Groot charterboek der graven van Holland, van Zeeland en heeren van Vriesland, iv. Ed. F. van Mieris. Leiden, 1756.

Gross, L. 'Ein Versuch Herzog Friedrichs von Tirol zur Erwerbung von Brabant.' *MIOG* xli (1926), 150–8.

Gruel, G. *Chronique d'Arthur de Richemont*. Ed. A. le Vavasseur. SHF. Paris, 1890.

Grüneisen, H. 'Die westliche Reichstände in der Auseinandersetzung zwishen dem Reich, Burgund und Frankreich bis 1473.' *RV* xxvi (1961), 22–77.

Grunzweig, A. 'Quatre lettres autographes de Philippe le Bon.' *RBPH* iv (1925), 431–7.

——. 'Un plan d'acquisition de Gênes par Philippe le Bon, 1445.' *MA* xlii (1932), 81–110.

——. 'Le roi d'armes des Ruyers.' *RBPH* xxv (1946–7), 343.

——. 'Namur et le début de la Guerre du Bien Public.' *Études d'histoire et d'archéologie namuroises dédiées à Ferdinand Courtoy*, 531–64. Publication extra-ordinaire de la Société archéologique de Namur. Namur, 1952.

——. 'Philippe le Bon et Constantinople.' *Byzantion* xxiv (1954), 47–61.

——. 'Le Grand Duc du Ponant.' *MA* lxii (1956), 119–65.

——. 'Correction d'un passage des "Mémoires" de Comines.' *MA* lxxii (1966), 511–30.

Guichenon, S. *Histoire généalogique de la royale Maison de Savoie*. 4 vols. Turin, 1778–80.

Gysels, G. 'Le départ de Jacqueline de Bavière de la cour de Brabant, 11 avril 1420.' *Miscellanea historica in honorem L. van der Essen*. Brussels, 1947.

Halecki, O. 'Gilbert de Lannoy and his discovery of East Central Europe.' *BPIAA* ii (1943–4), 314–31.

Hansen, J. *Westfalen und Rheinland im 15. Jahrhundert*. 2 vols. Leipzig, 1888, 1890.

Hanserecesse. Die Recesse und andere Akten der Hansetage von 1256 bis 1430. Ed. K. Koppmann. 8 vols. Leipzig, 1870–97.

——. *Von 1431 bis 1476.* Ed. G. von der Rupp. 7 vols. Leipzig, 1876–92.

Hansisches Urkundenbuch. Ed. K. Höhlbaum and others. 11 vols. Halle, Leipzig, etc., 1876–1939.

Hautcoeur, E. *Histoire de l'église collégiale et du chapitre de Saint-Pierre de Lille.* 3 vols. Lille, 1896–9.

Haynin, J. de. *Mémoires.* Ed. D. Brouwers. 2 vols. Liège, 1905, 1906.

Heimpel, H. 'Karl der Kühne und der burgundische Staat.' *Festschrift Gerhard Ritter,* 140–60. Tübingen, 1950.

Helbig, H. 'Fürsten und Landstände im Westen des Reiches im Übergang vom Mittelalter zur Neuzeit.' *RV* xxix (1964), 32–72.

Héliot, P. and A. Benoit. 'Georges de la Trémoille et la mainmise du duc de Bourgogne sur le Boulonnais.' *RN* xxiv (1938), 29–45.

Herbomez, A. d'. 'Le traité de 1430 entre Charles VII et le duc d'Autriche.' *RQH* xxxi (1882), 150–8.

Heuterus, P. *Rerum burgundicarum libri sex.* Antwerp, 1584.

Hexter, J. H. 'The education of the aristocracy in the Renaissance.' *JMH* xxii (1950), 1–20.

Hillard, D. *Les relations diplomatiques entre Charles VII et Philippe le Bon de 1435 à 1445.'* Unpublished thesis. Paris, École des Chartes, 1963.

——. 'Les relations diplomatiques entre Charles VII et Philippe le Bon de 1435 à 1445.' *PTSEC* (1963), 81–5.

Hintzen, J. D. *De kruistochtplannen van Philips den Goede.* Rotterdam, 1918.

Hirschauer, C. *Les États d'Artois de leur origines à l'occupation française, 1340–1640.* 2 vols. Paris, 1923.

Historia Gelriae auctore anonymo. Ed. J. G. C. Joosting. Arnhem, 1902.

Historical poems of the xivth and xvth centuries. Ed. R. H. Robbins. New York, 1959.

Historischen Volkslieder der Deutschen, Die. Ed. R. von Liliencron. 4 vols. Leipzig, 1865–9.

Hommel, L. *Chastellain.* Brussels, 1945.

——. *L'histoire du noble ordre de la Toison d'Or.* Brussels, 1947.

Houtart, M. *Les Tournaisiens et le roi de Bourges.* Tournai, 1908.

Houtte, J. A. van. *Bruges. Essai d'histoire urbaine.* Brussels, 1967.

Hozotte, M. A. 'Philippe le Bon et les institutions judiciaires, financières et militaires en Franche-Comté.' *PTSEC* (1934), 71–81.

Huguet, A. *Aspects de la Guerre de Cent Ans en Picardie maritime, 1400–1450*. 2 vols. Mémoires de la Société des antiquaires de Picardie, xlviii and l. Amiens, 1941, 1944.

Huizinga, J. *The Waning of the middle ages*. London, 1924. Translated from *Herfsttij der Middeleeuwen*. Haarlem, 1919.

——. 'La physionomie morale de Philippe le Bon.' *Verzamelde werken*, ii. 216–37. Haarlem, 1948. Reprinted from *AB* iv (1932), 101–39.

Hulin, G. 'Guy Guilbaut, conseiller, trésorier et gouverneur-général de toutes les finances de Philippe le Bon, et premier maître de la chambre des comptes de Lille.' *BSHAG* xix (1911), 329–41.

Hullu, J. de. *Bijdrage tot de geschiedenis van het Utrechtsche schisma*. The Hague, 1892.

Humbert, A. *La sculpture sous les ducs de Bourgogne, 1361–1483*. Paris, 1913.

Humbert, F. *Les finances municipales de Dijon du milieu du xive siècle à 1477*. Dijon, 1961.

Huydts, G. 'Le premier chambellan des ducs de Bourgogne.' *Mélanges d'histoire offerts à Henri Pirenne*, 263–70. Brussels, 1926.

IAB. L. Gilliodts van Severen. *Inventaire des archives de la ville de Bruges, 13e–16e siècle*. 7 vols. Bruges, 1871–8.

IAC. C. Mussely. *Inventaire des archives de la ville de Courtrai*. 2 vols. Courtrai, 1854, 1858.

IACB. M. Prinet and others. *Inventaire sommaire des archives communales. Série BB. Ville de Besançon*, i. Besançon, 1912.

IACD. L. de Gouvenain and others. *Inventaire sommaire des archives communales de Dijon*. 5 vols. Dijon, 1867–1900.

IACOB. C. Rossignol and others. *Inventaire sommaire des archives départementales de la Côte d'Or. Série B*. 6 vols. Dijon, 1863–94.

IADB. J. Gauthier. *Inventaire sommaire des archives départementales du Doubs. Série B*. 3 vols. Besançon, 1883–95.

IADNB. A. le Glay and others. *Inventaire sommaire des archives départementales du Nord. Série B*. 10 vols. Lille, 1863–1906.

IAEG. C. Wyffels. *Inventaris van de oorkonden der graven van Vlaanderen*. Ghent, no date.

IAEH. L. Devillers. *Inventaire analytique des archives des États de Hainaut*. 3 vols. Mons, 1884–1906.

IAG. P. van Duyse. *Inventaire analytique des chartes et documents de la ville de Gand*. 3 vols. Ghent, 1849–57.

IAGRCC. L. P. Gachard and others. *Inventaire des archives des chambres des comptes*. 6 vols. Brussels, 1837–1931.

IAM. P. J. van Doren. *Inventaire des archives de la ville de Malines.* 8 vols. Malines, 1859–94.

IAY. I. L. A. Diegerick. *Inventaire analytique des chartes et documents appartenant aux archives de la ville de Ypres.* 7 vols. Bruges, 1853–68.

ICL. A. Verkooren. *Inventaire des chartes et cartulaires du Luxembourg.* 5 vols. Brussels, 1914–21.

Inventaire de la 'librairie' de Philippe le Bon, 1420. Ed. G. Doutrepont. CRH. Brussels, 1906.

Isenburg, W. K. P. von. *Stammtafeln zur Geschichte der Europäischen Staaten.* 4 vols. Marburg, 1961–5.

Jansma, T. S. *Raad en Rekenkamer in Holland en Zeeland tijdens Philips van Bourgondië. BIMGU* xviii. Utrecht, 1932.

——. 'De voorgeschiedenis van de instructie voor het Hof van Holland.' *TG* xlix (1934), 444–53 and li (1936), 401–19.

——. 'Het oproer te Rotterdam, 1439, een tijdverschijnsel.' *TG* liii (1938), 337–65.

——. 'Het vraagstuk van Hollands welvaren tijdens hertog Philips van Bourgondië.' Gröningen, 1950. Reprinted in *Economisch-Historische Herdrukken. Zeventien studien van Nederlanders. Het Nederlandsch Economisch-Historisch Archief,* 55–73. The Hague, 1964.

——. 'Philippe le Bon et la guerre hollando-wende, 1438–1441.' *RN* xlii (1960), 5–18.

Jongkees, A. G. *Staat en kerk in Holland en Zeeland onder de Bourgondische hertogen, 1425–1477. BIMGU* xxi. Groningen, 1942.

——. 'Philips de Goede, het concilie van Bazel en de Heilige Stoel.' *TG* lviii (1943), 198–215.

——. *Het koninkrijk Friesland in de vijftiende eeuw.* Groningen, 1946.

——. 'Holland en der Gentse oorlog van 1452–1453.' *Handelingen van het zeventiende Vlaamse Filologen-Congress,* 63–7. Louvain, 1947.

——. 'De Pragmatieke Sanctie van Bourges in de Bourgondische landen. Het geval van de Sint-Baafsabdij bij Gent.' *Postillen . . . aangeboden Prof. Dr. R. R. Post,* 139–53. Nijmegen, 1964.

——. 'Philippe le Bon et la Pragmatique Sanction de Bourges.' *AB* xxxviii (1966), 161–71.

Jorga, N. *Notes et extraits pour servir à l'histoire des croisades au xve siècle. Troisième série.* Paris, 1902.

——. *Les aventures 'sarrazines' des français de Bourgogne au xve siècle.* Cluj, 1926.

José, M. *La Maison de Savoie. Amédée VIII.* 2 vols. Paris, 1962.

Jouffroy, J. *Ad Pium papam II de Philippo duce Burgundiae oratio.* Ed. Kervyn de Lettenhove. *Chroniques relatives à l'histoire de la Belgique sous la domination des ducs de Bourgogne. Textes latins,* 117–206. CRH. Brussels, 1876.

Journal d'un bourgeois de Paris, 1405–1449. Ed. A. Tuetey. Paris, 1881.

Juvenel des Ursins, J. *Histoire de Charles VI.* Ed. J. A. C. Buchon. *Choix de chroniques et mémoires relatifs à l'histoire de France. Anonyme chronique de du Guesclin, etc.,* 323–573. Paris, 1875.

Kauch, P. 'Le Trésor d'Épargne, création de Philippe le Bon.' *RBPH* ix (1932), 703–19.

——. 'Note sur l'organisation matérielle de la chambre des comptes de Bruxelles, 1404–1473.' *BSAB* (1945), 15–22.

Keen, M. H. *The Laws of War in the Late Middle Ages.* London, 1965.

Kerling, N. J. M. *Commercial relations of Holland and Zeeland with England from the late thirteenth century to the close of the middle ages.* Leiden, 1954.

Kervyn de Lettenhove. *Histoire de Flandre.* 6 vols. Brussels, 1847–50.

——. 'Programme d'un gouvernement constitutionnel en Belgique au xve siècle.' *BARB* (2) xiv (1862), 218–50.

——. *La Toison d'Or. Notes sur l'institution et l'histoire de l'Ordre, 1429–1559.* Brussels, 1907.

Ketner, F. *Handel en scheepvaart van Amsterdam in de vijftiende eeuw.* Leiden, 1946.

Kleinclausz, A. *Claus Sluter et la sculpture bourguignonne au xve siècle.* Paris, 1906.

Knetsch, K. *Des Hauses Hessen Ansprüche auf Brabant.* Marburg, 1915.

Knowlson, G. A. *Jean V duc de Bretagne et l'Angleterre.* Cambridge, 1964.

Kraus, V. von and K. Kaser. *Deutsche Geschichte im Ausgange des Mittelalters,* i. *1438–1486.* Stuttgart, 1905.

Krause, G. *Beziehungen zwischen Habsburg und Burgund bis zum Ausgang der Trierer Zusammenkunft im Jahre 1473.* Göttingen, 1876.

Kronyk van Vlaenderen van 580 tot 1467. Ed. P. Blommaert and C. P. Serrure. MVP. 2 vols. Ghent, 1839, 1840.

Kurth, G. *La cité de Liège au moyen âge.* 3 vols. Brussels, 1910.

Laborde, L. de. *Les ducs de Bourgogne. Études sur les lettres etc.* 3 vols. Paris, 1849–52.

La Broquière, B. de. *Voyage d'Outremer.* Ed. C. Schefer. Recueil de voyages et de documents pour servir à l'histoire de la géographie, xii. Paris, 1892.

Lacaze, Y. *Jean Germain.* Unpublished thesis. Paris, École des Chartes, 1958.

——. 'Un representant de la polémique anti-musulmane au xvᵉ siècle. Jean Germain, évêque de Nevers et de Chalon-sur-Saône.' *PTSEC* (1958), 67–75.

——. 'Philippe le Bon et les terres d'Empire, la diplomatie bourguignonne à l'œuvre en 1454–1455.' *AB* xxxvi (1964), 81–121.

——. 'Une page d'histoire marseillaise au xvᵉ siècle: l'incident vénéto-bourguignon de Porto Conte et ses suites, 1448.' *PH* lvii (1964), 221–42.

——. 'Les débuts de Jean Germain.' *MSHAC* xxxix (1968), 1–24.

——. 'Philippe le Bon et le problème hussite: Un projet de croisade bourguignon en 1428–1429.' *RH* ccxli (1969), 69–98.

Laenen, J. *Les archives de l'État à Vienne au point de vue de l'histoire de Belgique.* CRH. Brussels, 1924.

——. *Geschiedenis van Mechelen tot op het einde der middeleeuwen.* 2nd edn. Malines, 1934.

Lagrange, A. de. 'Itinéraires d'Isabelle de Portugal.' *ACFF* xlii (1938).

La Marche, O. de. *Mémoires.* Ed. H. Beaune and J. d'Arbaumont. SHF. 4 vols. Paris, 1883–8.

Lambin, J. J. 'Reddition de Zevenbergen à Philippe le Bon, duc de Bourgogne.' *MSAB* v (1837), 13–16.

Lambrecht, D. 'Centralisatie onder de Bourgondiërs. Van audiëntie naar Parlement van Mechelen.' *BGN* xx (1965–6), 83–109.

Lameere, E. *Le grand conseil des ducs de Bourgogne de la Maison de Valois.* Brussels, 1900.

Lannoy, B. de. *Hugues de Lannoy.* Brussels, 1957.

——. and G. Dansaert. *Jean de Lannoy le Bâtisseur, 1410–1492.* Paris, 1937.

Lannoy, G. de. *Œuvres.* Ed. C. Potvin, Louvain, 1878.

Laroche, L. 'Les États particuliers du Charolais.' *MSHDB* vi (1939), 145–94.

La Taverne, A. de. *Journal de la paix d'Arras, 1435.* Ed. A. Bossuat. Arras, 1936.

Lavirotte, C. 'Odette de Champdivers à Dijon.' *MAD* (2) ii (1852–3), 147–66.

Le Blant, E. *Les quatre mariages de Jacqueline duchesse en Bavière.* Paris, 1904.

Le Bouvier, G., dit le Héraut Berry. *Les cronicques du feu roy Charles septiesme du nom.* Ed. D. Godefroy. *Histoire de Charles VII*, 369–480. Paris, 1661.

Leclercq, M. *La politique navale méditerranéene de Philippe le Bon*. Unpublished thesis. University of Lille, 1958.

Lecoy de la Marche, A. *Le roi René*. 2 vols. Paris, 1875.

Le Févre, J., lord of St. Rémy. *Chronique*. Ed. F. Morand. SHF. 2 vols. Paris, 1876, 1881.

Leguai, A. 'Dijon et Louis XI, 1461–1483.' *AB* xvii (1945), 16–37, 103–115, 145–69 and 239–63.

——. *Les ducs de Bourbon pendant la crise monarchique du xve siècle*. Paris, 1962.

Lemaire, L. 'La mort de Philippe le Bon, duc de Bourgogne.' *RN* i (1910), 321–6.

Leman, A. 'La cour des ducs de Bourgogne à Lille.' *LFCL* xiii (1922–3), 293–306.

Lemmink, F. H. J. *Het ontstaan van de Staten van Zeeland en hun geschiedenis tot het jaar 1555*. Rosendaal, 1951.

Lenain, L. 'L'Église et l'État au temps des ducs de Bourgogne.' *RDT* (1953), 46–52.

Leroux, A. *Nouvelles recherches critiques sur les relations politiques de la France avec l'Allemagne de 1378 à 1461*. Paris, 1892.

Lespinasse, R. de. *Le Nivernais et les comtes de Nevers*, iii. *Maison de Bourgogne, 1384–1491*. Paris, 1914.

Lestocquoy, J. *Les Évêques d'Arras*. MCMP iv (1). Arras, 1942.

Letters and Papers Illustrative of the Wars of the English in France During the Reign of Henry VI. Ed. J. Stevenson. RS. 3 vols. London, 1861, 1864.

Lettres de Louis XI roi de France. Ed. J. Vaesen and E. Charavay. SHF. 12 vols. Paris, 1883–1909.

Lettres et mandements de Jean V, duc de Bretagne. Ed. R. Blanchard. Société des bibliophiles bretons. Archives de Bretagne, vols. iv–viii. 5 vols. Nantes, 1889–95.

Lettres et négotiations de Philippe de Commines. Ed. Kervyn de Lettenhove. 2 vols. Brussels, 1867, 1868.

Lettres, mémoires, instructions et autres documents relatifs à la guerre du Bien Public en l'année 1465. Ed. J. Quicherat. CDIHF. Mélanges historiques. Documents historiques inédits tirées des collections manuscrits de la Bibliothèque Royale, ii (2), 194–470. Paris, 1843.

Lewis, P. S. 'The failure of the medieval French Estates.' *Past and Present* xxiii (1962), 3–24.

Libelle of Englyshe Polycye, The. Ed. G. Warner. Oxford, 1926.

Liber Karoleidos. Ed. Kervyn de Lettenhove. *Chroniques relatives à l'histoire de la Belgique sous la domination des ducs de Bourgogne. Textes latins.* CRH. Brussels, 1876.

Lichtervelde, P. de. *Un grand commis des ducs de Bourgogne. Jacques de Lichtervelde.* Brussels, 1943.

Liebenau, T. von. *Die Beziehungen der Eidgenossenschaft zum Auslande in den Jahren 1447 bis 1459. Der Geschichtsfreund. Mitteilungen des historischen Vereins der fünf Orte Luzern, Uri, Schwyz, Unterwalden und Zug,* xxxii (1877), 1–106.

Lièvre, L. *La monnaie et le change en Bourgogne sous les ducs Valois.* Dijon, 1929.

Lippens, H. 'Saint-Jean de Capistran en mission aux États bourguignons, 1442–1443.' *AFH* xxv (1942), 113–32 and 254–95.

Lippert, W. 'La Bourgogne et la Saxe, 1451–1454.' *MSE* (n.s.) xxv (1897), 1–44.

Livre des faits du bon chevalier Messire Jacques de Lalaing, Le. Ed. Kervyn de Lettenhove. G. Chastellain, *Œuvres,* viii. 1–259. Brussels, 1866.

Livre des trahisons de France, Le. Ed. Kervyn de Lettenhove. *Chroniques relatives à l'histoire de Belgique sous la domination des ducs de Bourgogne. Textes français,* 1–258. CRH. Brussels, 1873.

Löher, F. von. 'Kaiser Sigmund und Herzog Philipp von Burgund.' *Münchner historisches Jahrbuch für 1866,* 305–419.

——. *Jacobäa von Bayern und ihre Zeit.* 2 vols. Nördlingen, 1862, 1869.

——. *Beiträge zur Geschichte der Jakobäa von Bayern.* 2 vols. Abhandlungen der historischen Classe der königlich bayerischen Akademie der Wissenschaften, x (1867), 1–111 and 207–336.

Looten, C. 'Isabelle de Portugal, duchesse de Bourgogne et comtesse de Flandre, 1397–1471.' *RLC* xviii (1938), 5–22.

Los, J. de. *Chronique.* Ed. P. de Ram. *Documents relatifs aux troubles du pays de Liège sous les princes-évêques Louis de Bourbon et Jean de Horne, 1455–1505,* 1–132. CRH. Brussels, 1844.

Lot, F. and R. Fawtier. *Histoire des institutions françaises au moyen âge.* i. *Institutions seigneuriales.* Paris, 1957.

Lousse, E. 'Portugal, Bourgogne, Angleterre au XVe siècle. Henri le Navigateur, Isabelle de Portugal et Philippe le Bon.' *La Nation Belge,* nos. 21–32 (1961–2).

Lousse, E. and others. *Assemblées d'États.* Louvain, 1965.

Mandrot, B. de. 'Les relations de Charles VII et de Louis XI rois de France avec les cantons suisses, 1444–83.' *JSG* v (1880), 59–182 and vi (1881), 203–77. Reprinted separately, Zurich, 1881.

Mandrot, B. de. 'Jean de Bourgogne, duc de Brabant, comte de Nevers et le procès de sa succession.' *RH* xciii (1907), 1–45.

Marc, J. 'L'avènement du chancelier Rolin, décembre 1422.' *MSBGH* xxi (1905), 323–78.

Marinesco, C. 'Philippe le Bon, duc de Bourgogne, et la croisade, ii. 1453–1467.' *BEP* (n.s.) xiii (1949), 3–28.

——. 'Notes sur quelques ambassadeurs byzantins en Occident à la veille de la chute de Constantinople sous les Turcs.' *AIPHOS* x (1950), 419–28.

——. 'Philippe le Bon, duc de Bourgogne, et la croisade, i. 1419–1453.' *Actes du VIᵉ Congrès international des études byzantines*, 149–68. Paris, 1950.

——. 'Les origines de la Toison d'Or et du Voeu du Faisan, 1454.' *Le Flambeau* xxxix (1956), 382–4.

——. 'Documents espagnols inédits concernant la fondation de l'Ordre de la Toison d'Or.' *CRAIBL* (1956), 401–17.

Marix, J. *Les musiciens de la cour de Bourgogne au xvᵉ siècle*. Paris, 1937.

——. *Histoire de la musique et des musiciens de la cour de Bourgogne sous le règne de Philippe le Bon*. Strasbourg, 1939.

Marle, R. van. *Le comté de Hollande sous Philippe le Bon*. The Hague, 1908.

Marot, P. 'Notes sur l'intrusion bourguignonne en Lorraine au xvᵉ siècle. Les Neufchâtel et la Maison d'Anjou.' *Annales de l'Est* xliv (1930), 21–36.

Marquant, E. *La vie économique à Lille sous Philippe le Bon*. Paris, 1940.

Martens, M. 'La correspondance de caractère économique échangée par Francesco Sforza, duc de Milan, et Philippe le Bon, duc de Bourgogne, 1450–1466.' *BIHBR* xxvii (1952), 221–34.

Maschke, E. 'Burgund und der preussische Ordenstaat. Ein Beitrag zur Einheit der ritterlichen Kultur Europas im späteren Mittelalter.' *Syntagma Friburgense. Historische Studien, Hermann Aubin zum 70. Geburtstag dargebracht*, 147–72. Constance, 1956.

Materialen zur österreichischen Geschichte. Ed. J. Chmel. 2 vols. Vienna, 1837, 1838.

Matthieu, A. 'Histoire du conseil de Flandre.' *AAAB* xxxv (1879), 171–460.

Matthieu, E. 'La reconnaissance par les États de Hainaut de Charles le Téméraire comme héritier du comté en 1465.' *BCRH* (4) xiii (1886), 225–42.

——. 'Les doléances du pays de Hainaut en 1450.' *BSBB* i (2) (1909), 38–45.

Maupoint, J. *Journal parisien*. Ed. G. Fagniez. *MSHP* iv (1877).

Mazeran, G. 'Essai sur la politique religieuse de Philippe le Bon dans les Pays-Bas.' *PTSEC* (1910), 147–51.

Meilink, P. A. 'Holland en het conflikt tusschen Philips de Goede en zijn zoon, 1463–1464,' *BVGO* (7) v (1935), 129–52 and (7) vi (1935), 49–66.

——. 'Dagvaarten van de Staten-Generaal, 1427–1477.' *BGN* v (1950), 198–212.

Mémoires pour servir à l'histoire de France et de Bourgogne. 2 vols. Paris, 1729.

Memorialen van het Hof van Holland, Zeeland en West-Friesland, van den secretaris Jan Rosa. Ed. A. S. de Blécourt and E. M. Meijers. Vols. i–iii. Rechtshistorisch Instituut, Leiden. Haarlem, 1929.

Memorieboek der stad Ghent. Ed. P. J. van der Meersch. MVP (2) xv. 4 vols. Ghent, 1852–64.

Merica, H. de. *De cladibus Leodensium*. Ed. S. Balau. *Chroniques liégeoises*, i. 221–308. CRH. Brussels, 1913.

Mirot, A. 'Charles VII et ses conseillers assassins présumés de Jean sans Peur.' *AB* xiv (1942), 197–210.

Mirot, L. 'L'État bourguignon-flamand au xvᵉ siècle.' *JS* (1942), 66–81.

Mitchell, R. J. *The Laurels and the Tiara. Pope Pius II, 1458–1464*. London, 1962.

Mollat, M. 'Recherches sur les finances des ducs Valois de Bourgogne.' *RH* ccxix (1958), 285–321.

Monget, C. *La Chartreuse de Dijon*. 3 vols. Montreuil-sur-Mer and Tournai, 1898–1905.

Monstrelet, E. de. *Chronique*. Ed. L. Douët d'Arcq. SHF. 6 vols. Paris, 1857–62. English translation by T. Johnes. 2 vols. London, 1840.

Moreau, P. E. de. *Histoire de l'église en Belgique*. 5 vols. Brussels, 1940–52.

Morembert, H. T. de. 'Jean Chevrot, évêque de Tournai et de Toul, vers 1395–1460.' *MAM* cxlv (1963–4), 171–220.

Morosini, A. *Chronique. Extraits relatifs à l'histoire de France*. Ed. and transl. G. Lefèvre-Pontalis and L. Dorez. SHF. 4 vols. Paris, 1898–9.

Muller, J. 'La représentation populaire dans le comté de Namur au début du xvᵉ siècle.' *Études d'histoire et d'archéologie namuroises dédiées à Ferdinand Courtoy*, 483–98. Publication extra-ordinaire de la Société archéologique de Namur. Namur, 1952.

Nelis, H. *Catalogue des chartes du Sceau de l'Audience*, i. Brussels, 1915.

——. 'Bâtards de Brabant et bâtards de Bourgogne.' *RBPH* i (1) (1922), 337–42.

Nelis, H. 'Fragment d'un registre de correspondance politique de Philippe le Bon.' *RBPH* x (1931), 594–605.

Niermeyer, J. F. 'Een vijftiende eeuwse handelsoorlog. Dordrecht contra de bovenlandse steden, 1442–1445.' *BMHGU* lxvi (1948), 1–59.

Nieuwe oorkonden betreffende den opstand van Gent tegen Philips den Goede. Ed. V. Fris. *ASHAG* vii (1906–7), 179–219.

Noomen, W., ed. *La traduction française de la Chronographia Johannis de Beka.* The Hague, 1954.

Odlozilik, O. *The Hussite king. Bohemia in European affairs, 1440–1471.* New Brunswick, 1965.

Oorkonden betreffende den opstand van Gent tegen Philips den Goede, 1450–1453. Ed. V. Fris. *ASHAG* iv (1901–2), 55–146.

Ordonnances des ducs de Bourgogne sur l'administration de la justice du duché. Ed. E. Champeaux. *RB* xvii (2, 3) (1907).

Ordonnances des rois de France de la troisième race. Ed. D. F. Secousse and others. 21 vols. Paris, 1723–1849.

Ordonnances franc-comtoises sur l'administration de la justice, 1343–1477. Ed. E. Champeaux. *RB* xxii (1, 2) (1912).

Oudegherst, P. d'. *Les chroniques et annales de Flandres.* Antwerp, 1571.

Oudenbosch, A. d'. *Chronique.* Ed. C. de Borman. Liège, 1902.

Particularités curieuses sur Jacqueline de Bavière, comtesse de Hainaut. Ed. A. Decourtray and L. Devillers. Société des bibliophiles belges. 2 vols. Mons, 1838, 1879.

Paston Letters, The. Ed. J. Gairdner. 4 vols. London, 1896–1900.

Pauwels, T. *Alia narratio de ducibus Burgundiae.* Ed. Kervyn de Lettenhove. *Chroniques relatives à l'histoire de la Belgique sous la domination des ducs de Bourgogne. Textes latins,* 264–328. CRH. Brussels, 1876.

——. *Historia de cladibus Leodensium.* Ed. P. de Ram. *Documents relatifs aux troubles du pays de Liège sous les princes-évêques Louis de Bourbon et Jean de Horne, 1455–1505,* 185–232. CRH. Brussels, 1844.

Payet, E. 'L'agression du Dauphiné par le prince d'Orange et la vérité sur la bataille d'Anthon, 11 juin 1430.' *Bulletin de l'Académie delphinale* (6) xxiv–xxvi (1957), xix–xx and 39–51.

Perier, A. *Nicolas Rolin, 1380–1461.* Paris, 1904.

Perrault-Dabot, A. *Le duc de Bourgogne Philippe le Bon et le Concile de Florence.* Paris, 1899. Reprinted from *MCACO* xiii (1895–1900), 199–214.

Perret, P. M. *Histoire des relations de la France avec Venise.* 2 vols. Paris, 1896.

Perroy, E. 'L'artillerie royale à la bataille de Montlhéry.' *RH* cxlix (1925), 187-9.

——. *The Hundred Years War*. London, 1951. Translated from *La Guerre de Cent Ans*. Paris, 1945.

Petit-Dutaillis, C. *Charles VII, Louis XI et les premières années de Charles VIII, 1422-1492*. E. Lavisse, *Histoire de France* iv (2). Paris, 1902.

Petri, F. 'Nordwestdeutschland in der Politik der Burgunderherzöge.' *Gemeinsame Probleme deutsch-niederländischer Landes- und Volksforschung*, 92-126. *BIMGU* xxxii. Groningen, 1962. Reprinted from *Westfälische Forschungen* vii (1953-4), 80-100.

Picard, E. 'La vénerie et la fauconnerie des ducs de Bourgogne.' *MSE* (n.s.) ix (1880), 297-418. Reprinted separately, Paris, 1881.

Piloti, E. *Traité sur le passage de Terre Sainte, 1420*. Ed. P. H. Dopp. Publications de l'Université Lovanium de Léopoldville, iv. Louvain, 1958.

Pinchart, A. *Histoire du conseil souverain de Hainaut*. MARB 8vo série, vii. Brussels, 1858.

Piquard, M. 'Étude sur la situation politique des archevêques de Besançon de 1290 à 1435.' *PTSEC* (1929), 193-201.

——. 'Charles de Neufchâtel, archevêque de Besançon de 1463 à 1498.' *BHPTH* (1932-3), 35-46.

Pirenne, H. 'Les dénombrements de la population d'Ypres au xve siècle, 1412-1506.' *VSW* i (1903), 1-32.

——. *Histoire de Belgique*, ii. 4th edn. Brussels, 1947.

Pius II. *Commentaries*. English translation by F. A. Gragg and L. C. Gabel. Smith College studies in history, xxii, xxv, xxx, xxxv and xlii. Northampton, Mass., 1937-57.

——. *Opera*. Basel, 1551.

——. *Orationes*, iii. Ed. J. D. Mansi. Lucca, 1759.

Plancher, U. *Histoire générale et particulière de Bourgogne*, 4 vols. Dijon, 1739-81.

Pocquet du Haut-Jussé, B. A. 'Deux féodaux: Bourgogne et Bretagne, 1363-1491, v and vi. Philippe le Bon et Jean V.' *RCC* xxxvi (1) (1934-5), 439-57 and 641-56. 'vii. Charles e Téméraire et François II, 1461-1473.' *RCC* xxxvi (2) (1934-5), 177-86 and 363-75.

——. 'Anne de Bourgogne et le testament de Bedford.' *BEC* xcv (1934), 284-326.

——. 'Le connétable de Richemont, seigneur bourguignon.' *AB* vii (1935), 309-36 and viii (1936), 7-30 and 106-38.

Poitiers, A. de. *Les honneurs de la cour*. Ed. La Curne de Sainte-Palaye. *Mémoire sur l'ancienne chevalrie*, ii. 171–267. Paris, 1759.

Post, R. R. *Geschiedenis der Utrechtsche bisschopsverkiezingen tot 1535*. BIMGU xix. Utrecht, 1933.

Pot, J. *Histoire de Renier Pot*. Paris, 1929.

Potter, F. de. *Geschiedenis van Jacoba van Beieren*. MARB. 8vo série, xxxi. Brussels, 1881.

Potvin, H. 'Hugues de Lannoy, 1384–1456.' *BCRH* (4) vi (1879), 117–38.

Poullet, E. *Mémoire sur l'ancienne constitution brabançonne*. Mémoires couronnés et mémoires des savants étrangers, xxxi. Académie royale de Belgique. Brussels, 1863.

Prarond, E. *Abbeville au temps de Charles VII, des ducs de Bourgogne, maîtres de Ponthieu, et de Louis XI, 1426–1483*. Paris, 1899.

Précis analytique des documents que renferme le dépôt des archives de la Flandre-Occidentale à Bruges. Ed. O. Delepierre and F. Priem. 1e série, 3 vols. Bruges, 1840–2, 2e série, 9 vols. Bruges, 1845–58.

Prims, F. *Geschiedenis van Antwerpen*. 11 vols. Brussels etc., 1927–49.

Proceedings and Ordinances of the Privy Council of England. Ed. H. Nicolas. 7 vols. London, 1834–7.

Proost, G. *De financiele hoofdambtenaren van de Burgondische hertogen voor de regering van Karel de Stoute*. Unpublished thesis. University of Ghent, 1959.

Prost, H. 'Les États du comté de Bourgogne des origines à 1477.' *PTSEC* (1905), 115–22.

Putnam, R. *A Medieval Princess*. New York, 1904.

Puyvelde, L. van. 'De reis van Jan van Eyck naar Portugal.' *VVATL* (1940), 17–27.

Quarré, P. 'La chapelle du duc de Bourgogne à Dijon "lieu, chapitre et collège" de l'Ordre de la Toison d'Or.' *PCEEBM* v (1963), 56–64.

Quarré-Reybourbon, L. 'Trois recueils de portraits aux crayons ou à la plume représentant des souverains et des personnages de la France et des Pays-Bas.' *BCHDN* xxiii (1900).

Quelques documents inédits sur l'élection des évêques d'Arras du xive au xviie siècle. Ed. E. Fournier. *Études historiques dédiées à la mémoire de M. Roger Rodière*, 121–37. Arras, 1947.

Quenson de la Hennerie, A. 'Le séjour de Philippe le Bon à Saint-Omer, le 15 août, 1448.' *RN* xii (1926), 149–61.

Quicke, F. *Les chroniqueurs des fastes bourguignons*. Brussels, 1943.

Rachfahl, F. 'Die Trennung der Niederlande vom Deutschen Reiche.' *WZGK* xix (1900), 79–119.

Raffalli, L. 'Des rapports entre le Parlement et les États de Franche-Comté du xive siècle à la conquête définitive de la province par Louis XIV.' *MAB* clxxii (1947-57), 380-93.

Recueil de documents relatifs à l'histoire de l'industrie drapière en Flandre, ii: *Le sud-ouest de la Flandre depuis l'époque bourguignonne*. Ed. H. E. de Sagher and others. CRH. 3 vols. Brussels, 1951-66.

Recueil de documents relatifs aux conflits soutenus par les Liégeois contre Louis de Bourbon et Charles le Téméraire, 1458-1469. BCRH xciv (1930), 245-353.

Regesta Imperii, xi. *Die Urkunden Kaiser Sigmunds, 1410-1437*. Ed. W. Altmann. 2 vols. Innsbruck, 1896, 1900.

Régestes de la cité de Liège. Ed. E. Fairon. 4 vols. Liège, 1933-40.

Régibeau, L. *Le rôle politique des Croÿ à la fin du règne de Philippe le Bon, 1456-1465*. Unpublished thesis. University of Brussels, 1956.

Reiffenberg, F. A. T. de. *Mémoire sur le séjour que Louis, dauphin de Viennois, depuis roi sous le nom de Louis XI, fit aux Pays-Bas, de l'an 1456 à l'an 1461*. MARB. 4to série, v. Brussels, 1829.

——. *Histoire de l'Ordre de la Toison d'Or*. Brussels, 1830.

——. 'Enfants naturels du duc Philippe le Bon.' *BARB* xiii (1) (1846), 172-87 and xiv (1) (1847), 585-97.

Reilhac, A. de. *Jean de Reilhac*. 2 vols. Paris, 1886, 1887.

Remy, F. *Les grandes indulgences pontificales aux Pays-Bas à la fin du moyen âge, 1300-1531*. Louvain, 1928.

Renouard, Y. 'Le grand commerce du vin au moyen âge.' *RBG* i (1952), 5-18.

Renoz, P. *La chancellerie de Brabant sous Philippe le Bon, 1430-1467*. CRH. Brussels, 1955.

Report on manuscripts in various collections, iv. Historical Manuscripts Commission. Dublin, 1907.

Richard, J. 'Les archives et les archivistes des ducs de Bourgogne.' *BEC* cv (1944), 123-69.

——. ' "Enclaves" royales et limites des provinces. Les élections bourguignons.' *AB* xx (1948), 89-113.

——. 'Le gouverneur de Bourgogne au temps des ducs Valois.' *MSHDB* xix (1957), 101-12.

——. 'Une assemblée de nobles bourguignons pour la défense du duché, 1426.' *MSHDB* xxii (1961), 125-33.

——. 'La Toison d'Or dans les deux Bourgognes.' *PCEEBM* v (1963), 47-52.

P

Richard, J. 'Les débats entre le roi de France et le duc de Bourgogne sur la frontière du royaume à l'ouest de la Saône.' *BHPTH* (1964), 113–32.

——. 'Problèmes de ressort au xvᵉ siècle: l'enquête de 1451–1452 sur la situation de Fontaine-Française.' *MSHDB* xxvi (1965), 217–27.

——. 'Les États de Bourgogne.' *APAE* xxxv (1966), 299–324.

——. 'La croisade bourguignonne dans la politique européene.' *PCEEBM* x (1968), 41–4.

Richter, F. *Der Luxemburger Erbfolgestreit in den Jahren 1438–1443.* Westdeutsche Zeitschrift. Extra vol. v (1889), 1–73. Reprinted separately, Trier, 1889.

Riemsdijk, T. van. 'De oorsprong van het Hof van Holland.' *Geschiedkundige opstellen aangeboden aan Robert Fruin*, 183–208. The Hague, 1894.

——. 'De opdracht van het ruwaardschap in Holland en Zeeland aan Philips van Bourgondië.' *VKAWL* (n.s.) viii (1906), 1–82.

——. *De tresorie en kanselarii van de graven van Holland uit het henegouwsche en beyersche Huis.* The Hague, 1908.

Roffin, R. *Le tonlieu du port de Gravelines.* Unpublished thesis. University of Lille, 1953.

Rompaey, J. van. *Het grafelijk baljuwsambt in Vlaanderen tijdens de boergondische Periode.* Verhandelingen van de koninklijke Vlaamse Academie. Letteren, lxii. Brussels, 1967.

Rover, R. de. *Money, Banking and Credit in Medieval Bruges.* Cambridge, Mass., 1948.

——. 'Oprichting en liquidatie van het Brugse filiaal van het bankiershuis der Medici.' *MKVAL* xv. Brussels, 1953.

——. *The Rise and Decline of the Medici Bank, 1397–1494.* Harvard studies in business history, xxi. Cambridge, Mass., 1963.

Rotuli parliamentorum, 1278–1503. 6 vols and Index. London, 1783–1832.

Roye, J. de. *Chronique scandaleuse.* Ed. B. de Mandrot. SHF. 2 vols. Paris, 1894, 1896.

Rozmital, Leo of. *Travels.* Ed. M. Letts. Publications of the Hakluyt Society. Second series, cviii. Cambridge, 1957.

Ruwet, J. *Les archives et bibliothèques de Vienne et l'histoire de Belgique.* CRH. Brussels, 1956.

Rychner, J. *La littérature et les moeurs chevaleresques à la cour de Bourgogne.* Neuchâtel, 1950.

Saintenoy, P. *Les arts et les artistes à la cour de Bruxelles.* MARBBA (2) v. Brussels, 1934.

Schanz, G. *Englische Handelspolitik gegen Ende des Mittelalters.* 2 vols. Leipzig, 1880–1.

Schneebalg-Perelman, S. 'La tenture armoriée de Philippe le Bon à Berne.' *JBHM* xxxix-xl (1959–60), 136–63.

Schneider, F. *Der Europäische Friedenskongress von Arras, 1435, und die Friedenspolitik Papst Eugens IV und des Basler Konzils.* Griess, 1919.

Schötter, J. *Geschichte des Luxemburger Landes.* Luxembourg, 1882.

Schwarzkopf, U. *Studien zur Hoforganisation der Herzöge von Burgund aus dem Hause Valois.* Unpublished thesis. University of Gottingen, 1955.

——. 'La cour de Bourgogne et la Toison d'Or.' *PCEEBM* v (1963), 91–104.

Septendecim diplomata et chartae, xi–xiv. Ed. H. C. Senckenberg. *Selecta juris,* vi. 473–94. Frankfurt, 1742.

Speierische Chronik, 1406–1476. Ed. F. J. Mone. Quellensammlung der badischen Landesgeschichte, i. 371–520. Karlsruhe, 1848.

Spufford, P. *Monetary problems and policies in the Burgundian Netherlands, 1433–1496.* Unpublished thesis. University of Cambridge, 1963.

——. 'Coinage, taxation and the Estates General of the Burgundian Netherlands.' *APAE* xl (1966), 61–88.

Stabel-Stasino, N. *Bijdrage tot de kennis van de Standenvertegenwoordiging in Vlaanderen en van haar verhouding tot de vorst, 1410–1427.* Unpublished thesis. University of Ghent, 1957.

Stahr, K. *Die Hanse und Holland bis zum Utrechter Frieden, 1474.* Marburg, 1907.

Stälin, C. F. von. *Wirtembergische Geschichte.* 4 vols. Stuttgart, 1841–70.

Stavelot, J. de. *Chronique, 1400–1449.* Ed. A. Borgnet. CRH. Brussels, 1861.

Stein, H. *Étude sur Olivier de la Marche.* MARB 4to série, xlix. Brussels, 1888.

——. *Charles de France, frère de Louis XI.* Paris, 1921.

——. *Nouveaux documents sur Olivier de la Marche et sa famille.* MARBL (2) ix (1). Brussels, 1922.

——. 'Un diplomate bourguignon du xve siècle, Antoine Haneron.' *BEC* xcviii (1937), 283–348.

Stengers, J. 'Les traités de Philippe le Bon et de Charles le Téméraire avec les Liégeois, décembre 1465–janvier 1466.' *Annales du xxxiiie Congrès de la Fédération archéologique et historique de Belgique,* iii. 741–8. Tournai, 1949.

Stouff, L. *Catherine de Bourgogne et la féodalité de l'Alsace autrichienne.* 2 parts. Paris, 1913. Reprinted from *RB* xxiii (2, 3, 4) (1913).

Stouff, L. *Contribution à l'histoire de la Bourgogne au concile de Bâle. Textes inédits extraits des archives de la Chambre des Comptes de Dijon, 1433.* Publications de l'Université de Dijon, i. Mélanges, 83–133. Dijon, 1928.

Struick, J. E. A. L. 'Het bewind van de gilden en de strijd om het bisdom in de stad Utrecht, 1455–1456.' *Postillen aangeboden aan Prof. Dr. R. R. Post*, 85–115. Nijmegen, 1964.

Surjous, J. M. *Isabelle de Portugal et les Portugais à la cour de Bourgogne.* Unpublished thesis. University of Lille, 1953.

Table chronologique des chartes et diplômes relatifs à l'histoire de l'ancien pays de Luxembourg. Ed. F. X. Wurth-Paquet. PSHIL xxviii (1873), 1–192, xxix (1874), 1–108, xxx (1875), 1–161, xxxi (1876), 1–134, and xxxii (1877), 1–66.

Tafur, P. *Travels and adventures.* Ed. M. Letts. London, 1926.

Terdenge, H. 'Zur Geschichte der holländischen Steuern im 15. und 16. Jahrhundert.' *VSW* xviii (1925), 95–167.

Terlinden, Le Vicomte. 'Les origines religieuses et politiques de la Toison d'Or.' *PCEEBM* v (1963), 35–46.

Thelliez, C. 'Un compromis pour la juridiction spirituelle en Hainaut entre le duc de Bourgogne Philippe le Bon et l'évêque de Cambrai, 1448–1449.' *RN* xl (1958), 375–80 and 428.

Thibault, M. *La jeunesse de Louis XI, 1423–1445.* Paris, 1907.

Thielemans, M. R. 'Une lettre missive inédite de Philippe le Bon concernant le siège de Calais.' *BCRH* cxv (1950), 285–96.

——. *Bourgogne et Angleterre. Relations politiques et économiques entre les Pays-Bas bourguignons et l'Angleterre, 1435–1467.* Brussels, 1966.

Toison d'Or, La. Cinq siècles d'art et d'histoire. Exposition à Bruges, 1962. Bruges, 1962.

Tourneur, V. 'Les origines de l'Ordre de la Toison d'Or et la symbolique des insignes de celui-ci.' *BARBL* (5) xlii (1956), 300–23.

Tournier, C. 'Le vin à Dijon de 1430 à 1560.' *AB* xxii (1950), 7–32 and 161–86.

Toussaert, J. *Le sentiment religieux en Flandre à la fin du moyen-âge.* Paris, 1963.

Toussaint, J. 'Philippe le Bon et le concile de Bâle, 1431–1449.' *BCRH* cvii (1942), 1–126.

——. *Les relations diplomatiques de Philippe le Bon avec le concile de Bâle, 1431–1449.* Louvain, 1942.

Trouvé, R. 'Enkele bijzonderheden over de Mechelse stadsfinanciën in de xve eeuw.' *HKOM* lvi (1952), 46–67.

Tuetey, A. *Les écorcheurs sous Charles VII.* 2 vols. Montbéliard, 1874.

Urkunden, Briefe und Actenstücke zur Geschichte der habsburgischen Fürsten, 1443–1473. Ed. J. Chmel. FRADA ii. Vienna, 1850.

Urkundenbuch der Stadt Lübeck. Ed. Verein für lübeckische Geschichte. 11 vols. Lübeck, 1843–1905.

Urkundenbuch für die Geschichte des Niederrheins. Ed. T. J. Lacomblet. 4 vols. Düsseldorf, 1840–57.

Urkundliche Beiträge zur Geschichte Böhmens im Zeitalter Georg's von Podiebrad, 1450–1471. Ed. F. Palacky. FRADA xx. Vienna, 1860.

Urkundliche Nachträge zur österreichisch-deutschen Geschichte im Zeitalter Kaiser Friedrich III. Ed. A. Bachmann. FRADA xlvi. Vienna, 1892.

Utrechtsche jaarboeken van de vijftiende eeuw, 1402–1481. Ed. K. Burman, 3 vols. Utrecht, 1750–4.

Uyttebrouck, A. 'Les origines du conseil de Brabant: la chambre du conseil du duc Jean IV.' *RBPH* xxxvi (1958), 1135–72.

Uytven, R. van. 'La Flandre et le Brabant, "terres de promission" sous les ducs de Bourgogne?' *RN* xliii (1961), 281–317.

Valat, G. 'Nicolas Rolin, chancelier de Bourgogne.' *MSE* (n.s.) xl (1912), 73–145, xli (1913), 1–73 and xlii (1914), 53–148.

Vallet de Viriville, A. *Histoire de Charles VII.* 3 vols. Paris, 1862–5.

Valois, N. *Histoire de la Pragmatique Sanction de Bourges sous Charles VII.* Paris, 1906.

——. *Le pape et le concile, 1418–1450.* 2 vols. Paris, 1909.

Van de Kieft, C. 'De Staten-Generaal in het Bourgondisch-oostenrijkse tijdvak, 1464–1555.' *500 jaren Staten-Generaal in de Nederlanden,* 1–27. Assen, 1964.

Van den Borren, C. *Geschiedenis van de muziek in de Nederlanden,* i. Antwerp, 1948.

Van den Nieuwenhuizen, J. 'Het onstaan der Staten-Generaal in de Nederlanden in 1464.' *TG* lxxii (1959), 245–50.

Vandenpeereboom, A. *Le conseil de Flandre à Ypres.* Ypres, 1874.

Vandeputte, F. 'Droits et gages des dignitaires et employés à la cour de Philippe le Bon, 1437, et de Charles le Téméraire, 1471.' *ASEB* xxviii (1876–7), 1–24 and 188–92.

Vander Linden, H. *Itinéraires de Philippe le Bon.* CRH. Brussels, 1940.

Van der Wee, H. *The growth of the Antwerp market and the European economy.* 3 vols. The Hague, 1963.

Vaněček, V. and others. *The universal peace organisation of King George of Bohemia.* London, 1964.

Vaughan, R. *Philip the Bold.* London, 1962.

432 BIBLIOGRAPHY

Vaughan, R. *John the Fearless*. London, 1966.

Veen, J. S. van. 'De laatste regeeringsjaren van Hertog Arnold, 1456–1465.' *WG* xiv. Arnhem, 1920.

Verlinden, C. 'À propos de la politique économique des ducs de Bourgogne à l'égard de l'Espagne.' *Hispania* x (1950), 681–715.

Vermaseren, B. A. 'Het ambt van historiograaf in de bourgondische Nederlandern.' *TG* lvi (1941), 258–73.

Vickers, K. H. *Humphrey, duke of Gloucester*. London, 1907.

Vlietinck, E. 'Le siège de Calais et les villes de le côte flamande.' *ASEB* xl (1890), 91–101.

Voigt, G. *Enea Silvio de' Piccolomini als Papst Pius II und sein Zeitalter*. 3 vols. Berlin, 1856–63.

Vollbehr, F. 'Die Holländer und die deutsche Hanse.' *PHG* xxi. Lübeck, 1930.

Warnsinck, J. C. M. *De zeeoorlog van Holland en Zeeland tegen de wendische steden der duitsche Hanze, 1438–1441*. The Hague, 1939.

Waurin, J. de. *Recueil des croniques*. Ed. W. Hardy. RS. 5 vols. London, 1864–91.

Weale, W. H. J. *Hubert and John van Eyck*. London, 1908.

Weiss, R. 'Humphrey duke of Gloucester and Tito Livio Frulovisi.' *Fritz Saxl, 1890–1948. A volume of memorial essays*, 218–27. London, 1957.

Werveke, H. van. 'De ekonomische en sociale gevolgen van de muntpolitiek der graven van Vlaanderen, 1337–1433.' *ASEB* lxxiv (1931), 1–15.

——. *Gent. Scherts van een sociale geschiedenis*. Ghent, 1947.

Werveke, L. M. van. 'De Engelschen in de ambachten van Oostburg en Ysendijke in 1436.' *ASEB* lxxiv (1931), 183–8.

Werveke, N. van. *Definitive Erwerbung des luxemburger Landes durch Philipp, herzog von Burgund, 1458–1462*. Luxembourg, 1886.

——. 'Notice sur le conseil provincial de Luxembourg avant sa réorganisation par Charles-Quint, c. 1200–1531.' *PSHIL* xl (1889), 253–382.

Wickersheimer, E. 'Un jugement astrologique de la paix d'Arras et le médecin Thomas Broun.' *XIIᵉ Congrès de l'Association bourguignonne des Sociétés savantes*, 202–4. Dijon, 1937.

Wielant, P. *Recueil des antiquités de Flandre*. Ed. J. J. de Smet. *Recueil des chroniques de Flandre*, iv. 1–442. CRH. Brussels, 1865.

Williams, E. C. *My lord of Bedford, 1389–1435*. London, 1963.

Windecke, E. *Denkwürdigkeiten zur Geschichte des Zeitalters Kaiser Sigmunds*. Ed. W. Altmann. Berlin, 1893.

Wylie, J. H. and W. T. Waugh. *The reign of Henry V.* 3 vols. Cambridge, 1914–1929.

Wyndham Lewis, D. B. *King Spider.* London, 1930.

Yans, M. *Histoire économique du duché de Limbourg sous la Maison de Bourgogne. Les forêts et les mines.* MARBL xxxviii (2). Brussels, 1938.

Zantfliet, C. *Chronicon.* Ed. E. Martène and U. Durand. *Veterum scriptorum amplissima collectio,* v. cols. 67–504. Paris, 1729.

Zilverberg, S. *David van Bourgondië, bisschop van Terwaan en van Utrecht. BIMGU* xxiv. Groningen, 1951.

Zuylen van Nyevelt, A. van. *Épisodes de la vie des ducs de Bourgogne à Bruges.* Bruges, 1937.

BIBLIOGRAPHY

Index

Rochefort, 222
Rochefort, Charles de, 129
Rochefort, the lord of, 329
Roeslelare, 90
Rolin, Anthoine, lord of Aymeries, 339, 386, 387
Rolin, Jehan, bishop of Chalon, Autun and cardinal, 215, 232
Rolin, Nicolas, ducal chancellor, and lord of Authumes, 5, 8, 66, 108, 165, 166, 168–70, 173, 178, 189, 190, 236, 267, 283, 328, 337, 340; and Charles VII, 100–1, 126, 352
Rolin, Anthoine, bastard of Nicolas R., 236
Rome, 5, 205, 206, 237, 272, 342, 363, 369; Hospital of St. Julian, 215
Ronse, 328
Roosebeke, battle of, 303, 332
Rosay, Pierre de, provost of Cassel, 220
Rosimbos, Jehan de, 13
Rosin, the bastard of, 361
Rostock, 92, 93
Rötteln, Wilhelm von, 173
Rotterdam, 33, 40, 76, 92, 303; P. the Good at, 42
Rouault, Joachim, marshal of France, 381, 383
Roubaix, Jehan, lord of, 86, 101, 179–84, 234, 264, 269–70
Rouen, 84, 374, 390
Round Table, Knights of the, 242
Roussillon, Girart de, 157
Rouville, Jehan de, vice-chancellor of Brittany, 374
Rouvres, 2, 149
Roye, 31, 381, 383; prebends, 234
Roye, Jehan de, 383
Rozmital, Leo of, 134, 151
Rubempré, affair of the bastard of, 374–5, 377, 379
Rupelmonde, 321, 322, 326, 332; castle, 344
Russia, 269, 364
Ruven, Claes van, 228
Rynel, Jehan de, 165
St. Adrian, 336
St. Andrew's cross, 39, 329, 389
St. Bernard pass, 363
St. Claude, 7
St. Cloud, 383–5

St. Denis, 383, 389
St. Eustace, 336
St. George, 37, 336
St. Géry's tooth, 129
St. Hubert, Order of, 293
St. Josse, shrine of, at Montreuil-sur-Mer, 73
St. Léger, Mauroy de, 12
St. Luke's painting of Our Lady, 130
St. Maartensdijk, treaty, 33, 34
St. Maurice, 336
St. Maurice, Order of, 212
St. Omer, 77, 114, 149, 338; abbey of St. Bertin, 124, 235 and see Fillastre; negotiations at, 27; P. the Good at, 135, 161, 235; provost, see Menart
St. Patrick's Isle, Lough Erne, 111
St. Pol, see Luxembourg
St. Quentin, 99, 116, 278, 355
St. Rémy, lord of, see Lefèvre
St. Riquier, 12, 17, 355
St. Trond, 395; treaty, 396, 397
St. Valéry, 13, 18
St. Victor, 336
Ste, Camelle, Jannot de, 394, 395
Ste, Paule, Digne, 361
Saintrailles, Poton de, 14
Saligny, Lourdin de, 234
Salins, salt-works, 240
Salisbury, Thomas Montague, earl of, 49
Sandwich, 67, 77, 110, 179
Sangatte, 79
Sanguin, Guillaume, 6
Santerre, 381
Santes, lord of, see Lannoy
Santiago de Compostela, 5, 180
Saône, river, 149, 362, 364, 365
Sardinia, 273
Sars, Bruyant de, 336
Saveuse, Philippe de, 12
Saveuse, the lord of, 329
Savoisy, Charles de, 5
Savoy, duchy, 132, 147, 212, 357
Savoy, Amadeus VIII, duke of, 7–8, 20, 64, 70, 71, 143, 163; ambassadors of, 21, 208, 210; as Pope Felix V, 212–15 passim
Savoy, Charlotte of, dauphine of France, 353–4
Savoy, Louis I, duke of, 347
Saxony, Anna, wife of Duke William of, 277, 278, 282

Printed and bound by CPI Group (UK) Ltd, Croydon, CR0 4YY

31/03/2025

14650407-0002